D1417566

PUBLICATIONS, LIBRARIANS AND LIBRARY E

Copyright © 1962 by the McGraw-Hill Book Company, Inc. All rights reserved. Printed in the United States of America. This book, or parts thereof, may not be reproduced in any form without permission of the publishers. Library of Congress Catalog Card Number 61-18053

HIGHER EDUCATION:
RESOURCES AND FINANCE

SEYMOUR E. HARRIS

Lucius N. Littauer Professor of Political Economy
Harvard University

McGRAW-HILL BOOK COMPANY, INC.   1962
New York   San Francisco   Toronto   London

HIGHER EDUCATION: RESOURCES AND FINANCE

TO McGEORGE BUNDY
who in eight years as Dean of the Harvard Faculty of Arts and Science contributed greatly to the advance of education in the nation and at Harvard

ABOUT THIS BOOK

CREDENTIALS

In writing a book on the economic aspects of higher education one is likely to be charged with excessive emphasis on material aspects. I am indeed concerned primarily with two problems: how to get more resources into higher education and how to use them more effectively. But we cannot discuss education in one compartment and economics in another. Any allocation of resources must be examined in relation to the increment or decrement of educational product.

In forty years of teaching, almost wholly at Harvard (with two years at Princeton immediately after I received my A.B. at Harvard), I have been much interested in educational issues.* I first became interested in the economic issues of higher education when I wrote a report for the Buck (then provost of Harvard University) Committee on General Education on the economic issues.

In the late 1940s I wrote a book, *How Shall We Pay for Education?*, in which I urged government to play an enlarged role, and, later, another book, *The Market for College Graduates,* in which I raised some questions concerning the supply of, and demand for, college graduates. This is a problem that requires continued examination.

But in this book I do not suggest a solution to our economic problems through the setting of standards which would keep the 1970 college attendance at, say, the current figure of 3½ million. This is a possible way out but on the whole has little appeal in the nation. Even if 25 to 50 per cent of our college students do not profit greatly from higher education, expenditures for their education—given our large resources and an adequate

* Over the years I have served on the following committees at Harvard in addition to being chairman of one of the largest departments: Educational Policy, General Education, Faculty on Athletics, Economics and Political Science Higher Degrees, Ph.D. in Social Sciences (Chairman), Size of the College, Fringe Benefits and Pensions and Retirement (University).

diversification of IHL (institutions of higher learning) and of curricula—in most cases undoubtedly yield a greater product than would be had from alternative expenditures by parents or siblings. Yet I was impressed by replies to a questionnaire I sent to a few hundred outstanding academic economists on the financial issues of higher education. Many commented on the small educational gains obtained by a large proportion of their students and would, therefore, at the very least have the IHL offer a high-grade product to one group and a low-grade product to another.

Earlier literature is vast; I should especially mention the reports of the Presidents' Commissions under Truman and Eisenhower, the important anniversary volume *Financing Higher Education: 1960–70* put out by the McGraw-Hill Book Company, Inc., and edited by Dexter M. Keezer, the numerous quality volumes put out by the Commission on Financing Higher Education (John Millett, Chief of Staff), the American Assembly volume on the Federal government and higher education, and reports of experts in most states. Here I mention especially the master plan of California and the Heald report for New York State. The reader will find literally hundreds of other references in this volume.

In the last year or two even while I was writing this book and the publishers were editing this volume, the output of books and articles dealing with the range of subjects with which I am especially interested has greatly increased. These writers have concentrated especially on such problems as the contribution of education to productivity, i.e., output per hour—the estimates of education's contribution have varied from 35 to 85 per cent of the total advance of productivity; capital investments in education—from 9 per cent of gross investment in 1900 to 34 per cent in 1956; the total costs of education—estimated as high as $47 billion in 1957–58 once allowance is made for income foregone, depreciation allowances and tax exemptions; on the analysis of private and social gains of education and comparisons of returns on investment in physical capital and in human capital as well as the case for favoring the latter rather than the former; and on estimates of the total years of education amassed by the whole population. These studies throw much light on the private and social gains of higher education as well as the costs, with large social gains pointing to the need of substantial government contributions to education, inclusive of higher education.*

* See especially Svennilson, Edding, and Elvin, *Policy Conference on Economic Growth* and *Investment in Education, Targets for Education* (in Europe), and *Organization for European Economic Cooperation* (OEEC), 1961; T. W. Schultz, "Capital Formation by Education," *Journal of Political Economy,* pp. 571–583, and "Investment in Human Capital," *American Economic Review,* March, 1961, pp. 1–17; essays in a forthcoming volume by the Office of Education (Selma Mushkin, ed.) by A. M. Rivlon, H. P. Miller, R. C. Blitz, R. S. Eckaus, T. W. Schultz, M. J. Bowman, T. J. Mills; R. M. Solow; "Technical Change and the Aggregate Production

THE WRITING OF THIS BOOK

A generous grant of the Ford Foundation enabled me to spend the major part of my time in the last four years on this study. The foundation gave me complete freedom in the writing of this book, an important fact since ideological issues cannot, try as one will, be completely erased. Their support enabled me to cover a large part of the literature on this subject; to have twenty months completely free of other responsibilities; to visit college administrators of more than one hundred IHL for periods ranging from two hours to two days at each IHL; to send out questionnaires to hundreds of economists, the presidents, deans, registrars, and treasurers or business officers of more than two hundred IHL; and to have the assistance of a remarkable group of Harvard seniors and graduate students in arts and science and the Law School. Their help was especially valuable in the analysis of the questionnaires.

In visiting IHL and sending questionnaires I tried to get a good sample of different types of IHL—large and small; North, South, East and West; public, independent, and church-oriented; universities; four-year liberal arts colleges; women's, men's, and coeducational colleges; junior colleges; and urban universities.

The questions put to the officials of these IHL, both in the questionnaires and in meetings, concerned, for example, the following: attitudes toward pricing; the objectives of scholarships and loans; sources of revenue and allocation of resources; plans for the next ten years in all vital fields, but especially enrollment (and relation to unit costs); financing and manner of increasing productivity; use of cost studies and new methods of teaching; faculty salaries, average by ranks, by departments, ages by ranks, fringe benefits, faculty/student ratios; manner of managing productive funds, inclusive of accounting methods; financial interdependence of departments.

The current volume is not small. I wish it could have been. But the problems are large and numerous. I have tried to cover the major issues here. The impatient reader can get a quick summary in the opening chapter. The reader interested in my views on enrollment and the *special* problems of different types of IHL and of individual IHL will have to wait for another volume. Here I present what I learned from my questionnaires and

---

Functions," *Review of Economics and Statistics,* August, 1957, pp. 312–320; W. P. Hogan, *ibid.,* November, 1958, pp. 411–413; S. Fabricant, *Basic Facts on Productivity Change,* National Bureau of Economic Research, 1959; J. W. Kendrick, *Productivity Trends in the United States,* National Bureau of Economic Research, chap. 4, 1961; Gary Becker's promising work for the NBER; J. Vaizey's brilliant new book on the *Economics of Education;* E. F. Denison's forthcoming book, *Economic Growth in the United States.*

visits in a general way; the diagnosis for classes of IHL and individual IHL awaits another volume.

In four years of preparation I have written and presented at least a dozen papers. These give some impressions of my views.* But over the four years my conclusions have also changed. This book is a new product.

A writer is always confronted with a personal problem: is he *not* to check his results with others and present a clear-cut version of his views, or is he to submit his ideas to the examination of others with the result that the position of 1957 is substantially modified by 1961, not alone because of further examination of evidence, but also because of the impact of the ideas of others? One of my most distinguished colleagues and one of the world's greatest social scientists would never allow another to read his manuscript. I have preferred the other approach, that is, exposed myself to the views of others.

For example, I started in 1957 with a strong preference for the free market approach—charge according to the capacity to pay, subsidize the able and impecunious, and depend substantially on higher fees. But I spent several days with a Committee of University Presidents of the American Council for Education, a day with a group of university presidents assembled by the Ford Foundation, two full days with fifty presidents of

---

* Among my writings during this period:

1. "An Essay on Broad Issues in Financing," in Dexter M. Keezer, ed., *Financing Higher Education, 1960–70*, McGraw-Hill, 1959.

2. "Student Credit Could End Colleges' Financial Plight," *College Board Review*, Winter, 1959.

3. "Future Demand for College Graduates," in *Planning College Policy for the Critical Decade Ahead*, College Entrance Examination Board, 1958.

4. "Higher Education on the Cuff," *National Parent-Teacher Magazine*, March, 1960.

5. "The Economic Aspects of a Memo to a College Trustee," *The Journal of Higher Education*, November, 1959.

6. "Is Higher Tuition the Answer?" in *Financing Higher Education*, no. 4, Southern Regional Education Board, November, 1959.

7. "The Economics of Harvard," *Harvard Alumni Bulletin*, Feb. 20, 1960.

8. "Faculty Salaries," *American Association of University Professors Bulletin*, Winter, 1957.

9. "College Salaries, Financing of Higher Education, and Management of Institutions of Higher Learning," *ibid.*, Summer, 1958.

10. "Charging the Student Tuition on the Basis of Costs," *Educational Record*, January, 1959.

11. *Higher Education in the United States: The Economic Problems*, (S. E. Harris, ed.), especially "Introduction," Harvard University Press, 1960.

12. *More Resources for Education*, (John Dewey Lecture) Harper, 1960.

13. Paper to Presidents, State Universities, Higher Education: Economic Problems of the 1960's in *Transactions and Proceedings, National Association of State Universities*, 1960, pp. 24–42.

the land-grant and state universities, about a hundred days visiting with college presidents and other officials, at least twenty additional days with groups of high officials of IHL at symposia, eight solid ten-hour days at a seminar on higher education for which I was responsible. In addition I discussed these problems with governors, officials of the HEW, congressional committees, state budget officers, admissions officers, and others. All these meetings had an impact on me. I find myself less committed to the *heavy* reliance on higher fees than in 1957.

THE CONTENTS

In Part One (after the Summary) I present three introductory chapters, the first largely historical to give some idea of the trends since the early part of the century, the second an attempt to project the higher education budget to 1970, the third a study of trends of enrollment, income, endowment, scholarships, and faculty structure for 8 Ivy League and 6 other private universities, 10 outstanding women's colleges, 20 outstanding liberal arts colleges, 40 large urban universities, and 23 large Catholic universities. One conclusion emerges: the highest-quality IHL are losing ground.

Parts Two to Four treat the pricing problems, including scholarships and loans. I believe that by 1970 students will pay a larger part of the bill than they did in the 1950s. One reason for this is the large financial problems facing IHL in an age when resistance to state taxes grows. An examination of tuition trends in four recent years reveals that a continuation of such trends for the 1960s would mean about a 100 per cent rise of tuition for both public and private IHL.

Yet this may be too pessimistic, at least for the public IHL. A continuation of the trends of state support during the 1950s (corrected for prices) points to a rise of state and local government aid of about $3 billion in the 1960s, a substantially larger contribution than I guess for my 1970 budget. (This of course leaves out of account rising opposition to state and local taxes.) It is possible also that by 1970 the Federal government might contribute to IHL at least $1 billion in addition annually for nonservice purposes. With these gains, tuition in public IHL at least might not rise relatively more than per capita incomes, the best index of ability to pay.

Society gains from having an adequate number of college-trained members. This is the argument for public subsidies. But it is also the argument for charging what the traffic will bear and diverting a large part of the additional tuition revenue to scholarship funds for the able and impecunious. A $200 tuition bill for a $1,000 education in a public IHL is not enough for the farm boy who forgoes income earned and has to pay $1,300 in cash each year for his education, even with a $200 tuition. On paper the best solution seems to be higher fees and more aid. But, as a result of much conversation, I discovered that one cannot be certain that state legislatures will not use the new tuition money to relieve the taxpayer.

Much more can be done through scholarship and loan programs. In this book I suggest new programs, point out wastes in the old, estimate the magnitude of adequate outlays. From a financial viewpoint scholarships are especially important because they make possible rises in tuition income which are a multiple of the costs of the scholarships. Loans contribute in the same manner, and they help democratize higher education, since financial burdens are spread over much longer periods and hence higher education is made available to many otherwise not able to finance it. Moreover, credit is a means of diverting more resources into higher education, and since payments come after the act, the burden of financing charges is reduced as incomes steadily rise. Prefinancing is even less costly, since interest works for the student rather than against him. But prefinancing is not likely to be as important as postfinancing.

Part Five: Governments' contributions are important, though their share might decline in the next ten years even if their dollar contribution is doubled by 1970. But even more may be forthcoming. On state aid, my major contribution is an examination of the burdens, capacity, efforts, and achievements of 48 states, one by one. The statistical problems are most troublesome. But I checked my results with 150 university presidents (and other college officials), state budget directors, and heads of state coordinating boards, regents, etc. All that I can claim for my results is a *rough* indication of the ranking of the states on these criteria, in turn related to an examination of numerous variables.

A small proportion of IHL depend substantially on endowment-fund income to pay their bills. At Harvard, for example, roughly one-third of the income is from endowment, one-third from current gifts, and one-third from fees. (I leave out of account organized research.) But for most IHL current gifts are more important than endowment, and increasingly so.

In Part Six I stress the declining significance of endowment-fund income, related to rising enrollments, increased importance of other sources of income, the rising price and income levels. I also examine the mistakes of management and propose accounting methods that might bring larger returns on endowment.

This part also includes the results of a questionnaire addressed to 50 IHL with the largest endowment. I sought the answer to the following questions: class, education, grades, occupation of the 24 largest donors of each IHL over a recent period. I also compared needs in relation to purposes of gifts; sources of gifts for different types of IHL; the relation of numbers enrolled and number of alumni as factors determining economic status; the IHL command of the philanthropic dollar; the relation of results to type of financial management.

Costs and economies are the subject matter of Part Seven. IHL are not as efficient as they ought to be, which in part is the result of the manner of organization. The faculty are co-managers, not really employees. They, more than the administration, are responsible for the wastes and the reluctance to adopt improved techniques in higher education. To a large extent IHL share in the inefficiencies of nonprofit organizations, of large units, and from the peculiar relation of faculty and administration.

Cost studies, their possibilities and abuse; proliferation of courses; excessive number of small courses; inadequate use of plant; ignorance of the economies of size and location; lack of coordination among public IHL; excessive duplication; wastes in admission policies—these are some of the issues fully discussed in this part.

Replies to one questionnaire revealed that there is widespread ignorance of the factors that should determine the opening of new colleges and also their location. Incidentally, I studied the location of colleges in relation to the distribution of population.

My final part is devoted to the economic status of the faculty. Since before World War II they have experienced a serious relative deterioration in economic status. Had they maintained their relative prewar status they would have had $6 to $7 billion more income in a sixteen-year period. What is important is that income be high enough to assure the flow of additional teachers of quality needed in the years to come. This does not necessarily mean a rise of pay of 100 per cent in ten years. Continuance of trends of the last few years promises a rise of these proportions, though in the meanwhile other incomes may rise by about 30 per cent and hence the *relative* gains may not be enough.

But there are some reservations to the 100 per cent rise indicated. One is the large gains in fringe benefits; others are the declining average age of teachers, the greater growth of below average IHL, the trend toward less training of teachers and hence to that extent support for reduced rewards, the rise of outside income and the decline of work loads; and finally there is the question of base period. Professors have lost somewhat less on the basis of 1929 income than on that of 1939.

ACKNOWLEDGMENTS

First, let me say that it is impossible for me to mention by name the hundreds of college administrators and public officials who gave generously of their time in my visits to more than 100 IHL and in patient replies to my endless questionnaires. The college presidents left with me an impression of dedicated men and women of unusual intelligence, and skillful workers at tasks that are as demanding as any.

Messrs. Irwin I. Boris, Alan Brown, Kenneth Deitch, Alan Lefkowitz,

Julius B. Levine, Robert Repetto, all students at Harvard University, served as research assistants, as did Miss Elizabeth Niebuhr of Radcliffe College and Mrs. Joan Eckstein and Mrs. Eliot C. Nolen. Roderic C. Hodgins gave me editorial help in an early stage of the manuscript. I have had much important secretarial and executive help from the late Mrs. Anna Thorpe, Miss Lillian Buller, and Miss Mary Watson. Mrs. Elizabeth May typed the final version of the book with unusual skill. To all these I owe much.

Among my student research assistants, Richard N. Cooper (at present writing with the President's Economic Council), Paul A. David (at Stanford University), James R. Duffy (a practicing attorney), Reginald Green (at Yale), Saul Hymans (at the University of California at Berkeley), and Daniel Khazzoom (on the Harvard staff) deserve special mention for their rare intelligence and large contributions. Richard E. Sylla was responsible for the preparation of the Index. The contributions of Peter Kenen of Columbia and Edward Budd of Yale will be evident in a later volume.

My wife, Ruth B. Harris, helped as always, contributing directly to the improvement of the manuscript and also indirectly by shouldering many time-consuming chores for me. She also read the proofs.

I, as well as this volume, profited from my seminar in higher education, well attended by first-class college administrators, government officials, and college faculty, for which that unusual innovator in higher education, Philip Coombs, formerly of the Ford Foundation, now Assistant Secretary of State, was largely responsible. In helping to conduct that seminar and clarify my views, Dean (then) McGeorge Bundy, Dean Vernon Alden of the Harvard Graduate School of Business Administration, and Professor David Riesman were especially helpful.

My greatest debt is to Alvin Eurich of the Ford Foundation who supported this project and gave me complete freedom in its management. He also has greatly influenced the trend of higher education as a result of his persistent emphasis on the need of planning and exposure to new methods of teaching and organization.

Seymour E. Harris

CONTENTS

Contents

170 POINTS BY WAY OF SUMMARY AND EMPHASIS

COST TRENDS (Chapter 1)

1. *Rise of Expenditures.* Over a period of sixty to seventy years, educational and general expeditures for higher education have risen much more than gross national product, the best measure of the size of our economy.

2. *Expenditures Corrected for Prices.* Since the price of higher education has risen much more than general prices, the gains of education vis-à-vis GNP are not so great as they at first seem.

3. *The Lag of Unit Expenditures.* But the rise of expenditures per student has not nearly matched that of per capita income. Hence the standards of higher education have not risen *pari passu* with those of the economy.

4. *Gains a Maximum without Inflation.* On a per student basis the largest gains seem to come in periods of growth, without inflation—e.g., in the 1920s.

5. *Why Costs per Student Rise.* Continued rises in per unit costs in stable dollars over this period of sixty to seventy years—despite the trend toward low-cost education and the increased size of the unit, a factor tending to reduce costs—may surprise many. Among the explanations are the rising standards in the economy which spill over to higher education through competition for goods and services, the difficulties confronting higher education in matching productivity gains in the economy, the rising proportion of students in the upper two years and graduate work, and the change in the product—e.g., the use of expensive equipment, provision of health, social activities, research.

6. *Recent Gains in Expenditures and Needs in the 1960s.* We need rises of 140 to 150 per cent in expenditures in the 1960s. At the rate of rise (in stable dollars) from 1950 to 1958, it will take twelve (not ten) years to achieve our objectives.

THE 1970 BUDGET (Chapter 2)

7. *How Much?* Operating expenses in 1960 dollars should require $9 to 10 billion as compared with around $4 billion in 1960. Rise of enrollment, increased pay levels, and matching the rise in the standards of the economy are especially relevant.

8. *Where Will the Money Come From?* I suggest a large absolute increase from all sources, but especially from government and tuition, and a

large relative rise in tuition. This projection is based largely on the most likely sources of income.

9.   *Cutting Down Substantially the Share of Tuition below the Proposals in the Budget.* This is possible if strong pressures are put on government and private donors. In the country the ideology of many favors this approach.

10.   *Can We Achieve a Goal of $9 to $10 Billion by 1970?* The rise in stable dollars per resident student need be only a little more than one-half that achieved from 1940 to 1958, and general and educational income (total) need rise only 7.75 per cent per year in these years compared to 6.75 per cent from 1940 to 1958.

11.   *Is Our Proposed Budget Inflated?* Once allowance is made for the trend toward low-cost curricula, for movement from high-price to low-price IHL,* increased numbers of part-time students, and possible economies, the budget can be cut or standards improved further.

A STATISTICAL SURVEY OF SPECIAL CATEGORIES OF IHL (Chapter 3)

12.   *Relative Losses of High-quality IHL.* A survey from 1928 to 1956 reveals large *relative* losses for the Ivy IHL, other *outstanding* private universities, women's colleges, and liberal arts colleges. The Ivy League, however, continues to gain in endowment and especially endowment per student. Large urban and Catholic IHL reveal a serious deterioration in the proportion of high-ranking faculty.

THE TUITION PROBLEMS (Chapter 4)

13.   *Tuition Rates Depend in Part on Investments of Society in Higher Education.* Large incomes of graduates relative to investment in higher education point to underinvestment. Whether tuition rises 40 per cent by 1970 (little more than per capita income) or 100 to 200 per cent will depend on the success in obtaining additional resources from public and private contributions.

14.   *Rising Demand and Pricing.* College administrators face three alternatives: (*a*) match higher demand with *higher prices*—a likely outcome when financial needs are great and excess capacity low, but unfortunate in the resulting change of student body; (*b*) accept gains in *improved quality* of students—available to IHL with adequate financial resources and little excess capacity; (*c*) accept *larger numbers* at roughly unchanged quality—especially when excess capacity prevails.

15.   *Dominant Sellers Do Not Determine Prices*—suggested by similarity of ratio of tuition in private IHL to public IHL on West Coast and in Northeast despite large differences in proportion of public enrollment.

16.   *Tuition and Costs.* Tuition should not be based on costs. But variations in charges to some extent reflect costs—e.g., medicine, and where public and private gifts are not available. One curriculum costs more than fifty times that of another in one university; but charges vary little.

17.   *Tuition and Social and Private Gains.* Social gains point to low tuition; private, to high. Variations in tuition in different curricula reflect varying importance of social and private gains.

* IHL = *Institutions of Higher Learning*

TUITION AND COSTS OF IHL (Chapter 5)

18.   *Rise of Tuition.* On the basis of tuition income per student, corrected for rise in scholarship aid, tuition rose only by $100 from 1930 to 1956. In a period when prices rose almost 100 per cent and per capita income (the best test of capacity to pay) 136 per cent, tuition rose only 56 per cent. College instruction became a bargain item. Subsidies per student rose by $400 exclusive of capital costs.

19.   *Public versus Private Tuition.* Despite somewhat larger rises for the former in recent years, the 4 to 1 ratio of private to public fees has not materially changed in the last generation.

20.   *Tuition and Joint Costs.* Charging costs, even if desired, are not easily achieved, in part because of the difficulties of accounting. But at any rate, IHL, unlike business, do not systematically increase charges equal to additional costs. The graduate students in arts and science may cost three times as much (marginal) as undergraduates, but their tuition will be equal to, or less than, that for undergraduates.

21.   *Tuition and Enrollment.* To estimate the financial results of rising enrollment one has to consider the rise of costs per student (marginal) in relation to the increased tuition. On one estimate, where tuition is about two-thirds of costs, a rise of enrollment is likely to pay. But net results vary in the short run over the long run. The crucial issue is what costs rise and how fast. The public IHL with low tuition find rising enrollment especially costly. Rising enrollment is more costly than it otherwise would be because of *declining* yield of endowment per student with rising enrollment.

22.   *The "Rigged" Market.* Where IHL are homogeneous, tuition rises tend to be similar.

23.   *Tuition and Size of IHL.* Tuition tends to be higher for large than for small IHL. One reason is that the smaller IHL are *generally* of lesser quality. It would be expected that costs, and hence tuition, would be less for large than for smaller IHL.

A SPECIAL STUDY OF TUITION CHARGES (Chapter 6) (Based on 152 returns of S. E. H. questionnaire)

24.   *Trends of Tuition, 1939 to 1959.* Some cyclic factors; lag behind GNP by one year.

25.   *Endowment per Student and Tuition (85 IHL).* Generally higher endowment, higher tuition.

26.   *Ratio of Number of Independent to Public IHL.* Tuition tends to be higher where number of private IHL is larger relative to public. But note here personal income tends to be higher where private IHL are numerous also, and large numbers of prestige IHL are located where demand is strong.

27.   *IHL with Religious Affiliation.* Clearly tuition tends to be low for these IHL. The explanation is partly the low-income families involved, declining demand for the product, and dependence on current gifts and cartellike behavior that preclude increases in tuition.

THE PRICING OF COLLEGE SERVICES (Chapter 7)

28.   *Competition Is a Factor.* Competitors (e.g., Williams, Swarthmore, and Amherst) must not get too far out of line.

29.   *Competition of Public IHL Concerns Many Private IHL.* Though the Northeast had nine to ten times as many resident students relatively in private as in public IHL as the West, relative tuitions were almost identical. But competition in numbers (capacity) and in quality of public IHL was greater in the West.

30.   *Social Values Influence Relative Tuition Rates.* For example, in public IHL tuition in other independent *professional* schools was 3 times as high as in teachers' colleges; and in private, 2½ times that for theological students.

31.   *Product Differentiation.* Students tend to pay more where they estimate the value of the product as high. But the product is not easily measured. Inputs vary and outputs are subject only to crude measures.

32.   *Limits on Charges.* Excessive weight to social values may mean IHL *A* charges $200 for liberal arts and $1,000 for a business course; but IHL *B* may then charge $500 for business and attract students from *A*. Costs also have to be covered from *all* sources, though limitation of student resources restricts cost pricing. In public health at Harvard costs (inclusive of research) are $13,540; in law, $1,720. But tuition covers only 7 per cent of the former and 66 per cent of the latter.

THE LEVEL OF TUITION RATES (Chapter 8)

33.   *Ideology.* Both public and private IHL have had a long tradition against high tuition rates. Concern for the poor boy or girl, fear of depressing standards (through appeal to the affluent with rising fees), and instability of tuition income contributed to the espousal of low tuition.

34.   *Trend Is Upwards.* Both in dollars and in relation to IHL income, tuition tends to rise, though not in relation to capacity to pay. On the one hand the public IHL tend to seek for low fees, and the taxpayers for high.

35.   *The Ultimate Outcome.* This will depend in part on the resources of each state, competing demands of other services, traditions of public higher education, and the ideological struggle between taxpayers and those seeking greater public service.

36.   *Discriminatory Pricing.* Much can be said for charges based on capacity to pay and ability. But an adequate program on these lines is thwarted by competition among IHL. The IHL that charges full costs, say, for 25 per cent of its students will lose many of its students to others or will depress standards. High tuition financed by loan financing is a possible way out.

37.   *The Resources Are There for Low Tuition.* Two per cent of the rise of GNP in the 1960s would pay the entire tuition bill. The issue is: how will the additional $200 to $300 billion of GNP be used?

HIGHER TUITION AND ABILITY TO PAY (Chapter 9)

38.   *Trends.* Tuition rises more than capacity to pay since the Civil War, but less since before World War II.

39.   *Mitigation of Rising Tuition.* In the late 1950s a doubling of tuition would mean a rise of all costs of 20 per cent, inclusive of income forgone, by 10 per cent. Other costs rise less than tuition; but in so far as they also rise, the increase in costs will be more than 20 and 10 per cent respectively.

40.   *The Peculiar Market.* As price (tuition) steadily rises, purchases increase: rising population, increasing incomes, changing attitudes toward higher education, and improvement in product are relevant.

41.   *Discretion in the Product Purchased.* By choosing among types of IHL, location, types of curriculum, the student can offset to some extent the rise in the price of product.

42.   *Tuition and Aid.* Rising aid tends to offset increased tuition.

THE CASE FOR HIGHER TUITION (Chapter 10)

43.   *Shortage of Resources.* This is one of the strongest arguments for higher tuition.

44.   *Equity.* The student gains, and hence he should pay a substantial part of total costs. My estimate is that the lifetime differential for a *college graduate of 1960* should be about $200,000—this is subject to some reservations. A precise valuation of social versus private gains is not possible.

45.   *Improved Financing.* Long-term credit financing, even over as much as forty years, would help greatly. The burden of financing is reduced as per capita incomes steadily rise. But interest is a burden. Nevertheless, 1 to 2 per cent of lifetime income could finance loans of $1,000 per year. But prefinancing at twenty years (4 per cent interest) would cost only $155 a year as against $425 for postfinancing with a five-year moratorium. With prefinancing, interest works for, not against.

46.   *The Views of Economists* (Returns of 220 questionnaires from outstanding economists). They agree that total effects on enrollment of a 100 per cent rise of tuition by 1970 would be small. Net effects would depend on growth of per capita income and aid. But the average student would come from higher-income families; substantial numbers at the margin economically would be excluded; the trend would be toward public IHL, toward IHL located near home, against Negroes, women, and nonresident students in state IHL, and against IHL in poor regions. The private IHL would tend to have a bimodal distribution: very rich and very bright. The second-rate private IHL would be destroyed according to some and helped in the views of others.

SCHOLARSHIPS: PRELIMINARY CONSIDERATIONS (Chapter 11)

47.   *Attitudes of Public versus Private IHL.* Private IHL favor scholarships, in part because scholarships facilitate increases of tuition and hence increase of revenue; public IHL generally oppose them, because scholarships increase costs and reduce competitive advantage of public IHL in attracting able students.

SCHOLARSHIPS AND CHOICE OF COLLEGE (Chapter 12)

48.   *Choice of College by Best Students.* In one year private IHL attracted eight times as many National Merit Scholars relative to enrollment as

public IHL. Twice as many of these scholars, relative to region of origin, went to Northeastern IHL as to Southern IHL.

49.   *Scholarships Related to Tuition and Migration?* Under the original GI Bill, the student could choose highest-priced IHL without additional costs to himself. Hence migration to prestige IHL and regions, with losses of talent by the South and West. Later legislation put the burden of higher costs on the student, and also increasingly the choice of student on the IHL—with reduced pressures to migrate.

50.   *Allocation by States Rather than on a National Basis.* The National Merit now allocates by states. Hence in one year many New York high school students were excluded even though test scores exceeded those of any winner in some other states.

MORE VIEWS ON SCHOLARSHIPS (Chapter 13)

51.   *Failure to Push Federal Scholarships.* Fear of rising costs, of loss of able students by the West and South, and of waste in manner of allocating and amounts contributed to the failure of a program in 1958.

HOW MUCH FOR SCHOLARSHIPS? (Chapter 14)

52.   *Subsidies of Low Tuition versus Scholarships.* The former amounts to about $3 billion as against $100 to 150 million available for scholarships. But the latter is of great importance in saving the able but impecunious and making possible higher tuition incomes.

53.   *How Much Is Needed?* I estimate approximately $400 million per year now and $1 billion by 1970. Other estimates put the current figure at from $600 million to $2,500 million. I estimate that a system like the British (scholarships to 75 per cent to cover all costs and based on need) would cost $2.5 billion yearly here. But note that cost of higher education is much greater vis-à-vis personal income in Britain than here and the average standard of living much lower. (An ideal arrangement would be to collect $2 billion in addition annually in tuition out of higher rates by 1970 and distribute the $2 billion on the basis of need and ability.)

54.   *The Havighurst Study.* Of the upper quarter of intellectual ability, 75 per cent of those in the highest one-third in economic status graduate from college; of the second third, 28 per cent; of the third, 18 per cent.

WASTE OF SCHOLARSHIP FUNDS AND THEIR COST TO IHL (Chapter 15)

55.   *Wastes.* Relevant are restriction of scholarships to particular name, region, occupation of father; excessive emphasis on subject to be studied; payments in excess of need; stipends too low to be effective; unacceptable objectives as guides in choice; unreliability of tests (difficulty of measuring motivation, emphasis on 100-yard dash, not marathon, failure to exclude environmental factors).

DISTRIBUTION OF SCHOLARSHIPS AND FELLOWSHIPS (Chapter 16)

56.   *Competition of Public and Private.* A study for eight states shows that by providing relatively large stipends and many more scholarships relative

to enrollments, the major private universities in a state offset the tuition advantage of the major public university.

57.   *Regional Distribution.* The Northeast is especially favored in its proportion of scholarships and fellowship money. And fellowships are heavily concentrated in a dozen states and IHL.

58.   *Fellowships by Fields.* Tend to be large and numerous especially in physical sciences, though the difference is explained in part by the larger number of Ph.D. candidates in these fields.

59.   *Scholarships in Relation to Quality.* The more talented students seem to get more of the scholarship money, but the differences in quality are not as great as might be expected, and the scholarship holders of IHL in the College Scholarship Service (largely leading IHL in the Northeast) show much lower aptitude scores than the National Merit winners.

60.   *Scholarship and Residence.* Stipends do not vary as much as might be expected for commuters as against resident students.

61.   *Scholarships and Tuition.* Scholarships tend to rise more than tuition, and stipends per student, despite the large rise of number of scholarships, generally rise more than tuition per student (not necessarily more than total costs per student).

62.   *Rise of Scholarships and Tuition Income.* Increased scholarship money is a condition for large rises in tuition income. From 1940 to 1961 tuition increased by $1,050 million and scholarships by $125 million, a high multiplier for tuition.

APPENDIX: SCHOLARSHIP FUNDS

63.   *Over Long Periods.* Scholarship money does not seem to have risen as much as total budgets of IHL, but in the last generation the rise has exceeded that of total budgets.

64.   *Pressure on General Funds.* In recent years scholarships have come increasingly from general funds of IHL, though outside contributions also are of increasing importance.

65.   *An Analysis of Ivy, Other Universities, Liberal Arts, Women's Catholic and Urban Colleges.* The last two have especially gained relatively since 1940. But the Ivy and other outstanding universities, women's colleges, and liberal arts colleges on the average still have somewhat higher stipends and about three times as many (relatively) helped as the Catholic and urban IHL.

LOANS: VIEWS OF ECONOMISTS (Chapter 17)

66.   *Various Proposals.* Loans by private interests, with repayments to be related to excess income associated with higher education; loans by government to correct underinvestment in higher education; greater recourse to loans to increase the reservoir from which students are drawn for occupations where rewards greatly exceed costs—these are among the proposals.

67.   *Pros and Cons.* Greater use of government loans and guarantees, repayments related to varying income and responsibilities; rates of interest below market—these would help. The student, through loans, should also have an opportunity to second-guess the scholarship boards, and there should be

greater publicity and improved administration for loan programs. Against loan programs: some objected because they enable public and parents to shirk responsibilities, and others because of the increased pressures for inflation with a rising debtor class.

STUDENT LOANS: BROAD ISSUES (Chapter 18)

68.   *Growth:* In the past student loans were relatively unimportant, but their use is increasing, especially because of influence of the Federal program.

69.   *Relation to Resources.* Loans make possible larger claims on the resources of the nation—e.g., cf. consumer credit.

70.   *Relation to Scholarships and Tuition.* Loans make for more productive use of scholarships and make possible higher tuition without adverse effects on structure of student body.

LOANS: HISTORY AND PROPOSALS (Chapter 19)

71.   *Breakdown by Types of IHL.* There have been great variations in percentage of resources for loans.

72.   *Blocks.* Poor administration, harsh terms, student preference for scholarships all keep down the use of loans.

73.   *Proliferation.* In recent years there have been many advances, especially the Federal program.

EXPANSION OF LOANS (Chapter 20)

74.   *Possibilities.* At Harvard loans rose from 2 per cent of scholarship money to 28 per cent in ten years.

75.   *Federal Guarantee.* This would help.

76.   *Federal Loan Program an Economical Approach.* A ceiling of $1,000 per year, a ten-year loan, and a 2 per cent rate would cost the Treasury $65; for twenty years, $115. Costs would be 6½ and 11½ per cent of a $1,000 scholarship.

COMPETITIVE ASPECTS OF STUDENT AID (Chapter 21)

77.   *Eleven Prestige Private and Four Outstanding Public IHL.* The 11 generally provide more scholarships, higher stipends, more employment and loans, thus reducing competitive advantages of the public IHL. In graduate aid, however, public do much better.

78.   *Four Prestige Private IHL.* Large variations in per student scholarship and loans.

A PROGRAM FOR STUDENT CREDIT (Chapter 22)

79.   *A Massive Loan Program.* One thousand dollars per year for a period as long as forty years at low rates of interest.

80.   *Advantages.* To the student: distributes costs over a long period—could even be cut to 1 per cent of lifetime income. Exploits the growth process —as *average* per capita income over period of loan—is at least twice that at time of incurring debt.

To IHL: contributes funds that make possible an adequate tuition policy—should alternative resources not be made available.

To society: makes possible a larger command of resources.

81.   *Prefinancing.* Costs less, since savings are compounded: interest contributes rather than costs as in postfinancing. But prefinancing is not likely to play a large part.

FEDERAL AID TO HIGHER EDUCATION (Chapter 23)

82.   *How Much?* More could be made available out of growth, though much depends on competing demands. On my scale of priorities an increase of genuine aid (not payment for services) should be a minimum of $1 billion by 1965 and substantially more by 1970.

83.   *Tax Exemption.* This constitutes about $350 million yearly to IHL, and wider use of fringe benefits would increase the take.

84.   *Manner of Aid.* In general, loans are least costly; construction aid is greatly needed; scholarships on a large scale would help.

85.   *Tax Concessions.* Tax credits, larger exemptions, and equalization of tax burden of contributors, irrespective of income, have been proposed. I would support these in that order. Giving a low-income contributor as large a tax offset as the highest-bracket donor (say 90 cents on the dollar instead of 20 cents) would be wasteful in that the government would needlessly lose revenue and the gains to the taxpayer would not result in substantial increases of gifts. Generally all these tax concessions are wasteful, since they are given whether need is present or not.

86.   *Recovery of Cost.* In research outlays and ROTC, IHL are treated unfairly. Why should a private recipient of a research grant be allowed to write off a building in ten years and an IHL be allowed write-offs on a fifty-year basis?

87.   *Conflicts of Views.* The difference of approach between public and private IHL on the *kind* of aid and on the availability of aid increases the difficulty of obtaining adequate Federal aid.

STATE EXPENDITURES ON HIGHER EDUCATION (Chapter 24)

88.   *Trends.* The trend is upward, relative to all state expenditures, in the twentieth century except in the interwar period. Increasing competition of highways and social security is, however, relevant. Rising priority of higher education is also important.

89.   *Regressivity of State and Local Tax Revenues.* In a recent year 83 per cent of revenues of Federal government were direct taxes; for state and local government, only 17 per cent. Hence transfers from poor (taxpayers) to relatively affluent students at IHL.

90.   *Fiscal Trends, Federal versus State and Local Government.* Increasing *relative* expenditures and debt of state and local governments are factors tending to increase support of Federal aid.

91.   *Trends in State Outlays and Potential State Contribution.* At the 1950-to-1959 rate of increase, state expenditures on higher education would rise by more than $4 billion by 1970; and allowing for price increase from 1950 to 1959, the gain for the 1960s would be $2.8 billion in stable dollars, a substantially larger increase than I suggested in my budget.

92.   *Ten High and Ten Low Per Capita Income States.* Low-income states have a much larger percentage of population in the college-age group; state outlays relative to personal income are more than 50 per cent greater than for rich states; per cent of enrollment in college-age population only half as great; educational expenditures per member of college-age population, about 40 per cent as high as for rich states; and educational expenditures per resident student about 80 per cent as high. The advantage of the rich states is even greater for private IHL. Thus private enrollment as per cent of college-age population is three times as great relatively in the rich states.

93.   *Recent Trends in Expenditures by Economic Status.* Percentage of income spent by states on higher education rose much more for poor states from 1950 to 1957.

94.   *Largest and Smallest States by Population.* The smallest states spent 2½ times as much in relation to personal income for state IHL as the largest states. This is partly due to lack of tradition for public higher education in some heavily populated states and partly because of high unit costs in lightly populated states.

SOME ASPECTS OF DIFFERENTIALS IN HIGHER EDUCATION AMONG STATES (Chapter 25)

95.   *Inclusion of Organized Research in Costs of Higher Education.* It is not clear that they should be excluded, though I have done so in this chapter. Exclusion modifies rankings greatly for a number of states (e.g., California).

96.   *Difference Made by Inclusion of Local Government Expenditures on Higher Education.* Rankings of several states substantially are affected by inclusion (e.g., California, New York).

97.   *Difference Often Made by Exclusion from State Budgets of Such Items as Student Fees, Endowment Income.* Frequently only state appropriations, not expenditures of public IHL, are given.

98.   *Twelve Poor and Twelve Rich States.* A study of these states for 1957 confirms the study for 1950. In the rich states much less is spent vis-à-vis personal income, but more per member of college-age population; but though ranking low on college-age population, these states rank very high on expenditures per enrollee.

99.   *Ranking Expenditures of States on IHL as Percentage of Personal Income, 1952–1958.* In states where territory is large, population sparse, per capita income below average, and tradition of higher education strong, the expenditures vis-à-vis personal income are very high. Of the top 10 states only Minnesota does not meet this test. The 40th to 48th rankings belong primarily to high-income states with heavy concentrations of population.

100.   *Rank per Capita Income and State Taxes per Capita.* Note the consistent association of 12 states in 1957 with highest per capita income with high state taxes per capita. Six also were among highest 12 in state taxes per capita.

101.   *States with Highest and Lowest Expenditures per Member of College Age and per Enrollee in Public IHL.* Five Southern states and five from the Northeast contribute the lowest amounts. Lack of resources in the South and an absence of tradition for higher education in the Northeast are relevant.

Yet five Southern states spent 3.42 per cent of state and local revenue, and five Northeastern states only 1.65 per cent. But per enrollee the latter perform much better than the five Southern states—for the Northeast has relatively few students in public IHL.

HIGHER EDUCATION: BURDEN, CAPACITY TO FINANCE, EFFORT, AND ACHIEVEMENTS, STATE BY STATE (Chapter 26)

102.   *The Meaning of the Comparisons.* Ranking states on the basis of at least 12 variables that measure burdens, capacity, effort, and achievements requires considerable caution. In particular such questions as the following arise: What are the relevant expenditures for higher education; what items are excluded inappropriately from state figures? Is it correct to exclude local expenditures and taxes? What is the relevance of net migrations in or out? How are adjustments made for part-time students and high-cost students, e.g., medical?

The resultant tables should be read with these reservations in mind. If they are, I believe the tables based on my calculations, with the help of 150 university presidents, higher-education boards, and state budget officers, will throw some light on the achievements or lack of them for the 48 states.

DIFFERENCES AMONG STATES: DETAILS FOR 48 STATES (Chapter 27)

103.   *Factors Determining Rankings in Burden, Capacity, Effort, and Achievements.* Many are relevant. Thus burdens are measured by the relation of college-age population and total population and unit costs of higher education in relation to per capita income. Since unit costs are tied largely to national forces, and per capita income to a substantial degree to local factors, burdens tend to be high in poor states (e.g., the South) and low elsewhere. Efforts are also high in low-income states. But much depends on tax structure, distribution of state and local taxes, growth of economy, and allocation of funds among education, higher-education, and other services. Effort in turn depends on capacity—e.g., per capita income and tax receipts in relation to college-age population. Achievements depend on burdens, capacity, and effort. The best measures of achievement are given by the ratio of college-age population at IHL, the proportion at public IHL, and the expenditures per student. (Variations in the last are offset to some extent by differences in costs.) Numerous factors influence the net results: where states are small and enrollment therefore small, both taxes per capita and unit costs in higher education tend to be high. (Achievement is less than it seems to be.) Where states are large and enrollments—especially in lower divisions—high, unit costs are low (e.g., California). The underachievement is overdone. To measure the achievements accurately, we should allow for expenditures not related to instruction, correct for part-time and for high- and low-cost enrollments(e.g., medical versus junior college), items excluded from state budgets, deduct for net in-migration (subsidizing others) and add for net out-migration (exploiting others).

MANAGEMENT: VIEWS AND HISTORY (Chapter 28)

104.   *Trends.* Investments in equities became important only after 1830s; in bonds, after the Civil War; there was slow response of investment policies to inflation.

THE CASE FOR COMMON STOCKS (Chapter 29)

105. *Why Larger Returns from Common Stocks?* Corporations are run for stockholders; equities rise in value in response to inflation and growth.

106. *Capital Gains Not Inviolate.* I argue here that the advantage of common stocks rests partly on capital gains; and to make possible an appropriate investment policy, the treasurer should be allowed to spend capital gains.

107. *Growth Stocks and the Present Generation.* Large investment in growth stocks cuts current income and penalizes the current generation of students and faculty unless income distributed exceeds that on nongrowth (this actually happened in 1950s for some IHL) and unless IHL can sell stocks and spend the gains.

108. *Investment in Equities and Inflation.* Since IHL have to pay higher prices for goods and services as inflation proceeds, they need equities to protect themselves against rising prices. The record shows that they have done reasonably well in thus protecting themselves since 1940, though the movement into equities might have been more rapid.

FORMULA INVESTMENT POLICIES (Chapter 30)

109. *Failure of Formulas.* An attempt to substitute rigid rules for judgment had to fail, especially since the theory is based largely on domination of cyclic movements and leaves out of account inflationary and growth trends.

HOW TO MANAGE ENDOWMENT (Chapter 31)

110. *Results Vary with Type of Management.* The worst results are shown where responsibility lies with a subcommittee of the board.

111. *A Central Organization.* For the small IHL a central management board might well be the most economical and most profitable approach, though some legal objections have been raised.

THE EFFECTIVE USE OF ENDOWMENT FUNDS (Chapter 32)

112. *The Case for Entry of New Funds in Relation to Book Value in Funds of Rising Values.* In this way current gifts, which more nearly reflect current educational needs, receive a larger part of income than if entered in relation to market values.

113. *Bargain Professorships?* Where need is great and the market not likely to be spoiled, a university may accept (say) $250,000 rather than $500,000. But universities should also consider that a generation from now costs may be twice as high and hence involve IHL in large commitments.

THE DECLINE OF ENDOWMENT (Chapter 33)

114. *What Explains the Decline?* Inflation, growth of economy, increased student body, deficient management, and large rise of current gifts and other sources of income. In particular, under financial stress, there is a tendency to rely on gifts which meet *current* problems more adequately.

115. *Wisdom of Reliance on Endowments.* From Adam Smith on, many have held that recourse to endowments reduces response to needs of society

and impairs motivation. In their view it is better to seek help periodically. But endowment yields continuity and greater freedom from unwanted pressures.

CORPORATE AND OTHER BUSINESS GIFTS (Chapter 34)

116. *Growth and Academic Problems.* As these gifts become more important, the IHL have increasingly to be on guard against attachment of unacceptable conditions.

HIGHER EDUCATION'S SHARE IN THE PHILANTHROPIC DOLLAR (Chapter 35)

117. *The Trend Downward.* Other claims have tended to become relatively stronger, but in the 1950s the trend seems to have turned in favor of IHL.

TRENDS OF ENDOWMENTS AND GIFTS (Chapter 36)

118. *Variations in Trends.* Largest gain of endowment has been in Ivy League colleges over twenty-eight years (345 per cent); the smallest, Catholic (68 per cent).

119. *Relation of Gifts to Enrollment.* Major private universities receive almost twenty times as much as urban universities. Much depends on the ratio of students (cost factor) to alumni (potential gift factor).

120. *Gift Structure.* Sources of gifts vary greatly by type of IHL, and gifts vary greatly vis-à-vis budgets of IHL—e.g., instruction gifts equaled 40 per cent of its relative position in the budget; gifts for student aid equaled 3½ times its importance in the budget.

TECHNIQUES FOR RAISING MONEY (Chapter 37)

121. *Potentialities of the Alumni Drive.* These are suggested by the rise of proportion of college-age population and increased effectiveness of drives. By 1970 alumni drives might yield $700 million per year—with each alumnus giving but ⅛ of 1 per cent of income.

A SURVEY OF LEADING DONORS OF HIGHLY ENDOWED COLLEGES AND UNIVERSITIES (Chapter 38)

122. *The 456 Large Donors to American IHL.* Their records at college are much above average; they are predominantly graduates of their colleges; they attended graduate schools much more than all students; and they are predominantly businessmen.

THE STRUCTURE OF INVESTMENTS (Chapter 39)

123. *The Increased Interest in Equities.* This is explained in no small part by the rise of stock prices. Without changes in purchasing policies the ratio of equity investments greatly increases as stock prices rise.

RETURN ON INVESTMENTS (Chapter 40)

124. *The Trend Is Down.* Since the 1920s the return on investments has tended to decline. But these results are subject to reservations: changing book values, capital gains, incomparability of results over years.

125.   *Differences among IHL.* Unorthodox investing, structure of investments, size of IHL, impairment of freedom to operate, quality of management
all affect the results.

SOME DETAILS ON HISTORY (Chapter 41)

126.   *For Seven IHL, Investment Policies and Results Vary.* Much depends on holdings of equities in 1929, interest in growth stocks, penchant for
industrials.

THE PROBLEM OF COSTS (Chapter 42)

127.   *Neglect of Cost Studies.* IHL tend to underexploit cost studies, in
part because pricing is not related to costs as in profit organizations. But cost
studies serve many useful ends—e.g., they justify budgetary demands, explain
to students the size of subsidies, give indications of efficiency of operations,
and set prices where cost considerations are dominant.

128.   *Dangers of Cost Studies.* Comparisons, especially among IHL, are
fraught with danger. High unit costs do not necessarily mean waste; more likely
they may suggest high-quality education.

129.   *Allocation of Costs.* Where the product is joint, the difficulties are
great. But allocations, especially of overhead, are useful, and the manner is a
matter of judgment.

130.   *Costs of Old and New Programs.* There is a tendency to consider
high costs of new programs but to neglect costs of old programs.

CASE STUDIES ON COSTS (Chapter 43)

131.   *Decisive Factors.* Size of classes, teaching load, relative numbers
in lower, higher, and graduate divisions, level of salaries and structure of pay,
and size of the unit are among the important factors. Note lower-division,
upper-division, and graduate costs per unit are roughly 1:2:6.

132.   *Warning!* "Cost accounting can disclose which courses, departments,
or divisions are high cost per student hour, but cost accounting cannot decide
whether the courses should be offered or abandoned."

ECONOMIES THROUGH THE CURRICULUM AND INSTRUCTIONAL METHODS (Chapter 44)

133.   *Small Class versus Large Class.* Innumerable controlled experiments,
inclusive of some that test beyond the usual objective tests, reveal either that
results are equal in large and small classes or that the large class yields better
results. Indeed, some of the gains of small classes may escape measurement.

134.   *Student-Teacher Ratios.* (*STR*) The trend *in recent years* is upward
through larger classes, more independent work, elimination of unnecessary
classes, less formal requirements. But on many points teachers still oppose the
rise of STR.

135.   *Proliferation of Courses.* In fifty years, a study by the author reveals
a rise of graduate courses several times as great as for undergraduate, two
times as many graduate courses as undergraduate vis-à-vis enrollment currently,
and a downward long-term trend of STR.

136. *Economies in the Classroom.* Aside from course control and size of class, other aids are more independent work, use of machines, concentration of the able and experienced faculty on the larger tasks (inclusive of larger enrollments per course). The alternative, with limited talent available, is a great deterioration of teaching standards.

137. *The Problem of Numbers.* An increase of STR, as suggested above, will help. But the problem must be related to other persistent educational problems: equality of opportunity, effective motivation for students, a balance between independent work and guidance, fitting the subject to the learner by a precise analysis of the learning process, avoidance of excessive compartmentalization of education, modification of the current courses and credit system, and greater recourse to achievement tests.

SOME GENERAL ASPECTS OF ECONOMIES (Chapter 45)

138. *Rising Unit Costs.* Explained by increasing *real* pay, additional services, higher costs of instructional equipment and plant, declining work loads, proliferation of courses, inability to match the rising productivity of profit-making employments and yet having to face the competition of business in rising levels of pay and prices for services and materials. The opposition of faculty to new methods of teaching, the fear of technological unemployment, and the absence of an employer-employee relationship in IHL are also relevant.

THE BROADER ISSUES (Chapter 46)

139. *Inefficiencies and Public Relations.* Administrators fear exposure of wastes as a factor likely to cut new funds. But the quest for truth applies here as elsewhere.

140. *Wastes.* Failure to match students with appropriate college; the inadequate product for 45 per cent with IQs of less than 110 seeking college, according to one sample; excessive attrition in college, especially of the able; the tendency to neglect past costs and concentrate on use of new resources; the failure to tie budgets and admissions to the objectives of the IHL; the failure to measure the product of IHL and also to identify talent; the tendency to give the same education to the talented and nontalented; the failure of trustees to study the budgetary implications of policy in the current and later years— these are among the problems relevant in a study of productivity of IHL.

DETAILS ON ECONOMIES (Chapter 47)

141. *Location and Duplication of IHL.* A study of location reveals much waste resulting from political and local pressures. We need more studies on the manner of reconciling the goals of minimum excess capacity and minimum costs of travel and living away from home by students. Larger contributions by local taxpayers to public IHL might discourage excessive duplication, i.e., too many units. Consider the excessive pressures of state colleges to introduce Ph.D. programs in many states.

THE OPTIMUM SIZE OF THE INSTITUTION (Chapter 48)

142.   *Educational and Economic Issues.* The IHL with less than 1,000 students is generally to be justified on presumed educational gains, not on economies of operation. But a very small IHL suffers from inadequate curriculum as well as high unit costs.

143.   *Optimum Size.* An IHL that is too large can experience rising costs as well as educational liabilities. Numerous studies are available on optimum size of different types of IHL.

144.   *Expansion Guides.* Estimate the rise of costs and that of revenue with proposed increases of enrollment. Where housing is required, and especially at high standards, this is a deterrent to expansion.

PLANNING (Chapter 49)

145.   *And Excessive Duplication of Public IHL.* Here the explanation of waste is in part the unpopularity or weakness of central coordinating boards. Large discretion to boards of individual IHL also means variations in standards (e.g., California) and curriculum.

146.   *Deficiencies of Planning.* Many IHL operate on an *ad hoc* basis and fail to plan for enrollment, provision of necessary faculty, equipment and buildings, finance, and improving productivity. (This chapter contains the results of a questionnaire on enrollment planned by 161 IHL: by size, by income areas, by controls, and undergraduate and graduate students.)

COOPERATION AND COORDINATION (Chapter 50)

147.   *Fruits of Cooperation.* Sharing courses, curricula, faculty, buildings, and research projects is increasingly common. The fruits are especially large in the interregional compacts or in such constellations as the Claremont colleges where cooperation induces a reduction of unit costs for the relevant colleges and makes possible improved instruction.

PLANT LOCATION AND UTILIZATION (Chapter 51)

148.   *Proximity to IHL and Attendance.* Time and again it is shown that the proportion of college age at college varies with the proximity to a college. Thus in Michigan the proportion at college in counties with IHL was twice as great as in those with no IHL. But low economic status in the latter is also relevant.

149.   *Small Number of Recent New IHL, Notably in Liberal Arts Colleges.*

150.   *Inadequate Analysis of Markets for New Colleges and Schools.* My questionnaire reveals that only in about one-half of the instances were any serious attempts made to study the market.

151.   *Enrollment Goals of New IHL or New Schools.* Goals generally stressed educational, not economic issues. Respondents to questionnaire were often unaware of a relation of costs and size of student body.

152.   *Choice of Location.* Questionnaire shows most important was availability of students and site or buildings. Donors had little influence.

153.   *Professional Schools in Standard Metropolitan Districts in the United States.* In rich states professional schools tend to be concentrated in large metropolitan areas. Utilization is high in medical, lower in law and graduate schools. In low-income states, there are more dispersion and more excess capacity.

154.   *High Unit Costs.* For example, in graduate arts and science, much is to be said for concentration and subsidization of transportation and similar costs; in law and business, dispersion is justifiable.

155.   *New IHL.* Surprisingly small in postwar period. Growth, as in the economy, tends to be obtained through expansion of existing units. Nor is the number of new entries highly correlated with population trends and income. New England has the largest increase in new units.

156.   *Per Cent of State Enrollment in re Per Cent of State Population by Counties.* In general, a favorable index (greater than 1) falls to counties with large population centers—e.g., in Massachusetts Suffolk (Boston) this index is 2.7 and Essex (small), 0.2. But on a national basis, this pile-up not so clear— in part because many IHL (e.g., public) are in sparsely populated areas. But the 10 largest cities average 1.67 (only one with an index of less than 1).

157.   *Underutilization of Plant.* Study after study shows the need of longer periods of classroom use daily and annually, and also that studies of utilization are necessary. By 1970, savings as large as $1 billion a year are possible.

TELEVISION (Chapter 52)

158.   *The Gains.* Especially important is the more effective use of able and scarce faculty. Television will not solve the problems of shortage of resources, inadequate faculty, poor instruction, etc. But properly used it should help substantially.

FACULTY STATUS (Chapter 53)

159.   *The Decline of Economic Status.* Over a period of fifty years faculty pay has fallen relative to the levels in the economy and other professions. Since 1940 there has been an absolute and relative decline. In a recent period of seventeen years, had their pay kept up with the rise in the cost of living, they would have gained $6 to $7 billion.

160.   *Changes in Structure of Pay.* In periods of stress the pay of low ranks tends to rise vis-à-vis that of high ranks, and the range of pay tends to narrow excessively.

161.   *Trends in the Late 1950s.* These point to a doubling in less than eleven years for a picked sample of 188 IHL, but a larger universe points to twenty-three years.

162.   *Reservations on Pay Trends.* Work loads tend to fall; promotions to be accelerated; average age to decline; proportion of higher ranks to rise. All these point to the need of a somewhat smaller rise of pay than indicated by crude figures of average pay of each rank. (Average pay for all ranks would reflect variations in proportions at each rank).

163. *Why the Deterioration?* Inadequate resources; the greater pressures of nonacademic workers; the rising burden of capital plant; inefficiencies; the lack of organization of college faculty (cf. public school teachers)—these are among the explanations.

164. *How Much Should Salaries Rise?* They should rise sufficiently to assure the flow of talent required, both in numbers and quality. Numerous experts propose a 100 per cent rise in five to ten years. In ten years even a 100 per cent rise would leave faculty in a deteriorated position vis-à-vis 1940. When allowance is made for accelerated promotions, outside work, reduced work loads and preparation, and expansion of low-quality IHL, the rise might well be less than 100 per cent. Much will depend on resources available and increased productivity.

165. *Merit versus Scale Increases.* IHL tend to waste resources by depending too much on across-the-board increases in pay. Early and excessive tenure appointments may also be costly. In inflationary periods, across-the-board increases or at least rises in minimum are necessary. But limiting these increases results in greater use of merit rises.

166. *Outside Pay.* Inadequate income, need for outside relations for improved teaching and research, and competition among IHL account for increased recourse to outside activities. The average outside income is not large but should be a factor in deciding how much salaries should rise. Many abuses prevail.

167. *Pay and Economies.* More effective use of faculty through elimination of excessive courses, allocation of faculties on the basis of abilities (e.g., a research man for research), maintaining optimum size of college, etc., would facilitate higher pay. Advancing the retirement age increases costs of faculty, though with inadequate numbers this policy may be justifiable.

168. *Fringe Benefits.* These are of increasing significance, but many IHL neglect them even when they are costless to the IHL—e.g., group insurance. They benefit faculty because of tax gains and distribution of costs among large numbers and over time. They are often a means of putting part of costs on government.

169. *Annuity Programs.* These are generally inadequate because they do not allow for the fact that average incomes are likely to increase by 100 to 300 per cent in the forty years elapsing from entry to retirement.

170. *The Problem of Supply.* Here increased productivity, use of part-time faculty and women, rising economic status of faculty, improved marketing organization all will help.

PART ONE

INTRODUCTORY

Chapter 1

SOME HISTORY

SUMMARY

To the reader who is allergic to history and dull statistics, I offer this summary. I hope, however, that the reader will stay with this chapter, for the historical trends are suggestive not only of the problems of yesterday but also of those of today and tomorrow. These statistics carry us from 1889–90 to 1958 or 1960. I should warn the reader that the statistics before 1919 are not as reliable as those since 1919. But they are adequate to provide rough guides. The statistics offer a take-off for a study of unit costs in the latter part of this chapter.

Over a period of seventy years enrollment in colleges has increased to 22 times that of 1890, educational income per student to 8+ times, and all income of higher education to 175 times.

In successive ten-year periods beginning in 1869, the percentage rise of resident enrollment was 126 (1870s), 36 (1880s), 52 (1890s), 50 (1900s), 69 (1910s), 84 (1920s), 36 (1930s), 78 (1940s), and 28 (1950s). In several of these decades the rise of enrollment exceeds the 70 per cent conservatively anticipated for the 1960s (100 per cent from 1957 to 1970). But the largest rise in numbers for any ten years was 1.2 million in the 1940s. The expected gain in the 1960s is about 2.7 million.

Expenditures on higher education in general rose more than in the economy as measured by the gross national product (GNP); but once allowance is made for the greater rise in the price of educational services (suggested by the greater increase of tuition than of prices), then the gains of educational income vis-à-vis GNP are substantially reduced.

A more significant comparison is that of the income *per resident student* and GNP per capita, for the former rose only about one-half as much as the latter. Here the advantage lies with the economy; that is to say, the advance of higher education per student did not reflect fully the gains of the economy.

The major gains of education as measured by the relation of per resident income against per capita GNP were recorded in the 1920s and the 1950s. In these years also the real educational income (that is, corrected for prices) rose greatly.

The moral of this seems to be that colleges do best when the economy is growing substantially and prices are not rising greatly. In the 1940s, a decade of great growth, little gain was shown for colleges as measured by real income per resident student, the explanation being the large inflation and the war. As might be expected, in the years 1890–1920, the 1930s (depression), and the 1940s (inflation), the rise per resident student of educational income lagged behind that of per capita GNP.

Of special significance is the period 1950 to 1956. The rise of educational and general income in these six years was but 40 per cent, corrected for prices, a rate of rise not adequate to yield a needed gain of 150 per cent (stable prices) of educational and general income in ten to twelve years. (This was a period of no net change in enrollment.) Does this mean that our goal of 150 per cent gain in income in stable prices is hopeless? Not at all. In the two years 1954 to 1956, a period of rising enrollment, the increase of per resident student income vis-à-vis GNP per capita was more than adequate to yield the required funds if GNP increases as expected and if the trend of gains of educational and general income per student continues to 1970. The experience from 1953–54 to 1957–58 if continued for fourteen years would easily yield a rise of 150 per cent—educational income at stable prices. (See Table 1-3.)

One of the puzzling aspects of the historical statistics is that the cost per resident student has risen substantially more than the price level. In some respects this is unexpected because the average college today is much nearer an optimum size (minimum unit costs) than sixty to seventy or even thirty years ago, and the trend is disproportionately toward the low-cost curricula.

But in view of the rising standard of living of the nation, it would be expected that the colleges would reflect these gains, that is, in the rise of per resident educational and general income in stable dollars. That the colleges have not reflected these national gains fully may be explained by an unwillingness of the nation to support its colleges as much as other services and markets.

The fact that costs of higher education per unit rose more than prices, aside from the above considerations, is the result of the change in the product, the higher costs of buildings and equipment, the trend to costly graduate work, the increasing emphasis on research, extension, and related activities. Relevant also is the unavailability of many economies of technology and management that competitive enterprises exploit. (More on this later.)

TRENDS IN HIGHER EDUCATION AND THE ECONOMY[1]

Over the years enrollment in IHL has increased much faster than population. In fact, in ninety years the rate of increase in enrollment has been fifteen times as great as in population. Even since 1929, when the proportion of enrollment to population was 0.90 per cent, the rise has been striking. By 1959–60 the percentage had increased to 1.89. Table 1-1 gives the increases in population, enrollment, faculty, the percentage of women in the student body, the number of institutions, the number of students per institution, and student/faculty ratios for 1869–70, 1929–30, 1955–56, and 1959–60. At the outset I should warn the reader that for all kinds of reasons the trends can be held to be only roughly accurate, especially before 1900.

TABLE 1-1

Population, Numbers of Institutions of Higher Learning, Faculty, Enrollment, and Related Variables, 1869–70, 1929–30, 1955–56, and 1959–60

Year	Population (millions)	Resident enrollment (thousands)	Enrollment, per cent of population	Faculty (thousands)	Student-faculty ratio	No. of institutions	Students per institution	Women in residence, per cent
1869–70	40	52	0.13	5.55	9.4	563	98	21
1929–30	123	1,101	0.90	82.39	13.4	1,409	781	44
1955–56	168	2,661	1.58	301.60	8.8*	1,858	1,420	34
1959–60†	180	3,402	1.89	261.88	13.0			

* The figure is increased to 14 to 1 if assistants are eliminated and adjustments made for part-time teachers and students.

† 1960 enrollment figures from R. Walters, *Four Decades of U.S. Collegiate Enrollments Faculty,* from National Education Association, *Teacher Supply,* 1960–61, p. 52.

Source: See Table 1A-1.

Aside from the rise of population a few other items in this table should be noted. The increase in the number of institutions has been only from 563 in 1869–70 to 1858 in 1955–56, or just over 200 per cent. But with such a large expansion in the number of students, the student body per institution has increased from 98 in 1869–70 to 781 in 1929–30 to 1,420 in 1955–56. These figures are of great significance in understanding the unit costs of higher education. Obviously at an enrollment of 781 or 1,420 the cost per unit should be much smaller than at an enrollment of 98.

Another important ratio is that of students to faculty. This ratio seems to have fallen since 1929, a factor causing higher unit costs. But we cannot be sure of this, because the faculty consists of part-time and full-time members, as does the student body. If the ratio of part-time teachers rose more than that of part-time students, then the trend of the ratio of students to teachers would seem to have fallen less than it actually has. We do know that this ratio, on the basis of *full-time equivalents,* was 14 to 1 in 1955–56. There is some evidence of a rise in this ratio for the last few years.[2]

Table 1-2 also shows trends that may throw light on current problems. The proportion of educational and general income to GNP, the best measure of the output of the nation, has steadily risen from 0.23 per cent in 1889–90 to 0.51 in 1929–30 and to 0.70 in 1956–57. Our later estimates will indicate that in order to obtain the necessary funds by 1970 at current price levels, this proportion of educational outlays to GNP would have to increase by more than 80 per cent to 1.30. That is to say, we expect a GNP of at least $700 billion and current educational expenditures for colleges and universities of about $9 billion, or 1.30 per cent of the GNP.[3] Should we add capital outlays, the total rises to about 0.80 in 1956 and 1.50 in 1970; the rise is 0.80 to 1.50, exclusive of capital costs, from *1957–58* to 1969–70.

These figures may, however, give an exaggerated view of the success of colleges and universities in attracting additional services. Prices of college services have gone up much more than the general price level. In ordinary markets a rise of prices points to a smaller product for a given outlay in dollars. In the market for college services, variations in the price charged (tuition) are of less significance as an indication of the real resources made available, because tuition represents only part of the price of the product. From 1860 to 1933 tuition charges increased about seven times as much as prices, and in the forty years ending in 1948, for 24 identical institutions the increase of tuition was roughly twice the rise of prices. Moreover, index numbers on cost of education generally show a rise greater than the general index. Hence if we consider the *real resources* available to higher education, that is, the actual goods and services rather than their money equivalent, we find that the increase in the proportion of educational and general income to GNP is substantially less than suggested by Table 1-2. The figures are sufficiently rough to exclude any very precise conclusion here, but the proportion of educational and general income[4] to GNP has not increased over the last seventy years as much as the crude figures suggest. Quality changes are, however, excluded from these calculations. If we allow for an improvement in quality, I conclude that higher education may well absorb a larger share of GNP than it did seventy years ago but probably not so much as is suggested by the table. (More later on the measurement of quality.)

Another approach is to estimate the educational and general income per resident student and to compare these totals with the increase of prices (see Table 1-2). Here again the rise of educational and general income per resident student has been roughly about twice as large as the increase in consumer prices. Hence we infer that the higher education product per student has roughly doubled in seventy years. A relative rise of tuition greater than the rise of revenue per resident student points to an increased relative significance of tuition income. (Earlier figures suggest a larger rise of tuition than of income per resident student.) Allowing for the rise in number of part-time students, a phenomenon explained in part by the rising population in metropolitan areas, I would conclude that the educational and general income per full-time resident student has increased more than is suggested by Table 1-2.

TABLE 1-2
Higher Education, Income in Relation to GNP and Other Variables, 1889–90 to 1957–58

Year	Education and general income, per cent of GNP	Consumer prices (1923 = 100)	Resident enrollment (thousands)	Education and general revenue per resident (dollars)	Value of physical property (millions of dollars)	Endowment (millions of dollars)
1889–90	0.23	48	157	137	95	579
1919–20	0.28	108	598	289	741	569
1929–30	0.51	98	1,101	439	1,925	1,512
1939–40	0.58	85	1,494	382	2,753	1,764
1949–50	0.66	142	2,659	689	5,275	2,644
1953–54	0.63	158	2,407	979	8,033	3,313
1956–57	0.70 (est.)	163	3,200 (est.)	1,000 (est.)	10,000 (est.)	
1957–58	0.84 (est.)	166	3,376 (est.)	1,060 (est.)	11,180	4,647

Source: U.S. Census, *Historical Statistics of the United States, 1789–1945*; HEW, *Statistics of Higher Education: Receipts, Expenditures and Property*, and *Faculty, Students and Degrees*, various issues; *Economic Report of the President*, January, 1959. Estimates and computations are mine; from Dexter M. Keezer (ed.), *Financing Higher Education 1960–70*, McGraw-Hill, 1959, pp. 72–74; and HEW, *Memo to the Board*, 1960 series no. 4, 1960.

Another relevant factor in interpreting the increase of educational and general income (and expenditures) per resident student is the value of physical property. This table reveals that, whereas the value of physical property was about one-sixth of endowment in 1889–90 and about 1¼ times as much as endowment in 1929–30, by 1956–57 the value of physical property was about 2½ times endowment. (Endowment is at book value; market value is substantially higher.) Whereas endowment yields income, physical property requires large maintenance expenditures. Under the general and educational budget, maintenance and operation of physical plant costs about 12 per cent. The expansion of plant suggests higher outlays for plant as well as larger maintenance costs, and therefore rising unit costs.

This increase in cost per resident student, when corrected for price level changes, has not been uniform over the whole period. In fact, if we take more detailed figures from 1889–90 we find that the rise of educational income in stable prices was marked only in the 1920s and since 1949–50.

This particular problem can be understood better if we consider the percentage increase of educational expenditures per student with the income per capita. Table 1A-1 shows that only from 1919–20 to 1929–30 and from 1949–50 to 1957–58 does the increase of the educational income per resident student exceed that in income per capita. These are the periods when higher education gained more rapidly than the economy generally. In all other periods the opposite was true.

We can draw still another obvious conclusion from this table: institutions of higher learning do not perform well in inflationary periods. The largest gains were made from 1919 to 1929 when prices were relatively stable and the economy prosperous. From 1939 to 1949 the reader will note a rather disappointing trend, with national income per capita rising almost twice as much as educational income per student. Since 1949–50, despite a modest inflation, the gains for education exceeded those for the economy. This was a period in which the colleges and universities managed to mobilize private and public resources as well as to raise their tuition substantially. Income per resident student rose by two-thirds from 1950 to 1958; GNP per capita only by 50 per cent.

BROAD LINES OF EXPENDITURES AND GROWTH OF THE ECONOMY, 1889–1960

In Table 1A-1 I present some relevant statistics on finance, national income, and prices, 1889–90 to 1959–60.

Over the last seventy years or so, the resources going into higher education have greatly increased. With resident enrollment in 1959–60 twenty-two times that of 1889–90 and educational and general income per resident student more than eight times, the total educational and general income was about 175 times as high in 1957–58 as in 1889–90. Not only was the educational income per resident student rising, but even when corrected for the increase in price, outlays per student had roughly doubled.

In one respect, however, the results were disappointing: the increase of educational income per resident was less than one-half that of the gains of national income per capita. In this sense the standards of higher education were not keeping up with the rise of national economic standards. That the rise of general and educational expenditures vis-à-vis GNP occurred despite the lag in income per resident student is explained by the large rise of enrollment.

Table 1-3 summarizes a larger Table 1A-1. Comparisons are available for the years 1889–90 to 1953–54 (64 years); 1929–30 to 1953–54 (24 years) and 1953–54 to 1959–60 (though for some variables only for four years, that is, 1953–54 to 1957–58).

TABLE 1-3

Percentage Rise of Enrollment Income, Cost of Living, and Other Variables,
1889–90 to 1953–54, 1929- 30 to 1953–54, and 1953–54 to 1959–60

Variable	1889–90 to 1953–54	Annual rise	1929–30 to 1953–54	Annual rise	1953–54 to 1959–60	Annual rise
Resident college enrollment.....	1,433	22	119	5	41	7
Education and general income...	10,863	17	388	16	60*	15*
National income..............	747	12	281	12	36	6
Educational and general income per resident student.........	615	10	122	5	17*	4*
National income per capita.....	1,390	22	190	8	24	4
Rise of cost of living..........	229	3.6	60	2.5	7½	1.2

* To 1957–58, not 1959–60.
Source: See Table 1A-1.

Here are some points to be stressed. (The trends for the whole period are to be considered only roughly accurate.)

In this summary, the three periods are referred to as long, medium, and recent short.

1. *Average Percentage Rise of Resident Enrollment.* The largest percentage increase was for long, the recent short, and then medium (22, 7,5). From higher plateaus, the percentage increases tend to flatten out—all the more significant are the gains for 1954–1960.

2. *Educational and General Income.* Roughly equal relative rises per year, suggesting very large gains in recent years.

3. *Relative Gains of Educational and General Income Vis-à-vis National Income* (GNP). The former rises more, relatively, and especially for the recent short period.

4. *Relative Rise of Educational and General Income per Resident Student and GNP per Capita.* This comparison is of more significance than the preceding one, for it reveals the rise of standards in the economy and in higher education. Here the best record is made in four recent years; in the long period, the per capita gains of higher education are only 45 per cent those of the economy.

5. *A Correction for the Rise in the Cost of Living.* For the long period, per capita income per resident student rose 2.8 per cent as much

as the cost of living; for the medium period 2.0, and for the recent short period 3.3. Hence the smallest losses related to inflation is for the period 1954–1958.

SOME DETAILS BY PERIODS

Enrollment

The rise of resident enrollment seemed to average around 70 to 80 per cent per decade in recent decades except in the 1930s. In the last three decades under consideration, the average was 90 to 95 per cent per decade; for 1919 to 1929, 84 per cent; for 1929–30 to 1939–40, only 36 per cent (a reflection of the Depression); and from 1949–50 to 1955–56 there was little change, a fact to be explained by the large number of over-age veterans in IHL in 1949–50. But in the 1950s it was 743,000—only 28 per cent. The rise from 1939–40 to 1949–50 is inflated by the large influx of over-age veterans. All in all, the most spectacular relative rise occurred in the twenties, with an 84 per cent increase from a high level; the most spectacular absolute rise was in the forties, with an increase of 1.16 millions.

Enrollments versus Degrees

In general, the ratio of degrees to resident enrollments has tended to rise since 1919–20. In successive ten-year periods ending 1929–30, 1939–40, and 1949–50, the increase of degrees relative to that in enrollment was 180, 147, and 169 per cent, respectively, in each instance relative to the year ten years earlier.

This relative rise of degrees to enrollment reflects a reduced rate of attrition as well as the rise in the number of graduate degrees, which often require less than four years of work. Since this trend means that a smaller proportion of students are enrolled in the freshman and sophomore years and a larger number in the upper classes and graduate curriculum, the result is higher costs per average year of study. (See later.)

Educational and General Income

In every decade the growth was impressive in current dollars—with the exception of the thirties when the increase was but 18 per cent. (From 1919–20 to 1929–30 the rise was 179 per cent.)

What is more significant than the rise in current dollars is the increase corrected for price changes. Once this correction is made, the gains for the first *thirty* years are 210 per cent; in the 1920s, 207 per cent; in the 1930s, 36 per cent; and in the 1940s the gain in current dollars of 221 per cent is reduced to 92 per cent in stable dollars. Again, the most striking advance was in the 1920s, although the advances in the later 1950s were reassuring.

TABLE 1-4

Per Year Percentage Gains of Educational Income in Stable Dollars

1889–90 to 1919–20 = 7
1919–20 to 1929–30 = 21
1929–30 to 1939–40 = 4
1939–40 to 1949–50 = 9
1949–50 to 1953–54 = 3
1953–54 to 1957–58 = 12

EDUCATIONAL AND GENERAL INCOME PER RESIDENT STUDENT

In current dollars the increase was from $137 in 1889–90 to $979 in 1953–54. But in dollars of stable purchasing power the rise was from $457 to $979, or about 115 per cent.

In the first thirty years under consideration, the rise in prices exceeded that in income per student, and hence there seemed to be a deterioration. But again in the twenties the progress was striking, an increase per student of 52 per cent being accompanied by a price decline. In contrast, in the thirties the dollars in stable purchasing power available per student in 1939–40 did not exceed the 1929–30 total. In the 1940s, a gain of 80 per cent in current dollars was virtually wiped out when corrected for a rise of prices of 67 per cent. In the years 1949–50 to 1953–54, the gains were substantial: 27 per cent in real dollars per student in four years. In the next four years the improvement was small, a fact explained by the substantial increase of enrollment.

TABLE 1-5

Percentage Change Per Year Real Educational Income Per Student

1889–90 to 1919–20 = −0.6
1919–20 to 1929–30 = +6.7
1929–30 to 1939–40 =   n.c.
1939–40 to 1949–50 = +0.8
1949–50 to 1953–54 = +6.7
1953–54 to 1957–58 = +1.3

GROWTH OF HIGHER EDUCATION AND OF THE ECONOMY

We have indicated above that the resources made available to each student have not grown as much as the resources available to the average American. In the first thirty years under consideration, for example, the rise of income per resident student equaled but 39 per cent that of income per capita—though total educational income rose substantially more than income. In the 1920s and in 1949–50 to 1953–54, the rises of educational income per student were 52 and 42 per cent, respectively, as compared with rises of income per capita of 35 and 21 per cent. In the 1940s the gain per student was but 80 per cent compared with a gain of 149 per cent per capita, but the record was better in the 1950s.

It is interesting that higher education falls much more behind the economy in inflationary periods than in the Great Depression—a relative decline of 8 per cent in the thirties and of 28 per cent in the forties. But this does not mean IHL are in better financial shape in periods of depression.

TABLE 1-6

Percentage Rise of Educational Income Per Resident Student to Percentage Rise of National Per Capita Income

1889–90 to 1919–20	=	39
1919–20 to 1929–30	=	149
1929–30 to 1939–40	=	(260)*
1939–40 to 1949–50	=	54
1949–50 to 1953–54	=	200
1953–54 to 1957–58	=	129

* Larger decline (−13 and −5).

In Table 1-7 I have added some comparative figures for 1950 to 1956. These figures are of some interest because they throw some light on possible future growth.

TABLE 1-7

Variable	Annual rise, per cent		Total rise 1950–1956, per cent
	1950–1954	1954–1956	
Enrollment..	$-2\frac{1}{4}$	$+5\frac{1}{2}$	n.c.
National income (GNP).............................	$7\frac{1}{2}$	$6\frac{1}{2}$	48
Educational and general income.....................	$7\frac{1}{2}$	11	57
National income per capita.........................	$5\frac{1}{4}$	5	34
Educational and general income per resident student.....	$10\frac{1}{2}$	$5\frac{1}{2}$	57
Consumer prices...................................	3	$\frac{1}{2}$	13
Endowment..	$6\frac{1}{4}$	8	45
Physical property.................................	13	9	80

Source: See Table 1A-1.

In six recent years general and educational income rose by 57 per cent (much more in the last two than in the first four years). But when corrected for price rise, the gain is only 40 per cent. At this rate an increase of about 140 per cent of current income from 1958, the estimated need by 1970, would not be attained before 1973. By 1970 the increase would be 100 per cent.

At the greater growth of 1950 to 1958 (educational and general expenditures rose by 30 per cent from 1956 to 1958), the 140 per cent growth would be attained by 1972. On a per capita basis, the gains are roughly the same as for total educational income, since enrollment did not rise from 1950 to 1956. But since about half the rise of income for the 1960s is associated with an increase of enrollment, the prospects do not seem bad if the pace of recent gains with stable enrollment can be inflated for a doubling of enrollment from 1958 to 1970. But in the years 1954 to 1956 educational and general income per resident student (in stable dollars) rose by 5 per cent, and that is substantially less than the required rate for the next ten years. But from 1953–54 to 1957–58 the increase per student was 38 per cent (28 per cent when deflated for the rise of prices). At this rate it would require fourteen years to double the general and educational income at stable prices.

In one other respect the prospects seem good. The rise of general and educational income exceeds that in GNP and a fortiori on a per capita basis (education vis-à-vis national income per capita). In fact, in the years 1954 to 1956 the relative gain of income per resident student to income per capita is greater than that required in the next ten to eleven years to achieve our objectives. These relative movements are remindful of the favorable experience of the 1920s. The improvement in the years 1953–54 to 1957–58 as measured by income per resident student in stable dollars, if sustained for twelve years, would yield more than 140 per cent additional revenue—on the assumption of a rise of 80 per cent enrollment.

RISING UNIT COSTS

Let us consider in greater detail the perplexing problem of the increasing unit costs in higher education, a problem dealt with more fully later. The over-all upward trend is all the more surprising in view of the increased enrollment per institution and the relatively large rise for large urban, Catholic, and junior colleges, which are usually low-cost units.

For example, as we note in Table 1-9, the proportion of first professional and bachelor degrees in business and commerce and in education to all such degrees rose from 0.6 per cent in 1901–1905 to 19.6 per cent in 1926–1930 and to 33.8 per cent in 1952–53. These are relatively low-cost degree programs, because little laboratory work is required and classes are large. In the health field, a relatively high-cost operation, the percentage dropped from 33.2 to 9.5 and to 6.0 in these three periods. We do not have similar figures for junior colleges, but we know that in 1919 there were only 8,000 students in junior colleges; in 1939, 150,000; and in 1955,

335,000 (resident degree-credit students). This is a rise much beyond that of the average enrollment, and on the whole costs of operation in junior colleges are lower than in colleges generally.

Then why have the IHL experienced such large increases of unit costs even when allowances are made for the rise of prices?

One possible explanation is an increase in the number of faculty in relation to students.[5]

TABLE 1-8

Percentage Rise, Higher-educational Income Per Capita and National Income Per Capita

Income	1889–90 to 1919–20	1919–20 to 1929–30	1929–30 to 1939–40	1939–40 to 1949–50	1949–50 to 1957–58
Education..........	+111	+52	−13	+ 80	+54
National..........	+283	+35	− 5	+149	+36

Source: See Table 1-2 sources.

TABLE 1-9

Percentage First Professional and Bachelor Degrees, Various Fields (Not All)

Field	1901–1905	1926–1930	1952–1953
Health fields.................................	33.2	9.5	6.0
Business, commerce, and education...............	0.6	19.6	33.8
Natural science, social science, and humanities.......	42.4	39.9	33.0

Source: D. Wolfe, *America's Resources of Specialized Talent*, 1954, table B-1.

TABLE 1-10

Percentage Rise of Enrollment, Faculty, Courses (All) and Courses (Graduate), 11 IHL, 1956 in Relation to 1900

Enrollment.................... 374
Faculty...................... 530
Courses (all)................. 330*
Courses (graduate)............ 790†

* 9 IHL
† 4 IHL
Source: Computed from catalogues.

A second, related explanation is the rise in the number of courses given by the colleges, particularly in the graduate field where the courses are likely to be small.

I made a study of the rise of enrollment, the increase in the number of faculty, and the increase of courses in the eleven following institutions for the years 1900, 1925, and 1956: Brown, Columbia, Harvard, Mt. Holyoke, Princeton, Smith, Swarthmore, Vassar, University of Wisconsin, Williams, and Yale.[6]

Another explanation of the increased unit cost is that the nature of the product is gradually changing. A larger part of the educational process includes such items as intercollegiate athletics, medical care, counseling, and public relations. This is apparently what the clientele wants, and this is what the colleges generally provide.

Another vital factor is the increased costs of administration. Actually, from the published figures from the Office of Education, the rise is not nearly as great as one might expect. Under general and educational expenditures the increase was from $43 million in 1929–30 to $358 million in 1955–56, but only from 11.4 to 12.8 per cent of total general and educational expenditures. (For 1957–58 the rise was to $478 million or 13.2 per cent.) This is a surprisingly small rise in ratios, considering the widespread view that administration has greatly increased its demands on the college budget. One explanation of this small rise is undoubtedly the fact that the average size of the college has increased, a factor making for lower relative administrative costs. I shall show elsewhere that the relative costs of administration tend to be high for the small colleges—and even today two-thirds of our colleges have enrollments of less than five hundred —and less for the larger institutions. Since the average size of the unit has increased since 1929–30, it might be expected that the relative costs of administration for this reason would tend to decline.

Still another factor that tends to raise unit costs is the increased importance of extension courses and organized research, both of which are generally classified under general and educational expenditures. Research is especially important. The increase for extension and public services has been from $25 to $178 million, and for organized research from $18 to $734 million from 1929–30 to 1957–58, or an increase for organized research from 4 to 20 per cent of total educational and general expenditures. Here again we have what we might call a change in the product. How much of organized research should be included in the educational program is a difficult problem. Obviously the large institution, particularly the university, now participates to a larger extent than in the past in the provision of research. Estimates of the ratio of tuition to costs tend to exaggerate the subsidy to students for this reason. One of the issues we shall discuss later is the allocation of organized research as part of the instructional expenditures. To what extent should the research expenditures of the faculty, especially if they are not closely related to teaching responsibilities, be allocated to institutional costs? It is clear that the university today devotes a larger part of its resources and activity to research than it did even twenty-five years ago. Hence this rise in unit costs does not mean or suggest greater inefficiency, but rather a change in the kind of job being done by the average institution.

Still another item in the budget, organized activities as aids to instructional departments, also suggests a change in the functioning of the college and university. Included in these items are " . . . the conducting of a laboratory, of demonstration schools, medical schools, hospitals, dental clinics, home economics cafeterias, agricultural college creameries, college-operated industries, and other activities closely connected with the instructional program but not actually integral parts of it."[7] This item also has increased substantially from $27 million in 1939 to $239 million in 1957–58, or from 5 to 7 per cent of expenditures in this short period. Costs of these three items, not always closely related to regular college instruction, rose from $90 million in 1940, or 17 per cent of general and educational expenditures, to $1,152 million in 1957–58, or 32 per cent.

These items are largely under the control of the *universities*. Whereas 60 per cent of all expenditures are incurred by the universities, they account for about 80 per cent of organized research, almost 80 per cent of extension, and close to 80 per cent of the related activities. I should add that the last item belongs to the instruction process to a greater degree than do the other two items; but it also reflects a change in the product.

Three other factors help to explain the rise of unit costs. The first is the increase in the number of degrees relative to enrollment. The dropouts tend to decline, and instruction costs are higher in the junior and senior years. In comparison to the freshman and sophomore years, the relatively low-cost years of instruction, a rise in the number of students who continue until graduation is likely to raise unit costs. For example, the proportion of those receiving degrees in a single year to enrollment in 1889–90 was 10 per cent; in 1919–20, 11 per cent; and by 1955–56, 14 per cent. These figures give some indication of declining attrition; a relatively larger proportion tend to graduate these days. But part of this gain must be associated with the increased importance of graduate courses that require less than four years, and hence a rise of the numbers in these courses, relatively speaking, would tend to increase the proportion of graduates to enrollments. Second degrees (e.g., M.A.s) increased from 7 per cent of bachelor and postprofessional degrees in 1889–90 to 19 per cent in 1955–56. (The increased importance of the junior college tends to raise the proportion of degrees to enrollment. But the junior college tends to reduce unit costs.)

The second point is that the proportion and numbers in graduate instruction have increased greatly over the years. This is of course much more expensive than undergraduate instruction. The numbers involved are still not very large compared to the undergraduate enrollment, but they do contribute toward higher costs. From 1½ per cent of the total in resident enrollment in 1889–90 the graduate student proportion rose to 4⅓ per cent in 1929–30 and 9 per cent in 1955–56. If the average graduate student cost two to three times as much as the average undergraduate, it is clear that the increase in graduate students may be a substantial factor in explaining the rise of educational costs over this long period.

A third factor is the increased mass of materials to be covered and the rising costs of plant and equipment, inclusive of laboratories. Related is the improved product, we hope.

* * *

What can we say by way of conclusion? It is clear there has been a very large rise of enrollment in the last eighty or a hundred years as compared to the rise in population. It is also evident that the proportion of GNP going to higher education in current dollars has substantially increased. But once we allow for the greater relative rise in prices of college services, it is not clear that the proportion of educational income to GNP has risen as much since 1889–90 as might be inferred from the crude figures. This is disconcerting when one recalls that the outlays in the next ten years must increase to a point where the proportion of general and educational income to GNP must rise from 0.80 per cent to about 1.50 per cent.

The rise of costs per resident student, twice as large as that in prices over this period of seventy years, is rather disturbing. This increase has occurred despite the fact that the average size of the institution has increased many times, a factor tending to reduce unit costs. Other factors making for lower unit costs have been the growth of the junior colleges and the disproportionate gains of Catholic and urban universities that on the whole have low unit costs. Another factor tending to reduce the unit costs is the larger proportion of part-time students.

But we should stress the point that in this period of seventy years a rough calculation yields the result that per capita income in stable prices rose by three times. The corresponding rise of income per student was not one-half as great. In other words, the college product did not improve nearly as much as might be inferred from the rise of real per capita income. We should, however, allow for two factors: one is the trend toward lower-cost education already mentioned; the second is that IHL probably do not profit nearly so much from rising productivity as the nation does. The first accounts in part for the slower rise of unit income in higher education; but the second, i.e., low productivity, tends to raise unit income (used interchangeably here for expenditures) in higher education, and hence an allowance for this would suggest that, despite the relatively low productivity (and higher unit costs), the unit costs in higher education were low vis-à-vis the rising standards of the economy.

* * *

Then what explains the rise of unit cost? One very important factor is that the college of today is a different type of institution and offers a different kind of product from that of twenty-five or fifty or seventy-five years ago. Research, extension services, organized activities related to instructional departments, graduate work—all these have tended to become more important. The *pure* element of education plays a much smaller part in the average institution than was true twenty-five or seventy-five years ago.

Further factors making for higher costs are the rise in the number of faculty relative to students, and (related) the continued increase in the number of courses, though this increase has not been as great as that in the rise of enrollment. This would hardly be expected, for the increase in the size of the average college from just a few hundred to close to fifteen hundred would suggest a very large decline in the number of courses relative to enrollment.

Obviously the latter factors weigh more heavily than the former, and the net result has been not only a substantial rise in unit costs per student but a rise greatly exceeding that in the price level.

Another relevant factor is that productivity does not rise in the colleges as in the economy generally. Assembly-line methods are not practical in higher education. The result is that as incomes rise in manufacturing and other services, higher education must reflect these increases by offering higher rewards to those in the employment of higher education. Hence the rise of productivity which is reflected in the higher incomes in the productive industries and services is measured in higher education by rising costs and therefore higher prices. As we shall see later (Chapter 53), academic men and women do not accept new methods tending to reduce costs with great enthusiasm. That the college is not a profit-making institution also results in less interest than private enterprise takes in cutting costs. Finally, we would expect that the rising standards of the nation, reflected in the increase of per capita income of about 300 per cent in stable prices, would spill over to some extent into higher education.

FOOTNOTES

[1] See Table 1A-1.

[2] Later discussion, in Chap. 53, "Faculty Status," lends support to the theory of a rise in the faculty-student ratio. Cf. National Education Association, *Teacher Supply . . . 1960–61*, 1961, p. 52.

[3] The Rockefeller Report (*The Challenge to America: Its Economic and Social Aspects*, 1958, p. 72) estimates GNP at $642 billion in 1967 on the assumption of an annual rise of 4 per cent, the gains in the years 1947–57.

[4] Educational and general income includes fees, government appropriations, gifts, endowment income, etc., but not auxiliary enterprises or student-aid income, and the corresponding expenditures relative to administration, instruction, research, library, plant operation, extension, and public service.

[5] See Chap. 53, "Faculty Status," for some details.

[6] Cf. Chap. 44 for details.

[7] HEW, *Statistics of Higher Education: Receipts, Expenditures and Property, 1953–54*, p. 52.

APPENDIX

TABLE 1A-1

Trends of Finance in Higher Education, National Income, and Prices, 1889–90 to 1959–60

Variable	1889–1890	1919–1920	Percentage change 1889–90 to 1919–20	1929–1930	Percentage change 1919–20 to 1929–30	1939–1940	Percentage change 1929–30 to 1939–40	1949–1950	Percentage change 1939–40 to 1949–50	1953–1954	Percentage change 1949–50 to 1953–54	1955–1956	Percentage change 1953–54 to 1955–56	1959–1960	Percentage change 1955–56 to 1959–60
	(1)	(2)	(3)	(4)	(5)	(6)	(7)	(8)	(9)	(10)	(11)	(12)	(13)	(14)	(15)
Resident college enrollment (thousands)†	157	598	+280	1,101	+84	1,494	+36	2,659	+78	2,407*	−9	2,661	+11	3,402	+28
Degrees (thousands)†	15.5	48.6	+214	122	+151	186.5	+53	432	+132	357	−17	379	+6		
Educational and general income (millions of dollars)	21.5	173	+704	483	+179	571	+18	1,834	+221	2,357	+29	2,882	+22	3,762ᵃ	+31ᵃ
Educational and general expenditures (millions of dollars)†	.....	.....	.....	378	.....	522	+38	1,706	+227	2,288	+34	3,525	+22	3,634ᵃ	+3ᵃ
Educational and general income per resident student (dollars)†	137	289	+111	439	+52	382	−13	689	+80	979	+42	1,083	+11	1,154ᵃ	+7ᵃ
Value of physical property (millions of dollars)†	95.4	741	+677	1,925	+106	2,753	+43	5,273	+92	8,033	+52	9,485	+18	11,180ᵃ	+18ᵃ
Endowment and other nonexpendable funds (millions of dollars)†	78.8	569	+622	1,512	+166	1,764	+17	2,644	+50	3,313	+25	3,837	+16	4,648ᵃ	+21ᵃ
National income (GNP, millions of dollars)†	9,410	61,000	+548	95,000	+56	97,400	+3	279,000	+186	364,000	+30	412,000	+13	496,000	+20
National income (GNP) per capita (dollars)†	150	575	+283	774	+35	740	−5	1,846	+149	2,242	+21	2,467	+10	2,771	+12
Consumers prices (1923 = 100)†	48	107.8	+125	98	−9	85	−13	141.7	+67	158	+12	159.5	+1	161.9	+1½

* Interpolation 1951 to 1956 estimates and related to annual figures of fall enrollment of HEW.

† Columns 3, 5, 7, 9, 11, 13, 15 = percentage changes.

ᵃ = 1957–8.

Sources: HEW, Statistical Summary of Education, 1951–52, 1955, and Summary of 1953–54 Financial Statistics of Higher Education, 1956; ibid., Statistics of Higher Education, 1955–56: Receipts, Expenditures and Property, 1955–56, 1959, and Faculty, Students and Degrees, 1955–56, 1958; Economic Report of the President, January, 1957, 1960; and U.S. Department of Commerce, Historical Statistics of the United States, 1789–1945, 1949; also see Office of Education: Memo to the Board, 1960, series no. 4; National Education Series, Teacher Supply . . . 1960–61, Research Report 1961–R12; and R. Walters, Four Decades of U.S. Collegiate Enrollments, 1960.

Chapter 2

THE 1970 BUDGET[1]

Toward the end of this chapter I present a budget and projected enrollments for the years 1929–30 to 1969–70. This is a budget of $9.2 billion by 1969–70, and $9.8 billion if allowance is made for the rise of scholarships. The educational and general budget for 1957–58 was $3,650 million. Hence the increase over 1957–58 is $6.2 billion, or about 170 per cent. Since enrollment is expected to rise by more than 70 per cent, it can be assumed that less than one-half of the rise is to be associated with increased enrollments.

Even the estimate of $9.8 billion may well be too low, first, because we are discussing operating budgets only. The capital budget may well be of the order of $1.5 billion per year, an amount at least 50 per cent above the 1959 outlays. Economies may cut this figure. At any rate we should keep in mind the point that we may need for capital purposes in the next ten years about $½ billion additionally over and above what is now available per year. Second, we have assumed no inflation. A more realistic estimate is a 20 per cent inflation in ten years and hence a total operating educational and general budget of $11,760 million.

But let us revert to the $9.8 billion budget on the no-inflation assumption. Where is this money to come from? Table 2-1 gives the picture. In general the relative contribution of tuition is likely to increase, that of government to decline, that of endowment and gifts also to fall. Yet the dollar incomes from government and philanthropy will more than double.

Resources of these proportions may not be forthcoming. If they are not, then enrollment may suffer; but the net effect is more likely to be a decline in the quality of the product. I am also aware that, although increased cash resources are required, the rising flow of cash may largely yield inflation rather than genuine resources if, for example, the flow of personnel of ability is not accelerated.

This is not a forecast of what is going to happen; rather, it is an attempt to estimate what the sources of income should be if the budget

20

rises from \$3.6 to \$9.8 billion in twelve years. Many will contend that I am relying too heavily on tuition. Government may make larger contributions than I estimate; if so, the rise of tuition need not be so large as I here suggest. On the assumption that resources from state and local taxes rise *pari passu* with GNP, the contribution of these units may increase by several hundred millions above my estimates.

TABLE 2-1
Sources of Funds, Institutes of Higher Education

	1957–58		1969–70	
	Millions of dollars	Per cent	Millions of dollars	Per cent
Tuition....................................	904	25	3,800	40
Government................................	1,752†	48	3,700	38
Endowment income and gifts....................	578	16	1,200	12
Other (scholarship fund from various sources, etc.)...	416	11	1,100	11
Total..................................	3,650	100	9,800	101*

* Percentages do not add to 100 because of rounding.
† A revised figure is close to 2 billion.
Source: See Table 2-4.

I have argued frequently on the practicability and equity of higher tuition fees. This increase of \$2,900 million in tuition income seems less frightening if allowance is made for the \$800 million associated with rising enrollment at current fees and the \$530 million of additional scholarships.

The major part of the rise in government funds projected is in Federal government funds. But of this increase about a billion is for research, with research income from Federal government accounting for 13 per cent by 1969–70 as compared to 5 per cent in 1939–40 and 12 per cent in 1955–56.* State and local government income is to rise by about \$600 million, or 60 per cent, and endowment income and gifts would roughly double. An increase of \$1,000 million may well be achieved. Then governments share would rise to 42 per cent and tuitions decline to 36 per cent.

Expenditures rise primarily because of the doubling of enrollment and of salaries and related instructional outlays. With a trebling of costs, it is assumed that administration's share would drop from 12 to 10 per cent

* On some estimates, the Federal contribution would be much larger. Thus in the forthcoming Mushkin volume (HEW), the estimated Federal research payments in 1970 to IHL would be \$3.5 to \$4 billion—my projection for *all* research is only \$2.1 billion.

and research's share (government-financed and other) would rise from 5 per cent in 1939–40 to 18 per cent in 1955–56 and 23 per cent by 1969–70. The assumption here is that research is going to play a much larger part in university activities and that, as currently, almost two-thirds of it will be financed by the Federal government.

In earlier versions of these estimates I included as a factor making for higher outlays the sharing by higher education in the gains of the economy. That is, if the average standard of living of the population improves by 30 per cent in ten years, similar gains should be allocated to higher education. In a sense that is what I assume here.

TABLE 2-2
Average Cost per Student, Assuming No Inflation

Year	Cost
1957–58	$1,070
1969–70	1,520

Table 2-2 reveals that unit costs rise by more than 40 per cent. That unit costs will not rise more, despite the large increase in faculty pay assumed so far, may be explained in part by the failure of other costs to rise as much and by the tendency of students to shift to low-cost institutions. But the trend is consistent with our history, and especially so in view of the current underpayment of faculty now to be corrected.

This rise of 40 per cent is the result of the large increase in faculty salaries and smaller increase in other costs. But it should be noted that, against this rise of 40 per cent per unit cost, productivity in the economy should rise by more than 25 per cent. Hence the net rise over the general gains of the economy are not large when considered against the rise of pay and instruction needs. But the relative increased budget for *all* students amounts to about four times the expected improvement of GNP. Here especially relevant is the rise of enrollment.

We might expect economies associated with large rises of enrollment in periods of excess capacity. But even though large rises of enrollment occurred in the 1950s, real costs per student continued to rise, and in the 1960s excess capacity will not be large.

Economies, as we shall suggest later, may well yield gains of $1 billion to $2 billion per year by 1970. If that should happen, then the quality of the product might improve further, or the demands made on the student and taxpayer might be reduced below our projections.

We should perhaps distinguish between economies and savings. An economy might, for example, be better use of classrooms or elimination of unnecessary or high-cost courses without any serious effect on the quality of the educational product. A saving might result from the trend toward two-year colleges, for example, not that they are necessarily cheaper than the first two years of a four-year college, but rather that a much larger proportion will be in those institutions. (We have already allowed for this type of saving.)

But there are other types of savings. For example, with the large rise of demand for teachers in the next ten years, the colleges are likely to command disproportionately young and non-Ph.D. teachers. Hence, a doubling of salaries might result in an over-all increase of salary costs of 75 per cent in 1970. Such savings might amount to as much as $600 million. The result is a likely deterioration of product; but $600 million less resources would be required. I consider this a saving because I assume that the younger teachers would do a less effective job. If the product is identical and expenditures are cut by $600 million, there is a genuine economy.[2]

ECONOMIES

Economies require further discussion. Here is a sample illustration of the possibilities of economies:[3]

Current Situation, Data of 1955–56	
Full-time enrollment equivalent..................	2,300,000
Full-time equivalent faculty.....................	152,000
Student-teacher ratio...........................	15 to 1
Proposed Rise in Student-Teacher Ratio	
Increase the ratio to...........................	20 to 1
Needed teachers at 20 to 1 ratio (full time)........	115,000
Estimates of Savings	
Savings in teachers...........................	37,000
At salaries double 1959 in 1970, per teacher.......	$13,000
Economies (37,000 × 13,000)...................	$481,000,000
Economies at enrollment of 1970 (2.3 × 1956).......	$1,106,000,000

These statistics give an exaggerated view of the savings. There will be disproportionate reduction of low-income faculty, and in the large university the faculty does research as well as teaching. Organized research in a recent year accounted for about one-sixth of all general and educational expenditures. For these reasons I would be inclined to estimate these savings at about $800 million; substantial savings are certainly possible.

I do not mean to suggest that we have dealt with all aspects of this problem. For example, organized research is becoming a larger function of institutions of higher learning (IHL). This trend may well continue. The rise has been from $18 million, or 5 per cent of educational and general expenditures in 1929–30, to $375 million, or 16 to 17 per cent in 1953–54, which is an average increase of ½ per cent per year. If the rate of rise from 1929–30 to 1953–54 should continue, by 1970 the percentage will be roughly 25, or more than $2 billion. Indeed the net result will be an increase, not of about $800 million, as is suggested by a trebling of all expenditures, but $2 billion, or an additional $1.2 billion. (My estimate here is outlays of $2.1 billion.) This is not an unreasonable assumption.

But other assumptions are possible. One is that the research function will increasingly be assumed by government and industry directly. Another is that the growth of research will be at the expense of instruction.

I can envisage other savings, as adumbrated above, resulting from the changing structure of higher education. Low-cost operations tend to become relatively more important. The undergraduate business and educational schools, the junior college, and the large urban university grow disproportionately; all of them are low-cost operations; and the high-cost Ivy League, select women's and men's liberal arts colleges, and professional schools of leading universities become less important.

My projections of enrollment are conservative. A rise of enrollment up to 6 million in ten years results from a rise in the ratio of college-age population at college by $\frac{1}{2}$ per cent per year, as compared to 1 per cent since 1939–40 and 2+ per cent per year from 1951–52 to 1955–56, and the latter despite the reduction of veteran enrollment. The largest rises in this ratio have occurred since 1919, and especially in the last few years. (The ratios to population aged eighteen to twenty-one were 4 per cent in 1900, 12 per cent in 1930, and 35 per cent in 1956. Need I add that a substantial proportion are aged seventeen and in excess of age twenty-one.) In view of the widespread policy of providing IHL within commuting distance of most students, the large growth of the junior college and the strategically located public four-year college; the great expansion of the urban university; the continued relative rise of discretionary expenditures per family and the growing tradition of higher education; the improved methods of financing students through employment, scholarships, and loans; the almost certain relative gains for women and Negroes, now underrepresented; the rapid expansion of graduate study; the reduction of dropouts; the increased diversification of IHL—all these point toward steady gains in the percentage of college-age people at college.

In an essay for the forthcoming HEW (Mushkin) volume, Louis H. Conger, J., shows that the college attendance would rise as follows:

```
000s
1960 = 3,570
1970 = 6,936    Projection I—continued rise in proportion of college-age
      population in IHL as in past
1970 = 5,188    Projection II—constant rate projection
1970 = 5,940    Projection III—based on fathers' educational achievement
```

The importance of the rising proportion (Projection 1) is suggested by the fact that if college attendance rates had remained constant from

1950–52 to 1958–60, the number of men enrolled would have increased by only 8 per cent, and the number of women by less than 1 per cent. Actually, the number of students rose by 40 per cent.

Projection 1 is based on the following trends:

Per Cent Civilian Non-institutional Population Aged 16 to 34 Enrolled in College

Average, 3 years	Years				
	16–17	18–19	20–24	25–29	30–34
1950–1952	3.5	20.7	14.2	4.7	1.3
1958–1960	3.3	32.7	19.3	8.4	3.0
1970	3.3	43.7	25.1	11.9	4.7

Source: L. H. Conger, Jr., *Projections of College Enrollment,* forthcoming HEW volume. Of particular interest is the large proportion at IHL aged 25–34.

Note especially the tendency of those attached to the labor market and studying part time to increase disproportionately. In my estimates I have assumed that they would be part of the 6.4 million. But a large rise in the proportion of part-time students, say from the current 22 to 30 per cent, would mean a rise of part-time students of 1,130,000 and an enrollment probably substantially in excess of 6.4 million.

The trend toward low-cost units needs more elaboration. Thus the rise of enrollment from 1928 to 1956 (my compilation and calculations) was as follows for the high-priced units:

```
8 Ivy League........................................  41.8
6 other outstanding private universities.................  29.8
10 outstanding women's colleges.............  No net change
20 outstanding liberal arts colleges...................  46.8
```

Against these increases note a rise of 141.8 per cent in all institutions, an increase from a very small beginning to 452,000 in the junior colleges by 1955–56, a 79.9 per cent increase for 40 large urban IHL, and an 87.4 per cent increase for 23 large Catholic institutions. The large rise for *all* IHL as compared to the separate categories is explained in part by the tremendous increase in junior colleges and also by large rises in public institutions generally. It is also explained by the fact that the over-all figures include old *and new* institutions, whereas the above table covers only *identical* institutions in both years.

The significance for the future budget lies in part in the continued *relative* losses for the high-cost operations. Increasingly the trend is toward the low-cost institutions: the junior college, the commuting (street-car) institutions, and the urban colleges. It is likely that the less-favored and the low-cost IHL have large amounts of excess capacity and that the many IHL in small towns have much excess. They especially may gain from the rise of enrollment. At current costs the $500 unit-cost operations are gaining at the expense of the operations costing $1,500 to $2,500.

Let us give one example of the possible trends: the junior college today costs about $600 per student, as compared to an over-all average of about $1,000. From almost nothing in 1929 the junior college has increased its enrollment to 450,000, or 17 per cent of the total, in 1956. A rise to 25 per cent of total enrollment by 1970, in view of the current planning for commuting colleges, is a conservative projection. At a 6-million enrollment, an addition of 8 per cent is roughly 500,000 additional enrollment beyond what might be expected on the basis of 1956 structures of enrollment. At cost differentials of 1970, the savings might well be about $250 million. This estimate includes an allowance for the larger proportion of part-time students in junior colleges, and note that it is based on the *relative* rise of numbers in these institutions, not on any substantial difference between unit costs in junior colleges and those in the first two years in four-year colleges. In addition, there are the savings related generally to the drift to the four-year commuting college, a drift accentuated by the growth of the metropolitan area.

This shift toward the commuting college involves savings of another type adumbrated above: the proportion of part-time students greatly increases. For example, HEW (Health, Education, and Welfare) estimates the proportion of part-time students in 1955–56 in undergraduate instruction at 22 per cent.[4] But in the junior colleges the proportion of part-time students was 40 per cent, or almost twice as great relatively. For the junior college and urban institutions generally, this means reduced costs of hundreds of millions.

Our estimate of increased costs—say, from $4 to $10 billion, or 150 per cent—may seem unrealistic to many. But in stable dollars the rise per student for educational costs was close to twice as large from 1919–20 to 1953–54 as we anticipate from 1958 to 1970. This increase for the twelve years 1958 to 1970 is roughly 4½ to 5 per cent per student in stable dollars as compared with a likely rise of about 3 per cent in GNP per capita in stable dollars. In view of the fact that salaries of faculty ought to double and in view of the large backlog in construction, a rise of expenditures per student 50 per cent (roughly) in excess of the national gains is surely not excessive.

Some may question the need of a doubling of salaries. This is an issue we discuss more fully elsewhere. But perhaps of relevance here is the fact that by the late 1950s faculty salaries had declined, vis-à-vis income of the able working population, as much as 50 per cent for high ranks and somewhat less for lower ranks. Even a doubling of faculty salaries by 1970 and a rise of income of other groups by 25 per cent (stable prices) would leave faculty salaries about 10 per cent less than compensation of others compared to 1930. Even this may be held to be inadequate when it is realized that faculty numbers may have to increase by 100 per cent—several times the rise for the whole working population and much more than that for the professions.

Where are the additional funds to come from? Table 2-1 reveals that a rise of $2,900 million in tuition would account for 40 per cent of income in 1970 as against only 25 per cent in 1958. Government, with outlays of $2,000 million additionally, would nevertheless reduce its share from 48 to 38 per cent. The largest rise here would be $800 million for Federal research, a gain not to be put down as aid but rather as payment for services rendered; for the states, $700 million; and for local governments, $70 million. Federal government would add about $300 million, exclusive of research.

It is certainly conceivable that the Federal government nonresearch contribution may rise to $1,000 million by 1970 as compared to $500 million assumed here. Much depends on the rate of growth of the economy, the political situation, competing demands on government, particularly for the cold war, other welfare claims, and especially the manner of coping with the additional $11 billion needed for public school education.

My estimate of $1,200 million (a rise of about $600 million) from endowment incomes and gifts may be low. Over a recent period of four years the gains have amounted to $65 million per year. A twelve-year average gain even of $65 million, surely a figure that might well be exceeded, would provide $780 million additional, or $1,350 million in all. Vigorous efforts to obtain gifts and a continuance of our growing income might well yield a total of $1,500 to $2,000 million by 1970. At expected GNP of 1970, the yield of gifts alone should increase about $200 million without any improvement of efforts and techniques. The Council for Financial Aid to Colleges looks forward to gains of $1,050 million in the twelve years ending 1970, or a yield of $1,650 million in all. The council's estimate may be a little on the optimistic side. They found that gifts, exclusive of the Ford faculty grant, in the years 1955 to 1957 rose by $300 million. But the HEW's estimate is a rise of $328 million in the six years from 1949–50 to 1955–56, or a little more than $50 million per year. Moreover, 25 per cent in 1950 and 33 per cent in 1956 were fund increases from which income alone was usable.

Hence I would conclude that a rise of $600 million in twelve years (50 × 12) is a minimum and of $1,200 million (100 × 12) a maximum. (These are at 1960 prices.) Since about one-third is in the form of new endowment funds, actually a gain of $1,200 million of income annually by

1970 would involve a rise of gifts by 1970 of about $1,600 million ($1,600 — 500 [endowment] + 100 million additional income from $2 billion of additional endowment).

My projections are not in agreement with some others. For example, the Council for Financial Aid (apparently with the approval of Millett) proposes[5] for 1969 the distribution given in Table 2-3. My reasons for putting a heavier burden on tuition will be evident later; and related is the case for not putting such a heavy load on government.

TABLE 2-3
Income, IHL, Per Cent

Source	Council	S. E. H.
Tuition...................	21	40
Government..............	50	38
Gifts and grants...........	21 ⎫	12
Endowment..............	3 ⎭	
Miscellaneous.............	5	11

The council's projection of 21 per cent from gifts and endowment seems very optimistic.

It is of course conceivable that government will pay half the bill, that is, about $5 billion in 1970 as against a little more than one-third that amount in 1958. But unless the Federal government intervenes to a much greater degree than now seems likely, not only in education, but also in other services, it seems unlikely that state and local governments would in fact increase their contributions adequately to raise government's contribution to 50 per cent. A relevant factor, of course, could be the pressures exerted by students and alumni. That enrollment is likely to rise relatively more in regions where public institutions are dominant means both greater burdens on government and also greater pressures. Should the contributions of philanthropy rise by $1 to $2 billion instead of $600 million, I estimate that then to that extent students and government might be relieved.

A rise of current expenditures from $3.8 billion in 1958 to $9.2 billion (in 1958 prices), or a rise of 150 per cent, may seem to many a visionary projection. But it is not. Table 2-8 gives the trends since 1929, with corrections for price changes. What is striking is that the percentage of rate of rise (1) *per resident student* from 1958 to 1970 need be little more than one-half that from 1940 to 1958 and (2) total educational and general income need rise 7.75 per cent (compounded) from 1958 to 1970 against 6.65 per cent from 1940 to 1958. In view of the increasing awareness of the financial problems in higher education, in view of the larger expected rise of population—4½ per cent compounded 1940–1958 and 5½ per cent 1958–1970—and in view of the continued growth of the economy, the $9 to $10 billion should become available.

Perhaps the most troublesome problem is the source of this additional income. I am inclined to believe that the share coming from tuition will rise

TABLE 2-4

Current Income of Institutions of Higher Education, 1930–1970

(In millions of dollars)

Item	1929–30	1939–40	1953–54	1955–56	1957–58	1969–70
Educational and general income:						
Student fees...............	144.1	200.9	554.2	725.9	904.3	3,800*
Federal government:						
For veterans' education....	.....	.....	44.4	15.6		
For research............	†	†	282.4	355.6	534.9	
For other purposes........	20.7	38.9	92.8	122.7		
State governments..........	150.8	151.2	751.6	891.6	1,086.1	3,700‡
Local governments..........	†	24.4	88.2	106.9	130.7	
Endowment earnings.........	68.6	71.3	127.5	145.0	166.6	
Private benefactions.........	26.2	40.5	191.3	245.5	411.0	1,200§
Sales and services...........	†	32.8	165.5	192.4		
Other educational and general	72.7	11.4	58.6	80.5	346.1	500
Subtotal, educational and general...............	483.1	571.3	2,356.5	2,881.8	3,579.7	9,200
Student aid income...........	†	†	32.9	53.0	70.0	600
Subtotal, education, general, and student aid................	483.1	571.3	2,389.4	2,934.8	3,649.7	9,800¶
Auxiliary enterprises income.....	60.4	143.9	576.8	694.0	NA	NA
Other current income...........	11.0	†	....	....	NA	NA
Total current income.........	554.5	715.2	2,966.3	3,628.8	NA	NA

Note: Figures are rounded and do not necessarily add to totals.

NA: Not available.

* Calculated from 900, current fees + 800, for 90 per cent rise of enrollment + 2,550, tuition rate increase (4 million at 375 = 1,500; 2 million at 525 = 1,050) = $4,250 million. Deduct $450 million for rise of part time and increased percentage in low-cost units.

† Data not reported separately.

‡ Federal (research) = 1,300; Federal (other) = 500; state = 1,700; local = 200.

§ Endowment = 300; gifts = 900.

¶ Educational and general and student aid, in 1969–70 dollars (assumption, 20 per cent inflation ten years) is $11,760 million.

Source: Office of Education, 1930–1960; Council for Financial Aid to Education, 1958; and estimates of the author.

substantially, and from government, decline. But I would much prefer that the share of government and private philanthropy should not be reduced. In view of the growth of our economy and rising tax receipts (without any change in tax structure), there is much to be said for an increase in the

TABLE 2-5

Current Expenditures of Institutions of Higher Education, 1930–1970

(In millions of dollars)

Item	1929–30	1939–40	1953–54	1955–56	1957–58	1969–70
Educational and general expenditures:						
Administrative and general expense	42.9	62.8	290.5	358.4	NA	1,000.0
Resident instruction	221.3	280.2	966.8	1,148.5	NA	4,600.0
Organized research	18.0	27.3	374.9	506.1	NA†	2,100.0
Extension	25.0	35.3	114.7	141.1	NA⎱	300.0
Libraries	9.6	19.5	73.4	86.1	NA⎰	
Plant operation and maintenance	61.1	69.6	280.0	326.3	NA	700.0
Related activities	*	27.2	188.0	222.3	NA	500.0
Subtotal, educational, and general	377.9	522.0	2,288.4	2,788.8	3,700.0	9,200.0
Student aid expenditures	*	*	74.8	96.2	100.0	600.0
Subtotal, education, general, and student aid	377.9	522.0	2,363.2	2,885.0	3,800.0	9,800.0
Auxiliary enterprises expenditures	*	124.2	539.3	639.7	NA	NA
Other current expenditures	129.2	28.5	*	*	NA	NA
Total current expenditures	507.1	674.7	2,902.5	3,524.7		

* Data not reported separately.

† $846 million in 1960 from Federal Government (estimate of National Science Foundation).

NA: Not available.

Note: Figures are rounded and do not necessarily add to totals.

Source: Office of Education, 1930–1960; Council for Financial Aid to Education, 1958; and estimates of the author, 1970.

TABLE 2-6

Explanation of Increase of Tuition Income of $2,900 million

(In millions of dollars)

Increase of enrollment		800
Higher fees:		
Public, 4 million at $375 ($150 to $525)	1,500	
Private, 2 million at $525 ($600 to $1,125)	1,050	
Gross tuition increase		2,550
Total increase		3,350
Reduction of $450 million associated with a disproportionate increase of junior college students:		
500,000 with saving of $400	200	
Additional students saving because 40 per cent of junior college students are part time (others are 20 per cent part time) = 100,000 × 300	30	
Other savings resulting from movement to lower-cost IHL	220	450
Net tuition increase		2,900

contribution of government, especially Federal government. Should the Federal government increase its subsidy by $500 million (possibly $1 billion inclusive of construction) above the amounts so far assumed, and state governments by $500 million, then the tuition share would rise from 25 per cent in 1958 to less than 30 per cent in 1970—a rise of tuition rates roughly of only 50 per cent. We might do even better than this. The

TABLE 2-7

Educational Income, Total per Resident, Current and Stable Dollars, and Enrollment
(Compounded), 1930, 1940, 1958, 1970

Item	1930	1940	1958	1970 (est.)
Educational and general income (millions of dollars). . .	483	571	3,762	9,200
Enrollment (thousands).	1,101	1,494	3,376	6,443
Educational and general income per resident student (dollars).	439	383	1,117	1,412
Educational and general income at 1930 prices (millions of dollars).	483	680	2,175	5,323
Educational and general income per resident student at 1930 prices (dollars).	439	466	646	816

Source: HEW, *Statistics of Higher Education, 1955–56: Receipts, Expenditures and Property* and *Memo to the Board*, 1960 Series, no. 4; and my estimates and calculations.

TABLE 2-8

Rise in Educational and General Income, Total and per Resident Student (Corrected for Prices)
and Enrollment, 1930–1940, 1940–1958, 1958–1970

Period	Per cent annual rise (compounded)		
	General and educational income per resident student	Total educational and general income	Enrollment
1930–1940	0.84	3.90	1.7
1940–1958	3.65	6.65	4.5
1958–1970	1.90	7.75	5.5

Source: My calculations from earlier material.

additional offers of Federal government, state, and local governments and private philanthropy might increase by $750, $500, and $250 million, respectively, beyond my projections. Then the tuition share would not increase, and government's share would decline only slightly from its 1958 level.

The share of tuition and private philanthropy has tended to fall since 1930, and of government to rise.

The response to demands for larger state contributions will depend in part upon the varying pressures of rising enrollments. When public enrollments are larger, the demands become more vocal. In the forthcoming HEW volume (Miss Mushkin, ed.), it is revealed that the percentage *of the total increase* of enrollment for 1959–60 for public IHL varies from 100 per cent for three states to 31 per cent for New York; and the percentage *rise* for public IHL from 178 per cent for New Jersey to 15 per cent for Alabama.

TABLE 2-9

Source of Funds, Educational Income of Higher Education, 1930–1970, Per Cent

	1930	1940	1958	1970 (est.)
Tuition..........................	30	28	25	40
Government......................	35	33	53	38
Endowment income and gifts........	20	20	13	12
Other...........................	15	19	9	10

Source: Earlier tables—my calculations and estimates.

How much government will contribute will depend also on resources made available from private sources inclusive of tuition. That the ratios of resources made available for elementary, secondary, and higher education per student respectively varied from 1:1.9:5.8 in 1940 to 1:1.9:4.2 in 1950 reflects the difficulties confronting higher education.* And this occurred despite the very large rise of enrollment in IHL from 1.4 to 2.6 millions. No wonder that college salaries have responded much less than school pay to increasing standards of living and that a rising burden is being put on government.

The possibilities of expansion of state outlays are suggested by the recent California Master Survey.

Public IHL California

Expenditures	$ mill.
1948–49	113
1957–58	413
1970–71	758
1975–76	959

Source: Master Plan: *The Costs
of Higher Education in
California, 1960–1975,*
1960, pp. 18, 97.

These vast outlays—the 1976 estimate equals roughly *all* state expenditures for IHL in the late 1950s—assume no rise of costs per student.

* I owe these ratios to Richard Eckaus.

FOOTNOTES

[1] Parts of this chapter were published in the McGraw-Hill fiftieth anniversary volume, Dexter M. Keezer (ed.), *Financing Higher Education: 1960–70,* 1959, and *in Bulletin of the American Association of University Professors,* Summer, 1958, pp. 589–595.

[2] *Cf.* HEW, *Ten Year Objectives in Education,* 1961, pp. 44–46.

[3] Calculated from HEW, *Statistics of Higher Education, 1955–56, Faculty, Students and Degrees.*

[4] *Ibid.*

[5] Keezer, *op. cit.,* p. 171.

Chapter 3

A STATISTICAL SURVEY OF INSTITUTIONS BY SPECIAL CATEGORIES*

I think this classification, which deals with income, enrollment, student aid, endowment, and faculty structure, throws some additional light on the problems we are discussing. State IHL are not included in this survey. I present Tables 3-1 through 3-5 for a number of variables. In these particular tables I have included only an average of all cases in each category. That means that in some instances the same institutions are not included in all years. I have, however, compiled another table, not reproduced here, which gives the averages of colleges represented for all three years (referred to as comparisons of identical IHL). Where there are large differences, I shall note them.

First, Enrollment. All these groups seem to lose in relation to the total rise of enrollment from 1928 to 1956, but the losses are not nearly so large if the comparison is made with the average per institution. It is certainly clear that the first four groups, which represent the cream of our universities and colleges (aside from many outstanding state universities), have lost ground substantially in their percentage of the total college population. In particular, women's colleges have had no increase from 1928 to 1956, although when identical colleges are compared over this period, the increase becomes 18 per cent.[1] The rise of Catholic colleges over this period for identical institutions is not 87 but 125 per cent. The large relative gains are made by the large urban universities, large Catholic institutions, and public institutions including junior colleges (not listed here). The quality of the urban and Catholic institutions is indeed improving, but they are not quite at the level of the top four groups in Table 3-1. In the sense that the best institutions take a smaller share of the students, there has been a deterioration of higher education as a whole. Some of us fear

---

* A statistical survey of 8 Ivy League universities, 6 other private universities, 10 outstanding women's colleges, 20 outstanding liberal arts colleges, 40 large urban universities, 23 large Catholic institutions.

that under the pressure of numbers this trend will continue, a result that may reduce financial needs below those estimated earlier.

I Now Turn to Current Income. Here again the rise for the average Ivy League university and the 10 women's colleges has been less than the total rise of income, which was more than 500 per cent during this period.* But compared to the 40 large urban and 23 large Catholic institutions, the Ivy League schools have done well. Their record is not, however, nearly so good when the comparison is made with identical institutions in each group over the years, for the large urban schools then show an increase of

TABLE 3-1
Enrollment*

| College groups | Average of all cases | | | | | |
| | 1928 | 1940 | 1956 | Percentage rise | | |
				1928–1940	1940–1956	1928–1956
Total U.S. (thousands)........	1,101†	1,494	2,661	35.8	78.4	141.5
Average per inst., U.S........	781†	875	1,432	12.0	63.8	83.2
8 Ivy League..............	6,949	7,839	9,832	13.0	25.5	41.8
6 other private universities....	6,070	4,904	7,899	−19.3	59.4	29.8
10 women's colleges.........	1,132	982	1,137	−13.2	15.3	0.5
20 liberal arts..............	641	701	942	9.4	34.2	46.8
40 large urban.............	6,175	7,438	11,067	20.4	48.5	79.4
23 large Catholic...........	2,677	2,632	5,009	− 1.7	90.0	87.4

* Excluding summer and extension schools.
† This figure is for the year 1930.
Source: *American Universities and Colleges,* 1928, 1940, 1956. (Compiled and calculated by S. E. Harris.)

604 per cent, and the large Catholic institutions, one of 684 per cent. Six other private universities have made a particularly impressive record in their increase of current income during this period. Their rise, despite a relatively small increase of enrollment, is 1,025 per cent. Undoubtedly a large part of their outlays goes to research and similar objectives. Women's colleges are clearly losing ground with an increase of 173 per cent (or 205 for identical colleges) as compared to a rise of more than 500 per cent for all IHL.

In student aid, the Ivy League, 6 other private universities, and 10 women's colleges seem to have a considerable lead. But the 20 liberal arts colleges make up for their smaller average aid by helping a larger per-

* Not shown in table. Based on HEW estimates.

centage of their students. The 40 large urban and 23 large Catholic universities and colleges have improved their position since 1940, particularly if identical institutions are compared. But the last two groups help a relatively small percentage of the students as compared with the first four groups, though the urban and Catholic institutions have increased their aid per student relatively more than the other groups since 1940.

TABLE 3-2
Current Income*
(In millions of dollars)

| College groups | Average of all cases | | | | | |
| | 1928 | 1940 | 1956 | Percentage rise | | |
				1928– 1940	1940– 1956	1928– 1956
8 Ivy League...............	5.03	7.22	22.80	43.5	215.0	353.0
6 other private universities....	2.07	4.86	23.30	135.0	380.0	1025.0
10 women's colleges.........	0.97	1.26	2.66	29.0	112.0	173.5
20 liberal arts..............	0.31	0.66	1.83	116.0	180.0	500.0
40 large urban.............	2.49	3.07	10.82	23.6	252.0	335.0
23 large Catholic...........	0.72	0.87	3.50	21.4	302.0	389.0

* Current income includes income from endowment and gifts, student fees, and other small sources.
Source: *American Universities and Colleges*, 1928, 1940, 1956. (Compiled and calculated by S. E. Harris.)

The 10 women's colleges have a somewhat higher average of aid, perhaps because they have had high charges, and they have therefore been more disposed to practice discriminatory pricing than some of the other colleges. In general, it may be said for many of these colleges, particularly for the Ivy League and probably for other groups, that in view of the improved administration of aid the scholarship dollar goes much further than it used to. The increase of aid per student from 1940 to 1956 is less on the average than that of tuition and probably less than the average of all costs. But note that a larger percentage of the students are helped, and much greater attention is paid to needs of students. When allowance is made for the large percentage of the student body aided as well as the average amount provided and consideration is given to the much more careful job done in providing help where needed, the scholarship and other aid programs have clearly advanced since 1940. The improvement is even greater when allowance is made for the large expansion of aid not in control of IHL, for example, that given by the various foundations and hence not included in this survey.[2]

Now I Turn to Endowment. Despite a tendency for endowment to play a much smaller part in financing higher education, it is clear that endowment is still a very important matter for a limited number of institutions. The percentage increase of endowment for the 8 Ivy League schools was nearly twice the average increase for all institutions. The others have not done nearly so well; and even the 6 other private universities, with their very large budgets, have not performed as well as the 8 Ivy League universities. Note that the record of the 10 women's colleges is exceptional. The large urban and large Catholic institutions have experienced rises that roughly correspond to that for the whole nation, when identical institutions are compared.

TABLE 3-3
Student Aid

College groups	Average of all cases			
	Per cent of students aided		Dollars per student aided	
	1940	1956	1940	1956
8 Ivy League...............	14.5	20.0	412	720
6 other private universities....	11.5	14.2	521	786
10 women's colleges.........	18.9	21.4	600	872*
20 liberal arts.............	25.5	28.0	329	572†
40 large urban.............	6.4	6.5	338	685
23 large Catholic..........	3.0	6.4	304	609

* Sarah Lawrence College excluded because of a disproportionately large figure.

† Bard excluded in the average because it had an extremely large figure which threw off the average disproportionately. (An error is suspected.)

Source: *American Universities and Colleges,* 1928, 1940, 1956. (Compiled and calculated by S. E. Harris.)

When the comparison is made of endowment per student, the Ivy League schools have an even better record. Their increase is about nine times as great as the average for the nation, whereas other private IHL scarcely exceeded the national average. Ten women's colleges experienced a rise of only 71 per cent, and *identical* large urban and large Catholic institutions, 76 and 63 per cent, respectively.

I Finally Turn to the Structure of the Faculty. This is of interest because standards as well as levels of faculty pay are related to the proportion of full professors and associate professors. When institutions reduce the percentage of their full professors, they tend to deteriorate their standards. They depend more largely on younger members of the faculty. A table (not reproduced) shows that the proportion of full and associate professors

TABLE 3-4
Endowment
(In millions of dollars)

College groups	Average of all cases					
				Percentage rise		
	1928	1940	1956	1928–1940	1940–1956	1928–1956
Total U.S....................	1,372*	1,764	4,000†	28.6	127.0	192.0
8 Ivy League................	21.5	52.6	95.4	147.0	81.8	345.0
6 other private universities......	24.9	35.4	51.6	44.4	45.0	107.0
10 women's colleges...........	4.4	5.1	10.2	15.9	98.0	132.0
20 liberal arts...............	3.5	5.6	9.4	61.0	66.0	170.0
40 large urban...............	9.8	15.5	22.6	57.0	46.8	130.0
23 large Catholic.............	1.6	1.3	2.7	−18.7	111.0	68.0

* This figure is for the year 1930.
† This figure is an estimate.

TABLE 3-5
Endowment per Student

College groups	Average of all cases					
				Percentage rise		
	1928	1940	1956	1928–1940	1940–1956	1928–1956
Total U.S....................	1,245*	1,180	1,500†	−5.2	27.1	20.5
8 Ivy League................	4,326	8,334	12,103	93.0	45.5	180.0
6 other private universities.....	6,168	9,397	7,738	52.0	−17.6	26.0
10 women's colleges..........	4,501	4,864	7,704	8.0	60.0	71.0
20 liberal arts...............	6,247	7,500	9,765	20.7	30.1	56.2
40 large urban..............	1,590	2,080	2,050	30.8	−1.5	28.9
23 large Catholic............	606	490	542	−19.1	10.6	10.6

* This figure is for the year 1930.
† This figure is an estimate.
Source: *American Universities and Colleges*, 1928, 1940, 1956. (Compiled and calculated by S. E. Harris.)

is roughly unchanged over twenty-eight years for the Ivy League. But the 6 other private universities have experienced a substantial fall in the proportion of full professors. This may be explained in part by the growth of research programs. It is also explained by a rise in the percentage of associate professors. The proportion for women's colleges has not changed considerably, but there has been a substantial decline of full professors in the 20 liberal arts colleges, which is only partly made up by a rise in the percentage of associate professors. The decline of full professors is especially marked in large urban and large Catholic institutions. Here, where enrollment has been rising greatly and costs increasing, the response has been to depend upon a younger faculty. It should be pointed out, however, that a rise in the rate of growth of enrollment would lead us to expect some tendency in this direction.

FOOTNOTES

[1] By "identical colleges" I mean those colleges for which figures are available for all three years.

[2] The problem of aid is discussed fully in Chap. 11.

PART TWO

PRICING

Chapter 4

THE TUITION PROBLEM

SOME INTRODUCTORY REMARKS

A writer comes to certain conclusions and then writes his book. He can proceed by working on his own, using printed materials for the most part. He is likely to end up with a program, after several years, not unlike one that might have been forecast almost at the beginning.

My experience has been somewhat different. In 1957 I was convinced, in fact because of theoretical and practical experience with state government, that the solution for the problems of both public and private IHL was large increases in fees. This position troubled me, because my general ideological position was favorable toward public aid and equality of opportunity. Yet high tuition would discourage the underprivileged.

In a period of three years my views underwent considerable change. In this period I visited 120 IHL and attended at least 10 conferences on higher education. For example: I spent several days with a group of university presidents under the auspices of the American Council of Education; spent three weeks at Southampton (Merrill Center) at two higher-education conferences of educators and others, one sponsored by the McGraw-Hill Book Company, Inc.;[1] spent a week at a conference sponsored by the Manpower Commission of Columbia University; attended a conference on Federal Aid to Higher Education by the American Assembly;[2] and, most important, spent a few days with the state university presidents at their annual meeting in May, 1960.[3]

In addition there were several conferences, sponsored by the Ford Foundation, with college administrators, and nine days at a seminar on the economics of higher education,[4] and visits to 120 colleges and universities, generally with the head of the institution, the treasurer and the academic dean. These lasted from a few hours to a few days. In all I estimate about one hundred forty days spent on visits and conferences.

These meetings considerably affected my views on the financing of higher education. My general position had been strongly in favor of substantial rises in tuition. I supported this conclusion on the grounds of ability to pay—e.g., a rise of per capita disposable income of $1,100 since before the war against an increase of tuition of little more than $100; on the larger lifetime gains of the college graduate over others—e.g., a $200,000 advantage for current graduates;[5] on the assumption of improved methods of financing higher education that would eliminate the sting of higher tuition and that through longer periods of payment and rising incomes would reduce the burden.

This position does not mean an unawareness of the social gains of higher education which justify large payments by government, nor does it mean tuition equal to costs. What is proposed here is a continuance of subsidies by government and private philanthropy, and even increases. But it is also assumed that these categories would not provide all the additional resources needed. Far from it.

By 1960, I had substantially changed my position under the constant hammering of the low-tuition school. I hope that my willingness to listen to argument will not leave me as regretful as I have been for twenty-six years for having shifted my position on some aspects of New Deal economics under the persuasive power of a brilliant and older colleague and coauthor of the *Economics of the Recovery Program* (1934).

I realize now, more than I did before, the importance of the image of the public institution as the home of the impecunious but worthy. I realize now that out of the growing economy, to avoid any large increases in tuition, many states should be able to increase their contributions, as should the Federal government. Yet even this will require strong efforts by students, alumni, and public-spirited citizens. The more economical the operations, the more equitable the tax system, the more the rate of growth, the less the numbers seeking higher education, the more likely the budgetary problem will be met without increases in tuition by 1970 of 100 to 200 per cent. Once the country and the taxpayer are adequately briefed on the gains of higher education for the individual and the nation, it is certainly possible that we could keep our tuition from rising more than 40 per cent by 1970 (stable prices), a rate not greatly exceeding the gains of per capita income. Then tuition would increase only by about $75 by 1970 for students in public institutions, and less than $300 in private institutions. Then, instead of yielding $3 billion additional income by 1970, tuition would yield only about $1.5 billion additional, the major part associated with rising enrollments.

But we should stress the point that in the years 1954 to 1958 tuition rose about one-third in both categories of institutions, and at that rate there would be more than a doubling in tuition by 1970 (e.g., at $400 in public and $1,600 in private institutions). Hence, whatever our views about what should be done, the pressures of taxpayers may yet raise tuition by 100 per cent by 1970. This would indeed be unfortunate. A 50 per cent rise might well be a happy compromise—that is, 4 per cent compounded per year for ten years. This would not be much out of line with rising capacity to pay, enhanced by improved financing methods, and might be achieved by an intensive educational program.

In general, government has under- rather than overinvested in education. The best evidence of this is a long-term rise of output about three times as great as input of labor, management, and capital. What is the explanation of this other than the much larger rise of investment in personal capital (education) than in impersonal capital since 1900? Some economists have estimated that about 90 per cent of the gains of productivity are associated with technological advances, a product primarily of education. This may indeed be too high. Incidentally, Gary Becker, in a paper to the American Economic Society in December, 1960, argued that the return on education did not exceed that on corporate capital and hence, aside from external gains (e.g., the contributions of scientists), there was no evidence of underinvestment in education. But this leaves out of account the important nonmaterial gains of education.

Throughout this volume we refer to social and private benefits from higher education, and our problems of financing in relation to these benefits. The benefits to society stem from filling needs for professionally trained men and women, contributing manpower generally needed for defense, education, and the like; providing the scientific and educational resources so essential for growth and hence for defense and welfare; and assuring the nation the cultural standards deemed essential. For the individual, the emphasis is on income gains and on its nonmaterial contributions of education, e.g., increased ability to think and communicate, and a rising desire for knowledge.

In general, people underinvest in education, a fact suggested by the large excess of income available to the college-trained over the cost of the investment (cf. Becker). In a perfect market the individual capable of meeting minimum standards would estimate the monetary and other gains of higher education against the costs involved, i.e., monetary outlays, income forgone, postponement of marriage, etc. But the market is imperfect. Ignorance related to deficient vocational guidance; irrational weighting of costs and benefits; consideration of noneconomic issues, e.g., preference for work over study, desire for early marriage; inadequacy of finances for education—these are among the factors that explain the underinvestment in higher education.

Availability of resources often has the result that those with relatively low intelligence and hence with relatively small gains from higher education obtain a college training and the highly intelligent with small resources and family responsibilities do not achieve a college education. We shall discuss alternatives later, but it is of some interest that only three-fifths of the most promising 5 per cent of high school graduates earn college degrees; only 90 per cent of those in the top 2 per cent and two-thirds of those in the top 10 per cent go to college; and one-half of the high quarter in high school do not go to college.[6]

The big issue is, what can be done to increase the investments in higher education? Obviously, improved methods of financing and better vocational guidance would help encourage those going to college who would gain more than the costs. Reduced tuitions, loans below cost, and more and better scholarships would all help.

Government should weigh the returns on alternative expenditures. Where the dividends on outlays on higher education exceed those elsewhere, the government properly increasingly subsidizes higher education. Beyond this the government may favor higher education through outlays financed by increases in taxes, thus converting private into public spending.

Where the gains are primarily society's these policies are clearly appropriate. But what if the gains are primarily private? Then the burden might well be put on the individual, and he might be required to assume the entire costs. But even this is not acceptable, for we are wedded to a theory of equality of opportunity. The poor boy should also have an opportunity to achieve these private gains. It is, however, difficult to envisage a situation where the gains are exclusively private. Even if the income gains accrue to the individual, society gains from higher incomes yielding more taxes and more outlays for defense and welfare. When the benefits are joined, welfare economics has as yet not provided us with the answers of the ratio of public and private benefits. An interesting example is medicine. The private gains are very large—I estimate a lifetime income for a doctor who graduates in 1960 at about $1.5 million. Then why not put the financing burden on him? But even here society has an interest. Doctors are scarce, and pay-as-you-go financing or long-term borrowing at cost may discourage many potential doctors.

On the theory that the gains are private, not public, Milton Friedman would treat underinvestment and market imperfections, with government equity investments in higher education. The costs of such investments to private lenders would be high enough to discourage potential borrowers. Enslavement (a counterpart of mortgage) is not possible, and risks of inadequate future income for any individual are too great. Hence the case for government investment, with the government receiving a percentage of income of the borrower who meets minimum standards.[7] Administration costs are relatively low for the big lender, and government can reduce risks through large operations.

In the remainder of this chapter I discuss a few general issues more fully treated later: tuition in relation to the product of the IHL; the relation of price changes and enrollment; gains of higher education, private and social; the practicability of higher fees.

PECULIARITIES OF THE MARKET

The price of higher education is a matter of public record: each college and university prints its tuition rate in firm black print in a catalogue. If the product for sale were an automobile instead of an education, the figure behind the dollar sign would be the result of a comparatively small number of factors, notably the product's cost to the manufacturer and demand for the product, which in turn are related to the prices charged by competitors. The figure in the college catalogue represents a much more complex situation.

Tuition charges are the result of a curious mixture of factors in the minds of those who set them. Some of the feelings are contradictory— such as their good will toward the student but an understandable reluctance to see the institution go broke. The price on the catalogue page is the result of a compromise among many such considerations. This compromise varies from institution to institution, but in general it makes learning a bargain.

Consider first the consumer of higher education—the young man looking about for a college to attend. Will the institution with tuition of $1,000 be correspondingly better for him than the $500 institution or the $250 one?

In his perplexity, the potential student may consult an educational counselor and discover that youth has no monopoly on bewilderment. The counselor will perhaps have information about the worth of a particular institution, such as its accreditation, the number of Ph.Ds on its faculty, its graduates in *Who's Who,* the average income of the men it has trained, and other indications of excellence, but these may not have any direct bearing on the question of whether or not school Alpha is justified in charging twice as much as school Beta. The average vocational guidance officer will probably not even have the information listed above, but only some general views. He may get some help from numerous guidebooks such as Hawes's *Guide to Colleges* or Babbidge's *Student Financial Aid.*

Despite any professional advice which the young man receives, however, the final decision rests with him. Necessarily, he will make this decision without adequate knowledge.

A similar confusion exists within the institutions which the young man is considering. This confusion is compounded by the awkward fact that tuition rates do not obey the laws which govern pricing in the commercial world. Here are a few examples of the difference:

1. Dominant sellers of education do not determine its price as in other

markets. In the Northeast, the ratio of students in private institutions of higher learning to students in public institutions is roughly 4 to 1; in the West, 1 to 4, or a *relative* ratio sixteen times as great for private enroll-ment in the Northeast as compared to the West. One might expect that private institutions in the West would be forced to lower their prices to compete with the larger proportion of institutions supported by the tax-payer, but the ratio of tuition rates of private to public IHL in the West, despite this heavy competition, is nearly identical with that in the North-east.

2. Tuition rates in different fields are not closely related to costs of instruction in that field. In one university, the cost of training a student in the medical school in a recent year was fifty-five times as great as that of training a student in the business school. The difference in tuition rates was not remotely comparable to this difference in cost.

3. A rise in price does not necessarily mean a reduction in sales. As our survey since the Civil War shows, the rule is higher prices and *more* sales. For generations, the increase of tuitions far exceeded the gains of prices and often per capita income, yet enrollment has risen steadily, even in the Great Depression, when tuition rates rose despite reductions in prices and per capita income. But rises in tuition affect the make-up of the student body.

4. There are two distinct types of institutions selling education in the open market: public institutions, whose tax support makes it possible to keep tuition and fees low, and private institutions, which, without much government aid, generally have to charge higher prices.

The effects of low fees in public IHL are important, for the extent to which tuition will rise as costs increase depends in no small part upon the policies of public institutions. Those speaking on behalf of these insti-tutions protest rising fees, arguing that the state university was created to serve poor boys and girls. This is true, but the situation has changed radically since the day in which most of these schools were founded. The college graduate does not turn predominantly to the low-paying occupa-tions of the ministry, teaching, and farming, as he did a century ago.

If public institutions keep their fees at substantially the same level over the next ten or twelve years, they will absorb perhaps 75 per cent of en-rollment in higher education. Expansion of these proportions might seri-ously damage many private colleges and universities. This projection is based on the record of the years from 1948 to 1958, when enrollment in all institutions of higher learning rose by 35 per cent and the public in-stitutions accounted for 82 per cent of this increase, raising their share of the total number of students from 51 per cent to 59 per cent. A continu-ance of this trend, strengthened by the increased pressure on government to assume responsibilities for the rising demand, would increase enrollment in public institutions to about 4½ million out of a total of 6 million by 1970.

I do not recommend that private institutions press for higher tuition in public institutions as a means of saving their own economic lives, still less that they should lobby against appropriations for public institutions, as has sometimes been done in the past. Former Chancellor Kimpton of the University of Chicago, in an address on November 11, 1959, said:

The inability of a private institution to raise its tuition has varied inversely with its proximity to strong public institutions. It was only natural, therefore, that presidents of private institutions, singly and collectively, should suggest to the heads of neighboring public universities that they should raise their tuition rates, thereby reducing this ominous competition.

If private institutions are to survive, they must do so by offering a product which is *different* from the product of the state institution and which the public will buy because it believes that the difference in product is worth that in price. The case for higher tuition in public institutions rests largely on fiscal considerations, the excessive tax burdens which would result if current tuition rates are maintained at state colleges and universities— especially in view of the additional burden of public school education of an estimated $11 billion by 1970, a burden likely to fall on state and local governments almost exclusively.

FEES AND SOCIAL VALUES

Present tuition fees reflect social values, to some extent, in that divinity students and future teachers pay little, technological students relatively much. The effect of these social values is particularly clear in one first-class university which has five schools with a large emphasis on "social values" and two others which do not. In the first group of schools, tuition fees cover from 9 to 27 per cent of the university's costs; in the second group, from 52 to 58 per cent.

If the taxpayer wants to support some branches of education at state universities more heavily than others on the ground that he considers these fields of great social worth, he is free to do so by paying for 90 per cent of the cost of the student's education from his own pocket and letting the student pay 10 per cent. At Harvard I discovered costs per student as high as $14,000 (in public health) and less than $2,000 in law, yet tuition fees vary little. In almost *all* universities the tuition rates for law and medicine are comparable, despite the fact that training doctors is much more expensive than training lawyers.

These social factors are not entirely free from influence by costs. It is an interesting fact that, whereas the ratio of tuition in private to public institutions is 4 to 1, in medicine it is 2 to 1. These higher fees for medical training in the public schools undoubtedly reflect higher costs, though in part also the comparatively high earnings of doctors and the competition to enter medical school.

TUITION VERSUS COSTS

Tying tuition to costs can easily be carried too far. One unfortunate result would be choice of courses of study on the basis of costs rather than interest, capacity, and needs. Who, for example, would propose tuition in the ratio of 1 to 3, 1 to 6–7 and 1 to 24 for instruction in lower division (1), higher division (3), graduate (6–7), and graduate research (24) because costs at different levels vary in these ratios in one university; or who would suggest that because instructional costs are five times as high in schools of medicine as in other schools in 17 universities, their tuition rates should be five times as high?

Tuition does, nevertheless, to some extent reflect differences in costs. In a recent year variations in tuition were substantial—e.g., $105 to $397 (averages) in different types of schools (public), and $250 to $701 in private institutions. To some extent, pricing policy yields to financial pressures and deviates from policies tethered to social objectives.

This picture of present policy of fixing tuition fees makes one thing very clear: as costs rise, the pressure on IHL is to increase their tuition. It is not easy to measure average costs, but the college administrator need only know that gifts, capital income, and government appropriations will not cover total costs in the future. The alternatives to higher tuition fees are more efficient operation, a lower quality of education, a failure to satisfy the growing demand for college education or recourse to other sources of income.

PRACTICABILITY OF HIGHER FEES

Some factors that suggest the practicability of higher fees are the following:

In the past, administrators have assumed that tuition should be tied to the price level. This has only an indirect bearing on the ability of the student, or the student's parents, to pay. Per capita income rises faster than prices, and hence, in so far as tuition is tied to capacity to pay, per capita income, not prices, is the relevant measure.

The demand for higher education will, if nothing else does, reflect the growth in numbers of people of college age—especially important in the next ten to fifteen years.

Tuition charges are only part of the total cost of education to the student. If tuition should rise by 100 per cent, say, by $500, then the rise would be but roughly one-fourth of all costs ($1,800), assuming no rise in room and board charges (although these might actually rise somewhat), and only about one-eighth of costs inclusive of income forgone.[8] Actual percentage rises for all costs would be higher because of increases in other expenses.

The additional expense need not all be paid at once. The longer colleges are able to extend the period of payment of tuition, the less burdensome a rise in tuition will be.

Scholarships and loans, discussed elsewhere in this book, can also ensure that colleges will not be forced to turn away able students with modest means. In recent years the relative growth of total student aid has exceeded the relative growth of tuition.

In other words, when attention is given to the *total* costs to the student, to the possibilities of revolutionary changes in the methods of financing higher education, notably through lifetime financing, to the possibility of helping poor and able students through scholarships as well as loans, and to the possibility of cooperation among competitors in this field, we might then find that substantial rises in tuition would make the financing of higher education possible without excessive appeal for help from any one group and without substantial deficits. But any attempt by private IHL alone to raise tuition greatly which does not take these factors into consideration will leave private IHL facing serious competition from state institutions, where tuition is only about one-quarter as high as in private institutions and where there does not at present seem to be any strong disposition to increase tuition substantially even if the percentage rise is large.

There are, in fact, alternatives to this oversimplified strategy of higher pricing. In a period of excess demand, the college administrator can choose between absorbing the increased interest in his product in higher prices or in an improvement in the quality of the purchaser, i.e., the student, or, of course, in something of each. This "quality," of course, is defined as the institution in question chooses to define it. In my opinion, institutions in a sound financial position which are not overeager to expand should absorb the gains of a rising market primarily in an improved product—a more discerningly chosen student body. For others the way out would seem to be increased enrollment rather than large rises of tuition. When there is much excess capacity and small classes, it is possible to increase enrollment at current tuition and improve the financial situation. But many IHL, under financial pressure, will absorb the gains of an improved market, not in higher-quality students, but in higher prices.

Whatever the solution, the competition for students between public and private institutions will certainly be affected. Friends of private institutions may be realistically concerned by competition from state colleges and universities. But legislators and governors, sensitive to the demands of taxpayers, will probably not allow the cost of higher education to rise from roughly 5 per cent of the total budget of states today to 12 per cent in the next ten to twelve years (my estimate, assuming that tuition stays constant and higher costs are absorbed primarily by higher taxes).

CONCLUSION

Tuition rates for all institutions of higher learning, both public and private, must be raised. The real issue is how much. The *way* in which these tuition charges can be raised will be discussed later, but one simple idea can be discarded at once—that tuition charges can be based on costs alone. If this were done, concentration in classics (for example) would end, and medical schools would be forced to accept only students from wealthy families, ruling out the poor but able students. In a college of a famous university, faculty salaries charged to the college in relation to fees received varied from 36 per cent in a civilization course, to 4,335 per cent in Chinese and Japanese. Imagine charging on the basis of costs! I believe that it is possible to preserve education from either a weakening lack of funds or from such painful increases in the financial burden to students that education becomes the privilege of the rich alone.

Nevertheless, in view of the fact that the ability to pay would be greatly increased if financing methods were changed and that the college student receives a large advantage compared to the noncollege student in income received, I urge that there is a case for higher tuition. But the large social product militates against high fees. We want a system that will take into account the resources currently available to students and a system that would make it less necessary for students to work while at college and to pay their college bills in part through loans, that is, out of the rising income of the future rather than from the low income of the past, as is so largely done now.

Hence, because of rising family income and the needs of IHL in relation to alternative sources of income, I envisage higher fees. But it would be most unfortunate if rising fees were to exclude students of adequate quality. The public institutions are likely to remain the haven of the poor and deserving youths who are frightened either by high costs or substantial use of credit. The private IHL, through the use of financial aid, will be able to enroll a much smaller proportion of these young men and women. It is, therefore, important that government at all levels make increasing contributions to higher education. Governments will, as we shall see, be better able to do this as their incomes rise, their tax systems become less regressive, and competing demands are kept in check. But the contributions of state governments will vary in accordance with rates of growth, types of tax systems, traditions of public higher education, and the like. To some extent the Federal government may be able to neutralize the effects of inadequate income and high needs at the state level.

FOOTNOTES

[1] Dexter M. Keezer (ed.), *Financing Higher Education: 1960–70*, McGraw-Hill, 1959.

[2] *The Federal Government and Higher Education*, 1960.

[3] *Transactions and Proceedings of the National Association of State Universities in the United States of America*, 1960.

[4] Published as *Higher Education in the United States: The Economic Problems*, Harvard University Press, 1960.

[5] Reservations later.

[6] See D. Wolfle, *America's Resources of Specialized Talent*, 1954, chap. 6 (especially p. 150). and chap. 9; B. S. Hollinshead, *Who Should Go To College*, 1952; C. C. Cole, *Encouraging Scientific Talent*, 1955; and the discussion of my tutee J. B. Levine in his honors thesis on "Student Subsidization in American Institutions of Higher Education," 1960, pp. 151–163.

[7] M. Friedman, "The Role of Government in Education," in R. A. Solo (ed.), *Economics and the Public Interest*, 1955, pp. 123–145.

[8] See Chap. 8 for further discussion.

Chapter 5

TUITION AND COSTS

PRICING PRACTICES

Tuition is in a sense a price for services rendered. Like any price, many factors bear on its determination. In a later chapter I shall discuss the effect of competition among institutions on the levels of tuition, but here I would like to consider another important variable, the costs associated with the services of IHL. Colleges and universities are in the somewhat unusual position of having major sources of income other than the "price" of their product. Nonetheless, tuition income is a very important source of funds to IHL, accounting on the average for 43 per cent of total educational and general income in 1940, 51 per cent in 1950 (inflated by GI Bill), and 35 per cent in 1957–58. It is of interest that the ratio tends to fall, though 1950 is not a good base, since tuition paid by the government tended to raise the ratio of tuition to educational and general income. Tuition paid by the government in that year covered 44 per cent of all tuition.[1]

Also of some interest in these figures is the failure of tuition to rise relative to all educational income in the years 1955–56 to 1957–58. Yet in these years, large increases in tuition occurred.[2]

Like the businessman, the college administrator must balance his accounts. What cannot be obtained from capital income (or consumption of capital) or gifts or government appropriations must be obtained from tuition. A substantial part of costs must be covered by tuition; and when costs rise more than nontuition income, the relative contribution of tuition must rise. Many colleges can put the day of reckoning off by borrowing or, as they did especially in the 1930s and 1940s, by living on capital. In some cases endowment was consumed; in many colleges the consumption of capital took the form of undermaintenance of capital plant. In general, IHL do not put aside more than 2 per cent for depreciation of plant—an unusually small allocation, suggesting capital depreciation and overstatement of income.

Here I emphasize the point that college authorities may have to increase tuition relative to costs, not because nonprofit institutions operate like

54

business and must cover costs with fees—in fact, they need not cover all costs in this way—but because the services required will deteriorate otherwise. This again is on the assumption that government and private philanthropy do not greatly raise their contributions and substantial economies are not achieved.

I hasten to add that the discovery of costs is not always easy. Of course, the college administrator in this context may not need to know too much about costs of his institution; all he needs to know is that he needs to increase tuition in order to recover a larger part of total costs.[3] A failure to do so would mean either a deterioration of standards, curtailed enrollment, or bankruptcy.

Still, the determination of costs is helpful, even if it is conceded that tuition should not be based on them. We then know the size of the subsidy to students, and they will be more aware of their indebtedness. Moreover, knowledge of costs is useful in trying to raise funds from alumni, and as tuition goes up, the parent and the student want to be convinced that tuition does not exceed costs. [This does not mean, of course, that institutions in great demand might not charge a tuition exceeding the costs in a particular school, using the proceeds to subsidize others. In fact, the extension work of one major university yields a substantial surplus which is used to offset deficits in other schools. A study of New York University (*New York University Self-study,* 1956) comments on the surplus produced ". . . by a large number of fee-paying students in low-cost instructional areas" and the failure to plow back these earnings in order to improve standards.]

The problem of allocating costs out of a total budget to different departments and schools is a formidable one. In the simple liberal arts college it is relatively easy to estimate costs for the average student. Difficulties arise when the college or university produces joint products. How should outlays on research be allocated? Those on library expenditures? Pay of professors who teach in more than one department of the university? How should the costs of buildings, heating, and general overhead be allocated? In a division of expenditures between the college and the graduate school of arts and sciences, especially serious problems arise. Most will concede that the costs of education are much higher in the graduate school than in the arts and science college, partly because of the greater interest of the high-priced teachers in graduate instruction and partly because of the numerous small classes. But what part of the research done by a professor who teaches in both should be allocated to the college and what part to the graduate school?

These are tough problems, but businesses which turn out many more different products than colleges manage to allocate costs with reasonably satisfactory results. Many studies have been made on the cost per course or the cost per credit hour and the like. In addition we have a number of studies, including one by the University of Chicago, giving the amount of time a faculty member devotes to undergraduates, to graduates, and to research. The costs at the University of California, three surveys of medical school costs, where jointness is paramount, and many other cost studies are available. Business officers of IHL have found techniques for allocating direct and indirect costs among the services provided. Of course, the allocation is partly a matter of judgment, and different accounting methods sometimes yield different results. Nonetheless, we have had a long history in this field and have achieved reasonably good results.

In industry the pricing of a genuine joint product—when the product is produced inevitably in fixed proportions, as with cottonseed produced jointly with cotton—depends on the relative demand for the two products. When demand for one of the joint products is favorable, that product contributes the larger part of total costs.

But when the conjunction of the two products is not inevitable and additional costs must be incurred in producing the second product, a firm will seek to recover at least these additional costs in its pricing policy. Colleges and universities often do not do this. The *additional* cost of operating a graduate school of arts and sciences may well be (say) $2,000 per student; but the institution may charge only $1,000 in tuition. This pricing is motivated partly by the desire to attract able students, and generally these students are unable to pay fees based on additional costs.

In a similar manner the average medical school may cost $4,000 per student per year (though substantially less when research and other costs not relevant to instruction are excluded). Yet the usual charge in private schools is about $1,100 and in public schools about half this figure. Medical schools report costs of teaching varying from $1,000 to $15,000, half of them having costs between $2,000 and $4,000 per year. Here again the fear of excluding able applicants at fees based on costs is relevant. In 1956–57 tuition income covered only 18 per cent of operating expenses of medical schools. But a large part of expenses should not be charged to medical undergraduates.

In contrast to the medical schools, summer school tuitions generally cover at least the additional costs involved and frequently are high enough to cover part of the overhead. In this manner, many IHL require summer schools to pay part of the expenses of the regular semester. The contributions of the summer school are not usually considered important enough from an educational viewpoint to warrant deficits.

TUITION IN RELATION TO COSTS

The capital costs for a plant at book value of $11.2 billion and at least $20 billion of replacement value are estimated to exceed all tuition payments. At forty years' amortization and a 4 per cent rate of interest, the additional costs would be about $1,300 million per year, $500 per student. Hence over-all, the students' contributions are just about matched by unrevealed capital costs. This is subject to one reservation: part of these capital costs are charged to students through room and board charges; once allowance is made for these, the concealed capital costs would almost equal tuition payments.[4]

VARIATIONS IN TUITION

It is scarcely necessary to add that the tuition as a ratio to educational income (exclusive of these capital costs) varies greatly from college to college. For example, in the 60-college study for 1953–54, the minimum of student fees as a percentage of educational and general income was 5.7 per cent, and the maximum, 89.4 per cent. For the 11 men's colleges the median was 50 per cent; for the 11 women's colleges, 59 per cent; for all 60 colleges, 63 per cent; and for the 38 coeducational colleges, 66 per cent. Variations among the Ivy colleges and others are also large. The differences are evidently due in part to varying kinds of accounting.

President Griswold of Yale noted in one of his recent reports that tuition accounts for only 25 per cent of educational costs, a ratio roughly equal to that for public institutions. At Wesleyan in 1955 student fees were 26.9 per cent of income and student aid 9.3 per cent of expenses. In other words, the net income from students was but 17 to 18 per cent of expenses (*Financial Report, 1955*).

According to statements issued by presidents of leading private universities, the percentage of tuition to *educational* costs in 1954–55 was as shown in Table 5-1.

TABLE 5-1*

Princeton	42	Chicago	27
Stanford	48	Cornell	44
Yale	40	Harvard	34

* Figures are adjusted to some extent to make them comparable. The Yale figure is higher than the one shown above because of the elimination of some costs in this table.

Source: *The New York Times*, June 25, 1956.

One will also find large differences in the ratio of tuition to educational expenditures in the same institution: for example, the ratios for Harvard of tuition to relevant expenditures are as shown in Table 5-2.

In Table 5-3 I compare the ratio of tuition to educational and general expenditures (organized research and public services deducted). As might be expected, public fees are relatively low. But there are some differences among types of school—note the low tuition in theology—here the social gains may be held to be relatively large. The large rise for 1960–61 raises some questions, especially since the rise for individual categories does not justify the over-all increase.*

Large differences are to be found among institutions within any one category. Cooper Institute, for example, charges no tuition or fees, and first class private technological schools set tuition at $1,200 or more. Even

TABLE 5-2*

Field	1954–55	1958–59
Arts and science...............	47	45
Medicine......................	18	19
Public health..................	9	7
Law..........................	58	66
Business......................	52	44
Education.....................	27	40
Divinity......................	22	24

* *Financial Report to the Board of Overseers for the Fiscal Year 1954–55*, pp. 10–13. (See the Appendix to this chapter for the corresponding figures including expenditures on research.) For 1958–59, see my article "The Economics of Harvard," *Harvard Alumni Bulletin*, Feb. 20, 1960, p. 382.

TABLE 5-3
Ratio of Tuition to Educational and General Expenditures by Type of Institution, 1955–56, and Tuition, 1959–60, 1960–61

Type of institution	All, per cent	Public, per cent	Private, per cent	1959–60		1960–61	
				Public	Private	Public	Private
All.................	35	...	...	$168	$615	$206	$ 859
Universities..........	...	19	52	241	853	249	973
Liberal arts..........	...	17	66	162	659	138	784
Teachers colleges.....	...	19	...	170	552	174	549
Theology............	...	...	26	....	306	....	343
Technological........	...	10	46	220	860	218	1,040
Junior colleges.......	...	13	67	127	490	134	516

Source: HEW, *Statistics of Higher Education 1955–56: Receipts, Expenditures and Profits, 1959*; my calculations; and HEW, *Higher Education; Planning and Management Data, 1959–60*, Table 21; *Ibid.*, 1960–61, Table 23.

in the same type of institution—e.g., private liberal arts—tuition will vary from a few hundred dollars to $1,500 or more. Among the land-grant colleges, tuition and fees at the Universities of California and Minnesota in 1957–58 were about 13 per cent of educational expenditures minus those

* I have since been informed that the large rise for 1960–61 is explained by the introduction of a weighting procedure.

for extension, public services, and organized research, but 34 per cent for the University of New Hampshire.[5]

A comparison of tuition income with faculty salaries is of some interest. In 1955–56 the average faculty member's salary over the whole country was $5,200. In the same year average tuition (estimated) was $350, or only 7 per cent of average faculty pay. At a ratio of 14 students per faculty member, tuition would nearly cover the costs of faculty pay, although, of course, outlays on instructional and departmental research (of which faculty pay forms the major part) account for only 42 per cent of educational and general expenditures. The relation of faculty pay to tuition also varies among institutions.

RELEVANCE OF THE RELATION OF TUITION TO COSTS

The larger the ratio of tuition to costs, the more likely that a rise of enrollment will increase revenues more than costs. But, when for example, tuition is only 25 per cent of costs, an increase of enrollment is likely to be costly to the IHL. In institutions where tuition covers a small part of costs, the college administrator should not at the same time complain of *both* the reduction of enrollment and the large subsidies paid to students.

TABLE 5-4

Cost item	Millions	Per cent
Total.....................................	$2,288	
Instruction and departmental research.............	966	42
Administration................................	291	13
Organized research*..........................	375	16
Extension and public service*....................	115	5
Plant operation and maintenance.................	280	12
Libraries.....................................	73	3
Activities related to educational departments.......	188	8
Scholarships, fellowships, and prizes..............	75	3

* May be excluded since financed separately and irrelevant for tuition.
Source: HEW, *Statistics of Higher Education, 1953–54: Receipts, Expenditures and Property.* My calculations.

One investigator estimated that fixed costs (for example, cost of building maintenance) were 50 per cent of costs, and sticky ones about 25 per cent of costs. Hence an institution with tuition covering more than 50 per cent of costs would do well to increase enrollment—on purely financial grounds.

For 1953–54 Table 5-4 gives educational costs for all IHL. If instruction is 42 per cent of educational costs, then, to cover additional costs out of additional tuition related to rising enrollment, tuition must cover at least 42 per cent of these costs. This is on the assumption that instructional costs rise *pari passu* with increased enrollment. In the short run they clearly do not—as recent history has well shown. In the future, with a rise in the student/faculty ratio as enrollment rises greatly and faculty becomes difficult to find, instructional costs might not rise as much as they otherwise would.

Assume the percentages of marginal costs (that is, additional cost per additional student) to average costs given in Table 5-5. Tuition was 26

TABLE 5-5

Cost item	Millions	Marginal/average costs,* per cent
Instruction...........................	$966	80
Administration......................	291	25
Plant operation and maintenance......	280	40
Libraries...........................	73	50
Activities related to education.........	188	75
Scholarships........................	75	75

* The number "80" opposite "instruction," for example, means that the additional cost of instruction for one more student is 80 per cent of the average cost of instruction for all students. For plant operation, of course, the ratio is much lower: a building must be heated whether all its classrooms are used or only some of them.

per cent of all educational and general expenditures but 35 per cent of the relevant (i.e., excluding organized research and extension) educational expenditures.

On the basis of assumptions made in the preceding table, the marginal costs are 63 per cent of relevant average costs. Hence if tuition exceeds 63 per cent of relevant costs, IHL would gain financially from rises in enrollment.

But we should emphasize that:

1. We need more information about average and (especially) marginal costs.

2. The relation of tuition to expenditures and of marginal to average costs varies from institution to institution.

3. This ratio of marginal to average costs varies over time, and the marginal cost (per unit) will vary with the size of the increment of enrollment.

4. We have not given any consideration to the capital costs involved in building new plant in response to additional enrollment. A rough esti-

mate suggests that inclusion of capital costs would raise marginal costs by 13 per cent of relevant average costs, that is, to 76 per cent.[6]

In this discussion I have not included capital charges as part of costs. Yet under the pressure of rising enrollment and shortage of academic buildings in several states, e.g., Iowa, Michigan, and Indiana, serious attention has been given to the financing of academic buildings through tuition fees. At Michigan State, for example, the authorities proposed the use of 10 per cent of fees to amortize buildings over a thirty-year period.[7]

Another aspect of this problem needs elaboration. Why, despite higher costs of graduate instruction, is the charge for graduate (arts and science) instruction equal to, or frequently less than, for undergraduate instruction? One reason may be merely that social product is higher here—e.g., the need of teachers. But in part the explanation probably lies in the high elasticity of demand for graduate instruction: competition is keen and resources of students low. They are greatly influenced by variations of costs of $100 or $200.

ENROLLMENT AND ENDOWMENT YIELD

On the issue of marginal and average costs, a word should be said about endowment. As enrollment rises, the contribution of endowment (and current-gift) income per student declines (though in part this may be made up later as gifts increase with a larger alumni body). Rises of enrollment, increases of prices, and reduction of yield explain the decline of endowment income per student and as a proportion of all income in recent years. These declines reflect, first, a rise of enrollment and, second, the increase of prices.

Endowment funds and the income from these funds play a much smaller part in the financing of education than in the past. (I shall dwell on this problem only briefly here; the main discussion of it comes later.) As can be seen from Table 5-6, the amount of endowment income per student in stable dollars declined by about 45 per cent from 1929–30 to 1957–58. Unusual efforts for a few years reversed the trend, and, despite a substantial increase of enrollment, the endowment earnings in stable dollars per resident student rose by $15 in the eight years from 1947–48 to 1955–56. But the decline then resumed. The trend is in the direction of gifts. Through the use of current gifts, income can be had more nearly in accordance with the needs of the institution today, rather than with the needs as they were conceived (say) fifty years ago. One of the disadvantages of endowment is that the money for the future is received on the basis of present needs rather than future needs, and adjustments of outlays to current requirements are often hampered by issues of morality and law. The disadvantage of endowment does not apply to unrestricted gifts or where

TABLE 5-6
Endowment, Endowment Earnings, Total and Per Student Current and Stable Dollars

	1929–30	1939–40	1947–48	1953–54	1955–56	1957–58
Endowment funds (millions of dollars)...............	.....	1,686	2,385	3,196	3,837	4,647
Endowment earnings, current dollars (millions).........	68.6	71.3	86.7	127.4	145.0	181.6
Endowment earnings, stable dollars (millions, 1947–48 = 100)...............	93.7	119.4	87.0	110.8	129.6	148.9
Endowment earnings, per student, current dollars......	62.33	47.72	33.13	50.69	54.55	53.79
Endowment earnings, per student, stable dollars.......	85.15	79.93	33.25	44.08	48.88	44.05

Source: HEW, *Statistics of Higher Education: Receipts, Expenditures and Property, 1953–54, 1955–56, 1957–58 (Preliminary) 1959, 1960.* (My computations.)

the college administrator can adjust to maldistribution of endowment funds through reallocation of other funds.[8]

TUITION AND THE SIZE OF THE INSTITUTION

At a meeting of deans of admissions in 1958, the deans emphasized the widespread preference among students for IHL with high tuition. In part this preference results from the prestige of such institutions and in part from a general view that where the price is high, service is better. This may be true in a general way, but we must not forget that there are first-class institutions, public and private, that charge low tuition. Rice Institute charges no tuition. As we shall see later, the institutions with large endowments tend to charge high tuition. They are frequently the IHL with prestige and high-quality education.

It is surprising that tuition, at least in the private IHL, should be highest in the largest institutions. As enrollment rises up to a certain point, certainly up to 1,000 students, unit costs tend to decline because of the spreading of fixed overhead costs over a larger number of students.[9] Higher tuition prevails in the largest institutions, even though we should expect costs in these institutions to be low just because they are large. Here we have an apparent inverse correlation: the lower the cost, the more the tuition. The explanation is, perhaps, a better faculty and plant in larger institutions, though this is not invariably so.

There can be no doubt about the facts. In a study of 193 independent liberal arts colleges, fees for institutions reporting 1,000 or more students averaged $294 in 1930. As the number of students declined, tuition also dropped until, at institutions with less than 200 students, tuition averaged $159. Many of these institutions undoubtedly provide poor instruction, since unit costs for a good education must be high for small institutions. To some extent these small institutions offset low tuition rates with gifts and capital income. In this same study it was shown that for institutions with enrollment of more than 1,000, private benefactions for current purposes were 1.7 per cent of receipts, but for the smallest institutions, 16.8 per cent. The percentage of gifts tends to vary inversely with the size of the enrollment.

In a study of 60 colleges (*A Second Look at the Sixty College Study,* 1960), the median percentage of tuition to educational and general income was 42.7 per cent in 1957–58 for IHL with enrollments of 200 to 600, and 58.6, 70.9, and 66.1 for those with enrollments of 601 to 1,000, 1,001 to 1,400, and 1,401 and up, respectively.

Total educational and general expenditures for 193 IHL per student were $428 in institutions with an enrollment of more than 1,000 and declined to $306 for institutions with enrollment from 400 to 599. For the next two groups, institutions with 200 to 399 students and those with less than 200, the average expenditure rose to $332 and $384. At the last point undoubtedly the uneconomic size of the institution makes it necessary not only to reduce the quality of the education but also to increase the unit cost. I hasten to add that there are many institutions, e.g., Haverford, where enrollment is small and unit costs and quality high.

Finally, the HEW study, *Planning and Management Data, 1957–1958,* supports these statements. My generalizations relate to private rather than to public institutions. Public institutions, less sensitive to costs, tend to charge roughly similar fees regardless of size. There is indeed a tendency to charge somewhat less in the smaller institutions, but the differences are not large. In the private institutions, beginning at enrollment below 200, the tuition is $365 and rises to $963 for enrollments of 20,000 or more.

In 1959–60, tuition in public IHL varied from $162 in liberal arts to $468 in other professional fields; private, from $306 in theology to $860 in technology. Note that the highest-price institutions are not here the large ones. But an over-all classification by size yields a consistent rise from $138 for institutions with less than 500 to $216 for those public IHL with enrollment in excess of 10,000. The respective figures for private IHL are $510 to $876 ($918 for those with 5,000 to 9,999).

Charges are smaller in the small institutions even though one would expect, at the same level of performance, higher costs at the smaller institutions. In support of 65 small colleges, A. T. Hill points to an average total cost of $1,500 for public IHL, $2,000 for private IHL, and only $850 for the 65 designated small colleges, largely unaccredited. Here quality is relevant. Ostheimer also classifies colleges in the East on the basis of tuition. The highest-quality institutions in the East average $801; the next highest, $601; and the lowest, $594. In this connection, total costs are more significant than tuition alone. For example, Mabel Newcomer shows that the excess of costs in 33 women's as against 24 men's

TABLE 5-7
Fees, Public and Private, 1957–58

Enrollment	Fees	
	Public	Private
Continental United States........	$155	$526
Below 200....................	167	365
200–499.....................	145	470
500–999.....................	154	551
1,000–1,999..................	139	623
2,000–4,999..................	158	638
5,000–9,999..................	168	687
10,000–19,999	181	790
20,000 and more.............	190	963

Source: HEW, *Higher Education: Planning and Management Data, 1957–58*, p. 68; also see *Bulletin of the Association of American Colleges*, vol. 18, 1932, pp. 434–435; *A Study of Income and Expenditures in 60 Colleges, a Summary of Full Year, 1953–54*, pp. 26–27. See 1958–59 issue, HEW, p. 73, for more recent data.

colleges stems primarily from an excess of room and board charges in the women's colleges.[10]

TRENDS IN TUITION

Tables 5A-1 through 5A-9 show the trend of tuition over the years. Elsewhere I have pointed out that tuition from the Civil War until World War II increased much more than prices or per capita income.

Table 5A-4 shows substantial rises of tuition since 1928–29, and a somewhat larger relative increase for public IHL. By 1959–60, tuition and fees in private IHL were only 3.75 times as high as in public, as compared to 4 to 1 or higher ratio in earlier years. Yet a comparison for 229 IHL revealed rises of 33.5 per cent for public IHL and 34.0 per cent for private from 1954–55 to 1958–59.[11] (But from 1957–58 to 1959–60 the respective increases were $71 for public and $86 for private, the public fees then rising from 23 to 27 per cent of those for private IHL in the period of 1928–29 to 1959–60.) Undoubtedly large pressures were being exerted by taxpayers and politicians to make the student pay more. Good examples of this pressure are reflected in a *Resolution of the Texas Commission on Higher Education* (March 9, 1959) that tuition should equal 20 per cent of the general revenue and tuition appropriations, and in a rise in tuition at the University of Mississippi from $92 to $125 per semester in order to make possible temporary increases in salaries, which would enable the institution to hold their professors for another year. In 1959–60, however, the percentage rise for public IHL was but 2½ per cent as against 5 per cent for private.

Millett's results based on an unpublished study of 216 IHL suggest a larger relative increase for public vis-à-vis private than the other studies. Charges for public IHL rose from one-third of private in 1930 and 1940 to almost one-half in 1950. His results give a much higher figure for public, and a much lower one for private, than Conrad's and those of other studies. Figures for the 1950s are rather confusing. I find an equal rise of 33 per cent for four recent years. But the HEW and Miss Mushkin find respective rises of 47 and 36 in the years 1953–1960 for private and public IHL.

TABLE 5-8
Dollars per Student

	Private		Public	
	Conrad	Millett	Conrad	Millett
1940	328	224	70	71
1950	468	372	109	177

Source: See source for Table 5A-5 and J. D. Millett, *Financing Higher Education in the United States,* 1952, pp. 300–301.

Table 5A-5 reveals trends in tuition rates per student from 1940 to 1955. Here the over-all rise is 85 per cent; but 89 per cent for public and 83 per cent for private IHL. These results are for tuition in 196 IHL as revealed by catalogues. In general this table shows roughly similar relative increases for different types of institutions within the public and private universe. One important exception is public liberal arts where tuition rose by 145 per cent—in part explained by the very low charges—$29 in 1940 and $71 in 1955. In public technological institutions the rise was only 59 per cent—possibly explained by the small sample and also the need for the technically trained.

How uniform have increases been? One study of 43 *well-known* colleges and universities revealed a general rise of 93 per cent from 1946–47 to 1957–58. Only nine of these institutions had increases of less than 75 per cent. Similarity of rises reflects similar problems and the tendency of competitors not to get out of line too much. The relatively small rise of several may be explained in part (1) by the fear of state competition, as for Stanford and Chicago, (2) by the competition of coeducational institutions, as for Bryn Mawr and Vassar, and (3) by the relatively high tuitions in 1946–47, as for the Massachusetts Institute of Technology. (This might also be part of the explanation of the small Bryn Mawr increase.) Another explanation may be simply a reluctance to increase fees which prevails even among private institutions. Only four institutions increased their tuition by more than 125 per cent, the highest being Harvard with 154 per cent. Part of the explanation here is the low tuition at Harvard in 1946–47. Harvard's tuition was $415 as compared with an average of $463 for all 43 institutions. In 1957–58 Harvard's figure was $1,056 against an average of $895, and there was a further increase in 1958–59 and in 1960–61.[12]

The study of 422 institutions by C. W. Hoff revealed a median increase of tuition from 1941–42 to 1951–52 of 50 per cent (the mean increase was 66). The lowest percentage increase for a study of 237 institutions was 7, and the highest, 489.[13] This does not suggest as close an agreement as existed among the earlier 43 institutions considered. In part the explanation is that this is a much less homogeneous sample than the one above.

RESIDENT AND NONRESIDENT FEES

In an analysis of public institutions, we should comment on the relation of resident and nonresident fees. In recent years nonresident fees have tended to rise more than resident fees. Thus from 1940 to 1950 resident fees in public universities rose by 54 per cent, nonresident by 81 per cent; for complex colleges, 45 and 65 per cent respectively; for teachers colleges, 42 and 56 per cent. The differential had risen from $66 in 1939–40 to $171 by 1954–55, and by 1959–60 the average fee for resident students in 438 public *undergraduate* institutions was $175; for nonresidents, $384.[14]

A study of public institutions in 12 Middle Western states reveals substantial differences in fees between resident and nonresident; larger rises for the latter in the years 1947–1957; and substantially higher fees in *larger* than in all public IHL in these states: $166 and $299 for resident and nonresident undergraduates in 1957 for the 12 Middle Western states; but $207 and $452 respectively for 22 large institutions in these states.[15]

Public institutions tend to discourage out-of-staters because of the pressure of numbers within the state. The local taxpayer does not want to subsidize outsiders. Yet it is not always clear that on a pure cost basis these decisions are justified—aside from the educational gains of free entry. The issue is, not average, but marginal costs. When, for example, marginal costs are less than, say, $500 today for large institutions, a tuition of $500 means a loss of revenue. But the institution may gain on those who enter paying, say, $500 where marginal costs are, say, $400. Hence the net gain of the higher fees is measured by the excess of fees over additional costs of those in residence, against the losses resulting from the nonentries who might have paid more than marginal costs if fees were lower.

Large relative increases for nonresidents do not seem to have reduced the percentage of nonresidents—in part because fees constitute a small part of total costs.[16] The proportion of nonresidents is not large. In 11 Middle Western states they averaged 17 per cent.[17]

TUITION AND PER CAPITA INCOME

What is especially significant is the relation of rises in tuition to those in per capita disposable income. The latter measures well changes in capacity to pay. Table 5A-6 gives relevant figures for the years 1939–40 to 1955. From 1939–40 to 1949–50, per capita disposable income rose by 136.5 per cent, and tuition in public and private institutions by 56

TABLE 5-9

	Per cent
Rise of tuition	35
Rise of per capita disposable income	23

Source: Various issues of *Planning and Management Data* and *Economic Report of the President, 1960.* (Estimates of 1960 income based on Department of Commerce estimates of third quarter.)

and 43 per cent. Tuition had indeed become a bargain. In so far as students increasingly came from more modest homes, this generalization is subject to a reservation; but for another reason these comparisons understate the increased cheapness of a college education: the largest rises of income in the 1940s occurred to the lower-income groups.

From 1949–50 to 1954–55 tuition tended to rise more than per capita income—a rise of 20 per cent in per capita disposable income and 21 per cent in tuition for the publicly controlled, and 28 per cent for the privately controlled, IHL respectively.

What about more recent years? From 1954–55 to 1959–60 I estimate the percentages shown in Table 5-9.

Tuition rose in these five years more than per capita disposable income. A study of identical institutions, and hence an especially significant study, revealed the data shown in Table 5-10.

TABLE 5-10
Per Cent Increase in Undergraduate College Costs

	1928–1960	1948–1956	1950–1960
14 large private........	278	36	40
20 large public:			
Resident.............	222	30	39
Nonresident..........	338	30	31

Source: *Acceleration in Costs of Attending College*, release by American Council on Education, 1960.

The rise of tuition for *196* (identical) IHL by 1957 had exceeded the increase in cost of living but was much less than the rise in per capita incomes.

TABLE 5-11
Median Income of Heads of Family, Aged Thirty-five to Fifty-four, the Cost of Living, and Mean Institutional Tuition Charges, 1957
(1939 = 100)

Income............................ 380
Cost of living...................... 202
Tuition, public IHL................... 215
Tuition, private IHL.................. 239

Source: L. G. Lewis, in *College and Business*, December, 1959.

I am not sure that the studies discussed above give the only relevant approach to the increase of tuition. It is possible to use other approaches which reveal relatively smaller increases of tuition than, for example, the rise given by Conrad and Hollis of more than $150 from 1940 to 1950.

The usual approach is to compare tuition at various types of institutions in, say, the 1930s and 1956. Such studies may reveal a rise of tuition in private institutions of about $300 and in public institutions of $117. But there is another approach which seems to me to be at least as relevant. I compare the increase of operating costs per student, of tuition (tuition divided by number of students), and of family income *after taxes* from 1929–30 to 1955–56. What do I find?

Rise of family income... $3,000
Rise of tuition per student minus increase of scholarships per student........ 100
Rise of operating cost... 500
Rise of subsidy, per student.. 400

These figures point to a considerable easing of the burden of tuition upon the family finances and a substantial rise of subsidies. One may be surprised at the small rise of tuition shown, namely, about $100 net. The explanation lies largely in the fact that a much larger proportion of students *now* go to IHL where tuition is relatively low. Another factor is that scholarship funds per student have increased by about $30 in twenty-six years and should be deducted from gross tuition. Consider, for example, the effect of the large rise of enrollment since 1929–30 in junior colleges generally free of any tuition, the growth of urban universities and Catholic institutions, and the reduction of the relative enrollment in the Ivy League and other high-tuition groups mentioned above. Consider, for example, the effects on tuition trends of 400,000 additional students at junior colleges who are now paying substantially less than $100 and who otherwise might be paying an average of at least $400. Consider also the relative rise of enrollment in public institutions where tuition is about one-quarter that in private institutions. In the 1950s, the gain in enrollment seemed to go to public institutions about 4 to 1. Once we allow for these diversions to low-tuition institutions, the net effect of *this factor* is to reduce rather than increase tuition.

This result is subject to one reservation. Undoubtedly the proportion of part-time students has increased since 1930. To the extent that this is true, the rise of tuition is understated, but not by much, since even today part-time students are less than one-quarter of the total.

In summary, the last few sections reveal large increases in tuition, especially by the later 1950s when the average rise seems to approach 100 per cent over a period of twenty years. But the results vary greatly according to the type of institution, the years covered, and the sample. Over much longer periods, it seems that faculty salaries have not kept up with the rise of tuition. But again I remind the reader that from a study made of tuition, not by comparing institutions and their charges as most of these studies do, but by comparing national tuition income, number of students, and scholarship funds, the rise of tuition is little more than $100 from 1940 to 1956.

MISCELLANEOUS TRENDS

A few miscellaneous details concerning tuition trends may be of some interest. It is often assumed that tuition income should at least finance academic salaries. At Amherst, Nelson discovered that from 1904 to 1956–57 tuition rose from $110 to $800, or a rise of 6 to 7 times; but faculty salaries increased only 2½ times, the result being that in stable dollars salaries were less in 1956–57 than in 1904.[18]

At Harvard College tuition rose from $150 in 1900 to $1,000 in 1957. The excess of cost over tuition for four years varied from $2,770 in 1915 to $4,403 in 1931 and $3,600 in 1957. (All in 1957 dollars.) A more recent study by the author revealed an average tuition of $1,200 and costs of $3,600 in the university. Six outstanding land-grant colleges had costs equal to about one-half those of Harvard.[19]

Large variations are to be found even for liberal arts colleges in the state universities: the extremes were $60 for Texas and $420 for New Jersey (see Table 5A-1).

Tuition varies by type of institution. One source for 1953–54 (Table 5A-2) reveals variations in fees from a minimum for Federal, state, or municipal colleges of $133 to a maximum of $549 for nondenominational liberal arts colleges. Costs vary from $661 for Catholic universities to $1,065 for professional and technical schools. The largest dollar subsidy is by state universities, and the smallest by Catholic universities.

In 1959–60, according to *Planning and Management Data,* 1959–60, the minimum of tuition and fees was $162 for public liberal arts colleges, and the maximum, for private technological colleges, $860. The average varied from $210 and $787 for North Atlantic public and private IHL respectively to $123 and $443 for the Southeast.

Finally, we know that costs greatly exceed tuition. For example, in Pennsylvania an official estimate puts costs at $1,300 per student, and tuition at $550. But what is more interesting is that it costs much more to graduate *one* student of low ability than one of high ability, for there is much attrition for the former. In a study (1959) by the Joint State Government Commission of Pennsylvania for *Pennsylvania High School Seniors,* it was discovered that it cost $22,200 to produce a graduate of the third stanine, and only $5,500 for one from the higher level of intelligence in the fifth stanine.

ENROLLMENT AND COSTS

In the preceding sections I have considered the relationship between tuition and the size of IHL, and some of the more important trends in tuition in recent years. As I have emphasized earlier, tuition is not determined exclusively by the costs of education, nor should it be. But costs certainly have a bearing on the financial policies of IHL, and if other sources of revenue do not materialize to cover rising costs, higher tuition is the only alternative to severe financial distress.[20]

But what of the future? How can we expect costs to change as enrollment increases from its present level of about 3½ million?

Tuition policy should be related to the effects of changing enrollment upon the costs per unit. In a static economy (in which all other variables remain unchanged) a rise of tuition tends to cut enrollment somewhat. But an actual increase in charges is consistent with a rise of enrollment because of rising income and the higher demand for a college education. With the rise of tuition there has also been an increasing demand. Should tuition rise in a period of falling demand, then the effects on enrollment might be more serious. But even in the 1930s, when tuition rose about 20 per cent in the face of a decline of prices and per capita incomes of about 20 per cent, enrollment rose by about 35 per cent.

Tuition continued to be a bargain in the 1930s, since the charges were only a part of educational costs. Though the ratio of tuition to educational costs per student rose in the thirties, even in 1939–40 one writer estimated that per student educational costs were $382, and tuition for liberal arts students in state institutions in 1936–37 was $76 and average fees in private universities and colleges $306 and $255, respectively.[21]

Despite the substantial increases of tuition in the 1950s, the ratio of tuition to *relevant* educational and general expenditures declined from 43 per cent in 1940 to 35 per cent in 1958. In relation to prices, tuition has become cheaper; that is, the purchasing power of tuition has fallen; and in relation to per capita income, which has risen about $2\frac{1}{2}$ times as much as tuition, the student charge has indeed become a bargain. Hence, it is not surprising that despite a rise of tuition, estimated by Conrad and Hollis at about 85 per cent from 1940 to 1955, enrollment had increased about three-quarters. Actually, as I show elsewhere, tuition income weighted by enrollment yields a net rise of tuition of only about $100, a percentage increase of about 40 per cent from 1940 to 1956. Prices rose by 93 per cent in this period.

It might be expected that with tuition accounting for but 35 per cent of educational expenditures, large rises in tuition rates bringing reductions in enrollment or moderating the rises would result in a financial advantage for the institutions. But this is not necessarily so. We must distinguish the average from the marginal costs, that is, the average cost from the additional cost associated with the enrollment of an additional student. Where the costs are largely fixed and additional enrollment means merely an additional record card in the dean's office, with no additional outlay for plant, instruction, and other major expenses, then a rise of enrollment would increase revenue more than it would raise expenses, resulting in a net financial advantage for the college.[22]

Obviously, the net effect of a rise of enrollment in increasing outlays will depend on a number of factors. Where much excess capacity exists in both plant and manpower, the marginal costs are likely to be small. Furthermore, in the short run the possibility of increasing enrollment without increasing outlays is more likely than in the long run. In the early postwar period, with a rise in enrollment but with relatively fixed educational resources and excess capacity, marginal costs frequently rose less than the additional revenue from additional students. This was especially true where tuition was a large part of income. The government even accused state IHL of financing new buildings out of GI tuition. The larger the fixed costs, the less the additional costs with rising enrollment; even variable costs, such as faculty pay, may be inflexible in the short run. In so far as the authorities keep costs down, as they have teachers' salaries in recent years, then the additional costs associated with higher enrollment may be kept down.

In this connection let us look again at the expenditure of IHL for 1953–54 (see Table 5-4). Total educational and general expenditures amounted to $2,288 million. Of this, instruction and departmental research outlays were $966 million. If these expenditures rise *pari passu* with enrollment, then the added costs of additional students would exceed the increase of revenue, and IHL would suffer financially, for these outlays are 43 per cent of the total and tuition was providing for only 26 per cent of costs. In addition, other expenses also change with enrollment.[23]

Thus, administration accounts for outlays of $291 million, or 13 per cent. Additional enrollment would raise these outlays per additional student less than average costs, but some increase would be necessary.[24] Organized research requires $375 million, or 15 per cent. (I have excluded these from the table.) These outlays need not rise significantly with increased enrollment; and in so far as they do, they are likely to be financed largely out of special resources. In fact, these outlays, as well as $115 million for extension and public services, which are financed out of special charges, should be excluded from our costs. Hence only instruction ($966 million), plant maintenance ($280 million), library ($73 million), administrative ($291 million), and other educational expenses ($188 million) should be considered as relevant. These items amount to $1,798 million, or 78 per cent of educational and general expenditures. We may conclude therefore that the tuition is not 26 but 33 per cent of total relevant educational expenditures. To the latter figure may be added $75 million for scholarships and prizes, making the total of relevant outlays 81 per cent and the ratio of tuition to educational outlays 32 per cent.[25] On the assumptions regarding marginal costs made earlier in the chapter, the *rise* of unit costs with increased enrollment would be 63 per cent of the relevant unit costs, and 50 per cent of the average educational and general expenditures.

Tuition is equal to 32 per cent of relevant costs; marginal costs of additional enrollment are equal to 50 per cent of average costs.[26] Thus, on these estimates, where tuition finances more than 63 per cent of relevant costs, or 50 per cent of all average educational costs, IHL would gain from increased enrollment. But we should allow for the reduced yield of endowment income as enrollment rises. Where tuition is a very large part of total revenue, say, 75 per cent or more, the institution can look forward to a substantial gain.

It is of some interest that the California master survey urged that nonresident students pay " . . . tuition sufficient to cover not less than the state's contribution to the average teaching expense per student . . . ." Apparently this is considered the marginal cost.[27]

Clearly the private institutions are more likely to gain than the public, since tuition is a small part of costs in the latter. In the discussions of Federal scholarships in 1958, it was the public institutions with their low tuitions which complained of the burden of high marginal outlays which would be necessary if new scholarship holders enrolled. Obviously, the rise of unit costs will vary according to the percentage rise of enrollment and the period during which the rise in enrollment takes place. Should backlogs of construction be made up and faculty salaries rise under this pressure, then marginal costs would rise more, although it is not clear that these are properly all marginal costs.[28]

In the early years after the war, when enrollments rose rapidly, the response was largely to hire temporary and young help and to increase the size of classes; at the time the increase in enrollment, due partly to the return of veterans, was profitable to many institutions, especially to those that financed most of their expenses through tuition fees. But this type of gain is much more likely over short periods than long, because of the need over long periods for additions to physical plant and tenure appointments as enrollment rises. In some respects, especially when they are financed out of special gifts, these outlays are not relevant, but in the area of auxiliary enterprises, such as dormitories where capital costs are met out of charges, the result would be higher charges.

IHL are also confronted with large rigid costs, such as permanent staff, large plant, and administration outlays, even when enrollment declines. Hence the IHL are likely to experience losses of revenue which are not offset by equal declines in costs. Roosevelt College, for example, faced this dilemma after the postwar "bulge" in enrollment. A reduction of receipts by one-third required heavy cuts in staff.

ECONOMIES

This discussion of costs has assumed that the present structure of costs does not change radically as enrollment rises. But in the view of the author, much more attention should be paid to possibilities of reducing some of these costs. One of the really striking characteristics of the American economy in the last century has been the great rise in productivity. Much of this rise, of course, has been related to the introduction of new and improved machinery in industry, and there are few ways of doing this in higher education. Still, important improvements can be made. Even if the output per man rose by 1 per cent per year in higher education, compared with a national average of 2 per cent per year, costs of all IHL would be reduced about a billion dollars per year after ten years.[29]

Among the issues that should be studied with great care are the ratio of students to faculty and the improved use of physical facilities. There is nothing sacred about the ratio of fourteen students to one member of the faculty. This ratio can be changed by reducing the number of courses or by alternating them, thereby making it possible to increase the size of classes. Nor has study after study shown that there is anything sacred about a section of 25: they have shown that a lecture to 100 by a good lecturer can produce much better results than four sections of 25. Indeed very small groups, say, tutorial groups, may be a very effective form of instruction, though expensive. Such groups do stimulate students to think, to write, to stand up in argument, offering them an opportunity to confront difficult problems. But the idea that teaching a class of several hundred is not effective when properly done has not been supported by numerous controlled experiments. In other words, there is much folklore in the matter of the size of classes, as well as in the number of classes. Though he oversimplifies the problem, there is much truth in Ruml's suggestion that the way to get salaries up is to double the size of classes and reduce the total number of classes.

Since universities are self-governing organizations, such reforms in higher education must come from the faculty, with the faculty participating in the final decisions made. The faculty should become aware of the relation between number and size of classes and their own pay. If they are ready to make the sacrifices in their standard of living in order to sponsor an excessive number of classes, they should at least know what the facts are.

In many instances in recent years an increase in the use of classrooms from twenty to forty or forty-four hours a week has reduced considerably the need for additional physical plant. Football and student employment sometimes make these adjustments difficult, but as a number of state university studies have shown, much can nevertheless be done to increase space utilization.

One of the striking facts about higher education is the increase in the value of physical plant from $2 billion to over $11 billion in a period of thirty years. Even these figures underestimate the rise, because physical plant is generally carried on the books at its original cost. Replacement costs probably exceed $20 billion. Such physical assets, of course, involve large annual maintenance expenditures. The value of plant has risen much more than endowment in these years. Whereas endowment yields income, plant of course involves additional expenditures.

Another trend in higher education has been the tendency to introduce a larger proportion of what might be called nonessential elements of higher education into the educational product. In other words, a "college education" contains less of what we generally refer to as education and contains much more of the joint product—medicine, employment aid, college athletics, dormitory facilities, food, recreational facilities, and the like. The result is a much higher cost for education than would otherwise be necessary. For many institutions and families this does not involve a great burden and makes education more appealing and perhaps more effective. But as costs rise and financial problems become more serious, we should become more conscious of these mixed elements in our educational bill of fare. With the development of the junior college and the tendency for enrollment to rise in the large metropolitan areas where the population tends to grow, the importance of these additional services is likely to decline and to that extent the financial problems will become less serious.

In this connection, for example, one might suggest that a college—and a superior one—could be set up with, say, 15 outstanding teachers (one in each department) at a salary of $20,000, and 15 assistants at a salary of $10,000. In addition, perhaps 1,000 students could be accommodated with a plant costing about $2 million. This would give us just the bare essentials of higher education. I wonder if there is not an opportunity for this kind of development, and I suppose to some extent the proposed New College in the Connecticut Valley reflects trends of this kind. Certainly this is more in accordance with education in European universities.

Interesting experiments in the Connecticut Valley and Hofstra College are relevant here. The latter plans an experimental college with students protected against diverting effects such as the automobile and too many extracurricular activities. The four Connecticut colleges under the planning of representatives from each also hope to found a liberal arts college with high standards and low unit costs. But Barber of Amherst finds the raising of a few million dollars for a new college a major obstacle. Potential donors seem to be tied to existing institutions. There certainly should be a way for an institution of this type to be launched in our wealthy country.

As one studies the trends of higher education, it becomes increasingly clear that nonresidential higher education becomes increasingly important. Economies result for both students and the colleges. But the product is deteriorated to some extent when the student lives at home. It has been said that " . . . the Oxford graduate receives half his university education from the dons, and the other half from his fellow-students."

There ought to be a careful investigation of the optimum size of an IHL. I mean optimum from the viewpoint of the minimum unit cost. I do not for one minute suggest that this should be a decisive matter, but it would be well to know what the facts are. Even today we have about 500 institutions with enrollments of less than 200, and almost 600 institutions with enrollments from 200 to 500. These 1,100 institutions are almost two-thirds of the total, although of course they account for a much smaller percentage of total enrollment. It is quite clear from numerous studies, including the 60-college study, that institutions of this size are expensive. It would therefore be well for all institutions to make estimates of how much unit cost would decline (or increase) with a rise of enrollment of 100, 200, 300, etc., students. In going over the country I find that very few colleges have made studies of this kind. Also required would be an examination of the additional dollar costs for faculty, plant, libraries, and administration for increases in enrollment of X, Y, and Z.

There is a good deal of talk about both expanding existing institutions and founding new ones. It would be well, before a new institution is founded, to make a careful survey, as a businessman would of the consumers of a new product, of the possibilities for getting an enrollment that would yield the lowest unit cost. The institution to be founded should also take into account the labor market, other costs in the area, and the cost of transportation for the student who is expected to enroll.

At the present time, the founding of colleges, and especially schools within colleges, is done on a most nonscientific basis. In discussing this issue with the head of the Catholic Education Association I discovered that a Catholic bishop who wants to establish a college tries to estimate what the probable enrollment would be, what resources are available, and where additional resources would be found. He then appeals to one of the orders to provide the necessary faculty members and whatever additional finance is required. The order then determines whether the requisite faculty is to be had in this area; on the basis of such decisions a new college is established.

In view of the present crisis in educational finance, particularly in state institutions, there is a great deal of pressure on the part of legislatures and others to examine the present location of schools, to compare costs of schools doing similar jobs, and thereby to put the costs of higher education on a more scientific basis. Most states now have, or are in the process of establishing, a general integration board and/or an official with over-all powers of varying degrees vis-à-vis all public IHL which is presumed to take into account the available facilities in both public and private institutions. Whenever a proposal for a new institution is made, this board decides that the public institution should not be established unless a need for it can be shown. Excessive competition is then somewhat reduced. In this connection it would be helpful to examine the cost per student of introducing a new public institution as against the cost of providing resources such as scholarships to private institutions already in existence. Where there is excess capacity, it would often be cheaper to give subsidies to private institutions in the form of building or scholarship aid rather than set up new public institutions.

In this connection the practice of the private Association of Claremont Colleges in California is of some interest. In the rapid growth of the Pomona area in the 1920s the Pomona College authorities decided not to expand lest the college become too large. Instead it was decided to start new units of a few hundred students when this was deemed expedient. In this manner the new unit can lean on the old units, and the additional costs required, say, for 200 additional students can be revealed. At the same time the new small unit can show in the economies (1960) of five colleges co-operating, with a total enrollment of 2,200.

In later chapters the issues of costs and economies are discussed much more fully.

SUMMARY

Here are several conclusions to be drawn from this chapter.

1. The trend in the last generation is for tuition income to fall in relation to general and educational income and even more in relation to per capita income, the best index of capacity to pay.

2. But the relative decline must be adjusted for two items: first, the exclusion of capital charges of about $300 to $400 per student, an exclusion which results in overstatement of the tuition contribution; second, the inclusion of expenditures not primarily to be tethered to instruction. Their inclusion reduces the relative contribution of tuition less than the first factor results in overvaluation of tuition.

3. From various sources, the conclusion is drawn that tuition in public IHL tends to rise relatively more than in private IHL, in the 1940s though probably not in the 1950s, and nonresident fees in the former more than resident.

4. Does it pay to increase enrollment by keeping tuition down? It is necessary to weigh the rise of costs with a given increase of enrollment against the additional revenue received. Some crude estimates are presented in the text. Generally, the larger the excess capacity and the higher the tuition in relation to total costs, the more likely financial conditions would improve with increases of enrollment.

5. Any disposition to keep tuition down and enrollment up on the theory that the gains of tuition with increased enrollment would exceed those of costs is to be put against the reduced yield of endowment income per student. In real dollars per student, despite large increases, endowment plays a declining part, and in relation to costs per student, the contribution of endowment per resident student declines even more. Hence when a college depends heavily on endowment, its finances may deteriorate even if,

with increased enrollment, additional tuition more than offsets the rise of costs.

6. Tuition has tended upward, especially in the 1950s after a serious lag in the 1940s. But how much depends on the series studied and method used. Here we suggest one method which shows surprisingly small increases from 1930 to 1956 in relation to the rise of cost and of per capita income after taxes.

7. A preliminary study of economies is relevant here. As an alternative to higher tuition, it is possible to reduce unit costs and in this manner raise the ratio of tuition to costs.

FOOTNOTES

[1] I deduct organized research, public services, and extension from the total educational and general expenditures.

[2] Figures from HEW, *Statistics of Higher Education, 1955–56: Receipts, Expenditures and Property,* and *Income, Expenditures for Nation's Colleges,* 1960 Series, no. 4.

[3] The problem of ascertaining costs is discussed more extensively in Chap. 42.

[4] HEW, cf. *College and University Facilities Survey,* 1959, p. 19.

[5] Calculated from *Statistics of Land-grant Colleges and Universities, 1958,* table 21.

[6] This estimate was obtained as follows:

Value of property of IHL in 1953–54...................	$11.3 billion
Deduct one-third for income-yielding property. Hence......	$7.6 billion
Average per student in 1953–54......................	$3,000
Assume addition of two-thirds of value of existing plant per student for each additional student..................	$2,000
Finance conservatively at 4 per cent over 50 years.........	$93
Average cost of relevant educational expenditures per student, 1953–54..................................	$720
% $93 / 720$.......................................	13%

($720 = Educational expenditures per student)

[7] J. W. Hicks, *Student Fees for Academic Buildings: A Preliminary Analysis,* 1959, pp. 7–10. (Mimeographed.)

[8] These issues are discussed more fully in later chapters.

[9] I shall deal with this problem further in Chap. 7.

[10] M. Newcomer, *A Century of Higher Education for Women,* 1959, pp. 155–167; A. T. Hill, *The Small College Meets the Challenge,* 1959, p. 114; C. Ostheimer, *Student Charges and Financing Higher Education,* 1953, *passim.*

[11] HEW, *Higher Education: Planning and Management Data, 1958–59,* p. 72.

[12] Council of Financial Aid to Education, *What Price Tuition?* pp. 4 and 5.

[13] C. W. Hoff, "422 Colleges Report," *College and University Business,* vol. 12, no. 5, May, 1952, pp. 19 and 20.

[14] J. D. Millet, *Financing Higher Education in the United States,* 1952, p. 297; H. S. Conrad and E. V. Hollis, "Trends in Tuition Charges and Fees," *The*

Annals, Higher Education under Stress, September, 1955, p. 156; and *Planning and Management Data, 1959–60,* p. 49.

[15] See Tables 5A-7 to 5A-9.

[16] The Council of State Governments, *A Report on Enrollments and Fees at State Colleges and Universities in the Midwest,* prepared for the Midwestern Interstate Committee on Higher Education, Chicago, 1958, p. 8. (Mimeographed.)

[17] *Ibid.*

[18] *The Relationship between Faculty Salaries and the Long-run Economic Problems of Privately-Endowed Higher Education,* report to the Amherst chapter of the AAUP, Dec. 13, 1957. (Mimeographed.)

[19] S. E. Harris, "The Economics of Harvard," *Harvard Alumni Bulletin,* Feb. 20, 1960.

[20] An exception must be made if economies of operation sufficient to offset the rising costs can be achieved. Something will be said of this in the next section, and more in Part Seven.

[21] Millett estimates that with a rise of enrollment of 10 per cent, costs rise 5 per cent. Hence, marginal costs are 50 per cent of average costs. Cf. *op. cit.,* pp. 271–272.

[22] On pp. 59–61 I have estimated what some of the relationships between marginal and average costs might be.

[23] The structure of costs varies, of course, among institutions. Thus, for 60 liberal arts colleges the following may be classified as overhead expenses and hence rather insensitive in the short run to changes in enrollment:

Percentage Costs, 60 Liberal Arts Colleges, 1953–54

Cost item	Median	High	Low
General administration.	9.1	18.4	4.6
Public services and information.	5.4	9.4	1.4
General institutional.	3.5	12.9	1.5
Libraries.	5.0	9.5	1.9
Plant operation and maintenance.	16.0	26.8	6.6
	39.0	77.0	16.0

Source: National Federation of College and University Business Officers
Associations, *A Study of Income and Expenditures in Sixty Colleges:
A Summary Report, Year 1953–1954.*

These of course are not rigidly fixed costs. They will vary some with enrollment and especially with the passage of time. What is surprising is the wide range in the categories between median, low, and high.

[24] It will be recalled that administrative costs tend to fall with increases of enrollment within a wide range.

[25] All education outlays of $2.29 billion divided into tuition of $600 million-26 per cent. All relevant educational outlays of $1,873 million divided into $600 million-32 per cent. This estimate of tuition is lower than that of the Commission on Financing Higher Education.

[26] See footnote 21.

[27] *A Master Plan for Higher Education in California, 1960–1975,* 1960, p. 22.

[28] Thus we can summarize the calculations:

	Per cent
All general and educational costs	100
Relevant general and educational costs (costs that respond to higher enrollment)	81
Tuition as percentage of general and educational costs	26
Tuition as percentage of relevant general and educational costs	32
Estimated marginal costs in relation to relevant average costs	63
Estimated marginal costs in relation to all general and educational average costs	50

Hence where tuition covers more than 50 per cent of general and educational average costs, there is a possibility of gain for IHL with a rise of enrollment.

[29] See Chap. 44 for a more expansive discussion of economies.

APPENDIX

TABLE 5A-1

Amount Charged All Students Annually for Liberal Arts by State Universities,* 1953–54

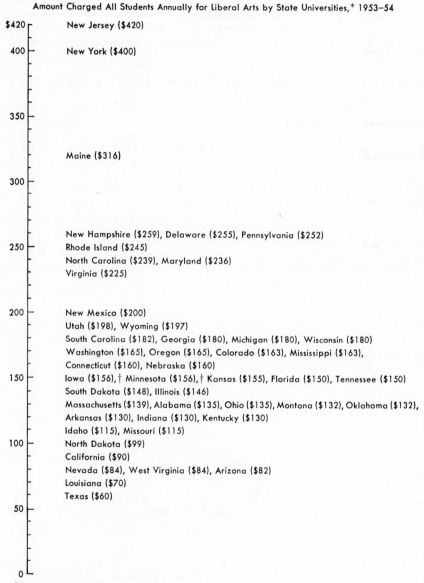

$420 — New Jersey ($420)

400 — New York ($400)

350 —

Maine ($316)

300 —

New Hampshire ($259), Delaware ($255), Pennsylvania ($252)
250 — Rhode Island ($245)
North Carolina ($239), Maryland ($236)
Virginia ($225)

200 — New Mexico ($200)
Utah ($198), Wyoming ($197)
South Carolina ($182), Georgia ($180), Michigan ($180), Wisconsin ($180)
Washington ($165), Oregon ($165), Colorado ($163), Mississippi ($163),
Connecticut ($160), Nebraska ($160)
150 — Iowa ($156),† Minnesota ($156),† Kansas ($155), Florida ($150), Tennessee ($150)
South Dakota ($148), Illinois ($146)
Massachusetts ($139), Alabama ($135), Ohio ($135), Montana ($132), Oklahoma ($132),
Arkansas ($130), Indiana ($130), Kentucky ($130)
Idaho ($115), Missouri ($115)
100 — North Dakota ($99)
California ($90)
Nevada ($84), West Virginia ($84), Arizona ($82)
Louisiana ($70)
Texas ($60)

50 —

0 —

* Vermont is omitted as nonpublic for liberal arts.
† Median—$156 (Iowa and Minnesota).
Source: State University of New York, *Crucial Questions about Higher Education*, 1955, p. 35.

TABLE 5A-2
The Gap between College Tuitions and Fees and the Per Capita Cost to the Institution

Institutional group	Number replying	Average tuition and fees, 1953–54	Average cost of operations per full-time student, 1952–53*	Cost per student to institution above his payments, 1952–53**	Percentage rise, 1947–48 to 1952–53
Church-related colleges, non-Catholic..	125	$414	$ 808	$344	104
Catholic colleges..................	85	440	702	239	73
Federal, state, or municipal colleges...	113	133	798	636	61
Nondenominational, independent liberal arts colleges................	184	549	1,060	397	98
Independent universities.............	66	538	932	515	100
State universities..................	54	167	911	730	143
Catholic universities...............	21	466	661	225	200
Church-related universities, non-Catholic	26	368	711	279	102
Professional and technical schools.....	80	479	1,065	649	27

* The "average cost of operations per full-time student, 1952–53" is based upon the individual institution's total expenditures, including educational, research, extension, and general expenditures. Those for research and extension account in part for the relatively higher "cost per student . . . above his payments" in the case of Federal, state, or municipal colleges and the state universities.

** The cost per student above payments (col. 4) is not clearly indicated by table.

Source: Council for Financial Aid to Education, *What Price Tuition?*, November, 1957, p. 2. Based on the college and university survey conducted by the CFAE in 1954.

TABLE 5A-3
Student Fees, as Per Cent of Educational and General Income, 1953–54

Colleges	Median	Minimum	Maximum
All...........................	63.3	5.7	89.4
11 men's colleges................	49.8	33.4	74.9
11 women's colleges.............	59.3	30.4	81.0
38 coeducational colleges.........	65.6	5.7	89.4

Source: *A Study of Income and Expenditures in Sixty Colleges*, pp. 52–53.

A number of Ivy colleges and other prominent colleges yield the following for 1954–55:

Ratio of Tuition to Educational Costs, Per Cent

Princeton................................. 42
Stanford.................................. 48
Yale...................................... 40 (operating expenses)
Chicago*.................................. 11 (27)
Cornell†.................................. 44

* The Chicago statement reveals some of the difficulties. Government contracts account for 23.2 per cent of income (not all inclusive); medical patient fees = 22.7 per cent; endowment = 13.6 per cent; gifts = 14.3 per cent; auxiliary = 10.4 per cent. Should we deduct government contracts, patient fees, and auxiliary activities, the ratio of tuition fees to income becomes 27 per cent.

† The Cornell figure is raised from 30 to 44 per cent by eliminating income from auxiliary enterprises.

Source: *The New York Times*, June 25, 1956. Statement by eight presidents on guiding principles for industrial gifts.

Harvard's figure for tuition is 23.8 per cent. But if income from auxiliary enterprises inclusive of research is eliminated, the figure is raised to 34 per cent.

Of interest is the contrast between different schools at Harvard:

School	Ratio of tuition to income, per cent	Exclusive of research contracts
Arts and Science...............	43	47
Medicine.....................	18	18
Public Health.................	8	9
Law.........................	58	58
Business.....................	47	52
Public Administration...........	14	19
Education....................	26	27
Divinity.....................	22	22

Source: Harvard University, *Financial Report to the Board of Overseers for the Fiscal Year 1954–55,* pp. 10–13.

TABLE 5A-4
Tuition, Various Years, by Types of Institutions

Year	Public institutions	Private universities	Private colleges
1928–29	$ 63	$276	$228
1936–37	76	306	255
1957–58	139	701	553
1959–60	210	787	

Source: HEW, T. Arnett, *Recent Trends in Higher Education in the U.S.,* New York General Education Board, 1940, Table 6; and HEW, *Higher Education: Planning and Management Data, 1957–58,* p. 68, and ibid., *1959–60,* p. 48.

TABLE 5A-5

Tuition Rate per Student in 196 Higher-educational Institutions, by Type of Control and by Curricular-organizational Classification, 1939–40, 1949–50, and 1954–55

(Catalogue study)

Type of control and curricular-organizational classification	No. of institutions	Tuition rate per student			Amount of increase			Percentage increase		
		1939–40	1949–50	1954–55	1940 to 1950	1940 to 1955	1950 to 1955	1940 to 1950	1940 to 1955	1950 to 1955
All institutions.............	196	$165	$249	$305	$84	$140	$56	51	85	22
Publicly controlled.............	120	70	109	132	39	62	23	56	89	21
Privately controlled.............	76	328	468	599	140	271	131	43	83	28
Publicly controlled:										
Universities.........	69	83	123	158	40	75	35	48	90	28
Liberal arts colleges.........	19	29	56	71	27	42	15	93	145	27
Technological schools.........	4	104	151	165	47	61	14	45	59	9
Teachers colleges.........	17	61	92	108	31	47	16	51	77	17
Other professional schools.........	1	72	103	137	31	65	34	43	90	33
Junior colleges.........	10	10.74	15.77	18.27	5.03	7.53	2.50	47	70	16
Privately controlled:										
Universities.........	57	327	465	600	138	273	135	42	83	29
Liberal arts colleges.........	14	294	426	525	131	231	99	45	79	23
Technological schools.........	5	389	598	736	209	347	138	54	89	23

Source: H. S. Conrad and E. V. Hollis, "Trends in Tuition Charges and Fees," The Annals, Higher Education under Stress, September, 1955, p. 149.

TABLE 5A-6

Comparison of Tuition Rates and per Capita Disposable Income, for Specified Years
Between 1939–40 and 1954–55

School year	Amount			Dollar rise			Per cent increase		
	Per capita disposable income*	Tuition rate per student		Per capita disposable income*	Tuition rate per student		Per capita disposable income*	Tuition rate per student	
		Publicly controlled institutions	Privately controlled institutions		Publicly controlled institutions	Privately controlled institutions		Publicly controlled institutions	Privately controlled institutions
1953–54	$1,564	119†	502†						
1954–55	1,569	132†	515†	5	13	13	0.3	10.9	2.6
1949–50	1,310	109‡	468‡						
1954–55	1,569	132‡	599‡	259	23	131	19.8	21.0	28.0
1947–48	1,226	55¶	188¶						
1954–55	1,569	77¶	257¶	343	21¶	69	28.0	38.0	37.5
1939–40	554	70	328						
1949–50	1,310	109¶	468¶	756	39	140	136.5	56.0	43.0

* Figures on per capita disposable income are based on data in *Economic Indicators* (April, 1955, and earlier issues), published by the U.S. Government Printing Office. The figure for 1954–55 is an estimate based on data for the last half of calendar year 1954 and the preliminary estimate for the first quarter of calendar year 1955.

† Based on a questionnaire study by the Office of Education.

‡ Based on a catalogue study by the Office of Education.

§ Based on a questionnaire study by W. R. Bokelman. Figures give tuition per institution, on a semester or quarter basis. Other figures in these columns give tuition per student, on an academic-year basis.

¶ Based on unrounded tuition rates for 1954–55 and 1947–48.

Source: H. S. Conrad and E. V. Hollis, "Trends in Tuition Charges and Fees," *The Annals, Higher Education under Stress*, September, 1955, p. 154.

TABLE 5A-7

Average Fee for All Institutions, Midwest State Colleges and Universities, 1947, 1952, 1957

Year	Undergraduate			Graduate		
	No. of institutions	Resident	Nonresident	No. of institutions	Resident	Nonresident
1947	66	$ 93	$156	35	$104	$178
1952	67	114	199	39	128	238
1957	72	166	299	48	184	339

Source: The Council of State Governments, *A Report on Enrollments and Fees at State Colleges and Universities in the Midwest*, prepared for the Midwestern Interstate Committee on Higher Education, Chicago, 1958, p. 6. (Mimeographed.)

TABLE 5A-8

Average and Median Fee for 22 Large Institutions, Midwest State Colleges and Universities, 1947, 1952, 1957

Year	Undergraduate				Graduate			
	Resident		Nonresident		Resident		Nonresident	
	Average	Median	Average	Median	Average	Median	Average	Median
1947	$113	$115	$223	$219	$111	$115	$210	$214
1952	140	147	303	314	139	147	278	294
1957	207	214	452	482	207	214	405	462

Source: See Table 5A-7.

TABLE 5A-9

Median Increase in Fees between 1947–1957 and 1952–1957 in Terms of Current and Constant Dollars

	Resident				Nonresident			
	Current dollars		Constant dollars		Current dollars		Constant dollars	
	1947–57	1952–57	1947–57	1952–57	1947–57	1952–57	1947–57	1952–57
Undergraduate	79%	45%	45%	35%	90%	45%	53%	35%
Graduate.....	82%	51%	47%	41%	90%	49%	53%	39%

Source: See source for Table 5A-7.

Chapter 6

A SPECIAL STUDY OF TUITION CHARGES[1]

Of the 152 institutions which responded to the questionnaire addressed to their financial officers by the author of this volume, 128 supplied information relating to their tuition charges which was presented in an unambiguous and comparable form. The data assembled from that questionnaire presumably relate simply to tuition and general academic fees charged by these institutions. In those cases where the charges were stated, or appeared, to include nonacademic fees or room and/or board charges, or were presented as charges per credit hour, etc., the responses were discarded. The tabulations thus represent changes in annual tuition and academic fees.

THE ISSUES

The questions which it seems worth while to ask in regard to this data are of the following sort: If the tuition charges can be regarded as some component of the price charged by IHL for their services, what pattern of fluctuations can be observed in these price movements? Is some cyclical movement apparent over the period between 1939 and 1959? Is there any relationship between the pattern of changes in this "price" series and that in other price and income series in the economy? Is there any marked difference in the pattern of changes of tuition exhibited by different groups of IHL? These questions have been couched in terms of price changes rather than cost (of higher education) changes. It must be emphasized that the means calculated for the total 128 IHL reporting over the twenty-year period cannot in any sense be construed as an index of tuition costs. This is the case primarily because the tuition changes have not been weighted with the enrollment figures for the corresponding institutions in each year.

It appears that the mean tuition changes of all 128 IHL display a rising trend over the 1939–40-to-1958–59 interval. If the war years are excluded, the trend is somewhat less marked; indeed, starting in 1945–46, the trend

87

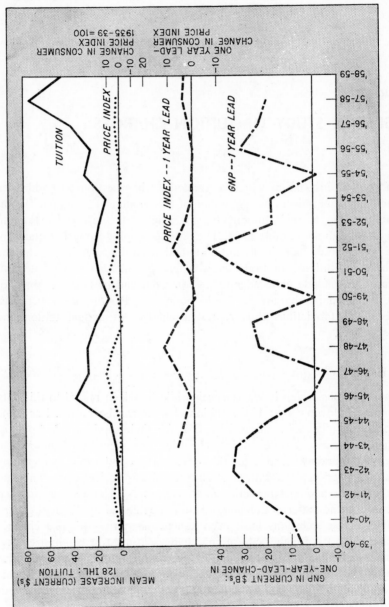

Chart 1. Year-to-year changes in tuition, GNP, and the consumer price index.

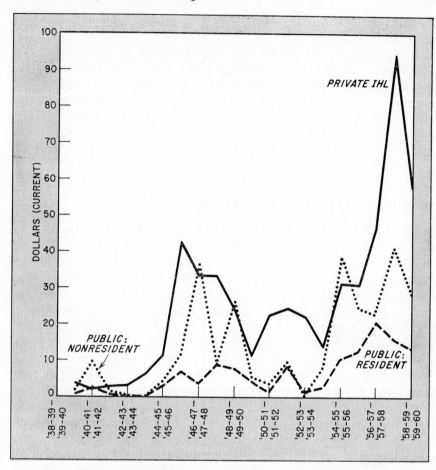

Chart 2. Breakdown of tuition changes by type of IHL.

appears to be mildly parabolic. Some cyclic pattern emerges over the twenty-year period, with peak changes occurring in 1945–46 (related undoubtedly to the GI Bill and expansion of enrollment), 1951–52, and 1957–58, and troughs occurring in 1949–50 and 1953–54. This pattern does not seem unrelated to the movements of the general level of activity in the economy and the changes in GNP (in current dollars) over the period since the war. There appears to be some tendency for tuition changes to lag one year behind the movements of the consumer price index, although after 1955 the magnitude of the changes is no longer proportional—the changes in the price index become damped, while those in tuition become more volatile. Similarly, the tendency for tuition changes to lag one year behind the changes in GNP, as far as turning points go, becomes obscure after 1955, when the rise of GNP declines, but tuition increases continue to rise to 1957–58. (The tendency of tuition is to rise more than per capita disposable income in the 1950s.)

The sample of 128 divides into 96 private and 32 public IHL. The differential in tuition changes between public and private (resident) IHL is what would be anticipated, although it is interesting to note that the two patterns of change are not markedly dissimilar.[2] Also intriguing is the erratic behavior of the nonresident tuition changes. These latter do not display the same rising trend in the postwar years which appears in the other two series. The amplitude of change seems much greater for non-resident tuition.

TUITION IN RELATION TO FOUR FACTORS

There is a second set of questions which can be addressed to the data. In Chapter 3 the performance (or experience) of different groups of IHL, all of which were private, are examined with respect to enrollment, current income, student aid, endowment per student, and faculty structure. The classification of colleges, while appearing intuitively reasonable, was not such as to permit any strong statements of causal connection between the nature of the colleges in the group and their experience with respect to the different variables. In particular, although one might say that Ivy League colleges, being located in a particular part of the country and enjoying "prestige," might be expected to have done better than the general average with regard to their endowments and their faculty structure, the categories "other private universities" and "liberal arts" are not prima facie mutually exclusive, nor indicative of what factors might render their experiences diverse. The same might be said of the category "large urban," save that one might anticipate that urban location and size played some (unspecified) role in the pattern of enrollment and student aid, as well as current income, exhibited by this group. Without laboring this point further, it can be said than an arrangement of a fairly large group of private IHL with respect to a *number* of characteristics could throw some light on the effect which different factors play in determining the differences in the values of *one particular* variable between one IHL and another. The formal distinction between this procedure and that followed in the statistical survey of Chapter 3 is simply that here we use a number of characteristics to group the values of a single variable, while in the survey in Chapter 3 one classification is used to group the values of a number of variables.

We have data on one variable, namely, the tuition charges (plus academic fees), for 85 of the 96 *private* IHL responding to the questionnaire. What we shall try to do is to determine whether or not four factors, which can be used to classify the members of the sample of 85 IHL, have a marked effect upon the level of their tuition charges.

The first of our four factors is the per capita endowment of the institution. One simple hypothesis might be that schools which have a high endowment per student are under less pressure to raise current income by high tuition charges. On the other hand, it could be suggested that schools which start with a moderately high per capita endowment find that by charging moderately low tuitions they can increase enrollment and current income; rising enrollment results in a decline in their per capita endowment. Thus, a priori, it does not seem clear that we should find a predominant number of low-tuition institutions among the group which have a high per capita endowment, or among the group of schools which have a low per capita endowment. If the latter were the case, we would have to conclude that the level of endowment per student had no clear-cut effect, that as far as their tuition charges were concerned, the two groups of IHL were essentially indistinguishable. Primarily, of course, we are interested in finding whether or not there is any such effect at all. If the presence of an "endowment effect" is established, we can then go on to analyze its nature.

. The second factor which shall be considered is the effect of the competition of low-tuition public schools upon the charges of private IHL. There are a number of difficulties in this connection—essentially those arising from ambiguities in the relationships between market structure, market power, and market behavior—which ensure that our attack on this problem can at best be rather indirect. The principal problem is that we cannot find a single-dimension measure of the degree of competitive pressure faced by IHL.[3] The simplest and operationally most feasible hypothesis we can offer is that the relative enrollment capacities of private and public IHL within an area—which is but one dimension in the structure of the market—imposes some restrictions on the range in which private IHL in that area can set their tuition charges. That is to say, a private institution in a state whose public colleges and universities can accommodate four times as many students as can be handled by private institutions in the state will be under greater pressure to prevent the differential between tuitions in public and private institutions from widening than will a private institution located in a state where public and private IHL divide the total enrollment capacity equally. This hypothesis, then, does not take into account the extent of competition between the private institutions in an area but focuses on the common constraint to which all private IHL tuition decisions in the area are more or less subject. Again, rather than attempt to test a specific form of the foregoing hypothesis, we shall initially examine the data to see if the assertion of the presence of any such "capacity effect" is warranted. Elsewhere I noted that an over-all examination *by regions* does not seem to yield the conclusion that, where enrollment in public institutions is relatively large, fees of private institutions tend to be relatively low. Undoubtedly one reason for this is the fact that, where the competition of public IHL is especially strong (i.e., the Far West), incomes also are very high.

The other two factors which shall be examined for their effects on the level of private tuition are the geographical location of the particular institutions and the presence or absence of affiliation with a religious organization. Classification of the 85 colleges and universities according to regional location is a rather omnibus device. Where regional differences in income and prices are pronounced, a corresponding regional classification would merely be an indirect method of assessing the effects of these factors. Obviously, to the extent that there is marked similarity between the component numbers of the regional groups and the groups (of IHL) constructed with respect to the other three factors mentioned, the regional factor will have added nothing new to our analysis. This last is but one aspect of a broader problem which applies equally to all the four factors we are considering and which is referred to again below.

The initial hypothesis which lies behind the grouping of the 85 institutions according to their affiliation with a church body, like that underlying the regional classification, is best left unspecified. We only suggest here that there may be some relationship between the existence of an affiliation with a religious society and the nature of such affiliation, and the level of tuition which is decided upon by the institution's administrators. It will only be really possible to affirm such a hypothesis if it can also be shown that the observed "affiliation effect" on tuition cannot be imputed to some other factor which is highly correlated with affiliation status in our sample of 85 IHL, for example, lower incomes of families sending children to denominational colleges, in turn related to the large numbers of these institutions in low-income areas. However, since it would hardly be feasible to examine *all* the relevant factors, were it within the competence of this investigator to isolate them, we will have to be content with satisfying ourselves that affiliation status is not highly correlated with one or more of the other three factors of classification. Thus, it must be borne in mind that affiliation status, like regional location (and to a lesser degree endowment per student and private versus public enrollment capacity), represents a catchall for the unenumerated variables which are highly correlated with it.

It is necessary to devote a few words to the manner in which the individuals in our sample have been grouped according to each of the four variables.

1. The five groups set out under the heading "Per capita endowment" in Table 6-1 for 1940 and 1956 represent a division of the distribution of that variable for the 85 IHL into something like "very low," "low," "average" (group 3), "high," and "very high."

2. In the foregoing discussion, the hypothesis concerning the effect of

"competitive pressure" of public colleges and universities upon the tuition charges of private institutions was formulated with respect to the relative enrollment capacities of privately and publicly controlled institutions within a given state. Unfortunately, we cannot readily obtain data giving total enrollment in IHL *by control and by state* for 1940 and 1956. We have, however, the *number* of private and public IHL in each state for these dates. If the ratios of the number of private to the number of public educational "plants" is well correlated with the ratio of private to public "plant capacity," we could establish class limits based on the distribution of the former ratios and thus test the "capacity effect" hypothesis indirectly. The correlation between the ratios of private to public enrollment and the ratios of the number of private to the number of public IHL turns out to be satisfactorily high for 1947–48, when data for both are available. Proceeding on the not implausible assumption that this would also be the case in 1940 and 1956, the five groups shown under heading II in Table 6-1 were set up in a fashion analogous to that followed in establishing the per capita endowment groups.

3. The regional grouping shown in Table 6-1 is self-explanatory. It was arrived at by aggregating several of the adjacent Census Bureau "Regional Divisions" to achieve a (numerically) more balanced distribution of the 85 IHL among the resulting six groups, without totally obliterating regional distinctions.

4. In establishing the four groups appearing under the last heading in Table 6-1, we depended upon the ACE guide, *American Colleges and Universities* (1956). Those classified as "loosely affiliated" were non-Catholic affiliated institutions whose governing boards were not wholly or partially *chosen* by the governing body of a religious society. The third group, thus, comprises non-Catholic affiliated IHL which are partially or completely controlled—to the extent that the governing board exercises effective control—by a church body.

While the four hypotheses set out above were stated in a positive form, e.g., religious affiliation status has an effect on the level of tuition, we shall make use of the technique of analysis of variance to test their converse, i.e., religious affiliation has no effect on tuition. It is now proposed to present briefly the results of these tests, to discuss the nature of those "effects" which are found to be significant, and finally to offer some comments and cautions regarding the interpretation of our findings.

RESULTS OF TESTS

The two sets of results we consider are those of the analysis performed on the 1940 and 1956 tuition data. Corresponding to each of the dates, 85 IHL were arranged in two different sets of groups according to their position in the per capita endowment distribution in these years. Similarly, changes in the position of an institution's state in the distribution of the ratios of the number of private to public IHL gave rise to some reshuffling of the 85 colleges and universities between the groups established under this heading. The constituents of the groups under headings III and IV in Table 6-1

TABLE 6-1

Mean Tuition Charges of 85 Independent Colleges and Universities Arranged in Groups according to Four Factors of Classification

	Tuition (current dollars)		No. of IHL in group	
	1940	1956	1940	1956
I. Per capita endowment:				
1. $0–999	288	621	19	17
2. $1,000–2,999	281	628	29	23
3. $3,000–4,999	301	573	16	14
4. $5,000–9,999	326	706	11	17
5. $10,000 and above	405	884	10	14
II. Ratio of private to public IHL in state:				
1. 0–0.99	378	713	10	11
2. 1.00–1.49	245	459	11	5
3. 1.50–2.49	335	542	15	22
4. 2.50–3.99	323	853	14	18
5. 4.00 and above	323	688	35	29
III. Geographical region:				
1. New England and Middle Atlantic	383	800	32	32
2. South Atlantic	333	654	12	12
3. East and West South Central	156	354	4	4
4. East North Central	278	608	15	15
5. West North Central	248	500	11	11
6. Mountain and Pacific	355	719	11	11
IV. Religious affiliation status:				
1. Nondenominational	383	786	44	44
2. Non-Catholic, "loose affiliation"	254	542	13	13
3. Non-Catholic, "tight affiliation"	278	606	16	16
4. Catholic affiliation	256	504	12	12
Grand mean	325	675		

naturally remained the same for both years. Table 6-1 shows the numerical distribution of the 85 IHL between the groups for the 1940 and 1956 classifications.

Analysis of the 1940 data showed that the only significant "effects" on tuition charges were those ascribable to the religious affiliation status of the institutions in the sample.[4] By contrast, in the 1956 data all four hypothesized "effects" are found to be significant. Again, the effect of affiliation status proves to be the most pronounced. The enrollment capacity and regional effects appear to be of roughly equal strength, while the per capita endowment effect—though significant—is the weakest of the four.

In the first two columns of Table 6-1 appear the mean tuition charges (in 1940 and 1956) of the groups resulting from the four successive classifications of the 85 colleges and universities in the sample.

Our original remarks regarding the influence which a school's endowment might have on its tuition charges suggested that the relationship between the two was roughly linear but raised the question of whether they were negatively or positively associated. It appears that the nature of the association is positive: for those schools which have a per capita endowment between zero and $4,999, the average tuition charge lies below the grand mean, while the mean tuition for schools whose endowment per student is greater than $5,000 is higher than the grand mean. However, while a major portion of this curve is positively sloped, there is a range—from $1,000 to $4,999 per capita endowment—over which mean tuition falls as per capita endowment increases, although within this range group mean tuition still lies below the over-all mean. Thus, in the range of per capita endowments of less than $4,999, there is no statistical justification for the notion that IHL with relatively low per capita endowments will attempt to raise current income by charging relatively high tuitions, and vice versa.

We are led to ascribe the significant "per capita endowment effects" to the great difference between the grand mean and the mean tuition charged by that group of schools with per capita endowments amounting to more than $10,000. The high tuitions of these institutions clearly are not a function of their per capita endowments: both are related to other common characteristics of these colleges and universities. Of the 14 IHL in this group 10 are located in the New England and Middle Atlantic states. Of those 10, 4 are Ivy League schools (Harvard, Yale, Princeton, Dartmouth), and at least 9 would have to be counted as among the so-called "prestige" schools. The 4 institutions not located in the Northeast (Cal Tech, Scripps College, Oberlin, and Emory) are all schools which enjoy regional and national prestige.

It is possible that while per capita endowment does not, at one point in time, affect the *level* of tuition charges in a fashion which would lend support to the hypothesis of negative association, its effects are exhibited over the course of time in the pattern of tuition changes. High per capita income from endowments may act as a buffer between rising costs and tuition charges, permitting those institutions which enjoy them to allow a greater gap to develop between their income from tuition and their current expenses before they finally increase tuition charges. Schools with low per capita endowments, on the other hand, would be forced to keep their tuition increases more closely in line with rising expenses from year to year. Were this the case, we should expect to find that the mean tuition increment of low per capita endowment institutions was lower than that of schools with high per capita endowments *but* that the frequency of tuition changes was greater for the former group of IHL. However, a series of statistical tests of the latter part of this hypothesis forces us to reject the notion that—at least as far as the 85 institutions in our sample are concerned—there is a significant degree of association between high per capita endowment and low frequency of tuition changes, and vice versa. Since this is the case, there is not much point in testing the first part of this alternative hypothesis.

Thus, despite the fact that a grouping of IHL according to their per capita endowment results in at least one group mean tuition charge which is significantly different from the over-all mean—that for the highest per capita endowment colleges and universities, we have not been able to find support in our data for a theoretical hypothesis relating the level of tuition, or the frequency of tuition changes, to the per capita endowment. In the light of these findings it seems reasonable to argue that those institutions which have low endowments relative to their full-time enrollment depend so heavily on current gifts that it is the behavior of this variable rather than the former which would be most likely to affect tuition charges. The 60-college study does not reveal, however, clear inverse relation of percentage of endowment income to percentage of gift income.[5] On the other hand, those institutions which enjoy relatively large endowments display an associated set of characteristics which in their combined effect are conducive to high tuition charges.

We turn now to the effects of the relative enrollment capacities of private and public IHL in individual states upon tuition charges. As we move in 1956 from the group of IHL in states where the ratio of private to public institutions is between 1.50 and 2.49 to the group for which the ratio lies between 2.50 and 3.99, there is a significant increase in the mean tuition charge. This finding is happily congruent with our tentative hypothesis that the level of tuition is a positive function of the relative enrollment capacity of private (against public) institutions in the state. Yet, if this hypothesis is taken to imply that the function is purely linear, it cannot be accepted: the drop in mean tuition of $165, as we pass into the group of IHL for which the ratio of private to public institutions is higher than 4.00, is also significant.

A fairly straightforward interpretation of this nonlinearity is available. Since there is probably a moderate level of private tuition charges below which the cross elasticity of demand for public higher education is negligible—that is, a level below which potential entrants do not shift in large numbers to public IHL as their tuition declines—private institutions, which share a very large proportion of the total enrollment capacity in a given area, are forced to compete more intensively among themselves to fill up their enrollment registers out of a fairly fixed demand for private higher education. We can render this explanation more realistic by recognizing that the market for private higher education is not segmented along state lines, that private institutions in the position sketched out above can tap the pool of demand for the kind of higher education they offer in other areas. To do this, they must offer a sufficiently favorable tuition differential to overcome either the competition offered by private schools in the student's home state or the transportation costs (and possibly higher living costs) incurred by moving away from home, or both.

On another point our findings with respect to the "enrollment capacity effect" support the general conclusion reached elsewhere in this book that " . . . the public schools in New England do not offer such serious competition to the private schools as is found elsewhere in the country." The states whose private colleges and universities comprise the 18 members of group 4—which shows the highest group mean—are Connecticut, Massachusetts, Vermont, New York, New Jersey, and Kentucky.

This denouement presents a temptation to dispense with the explanation which was offered for the nonlinearity of the "enrollment-capacity effects" as being unnecessary. If among the 18 members of group 4 we find Amherst, Barnard, Bennington, Cornell, Harvard, Princeton, Sarah Lawrence, and Yale, why not put down the peak mean tuition displayed by group 4 to the fact that the states which fall into this group are also those in which the number of "prestige" schools are relatively high and whose median incomes are above average? However, it may justifiably be argued that we cannot continue ascribing all significant deviations from average tuition charges to the effects of a number of "prestige" institutions without ever considering the anatomy of a "prestige" college or university. Here are some characteristics of a number of so-called "prestige" schools as revealed by this study: we have found them congregated in the highest group under the per capita endowment classification, in the next-to-highest group under the relative-enrollment-capacity classification, and in the high-median-income regions of the Northeast and Pacific Coast. Although it is perhaps obvious, it is certainly more instructive to ascribe the high tuition which they charge to the peculiar combination of these and other factors than to the fact that a certain "prestige" is attached to having attended them. Among the other factors are undoubtedly distinguished faculty and superior plant, though it is not necessarily true that prestige follows these variables closely.

In the course of the foregoing discussion, regional differences in mean tuition charges have been alluded to. The highest tuition regions which emerge from our sample are the New England and Middle Atlantic states—

what the Bureau of the Census calls the Northeast—and the Mountain and Pacific states, in that order. Of the 11 institutions comprising the last-mentioned group, only 1 was not located in the Pacific states, and of the 10 which were, 6 were in California. It is clearly this Californian group which pulls the average tuition for the Mountain and Pacific states above the over-all mean.[6] The national sample in *Planning and Management Data, 1958–60* yields somewhat different results, though unfortunately West and Southwest are combined. For private IHL average tuition in 1959–60 was $787 for the North Atlantic, $573 for the Great Lakes and Plains, $443 for the Southeast, and $554 for the West and Southwest.

On a general level, it is worth while to consider the implication of the fact that the analysis of variance performed for 1956 data revealed significant "region effects," while that for 1940 data—the grouping remaining the same for both cases—did not. If we are prepared to impute a substantial part of the regional differences in private IHL tuitions to regional variation in median income, it would seem that, in the period since 1940, tuition charges of private colleges and universities have come to reflect such regional income differences more closely. (In a later chapter we shall see that the expenditures per student in public IHL tend to be high in low-income regions vis-à-vis per capita income in these regions.) But the analysis of the preceding chapter reveals that tuition did not rise nearly as much as per capita disposable income from 1940 to 1956.

Only for the last of our four sets of factors, that of religious affiliation status, are we in a position to compare the nature of significant effects at two points in time. Unfortunately, as the effects of religious affiliation are likely to remain more stable over time than those of the other factors, such a comparison is perhaps the least interesting of the four possibilities.

The marked difference between the average tuition charges of institutions which have no religious affiliation and the affiliated colleges and universities is apparent. In both 1940 and 1956, the group mean tuition of the non-denominational schools lay significantly above the over-all mean charge, while the average for the loosely affiliated non-Catholic institutions and that of the schools with a Catholic affiliation was significantly lower than the over-all mean.

Why are tuition charges lower in groups 2 and 4 than in the general average? It is quite likely that a large number of these institutions pursue a policy of maintaining low tuitions, depending more and more on other sources of income to cover their rising costs. In this regard, there are at least two peculiarities of the position in which such schools find themselves which are worthy of mention: First, the market faced by an IHL affiliated with a religious society is more restricted than that confronting a non-denominational school. Consequently, oligopolistic contact between institutions affiliated with the same religious organization is probably stronger than between a random selection of the nondenominational colleges in a given area: a small number of institutions which were reluctant to increase their tuitions, appropriately distributed by affiliation, would thus constitute a stronger stabilizing force than would an equivalent number of non-denominational colleges and universities. The reasons why such institutions show reluctance to increase their tuitions need not be—and a reading of their responses to the questionnaire indicates they are not—substantively different from those of other colleges and universities. The restraints on tuition increases are simply stronger. Undoubtedly a downward trend in their relative command of the market is also relevant here. Second, the existence of a religious affiliation constitutes an effective medium through which institutions so situated can appeal for current gifts. Undoubtedly, not all denominational schools are equally successful in such appeals, but it is true that since they are on the whole less well endowed than the non-denominational colleges and universities (in our sample), they are more dependent than the latter on current gifts as a source of income.[7] In general IHL with low tuition and small endowment tend to rely more heavily on current gifts, though the evidence is a little mixed on this point.

It only remains to append a final word of caution concerning the interpretation of the results of the latter part of this study. The analysis of variance and the other statistical techniques employed have treated the 85 sets of responses as a sample from the population of private colleges and universities in the United States. Thus, on purely technical grounds it would appear to be valid to draw inferences from the sample to the entire population. However, on equally technical grounds, the nonrandom character of the sample would inveigh against such a procedure. There is, on the other hand, a counterargument to the last point which does carry some force. While the sample of 85 is admittedly not a random one, with respect to the entire population, it is quite representative of the upper echelons of IHL in America. To the extent that one believes that the type of IHL not adequately represented in the sample strive to emulate those which are, and in so far as it is with reference to the behavior of the latter group that policy recommendations are framed, the pertinence of whatever conclusions have emerged from this study does extend beyond the scope of the limited sample of colleges and universities upon which it is based.

FOOTNOTES

[1] I am greatly indebted to an unusually able research assistant, Paul David, now Assistant Professor at Stanford, who compiled the results of the questionnaires upon which this chapter is based and analyzed them.

[2] Cf. earlier discussion.

[3] Further, could such a measure be established, it would be questionable to assume that a given "degree of competitive pressure" imposed a uniform constraint

on the pricing of the academic services performed by all colleges and universities faced by it.

[4] To save space, I have not presented table 2.

[5] *A Study of Income and Expenditures of Sixty Colleges: A Summary Report, Year 1953–54,* pp. 26–27.

[6] Thus, if we consider the isolated case of California, where the ratio of private to public institutions is very low, we could either argue that the high median income of the state swamps the depressing effect of relatively low private enrollment capacity upon private tuition charges or that in situations in which the ratio of private to public enrollment capacity is extremely low, the inelasticity of demand for private higher education becomes operative, permitting private institutions to charge high tuitions. The two arguments are not really alternatives but are complementary, as high median income serves to reinforce the demand for private higher education.

[7] It is the author's opinion that the institutions affiliated with the Catholic Church are probably more successful than those of any other affiliation in raising income from current gifts. Two pieces of evidence tend to corroborate this supposition: (1) Of the 17 IHL in the sample which were in the lowest per capita endowment group in 1956, 12 were schools with some religious affiliation, and of those 12, 8 were affiliated with the Catholic Church. Hence, the need for current gifts. (2) Of the 12 IHL with Catholic affiliation included in the sample, 8 stated in their responses to the questionnaire that, in effect, they depended on current gifts to keep their tuitions from increasing. Only 4 of the 13 non-Catholic "loosely affiliated" schools in the sample made similar responses.

Chapter 7

THE PRICING OF COLLEGE SERVICES

Since tuition generally covers such a small part of the total costs of education and at the same time colleges and universities are finding themselves increasingly in financial difficulties, why is it that tuition has not risen to fill the gap between revenue and costs? The answer lies, I think, in a number of other variables affecting university pricing policy even as much as costs, the most important of which is competition among the colleges and universities. The high school senior searching around for a prospective college in 1960 may choose from among over nineteen hundred different institutions. Clearly tuition policy is going to affect his choice, and the college which wants to attract outstanding students—indeed, any students at all—is acutely aware of the tuition policies of its close competitors.

COMPETITION AMONG IHL

Competition among colleges is, of course, restricted by various considerations. Princeton, for example, does not compete with Holyoke Junior College or with William and Mary, or with Vassar, or, seriously, with the University of New Mexico. But there are restrictions on Princeton's freedom of action. For each college must watch her close rivals, in this case (say) Harvard, Yale, or Dartmouth. The son of a Princeton man may go to Princeton even if her charges are $1,000 more than Yale's, but most students would prefer Yale at $1,000 tuition to Princeton at $2,000, and vice versa. Even in the Ivy colleges, after all, the family income which backs a student is likely to average around $15,000. Princeton's product is uniquely Princeton's, but the difference is not great enough to yield a $1,000 advantage, given the resources and the spending pattern of the usual undergraduate. A Yale education, with frequent weekends away, probably would be preferred to Princeton without the weekends. The average student, that is, would react to any large differentials between these close rivals; even a difference of $500 out of *total* costs of around $4,000

to $5,000 (including income forgone) would undoubtedly result in sub-
stantial shifting.

As a result, Ivy League colleges try not to get out of line with one
another. If one college lags in raising its tuition rates, the others tend to
wait until the laggard catches up. (This actually occurred in the thirties
and forties.)

The Ivy college must also take notice of the pricing practices in the first-
class small liberal arts colleges, such as Swarthmore, Oberlin, Amherst,
Wesleyan, Williams, and Bowdoin. A difference of $500 between Prince-
ton and Amherst may well divert traffic from New Jersey to Massachusetts.

Like the Ivy colleges, other institutions determine their fees in relation
to their immediate competitors. In addition the policy of the state university is often decisive. Bowdoin, for example, is in competition with many
first-class liberal arts colleges and to a lesser extent with the Ivy colleges,
but it must also compete with the University of Maine. In Nebraska, the
position of the small liberal arts college is even tougher. The state university's $100 tuition fee looks especially inviting after several years of
drought. Stanford, with a tuition charge in excess of $1,000 competes
with an equally good school at Berkeley with fees of about $100. Nor is
Columbia exactly unconcerned that the municipal colleges of New York
provide a good education without tuition. Engineering schools, women's
colleges, and every other kind of institution whose specialty is this, that,
or the other thing watch each other closely and often regard tax-supported institutions with apprehension. Even if with unusual demand there
is no question of unfilled vacancies, the competition is felt in the quality
of the students applying.

Institutions such as the Ivy colleges, which seek a student body with
some geographical balance, feel competition from state universities in
more distant parts of the country; this is particularly true in the South,
Middle West, and Far West. In general, Ivy colleges charge about $1,000
more tuition than the large state institutions and undoubtedly lose students as a result, but generous aid policies and prestige keep the Ivy colleges on a reasonable competitive footing.

The prestige of these institutions does little good for the excellent private colleges in the center of the country. The head of a major private institution in the Middle West told me that the children of wealthy parents
go either to the East Coast or West Coast colleges. This situation may
change as state universities continue to improve their product. The advantage which the Ivy schools possess in their aid policies may gradually
vanish, too. The administrators of Pennsylvania State University, disturbed
by the loss of able students to private institutions offering attractive
scholarships, are seeking funds to provide equally attractive scholarships
of their own. Their example will probably not pass unnoticed. The Elliot
Congressional Committee hearings in 1957 showed that authorities in

many Western states resent all scholarships, public or private, which attract their best students to Eastern prestige institutions. But there is general agreement that a differential of $2,000 in tuition between major private and public institutions would largely stop the flow of students from Western and Southern states with good public institutions.

In this connection the reader may be interested in the results of a study, "Economics of Harvard," which I published in the *Harvard Alumni Bulletin* (February 20, 1960). My guess is that tuition of the prestige Eastern institutions by 1970 will be at least $1,750; and I assume no inflation. This rise would roughly be matched by an expected rise of per capita income of 35 per cent (no inflation).

Here are some conclusions from this article:

The average *cost* of an education at Harvard (without organized research excluded) was $3,690 in 1958–59.

The average charge (tuition) was $1,200.

This average cost was $3\frac{1}{3}$ times the average in the country and 2 times that of six outstanding land-grant colleges.

Despite the low average of tuition in the country (roughly $400) and the high tuition at Harvard ($1,250), the subsidies to the average student in the country were but $700, and at Harvard $2,440. This undoubtedly explains in part the prestige and numerous applications for Harvard.

The costs and subsidies vary greatly; for example:

Public health costs = $13,540	Tuition = $ 930	Tuition costs = 7%
Law costs = 1,720	Tuition = 1,130	Tuition costs = 66%

The nature of the instruction and the small numbers account for high costs in public health. But allowance for heavy research outlays increases the tuition vis-à-vis relevant costs for public health students.

The differential in costs is made up for impecunious and able students by larger and more numerous scholarships than in the country over.

Average scholarship in the U.S. = $ 300 (est.)	With scholarship = 17%
Average scholarship in Harvard College = 1,350	With scholarship = 25%

But should Harvard's cost differential continue to rise, then by 1970 her competitive position would be seriously impaired unless gifts should greatly increase.

Competition between public and private institutions varies from region to region. In some states the public institutions are dominant: California is an example; in both Illinois and Michigan the state universities have managed to acquire a substantial majority of the scholarship holders who enjoy free access to both public and first-class private colleges. In Texas, a rise of tuition of $200 by Southern Methodist University was immediately felt in a substantial drop of enrollments. The State University is a serious competitor.

In other areas, it is not so clear that public institutions hold the field.

In conversations with the presidents of Southern and Western state universities, I find that their view is that because public IHL in the Northeast
charge high fees, the competition there with local private college rivals is
not so serious for independent IHL as in other parts of the country. It is
true that competition between public and independent colleges in the
Northeast is not so serious for the latter IHL as in some other parts of the
country, but this situation cannot be attributed to the high tuition rates of
public colleges in that area. For one thing, half of the $29 difference in a
recent year between the average charge for public colleges in the Northeast
($184) and that throughout the country ($155) can be explained by
larger per capita incomes in the former area. But, more significantly, the
rates for private institutions in New England show an even greater excess
over fees in public IHL than in the nation: $488 in the Northeast as
against $371 nationally.

TABLE 7-1

Average Student Charges Paid by Full-time Students in 547 Public and Private Universities
and Liberal Arts Colleges, by Geographical Region, 1950*

Geographical region	Average student charge	Per cent of students in public institutions
Total United States.......	$291	48.1
Northeast..............	495	19.7
Middle East............	419	23.9
South.................	242	53.7
Middle West...........	245	56.0
West..................	185	71.2
Southwest.............	144	69.2
Far West..............	215	62.8

* Each institution's charge weighted by the number of students; the
resident charge used for public institutions.
Source: R. H. Ostheimer, *Student Charges and Financing Higher Education*, A staff
study for the Commission on Financing Higher Education,
1953, p. 35.

Such figures, then, suggest that competition between public and private
colleges in the Northeast is more serious than elsewhere in the country,
high tuition rates of public institutions notwithstanding. Similar conclusions from percentage figures seem to confirm this conclusion. For the nation, average fees of public institutions in a recent year were 30 per cent
of the average for private colleges; in the Northeast only 27 per cent, the
lowest of any area in the country. As might be expected, the average student charge is highest in those regions where state institutions enroll small
numbers.[1]

Yet, as I have said, the general conclusion must be that the public colleges in New England do not offer such serious competition to the private schools as is found elsewhere in the country. The reason must be one independent of tuition practices. State institutions in the Northeast are of a _relatively_ lower quality than those in the Middle and Far West at least; also, they provide a relatively small number of openings. Although prices are low (relative to private IHL), entry is greatly restricted in these public institutions. With rising enrollments, it is probable that they will offer more competition to private colleges in the future, particularly if the latter raise their tuition greatly. The growth of junior colleges, too, will perhaps cut applications to private institutions in some degree.

Elsewhere, the competition of public institutions presses private institutions hard. This fact is shown by the proportions of students attending each type of institution as shown in Table 7-2. One might expect that in

TABLE 7-2
Percentage of Resident Enrollment, Private to Public, November, 1953, 1955

Region	1953	1955
All........................	85	78
Northeast...................	263	252
North Central..............	78	70
South.....................	62	58
West......................	29	25

Source: HEW, _Statistics of Higher Education: Faculty, Students, and Degrees, 1953–54_, pp. 88–89; ibid., 1955–56, pp. 115–17.

the Northeast the private institution would be the dominant factor in price setting, and in the West, the public institution. Yet though the Northeast had nine to ten times as many resident students in private institutions vis-à-vis those in public institutions as the West (263 and 252 as against 29 and 25 from Table 7-2), the relative tuitions are almost identical. From these facts we draw the conclusion that, unlike usual markets, prices are not determined by the largest sellers.

TABLE 7-3

Region	Tuition fees		
	Public	Private	Ratio of public to private
Northeast............	$184	$672	27%
West................	145	507	29%

PRODUCT DIFFERENTIATION

Thus far, we have examined the importance of competition in keeping the level of tuition charges low. There is another factor which must be taken into account when the extent to which tuition fees may vary is examined: the differentiation of the college product. If all education were the same, no college could persistently charge tuition radically different from the rest. But we have seen that large differences in tuition do persist; that they can do so may be attributed to the fact that all education is not the same and colleges often feel able to charge a higher amount for tuition because it is consonant with the demand for their particular college product.

The measurement of a college product is, however, extremely difficult; it can only be done in terms of what the college is trying to do. Obviously the objectives of Yale, Notre Dame, and Haverford are different; but how different? What is more, how can we measure the success of a college in doing what it has set out to do?

For their own purposes of appraisal, many graduate schools use the Graduate Record Examinations. These examinations can be used to find out what is in the student's head, although they do not reveal who put it there. First-class graduate schools rate colleges on this basis. They come to prefer graduates of particular colleges, even to the extent of not requiring Graduate Record Examinations of them.

Again, the number of Wilson or Rhodes scholarships won by undergraduates is considered a test of the college's merit. Many college administrators stress such tests, as well as the number of students they place in leading graduate schools and the professions. (This last criterion may lead to some educational irony. One president of a leading liberal arts college, boasting that 60 per cent of his students went on to graduate schools, then complained that few of his graduates became business leaders and hence large donors to the college.)

Another test of the college product is simply the wealth of its graduates. Here, at least, there is a concrete figure. College students *graduating in* 1960 may look forward to lifetime incomes of about $200,000 in excess of a high school graduate who did not go to college.[2] The differences among colleges show up in this measurement too. In 1947, graduates of the "Big Three" (Harvard, Yale, and Princeton) had annual incomes 20 per cent above those of graduates of other Ivy colleges and 56 per cent in excess of the median income of all college graduates.[3] Lest anyone be too quick to seize upon this measure as final authority, I must point out that the input of a college will certainly affect the output and that if certain colleges persist in skimming the cream of the nation's youth, they cannot claim that the financial success of their graduates is their work alone.

Some have proposed that the college contribution be measured by tests given to the students graduating, or to a good sample of them. If the tests were properly constructed, they might reveal a great deal about the quality of different colleges. This has not yet been done, but one by-product of our Selective Service System is a breakdown by field of study, if not by institution. In 1951, 339,000 college men took the draft-deferment test. The scores of different colleges are not known, but Henry Chauncy revealed in an article in *Science* (July 25, 1952) that the following percentages passed: all, 53 per cent; engineering students, 68; physical science and mathematics, 64; biological science, 57; social science, 57; humanities, 52; and education, 27.[4] It is probably not worthwhile to quibble over a few percentage points in the middle of the scale, but no one concerned with education can compare the second and last figures without a sense of dismay.

In recent years we have had studies of accomplishments of college graduates in the sciences and in other fields. For example, the Knapp and Greenbaum study concentrated on compiling a roster of American scholars based on achievement of a Ph.D. or Sc.D. or the winning of some fellowship, scholarship, or prize at a graduate level. On this basis the writers find that " . . . even the lowest ranking school of these top 50 is at least threefold better than the median for the whole distribution . . . ; while, on the other hand, the highest ranking schools are nearly 20 times more fruitful than the median institution in over-all production of male graduates of promise."[5]

This type of study does not exhaust the issues. A college with relatively small output of scholars may make large contributions to the world of medicine, business, and government. But surely parents, counselors, and those students who anticipate a life of teaching, research, and scholarship should be aware of this study and know, for example, the excellent record of such institutions as California Institute of Technology in turning out physical scientists, Swarthmore in producing social scientists, and Haverford in training scholars in the humanities, as well as of the 47 other outstanding institutions thus judged. Yet the results are virtually unknown to the schoolteachers, counselors, parents, and potential students.

Unfortunately, none of these measures is adequate, first, because they allow neither for differences in ability of the raw material entering the colleges nor for the varying degrees of what the business world calls "connections." The latter factor may not be too important. Wolfle and Smith have shown that college graduates earn incomes, long before the peaks are reached, from $1,100 to $2,500 more per year than high school students *of equal ability* who do not go on to college. The excess seems independent of the occupations of parents but rises with the quality of the men.[6] However, there is no allowance made here for the presumably higher motivation of those who go to college. Second, economic measures neglect the greater values of a college education, which are only in part reflected in income. I have said before that we want our students to learn how to think, to analyze problems, to show seasoned judgment in their treatment of issues, to use their imagination, and to learn how to communicate. We expect them to understand and enjoy cultural activities, and to develop a set of principles to help them in their personal behavior. If these objectives of a college education are unrealized, then the educational process has failed.

While discussing the subject of the product of educational institutions, it is probably worthwhile to challenge the assumption that a product exists at all. It is an article of faith with all of us in the teaching profession that our students are changed by what we tell them and that the change is for the good.

Some recent studies by Stouffer, Riesman, and Jacob have some bearing on this faith.

Jacob's study shows a striking failure of the college to influence the values of its students. Here is an excerpt from his book:[7]

We turn now to a more pin-pointed examination of curricular influences. A review of over thirty attempts to detect and measure the effect of particular courses upon student attitudes, beliefs and sometimes conduct suggests (1) that significant change is the exception rather than the rule; but that (2) some students have definitely changed opinions and perhaps values in the process of taking certain courses; (3) that the experimental design in most of these studies precludes a firm conclusion that it was the course that caused the change although a presumption that it did so is reasonable; (4) that the content and organization of these potent courses had little in common; but (5) most of them did deliberately set out to induce some sort of value change among the students. One should not conclude from these experiments however that there are "packages" of social science materials which when presented as the content of a "core course" would have any more distinctive influence upon the body of students than other materials which might be selected. . . .

It certainly comes as no surprise to a professor to discover that his students do not listen from time to time, but the lack of any communication whatever would be a bitter pill. I am somewhat relieved to be able to say that experts disagree on this point. Riesman and Stouffer hold that Jacob's position is overstated.

Even if we suppose that colleges do affect their students, there is some evidence that the change may not be all for the good. In a study of Vassar undergraduates, Sanford found the freshmen stable, contented, cooperative, hardworking, and eager; the seniors unstable, uncertain, fearful, uncooperative and unhappy. All this may be interpreted in various ways, and the first which springs to mind is the old saw about ignorance and bliss. The modern world is often disagreeable, and if Vassar has succeeded in impressing this fact upon her daughters, it has given them at least part of their money's worth. Robert Hutchins once said that the test of education is to unsettle the minds of young men.

In spite of the ambiguity and confusion resulting from an inadequate and conflicting set of criteria, it is nonetheless possible for a prospective student to make a reasonably sane decision about which college he will attend.

It would be my guess that the ultimate reason for a high school senior's choice of one college over another frequently has little to do with the process of education. Many students go where their parents went, even though the institution may have changed greatly and the student would be better off elsewhere. Many decide on the basis of location, wishing either the security of a college near home or the excitement of college life far away. Many choose the college that will offer fraternities, sororities, and good football. The author chose Harvard, not because of its vast library system or the above-normal income of its graduates or the number of distinguished names on its faculty, but because he overheard three track coaches discussing the relative merits of different universities and their unanimous decision was that Harvard was the place to go. This last consideration, incidentally, is not to be scorned too quickly. Many college administrators who are disturbed by the emphasis put upon intercollegiate athletics are nevertheless reluctant to reduce its place in college life, for they know that in doing so they will lose not only financial support (and hence need higher tuition) but more important, they will lose many able students who also value highly the athletic attractions of college.

A student might make a better choice of a college if he were at least aware of the rational criteria for decision. These might not crowd every thought of coeds and raccoon coats from his mind, but they would tend to make a selection a little less hit-or-miss. At present, sources for such information are generally either poor or nonexistent. Counseling is still at a primitive stage, and resources for it are inadequate. Much of the student's information comes from a high school teacher or principal, sometimes good, sometimes bad.

One step toward improving the structure of tuition rates in the United States would be to give the prospective purchaser of higher education some idea of what his money will buy for him. If counseling were extended and improved and if rational criteria in the form of tests were established to measure the accomplishment of a college in teaching its students, the student would be better able to pay his money and make his choice. Colleges can hardly expect to set reasonable prices on their services while their customers are buying in the dark. Possibly the provisions for improved counseling in the National Defense Education Act will be helpful.

TUITION AND SOCIAL VALUES

Price policy is not set in a manner to obtain maximum revenue. If it were, the colleges would auction off their places to the highest bidders, and they would charge, say, $4,000 for a concentration in classics or medicine as a means of eliminating costly instruction. IHL are interested primarily in contributing to the advance of knowledge and to training students, including meeting the needs of our society. In their pricing policies they have to take into account these objectives.

One might expect that IHL would charge less for training those greatly needed by the nation (teachers, for instance) and for those taking a liberal arts education, where material gains are not so clear, but would charge full costs, or even more than full costs, for those studying (say) business or applied research and use the profits of the latter to subsidize basic research. (I assume that the capacity to pay is there.) Colleges might even be justified in putting upon government, as the agency of the people, the costs of operating national libraries, museums, basic research, and the like. In this manner costs extraneous to the student's education would not be put upon the student or other resources of the IHL.

Unfortunately pricing on the basis of social objectives—e.g., $500 tuition for liberal arts and $1,500 for business schools—is possible only if the IHL behave like a cartel. Otherwise the colleges that reduce tuition for liberal arts would attract liberal arts students disproportionately and experience financial embarrassment, and the others by keeping tuition for business schools down would attract the business school students. The reality of competition prevents a pricing policy based on social objectives.

Yet the figures below suggest that social objectives are taken into account in pricing policies. For example:

TABLE 7-4

Schools	Average fees, 1957–58	
	Public	Private
Teachers colleges......................	$131	$566
Technological...........................	176	749
Theological............................	....	250
Other independent professional schools.....	397	602
All....................................	155	526

Source: HEW, *Higher Education: Planning and Management Data, 1957–58*, p. 68.

In general, fees for liberal arts schools and teachers colleges are low in public institutions, and clearly much below costs for divinity students in private ones. Charges for technological students are high, though *far* below costs in public institutions. Not only do students in other independent professional schools pay high fees in both public and private institutions, but the charge is two-thirds as high in public as in private institutions. For all fees public charges are but 30 per cent of those in private institutions. High fees in the other independent professional schools reflect not only an association of private gain for this kind of education but also the high costs involved in the instruction.

Nonpecuniary considerations are also evident in the tuition charges, college by college. I refer the reader to earlier discussion of variations in costs and tuition of Harvard.[8]

Again, Table 7A-1 reveals large differences in charges as compared to costs. For one university, business administration accounts for 8 per cent of instructional expenditures and 23 per cent of the students; medicine, for 19 per cent of expenditures and 1 per cent of the students. In graduate instruction (arts and science) at another university, the costs are 6 to 7 times as high per student vis-à-vis those in the lower division and 2½ times vis-à-vis those in the upper division. Yet graduate fees in arts and sciences are generally not higher but lower than undergraduate ones.

As we shall see in the next chapter, basing tuition policy on social values has a considerable tradition in this country.

SUMMARY

In view of the financial difficulties confronting IHL it is rather surprising that they have not increased tuition more. One important reason is the fear of losing students to competitors.

Yet rates vary greatly—from free tuition to charges in excess of $1,500. Students also take into account the ratio of tuition to costs. That, for example, a student may pay $1,000 for a $3,000 education and $400 for a $400 education should surely influence the parent and the student. To some extent such considerations are taken into account. They explain in part the penchant for the prestige institutions.

It is often assumed that the competition of the public institution is the dominant factor everywhere but in the Northeast, where public tuition is high. But actually the tuition differential between public and private institutions is higher in the Northeast than in the rest of the country.

Students will often select higher-priced rather than lower-priced institutions because of product differentiation, an item not easy to define or measure. Obviously the main interest is in what the college contributes. Then we have to take into account the input (student ability, motivation,

etc., at entry) and the output, the college's contribution being the difference. We do not have very good measures of output, in part because input
varies so and in part because of the difficulty of measuring output. The
contribution relates to what the college is trying to do—increase knowledge of the student? Teach him (her) how to think and communicate?
Teach a profession? Measures of some use but scarcely adequate are
income of graduates, grades on graduate records and tests, numbers
winning Wilson fellowships and similar competitions, percentage in *Men
of Science, Who's Who,* etc.

Another factor that seems to influence tuition rates is the social product
contributed. There is a tendency to charge less when social gains are
highest, e.g., divinity and education, and more when the private gains are
great, even though in some instances social gains are also relevant, e.g.,
medicine, engineering.

But we should not overstress the logic in the structures of rates. In an
official report for North Carolina public IHL much was made of the
irrational manner of setting rates within the state structure—differentials
were often not justified. The committee wanted a rational explanation of
the structure of rates.[9] And in New York State it was shown that institutions classified from high to low tuitions had the following percentages
of enrollment in the local community: 1, 36, 51, 77 per cent. In other
words, tuition tends to be high when appeals are to nonresident students.[10]

FOOTNOTES

[1] See the discussion in Chap. 6.

[2] This problem is discussed fully in Chap. 10.

[3] *They Want to Go to College,* pp. 178–179.

[4] *Science,* July, 1952.

[5] Knapp and Greenbaum, *The Younger American Scholar: His Collegiate Origins,*
1953, especially pp. 11–16.

[6] D. Wolfle and J. G. Smith, "Occupational Value of Education for Superior High-
school Graduates," *Journal of Higher Education,* 1956, pp. 201–213. In a study of
land-grant college alumni, Bridgman, a generation ago, found that high-ability college
graduates performed much better than non-high-ability graduates. (His measure of
performance was income, and of ability was age of entry.) The assumption is that
the more able enter college earlier. He also concluded that college graduates of
ability are the ones who notably gain from a college education. D. S. Bridgman,
"Earnings of Land-grant College Alumni and Former Students," *Journal of Engineering Education,* November, 1931, p. 197.

[7] P. E. Jacob, *Changing Values in College,* 1957, p. 107.

[8] *Financial Report to the Board of Overseers for the Fiscal Year 1954–1955,* pp.
10–13.

[9] "State Supported Higher Education in North Carolina," *The Report of the
Commission on Higher Education,* 1955, table 32, pp. 33, 75.

[10] *Report of Temporary Commission on Need for a State University,* 1941, p. 33.

APPENDIX

TABLE 7A-1
Percentage Distribution of Instructional Expenditures, Student Enrollments, and Degrees Granted at Two Contrasting Universities, 1949

Field	University A			University B		
	Percentage of instructional expenditures	Percentage of student enrollment	Percentage of degrees granted	Percentage of instructional expenditures	Percentage of student enrollment	Percentage of degrees granted
Arts and sciences....	19	30	25	30	22	37
Agriculture..........	11	8	6			
Business administration	8	23	26	14	52	25
Education...........	12	15	15	2	2	5
Engineering.........	10	14	12	14	4	5
Law..............	1	2	2	3	2	5
Medicine...........	19	1	2	7	3	3
Other..............	20	7	12	30	15	20
Total.............	100	100	100	100	100	100

Instructional Expenditures per Full-time Student Equivalent at University C, by Field and Level of Study, 1950

Field	Lower division	Upper division	Graduate classes	Graduate research
Arts and sciences........	$134.10	$353.87	$ 873.53	$3,248.17
Business..............	89.91	152.26	380.65	1,312.00
Dentistry.............	....	416.77	1,496.81	
Education.............	333.32	661.22	538.38	1,827.99
Law.................	....	....	287.55	
Medicine.............	....	....	1,723.83	
Music................	489.65	440.26	611.41	
Agriculture...........	291.34	317.55	411.04	451.26
Engineering...........	434.35	383.53	618.60	2,850.38

Source: J. D. Millett, *Financing Higher Education in the United States,* 1952, pp. 145, 146.

Chapter 8

THE LEVEL OF TUITION RATES

TRADITION OF LOW RATES

In recent years private institutions seem more disposed to raise tuition than public institutions, though with the increasingly weak position of state and local governments tuition in the 1950s rose more relatively in public than in private IHL. Pressures are great also on private IHL.

But it would be a mistake to assume that private IHL have not had a long tradition of low tuition rates. For example, President Woolsey of Yale stated in 1850: "Yale ought to look for its means of advancement not to an increase in the price of tuition but to the liberality of its graduates and other friends."

A president of Ohio Wesleyan late in the nineteenth century wrote: "As we have seen, the University has no income from tuition fees. . . . The Ohio Wesleyan aims to make education as nearly free as possible. With no revenue from the fees of students the institution relies on the endowment for the support of the faculty."

In 1829 the president of Augusta College, Kentucky, announced that " . . . all students who find it inconvenient to pay their tuition fees are admitted gratis."

The fact that education grew up along the lines of an advancing frontier has contributed to the maintenance of low fees. Colleges, established as soon as there were permanent settlements, profited from the accumulation of wealth. Facilities were simple, faculty pay was low, and students attended only if fees were low.

A statement of 1856[1] reads:

At Yale College the rate of tuition is fixed at a price much lower than is paid in academies and private seminars of learning; and from this low rate there are numerous instances, in cases of pressing indigence, where a part or the whole price of tuition is abated. Moreover, there are funds held in reserve for the express purpose of enabling poor pious souls of fair promise to secure the blessings of a liberal education. It is for the same great object . . .

114

that the salaries of its elders are fixed at a rate adequate only to a bare support, and often indeed, below what is required for the support of a family on a moderate scale of respectability.

Again, Frank A. Dickey, writing in the *Education Review* in 1915, said:

Reduced to its simplest forms tuition fees are of necessity nothing more than an attempt to furnish a sum which will enable an institution to give to its students what it could not, without such charges, afford to give. . . . The marvelous growth of wealth in this country and the willingness of people of means to give to the support of educational institutions has inclined authorities to prefer to hustle for gifts rather than to increase the rates to their students. This preference has been strengthened by the fear that education will be made too expensive and by the competition of rival institutions.

In the 1939 report of the University of Chicago (*State of the University*), President Hutchins said: "Depending on fees, if carried too far, may mean subservience to the whims of students and their parents."

In the twentieth century the pressure of competition from state institutions has tended to keep fees down. It is true, however, that increased costs have resulted in a substantial rise in fees. A study of 20 colleges from 1909 to 1934 shows an average increase of tuition fees from $47 to $173.[2]

In its famous report of 1947 the President's Commission on Higher Education strongly supported the view that tuition fees were too high. The Commission stressed the low average income of American families and the substantial rise of tuition since the late thirties. As a minimum measure they wished to reduce tuition at state institutions to the prewar level. In the view of the 1952 Commission on Financing Higher Education, however, tuition increases were necessary. But they were not in favor of allowing tuition to be charged exclusively on the basis of ability to pay.[3]

In short, there is a long tradition of low tuition rates, for many years strongly supported by private institutions but gradually being weakened by economic pressures. Public institutions with tax resources behind them are even more firmly attached to this low-tuition tradition. In an interesting analysis Riesman writes: "These [public] institutions help spread the ethos that even wealthy students need not pay the full cost of their education and that desirable students (not only athletes but sometimes debaters, scholars, and 'all-around' types) need not borrow more than the token amounts that present loan services can proffer." In 1961 Henry Commager urged free tuition for all college students. The stress was on needs of trained manpower and the social gains of higher education. The dean of the City College of New York reacted strongly against tuition in CCNY, no tuition being held to be a symbol of democracy.[4]

RELATIVE CONTRIBUTIONS OF STUDENT FEES

The trend of tuition has been upward since 1920 at any rate. By 1955 tuition had risen above prewar levels by 85 per cent, somewhat less than prices, substantially less than per capita income. My own estimates put the rise of tuition at less than the official estimates. In the 1950s tuition tended to decline in relation to general and educational income, a fact

TABLE 8-1

Tuition and Ratio of Tuition Income to General and Educational Income (GEI)
and to GEI Adjusted, per Resident Student, 1920 to 1956

Tuition item	1920	1930	1940	1950	1956	1958
Fees per resident student..........	$70	$131	$133	$265	$279	
Tuition income to GEI.............	24%	30%	35%	38%	26%	25%
Tuition income to GEI adjusted......	....	33%*	41%	50%	39%	

* Related activities estimated.

Source: Calculated from HEW, *Statistics of Higher Education, 1955–56: Receipts, Expenditures and Property*, and *Faculty, Students and Degrees*. 1958 estimated on basis of HEW preliminary figures.

TABLE 8-2

Ratio of Tuition and Fees to Current Income, Per Cent

Type of IHL	1922	1938	1950
Private IHL..........	38.2	....	45.1
Public IHL...........	12.1	15.0	19.0

Ratio of Tuition and Fees to General and Educational Income,
Per Cent

Private IHL:...................	62.5	
Universities		57.2
Liberal arts colleges		71.8
Nonsectarian universities......		52.4
Catholic universities..........		78.1
Public IHL:...................	25.1	
Municipal		39.2
State.....................		24.4

explained in part by the large veteran tuition payments in 1950, in part by the large rise of enrollment in the early postwar period without corresponding expansion of faculty and physical facilities, and in part by large gains of other types of income. Table 8-1 gives the relevant facts. Of some interest is the last row, which reveals a substantially higher ratio of tuition to general and educational income when the latter is adjusted for expenditures not clearly related to instruction—e.g., organized research, extension and public services, and related activities. By 1956, whereas tuition was 26 per cent of general and educational income, it was 39 per cent, or one-half more, when adjusted for these items. Perhaps the deductions are excessive, for related activities are largely aids to instruction. I should add, as I have before, that the rise of tuition may be understated to some extent, because the proportion of part-time students is probably rising.

The Commission on Financing Higher Education also shows an upward trend in a study of 100 public universities and 468 private universities and liberal arts colleges.[5]

In 1956, the proportion of tuition income to general and educational income *adjusted* was as shown in Table 8-3.

TABLE 8-3

Schools	Public	Private
Universities..................	21	76
Liberal arts.................	17	64
Teachers colleges...........	18	54
Technological...............	10	46
Theological.................	..	26
Other professional..........	12	68
Junior colleges.............	12	73

Source: See Table 8-1.

Tuition in public IHL vis-à-vis private is especially low in junior colleges, technological schools, and other professional schools. Low relative fees in the last two prevail, even though actual tuition tends to be high in relation to charges in other schools. But at the high costs, the high tuition is still low in relation to educational income.

OPPOSITION TO HIGHER FEES

It is likely that tuition will continue to rise both absolutely and in relation to the costs of higher education. The primary reason for this is the difficulty of increasing gifts, capital income, or tax receipts for higher education as rapidly as costs rise.

As one reads the many state reports on the future of higher education, one is very much impressed by the strong disposition to keep tuition fees down, particularly in those states where state universities are strong. In these matters one must distinguish the attitude of the state legislatures and governors from that of the college and university administrators. In general, the legislatures, sensitive to the protests of the taxpayer, are reluctant to increase taxes for education. Governors frequently side with the legislature, although by no means always. A reduction of appropriations for higher education in Michigan in 1958 exemplifies the concern of legislatures.

The conflict of views between university administrators and government is suggested, for example, by the inaugural address of Governor Dwinell of New Hampshire in 1955:[6]

The unwillingness or inability of many private institutions to expand, and the high standards which have prevailed at the state university, have attracted a large number of students from outside the original category . . . total expenditures of the state institution are steadily increasing, giving rise to the question as to what ultimate extent state money should participate in this situation.

In his inaugural address of 1957 Governor Dwinell said:[7]

The General Court has a continuing responsibility to the young people of our state through the university. Unfortunately, quality in education of necessity is largely determined by dollars and cents. Retention of qualified faculty depends on the university's ability to meet the competitive salary market. Despite the sum appropriated for salary increases two years ago, the university continues to fall behind comparable institutions throughout the country in compensation of staff. . . .

Without additional state support, the university cannot provide our youth with an educational opportunity equal to that enjoyed by young people elsewhere in the nation, or cannot provide the research and services which we have come to expect. However, I believe the charges by the university upon the student should be increased so as to share the added costs and that scholarships should also be increased, in numbers and perhaps in amounts, so that those students whose financial inability is clearly demonstrated can receive the help they deserve.

For the latter remarks Governor Dwinell was widely criticized in the state, particularly by those interested in higher education.

In his report for 1956–57, the president of the University of New Hampshire wrote as follows:[8]

This is why the University urged the General Court and the Governor last year to grant a respite from tuition rises since the University already stands near the top in the nation in this respect and since room and board charges have already been raised. The hold-the-line decision on fees will benefit interstate students throughout the current biennium but it may yet be necessary, as suggested by state officials, to increase out-of-state fees above the present $600 to balance the budget for 1958–59. During the hold-the-line interim for interstate students, future policy might well be considered, keeping in mind that whatever increases are proposed will be on top of the inescapably rising room and board costs and that the point of excess is reached when society begins to lose the services of minds undeveloped for lack of opportunity.

Here we see the contrast in views of a governor concerned with rising taxes and administrators of a state university concerned with rising tuition. Regents, often leaders in the business community, are frequently prepared to recommend higher tuition. Even with significant increases in the tuition of state universities, *additional* burdens on the state universities may well be $2 to $3 billion a year in ten years. It is unlikely that the taxpayer will accept this additional charge without trying to put a much larger burden on the students, although this will vary from state to state.

In Massachusetts there are similar divergencies of opinion. The report of the Special Committee on the Audit of State Needs (of which the author was a member), *Needs in Massachusetts Higher Education, Special Report* (March, 1958), and the Governor's report, *The Responsibility of the Commonwealth in Higher Education: A Message from His Excellency Foster Furcolo, July 1st, 1958,* stressed the point that much needed to be done in higher education in Massachusetts. Even the Governor's program would provide only 16,000 additional spaces in public institutions, although projected expansion of private institutions and increased demands for higher education in the state would require about 30,000 additional places in them. The Governor was reluctant to put any additional burden on local governments because of the very heavy taxes of local governments in Massachusetts. In addition, a state subjected to severe economic competition from its neighbors in industry is very reluctant to impose additional taxes at the state level. The Governor therefore proposed a $24 million bond issue which would cost $1 to $1½ million annually to finance, as a means of establishing nine junior colleges with enrollments of 7,000. The Governor's proposal would put the major burden of costs upon the students, although any municipality could assume part of this burden if it wished. But with tuition in public IHL $200, obviously the largest part of costs would have to fall upon government.

It was apparent in the hearings of July 10, 1958, before the Legislature Committee on Education that there was strong opposition to any program that would involve the state government in additional taxes. Total capital charges in the next three years, according to Governor Furcolo, should average $29 million a year, somewhat less than the national average. Yet even these relatively small charges, which could easily be financed from rising income, were not accepted by the legislature. If the total cost of higher education to state government rises by more than 200 per cent, as seems likely in the nation during the next ten or twelve years, the taxpayer may prove more vocal than those who seek higher education with unchanged tuition.[9]

It may be of some interest to quote the views of President Wells of

Indiana University and his colleagues. These educators have discussed the issue of meeting increased costs by reducing unnecessary expenditures. They argue that increased prosperity and higher per capita incomes will enable more and more students to go to college. But they add:[10]

This will be so of course only on the assumption that families' increasing ability to pay the out-of-pocket costs of maintaining students in college is not fully offset by increases in fees, tuitions and other such costs. Certainly no more during the next 15 years than in the past should there be an indiscriminate resort to higher fees and tuition as expedients for meeting the short-run financial needs of higher educational institutions. Particularly in the case of state institutions, it would be altogether perverse to let year-to-year changes in fees become a device by which state governments escape their responsibility to levy adequate taxes.

In general, college administrators of public IHL are against higher tuition, a conclusion that is drawn after examining hundreds of reports from all over the country. In their *And Bless the Coming Millions* the American Association of Land-grant Colleges and State University Association wrote that when

. . . ability to afford is more important than the ability to learn [this] leads to the growing demand that students and families should bear an increasing share of the cost of education . . . more and more the nation's leadership potential is lessened or lost by making personal financial ability the controlling factor.

For President Gideonse of Brooklyn College, free tuition was necessary to attract students to the socially necessary but financially unattractive professions. The recent official Survey of Higher Education in Michigan urged good education with the lowest cost to the student. Despite the state's financial plight, the University of Colorado *Financial Report* (1957) devoutly hoped for a cut in tuition. In New Mexico tuition was " . . . presently as high as could be managed" (letter to the author, March 26, 1958). An official report in Illinois (*College Enrollment in Illinois*) urged against " . . . establishing arbitrary scholastic requirements so that modest incomes are excluded." This violates the principles and traditions of public education.

In a report to the trustees (1957–58) the president of the University of Alabama warned against higher fees and pricing themselves out of the market. Prices were so high in Vermont that large out-migration of students followed (*Report of Committee for Study of Factors Involved in Higher Educaton of Vermont Youth*, 1953). *The University in a Changing World* (report of the University of Rhode Island, 1956–57), announced " . . . a basic aim of public higher education is freedom of opportunity regardless of financial or social status." In the *College and University Business*

(March, 1959), President Hannah of the State University of Michigan argued that concentration on finance was diverting attention from philosophical issues. A report of a coordinating committee (*Tuition and Fees at Publicly Controlled Institutions,* March, 1959) would not use " . . . higher fees as a means of controlling the size of enrollment."

This fear of higher tuition fees is shared by many who control private universities. For example, the Commission on Financing Higher Education in its very able report[11] makes clear its skepticism toward large increases in tuition for private institutions. One reason for this is the fear of the competition of public institutions; a second, the folly of relying too much upon a form of income (i.e., tuition) which is unstable because it depends upon enrollment; the third reason, the democratic argument: education must not be made too expensive for the poor but deserving students. On the other hand, the commission does point out that an increasing proportion of families have incomes high enough to support higher tuition.

A large majority of the official reports still continue to stress the theory that public institutions were established to provide education at low charge for students of modest means. This is a position not easily repudiated, though if the costs of higher education rise rapidly, the taxpayers may provide an answer. It is my view that the growing tax load will be a potent factor, modified, of course, by the tradition of public support as it varies from state to state.

For example, in California, with perhaps the greatest expansion of public higher education in the country, the tradition of free higher education is so strong and the income is so high and growing so rapidly that for many years students may receive almost free education in the state institutions. Who would believe that California can provide its rich program of public education at a cost in relation to the income of its people roughly equal to that of Vermont taxpayers for *their* public higher education? But many states are not going to have such easy sailing. Where private institutions are entrenched and are prepared to assume the responsibility of training only a small fraction of the additional students to be educated, and where the tax money appropriated for higher education is small, the pressure for higher tuition will be great. In states where higher public education accounts for only 20 per cent of enrollment, for example, an increase of enrollment of only 80 per cent in the next ten to twelve years may force state institutions to increase their accommodations 100 to 200 per cent. Under these circumstances the pressure to put part of the additional burden on the students is very great.

SUPPORT FOR HIGHER FEES

College administrators in private institutions are at times inclined to argue that the low tuition fees in the public institutions will destroy private institutions; this position can be carried too far. They should remember that the difference between costs of an education in public and private institutions to the student is only 20 to 25 per cent of all costs of a college education, not counting income forgone. The relative costs in 1956–57 were $1,500 to $1,600 for the public institutions, and $2,000 for the private. In other words, we must not concentrate only on tuition. But if tuition in private institutions rises greatly and public institutions maintain their current fees, the difference may become much more serious.

I am not sure that the tack taken by many administrators of private institutions is appropriate. They will not succeed in raising fees in public institutions by pleading that if these fees are not raised, private institutions may have to close their doors. It seems to me that a more appropriate argument, more justified in terms of the national welfare, is that the state and municipal institutions of higher education may not receive adequate funds from tax sources to keep tuition down as they have in the past. The low-income groups especially hit by state and local taxation are not disposed to absorb a rising burden of taxes for education. The additional bill of about $11 billion required for public school education is another force working in the direction of higher fees—unless the Federal government absorbs a large part of the burden, as does not seem likely in 1962.

Over the years private college administrators have supported higher tuition both on the ground that alternative resources for meeting rising costs and turning out a good product are not available and because (in the view of some) the public institutions are maintaining unfair competition. For example, in the Great Depression, President Turck of Center College asked, "Why should the state universities pauperize students? Why should they not pay a reasonable percentage of costs?"[12] He implied that these low rates in public IHL were offering serious competition to the private institutions.

Carter Davidson, the president of Union College, also defends current fees and by implication even higher fees. On the assumption that family, savings, vacation work, and work during college can provide $300 each, President Davidson argues that the major costs of higher education could be provided. The remainder could come from scholarships or loans.[13]

The rise in educational costs in the last 40 years, and especially during the last 10 years, has encouraged a different pessimistic philosophy which declares that it is impossible for young people from "middle class" families to consider going to college at all. This I consider a vicious untrue myth, a "legend of the insurmountable financial barrier," and therefore one that should be exploded.

Many college administrators contend that higher tuition is necessary in order to meet the costs of higher education. The following is from a report of the Board of Trustees of Sarah Lawrence College:[14]

Because of this experience in the past the board of Trustees has looked with interest at the proposals made by several distinguished public figures, among them Beardsley Ruml, Crawford H. Greenewalt and Dexter Keezer, that the public be made aware that costs in education have increased radically and that everyone who can do so should be asked by the private colleges to pay the full costs of his children's education through a radical increase in tuition fees. . . .

These basic questions in the financing of private colleges have been thoroughly discussed not only in the Board of Trustees but in the Committee of Sarah Lawrence Parents. There is general agreement among the committee members that all parents who can afford to pay the full cost of education should be asked to do so, with scholarship aid in the form of reduced tuition for those who cannot. This point of view is coming to be accepted in the private colleges in general and is the basic policy approach taken by the Parents Committee of Sarah Lawrence in their work for the annual Sarah Lawrence fund drive.

In a somewhat similar vein President Samuel Gould of Antioch College (then) wrote to the parents of his students that the institution faces serious financial problems, because tuition covers only 58 per cent of total costs:

When everything that accounts for student tuition falls below two-thirds of the expenses in education, the institution must recognize the fact that this is a danger signal. Although unnecessary expenditures have been reduced, the tuition is not adequate to take up the other operating costs and therefore an increase is necessary.

The president of one of the leading women's colleges informed me that the administration was gradually moving toward a position of tuition close to full cost. But he recognized that such increases, when out of line with rates in other institutions, would substantially change the composition of the student body.

In looking over the literature written by college administrators, then, as well as by studying the trends of tuition, one cannot overlook the fact that, because of the rising costs of higher education, there is a strong and increasing sentiment among private college administrators for higher tuition. Higher tuition is a condition for adequate service. There are also proposals from some private college interests to keep the tax appropriation for public institutions down and tuition up. In some states, Illinois and Indiana for example, representatives of private institutions have gone so far as to testify before the legislature against increased appropriations for the public institutions. This seems to me to be unwise policy on the part of private institutions, not only for the welfare of the public, but from their own position as well. Fortunately such behavior is rare.

* * *

In the past officials have tried to keep tuition as low as possible, in part because they felt that IHL should not become too dependent upon tuition and in part because the entry of the poor but able youngster should be assured. If the college depended primarily upon tuition, the result might be lowering of standards in order to get the required revenues from tuition.[15] For example, in accrediting IHL the Association of American Universities is clear on financing methods:

> Adequate financial support, by making the institution relatively independent of student fees, helps to relieve the institution of the temptation to accept or to continue on its rolls students of poor academic quality; it is a means of obtaining a stronger faculty, more ample facilities, and greater permanence in the maintenance of high standards . . . . In general, at least half of its income should be derived from stable sources other than student fees, preferably from endowment.

I think that these guides are out of date. In the Great Depression the loss of tuition was less than the loss of endowment income, and, except for a limited number of institutions, endowment is no longer very important.

Another factor of historical importance is that hundreds of colleges were founded by churches in an attempt on their part to increase membership and subsidize students of particular denominations. The churches were not primarily interested in meeting costs and offered generous grants to these institutions. As their own financial problems became more serious, they tended to desert their church-related colleges. But many of these institutions still operate at uneconomic levels and with serious financial problems.

AN EARLY PRESENTATION: TUITION TO BE GEARED TO COSTS

In the last ten years, in *The New York Times,* in *The Reporter,* and at various educational meetings, I have suggested full payment of the costs of higher education *by students able to pay.* As early as 1948 I had written:[16]

> *An ideal system might be a multi-price system: prices to be adjusted according to need and ability.* The able and needy student should pay nothing, and even receive subsidies to cover living costs; the wealthy and lazy or mediocre student (and the wealthy and able) should pay the full costs of his education. Others (e.g., the good, but not outstanding student) would pay various amounts from 0 to $1,000, depending on the institution and the student's economic status and ability. In this manner the leading privately endowed institutions might, on the average, raise their tuition from $350 to $600. Tuition would contribute around three-quarters of the total cost of private institutions as compared with more than one-half now.

> It is interesting that, despite the theoretical appeal of this price structure, college administrators have not shown any great enthusiasm for adopting it. Why?

First, price discrimination is difficult of administration. The present system is, however, a multi-price system: most students pay full tuition; a large proportion, say 20 per cent, pay less than full tuition; some pay $100 and less and others pay no tuition; and many receive as much as $600 in addition to tuition. In fact, in graduate instruction some fellowships exceed full costs of education and maintenance of the student and family. What is involved in these proposals is simply to charge up to costs on the basis of grades, promise, and ability to pay. *The system could be made to work. Doctors indulge in a similar type of price discrimination.*

A second objection [to full-cost tuition] is much more serious. A large proportion of the students may not be able to pay the additional charge. This may not seem serious when one considers the large demand for education in relation to the resources available. Why would it not be desirable to check demand by imposing the law of the market place? *Many persons, in fact, recoil at decisions of entry or non-entry on the basis of economic status. . . .*

A third factor under consideration by college authorities is competition. With education more expensive, the public will be encouraged to spend more on alternative commodities. That the American public does not value education as much as it might is suggested by a comparison of expenditures for education with those for cars, amusements, alcoholic beverages, tobacco, etc.

Fear of losing students to rival institutions is an even greater deterrent to increasing tuition fees. Not hampered by antitrust laws, the universities might, of course, solve this problem by agreed policy. One private institution fears the competition of others; private institutions fear that of state operated colleges; and one section of the country fears the colleges of another. Although each institution offers a differentiated product, its monopoly is only partial. A rise of $100 not matched by a similar increase elsewhere will indeed be reflected in losses to rivals.

But this kind of price discrimination would not, I realized, be easy to administer.

In an address at Brown University in 1927, John D. Rockefeller, Jr., suggested that IHL should seriously consider charging full costs to students with adequate resources. As a result of this suggestion, the General Education Board (Rockefeller) sent a questionnaire to 100 colleges and universities, asking if the college administrator approved of Rockefeller's suggestion. The result showed that 44 were unqualifiedly for the plan and 45 unqualifiedly against it.

The opposition was based on the following:[17]

(1) It is too difficult to administer; (2) it would result in discrimination against students with slender resources; (3) it would lower standards; (4) it is impracticable because of low tuition in state-supported institutions; (5) the institution has few students able to pay the full cost; and (6) it would result in a rich man's college. Those favoring the plan emphasized the difficulties in administration; the need of concerted action by other institutions in the same class or area; and the advisability of approaching the goal gradually.

In 1945 Friedman and Kuznets discussed the possibility of students' borrowing from investors for the purpose of financing their education and repaying out of income received in the students' later working life. These authors believed that the rates would have to be high because of the risks involved, though if many such contracts were made, the losses on some could be offset by the gains on others.[18]

Perhaps the least justifiable subsidy is that paid to medical students. The average net pay of a nonsalaried doctor in the later 1950s was more than $20,000, or about 4 times that of the average male professional or technical worker, twice that of the average college graduate, and approximately 3 times that of the average faculty member.[19] *Medical Economics* in 1962 estimated incomes of practicing physicians before income taxes, at $25,000.

In this connection, I quote several paragraphs from my 1952 article in *The Reporter*.[20]

Clearly, something must be done to strengthen the dangerously weak financial structure of medical schools so that they can turn out enough well-trained physicians to meet the nation's needs. In the past, the medical schools have lived off their parent universities, to a large extent, but the financial plight of the latter is bringing this source of help to an end. Over the last forty years the cost of a medical education has gone up by about ten times. According to their accounting, the medical schools subsidize the average medical student by about $2,000 a year, or $8,000 over a four-year course.

Where is the money to train the extra medical students going to come from? Not much can be expected from higher tuition fees, reductions in expenses, and increased endowment. And the pressure of the A.M.A. will probably continue to prevent Federal subsidies.

Why not make the future doctors themselves pay? Perhaps they couldn't all pay up during their student years, but why shouldn't they obligate themselves to pay for their educations on the installment plan? Doctors can look forward to quite comfortable average incomes, and the obligation would not turn out to be burdensome if each student agreed to pay two per cent of his income during his working life. The current crop of medical students can probably look forward to average lifetime incomes of more than 1 million dollars. At that rate, each could pay an average of $12,000 to his medical school after he began practicing. Many could afford to pay $2,000 during training, and the total of $14,000 should cover their expenses. It would not seem unfair to require a medical student to pay the full costs of his education, since he obtains a license to practise in a restricted field that may yield him a lifetime income of approximately a million dollars, two or three times the income of the average college graduate.* If the payments were deductible for income-tax purposes, the government would in effect be footing a large

---

* Ten years later, as a result of large rises in physicians' incomes, and rising productivity in the economy, I estimate lifetime income at $1.5 million for current graduates. (See my forthcoming book on *Economics of Medicine*.)

share of the bill without worrying the A.M.A. about government control of, or influence on, medicine.

One difficulty would have to be overcome. There should be agreement among the medical schools that students would pay according to average costs. Otherwise schools in strong financial condition would be able to entice the best students with the offer of cheap tuition.

It will, of course, take a number of years for the two per cent payments of physicians who benefit under the plan to mount up. In order to avoid the use of government funds which the A.M.A. finds so objectionable, this gap could be filled by voluntary contributions from practising physicians who have already benefited from the subsidization of medical schools in the past. . . .

In many ways, this plan is an improvement of Federal subsidies. Why should the average American wage earner subsidize a doctor who will make four times as much as he ever will?

RELATIONS OF TUITION TO COSTS

After years of further consideration I am less inclined to argue that students in large numbers should pay the full costs of higher education. There are resources available now which mean that the student does not have to pay the full cost. But costs rise, and IHL must attempt to close the gaps in their budgets, including those hidden deficits to which President de Kiewiet of the University of Rochester so persuasively calls attention— underpayment of faculty, inadequate administration, and plant and equipment: deficits " . . . floating like an iceberg with most of its bulk submerged and hidden from view."[21] The case for higher tuition should not be restricted to covering costs, but rather to the view that covering a larger part of costs is the only manner in which the colleges can perform well.

I do not think that IHL should strive, as businessmen do, to meet their costs or charge what the traffic will bear. IHL are, after all, nonprofit organizations serving a public function. If they set their fees on the basis of maximum profits or highest gross income, then of course many of them could greatly increase their charges. In the present state of demand, the high-prestige colleges might very well be able to double or treble their tuition and still fill their halls. Should these institutions go further and discriminate in their prices (on the basis of capacity to pay) to a greater degree than they do now, they could increase their revenue still more. Some parents, for instance, might be willing to pay as much as $10,000 to get their sons into Princeton. In fact, a high-prestige college could solve many of its financial problems by auctioning off the last 100 places each year to the highest bidders and guarantee that somehow the students thus attracted would be kept in the university for a designated period of time. (This is of course a facetious suggestion.)

Of course, few would support policies of this type. But the tradition of low tuition is nevertheless being undermined as costs rise and philanthropy and taxes are not equal to carrying the full burden of these higher costs. It is not necessary, because of other sources of income, for tuition to cover the full amount; and the real burden to the student of the higher tuition that will be necessary diminishes continually as incomes rise. To this matter I turn in the next chapter.

CONCLUSION

This country has had a long tradition of low tuition rates. But with increased enrollments and rising costs, the pressures to increase tuition are mounting—more in private IHL, where the traditions are less strong and financial strain greater, than in the public IHL. But even the latter, pressed by rebellious taxpayers, are being forced to yield. In fact, as we have seen, public fees had risen *relatively* more than private in the 1940s.

A case can be made out for higher fees as we shall see. But full-cost financing is out of the question. It is in fact not necessary. At present the $3\frac{1}{2}$ million students pay in tuition an amount equal roughly only to the capital costs, and none of the operating costs. Given the great wealth, income, and growth of the nation and the tens of billions spent on such items as alcohol, cosmetics, pleasure driving, etc., a case could be made out for low tuition. The resources are clearly there. It would require only about 2 per cent of the expected growth of our GNP by 1970 to stabilize tuition fees at their present levels. But it will take a vigorous campaign to convince taxpayers in many states and Federal taxpayers of the wisdom of stabilized tuition. The tremendous contribution of education to our economy would easily justify such diversions of tax money. What, more than education, accounts for a rise of our output three times as large as our input of labor, capital, and management since the Civil War?

FOOTNOTES

[1] This and preceding quotations from J. T. Cavan, "The Student and the Financing of the College: A Study of Student Fees, Students and Faculty, Affecting the Proportion of the Cost of Higher Education Borne by the Student," thesis deposited in the University of Chicago library, 1935.

[2] *Ibid.*

[3] *President's Commission on Higher Education in American Democracy,* 1947, I, pp. 27–28 and II, pp. 11–13; and *Report of the Commission on Financing Higher Education,* 1952, especially p. 138.

[4] David Riesman, "Essay Review: Who Will and Who Should Pay for Higher Education?" *The School Review,* the University of Chicago, Summer, 1958, p. 218; *The New York Times,* Feb. 26, 1961, Mar. 12, 1961 (my comment), Jan. 3, 1961 (my letter), and Jan. 10, 1961 (dean's reply).

[5] R. H. Ostheimer, *Student Charges and Financing Higher Education,* a staff study

for the Commission on Financing Higher Education, 1953, pp. 12–17. Cf. J. D. Millett, *Financing Higher Education in the United States,* 1952, pp. 300–301.

[6] *Inaugural Address of His Excellency Lane Dwinell, Governor of the State of New Hampshire to the General Court,* Jan. 6, 1955, p. 14.

[7] *Ibid.,* 1957, p. 10.

[8] *Report of the President of the University of New Hampshire, 1956–57,* p. 28.

[9] See the eloquent plea of Russell Thackrey, Executive Secretary, American Association of Land-grant Colleges and State Universities, for expansion of land-grant colleges at low fees, in a commencement address, *Needed: A New Revolution in Higher Education,* Reno, Nev., June 3, 1957. (Mimeographed.)

[10] "Needs, Resources and Priorities in Higher Educational Planning," *Bulletin of the American Association of University Professors,* September, 1957, p. 439.

[11] J. D. Millett, *op. cit.,* pp. 133, 134.

[12] *Bulletin of the Association of American Colleges,* March, 1933, p. 226.

[13] *College and University Business,* June, 1953, p. 17.

[14] *Sarah Lawrence and the Future,* 1957, p. 8.

[15] Part of the gains from higher tuition fees would have to be forgone in more generous scholarships. In the year 1958 scholarship funds, even generously and roughly estimated, and exclusive of those not under the control of IHL, do not greatly exceed $100 million per year, or about $30 per student. The average scholarship is around $250 and is received by less than 10 per cent of the students. Other estimates in recent years put the mean at $275 to $300 and per cent from 17 to 22. For a comprehensive discussion of scholarships, see Chaps. 11–16. Also see American Council on Education, E. D. West (ed.), *Background for a National Scholarship Policy,* 1956; C. A. Quattelbaum, *Federal Aid to Students for Higher Education,* Legislative Reference Service, 1956; and *House Committee Report No. 291, Readjustment Benefits: Education and Training and Employment and Unemployment,* 1956.

[16] S. E. Harris, *How Shall We Pay for Education?* 1948, pp. 199–201.

[17] T. Arnett, *Trends in Tuition Fees,* General Education Board, 1939, pp. 56–75.

[18] M. Friedman and S. Kuznets, *Income from Independent Professional Practice,* 1945, pp. 89–90 (NBER). Developing the Friedman-Kuznets position, Van Den Haag, in 1956, proposed that students be allowed to repay the costs of their education to IHL. Those who could afford to do so would pay while at college. Others would borrow and agree to pay, with interest charged on the basis of risks. IHL in turn might borrow to finance current losses (E. Van Den Haag, *Education as an Industry,* 1956, pp. 66–72).

[19] See P. C. Glick and H. P. Miller, "Educational Level and Potential Income," *American Sociological Review,* 1956; U. S. Census, *Income of Persons in the United States, 1955,* 1956, p. 24; and *Medical Economics,* October, 1956, p. 111. Cf. 1950 U. S. Census of Population, Special Report P–C No. 1B, *Occupational Characteristics,* 1953, pp. 107, 199.

[20] S. E. Harris, "Why the Government Need Not Subsidize Medical Schools," *The Reporter,* Feb. 5, 1952. But since 1952 the Federal government has greatly increased its contribution.

[21] C. W. de Kiewiet, "The Necessary Price of Leadership," *The Educational Record,* July, 1958, pp. 236–237.

Chapter 9

HIGHER TUITION AND THE ABILITY TO PAY

In conventional economic theory the principal determinant of the amount of any good purchased is assumed to be its price. We hear, for example, of the generator plants which are equipped to use both oil and coal. As the price of coal rises while that of oil does not, the plant will at some point shift to consumption of oil, and vice versa.

In the case of higher education, however, we have grounds for believing that its "price" to potential consumers—the tuition which students are charged—may not be the principal determinant of demand for education. We have already seen that many institutions fear a loss of desirable students if their fees get out of line with their competitors. But if all fees rise together, there may be no such loss of students at all. Despite the large and steady increase of fees from the Civil War on, enrollment continued to rise at a spectacular rate. In the years 1889–90 to 1951–52, enrollment rose about thirteen times, and yet in the years since 1860 tuition rose about thirteen times. In the more recent period of 1940–1955, tuition rose by 85 per cent (less according to my estimates); nevertheless, enrollment almost doubled. (Indeed in dollars of stable purchasing power there was a decline in the recent period, though over the whole period since the Civil War tuition increased much more than prices.)

Broadly speaking, there are two reasons for this apparently perverse behavior, apart from the rise in population: In the first place, although tuition has risen considerably, it has not kept pace with the rise in per capita income since the early part of the century. As incomes rise, a smaller proportion is required for the basic necessities of life, and more can be spent for other items, including higher education. We may add here that even apart from higher per capita incomes the demand for college education may be growing, because of an enhanced desire for learning for its own sake, because of an increasing awareness by employers that college-educated employees are the most promising, because of the expected gains of income and position by students, or simply because of the social attractions of campus life.

Ostheimer, in his *Student Charges and Financing Higher Education,* 1953, concluded that a rise of tuition of 25 per cent would result in a decline of enrollment of 5 per cent. But this in 1952 is a static analysis and excludes from consideration rising income and changes in the pattern of spending and in the proximity of colleges to residence of students.

Secondly, tuition is only a small part of the total cost to the student of going to college. The average cost of attending a public institution in 1956–57 has been estimated at $1,500, and for a private one, $2,000. Yet average tuition rates (in 1954–55) were but $132 and $599 in public and private institutions, respectively, or 9 and 30 per cent of total costs.[1] Thus even a doubling of tuition would raise the costs to a student going to a public institution by only 9 per cent, and those of one going to a private school by 30 per cent. In the excellent *Report of a Survey of the Needs of California in Higher Education,* the writers stressed the point that the main deterrent was not fees but other costs to students. Of course, if other costs rise also, these increases will be larger. But tuition has tended to outstrip other costs of attending college: in the 1940s the cost of education to the student rose by 50 per cent, but room and board charges rose only 25 per cent. Many IHL reduce the sting of higher tuition by containing the increase in other charges—often by cutting services. A common practice is crowding of dormitories and reducing maid and waitress service.[2] But they also increase costs to the students by raising fees for such services as medicine, unions, and athletics. In *A Master Plan for Higher Education in California, 1960–1975,* published in 1959 (pp. 199–200), the emphasis is on increases in such fees, since the California constitution excludes instructional fees in the university.

Higher tuition, then, is mitigated by the fact that on an average it is only a small part of the costs of attending college, and by high and growing family incomes. Let us consider each of these in greater detail. (Incidentally, the rise of tuition from 1940 to 1956 has not been equal to the increase of costs to the college, even when organized research, extension, and public services and related activities are excluded. Tuition rose by 85 per cent or less, and relevant costs by 119 per cent.)

COSTS OF HIGHER EDUCATION TO THE STUDENT

The major elements in costs to the student are (1) tuition, (2) other fees (generally included in estimates of tuition), (3) room and board, (4) miscellaneous other costs—transportation, clothing, recreation, etc.—and (5) income forgone. Tuition, especially in public institutions, is only a small part of the total. In an Ivy League college, where tuition may be $1,200, it is perhaps 50 per cent of the total costs to the student, exclusive of income forgone. But for the average in public institutions tuition comprises only 9 or 10 per cent of costs to students (excluding income for-gone); for all private IHL, 30 per cent; and for all IHL, about 20 per cent.[3]

In 1957–58 *all* tuition was 25 per cent of educational and general income, and 35 per cent of educational and general expenditures exclusive of public services and organized research.

Strictly speaking, one of the costs of going to college is the income which the student could have earned if he had been working full time instead of attending school. This is not an out-of-pocket cost which must be paid in cash, as room rent must be. But it certainly must figure in the decisions of many who must decide whether or not to go to college—particularly among those who have families to support. (On the other hand, there are many who never consider the question of forgone income; but it is relevant.)

When income forgone is added to student costs, then the ratio of tuition costs to all costs is reduced further.[4]

Thus:

Average tuition and other costs..........	$1,800
Income forgone.......................	2,400
Total............................	$4,200

Tuition, 1957–58, is estimated at $350, or 8 per cent of total costs. Hence if tuition were doubled, the rise of all costs would be less than 20 per cent and of all costs plus income forgone, only 8 per cent.

For an Ivy college with tuition of $1,200 and total costs of $2,500, a rise of tuition of $500 would raise outlays by 20 per cent, and all costs inclusive of income forgone, by 10 per cent.

THE RELEVANCE OF HIGHER TUITION

It is easy to exaggerate the significance of a rise in tuition unless one takes into account the over-all picture of cost. I have given some rough figures to indicate this. Hollis has shown that in 1952–53 tuition was only 6.9 per cent of total expenditures by students in public institutions and 30.5 per cent of total expenditures in private ones. Obviously a rise of a given percentage in tuition means a much smaller rise in *total* cost to the student, especially if one takes into account income forgone.[5]

Board and room, also important elements in total costs to the student, do not seem to have risen as much as tuition. At Yale, for example, according to a study by Edward Budd,[6] tuition from 1940–41 to 1952–53 rose by 70 per cent, board by 71 per cent, and dormitory charges by 41 per cent. Again, whereas total tuition rose from 1946–47 to 1957–58 by 93 per cent in 43 outstanding universities, the increase of tuition, room, and board for 6 colleges—male, coeducational, and female, namely, Amherst, Carleton, Connecticut College, Mt. Holyoke, Smith, and Wellesley—was only 48 per cent. These figures also point to the tendency of board to rise much less than tuition. Between 1946–47 and 1958–59, tuition rose from $400 to $950 at Oberlin, or a rise of almost 140 per cent. The rise of all costs to the student, however, was from $941 to $1805, or less than 100 per cent. The last of course includes room and board.

But we should add that since room and board charges rise—even if less than tuition—the sting of higher tuition hurts more because other costs rise.

For eight different types of colleges and universities the percentage increase in room charges from 1947–48 to 1954–55 was less than for tuition and fees in all but two groups. Generally the sum of board and room rises less than tuition.[6a]

TABLE 9-1

Percentage Rise in Tuition and Other Charges of IHL, 1947–48 to 1954–55

Charges	State universities		Private universities	Private liberal colleges	
	Enrollment >5,000	Enrollment <5,000		Enrollment <500	Enrollment >500
Tuition and fees........	30.3	37.4	34.3	37.7	37.3
Room charges..........	33.8	41.5	26.3	26.2	26.0
Board charges.........	21.8	22.9	26.0	22.4	25.6

In numerous institutions the authorities tried to keep down the total cost by not allowing the charge for room and board to rise as much as for tuition. This of course was done partly by deteriorating the product, that is, for example, doubling up in rooms, providing self-service in the dining hall rather than waitress service.

Even more significant is the tendency for aid per student to rise as tuition goes up. In other words, the rise of tuition is a gross, not a net, figure.

These remarks are confirmed by Budd's study of Yale. In 1940–41 the aid per student was $142, in 1953–54, $302, and the rise for *undergraduates* was from $160 to $374. Aid as a percentage of student income rose from 26 per cent in 1940–41 to 35 per cent in 1953–54. In this connection the aid given to graduate students is of some interest. Not only is graduate instruction much more expensive than undergraduate, but the tuition fees are largely paid for by fellowships. A study of graduate business schools revealed that roughly one-third were self-supporting. Another study showed that the children of professional parents *tend* to go to arts and science graduate work and about two-thirds require aid. Of the students in law, 55 per cent receive aid from parents, and only 24 per cent in arts and science receive any aid from parents. The latter come from lower-income groups. In the Yale Graduate School aid was 88 per cent of student income in 1940–41 and 73 per cent in 1953–54. Yale spent on student aid no less than 51 cents for each additional dollar of tuition received in 1953–54 as compared to 1940–41.[7]

Table 9-2 gives the figures from Harvard, not comparable to Yale's because they cover only undergraduates, describe different periods of time, and are on a total, not per capita, base.

TABLE 9-2

Harvard, Student Finance, 1949–50 to 1958–59

Rise of tuition	$2,606,000
Rise of gift aid	898,000
Ratio of increase of gift aid to tuition rise	34%
Rise of tuition per student	$650
Rise of scholarship aid per student	707

Source: Computed from *Harvard University News Release*, Apr. 11, 1958, and other sources. Assume roughly same enrollment and number of scholarship recipients in 1958–59 as in 1957–58; also cf. S. E. Harris, "The Economics of Harvard," *Harvard Alumni Bulletin*, Feb. 20, 1960.

On a national scale, the following is of some interest:

1939–40 and 1957–58

Student aid as percentage of tuition fees, 1939–40	5.0
Student aid as percentage of tuition fees, 1957–58	14.0
Ratio of rise of student aid (controlled by colleges) to rise of tuition fees (exclusive of government)	9.1%

Source: Calculated from HEW, *Statistics of Higher Education: Receipts, Expenditures and Property, 1953–54*, pp. 6–7, and *Memo to the Board*, 1960 Series, no. 4. The 1939–40 figure for student aid is my estimate.

In the years 1951–52 to 1955–56 the trend of scholarship aid has been upward and much more so, relatively, than the tuition charges. The validity of this statement is supported by Table 9-3. From 1951–52 to 1955–56, total student aid rose by 142 per cent; total tuition, only by 24 per cent; average tuition, by but 8 per cent; and average student aid, by 110 per cent. For one reason these figures understate the gains for student aid. Aid not under the control of the colleges is omitted here, and the rise of outside aid has been disproportionately large in recent years.[8]

Since writing the above the 1957–58 figures have become available. From 1953–54 to 1957–58, the rise of total tuition income exceeds that in student aid: 69 versus 37 per cent. But tuition per resident student declined by $11 (4 per cent); aid per student rose by $14 (8 per cent). The decline

TABLE 9-3
Student Aid, Total and per Student, and Tuition, Total and per Student,
1951–52 and 1955–56, Totals and Percentage Gains

Item	1951–52	1955–56	Gain, per cent
Tuition and fees.........................	$596 million	$742 million	24
Student aid............................	$39.8 million	$96.2 million	142
Tuition per resident student...............	$257.00	$279.00	8
Student aid per resident student...........	17.20	36.20	110
Student aid per scholarship student*.......	86.00	181.00	110

* I assume 20 per cent receive scholarships, on the basis of earlier studies.
Source: Computed from HEW, *Statistics of Higher Education, 1955–56: Receipts, Expenditures and Property and Faculty, Students and Degrees.*

in tuition per student was explained previously by the switch to junior colleges, public IHL generally and, perhaps, to some extent, a relative increase in the proportion of part-time students.

From these figures I conclude that the increase in tuition is mitigated when viewed from the level of *total* student costs and when allowance is made for student aid.[9]

VARIATIONS OF COSTS TO THE STUDENT

The total cost of going to college varies with the type of education, the region, the residence of the student, and other factors. Some issues are well summarized in a study by the HEW.

Table 9A-1, "Variations by Field and Region in Annual Costs of Attending College, 1952–53," reveals that students in the humanities, with a total cost of $1,577 in 1952–53, incur the maximum costs of attending college, while students in education, with $1,059, spent the minimum. The differences are explained by various factors. Most schools of education are public and therefore usually have lower tuition. Humanities, relatively expensive, are popular in prestige institutions. The differences are also explained partly by the fact that students in some kinds of college spend less than they do in others.

Another factor that affects total cost is the location of the college. In the Northeast the average cost was $1,676 and in the South $1,164. The cost in the West was only $1,209, explained in part by the dominance of the state colleges and universities. When allowances are made for the differences in per capita income, the cost of higher education *to the student* is still low in the South and West. Many prestige institutions, few junior colleges, and few public institutions help account for high average costs in the Northeast.

As might be expected, the costs also vary according to where the student lives. For students living at home the average cost in 1952–53 was $1,017, and for the student living in a club, fraternity house, or sorority house, as high as $1,655, a difference of $638, or more than 60 per cent above the cost for the student living in the parents' home.

In *Financing Higher Education, 1960–1970,* Millett gives the following costs per student:

Private liberal arts college.............	$2,260
Private university in a large city.........	1,500
State university in small city............	1,525
Municipal university...................	1,000

For students in public IHL who live at home the extremes were $700 and $717 in public junior colleges and technological institutions, respectively, and $2,112 for students in privately controlled universities living in club, fraternity, or sorority houses.[10] The corresponding figures today would undoubtedly be higher.

In a fairly large sample the state of New York in the early 1950s revealed for students all over the country differences in the cost by type of college. For example, for expenses in excess of $1,500 the percentage of students in nursing was only 4 per cent, in agriculture and technical fields 6 per cent, and in teacher education 7 per cent, but as high as 35 per cent in engineering and 37 per cent in arts and sciences. Fifty per cent of the students in agriculture, twenty-two per cent of the students in engineering, and twenty-four per cent of those in arts and sciences spent less than $900.[11] This survey also revealed that where tuition is higher, the student tends to live on the campus. For example, with tuition in excess of $700, 22 per cent lived at home and 78 per cent on campus.[12] The New York study also revealed that on the average tuition and fees accounted for less than one-third of the $1,910 of total expenditures by the average student at 15 private colleges in New York State for 1950–51.[13]

Of some interest is the comparison of annual college expenditures a century ago for 17 colleges, primarily private institutions. Restricting these outlays to instruction, room rent (including wood, lights, and washing), and board, we find that in the year 1958 instruction accounted for 30 per cent, board for 50 per cent, and room rent, etc., for 20 per cent. Room rent now for all private institutions accounts for 18 per cent, the percentage for board has dropped to 34, but tuition is now up to 48 per cent. Relatively, tuition has become a larger factor in the total cost over a period of one hundred years. This is, of course, a very rough estimate.[14]

These facts are significant for this reason: by going to institutions near home or by choosing particular curricula where students do not have strong preferences, or by choosing low-cost colleges, students can often get by with much lower costs than the average. But to some extent the discretion is limited. Costs (and incomes) are higher in the Northeast; certain curricula, e.g., medicine and engineering, are expensive; often the able student should select a school with high standards and high costs; and the student's residence may be far from a college fitting his need.

It is scarcely necessary to add that the structure of costs varies between public and private IHL, and room and board are about $50 higher in women's than in men's private institutions. Room and board are relatively the expensive items for students in public IHL.

TABLE 9-4

Percentage of Costs, 1959–60, Public and Private Institutions of Higher Learning

	Tuition	Total, %	Room				Board			
			Men	Women	Weighted mean	%	Men	Women	Mean	%
Public.....	$168	24	$168	$174	$170	24	$373	$372	$372	52
Private....	615	50	201	220	207	16	401	431	411	33

Source: Calculated from *Planning and Management Data, 1959–60.*

CAPACITY TO PAY

As mentioned at the beginning of the chapter, price—even "total" price, including all the other costs to a student—is not the only variable determining demand for higher education. Perhaps even more important is the level of income out of which these charges must be paid. Per capita income has risen tremendously in the United States, yet one of the first things to be observed about tuition rates for IHL since before World War II is that the objective has been to keep pace with the price level, not with per capita income. Even this limited synchronization has not been very effective. From 1940 to 1950 the increase in tuition was 72 per cent of the rise in the cost of living, *but only one-third of the rise in per capita income.* If we extend the period of comparison five years further, to 1955, the rise in tuition is nearly as much as that in the cost of living but, once again, only one-third as much as the increase in per capita income. This begins to threaten the financial position of IHL when we realize that the rise in tuition during this period covered only half the increase in the cost to the college of educating one resident student. Even after taxes, per capita personal income rose by 188 per cent, and tuition by only 85 per cent. In 1956–57 average tuition was about $300, and per capita income after taxes was $1,750, so tuition was only 18 per cent of per capita income. I remind the reader of an earlier discussion which showed that in the later 1950s, at least, tuition tended to rise more than per capita income.

The figures in Table 9-5 are of some interest. They show that the rise of tuition has not covered a substantial part of the rise of costs. Hence not only has capacity to pay increased, but the rise of costs has exceeded that of tuition.

TABLE 9-5
1940 to 1956

Rise in tuition per resident student......................................	$ 146
Rise in tuition per resident student, adjusted for rise of student aid.....	127
Rise in costs per resident student*..................................	273
Rise in tuition income...	539 million
Rise in general and educational costs*...........................	1,422 million

 * Adjusted for irrelevant costs.

 Source: See Table 9-3.

Obviously, the higher the family income, the greater the capacity to finance higher education. Both the number of children to be educated and the proportion of income available for education are relevant. At least in the early 1950s there was a smaller proportion of young men and women of college age than in 1940, and a larger proportion of income was available for education at the higher incomes of the 1950s than in 1940. In the future, however, we can expect a rise in the number of children per family to be educated.

In 1955, the proportion of all families with incomes in excess of $5,000 was 35.5 per cent; in 1940, the proportion with incomes of $3,000 or over was 17 per cent. I assume, allowing for price change, tax increases, and the other factors suggested above, that a $5,000 income in 1955 yielded a capacity to finance a higher education equal to that of $3,000 in 1941. From 1947 to 1959, according to the *President's Economic Report of 1960* (pages 132 to 133) personal income after taxes per family rose by $980 to $5,830 in 1959 prices, or 20 per cent. What is even more relevant is a rise of family income in current prices from 1947 to 1959 (after taxes) of $2,110 as compared to an average rise of tuition of less than $100.

We live in prosperous times, but education has not shared in this prosperity. Tuition takes a smaller part of family income than it did before World War II. In fact, as compared to before the war, the ratio of tuition to family income had fallen by close to one-half in the years 1950 to 1955. The proportion of families with incomes (in stable prices) in the higher levels increased greatly: those in excess of $5,000 rose from 13 to 35 per cent from 1929 to 1954, and those with incomes in excess of $6,000, from 28 per cent in 1947 to 39 per cent in 1958.[15]

By 1959, median personal family income was $6,470 before taxes and

$5,830 after taxes. At the age when children are likely to go to college, parents' incomes are about $600 above the median. At an income of about $6,500, over half the families should not have any great difficulties in financing higher education—on the assumption that one child is at college, that work and loans will also be available, and scholarships for one-half of the other 50 per cent.

But for those with incomes below (say) $5,000 to $6,000 there are problems. Charles McCurdy, the executive secretary of the Public University Association, has brought to my attention the problems of farm families in the Dakotas with incomes of $1,200 to $1,500 when confronted with higher tuition. *The New York Times* of April 20, 1958, commented on the middle-income family that sent a son to Princeton at a cost of $2,100 per year but could not afford to repair a leaky roof. I am sure that all those with incomes of less than $5,000 have serious problems and often even parents with incomes of $10,000 do not find financing a college education for their children easy. Moreover, we have been discussing the problem in terms of a flourishing economy. A depression or even a recession brings problems. For example, Sweet Briar College in 1931–32 had to increase its tuition from $800 to $1,000 to cover its costs. But applications dropped from 647 to 292.[16]

Relevant, the gains of incomes have been especially large for those in the lower-income groups. In dollars of 1950 purchasing power, the percentage rise of income for the lowest 20 per cent of families was 42 per cent; the next 20 per cent, 37 per cent; the next 20 per cent, 24 per cent; the next 20 per cent, 16 per cent; and the highest 20 per cent experienced an increase of only 8 per cent. (For further details, see Table 9A-2.)

TUITION AND INCOME OF FAMILIES OF COLLEGE STUDENTS

Unfortunately, we do not know much about the incomes of families of *students in colleges*. Yet this is a most relevant factor in the determination of tuition policy. Because scholarship applicants are required to present the details of their economic status, we know more about this limited class of families.

In a paper before the College Entrance Examination Board, William Fels, now president of Bennington College, said (quite rightly in my opinion) that there was a case for requiring financial statements from students in colleges *even if they do not apply for scholarships,* " . . . because most, if not all, colleges contribute in some measure to the cost of education of all students." He stated that those able to pay the full cost of education are not charged the full cost and certainly do not bear a proportionate share of the cost for those less able to pay.[17]

We have *some* evidence that incomes of the families of college students who do not receive aid are relatively high. For example, we have a study of a group of undergraduates who applied for financial aid at the University of Chicago in the autumn of 1950. This study compares the family incomes of students without aid, students with aid, unsuccessful applicants, students in the entering class, and in the general population. We also have parental occupation and other data for each of these groups. In this sample the students without aid had family incomes averaging $9,000; students with aid, $5,044; and unsuccessful applicants, $4,071. The average for the class was $5,950, against a family income of $3,000 for the general population. (The latter figure seems low.) Obviously the students without aid have incomes three times those of the general population and about 80 per cent more than students receiving aid.[18]

On the basis of this sample, the case for large amounts of student aid and low tuition is not great, especially if financing methods are improved. Students who get no aid come from professional and business families four times as often as the general population and in roughly the same proportions as students with aid. There are, of course, large differences in the educational achievements of parents of college students, compared with the general population.

In an HEW sample of 14,214 families for 1952, the writers found that 9.5 per cent of the students' families (heads aged thirty-five to forty-four) had incomes of $6,000 to $6,999. Of all families with heads aged thirty-five to fifty-four in the national sample, 9.4 per cent were in this income bracket. At incomes of $7,000 to $15,000 the figures were 23.0 and 14.7 per cent respectively, and at $2,000 to $5,000, 42.1 and 46.6 per cent respectively. Whereas those in the $7,000 to $15,000 income class supplied more than one and one-half as many students as its proportion of families and those in the $15,000+ class four to five times the numbers given by the proportion of its families, those in the less than $3,000 income class contributed only about three-quarters as many students as suggested by their proportion of families.[19]

In an HEW study, *Retention and Withdrawal of College Students* (especially pages 61 to 64), the writers find that the median income of all families of college students was $5,713 in 1953. At the top of the lowest quarter the figure is $3,988 and at the bottom of the top fourth, $9,287. Incidentally, the median figure for public institutions is given as $5,243 and for private at $6,570, the latter being about 25 per cent above that for public institutions. The incomes differ little on the basis of quality of the student.

For 1960 these figures should be raised by 30 per cent. By 1959, median family incomes (National Sample) were almost 30 per cent higher than in 1953. Hence the median family income will be about $7,500 and the bottom of the top fourth about $12,000. Obviously those in the top fourth need little help, and a large proportion of those in second quarter would not need much. Many of them are oversubsidized.

A number of other studies of individual institutions shed some light here. For example, Paul H. Buck (then Provost) presented an interesting analysis for Harvard.[20] According to this study, the median income of parents of the nonveteran, nonscholarship students in Harvard College in 1947 was $12,250, and for scholarship students the median was $4,950. The parental income of veterans was $7,400. Since 1947 the average per capita disposable income of the nation has increased by more than 50 per cent in dollars. Extrapolating from the 1947 figures, we might expect that the average Harvard College student's parental income would now amount to more than $18,000. This, of course, is subject to changing admissions policies which affect the type of student admitted since 1947.

Another study, made in Florida, reveals less satisfactory conditions; the income in Florida is substantially below the national average. In Florida during 1954–55, approximately 18 per cent of the students came from families with incomes of less than $2,500, and 37 per cent with incomes from $2,500 to $5,000.[21]

* * *

A few peculiarities may be noted about the relationship between income and higher education. According to the Florida study, the expenditures of students do not vary greatly in relation to income. For private white senior colleges the amount of current expenditures in 1954–55 was as follows:[22]

Incomes under $2,500	$1,344
$2,500–5,000	1,458
$5,000–9,000	1,527
Over $9,000	1,869
All family income groups	1,531

In other words, with a parental income under $2,500, the student spent $1,344; with an income over $9,000, he spent only $500 more.

A New York State study does not yield exactly the same results. This is based, however, on *planned* expenditures. Of families with incomes under $4,000, 46 per cent expected to spend less than $900; of families with incomes of $8,000 and over, only 18 per cent; of those who expected to spend $1,500 and over, only 15 per cent came from the group with family incomes under $4,000, and 43 per cent from those with incomes of $8,000 and over.[23]

Finally, let me say a word about the scholarship students. I shall deal with this problem more fully later on.

In Table 9A–4,[24] King shows that parental income of scholarship applicants at Harvard College class of 1960 at the 50th percentile was

$6,900; at the 90th percentile, $12,800. The median figure for scholarship applicants admitted with an award was $6,000, with outside aid $6,800, for those denied scholarships $10,700. Net *assets* of scholarship applicants in the Harvard class of 1960 were a median of $800 for those with a Harvard award, $1,000 for those with outside award, $16,000 for those denied scholarships. The 90th percentile for the last was $61,000.

Of 400 applicants admitted but denied aid, 175 registered without aid at Harvard, and the university discovered that the median family income of this group was $10,700 and the median net assets after all allowances had been made according to the College Scholarship Service (CSS) formula was $16,000. At Harvard only 18 per cent of the scholarship holders were from families of incomes below $4,000.

More generally, John Morse, treasurer of RPI, says that the average family income of applicants a few years ago for the 152 colleges which use the CSS service (representing about 50 per cent of all scholarship funds) was $7,800. Morse also points out that about 80 per cent of the holders of National Merit Scholarships, with an average grant of $625 and 25 per cent receiving $1,000 or more, select private colleges, where costs are higher than in public colleges. This suggests that a large number of students from fairly high-income families receive these scholarships. The CSS is contributing toward a reduction of this waste: a formula has now been set up by which the participating colleges can adopt similar standards for determining needs and deciding the amount of scholarships.[25]

Although there is wastage of scholarships, we should also realize that scholarships do not provide a large part of the necessary funds. Actually, about one-fourth of the students questioned in one survey received scholarships, and two-thirds of these received only 1 to 19 per cent of their expenses; 4.9 per cent received 20 to 30 per cent.[26] Another survey by HEW reveals that less than 10 per cent of the students (undergraduate) receive scholarships *from the college*. The Hollis survey, which includes *all* scholarships, puts the total at 16 per cent. Scholarships, exclusive of veterans' benefits, accounted for only 4.3 per cent of student income.[27]

* * *

SUMMARY

1. Rises in tuition increase total costs of going to college much less than is indicated by the percentage rise of tuition fees. Tuition is one of several joint costs. Inclusive of income forgone, a doubling of tuition increases costs by less than 10 per cent.

2. As tuition has risen in recent years, student aid has increased much more, and therefore relief has been had when it was most needed.

3. Costs of higher education vary greatly. A student can get by in a municipal or state institution while living at home at considerably less than $1,000 per year. To some extent discretion is available to a large proportion of students to keep costs at a minimum figure.

4. Prewar tuition has risen only about one-third as much as per capita income and about 40 per cent of the rise of costs, and hence a college education has become a cheap commodity. Trends of income, studies of income of parents of both scholarship and nonscholarship students, improved distribution of income—all these point to capacity to pay higher fees.[28] In the late 1950s, however, tuition tended to rise more than per capita income.

In general, the conclusion drawn from this chapter is that capacity to pay higher tuition has grown much more than the tuition charge since World War II. The inference may well be that this is an argument for higher tuition. Indeed, for many it is. But insofar as financing higher education was a burden and an obstacle to entry before the war, it may still be a great burden to many. And even though half the population may not face serious problems, the other half well may. Though it is well to stress the point that a rise of tuition means a much smaller rise of total costs, it is also well to note that higher tuition may be accompanied by rising charges for the remainder of the budget. In so far as students come from families with lower relative incomes in 1960 than in 1940, as might be suggested by the rise in the proportion of college-age population at college, then to that extent the financial obstacles are greater than are so far assumed.

In the public IHL an obvious solution is to charge higher fees and use a large proportion of the additional receipts for scholarships. In this manner, the students who can afford to pay would pay more, and others of ability would get not only a tuition remission but help in meeting other expenses. On paper this seems like an ideal solution. But after discussing this problem with governors, budget officers, and college presidents, I find that in practice there are often difficulties. State legislatures tend to use additional tuition income, not to pay higher salaries or offer more scholarships, but rather to cut their own appropriations for higher education. Evidence on this point was mixed, however, and varied from state to state. The average view seemed to be that skillful college administrators could generally assure us that at least part of these gains would not be offset by reduced appropriations.[29]

FOOTNOTES

[1] H. S. Conrad and E. V. Hollis, "Trends in Tuition Charges and Fees," *The Annals, Higher Education under Stress,* September, 1955, p. 149; and E. V. Hollis, "Costs of Attending College," *Higher Education,* April, 1957.

[2] Cf. R. H. Ostheimer, *Student Charges and Financing Higher Education,* a staff study for the Commission on Financing Higher Education, 1952, p. 72. Cf. also L. G. Lewis, *College and University Business,* December, 1959.

[3] Based on Conrad and Hollis, *op. cit.* (Figures adjusted for changes in the last few years.)

[4] Estimate of income forgone is a rough one. I start with the average income of families and unrelated individuals aged fourteen to twenty-four and deduct $500 for earnings while at college. The resultant figure is $2,400. See *Survey of Current Business,* July, 1957; U.S. Census, *Income of Families and Persons in the United States, 1957,* 1958; and *1950 Census: U.S. Census of Population, Occupational Characteristics,* 1956; cf. T. W. Schultz, "Education and Economic Growth," *Social Forces Influencing American Education,* 1961, p. 87: Schultz estimates income forgone in 1956 at $2,000.

[5] HEW, *Costs of Attending College,* Bulletin 9, 1957, p. 40.

[6] E. C. Budd, *Trends in Yale's Finances,* 1957. (Mimeographed.)

[6a] Cf. E. D. West, *Background for National Scholarship Policy,* American Council on Education, 1956, p. 14. A more limited study by Charles W. Hoff for 422 colleges shows that tuition rose from 1941–42 to 1951–52 by 66 per cent. The rise of board charges was 72 per cent and of room charges 60 per cent (*College and University Business,* May, 1952, pp. 19–26).

[7] Budd, *op. cit.,* part 3; see S. E. Harris, "Economics of Harvard," *Harvard Alumni Bulletin,* Feb. 20, 1960; also see *Collegiate Schools of Business,* 1955, pp. 65–66; and Gropper and Fitzpatrick, *Who Goes to Graduate School?* 1959, pp. 28, 56–61.

[8] See HEW, *Statistics of Higher Education: Receipts, Expenditures and Property; Financing Aid for College Students; Undergraduate, Graduate; Costs of Attending College; Higher Education Planning and Management Data;* and President's Committee on Education beyond the High School, *Second Report to the President,* p. 50.

[9] Cf. Chaps. 11–16 for full discussion of scholarships.

[10] HEW, *Costs of Attending College, op. cit.,* p. 37.

[11] State University of New York, *Crucial Questions about Higher Education,* 1955, p. 54.

[12] *Ibid.,* p. 50.

[13] *Ibid.,* p. 48.

[14] *School and Society,* vol. 57, January–June, 1943, p. 220.

[15] Material in the following few paragraphs from H. P. Miller, *Income of the American People,* 1955; Conrad and Hollis, *op. cit.;* U.S. Census, *Family Income in the U.S., 1954 and 1953; Income and Families in the U.S., 1957; Economic Report of the President, 1957; 1950 Census of Occupational Characteristics;* S. F. Goldsmith, "Income Distribution Changes in the Size Distribution of Income," *AER,* May, 1957, pp. 504–18; *Economic Report of the President, 1960.*

[16] M. L. L. Stohlman, *The Story of Sweet Briar College,* 1956, pp. 171–172.

[17] W. C. Fels, *Foundation of Scholarship Policy in College Admissions,* no. 2, paper delivered before the College Entrance Examination Board, 1955, p. 80.

[18] Part of this table is reproduced as Table 9A-3.

[19] HEW, *Costs of Attending College, op. cit.,* p. 47.

[20] "Who Comes to Harvard?" *Harvard Alumni Bulletin,* Jan. 10, 1948.

[21] W. H. Strickler, *Study of Costs Undergraduate Students Incurred in Attending Florida Institutions of Higher Education, 1954–1955,* 1956, p. 6.

[22] *Ibid.,* pp. 42–43.

[23] State University of New York, *op. cit.,* p. 55.

[24] Taken from Richard G. King, "Family Incomes as Scholarship Applications,

Harvard Class of 1960," for the *College Board Review,* King is former assistant director of the College Board and now assistant director of admissions and financial aid at Harvard College; and from R. G. Moon, Jr., *"Financial Aid—from Application to Award."* Also see *College Board Review,* Winter, 1957.

[25] J. F. Morse, "How and Why Scholarships Are Awarded," *College Admissions,* IV, pp. 83–85.

[26] HEW, *Retention and Withdrawal of College Students,* p. 67.

[27] HEW, *Costs of Attending College, op. cit.,* pp. 48–55; *Financial Aid for College Students: Undergraduate.*

[28] Some relevant statistics have been put in the Appendix.

[29] Cf. address by L. Kimpton, Nov. 11, 1959.

APPENDIX

TABLE 9A-1
Variations by Field and Region in Annual Costs of Attending College, 1952–53*

Fields of study	Per cent of degrees conferred†	Per cent of student sample, by region					Mean total current expenditure by each student per year, by region				
		Total	NE	North Central	S	W	Total	NE	North Central	S	W
(1)	(2)	(3)	(4)	(5)	(6)	(7)	(8)	(9)	(10)	(11)	(12)
Agriculture.......	2.9	4.2	1.5	3.3	5.6	5.6	$1,159	$1,365	$1,246	$1,046	$1,290
Biological sciences	3.4	4.0	4.8	2.7	4.9	2.7	1,308	1,581	1,317	1,216	1,088
Education........	19.0	22.5	14.2	20.6	27.8	23.0	1,059	1,270	1,148	974	1,033
Engineering......	9.2	10.8	12.7	12.4	9.0	10.6	1,315	1,503	1,331	1,241	1,156
Healing arts and medical sciences	7.1	6.6	4.4	9.7	6.2	5.9	1,292	1,584	1,277	1,273	1,103
Humanities.......	14.0	13.3	22.6	14.1	9.9	8.5	1,577	2,099	1,406	1,244	1,146
Physical sciences..	3.7	4.8	5.4	4.4	5.3	3.7	1,207	1,576	1,302	1,160	1,031
Social sciences....	25.6	27.3	28.2	22.9	26.8	33.8	1,404	1,682	1,293	1,293	1,424
Other..........	15.1	6.5	6.2	9.9	4.5	6.2	1,230	1,686	1,090	1,177	1,049
Total........	100.0	100.0	100.0	100.0	100.0	100.0	$1,300	$1,676	$1,262	$1,164	$1,209

* Percentage distribution of 15,231 students, by field of study, total and region, and mean expenditure for each group.

† Figures in this column are percentages of 331,924 earned bachelor and first professional degrees conferred in 1951–52. Comparisons of degrees earned in each field with the cross section of enrollments shown in column 3 indicate the general adequacy of the student sample analyzed in this table.

Source: Ernest V. Hollis and Associates, *Costs of Attending College,* HEW Bulletin 9, 1957, p. 35.

TABLE 9A-2
Average Family Personal Income after Federal Individual Income Tax Liability, for Quintiles and Top 5 Per Cent of Consumer Units, Ranked by Size of After-tax Income, 1941 and 1950

Quintile	1941		1950	Per cent increase in 1950 dollars, from 1941 to 1950
	1941 dollars	1950 dollars		
Lowest..................	450	750	1,060	41
Second..................	1,040	1,730	2,360	37
Third....................	1,680	2,790	3,440	24
Fourth..................	2,430	4,030	4,690	16
Highest.................	4,940	8,190	8,880	8
Top 5 per cent...........	9,070	15,040	14,740	−2
All incomes combined.......	2,110	3,500	4,090	17

Source: S. Goldsmith, G. Jaszi, H. Kaitz, and M. Liebenberg, "Size Distribution of Income Since the Mid-thirties," *The Review of Economics and Statistics,* February, 1954, p. 26.

TABLE 9A-3

Income of Families of Scholarship and Nonscholarship Students, Various Postwar Studies

Study	Median income			
	No scholarship aid	Scholarship aid	Scholarship applicants	All students
HEW sample, 14,066 students, 1952–53	$5,260	$4,323		
CSS, 152 IHL, 1956–57.............	......	....	$7,800	
University of Chicago, 1950.........	9,000	5,044		
Harvard University, 1947...........	......	4,950	......	$12,250
Harvard University, 1957 (class of 1960)	......	6,000	6,900	18,000*
	......	6,800 (outside scholarships)		

* Blow up 1947 estimate by rise of average income.

TABLE 9A-4

Family Incomes of Scholarship Applicants, Harvard Class of 1960

Percentiles*	Total schol. appl. group	Admitted—registered				Admitted—not coming			Rejected schol. appl.
		Harvard award	Outside aid†	Schol. denied	Sub-total	Schol. award	Schol. denied	Sub-total	
90	$12,800	10,000	11,600	17,100	13,400	10,900	15,300	13,600	12,200
70	$ 9,100	7,600	8,400	13,000	9,400	8,500	11,000	10,200	8,600
50	$ 6,900	6,000	6,800	10,700	7,000	6,600	8,500	7,700	6,600
30	$ 5,300	4,900	5,600	7,100	5,300	4,800	6,100	5,700	5,000
10	$ 3,200	3,000	4,100	3,800	3,500	3,600	3,600	3,600	3,000
No. of cases in sample..	1,662	250	81	155	486	101	216	317	859
Total no. of cases......	1,803	262	84	179	525	105	226	331	947
Commuter median.....	$ 5,100	4,900	4,500	5,600					
No. of cases in sample..	52	33	2	17					
Total no. of cases......	58	34	2	22					

* Per cent scholarship applicants with family incomes falling below the amount given for each of the various categories.

† This category includes scholarship applicants who were given stipendiary awards of more than $200 from such sources as National Merit, General Motors, or the NROTC Holloway program.

Source: Richard G. King, "Financial Thresholds to College," College Board Review, Spring, 1957, p. 22.

TABLE 9A-5
Tuition, Prices, and Per Capita Income, 1860–1955

Years	Percentage rise of tuition charge			Percentage rise of prices	Percentage rise of per capita income
1860–1933:					
East.....................	700			103*	146*
West.....................	520				
1907–08 to 1947–48:				161	411
24 Identical IHL...........	336				
1928–29 to 1936–37:	46 state institutions	38 private universities	116 private colleges		
East.....................	13.1	10.3	13.9		
West.....................	13.0	14.5	8.3	−20	−22
All......................	20.6	10.9	11.8		
1940–1950:					
All institutions.............	53				
Public..................	47				
Residential............	56†				
Nonresidential.........	80†			72	156
Private.................	54				
Universities...........	49				
Liberal Arts Colleges....	61				
1940–1955:					
All......................	85				
Public..................	73			91	237
Private.................	90				

* Comparison of prices and incomes over long periods of time are subject to serious errors.
† Unweighted average of 54 institutions.
Sources: T. Arnett, *Trends in Current Receipts and Expenditures . . . in the United States from 1927–28 through 1936–37,* 1939, and *Recent Trends in Higher Education in the United States . . . Universities,* 1940; R. H. Ostheimer, *Student Charges and Financing of Higher Education,* 1953; Seymour E. Harris, *How Shall We Pay for Education?* 1948; H. S. Conrad and E. V. Hollis, "Trends in Tuition Charges and Fees," *The Annals, Higher Education under Stress,* September, 1955; U.S. Census, *Historical Statistics of the United States, 1789–1945,* 1949; *Economic Report of the President,* January, 1957; J. D. Millett, *Financing Higher Education in the United States,* 1952.

Chapter 10

THE CASE FOR HIGHER TUITION[1]

The case for higher tuition can be summed up in a sentence: *In ten years' time the annual budget for higher education (educational and general) will roughly triple, rising from $3.7 billion in 1957–58 to at least $10 billion in 1968–70.* I make this statement on the basis of what I consider conservative estimates. This money must come from somewhere, and it does not seem likely, as Pusey pointed out, that it will be found without increased help from students and parents.[2] This is not a statement of a kind of financing I would like to see. I think the resources are available for putting the additional burden largely on government and private philanthropy. But the trends of the last five years in financing higher education suggest that it is not going to be easy to convince the taxpayers and the affluent of this viewpoint.

I should point out two things about this figure at once: First, this tripling of the cost of higher education does not represent any visionary idea of a future in which every filling-station attendant has a Ph.D.; this money will be needed to do on a larger scale approximately the same job which we are doing now, though it will reflect also the rising standards of the economy. Second, we can take no comfort from the idea that we will pay this bill with cheaper dollars. The estimate of a $6 to $7 billion rise is based on the assumption of no inflation whatever. If inflation continues at the rate of the 1950s of a little more than 2 per cent a year, we will have an additional increase of about $2 billion, that is, a rise of closer to $8 billion than $6 billion.

The reasons for this great increase are many, but a few stand out sharply. They have been discussed more fully in Chapter 2. First, enrollment in institutions of higher learning may be expected to rise by about 85 per cent in these twelve years; second, the underpayment of teachers must be corrected; and, third, the costs of construction of school buildings is steadily rising.

The doubling of salary is no small part of the total increase in costs.

149

All told, it will come to about $3 billion, compared to the *total* educational budget of $3.75 billion in 1959. This may well be the part of the total rise which is resisted most strongly by legislatures and trustees who set the salary patterns of universities, because this is not easy money to find. I hope I have made it clear that they resist such a rise at considerable peril to the educational structure as a whole.

It will not be a simple matter to raise this additional $6+ billion per year by 1970 which we must have in order to keep our universities and colleges running well. We can rid ourselves of a few inadequate ideas at once. Philanthropy is not likely to provide the additional sums needed by private IHL. The largest of the philanthropic organizations, the Ford Foundation, has total assets of about $2½ billion. If the directors of this foundation decided to abandon all other projects and go out of business, even these enormous resources would support the increased costs for only about three months in 1970. I estimate that the contribution of all private gifts and endowment income put together will only account for about a tenth of the additional sum required. (This might conceivably be an underestimate if improvements in methods of fund raising continue as in the recent past.)

Even state governments will probably not shoulder the load of students in their own public institutions unless tuitions rise. In ten to twelve years, there will be more than six million students in IHL. Public institutions will probably enroll about two-thirds of them, or more than 4 million. Inclusive of new capital, public IHL will require about $1,300 per year to finance each student.[3] Tuition at 1958 rates should yield roughly $600 million. A little simple arithmetic (4 million students at $1,300 each = $5.2 billion, less $600 million = $4.6 billion) shows a net cost of $4.6 billion which would have to be paid by the taxpayer. This would raise the contribution of states to higher education from about $1¼ billion in 1957–58, or about 6 per cent of the total state budgets now, to about $4½ billion, or about 17 per cent of the expected budget of 1970. I do not think it likely that this sort of increase will occur.

THE EQUITY ISSUE

Aside from the need of obtaining additional resources, what is the case for higher tuition? One point is that the student obtains material gains from his education and hence should pay higher fees. I do not contend that the major gain of higher education comes in higher income returns, nor that the major objective of higher education is to increase the income of those who attend college. But it is noteworthy that many college students are affluent when they go to college and can afford to pay more than they do now, and that after they graduate, the income of most former students rises so substantially that they can afford to pay the full costs over a longer period. I do not intend to give the impression that the larger income resulting from higher education is the result merely of the higher education. We know that the college graduates have higher aptitudes (IQ of 120 as compared to 100 for the population), and we know they experience many environmental advantages.[4] Certainly higher education contributes something to the student's development, including earning power, and the diploma is a ticket of admission to high-paying occupations.[5] Indeed we would even concede that the condition of a degree for entry is overdone and often tends to be undemocratic in excluding many without A.B.s who are competent for particular occupations.

There have been several estimates of the gains of income resulting from higher education. Some older estimates, independent of one another, generally run around $100,000. They are subject to some margin of error, and some questions are raised concerning their reliability.

It should be noted first that the supposed $100,000 advantage is not available today but over the lifetime of the graduate. We are not comparing present values but income as it arises. Note also that any increase of income is subject to tax deduction. For these purposes, however, I contend that the appropriate measure is the gross income, not income after taxation, since I regard taxes as one way of spending income, not a deduction from income. Finally, all these estimates are based on a comparison of lifetime income of all college graduates with noncollege graduates. But for these purposes a more appropriate index would be a comparison of the probable advantage of the *current* crop of college graduates over those who do not go to college. On this basis we estimate that the college graduate would have an advantage of about $200,000 or even more. This estimate is based on assumptions of rising per capita income in the next fifty years similar to past gains. It is, however, subject to change in the relative supply of, and demand for, college graduates. My guess would be that to some extent, because of the large output of college graduates, the advantage would be pruned. But against this, the inflationary trend would increase the *dollar* gains.[5a]

On the basis of *1949* incomes, the average lifetime income of the average man would be $133,000; of the high school graduate, $165,000; of the man with 1 to 3 years of college, $190,000; of the college graduate (average 4½ years, inclusive of graduate work), $268,000.

Hence, on the basis of 1949 incomes, a college education is worth $135,000 vis-à-vis the income of the average man and $103,000 vis-à-vis the high school graduate.

Against these gains, we should deduct the costs of a higher education. An allowance for the direct costs minus cost of subsistence whether at home or college and plus earnings lost while at college equal about

$9,000. The costs may be increased to from $20,000 to $40,000 (depending on rates of interest and life span assumed) if it is assumed that, had the student not gone to college, he would have invested this money until death, say, at age seventy-two. The more likely assumption is, however, that the funds would have been spent. (Personal savings in the 1950s are only about 7 to 8 per cent of income.)[6]

Let us consider the arithmetic, not on the basis of 1949 incomes (the above), but on the basis of 1980 income. In that year graduates of 1957 will have attained roughly the mid-point of their working life. I assume a rise of per capita income of 75 per cent in these twenty-three years, a total equal to a gain of 2½ per cent per year compounded.

Under these assumptions a college education for the 1957 crop can be estimated as worth about $200,000:

> Net figure on basis of 1949 and 1958 incomes = $ 95,000 (roughly)
> Add 102 × 95* (rise of income 1949 to 1959) =   96,900
>   Total = $191,900
>
> * This figure is obtained by assuming a 2½ per cent rise of per capita income per year and a working life of forty-five years. At the end of forty-five years this rate of growth yields a rise of 204 per cent. Hence the average is 102 per cent.

These results are subject to various reservations. The first is that, as Bridgman has pointed out, the gains of a college education fall much more to the able than to the mediocre.[7] The second is, as I argued in my book on the *Market for College Graduates* more than ten years ago, that the relative income of college graduates may fall substantially in response to rising numbers. Income differentials since 1920 confirm this point. But against this decline should be put any increase of income associated with inflation. The U.S. Census released some figures in July, 1960, that showed that the lifetime income of those with four or more college years had risen from $268,000 in 1949 to $347,000 in 1958. But the differential vis-à-vis high school graduates was roughly unchanged. Income of high school graduates had risen by $78,000. Hence the *relative* gains of the college-trained had been reduced.

We tend to emphasize the material contributions of higher education altogether too much; possibly parents and students do so more than those who dispense it. I am afraid that this discussion will be interpreted by some as lending support to the wrong kind of emphasis. Yet what the student gains materially—even if, as we hope, this is not the major product of IHL—is relevant in discussing our pricing program. Nor does this position mean that the gains of higher education are not in substantial part society's.

In this connection, we compare the $4,000 compensation of the average worker in 1959 with roughly $8,000 for the college graduate. The mean of the 1959 graduate over his working life should be about $16,000 ($8,000 + about 100 per cent of $8,000) and the lifetime income about $1 million if we assume moderate inflation. (This is subject to the reservation of reduced relative income as the supply of college graduates rises.) But even if the lifetime income were only $500,000, a strong case would still be made for higher charges, especially if improved methods of long-term financing make it possible to increase charges by (say) $1,000 a year, or a cost to the college graduate of about 1 or 1½ per cent of the lifetime income. (Actually the additional tuition required by 1970 should be substantially less than $1,000.)

I concentrate here on the material gains of higher education for the students. I do not deny substantial gains in which society has a major interest. Nor do I hold it is easy to measure the benefits, for much must be ascribed to varying capacities and environmental advantages of the college-trained.

But it is next to impossible to be precise on the relative gains to society and the individual. How can we measure the social gains of turning out greatly needed doctors against the $1.5 million lifetime income made available to doctors graduated in 1960? As difficult as it is to measure the costs of college training, it is much more difficult to measure the benefits. But some emphasis on the material gains should not be excluded merely because the results can only be rough. They are an essential element in policy making.[8]

While we are still discussing the issue of equity, I turn to the problem of raising tuition in public institutions. In the numerous official reports on the plans and programs of public institutions, one finds much argument to the effect that the state institutions were created to provide higher education for those with low incomes (see Chapter 8). This is now subject to numerous reservations. In the nineteenth century the theory was that a college graduate would become either a preacher or a teacher and hence a member of the low-income group. Indeed, the land-grant colleges were formed to provide vocational education, such as farming. But the average college student is no longer impecunious, and the graduate is often affluent. Hence this argument has lost some of its force, though the image of the state IHL open to the poor may be worth preserving until we find adequate substitutes through improved financing. In the present situation the low-income groups finance many in the high-income groups—those who go to state institutions of higher learning. This is due to the tax structure. Only about 9 per cent of the taxes of state and local governments in 1958 came from income and corporation taxes. Most of the taxes are on consumption and property and are regressive; that is, they put a greater burden on low incomes than on high incomes. The regressivity of the state and local taxes is an argument against heavily sub-sidized higher education, which amounts to the subsidization of the rich by the poor. (More on this in a later chapter.)

Nevertheless we cannot completely dismiss the original objectives of public higher education. We should provide higher education at prices that are commensurate with the ability to pay. The problem of higher tuition can be solved in part by providing generous scholarships or loans for those with low incomes. We can then charge higher tuition for the others. Of the additional $2 billion collected in tuition (say) the state governments might use one-fourth to one-half to help, with scholarships averaging $1,000, the one-fourth of the students who are able but lack enough money to go to college. This would be a much more effective use of state re-sources in higher education than indiscriminate subsidies to the haves as well as the have-nots. I refer the reader, however, to the earlier discussion of the difficulties of earmarking additional tuition funds and the pressure to use them as a weapon for cutting appropriations.

On the basis of these figures on expected income, it is perfectly plain that anyone with the talent and determination to go to college is making a grave financial mistake if he does not take advantage of the opportunity. Furthermore, we have seen in the previous chapter that rising incomes in-creasingly make it easier for people to go to college. Despite large rises in tuition, demand for higher education has increased tremendously. Lately the rise in per capita income has far outstripped the average rise in tuition. In addition, we have seen that the effect of a rise in tuition is mitigated by the fact that tuition is only a part of the total cost of going to college. For all these reasons I believe that a rise in tuition rates is practicable as well as equitable.

But it is also clear that at least one-half the students at college—and probably a larger proportion at public IHL—will continue to have financial problems. With higher tuition it would be unfortunate if ways were not found through scholarships, loans, and employment to assure entry to all on the basis of ability. In so far as additional aid is not made available —and financed in part by the rise of tuition—which would assure entry to all who deserve it, then the case for higher tuition is to that extent weakened.

HIGHER TUITION AND IMPROVED FINANCING

Even when we allow for current subsidies, the rise in tuition required to satisfy the needs of IHL will be considerable. In ten years, on my projec-tions, the cost per student will be at least $1,300 (1960 dollars), and the *present* average level of tuition covers only one-fourth to one-third of this amount. And despite the arguments adduced earlier, under the present methods of financing many families are going to find difficulty supporting their children through college under a regime of higher tuition rates.

At present, colleges insist on payment over a period of four years. Since the average family has an income of about $7,000, the burden of $2,000 a year for one child's higher education means four lean years for the child's family. To some extent this load can be lightened by the use of savings and of student jobs, but these are inadequate, and the students are often required to spend too much time at work. Scholarships, of course, make it much easier for those who hold them, and the use of higher scholarships as tuition increases involves a desirable form of price discrimination in favor of the impecunious student of ability.

But scholarship funds are not available in the required amount. The way out of this difficulty is to spread the financial burden to the family over a longer period of time. Already colleges are moving in the direction of more reliance on loans. In discussing this problem with the presidents of more than one hundred colleges in the years 1958 to 1960, I found that the tendency is to insist upon a larger use of loans as against scholarships. Loans are especially helpful for students who do not rate a scholarship. But they also make the resources for scholarships go further than otherwise would be possible.

One solution is to finance higher tuition by a lifetime financial program. The parents should insure the child at age one and assume that the direct costs of education will not be $1,800, the average at present, but at least $3,600 by the time the student goes to college. Adequate insurance of this type would solve all the problems. But in many instances the parents will not take these measures, and in many they cannot afford to do so. Therefore there should be postfinancing as well as prefinancing.

The postfinancing program should consist of a loan at reasonable rates of interest for a period of up to forty years, analogous to the house-mortgage type of loan, say, forty years at 3 per cent. The student would be allowed to borrow in so far as his resources (inclusive of savings for higher education) are not adequate to pay his (her) costs of higher education. Loans of $1,000 a year at present could be financed at a cost of around 1 per cent of the lifetime income of the student, and since there would be a tax allowance here, the net cost would be reduced further. Insurance against the death of the student borrower would raise costs to some extent, but inflation would reduce the percentage of costs of loan finance to lifetime income. Students unwilling to undertake this obligation for forty years could be allowed to repay in shorter periods. The most economical approach is pre- rather than postfinancing, for the interest rate works for the student rather than against him. Eckstein shows that twenty years of postpayment, after a five-year moratorium, at 4 per cent interest would cost $425 annually per $1,000 of tuition of four years.

Twenty years of prepayment at the same rate of interest would cost only $155 a year.[9]

It is absurd that in the present economy the average family is indebted more than $3,000 for housing and durable consumer goods and the average student at college is indebted less than $10 to his college and perhaps $20 to $30 in all. It seems foolish to allot so much credit to relatively unproductive purposes and so little to the most productive loan of all, a loan to finance higher education.

What is required to put across this idea is a good public relations program. At present the mother who is perfectly content to borrow to buy a car or to improve her home is aghast at the thought that her child's future should be mortgaged in this particular manner. The student and, especially, the parent must be convinced that it is not immoral to borrow for higher education and that this is the most productive and effective type of borrowing. It is also necessary to sell this program to life insurance companies and to banks. In my opinion, there has been much progress made along this front in the last few years. But I am not so optimistic as to believe that long-term financing will be achieved on an adequate scale in a year or two. Vigorous efforts will be required over a decade or longer.

Precollege and postcollege financing have different advantages. Precollege financing is effective in that the interest rate works on behalf of the student. If the saving is done through institutions that are allowed to invest substantially in equities, the amount of monthly saving required to finance higher education could be greatly reduced. Earnings on savings invested are an *addition* to the funds made available for higher education. In postfinancing interest is a *cost,* and for this reason prefinancing is desirable. But for another and perhaps more important reason, it is better to have postfinancing if a choice must be made. Under the insurance program at age one the funds come from the low incomes of the past, but under postfinancing the program is financed out of the rising incomes of the future. A student graduating in 1960 whose funds came from the insurance scheme was financed out of the average income of his parents in the years 1940–1960 (average = 1950), whereas under postfinancing the average income would accrue in 1985 (average of 1960 to 2010). In 1985 per capita income (even without inflation) should rise to about 135 per cent (2½ per cent rise compounded over thirty-five years) above that of 1950, since per capita real income has tended in the past to double about every twenty-five to thirty years. As this trend continues, therefore, by the time the student repays his last installment, his income may be close to 200 per cent above his parents' income at time of his graduation. In addition, inflation might increase the per capita income even more.[10]

Another way of looking at the problem is the following:

Better budgeting would greatly improve the resources available for higher education. Assume that each of the 43 million families wanted to send one child to college on the average. (Some would send two or three, others none.) The result would be an enrollment of about 4 million at any one time. Assume, again, an average cost of $1,800, roughly Hollis's estimate for 1956. Then total average costs over four years would be $7,200 per family. The median income of the family (at current incomes) is around $280,000 in a lifetime. Hence the cost would be 2.6 per cent of this lifetime income. At any one time the burden would be large if financed out of current earnings, say, $1,800 out of $7,000, or 26 per cent of current income. Over the working life of the family, the costs would be modest.

Hence, what is required is a budgeting or financing program. Through the use of insurance companies or other financial institutions, payment can be financed out of savings plus interest over twenty years. For example, 20 payments beginning at birth of $250 per year at a modest rate of interest (say, equal to the return on savings bonds of 1960) would yield around $7,000. In other words, *savings of 5 to 6 per cent of income in the first twenty years or so of the life of the future student would yield the total required for higher education at current costs.* In so far as the cost of higher education rises less than income, as it has in the past, expense would be reduced further relative to income. Even this is too pessimistic, for it should be assumed that the student can earn $500 in the course of the college year. That would cut the required savings to around 4 per cent of income over twenty years. We have been too optimistic. A parent looking forward would do well to assume costs of $14,000 for this infant. Hence savings would have to be somewhat larger; but since income would rise in the next twenty years also, the additional burden would raise costs to about 8 to 9 per cent.

But there is another approach. The *student,* rather than the parent, might pay the costs of college over his lifetime. (I am now discussing the total costs to the *student,* not the total educational costs to the institution.) Here the student would borrow the costs of his education—say, $7,000 minus $2,000 of earnings or savings, or $5,000, and pay this back over his lifetime.

In footnote 11 I have made the roughest kind of guess of the amount of college loans that would be required for a loan program that would revolutionize college financing currently.[11] I assume loans of $1,000 a year by 60 per cent of the students. I do not delude myself that this will come overnight. A generous estimate is $2.5 billion a year once the program is launched, and close to $10 billion gross (less than $5 billion net after repayments) by the year 2000. The amount required would be about 5 per cent of the annual rise of debt, say, by 1965 and similarly in the year 2000. At that time the GNP should amount to about $1,300 billion to

$1,400 billion (1960 prices), and hence new debt incurred would be about ⅓ per cent of GNP.

As I have said, this cannot be done overnight, but the institutional break is no greater than what has happened in consumer durable goods and housing. All that is needed is a campaign of similar proportions for investments that are much more productive than those which now account for the growth of debt by consumers. I am also aware of the theory that the low-income groups will not borrow because they are afraid to borrow, or the argument that a potential borrower is not impressed by average gains of incomes of the college graduate. He is uncertain that he can make it and hence does not want to be saddled by large debts. The college student also, it is said, must reserve his borrowing power to purchase a car and launch a family. These are all relevant arguments, though frequently overdone, as is another, namely, that the rise of private debt has grown much more than GNP in the 1950s and hence further increases are dangerous. But even within these limits changes in the structure of debt are possible.

On the issue of the attitude of those with low income toward borrowing, Table 10-1 is of some interest. It has often been said that credit

TABLE 10-1

Ratio of Regular Payments to Disposable Income, Per Cent

Income	Per cent
Less than $1,000	10
$1,000–1,999	24
2,000–2,999	24
3,000–3,999	32
4,000–4,999	39
5,000–5,999	43
6,000–7,499	45
7,500–9,999	44
10,000 and over	28
Modal..	33

Source: Committee on Banking and Currency, Subcommittee on Housing; U.S. Senate Study of Mortgage Credit, 1958, p. 7c; Cf. also S. E. Harris, The Incidence of Inflation or Who Gets Hurt? Study Paper 7, Joint Economic Committee Congress of the United States, 1959, pp. 80–81.

financing of higher education would be undemocratic. It would divide the college population into those who are in debt and those who are not. But Table 10-1 here suggests that this division pervades American life. In fact, 48 per cent of the population is now subject to regular payments on debt, and the families sending children to college, say, those with incomes of $3,000 and over, are accustomed to borrowing and financing debts.[12]

QUESTIONNAIRE TO A SELECT GROUP OF ECONOMISTS ON EFFECTS OF DOUBLING TUITION[13]

I sent a questionnaire to about 350 economists who might have something to say about issues of pricing of a college education. The most important question was what the effects would be of a 100 per cent rise of tuition by 1970. A rise of these proportions by 1970 would mean *additional* tuition income of approximately $2 billion, and hence, aside from the roughly $2 billion of tuition associated with current charges by 1970, the rise of tuition would provide $2 billion additional tuition income. Furthermore, $1 billion more would be available from the rise of enrollment at current prices. This increase of $300 per student, or 100 per cent, is to be compared with an expected rise of 30 per cent in per capita income. Should, as many anticipate, the result of this 100 per cent rise in tuition be that public IHL would take the increased enrollment, then the rise of additional income associated with higher fees would be only $1.5 billion.

Economists are notably diverse in their opinions on public issues, and this select group of respondents of 220 economists is, in this respect, truly representative. Among the replies to the first question, on the effects of a doubling of tuition by 1970, each opinion can be set against an opinion diametrically opposite. However, on the broad effects of such an increase, and indeed on some of the more precise effects, a numerical consensus can be distinguished.

For example, the respondents agreed that should tuition be doubled across the board as proposed, enrollment in all IHL in 1970 would not be so great as it would otherwise be. They agreed that the demand for higher education is inelastic; that is, a rise of price would not greatly reduce "purchases." The range of estimates of curtailment of prospective enrollment ran from 0 to 25 per cent. In order to arrive at such estimates, assumptions had to be made about (1) the growth of per capita disposable income over the same period and (2) the amount of additional scholarship and loan aid that would accompany the rise in tuitions. Since the former is expected to increase 25 to 35 per cent over the period, the rise in the *real* cost of education would be less than 100 per cent. Relevant also is the large lag of tuition behind per capita income in the last twenty years. A rise of tuition by 100 per cent by 1970 and a gain of per capita income of 33 per cent would result in 1970 in, roughly, an equal rise of per capita disposable income and tuition by 300 per cent over thirty years. Moreover, much depends on what happens to educational expenses other than tuition and fees, such as the costs of board and room, and the costs of opportunities forgone. With these costs taken into account, tuition charges constitute about one-tenth of the total costs of a college education for most students and, therefore, can increase considerably before the effect on enrollment becomes apparent.

Despite this consensus that the effect on enrollment would be rather small, many respondents were unwilling to accept the prospect of a doubling of tuition, either because it offended their image of the world as it ought to be, or their image of the world as it is. Aside from the issue of unequal opportunities for rich and poor, which will emerge later, there is apparently a widely held belief among a selected group of economists that the social benefits of higher education outweigh the private benefits, from which it follows that higher education should be a public responsibility and promulgated as widely as the conscience of the nation prescribes. Some economists, dealing in hard-headed reality, doubted that public institutions would be able to muster political support for such an extensive increase in their charges. Others doubted that private institutions would be able to double their tuitions and still retain a student body of comparable size and background. One doubted that a quasi scarcity should be attacked through pricing policy.[14]

To return for a breathing space to the somewhat clearer air surrounding the question of the actual effects of such a policy, we are pleased to find substantial agreement about the effects on the existing balance between public and private IHL, if indeed such a balance exists. Since the cost differential between public and private IHL is already large enough to sway many students, a doubling across the board, which would magnify the absolute differential, would undoubtedly inundate the public IHL under seas of economy-minded students and leave most of the private IHL high and relatively dry.[15] This, of course, does not include Harvard, Yale, Princeton, and other institutions of more or less comparable stature, whose waters will never cease. The values that lead parents to send their children to those "prestige" colleges are highly resistant to economic pressures, which, in any case, are not so important for these parents as a group.

This line of reasoning needs some qualification, however. In the first place, the increase in the number of college applicants between now and 1970 is expected to be sufficiently large to keep in use all available facilities, both public and private. It is unlikely that many private IHL, even among those of substandard quality, would have to close their doors for lack of students. They might even expand their enrollments in absolute terms. However, the bulk of the rise in the college population would in all probability seek out public IHL, where their expenses would be substantially less.

Economists associated with some of these public IHL disagree that such a generalization is reasonable. They point out that costs among public IHL differ quite widely: the big state universities of the Middle West, for instance, are much more expensive than local or community colleges, partly because many of their students are from out of state and most are residents on campus. These institutions too might find their applications declining as a result of the economic squeeze.

Some economists felt that conclusions could be drawn about the overall quality of higher education after a doubling of tuition, reasoning solely from this shift from private to public institutions, and quite apart from changes in the quality of applicants. Their conclusions ranged from "an educational gain" to "an educational loss," and were based on two general arguments: first, that the increased demand for public education would present a challenge to public authorities to improve educational facilities and, second, that the greater pool of applicants to public IHL would provide them more students of above-average ability. Their conclusions were thus based on their judgments as to whether public authorities would respond to the challenge in time and in sufficient scope and whether the greater pool of applicants to public IHL would outweigh the lesser pool of applicants to private IHL.

This latter argument borders very nearly on questions of changes in "types" of students resulting from a doubling of tuition, and to this we will now turn. At the outset we, like most of the respondents, must state that the answer to this question, especially with regard to changes in the quality of students, depends primarily on the extent of concomitant changes in scholarship and loan programs. If scholarship aid does not fully keep pace with the increase in costs, there will be a further "leakage" of superior students from the bottom financial stratum out of the college communities. If one assumes, on the other hand, commensurate increase in aid programs, certain results seem likely, at least in the eyes of the respondents. First, the economic bias of American higher education would be intensified. At all IHL, the average students would have wealthier parents than the average student before the rise in costs. (This need not follow, of course, for students helped if the proportion of students helped by scholarships and other aids increased and the average stipend rose at least as much as tuition.) Second, the better and more costly private institutions would find their students falling into an increasingly accentuated bimodal distribution comprised of the very rich and the very bright. They would tend to lose the young men and women of middling means and middling parts, who could not quite qualify for scholarships and could not quite afford to stay without them. These people would tend to slide down the educational scale to places which they could afford, or at which they could stand up in the competition for scholarships. Thus, thirdly, the public IHL would have applicants of higher quality than they had before the changes in tuition took place. On the other hand, several economists argued that this effect would be offset by the tendency for the poorly motivated students (whose demand for higher education would ostensibly be more price-elastic than the average) to slide down the educational scale also. There seems to be no a priori way to weigh these arguments.

Among the categories of students most likely to drop out of the market altogether, the economists mentioned, with varying frequency, poorly motivated students, students from the lowest-income classes, notably Negroes and others from low-income regions, those from non-Jewish middle-class families with no tradition of college attendance, those from large families, and women students. An interesting dissent was submitted by one respondent, who felt that the parents of women students are particularly prone to place primary importance on the status value of education and are wont to act as conspicuous spenders on their daughters' educations. He argues that they might be *more* likely to send their daughter to a college if its tuition were doubled. (This is a viewpoint which many deans of admission have impressed upon the author as held by students generally.)

The loss of marginal students (marginal in terms of motivation, not wealth) might be an educational gain. Moreover, the greater costs of education might increase the motivation of the students that remain. This must be balanced, however, against the effects of greater financial pressures on all students to work part time, or even, in the view of one respondent, to marry in order to be supported while in college.

The final consideration is the influence of the proposed doubling of tuitions on the regional distribution of colleges and college students. There was substantial agreement on this issue that (1) students from poorer regions would be "hurt" more, in that they would tend to drop out or fail to enter college in greater numbers, (2) the interregional flow of students would be diminished, and (3) the remaining flow would be directed to a greater extent away from the strongholds of private education, such as the Northeast, toward those of public education, such as the Far West. Respondents envisaged a plethora of local community colleges catering to commuting students, which would probably be of scarcely better quality than their present-day prototypes. (I do not share the low appraisal of community colleges of many of my colleagues.) A paradox arises in this respect, in that these community colleges, which would become more popular should tuitions be doubled, are just the colleges whose students would be hit hardest by the increase. The reason is, of course, that these IHL, along with cooperatives, cater to students on the financial margin. Much of their present enrollment might be squeezed out and their places taken over by the new, wealthier marginal student. (The trend toward attending colleges nearby, e.g., community and urban IHL, is already apparent, a fact explained by lower costs, the growth of large metropolitan areas, and the accompanying rise of facilities in these areas.)

On the other hand, some economists argued that the out-of-state students at public IHL would be least affected by the increase, because for them tuition represents but a minor proportion of total costs. This seems to be an argument about short-term effects, however, relating to the existing college population, not to the decisions of college students to come. Students from areas with few public educational facilities would be at the greatest disadvantage, faced with the choice of traveling to other state universities or attending private colleges at home. Not only does this apply to students from the Northeast, but also to Negro students from the South, which still has very limited higher educational facilities at their disposal.

In conclusion, the main points of agreement on these issues can be summarized as follows: a small drop in total enrollment, if any; a shift of the student population to public and to urban IHL; a wealthier student population, but not necessarily a more able one; and, a greater provincialism in college attendance, modified by the location of good public IHL.

GENERAL OBSERVATIONS ON PRICING

Having devoted seven chapters to the problem of pricing, I now turn to some general conclusions.

In our kind of society, the allocation of resources is determined for the most part by individual decisions. But through compulsory powers, government determines the allocation of about 20 per cent of our resources. Where the social net product exceeds the private net product, the case for government intervention is made. Hence the institution of free public school education from grades 1 through 12. Without government help, the resources devoted to elementary and secondary education would be inadequate. The nation cannot afford uneducated youth.

But why, many will ask, stop at grade 12? Why, in view of the great need for the college-trained, should we not offer free education and even subsidies for room and board for college students? Increasingly this point is being made, and the spread of community colleges points toward an extension of free education to grade 14; and in such states as California, we could almost say that free education is available to all high school graduates through grade 14, and for most high school graduates through grade 16.[16]

Why in the past has free education stopped at grade 12? One explanation is undoubtedly the difficulties of raising the necessary taxes; another prevalent view held until recently was that there were an adequate number of college-trained; another, that incomes were so low that the offer of free education would not suffice for most families which could not afford the other expenses and income forgone. But now with increased need for the college-trained, the greater general interest in higher education, the more productive and flexible tax system, and the marked rise in the standard of living, the urgency for government subsidies in higher education has increased.

The debate on the issue of rising tuition fees goes on. Those who support higher tuition rest their case partly on the presumed unavailability of other resources to the IHL and the greater relative rise of costs than of tuition since 1940; the large material advantages obtained by the college-trained, and hence, financing by beneficiaries; the small impact of higher tuition on *total* costs to the student; the alternative colleges available at low costs; the possibility of improving financing methods, so that at higher tuition rates opportunities may be increased rather than reduced; the large rises of family income as compared with the small increases in tuition over the last generation; the need of adequate charges as a condition of appreciating higher education.

Defenders of no tuition or low tuition are equally eloquent. They stress the large social product and consider the substantial private product largely irrelevant. They are opposed to the determination of numbers or those chosen on the basis of a pricing system. In view of our expected $200 billion or more growth of GNP in ten years, the resources for a free higher education are available. All that is necessary is for the public—and particularly government and philanthropists—to sense the large social benefits to be had from higher education. These defenders of an equalitarian principle, namely, equal opportunities for all, are not optimistic concerning improved methods of finance as weapons for inducing higher tuition. They do not want two classes of citizens, the debt-ridden and the others; they fear a widespread scholarship program which may bring a vast bureaucracy, means test, and political chicanery. Supporters of no tuition or low tuition might see in increased economies an alternative to higher tuition. But they are not disposed to press this issue.

In general the main opposition to higher fees comes from the public IHL. The alternative is more tax money. But the private IHL without this resource and with limited funds to be had from private donors have to press for higher tuition—and generally with great reluctance.

But the public IHL are also under great pressure to increase tuition. They are confronted not only with higher unit costs, as are the private IHL, but on top of that they do not generally have the freedom to restrict enrollment as do the private IHL. Their costs per student greatly exceed tuition charges.

Here it is not surprising that in the midst of this debate, in four recent years, tuition rose by one-third in both public and private IHL. In a ten-year period a rise of tuition at the rate of the years 1954–55 to 1958–59 means a doubling of tuition. Should tuition double in the next ten years, the rise would amount to about $170 for public and $800 for private IHL. The differential would then increase by about $600. For this reason, and also because of the general rise of demand without corresponding openings in private IHL, the country may well expect that public IHL will absorb most of the increase of about three million students in the 1960s.

In this connection, I was a little surprised at the lack of understanding of many college administrators of the relation of rising enrollment and financial condition of IHL. Often, it is true, the decision of size of entering class is determined on the basis of educational objectives primarily. But many college presidents interviewed by the author failed to grasp the difference between average and marginal cost. Concentrating on financial aspects, they decided to increase their enrollment only if tuition exceeded average costs. Of course they would have to weigh financial results with the change in quality of students as more are accepted. They often did not seem to realize that what was relevant was the comparison of *additional* tuition and *additional*—that is, marginal—costs. One college president said, quite appropriately, that we would gladly take more students if they would concentrate in classics, but if they choose to study in the sciences, the additional costs make this prohibitive. And many administrators with excess capacity realized the improved financial status with rising enrollment.

FOOTNOTES

[1] Part of this chapter (since revised) was given to the Planning and Policies Committee of the American Council on Education in June, 1958. A shortened version was published in the *Educational Record,* July, 1959.

[2] Speech to the American Council on Education, Oct. 10, 1958.

[3] I find average costs per resident student, exclusive of those irrelevant for higher education, in 1955–56 for public IHL were $750. I also estimate that unit current educational costs per student would have to rise by 40 per cent, or $300. This total of $1,050 should be increased by at least $250 for capital costs ($1 billion per year for more than 4 million students). Hence the unit cost would be about $1,300.

[4] But D. Wolfle and J. G. Smith have shown that for men of roughly equal ability, the income of college students greatly exceeds that of noncollege students (see "Occupational Value of Education for Superior High-school Graduates," *Journal of Higher Education,* 1956, pp. 38–39).

[5] Cf., for example, the views of the president of Stephens College, who is impressed by the high incomes of the college graduate: J. M. Wood, "The Stephens College Fiscal Policy," *Journal of Higher Education,* October, 1933, p. 353. In reply to my position Neiswanger expressed skepticism concerning the material gains of higher education, and also suggests that these are irrelevant considerations: W. A. Neiswanger, "Tuition Policy and Benefits Received," *Educational Review,* July, 1959, esp. pp., 194–195.

[5a] See my *Market for College Graduates,* 1949, esp. part I, Chaps. 1–3, 6.

[6] Estimate by P. C. Glick and H. P. Miller, "Educational Level and Potential Income," *American Sociological Review,* 1956; cf. T. W. Schultz, *Education and Economic Growth,* p. 79, where he estimates the gain at $137,000 for graduates of past.

[7] See S. E. Harris (ed.), *Higher Education in the United States: The Economic Problems,* 1960; also D. S. Bridgman in Office of Education Bulletin 9, 1930, and *Journal of Engineering Education,* no. 3, November, 1931, p. 175.

[8] Cf. *Research in Economics of Higher Education,* Office of Education, May 31–June 1, 1960. (Mimeographed.)

[9] See O. Eckstein in *Higher Education in the United States: The Economic Problems,* 1960.

[10] *Ibid.* Eckstein finds that prepayment for ten years at a rate of interest of 3 per cent would provide $4,000 for four years of college at an annual cost of $365 ($383 inclusive of insurance of parent). For twenty years of insurance and an annual rate of 5 per cent only $130 (and $143 inclusive of insurance) would be required. These figures suggest the wisdom of a twenty-year policy and not one under the control of savings banks that pay little.

[11] Obviously, not all students would have to borrow. With a median family income of $7,000 (and about $7,600 for the family at age of sending son or daughter to college), it is doubtful that more than 60 per cent would have to borrow.

Here are some very rough calculations of the sums required for a loan program of vast proportions and one which will not be achieved for many years:

I assume 60 per cent of families borrow $1,000 per year in 1960. Hence, 2½ million × $1,000 = $2.5 billion.

I assume that by the year 2000 the number of students would be 8 million and only 40 per cent need to borrow. (For incomes are much higher. Here average loans would be $3,000 per year. The average cost of higher education would be about $5,000 in 1960 prices.)

Hence, new loans equal (8 million × 40 per cent) × $3,000, per year—$9.6 billion. Average over 40 years = approximately $6 billion per year.

This seems like a large sum, but our GNP by the year 2000 should be around $1,300 to $1,400 billion, and the annual rise of total debt about $100 billion (in 1960 prices). The required sum would be only a small part of the rise of indebtedness; and by the year 2000 new indebtedness would be matched by repayments which would be a substantial part of new debts incurred.

[12] S. E. Harris, *The Incidence of Inflation or Who Gets Hurt?* Joint Economic Committee of Congress of the United States, Study Paper 7, 1959, p. 81.

[13] I am greatly indebted to the 220 able economists who took so much of their time, often writing brilliant essays in response to the questionnaire. I also owe much to Reginald Green who assembled the answers and contributed so much to their analysis.

[14] On the other hand, one economist said that under the circumstances he counted a doubling of tuitions a positive good, because it served to restrict enrollment to the numbers that could be accommodated by the supply of instructors available, at present and in the foreseeable future.

[15] On the other hand, one economist was of the opinion that second-rate private IHL are a kind of "inferior goods" and as such would be hurt less than better private IHL.

[16] H. S. Commager, (*The New York Times Magazine,* Feb. 26, 1961, and comment by S. E. Harris, *ibid.,* Mar. 12, 1961) strongly urged that the Federal government should assume the tuition charge. I suggested that tuition fees might rise and a large part be used for scholarships. Thus charges would more nearly match ability to pay.

PART THREE

SCHOLARSHIPS

Chapter 11

INTRODUCTORY: SCHOLARSHIPS[1]

PRELIMINARY CONSIDERATIONS

In the nineteenth century the college offered scholarships generally to enable a poor student of ability to go to college. In more recent years a scholarship has been used more for another purpose, namely, to enroll in a college the type of student the college wants. He is likely to be a man of quality but not necessarily one with high scholastic standing. In the competition for students colleges increasingly use scholarship funds in order to achieve the type of student body that the college considers desirable. Of late many have criticized the use of the scholarship as a recruiting device.[2]

According to the American Association of College Registrars and Admissions Officers, "Scholarships are best understood as recognition of scholarly or academic excellence. It is possible, however, to have scholarships that recognize excellence in a particular field; this field may or may not be one that has been officially regarded as academic; for instance, it might be physics or literature or music or athletics."

According to the Council of Financial Aid to Education, "A scholarship, rightly conceived, is a grant made to an exceptionally able but financially needy student which will help in substantial measure to close the gap between his or his family's available resources and the total annual cost to him of a college education."[3]

In a book on the economics of higher education scholarships perhaps should not occupy a very large amount of space. In all, as I have indicated earlier, scholarship funds *offered by the institutions,* inclusive of fellowships, prizes, etc., amounted to $131 million in 1957–58. In 1955–56, of $99 million available, endowment income, gifts, and government appropriations provided $53 million, or more than half; the remainder came from general funds. Of course this percentage varies. At Columbia in 1956, for example, endowed funds provided 29 per cent.[4] In relation to total educational and general expenditures of $3.6 billion in 1957–58, the sums involved are not large. Indeed, in relation to the total faculty salaries, scholarships and the like are of the order of about 10 per cent. Therefore the argument that the colleges in diverting, say, $50 million from other funds into scholarships debase standards of faculty pay is not a strong one. If all these diversions were eliminated, faculty salaries would rise only by about 10 per cent. And it is not clear that the sums saved would be available for faculty salaries. Furthermore, an increase in scholarships facilitates much larger rises in tuition.

In another sense scholarships are of great importance for IHL and especially the private ones. According to President William Fels of Bennington College, 155 member colleges of the CSS awarded 41 per cent of the undergraduate scholarships in dollar value. The remainder were distributed among 1,650 institutions.[5] According to Frank Bowles of the College Entrance Examination Board, 50 IHL account for half the scholarship money. The nine Ivy colleges accounted for about 8 per cent of the undergraduate scholarships and but 1.4 per cent of undergraduate resident enrollment.[6]

In the high-tuition institutions there is a tendency to tie the value of scholarships to the level of tuition. In other words, scholarships are a means by which tuition tends to be raised without discouraging poor students of ability. The reader will find a discussion elsewhere of Yale University, where in the last few years approximately 50 per cent of the additional funds received from tuition were diverted to scholarships.

Whereas President DuBridge of the California Institute of Technology finds in scholarships a financial advantage, in that they enable the college to increase tuition fees, representatives of the land-grant colleges take a somewhat different viewpoint. Their spokesmen often contend that the effect of a scholarship program is to enable the colleges to increase their fees and therefore make it more expensive to go to college. Instead of favoring, for example, a Federal scholarship or fellowship program, they prefer that the Federal government use the money to subsidize the institutions and therefore enable them to improve the quality of their product rather than the quantity: " . . . A federal scholarship program is likely to have the effect of inducing institutions to increase their charges to students, thus making college attendance more difficult for non-scholarship students and requiring still more additional scholarship aid."[7] Any rise of enrollment resulting from increases in scholarships is likely to be especially costly to public IHL, where tuition is a small part of costs.

Two other objectives of scholarships should not go unnoticed: First, use of the scholarship as a means of inviting the interest of the public in classroom achievements. For example, it has been suggested that there might be a Congressional medal for students who obtain Federal scholarships, with the result that students would be acclaimed for their scholarship even more than they are now for their athletics. Scientists especially have stressed this particular objective of scholarships. They therefore do not demand large numbers of scholarships, but an adequate number to interest students, the public, and those who manage our schools.

For example, President DuBridge testified as follows:[8]

If a scholarship program is widely advertised through the country it can attract the interest of students who might not otherwise hear about college opportunities. It can hold up a goal to even a boy on the farm in a remote suburban area who would not otherwise hear about college opportunities. . . .

It will dig out the students of high intellectual capacity who now may not think about going to college or who may be prevented by financial barriers. . . .

To my mind, however, possibly the most important aspect of a scholarship program properly conceived is that if the requirements for winning a scholarship are properly set, if they include a stiff examination, let us say, and if they include requirements that the student shall have had some good tough subject, like mathematics, foreign language, and other things, then if there are a lot of students around the country that are going to compete for scholarships, they will demand of their high schools that they get these subjects and that they get a good training in them. . . .

A second objective of the scholarship programs of late has been to divert students into areas where there seem to be great deficiencies of manpower. In fact, the important bills before the Congress in 1958 had elements of this particular objective in them. It is of some interest, however, that most of the experts, inclusive of those in the sciences, objected to these so-called "crash programs" and would not give special treatment, for example, to students who were going to concentrate on the sciences.

In the discussions of scholarships in the 1950s much attention has been given to the problem of the effect of an increased number of scholarships upon the institutions that receive the students obtaining scholarships. Since the colleges pay out more than they receive back in tuition per student, the view is widely held that a scholarship program aggravates the economic position of the institution. Hence many have argued that the institution should also have a supplement if it is asked to take on additional students. In many instances, especially under grants from foundations and corporations, donors have given the institution a supplement to make up for the difference between tuition and the cost per student. The fellowship programs under the National Defense Education Act and the Wilson Foundation provide this type of supplementary aid.

The issues are not as simple as they have been made out to be, however. For example, during the early postwar period, when IHL were receiving millions of GIs, the revenue received from the government as a rule exceeded the additional cost. One reason for this was of course that the institutions considered the excess of students above normal numbers temporary and were not prepared to provide facilities to match the increased number of students. In other words, there was excess capacity and also a disposition to crowd facilities, and the additional cost per additional student was less than the average cost for all students. Indeed, state institutions tended to raise their fees considerably, because as they enrolled more students, costs rose more than tuition: with tuition equaling but a small percentage of total costs, it was quite clear that if enrollment should increase, say, by 25 or 50 or 100 per cent, the additional cost per student would exceed the tuition that was being paid for the additional student. The state universities therefore met this particular issue by substantially increasing their fees for GI students, frequently up to the level of the nonresident fee. In many instances the government did not allow the nonresident fee, on the ground that it exceeded the cost of instruction.[9]

In the year 1961 the situation is somewhat different. Where institutions are operating with relatively *low* tuition in relation to total costs and where excess capacity is low, any substantial rise of enrollment as a result of scholarship grants would indeed involve losses to the institution. But colleges may profit if they simply accept these scholarships and allow holders of scholarships to squeeze out other students.

Another issue widely discussed is the question of the net contribution of scholarship funds. Obviously one of the major objectives is to attract able students with low economic status who otherwise would not go to college. Later on I discuss the whole issue of attrition of these able students, and I shall not dwell on this subject here. Undoubtedly attrition due to low economic resources is an important factor, though it is very difficult to say exactly how important it is. Low motivation, not tied to economic conditions, is of course also an important factor in discouraging students from going to college.

What troubles some is the point that many who receive scholarships would go to college even without the scholarships. In view of the small contribution of scholarships to total costs of the average student, there undoubtedly is much in this position. Follow-up studies, that show students who are refused scholarships and then go to college in any case, further support this position.[10]

In this discussion, I have neglected the problem of outside scholarship and fellowship funds, that is, the grants not under the control of colleges. These are important, and rough estimates based on Hollis's study point to an amount equal to one-half of the total under control of colleges, that is, one-third of all. But the proportion varies. Strong institutions attract these funds. At Columbia, for example, outside funds are not one-third but close to 60 per cent of the total. For the political science faculty, the outside funds are as much as three-quarters of the total; for law, only one-quarter.[11] According to the National Science Foundation study *Graduate Student Enrollment and Support in American Colleges and Universities,* the colleges in 1954 provided 65 per cent of all stipends for graduate students (fellowships and scholarships). The Federal government provided 19 per cent, and other sources provided 16 per cent. The median values were highest for the Federal government.

FOOTNOTES

[1] The reader will find a statistical compilation and discussion in the appendixes to Part Three which include material on amounts available for scholarships, sources, relation to total income (expenses), distribution among institutions, historical trends, and so on.

[2] J. D. Russell, *The Finance of Higher Education,* 1954, p. 233; and "Bidding on Brains," *The New York Times,* May 25, 1954.

[3] See the excellent book by D. D. West, *Background for National Scholarship Policy,* 1956, pp. 10–11.

[4] HEW, *Statistics of Higher Education: Receipts, Expenditures and Property, 1955–56,* p. 50; R. G. Moon, Jr., "Who Should Pay the Bill?" *College Board Review,* Spring, 1958, p. 21; *The Educational Future of Columbia University,* 1957, p. 225.

[5] W. C. Fels, "College Scholarship Service," *College Board Review,* May, 1954.

[6] My calculations.

[7] Hearings, House Subcommittee of the Committe on Education and Labor, *Scholarship and Loan Program,* 1958, part 3, pp. 1659 and 1664.

[8] *Ibid.* part 2, p. 922.

[9] *Readjustment Benefits: Education and Training and Employment and Unemployment, a Report on Veterans' Benefits in the United States by the President's Commission on Veterans' Benefits,* Staff Report, 9, part *B,* House Committee Print 291, 1956, pp. 75–79.

[10] R. G. King, "Financial Thresholds to College," *College Board Review,* Spring, 1957, p. 21 *et seq.;* and R. G. Moon, Jr., "Aid Program: From Application to Award," *ibid.,* Winter, 1957, p. 14 *et seq.*

[11] *The Educational Future of Columbia University,* 1957, p. 222.

Chapter 12

SCHOLARSHIPS AND CHOICE OF COLLEGE

FREE CHOICE AND GAINS OF PRESTIGE IHL

Before turning to the problem of the source of scholarship funds, I discuss one important issue that has been widely debated. Under most scholarship programs the student is given the choice of college. Of course, should Yale offer a scholarship, the student is ordinarily expected to study at Yale. But what if a foundation or a business corporation or the government offers scholarships?

In the past, under most scholarship programs—of the Federal government, foundations, or business corporations—the student could choose his college. The result has been a tendency for recipients of scholarships and fellowships from such sources to attend a limited number of prestige colleges and universities, a result especially likely where the scholarships are tied to costs. Leaders in the states which lose their able students especially to the prestige institutions of the Northeast are much annoyed by this tendency of scholarship programs to redistribute their able young men and women geographically. They feel that they lose talent badly needed at home and more important to them than to the more advanced communities of the Northeast with their higher incomes. The first volume of hearings of the Elliott Committee (House Committee on Scholarship and Loan Program, 1958), contains frequent comments and protests against a scholarship policy which causes this kind of migration.

NATIONAL MERIT SCHOLARS

In the nationwide competition for the Merit Scholars (financed by the Ford Foundation and 58 other foundations and corporations in 1957), there were 6,428 finalists in 1957 who were " . . . among the top one or two per cent of the nation's most promising high school seniors." The corporation awarded scholarships to 827, with an average stipend (related to need) of $648. Stipends varied from $100 to $2,200; grants to colleges ranged from nothing to $750, with a mean of $529 for private institutions and $144 for tax-supported IHL. In some respects, the college grants are surprising; for with low tuition, the tax-controlled institution may well incur larger additional costs than private ones in accepting the Merit Scholar.[1]

In Table 12-2, I list the 11 IHL which attracted the largest numbers of these Merit Scholars (based on 1956 results). These 11 institutions accounted for 41.7 per cent of the winners in 1956 and 35.5 per cent in 1957. Harvard, MIT, Yale, Princeton, and Stanford, the top five in 1957, enrolled almost one-quarter of the total. It is of some interest that no public institution was in the first 11 in 1956, though in 1957 the University

TABLE 12-1

National Merit Scholars and Undergraduate Enrollment, Per Cent in IHL, 1956

IHL ranking	Merit scholars	Undergraduate enrollment
Top*...................	10.5	0.2
Top 3†.................	19.6	0.5
Top 10‡...............	39.3	1.7
Top 20§...............	54.1	5.4
All others¶............	45.9	92.2

* Harvard (57 winners).

† Also MIT (31) and California Institute of Technology (18).

‡ Also Cornell (17), Princeton (16), Yale (16), Rice (15), Swarthmore (15), Radcliffe (14), Stanford (14).

§ Also Duke (13), University of Chicago (11), University of Michigan (9), Williams (8), Oberlin (8), Wellesley (7), Notre Dame (7), Iowa State (6), Northwestern (5).

¶ 249 other colleges enrolled winners.

Source: National Merit Corporation, Annual Report, 1956, 1957; and HEW, Statistics of Higher Education: Faculty, Students, and Degrees, 1953–54. (My computations.)

of Michigan tied for seventh place, with 19 winners. Actually, the 9 public institutions with 5 or more recipients accounted for 70 Merit Scholars in 1957. The 9 top private institutions had almost four times as many winners; although they account for only 1 to 2 per cent of resident enrollment, they had 31 per cent of the Merit Scholars. In relation to enrollment, the private institutions attracted seven to eight times as many Merit Scholars as the public IHL. These figures point to one conclusion of some importance: when outstanding students have free choice, they tend to select the private prestige institutions. Under the Merit program, stipends are related to needs; and since costs are lower in public IHL, the stipends also are lower. Hence the advantage of low fees means nothing to the students under the Merit program.

In 1956 the highest winner, Harvard, accounted for 10.5 per cent of the Merit winners as against 0.2 per cent of total undergraduate enrollment. Concentration of winners is also suggested by the fact that 54 per cent of them went to only 20 IHL. These institutions accounted for only 5.4 per cent of total undergraduate enrollment, as Table 12-1 shows.

To suggest the migration problem in more precise terms, I have com-

TABLE 12-2

National Merit Scholars, 11 Top Winners' Choices of IHL (1956),
Numbers and Per Cent, for 1956 and 1957

IHL	1956		1957*	
	Numbers	Per cent	Numbers	Per cent
Harvard..............................	57	10.5	63	7.6
Massachusetts Institute of Technology......	31	5.7	55	6.7
California Institute of Technology.........	18	3.3	19	2.3
Cornell..............................	17	3.1	21	2.5
Yale.................................	16	3.0	26	3.1
Princeton............................	16	3.0	27	3.3
Swarthmore..........................	15	2.8	16	1.9
Rice.................................	15	2.8	18	2.2
Stanford.............................	14	2.6	25	3.0
Radcliffe............................	14	2.6	15	1.8
Duke................................	13	2.4	9	1.1
Total—11 top (basis of 1956).........	226	41.7	294	35.5
Total...............................	542	....	827	

* In 1960–61, 1,111, or 35 per cent of all scholars, were resident in these 11 IHL, and they accounted for almost 40 per cent of the scholars that had graduated.

Source: Compiled and calculated from National Merit Scholarship Corporation, *Second Annual Report for the Year Ending January 30, 1957*, table 4, and 1960 report, table 5.

TABLE 12-3

Region	Nationwide resident college enrollment, 1953–54, per cent	Scholars originating in region, 1957, per cent	Scholars going to college in region, 1957, per cent
South..............	22	29	16*
Northeast..........	42	21	44*

* I was unable to identify the location of several institutions, and hence the results may be slightly off.

Source: Compiled and calculated from National Merit Scholarship Corporation, *Second Annual Report for the Year Ending January 30, 1957*, table 4; and *Statistics of Higher Education: Faculty, Students, and Degrees, 1953–54*, pp. 100–101.

pared statistics of Merit Scholars in 1957 for the Northeast and the South in Table 12-3. Some aspects of this material are striking. The South received about one-third more and the Northeast one-half fewer of the scholars than suggested by the percentage of resident college enrollment. Possibly an important explanation here is the large proportion of part-time students in the Northeast. In its contribution the South lost heavily. Whereas the South contributed 29 per cent of the Merit Scholars, only 16 per cent remained there. Institutions in the Northeast enrolled more than twice its percentage of winners—an indication of large migrations northeastward.

THE FEDERAL PROGRAMS

In the original GI Bill of 1944, the Congress allowed students tuition plus a subsistence allowance. This tuition allowance could be as high as $500 if the college charged that much. At that time $500 was more than most institutions charged, and students were inclined to select institutions with high tuition fees, often prestige institutions. (Under certain conditions the government would also finance tuition in excess of $500.)

Under the second GI Bill, (Public Law 550 of the 82d Congress), following the outbreak of the Korean conflict, the approach differed from that under Public Law 346, the legislation associated with World War II. In the post-Korean legislation the government did not compensate the institution for tuition but provided the student with a fixed sum of money to take care of his subsistence and tuition. It was as usual up to the student to select the college. The allowance for full-time institutional program was put at $110 per month for the student without dependents, $135 for the veteran with one dependent, and $160 if he had more than one dependent. Since the amount of money available was not large and the government did not offer to pay tuition, the student might be expected to a greater degree than before to select a college with low tuition.

In 1953 the Office of Education investigated the distribution of first-time male Korean veterans between public and private institutions and among institutions according to tuition charged. This investigation followed numerous protests that the policy under Public Law 550 (1952) would discriminate against the private institution.

Actually a significant difference emerged:

Full-time Students at Public Institutions, First Time, Fall, 1953
Per cent of Korean veterans.............. 63.1
Per cent of nonveterans................. 58.7

Here Korean veterans seem to choose public IHL (low tuition) in somewhat larger numbers than nonveterans. They also tend to prefer low tuition IHL more than nonveterans.

Korean veterans	Per cent of total
Per cent of all first-time students, fall, 1953	12.5
At tuition of less than $100	12.5
At tuition of $100–$299	13.5
At tuition of $300–$499	12.6
At tuition of $500 or more	9.7

Of course these figures do not reveal how much better the private institutions would have fared under the arrangements provided by the original GI Bill.[2]

This change in policy under Public Law 550 was related to some extent to the issues mentioned above, but apparently a more important influence on the change of policy was the difficulty of negotiating tuition fees with state institutions under Public Law 346.[3]

Under the National Defense Education Act of 1958, the fear of diverting students to prestige and high-tuition institutions is also evident. The distribution of loan funds among states on the basis of full-time enrollment and the repudiation of the scholarship program reflect the fear of migrations to the prestige institutions. (As I read these proofs early in 1962, President Kennedy is asking for a Federal scholarship program.)

PROTESTS AGAINST CURRENT PRACTICES

Undoubtedly the general practice of allowing the student free choice of a college tends to result in gains for prestige institutions. The amount of the subsidy is, of course, a relevant factor. Where the amount of money available for tuition is small, the result should favor the smaller and less well-known institutions. At any rate, recent scholarship policies which encourage the trek to the prestige institutions have caused a considerable volume of protest. Nowhere is this more clear than in discussions of scholarship policy under the proposed Federal programs of 1958 following the Sputnik crisis. In the 3,700 pages of evidence before the House and Senate Committees dealing with these problems, the issue of freedom of choice of students under the scholarship program received much attention.

For example, the representatives of the American Council on Education, spokesmen for institutions of higher learning, said to the Senate Committee:[4]

The objectives of a Federal scholarship program should be to offer the opportunities of college education to qualified students who would otherwise be denied it for lack of financial resources. Therefore Federal funds should not be used to encourage students financially able to attend an adequate institution merely to seek admission to other institutions at higher cost.

In other words, the position of the influential American Council on Education is that scholarships should be modest but adequate to make it possible for poor boys to go to colleges near their homes. If they want to go to prestige places far away, then it is their responsibility to obtain the additional finance. John Morse, the financial vice president of Rensselaer Polytechnic Institute said (in a letter to S. E. Harris of November 13, 1958):

The scholarships should be elastic according to need, but pegged to only one variable—the financial strength of the family. The two variable National Merit approaches (the other variable being the cost of the institution to which the scholar goes) give too great advantage to the strong, expensive, private institution.

Before the House Committee the representative of the American Council said:[5]

On the other hand, we have tried to make very clear here that if he could get additional scholarships from other institutions, or perhaps earn money himself, he ought to have the choice of going to another institution and not lose his Federal scholarship. In other words, let us suppose that he gets $800 from the Federal Government. Maybe he could go to a local institution for that, but if he wants to go to Princeton, or Harvard, or some other place, it might cost him $2,600. Let us suppose that he could get $800 or $1,000 from the institution and he could earn $600 or $700. If he is ambitious enough to do that we feel that he ought to be allowed to do it and should not be penalized by having anything taken away from him because he goes to a more expensive institution.

R. A. Morgan, director of the Purdue Research Foundation, took a similar position in discussing the issue of fellowships. He pointed out that although there are 67 institutions in this country giving Ph.D. programs in engineering, the present fellowships in engineering are going to about ten or fifteen of them.[6]

So it would be most desirable if the fellowship program could be broadened so that a larger number would be available through the schools themselves if the quality could be maintained, so that we would have these fellowships spread to 60 or 65 institutions rather than to ten or twenty institutions.

The last quotation reflects a widely presented view, namely, that to a considerable degree Federal scholarships and fellowships should be tied to either a particular state or a particular institution; i.e., the institution would get the money and could then offer the scholarship or fellowship itself. The student would not receive the money and then choose his college. The 1958 National Defense Education Act reflected this view in its fellowship program.

The representative of the American Council also said:[7]

I think the general opinion of the Council people has been that even though you step down further into what might be called the high ability of the population of some states, in [some] regions, than you would in others, it is wise to keep it by states, because, after all, you are only dealing with a very small per cent of the upper group, so that in any state or region, regardless perhaps of some lack of opportunities, you would not get unqualified people.

You probably know that there has been criticism of that sort of thing—that is of concentrating awards in certain areas in connection with even the Rhodes Scholarship awards and with the Fulbright awards.

In general, the representatives of the public institutions were not inclined to favor large scholarship programs. Undoubtedly this is explained in part by the fact that a large scholarship program might encourage students to go to private rather than public institutions. Public institutions have a large advantage in tuition charges, and a scholarship program of large proportions might reduce this advantage, diverting students from public to private institutions, especially to the high-prestige private institutions. The Merit Scholarship program confirms this fear.

Public institutions prefer to have additional Federal money put into operating funds of institutions rather than into student subsidies. Their position is based on the premise that as enrollment rises, they will require much additional money to maintain their present standards. Thus, after discussing the serious financial problems of state institutions, representatives of the Western Interstate Commission for Higher Education wrote:[8]

In this situation it would be a disservice both to higher education and to the students it is primarily designed to serve if the public were to believe that a large-scale program of financial aid to students provided any kind of solution to the tremendous problems of financing institutions of higher education.

This clash between the public and the private institutions or between the nonprestige and prestige institutions is a real one and should not be dismissed too lightly. One might expect that all presidents of prestige institutions would be in favor of the freedom of choice. But this is not so. For example, President DuBridge, of the California Institute of Technology, testified as follows:

I do not think God gave any particular state more brains than any other state. He may have given them more money but not more brains. There are just as many smart people in State A as in State B and the fraction of population having brains is probably about the same in the states. But the education systems vary for a variety of reasons. So I think this would justify a state allocation, so the best brains in each state would have a chance and not be handicapped because their particular state happens to have low educational standards and have not been able to afford better schools let us say.

Thus President DuBridge favors a state allocation of undergraduate scholarships. He would even go so far as to favor, with some modifications, state allocations at the graduate level.[9]

A clear distinction must be made between allocating the scholarships by state (or regionally)—President DuBridge's arguments apply to this—and allocating the enrollment of scholarship recipients by state, for example, by administering the scholarship program through the institutions. Because of the tremendous variation in quality among colleges, the second method might result in a considerable misuse of resources.

After discussing the Woodrow Wilson Fellowship program which he had directed, President Goheen of Princeton University testified as follows:[10]

The problem of these nominees wishing to go to a very few institutions was very acute for us, and I had enough chances to get around the country and to interview lots of academic people to be quite convinced that in many cases these judgments which took boys from, say, the Midwest to the Ivy League institutions were just simply judgments of prejudice. They had nothing to do with what the academic excellence of the institution was.

This quote from President Goheen does suggest that, even with allocations by states and free choice of institutions, there are problems. But this seems to me the best approach, especially if, as we note elsewhere, counseling is greatly improved.

Many have commented on the increasing attraction of prestige institutions for the able students. For example, Frank Bowles, head of the College Entrance Examination Board

. . . was immediately struck by the extent to which the proportion of superior candidates from the smaller colleges had shrunk while the candidates from the university colleges had increased in both number and quality.

This change in the quality of candidates for graduate work had occurred in eight years. The heads of the colleges thus losing in the competition are not happy about it.[11]

Undoubtedly, as has often been claimed, one explanation of this trend is to be found in the increase of scholarships and fellowships which are tied to the cost of going to the college of the student's choice. The result, since it makes no financial difference to the student, is that he tends to pick the high-cost institution. A tendency of the CSS (College Scholarship Service) institutions to tie their scholarships to need, in turn related to varying costs, further encourages this trend, as do the National Merit Scholarship Corporation (NMSC) scholarships. In fact members of the research staff of the NMSC have even claimed that the nonprestige institutions, by agreement to abide by the principle of basing stipends on needs and costs, further strengthen the position of the prestige "cartel."[12] The heavy concentration of scholarships in a limited number of IHL has often been observed. Three per cent of the colleges, that is, 60 institutions, accounted for thirty-four per cent of the scholarship funds. Whereas Yeshiva University had $352 per student, the University of California at Los Angeles had available only $6 per student. Here the writers might have pointed out that the tuition and fee differential in favor of UCLA was about $650. In this same year the average per student in the nation was about $30; but Yeshiva, Chicago, Johns Hopkins, Yale Vassar, and Harvard averaged $352, $268, $211, $198, $188, and $186, respectively.[13]

ALLOCATION OF AID ON NATIONAL OR STATE BASES

A related problem should not escape us. It was noted in the discussion of the NMSC that winners tend to concentrate in a limited number of *institutions*. The test used, an aptitude test, if applied on the same basis all over the country, would result in a heavy concentration of winners in a relatively small number of *states*. But the NMSC now allocates awards among states on the basis of their ratio of high school seniors to all high school seniors. Hence a student in New York State may not receive an award though his test grades may be much higher than a student in (say) Montana with a much lower grade. The theory behind the current allocation is that students should not be penalized just because of inferior schools and grades below the national level. Fred Hechinger of *The New York Times* observed what might happen if the distribution were on a national basis.

"The Westinghouse Science Talent Search provides a good indication of what happens if a test is given on an across-the-nation basis of merit. This year New York State captured 40.7 per cent of all Westinghouse prizes and honorable mentions."

A Western Dean observed that " . . . there were more students in New York State alone who scored higher on the test used in this scholarship program than did any student in the 16 lower states, and yet who did not get scholarships because they did not score high enough to get a New York scholarship. . . . "[14] Another support for the present procedure might be found in the inadequacies of the tests used, a subject which I shall discuss more fully later.

But I am not convinced the present procedure is the best from the national interest. Indeed some allowance should be made for inadequate preparation and even socioeconomic status, which are reflected in lower aptitude scores. Nevertheless, an equal distribution on the basis of high school seniors does mean that large numbers of Merit Scholars do not achieve as much in college and later as those who might have been selected on a national basis. Adequacy of training is one important ingredient of later achievement. A suggested compromise for distribution of Merit Scholars might be half on a national score and one-half allocated on a state-by-state basis.

Incidentally, on the basis of material published in the 1960 NMSC report, I find that scholars from the 10 poorest states (1957 per capita income) rose by 60 per cent from 1956 to 1960, and by 92 per cent in the 10 richest states. Hence, whatever the theory, the trends do not support the view of increasing attention to the poor states—part of the difference is explained by greater population gains of rich states.

RESTRICTIONS ON FREE CHOICE

Two other programs raise related problems. The National Defense Education Act (NDEA) fellowships are distributed with a view to getting wider representation of institutions for graduate work. Here the net result is that on the whole students are weaned away from the best graduate schools by the offer of generous fellowships by the government if the student elects to go to an institution which offers the NDEA fellowships. Here note that, just as a general program with free choice of student and fees tied to costs favors the prestige IHL, a public program that ties the stipend to the institution operates against the interests of the leading IHL. But there is a strong point to be made for the NDEA program. We need more capacity for turning out good Ph.Ds.

Under the Woodrow Wilson Fellowship program, a student receives a fellowship on the assumption that he is seriously thinking of teaching. He may choose his college—but not the college of his undergraduate study. By limiting the number of fellows that any one IHL can accept (at this time Harvard alone), the foundation has deprived students of their first choice, and the better institutions of providing the best instruction for the best students.[15]

Here is what Dean Peter Elder of Harvard said:

1) . . . To see to it that a sizable number of men are *not prevented* from going where they wish (if they can get admitted). To turn the coin around, any scholarship program which more or less *forces* (however tactfully) a first-class man to go to a place to study which, however *generally* good it may be, is not as good in that *particular* field as the place of the student's first choice is likely to do two serious harms. First, to the student, for he will not be as well educated as he might. Second, to the whole system of higher education, since without many of the ablest students present, institutions may find their special pinnacles of excellence being dulled down to meet a lower level. Each would be a *national* loss.

CONCLUSION

Many have been struck by the increased enrollment of able students in the prestige institutions. Their large command of scholarship resources, the increasingly effective use of these funds (e.g., through the College

Scholarship Service), their more aggressive seeking out of the able, the availability of outside scholarships and fellowships which are tied not only to need but also to the cost of attending the institution—all these have encouraged the flow of talent to prestige institutions, most of which are in the Northeast, and also the migrations generally from the South and West to the East.

Increasing awareness of the direction of movement has brought rising opposition to Federal scholarships or fellowships with stipends tied to varying costs of attendance, and restricting free choice to the students. A reflection of complaints by leaders in the South and West, inclusive of spokesmen for public IHL, is to be found in the change-over from methods of financing GIs under World War II to those used after the Korean conflict and in the NDEA fellowships. The NMSC scholarships, which are distributed on a state rather than a national basis, provide one approach toward reducing the concentration of scholars in the prestige institutions. When (say) Arkansas gains in Merit Scholars over New York through this approach, a choice of nonprestige institutions becomes more likely. In general, a case can be made against excessive flow of talent to the prestige IHL; but there is danger also in restricting students' choice too much and, through favoring the badly educated, in reducing the net contribution of higher education.

All this is related to a broader question treated later. The scholarship winners were often young men and women with backgrounds which provided them with intellectual experience and training and orientation toward higher education. "Few boys down from the mountains, or up from the wrong side of the tracks, are found on the scholarship lists." The system was likened to the Oxford system where " . . . 60 per cent of the students are on scholarship, but they still come from the privileged class." This kind of analysis was frequently found among the 220 answers from fellow economists. This was the type of young men and women that the West and South were not anxious to lose. Many would be future leaders.

FOOTNOTES

[1] National Merit Scholarship Corporation, *Second Annual Report, for the Year Ending June 30, 1957*, pp. 2, 15, and 23.

[2] See *Readjustment Benefits: Education and Training and Employment and Unemployment, a Report on Veterans' Benefits in the United States by the President's Commission on Veterans' Benefits*, Staff Report 9, House Committee Print 291, pp. 105–106; HEW, *Advance Summary of Final Data on Enrollment of Korean Veterans and Male Non-veteran Students, Fall, 1953*, Apr. 30, 1954. (Mimeographed.)

[3] For details on the issues arising from the Federal scholarships, see *Readjustment Benefits: . . .* , *op. cit.*, especially part 1, chaps. 3–5; and R. G. Axt, *The Federal Government and Financing Higher Education*, 1952, chap. 6.

[4] *Hearings on Science and Education for National Defense, Senate Committee on Labor and Public Welfare,* 1958, p. 406.

[5] *Hearings and Scholarship and Loan Programs, House Committee on Education and Labor,* 1958, p. 678.

[6] *Hearings on Science and Education for National Defense, op. cit.,* p. 819.

[7] *Hearings on Scholarship and Loan Programs, op. cit.,* p. 675.

[8] *Ibid.,* p. 459.

[9] *Ibid.,* p. 931.

[10] *Ibid.,* p. 1091.

[11] F. H. Bowles, "Patterns of Dominance and Choice," *College Board Review,* Spring, 1959, p. 6; and M. Mayer, "Colleges That Are Not Crowded," *Harper's,* February, 1959, p. 48.

[12] J. L. Holland and L. Kent, *The Concentration of Scholarship Funds and Its Implication for Education,* 1960.

[13] *Ibid.*

[14] "Education in Review," *The New York Times,* Nov. 8, 1958; *Hearings on Scholarship and Loan Programs, op. cit.,* pp. 529–533.

[15] Letter of Apr. 21, 1959, Dean Peter Elder to Sir Hugh Taylor, President of the Woodrow Wilson National Fellowship Program.

Chapter 13

MORE VIEWS ON SCHOLARSHIPS

A LIMITED PROGRAM?

In presenting its case for scholarship in 1958, the Eisenhower administration emphasized two aspects of this problem:

1. The administration wanted a program adequate to interest all students of high ability. In other words, there should be enough scholarships and fellowships to attract the attention of the able student.

2. The administration was anxious that the amount made available should not be so large that the other contributors would be discouraged or would withdraw. Partly for this reason they hit upon the total of 10,000 scholarships per year or 40,000 in all, and a much smaller number of fellowships.[1]

In a similar vein the American Council on Education urged a limited scholarship and fellowship program with relatively low stipends. Here again, as urged by representatives of state institutions, the program was intended not to discourage other contributors, and not to provide so many scholarships and fellowships that the cost of operation of IHL would greatly increase in a period of insufficient funds. They also felt that there should be incentives for students to go to college near their own homes. Others (e.g., Vice President John Morse of Rensselaer Polytechnic Institute) held that a Federal program would discourage others, and hence to be effective it must be very large.

In its Second Report to the President,[2] the President's Committee on Education beyond the High School estimated that

. . . it would be desirable for "effective scholarships" to be made available to as many as the top 20 per cent of qualified high school graduates, on the basis of need. Coupled with each scholarship should be a separate grant to the institution where the scholarship is honored, to make up at least a substantial part of the difference between the tuition and actual cost of educating the student. To finance such a program could require as much as three-quarters of a billion dollars annually by 1970 even without the institutional grant feature.

By "effective scholarships" the Committee meant scholarships which pay at least half the cost of tuition and maintenance, awarded on the basis of proved intellectual aptitude and achievement and permitting unrestricted use of the money not otherwise available to the student. Although the 1957 Committee views were similar to those of the President's Commission of 1947, the Committee's recommendations differed greatly from those of the 1947 Commission. The 1957 Committee concluded[3]

. . . that the Federal government should maintain only a residual responsibility for providing student financial assistance, i.e., only after all other groups, private and public, have made their contribution, and only in the light of well-defined overall needs periodically examined.

In its recommendations the Committee suggested recourse to credit and a strong effort on the part of private interests as well as state government to provide the necessary cash for scholarships. The task of the Federal government should be to fill a gap that the others could not fill, giving free choice of course of study and *reasonable* choice of institution to the student. It should make up the difference between tuition and cost of education to the institution wherever possible, basing this payment on average institutional costs in the nation. Here we see a compromise between those who would give the student absolutely free choice and those who would restrict choice to prevent the migration of students to prestige institutions. The report also limited subsidies to the institutions by restricting payments to the difference between tuition and average costs *in the nation*. Again, this is an attempt to appease those supporting low-tuition institutions.[4] It may also have the effect of encouraging high-cost institutions to achieve economies in operation.

The President's Committee made it clear that one reason for their recommendation of effective scholarships was the small proportion of scholarships which pay a substantial part of total expenditures by the student. One study had indicated that in 1950–1954 nearly three-quarters of the scholarships paid less than 20 per cent of total expenses. Another study reveals that in 1952–53 almost half of the scholarships equaled 14 per cent or less of total student income.[5] More recently, average stipends seemed to be about 70 per cent of tuition.

Obviously, another approach to the problem of inadequate resources of students is to keep down the costs of higher education, for example, by having the students go to college near their homes. There is a tendency to provide smaller scholarships to students who live near home, though the difference is not equal to the savings on costs.[6] In fact, I have heard many protests from college administrators in New York State that many of the New York scholarships have gone to students who live at home with relatively small outlays, thus enabling them to use this money for recreation and the like. But a recent study in New York showed that scholarship accounted for a relatively small proportion of student income.

It is not generally known how many students live at home. But one national survey revealed that 51 per cent of the students attended institutions 50 miles or more away from home, and 46 per cent attended institutions within 50 miles (3 per cent unknown). The total living at home was only 31 per cent.[7]

THE CASE AGAINST GENEROUS PROGRAMS

In summary: those who support a program of numerous scholarships, particularly by the Federal government and with relatively high stipends, are impressed by the low incomes of the average American family and the great burden that those with low incomes experience in obtaining a college education. Supporters of large numbers of scholarships at high stipends are inclined to emphasize the superiority of scholarships to work or credit facilities. They are not excessively fearful of further rises in Federal expenditures, or at least they put this type of spending high on the government's priority list.

The proponents of a program of a small number of scholarships and fellowships at relatively modest stipends are fearful of the cost to government of numerous high stipends and are impressed by the waste in the present system, which gives an excessive number of scholarships to students with high family incomes (more on waste later) and which fails to distinguish adequately between commuter and noncommuter costs. They question the necessity of a high stipend when students who apply for scholarships and are denied reappear as students without scholarships. Others insist that a scholarship system favors the profligate and penalizes the thrifty. These are important considerations for those who support relatively modest programs. Many who hold this view are also fearful, as we have already suggested, that a large Federal program will result in movements of students from poor states to the high-income states of the Northeast. They want a program that makes it more difficult for students to migrate in this manner, and they also fear that a large program will put heavy additional burdens on institutions of higher learning. In other words, they prefer a subsidy for operation or construction to large outlays for scholarships. They are, moreover, fearful that a Federal program will discourage state and private programs. Therefore, as John Morse has argued, a Federal program to be effective must be large.

In 1958 Congress, both the House and Senate, held hearings which required about four thousand pages to record and reflected the wisdom of hundreds of witnesses. The quality of evidence was unusually high. What strikes the reader of these hearings is the failure of those in favor of scholarships to present a strong case. Almost no one raised the issue, for example, that a scholarship program would make it possible to raise tuition and therefore to solve some of the economic problems of the IHL. (President DuBridge was a notable exception.) Nor was the point made that if scholarships were available from the Federal or state governments, IHL could divert a large part of the resources now used for scholarships to other purposes. Perhaps the most common argument in the literature, namely, that a scholarship program would save thousands of able students who now do not go to college, received relatively little attention.

In fact, most of the testimony was *against* a scholarship program. Congressman Gwinn took the extreme position that there was not a single boy who could not take care of himself. Coming from affluent Westchester County, he said, " . . . I do not know of a single boy in my community of superior quality that you talk about that has been deprived of a college education if he wanted it. I doubt if you do either. Do you?"

Representatives of the public institutions in particular were critical of any substantial scholarship program. I have given some of their reasons earlier. In discussing various bills before Congress in 1957, Russell Thackrey, Executive Secretary of the American Association of Land-Grant Colleges and State Universities, had been very critical of the large number of scholarship and fellowship bills. His argument, which he repeated in the later proceedings of 1958, was that a large percentage of able boys get to college (a larger percentage than is generally known), that a scholarship program would not attract the able boys who otherwise would not go to college, and finally that the real bottleneck is in facilities and in other resources, such as income for operation, and not in scholarships. He maintains that the issue is one of quality and not of quantity. The representatives of the land-grant colleges thought that what was necessary was a reduction of fees, not large numbers of scholarships. In fact, they argued that state universities already had a comprehensive scholarship program, shown by the low fees that they charge. They were critical of any program that would make it possible to increase fees, and they stressed the relation of more and higher scholarships to the rise of fees.

The Land-Grant College Association in 1956, despite its strong appeal for aid to the college, was willing to accept a scholarship program if it would meet certain tests: a maximum of $750, free choice, decentralized administration, etc. But in 1958 the Association again announced its opposition.[8]

In the words of I. D. Weeks, President of the University of South Dakota, too many students are getting the scholarship habit. He was troubled also that " . . . superior students are drained particularly from the Midwest to the eastern portions of the country. . . . " In the view of

President Weeks, the recent national scholarship programs have taken care of students who would have been taken care of in any case. And in view of the large influx of students, he could see no need for a scholarship program. He pointed out that in his own university of 2,207 students, there were 1,190 car permits. Preferring a loan program to a scholarship program, President Weeks also said that if a Federal program were introduced, then it should be administered on a state basis, therefore putting all states on an equal basis.[9]

For the president of the University of Utah, the crucial issue was that the Federal government was not compensating the universities adequately for ROTC and similar programs. If the Federal government would do this, then the state universities in turn could take care of scholarships and provide adequate resources for other purposes.

The dean of the faculty of Portland State College, representing the Oregon State System of Higher Education, testified that what concerned him was the very large increase of enrollment coming in the next ten years. The major problem in higher education, according to him, was " . . . to provide for these large numbers of young men and women who we know will be clamoring to get into college throughout the country." He was also concerned that if a scholarship program were administered like the National Merit program, rich states would receive a disproportionate number of grants.[10]

Nor was the opposition concentrated in the representatives of public institutions. For example, President Newsom of New York University in a very strong statement emphasized the increased cost to IHL associated with a scholarship program, the failure to provide scholarships for middle-income groups, and the large waste in that many who could go to college without scholarships go now and receive them.

However, it would be interesting to know what percentage of students now going to college on scholarships would attend if scholarship aid were not available. When I posed this question recently before a group of college and university administrators, the estimates given as answers ranged from 90 per cent to 30 per cent with an average of about 80 per cent. If such guesses have any validity, the large scholarship programs now in vogue make a difference of perhaps 3 or 4 per cent in the college enrollment of this country.

Chancellor Kimpton of the University of Chicago wrote:

It has been our pleasant custom in the past like the chorus girl to accept anything but abuse and we are paying a high price for our generosity in accepting generosity. We have accepted scholarships that cost us more to administer than we have received in tuition income; we have accepted billions that drained away from us our precious free money in order to equip and maintain them. . . .

Although he admitted that gifts of money for scholarships were an easy way of helping colleges and arousing support from the student, the parent, the corporation, the stockholder, etc., Chancellor Kimpton insisted that such gifts were not beneficial to the college.

"It varies from institution to institution, but to take an extreme case, the University of Chicago has an annual budget of $20 million and our tuition is approximately $5 million. That means we are paying 75¢ for every 25¢ the student pays or that industry pays if it is providing him with a scholarship.

J. Douglas Brown and Harbison in their excellent book, *High Talent Manpower for Science and Industry,* have also come out against the general scholarship. They oppose the wholesale method of providing scholarships, insisting that the retail method (e.g., against the Wilson or National Merit) is much more effective. They are also critical of the tests used to pick scholars. In their view the usual aptitude test may tell you who is going to win the 100-yard dash, but it tells you nothing about the capacity to last in a marathon. They are also concerned that these tests often divert students away from first-class small colleges. In their view selection of students as well as administration of the funds should be in the hands of individual colleges.

President Wilkinson of Brigham Young University of Utah was also opposed to a scholarship program. According to him,

Over 14 per cent of the students within the state received aid by means of a scholarship, which would be nearly 20 per cent if athletic grants were included, . . . nine per cent of the students received loans from the institutions, and that 39 per cent of the loan funds were not touched. . . . 18.8 per cent obtained part-time employment. . . . It would seem to me that there is no imperative need to demand of the Great White Father in Washington to further encroach upon traditional functions of the State and now start a colossal Federal scholarship.

In an able statement President Goheen of Princeton accepted the principle of scholarships. He did, however, emphasize that colleges need more and better teachers and increased physical facilities, and said that he hoped the Federal government would make some contributions toward improving facilities. He also favored adding to any scholarship program a $500 cost of education payment to the institutions. He seemed to go further in the direction of Federal aid on scholarships than most of the witnesses.[11]

* * *

In summary, college officials are not in agreement on the need for more scholarships, nor on the source of funds for a scholarship program. There are cleavages between public and private institutions, between low- and high-tuition IHL, between those fearful of Federal intervention and those seeking it. These disagreements help explain the poor case made for financial aid by representatives of the colleges before Congress in 1958 and probably help explain the absence of a Federal scholarship program even as late as 1961. A widespread view that scholarship resources are used at less than maximum effectiveness also contributed to the less than enthusiastic support of a Federal scholarship program. The loan program in the National Defense Education Act had a great appeal to the administration, though I suspect for the wrong reason—namely, that it involved a relatively small strain on the budget. In 1961 and 1962 President Kennedy urged a scholarship program, with a payment to the IHL which accepts the scholarship holder.

FOOTNOTES

[1] *Hearings on Scholarship and Loan Programs, House Committee on Education and Labor,* 1958, pp. 698–699.

[2] *Ibid.,* p. 54.

[3] *Ibid.,* p. 55.

[4] *Ibid.,* pp. 52–54.

[5] HEW, *Costs of Attending Colleges,* Bulletin 9, 1957, pp. 48, 55.

[6] R. G. Moon, Jr., "Aid Programs—from Application to Award," *College Board Review,* Winter, 1957, p. 17.

[7] L. G. Conger, Jr., "What a College Education Costs in New York State," *College and University Business,* November, 1952, p. 49; also see Lansing, Lorimer, and Moriguchi, *How People Pay for College,* 1960, p. 19.

[8] *Higher Education,* January, 1957, pp. 92–93, and January, 1959, pp. 83–84.

[9] *Hearings on Scholarship and Loan Programs, op. cit.,* pp. 308–311.

[10] *Ibid.,* pp. 529–533.

[11] For the discussion above see especially J. D. Russell, *The Finance of Higher Education,* 1954, especially chap. 10; *The Report of the Commission on Financing Higher Education: Nature and Needs of Higher Education,* 1952, p. 158 *et seq.;* HEW, R. F. Howes (ed.), *Federal Funds for Education, 1954–55 and 1955–56,* 1956; American Council on Education, *Higher Education and the Society It Serves,* pp. 95–100; E. West, *Background for a National Scholarship Policy,* p. 60; *Hearings on Scholarship and Loan Programs, op. cit.,* pp. 308, 310, 396, 430–431, 530–531, 737, 1081–1086, 1651, 1666, and 2071–2074. Also see L. A. Kimpton, "Industry Looks at Private Education," *College and University Business,* July, 1955, pp. 19, 20; Brown and Harbison, *High Talent Manpower for Science and Industry,* 1957, pp. 35–40; R. I. Thackrey, "Washington Report," *College and University Business,* September, 1957, pp. 35–36.

Chapter 14

HOW MUCH FOR SCHOLARSHIPS?

VARIOUS ESTIMATES

The proposal of President Eisenhower's Committee on Education beyond the High School, it will be recalled, recommended outlays of about $750 million. But the administration's Commissioner of Education, on the basis of an estimate of 70,000 who qualified for scholarships and did not receive them (duplication reduced the estimated number to 40,000), proposed outlays of about $10 million by the Federal government for one class, or $40 million in all. (Fellowships, $1,500 per year, ultimately were additional.)

If we assume the number of students entering college to be roughly one million, a figure not too far off in 1960–61, a program yielding 40,000 scholarships *per class* (not *in toto* as under the Eisenhower proposals) would provide 4 per cent of the entering students with aid. The New York State program has an objective of state scholarships for 10 per cent of the students. According to the Hollis study, 10 per cent of all students in 1952–53 received scholarships under the control of institutions, and 6.5 per cent received outside scholarships.

A number of authorities have hit upon the figure of 20 per cent as the appropriate figure for scholarships. Apparently, the current ratio is not far out of line with the proposed goals of the two presidential Commissions and other experts, e.g., Millett, Havighurst, Cole, although the administration bill of 1958 would have provided scholarships for only 1½ per cent of current enrollment. (The Kennedy proposal of 1962 provides for 1 per cent.)

The deficiencies lie in two other areas, namely, (1) the low stipends offered today—the Hollis study showed a median of $218 for college-controlled funds and $268 for other scholarships in 1952–53—and (2) the exclusion of 50,000 to 100,000 out of 200,000 able students each year who should go to college but who are excluded because of financial disability. We assume that the effect of more scholarships would be an improvement of quality, not a deterioration as was concluded by a British authority in discussing the effects of more aid on the quality of British students. It would require at least 100,000 additional scholarships for each class and 400,000 in all to save the 50,000 to 100,000. (It may require two stipends to save one high-quality boy or girl.) Hence through this approach the additional funds required would be, for example:

$300 in addition to, say, the 1958–59 estimated average stipend
   of $250 to $300, for 500,000 recipients...................... $150 million
400,000 additional recipients at $600, average stipend.......... 240 million

Total.. $390 million

This would mean roughly a tripling of scholarship funds. In ten to twelve years the total bill would be about $1 billion, or more than twice the current needs. (I assume a rise in average stipend with increasing per capita incomes.)

In a study for the Educational Testing Service, the following conclusion was presented:[1]

Among the boys who indicated that they would accept a science scholarship, a total of 329 failed to enroll in college. Very roughly, this would represent 65,000 high-scoring senior boys in the public school population of this country. The corresponding estimate for the number of high-scoring girls interested in non-science scholarships is 80,000.

These figures point to large losses of able students, simply because they cannot pay the bill. On the other hand, it should be emphasized, as Cole has, that the CSS sample is not typical of the country. According to a national sample, only an estimated 31 per cent of all high-ability secondary seniors lived in the Northeastern part of the United States, and in the CSS sample 66 per cent were in this category.

This report also concluded:[2]

Professional occupation and extent of education of the father was positively related to college plans. Factors related to money were important; students having more than two siblings were less likely to have college plans than those with one or no sibling, and those who expected the family would give a substantial proportion of support for college were more likely to have college plans than those who said they expected little support.

In this study, for example, where there were no other children in the family, 83 per cent of the boys in the high-scoring group had plans to go to college and only 68 per cent where there were three or more other children in the family. For girls the respective percentages were 67 and 54.[3] Here relevant are both economic and noneconomic factors.

One of the most interesting studies of these problems was done by Havighurst of the University of Chicago. In this study Havighurst gives the summary in Table 14-1 for students in the top quarter of general intellectual ability, namely, those with an IQ of 110 or more.

Havighurst then divides his 100 youths in the top quarter of general intellectual ability into three groups according to economic status. He finds that the attrition is especially great for those in groups II and III (Table 14-2). On Havighurst's estimates, 20 of the 80 in groups II and III do

TABLE 14-1

Estimates of the Educational Experience of 100 Youths in the Upper
Quarter of Intellectual Ability (IQ = 110+)

Educational experience	Total	Well motivated	Nonmotivated	Malmotivated
Complete a four-year college course........	33	33	0	0
Enter college but not complete a four-year course..............................	11	5	4	2
Finish high school but not enter college.......	46	15	16	15
Not finish high school.....................	10	0	4	6
Total.............................	100	53	24	23

Source: American Council on Education, F. J. Brown (ed.), *Approaching Equality of Opportunity in Higher Education*, p. 74.

TABLE 14-2

Economic Status and Educational Experience of Youths in the Upper
Quarter of Intellectual Ability

Economic status	Composition	Complete a four-year college course	Per cent of group completing a four-year course
I	20	15	75
II	35	10	28
III	45	8	18
Total...........	100	33	33

Source: American Council on Education, F. J. Brown (ed.), *Approaching Equality of Opportunity in Higher Education*, p. 75.

not graduate from college *even though they are well motivated*. About 100,000 scholarships a year would be required to save these students, at the population of the early 1950s. Another 50,000 scholarships would be necessary to take care of the 18 out of 100 in groups II and III now completing their college education but not receiving scholarships. Havighurst's estimate, then, is that 600,000 additional scholarships are needed for each four-year college generation, as compared to my estimate of 400,000. At an earlier period (the 1940s), according to Byron Hollinshead, Havighurst had estimated additional needs at only 2 to 3 per cent of the college-age population, and, at a cost of $500 per student, this meant outlays of about $120 million for 240,000 additional scholarships for 1960. But estimates of enrollment were low in the late 1940s, and aid per student is estimated at a higher figure in 1960.[4]

Havighurst is fearful that with the large inflow of students the colleges will tend to accept their students from families with high economic status and not trouble too much about the others. Impressed by the fact that those in economic-status group I with a reproductive index of about 0.8 in 1940 are now approaching an index of 1.0, Havighurst concludes that the rising fertility of the upper economic group will put more pressure on those with low economic status. He estimated that in 1970–1975, of the 24 per cent in economic group I, 90 per cent would graduate from college; in group III only 30 per cent would graduate.

In his final conclusion Havighurst envisages the following possibilities:[5]

1. A greater emphasis on selection in terms of ability
2. (Policy 1) plus a policy of increased financial aid and increased motivating efforts directed at poor but able students
3. Less financial aid and motivating efforts with poor but able students since it would be easier to fill the colleges with others
4. A large rise of acceptances and provision of financial aid and motivational efforts for needy but able youths

* * *

In summary, the case is strong for a scholarship program yielding close to $500 million currently and a billion dollars by 1970. Sums of these proportions would be needed to raise the average scholarship to an adequate level and save the able students who now (or later) do not get a college education because of financial need. A greatly improved loan program may keep these costs down.

NEEDS WITH HIGHER TUITION

By 1970 the average stipend should rise to $800 in order to keep up with rising per capita income. Hence $1 billion would yield about 1,250,000 scholarships at $800, or about 20 per cent of the expected enrollment. But even an average of $800 might be considered inadequate should tuition rise by 100 per cent by 1970. Some alleviation would be had, however, from the fact that 25 per cent or more of the students would be part time—presumably working and hence not in need of scholarships. (This saving applies also to 1960 and points to the availability of higher average stipends than $600 or lower costs.) Some savings might also be inferred from the fact that per capita incomes would rise sufficiently to raise a substantial number above scholarship needs. But costs might rise if scholarships were used as a carrot to induce part-time students to become full time.

Earlier we had indicated that scholarship aid rose relatively more than tuition. Part of the rise of student aid should be associated with increased numbers of scholarships as well as with a rise in the stipend. The earlier discussion does not make clear that a rise in the scholarship stipend should offset the increase not only in tuition but also in other costs. At least this is a tenable position so long as we assume that family income does not increase. In so far as it does rise, then the need for offsetting higher costs is reduced.

How much additional aid should accompany a doubling of tuitions? One economist answering my questionnaire presented an algebraic analysis of the amount of aid that would be necessary to keep the burden on the student constant as both tuition and disposable income (per capita, presumably) changed.

Let t = the ratio of tuition to disposable income

Let a = the ratio of aid to tuition

Then, to keep the burden (the ratio of tuition-less-aid to disposable income) constant implies that $t(1 - a)$ is a constant.

Let the new situation, after the rise in tuition, be indicated by primes. Then

$$\frac{1 - a'}{1 - a} = \frac{t}{t'} \quad \text{and} \quad a' = 1 - \frac{t}{t'}(1 - a)$$

If tuition rises by 100 per cent and disposable income by only 45 per cent, then

$$\frac{t'}{t} = 1.38 \quad \frac{t}{t'} = 0.725 \quad \text{and} \quad a' = 0.275 + 0.725a$$

Thus, if $a = 1.0$, a value of 1.0 would keep tuition-less-aid/disposable income a constant. Since tuition itself would double, aid would have to increase twofold.

A rough estimate for the nation reveals scholarship stipends equal to 100 per cent of tuition. But 14 institutions, private and mainly prestige, yield a stipend equal to 70 per cent of tuition. Thus with a doubling of tuition the stipend would have to rise by $155/70$, or roughly 120 per cent if stipends are to rise sufficiently to keep tuition-less-aid/disposable income constant. The lower the stipend/tuition relative to tuition, the greater the rise required. With the ratio only 0.10 and tuition doubled, stipends would have to increase sevenfold to maintain the ratio of tuition-less-aid to disposable income constant.[6] Not only would the *amount* of the scholarship grants have to increase more rapidly than the tuition rate, in so far as the ratio of stipend to tuition is less than 1, as demonstrated above, but also the *number* of scholarships would have to increase at least as fast, and preferably faster, than the increase in the college-age population, in order to maintain or broaden the base of higher education in the country. On the basis of these considerations, many economists replying to my questionnaire voiced some skepticism as to whether scholarships would in fact be made available in sufficient volume to preserve " . . . the democratic aspects of higher education." Should a sufficient volume of new aid money be provided, how much of the new tuition revenue would remain for application to professorial salaries and other worthy causes?

ECONOMIC AND NONECONOMIC FACTORS

So far we have indicated that large sums of money would be needed for scholarships and largely because of the losses of good students associated with inadequate financial resources. These gaps are important, even if in recent years there has been a tendency for noneconomic cause of failure to

TABLE 14-3

Graduates or nongraduates	Incomes			
	Under $2,000	Under $3,000	Under $4,000	$10,000 or more
Per cent of all graduates...........	4.3	10.3	23.3	24.0
Per cent of all nongraduates........	4.9	11.6	26.9	19.0

enroll, or attrition after enrollment—such as lack of motivation, early marriages, and the like—to receive more attention. A Wisconsin study reveals that of the top 25 per cent of high school graduates only 10 per cent of the boys and perhaps 25 per cent of the girls fail to go to college. Of those who do not go, lack of money is given as a major deterrent by one-third to one-half. These figures suggest that financial need accounts for a failure of perhaps 5 to 8 percentage points of the top 25 per cent of high school graduates (one-third to one-fifth) to go to college. Also of some interest here is the high correlation of college attendance and occupation of parents and especially education of parents—more so than income of parents.

An interesting program for increasing the attendance of students from modest backgrounds in New Mexico revealed the great importance of lack of motivation. But a similar program for mobilizing Negroes who otherwise might have failed to go to college showed substantial gains in attendance.[7]

Again, an HEW study reveals some differences in the ratio of college graduates to nongraduates according to income levels (Table 14-3), but the difference is surprisingly small.[8] In view of the relatively high income of scholarship winners, there is no doubt but that the largest losses occur in the very low-income groups. Here the need of aid is so great—often the boy or girl must go to work—that colleges make little attempt to offer aid to those most in need. Hechinger reports: "In an Eastern factory city, with a population of 180,000, the local high schools this year sent only 15 to 20 per cent of their graduates to college. A residential school only ten miles away sent more than 80 per cent."[9] Any attempt to make scholarships available to cope with the losses among the (say) 25 per cent of families with incomes of less than $4,000 would greatly increase the cost of scholarship programs.

ALTERNATIVE APPROACHES TO OPTIMUM AID

Other approaches to the optimum amount of aid are possible. Thus I estimate the average amount of scholarships per student for the 23 IHL with the largest scholarship funds (average per student enrolled at $100 or more) at $168 in 1955–56. For the 1960–61 enrollment of about 4 million, but excluding part-time students, the costs at this standard applied to the nation would be $600 million ($200 for 1960–61 average amount of scholarship money per student times 3 million).

According to Moon, an adequate aid program for the nation's students would cost $900 million. He obtains this figure by applying to incomes of families in the nation the CSS computational procedures for aid required for a student at different family-income levels. This estimate for 1959 is much higher than my earlier estimate.

How much scholarship aid would be required can also be related to the amount of loans and employment. In recent years these nonscholarship aids have become increasingly important. The more acceptable they become, the less scholarship funds will have to increase. But to some extent loans are a technique for reducing current burdens on families and reducing the need for employment while at college, rather than a substitute for scholarships. To this extent they should not be considered as substitutes for scholarships and fellowships.

One estimate is as shown in Table 14-4 for 1955–56.*

This compilation reveals that loans and employment account for 40 per cent more than scholarships and fellowships. Since 1940, the proportion of students at work has increased by more than 100 per cent. The figures in Table 14-4 are not inclusive, for they do not include loans and scholarships under outside control, and much employment is excluded.

---

* The 1957–58 estimate for aid (presumably scholarships and loans) is $131 million: HEW, *Memo to the Board*, 1960 Series, no. 4.

TABLE 14-4

(In millions of dollars)

Undergraduates or graduates	Scholarships	Loans	Employment
Undergraduates.............	65.74	12.46	65.93
	Fellowships		
Graduates................	18.24	4.99	35.01 (assistantships)
Total...................	83.98	17.45	100.94

Source: HEW, *Financial Aid for College Students: Undergraduate*, p. 2; *ibid.*,
Graduate, p. 2, 1957.

Moon has estimated total aid, inclusive of outside sources, in excess of
$300 million.[10]

One study reveals that colleges and universities tendered 66 per cent
of the scholarships offered to near-winners of the National Merit Scholarships; government agencies, only 10 per cent; business and industry, 6 per
cent; the remainder, 18 per cent, came from various sources. Outside
sources may well provide one-half additional scholarships and fellowships. Another estimate puts them at 40 per cent.[11]

SCHOLARSHIPS VERSUS LOW TUITION

How much is needed for scholarships depends also upon the tuition
policy. The largest subsidies result from tuition charges much below costs.
As I said earlier, one could even establish the position that the less than
$3 billion of educational and general expenditures (exclusive of organized
research and public services) are in fact all subsidy: tuition roughly offsets
capital costs not included here. Against about $3 billion of subsidies
inherent in the pricing policies, the $200 to $300 million of student aid of
all kinds is relatively unimportant. Its significance lies in the help given to
able young men and women who otherwise would not be able to go to
college, and the support given to required rises of tuition.

At any rate it can be argued that if current differentials in tuition
between public and private IHL continue to widen and the rise of enrollment is largely absorbed by public IHL, then to that extent the need for
scholarship money will be reduced. On the whole the position of public
IHL is in favor of across-the-board subsidies through low fees rather than
providing aid to the able and needy. Indeed any likely scholarship program
is not apt to provide aid for more than 25 per cent of the student body.
The average student can be helped only through low tuition charges.

Though the general position of public IHL is that adumbrated above, increasingly these administrators are asking for scholarships and fellowships. In part this new attitude stems from an increased awareness of the manner in which private IHL are weaning away the best students. For example, aside from the large New York State program, which provides scholarships for students in both public and private IHL, there are programs in Illinois, California, Massachusetts, and other states. Even among private IHL there is considerable interest in scholarships financed by government; for through these subsidies private IHL are able either to save on scholarship funds or attract more students. A vice president of the University of Wisconsin even goes so far as to advocate much larger scholarships based on the need for financial aid by top-ranking high school graduates who do not now attend college.[12]

A scholarship program is in fact a form of discriminatory pricing. The student receiving a scholarship of $300, with tuition at $400, in fact is charged $100; and the student at a prestige institution with a tuition charge of $1,200 who receives a $2,000 scholarship in fact pays minus $800. It is of course possible to differentiate charges on the basis of costs and ability to pay. At Bennington College, for example, full costs are charged (measured exclusive of income other than from student fees and endowment) to those who can afford to pay $2,650. The minimum payment is $1,050 for room, board, and health services. Tuition charges vary from zero to $1,600, depending on financial capacity of families.[13]

One of the economists replying to my questionnaire, relying on the experience of the Kent School, proposed a discriminatory pricing system under which the parents negotiate with the school concerning the charges to be made. This is a technique that is used in a sense through the CSS where scholarships are determined on the basis of need. But to apply the Kent technique on an individual basis in the modern college would be difficult indeed.

THE GRADUATE PROBLEM

Our discussion so far has been concerned with aid for undergraduates, though over-all figures include graduate aid. Since graduate students account for only about 10 per cent of the total students, aid is of less importance here. But when aid is given, it is relatively more likely to be in the form of employment. And fellowship aid per student is likely to be three times as high as the average scholarship in arts and science.

Graduate students depend primarily on stipends—according to the National Opinion Research Center of the University of Chicago, about two-thirds have stipends. Next in importance is work income of a spouse. Stipends at the graduate level are more frequent in public IHL than in private, and in natural sciences than in other fields. Apparently one-third of the graduate students in arts and science—these figures apply to this group—are worried about economic status. Larger and more numerous fellowships would shorten the Ph.D. training period and probably be to the financial advantage of students. With graduate work becoming increasingly important, and with about one-half the students married, and—at least in arts and science—with little help from parents, the financing of graduate students is likely to become increasingly difficult.[14]

EUROPEAN EXPERIENCE

Another approach to the aid problem is that suggested by European experience. In Great Britain credit is virtually not used, and the contribution of employment is small. In Germany loans are encouraged, but not nearly so much as in this country.

What is especially striking is the aid system in Great Britain where, on the basis of need, about 75 per cent of the students receive aid primarily from government. Under the British system, the student receives grants for tuition and maintenance. Termtime grants vary, however, with incomes of parents. At £525 income adjusted, the parent contributes £10; at £1,000, £77; and at £3,000, £357. (In Germany the 20 per cent best students receive grants that meet part of their expenses.)

TABLE 14-5

		Millions of dollars
One-third (1 million) incomes <$4,000 = full subsidy	= $1,700 =	1,700
One-third (1 million) incomes $4,001–$7,000 = one-half subsidy =	850 =	850
One-third (1 million) incomes $7,001 and higher = no subsidy	= 0 =	0
Total..		2,550
		(1,550)*

* The British procedure is to discourage work and even provide aid for the summer vacation. But should we allow $500 for employment earnings, then the cost of applying a modified British system would be roughly $1,550 million (deduct 2 million × $500).

What would be the dimensions of the costs of the British system to the United States? Before trying to answer this question I should say that in England the ratio of college population to total is less than one-tenth that of the United States; and also per capita income is 30 to 40 per cent that of the United States. The first point suggests the much higher costs of the British system if applied here; the second, that the case for government subsidies is much greater in Great Britain. Help is needed in Great Britain especially because costs of higher education are much higher in relation to income levels than in this country. Thus at Oxford or Cambridge, costs are £325 to £450, or an average of about $1,200. The average cost elsewhere is somewhat less, especially for those living at home. But the average seems to be about twice as high in relation to income as in the United States. At any rate the application of the British system, even if applied only to full-time students, might well cost the taxpayer $2.5 billion yearly currently, and much more by 1970. (This is a very rough estimate.)

Table 14-5 is a rough estimate on the basis of incomes of college families in 1952–53 and current costs.[15]

CONCLUSION

How much will be needed for scholarships depends on numerous factors: the recourse to loans and employment as substitutes for scholarships; tuition policy; the rise of total costs and of family income; the extent to which loss of capable students is explained by economic and noneconomic factors; the determination to help where it is most costly, that is, for the lowest third of families by incomes. Above all, we stress the point that student aid of $200 to $300 million today is indeed small compared to $3 billion of subsidies made available through pricing below costs.

Some estimates of required scholarship aid for 1960 follow. (The 1970 total would be twice as large to cover increased enrollment and a rise of stipends to match increasing incomes.)

Millions of dollars

1. The President's Commission on Education beyond the High School (roughly 750,000 at $1,000)... 750*
2. To save 50,000–100,000 able students now lost in each class.................... 400
3. Item 2 plus aid for students in need now in college, not receiving help........... 600
4. Monro's proposal, $500 for each student..................................... 2,000
5. Application of scholarships on the basis of CSS formula under which scholarships are allocated on basis of need as measured by family incomes.................... 900
6. Provision of scholarship funds for the nation equal to sums available per student in the 23 IHL with largest scholarship funds per student............................ 600†
7. Application of the British policy to the United States........................... 1,500‡
8. Eisenhower administration proposals, 1958................................... 16
9. Kennedy proposals, 1961 (average five years)............................... 30

* Presumably largely non–Federal government.
† Part-time students excluded.
‡ Part-time students excluded, and allow $500 for employment earnings.

My recommendation would be a rise of scholarships currently from less than $150 million (inclusive of outside scholarships and fellowships) to around $500 million now and $1,000 million by 1970. I believe that spokesmen for higher education generally would approve such a program if the grants, unlike those of the National Merit Corporation or the original GI or the British system, were not tied to costs varying with the institution. Tying the grants to the cost of attending different institutions would result in opposition of public institutions and private ones not greatly in demand. It would be hoped that nongovernmental sources would provide funds adequate to finance able students who would profit especially by going to the best institutions.

A simple but costly program, but one which avoids the issues raised by a means test to which many—including the House Committee on Labor and Education—objected in 1958, is a grant such as the one proposed by Dean Monro of Harvard, $500 per student. But this would be very costly.

I have not raised the issue here of additional income for IHL to match the increased costs of additional students resulting from new scholarship programs. Any such aid should be premised on (1) a resultant rise of enrollment; (2) the *additional,* that is marginal, costs involved per additional student, not average costs; and (3) the facts under (2) being related to the ratio of tuition to relevant costs and the amount of excess capacity.

As this book goes to press, New York State has approved a program that is likely to influence aid everywhere. The program provides a scholar incentive program yielding $100 to $300 for each student going to an IHL in the state, need being a relevant consideration. For graduate fellowships the amount would be $200 to $800. Large amounts are also made available for loans with maximum rates of 3 per cent, and ceilings of $1,800 a year and $7,500 in all. The number of Regent scholarships is to rise from 7,200 to 17,000.[16]

FOOTNOTES

[1] *Background Factors Relating to College Plans and College Enrollment among Public High School Students,* 1957.

[2] *Ibid.,* pp. ii and 84.

[3] *Ibid.,* p. 33.

[4] American Council on Education, F. J. Brown (ed.), *Approaching Equality of Opportunity in Higher Education,* pp. 74–76; cf. B. S. Hollinshead, "The Report of the President's Commission on Higher Education," *Bulletin of the American Association of College Professors,* Summer, 1948, pp. 257–258.

[5] In addition to the references already cited in this chapter, the following have been especially helpful: *Hearings, on Science and Education for National Defense, Senate Committee on Labor and Public Welfare,* 1958, pp. 816, 932; *Hearings, on Scholarship and Loan Programs, House Committee on Education and Labor,* 1958, pp. 18–19, 1859–61; ACE, *Background for a National Scholarship Policy,* pp. 22–37; Havighurst and Rogers, Appendix to Hollinshead, *Who Should Go to College?,* Columbia University Press, 1952; C. C. Cole, Jr., *Encouraging Scientific Talent,* 1956, pp. 57–85; W. G. Mollenkopf and R. E. Dear, "Characteristics of Recipients and Non-recipients of Financial Aid," *The Report to the College Scholarship Service,* 1957, especially pp. 5–10; C. C. Cole, Jr., "Scholarship Applications Today," *College Board Review,* Spring, 1957, pp. 17–20; J. D. Millet, *Financing Higher Education in the United States,* 1952, pp. 380–383; "The Report of the President's Commission on Higher Education," *op. cit.,* vol. II, *Equalizing and Expanding Individual Opportunity,* pp. 67, 68; President's Committee on Education beyond the High School, *Second Report to the President,* p. 54; Fred M. Hechinger, "To Bridge the

Scholarship Gap," *The New York Times,* Sept. 13, 1959; and Gene Curwan, *ibid.,* Sept. 23, 1956.

[6] I owe the formula to Walter Salant, a former student who answered the questionnaire addressed to economists. The average of tuition and scholarship stipends, though, is based on the following: *College Admissions,* II, 1955, p. 91; HEW, *Planning and Management Data 1957–58,* p. 68, and HEW, *Financial Aid for College Students: Undergraduate,* 1957, p. 2.

[7] J. K. Little, *A State-wide Inquiry into Decisions of Youth about Education beyond High School,* 1958, pp. 93–101; E. Paschal, *Encouraging the Excellent,* Fund for Advancement of Education, 1960, pp. 64–68.

[8] HEW, *Retention and Withdrawal of College Students,* 1958, p. 63.

[9] *The New York Times,* Sept. 13, 1959.

[10] R. G. Moon, Jr., "The Truly Representative College Student Body," *College Board Review,* Spring, 1959, pp. 23–24.

[11] D. L. Thistlethwaite, "College Scholarship Offers and the Enrollment of Talented Students," *Journal of Higher Education,* 1958, pp. 24, 421–425; R. G. Moon, Jr., *op. cit.,* p. 22; HEW, *Costs of Attending College,* 1957, p. 53.

[12] J. K. Little, "College Scholarships in Wisconsin," *The Educational Record,* October, 1959, pp. 351–352; *A Report of a Survey of the Needs of California Higher Education,* 1948, pp. 110–111; *Minnesota Commission on Vocational and Higher Education,* 1953, p. 32.

[13] W. C. Fels, "Charging the Full Costs of Education," *College Board Review,* Fall, 1958, pp. 17–18.

[14] See especially National Opinion Research Study, *The Financial Situation of American Arts and Science Graduate Students,* by J. A. Davis and others, 1960, pp. 1–6 (mimeographed); H. Rosenhaupt, *Graduate Students Experience at Columbia University,* 1940–1956, chap. 4; and Gropper and Fitzpatrick, *Who Goes to Graduate School?,* American Institute for Research, 1959, pp. 28–29, 43.

[15] Sir E. Barker, *British Universities,* 1949, pp. 10–11, 35; British Information Services, *Education in Great Britain,* p. 42; Central Office of Information, *Universities in Britain,* 1959, pp. 10–12; R. G. Moon, Jr., "German and English Student Aid—and Our Own," *College Board Review,* Winter, 1960, pp. 24–28; W. J. Bender, "A Critical Role for the Colleges," *College Board Review,* Fall, 1959, p. 8; and HEW, *Costs of Attending College,* p. 47.

[16] See *Meeting the Increasing Demand for Higher Education in New York State,* A Report to the Governor and the Board of Regents, November, 1960; *The Regents Proposal for the Expansion and Improvement of Education in New York State, 1961,* 1960, pp. 19–21; *The New York Times,* Apr. 12, 1961.

Chapter 15

WASTE OF SCHOLARSHIP FUNDS, AND THEIR COST TO IHL

In recent years many experts have held that scholarships often do not achieve their objectives. It is certainly clear that if the objective is to help the poor but able student, much money is wasted; but it is important to consider scholarships also in terms of the objectives of the institution. One writer gives the following reasons for offering scholarships:[1]

To honor with a prize academic performance and promise; to draw to a college an abler group of students than might otherwise be expected to enroll there; to strengthen the college's position in nonacademic areas which for one reason or another the college deems important; to reshape the student body from what it might normally be expected to be to one which more closely represents the ideals of the college; to attract students into particular areas of study and into particular careers; to lead them to accept employment in given industries and companies; to persuade the general population to buy products, presumably because of the goodwill engendered through the award of scholarships. There are others. Scholarships are used to equalize educational opportunities for all economic groups. They are used to enable private institutions to compete with given students of public institutions. They are used to fill empty dormitory beds at cut-rate.

The same writer points out that the College Board's Scholastic Aptitude Test score of 750 almost assures an applicant of some kind of national scholarship. But he adds: "Measurements of 35-23-35 and an imitation of Marilyn Monroe won a South Carolina girl several thousand dollars worth of scholarships in a recent contest in Atlantic City."

INDICATIONS OF WASTE

Would the student who receives a scholarship have gone to college whether he received it or not? A study of GI veterans indicated that about 80 per cent of the students would have gone even without GI help. Since

208

these are older students, we can infer that *less* than 20 per cent of an average sample of students would be induced to go to college as a result of scholarship. Thackrey, executive director of the land-grant colleges, suggests that a scholarship program would make a difference in only about 20 per cent of the students who go to college with a scholarship.

A Harvard survey showed that in one recent year the college admitted but denied aid to 400 applicants. "Of this group 179 registered without aid and we were somewhat startled to find that the median family income of this group was $10,700 and the median net assets after an allowance had been made according to the CSS formula was $16,000. Only 22 students in this group were commuters and their families had a median income of $5,600."[2]

For approximately 100 colleges in the CSS study, the percentages of students who were denied scholarships and yet enrolled in the colleges denying aid (these relate to those with yearly expenses of less than $1,500) were 22, 32, 24 and 30, respectively, for men's colleges, women's colleges, men in coed colleges, and women in coed colleges.

Though the institutions of the CSS provide scholarships for less than one-quarter of their students, a study of CSS applicants reveals that of a sample of 2,000 applicants denied scholarships 90 per cent of those who completed answers to a questionnaire, and 72 per cent of the whole sample, ended up in college. Of the 21,000 total applicants, less than 4,000 received scholarships, but 12,000 enrolled in CSS colleges, nevertheless. The sample of 2,000 above comes from the 9,000 who did not enroll in CSS institutions.[3] Hence the evidence is overwhelming that most students who apply for aid and do not receive it nevertheless go to college. I should add, however, that the CSS sample is from a higher-income group than in the nation generally.

The evidence is not all on one side. In a survey of Minnesota high school graduates of 1950, 58 per cent of the high-ability students who were not planning to go to college reported in high school that they would change their plans and attend college if they had additional sums of money. They defined adequate financial aid as one-half of their expenses, about $750. But a Wisconsin study referred to earlier shows that only 10 per cent of the boys of the top 25 per cent in Wisconsin were lost because of financial need.[4]

Another factor that suggests waste of resources is the fact that a substantial proportion of the scholarship students come from high-income groups. This again, however, must be considered in terms of the objectives of the institution. If the objective is to help the poor boy, obviously the large grants to relatively high-income groups are not justified. If, however, the objective is to obtain a well-balanced student body, inclusive of large numbers from successful families, then the scholarship is not wasted. For example, about 30 per cent of Harvard scholarships in a recent year went to families with incomes above $7,600. Yet in 1956 families with incomes above $7,600 would fall in the highest 20 per cent in the nation. (In 1956, $5,950 was the average family income in the nation, and in 1959, $6,470.)[5]

Again, in New York State in 1953 those students from families with incomes of $8,000 and over accounted for roughly 20 per cent of the scholarship winners; moreover, 40 per cent of the holders of scholarships in the over-$500 category were in this income class. The percentage receiving scholarships was almost identical for the $8,000+ and the $4,000— income classes.[6] In this same year the 90th percentile of family incomes was at the $7,400 level in the nation. The Hollis study also showed a large proportion of scholarships going to relatively high-income families.

A study from the Far West confirms the results of the CSS study. Eighty-eight per cent of the scholarship holders at Brigham Young University (total student body of 8,000) said they would have attended the university without scholarship, and 62 per cent of the rejected applicants for scholarships enrolled anyway.

Another factor which might suggest that scholarships are wasted to some extent is that scholarship applicants apply disproportionately to the high-cost colleges. Applicants for the CSS colleges were two to three times as numerous for the schools costing more than $1,700 than for those whose costs were less than $1,500. The explanation is largely that higher-priced colleges offer higher scholarships to offset the relatively high costs. Thus for CSS men's colleges with expenses of less than $1,500, the mean value of offer was $613; for those with expenses of $1,700, the offers of scholarships averaged $903.[7] The offers were in somewhat similar proportions for both men's colleges and women's colleges.[8]

TABLE 15-1

Applications in relation to costs, types of colleges	Less than $1,500	More than $1,700
Men's colleges............	2,525	9,633
Women's colleges..........	1,040	3,551
Coeducational colleges:		
Men...................	1,343	2,217
Women...............	1,278	900

Again, it has been pointed out that of the 827 students selected for Merit Scholarships in 1957, 37 per cent felt no need for financial assistance; another 262 (32 per cent) had financial need of $900 or less. The average need was $648. On the basis of these statistics it was calculated that

40,000 scholarships at $1,000, as proposed in the 1958 Hill-Elliott Bill (which proposed no means test and which failed to pass), would result in $80 million being spent in excess of needs in a four-year period.[9]

But I emphasize the point that it does not necessarily follow that scholarship money is wasted simply because a larger number of students apply to the high-cost colleges and because grants increase with the expense of the college. The issue really is: does the expensive college do a job that is commensurate with its higher cost?

Undoubtedly a scholarship that is adapted to the tuition and expenses of different colleges tends to result in a movement toward the high-cost colleges. There are many who object to this type of scholarship for just this reason. But Philip Coombs, then of the Fund for the Advancement of Education, argued[10] that a scholarship program

. . . should be neutral as to the student's choice of institution and as to the student's choice of major academic field. . . .

Now, to be neutral as to the student's selection of institution, the scholarship award must be related to the actual cost of attending the particular institution selected. Otherwise it is not neutral. To ignore this important consideration in determining need would be illogical and misleading and would be inequitable to the students and to various institutions.

It is of some significance that the Coombs principle, that is, scholarships related to need *and* the costs at each institution, is the British practice.

Another complaint about the distribution of scholarships arises from the intense competition among institutions for students. An able student from California who might go to Stanford goes to Yale. The California boy comes East and the Eastern boy goes to California, though of course the major movements are from West to East and South to North rather than from East to West and North to South. I do not mean that it is wasteful for a California student to go to Yale or to Princeton, but it is wasteful if he can get as good an education in California.

SIZE OF SCHOLARSHIP GRANTS AND RESTRICTIONS PLACED ON THEM

Many other complaints can be made about scholarship programs. One is that many of the scholarships are too small and, therefore, not effective. This is the view of the Committee on Education beyond the High School. President Charles Phillips of Bates, however, considers the real waste to be in scholarships in excess of $1,200. Waste may result from high as well as low grants.

In seeking diversity of backgrounds, colleges often in fact concentrate on similar backgrounds and hence tend to favor high-income groups both on admissions and scholarships. Moon has well said:

Attempts to achieve this geographic representativeness are well known. The college admissions officer visits public high schools in Scarsdale, Montclair, Evanston, Walnut Hills, Newton, Lamar Senior High in Houston, the best boarding schools from coast to coast, and—if sufficiently moved—he might stop at the local high school.

This procedure of course accounts in part for the tendency of scholarships to go frequently to boys and girls from high-income homes.

On the issue of the excesses of competitive bidding, Frank Bowles has had something of interest to say. He urged consideration of measures " . . . which would control the flow of applications and the timing of the various phases of the admissions operations"; early applications and acceptances; matching plans " . . . in which the candidates and colleges have the opportunity to make their choices in order of preference and report them to a central agency . . . "; also techniques for limiting the number of applications. But Bowles does not seem too hopeful of acceptance of such procedures by the colleges. Such programs could reduce costs of admissions and bring about improved choices of students and scholarship winners.

In a study of retention and withdrawal of college students, the author found that out of $103 million spent annually for scholarships, about one-quarter went to students who did not graduate:

. . . scholarship money was used to defray the expenses of students of marginal ability while students of demonstrated ability dropped out of college because of financial difficulties. . . . Would not the interests of individual institutions of higher education and of society in general be better served by the primary utilization of scholarship funds . . . to insure the retention of students of proven ability rather than for the purpose of attracting promising students?

Wilbur Bender, after serving for many years as dean of financial aids at Harvard, listed numerous shortcomings of scholarship programs: unduly restrictive terms which reduce the effective use of funds; restrictions on choice of college or mobility; excessive support for students in certain areas and inadequate support in other areas, the result being diversions of students to areas to which they do not necessarily belong; fixed stipends with little relation to need; grants that attempt to influence what a college teaches or the point of view of the recipient on social, political, or religious issues; use of scholarships for recruiting personnel for corporations; coverage of too wide an area, with resultant excessive numbers of applicants.

In a discussion of scholarship practices by a CSS subcommittee, the following conclusions were reached:[10a]

Financial aid should supplement what parent and student can provide;
Aid should be in the form of scholarships, loans, jobs, or combination;
Aid should not exceed financial need;
Computation concerning financial need should not be related to non-financial issues;
Intercollege consultation on form and amount of aid is supported;
When outside aid is available, the college offer should be adjusted;
Students should be expected to borrow part of aid though grants should not be contingent upon acceptance of loans (no compulsory loans).

In the Hollis study, the total range of student expenditures for 1952–53 was shown to be from $200 to $5,500 and the interquartile range was from $815 to $1,708. For students with total expenditures, say, of less than $815, that is, the lowest quarter, a scholarship of $100 or $200 may be of some importance.[11] (We should add that the small scholarships do tend to be concentrated in low-cost IHL, especially public ones. In Michigan the public institutions had twice as many grants at $50 to $99, and one-seventh as many at $300 to $499, as private IHL.)[12] But it certainly does seem that a larger average scholarship for a smaller number of students would be more effective.[13]

Some institutions seem to be on the right track. A sample of three Ivy League colleges, one other outstanding private university, seven high-quality technical institutes, and three good small colleges provided scholarships that averaged 71 per cent of tuition in 1952–53.[14]

One of the most unfortunate factors is the restrictions placed upon scholarships. Many of them are residential, that is, a student must come from a particular place, especially from a particular state. At Stanford scholarships are open to orphan brothers; well-known Ford scholarships are open to sons of Ford employees. The Union Carbide scholarships are not restricted to children of employees, but they are good only at colleges chosen by the company, and the students are supposed to be interested in business careers. George Westinghouse scholarships can only be used at the Carnegie Institute of Technology. Scholarships from the Mullins Company in Cincinnati, and Reliance Electric, Thompson Products, and Warner and Swasey in Cleveland require the holders to follow a work-study plan with the companies and local colleges.[15]

In discussing the relative advantages of corporate and Federal scholarships, the writers of a report for the Joint Congressional Committee on Atomic Energy point out that corporations tend to take into account the location of the company's plants, employment, markets, the institutional sources of its personnel, and the particular subject interest of the corporation. Federal grants, in contrast, would be in the public interest.[16]

Older institutions seem to be particularly hemmed in by restricted scholarships. Among the 1,100 or so grants at Harvard, for example, there are roughly 50 Harvard Clubs that offer one or more scholarships to applicants in their own area. In addition, descendants of members of 27 classes from 1802 to 1929 have a preference in certain awards; graduates of 13 schools or school systems have special claim; students with surnames of Anderson, Boxendale, Borden, Downer, Hudson, and Murphy have preferences; there are 70 scholarships for students from various towns, counties, states, and foreign countries, as well as one for someone from the territory served by the Chicago, Burlington and Quincy Railroad in Iowa; also several corporations offer scholarships with special conditions. Finally scholarships are available to descendants or relatives of various persons: from a fund established in 1643 for kinsmen of Lady Mowlson (Ann Radcliffe) of London, from one in 1687 for descendants of William Browne II, and from a 1949 fund for sons of widows residing west of the Appalachians.[16a]

ATTEMPTS TO REDUCE WASTE

Some progress has been made in eliminating confusion in the administration of scholarships. The excellent program of the CSS is an example; this rather effective program was organized by John Monro, then dean of scholarship aid at Harvard, and W. C. Fels, now President of Bennington College. As a result of this program much unwise competition is eliminated. There is a regular form for measuring the needs of students. Parents are asked to provide a great deal of information about income, capital assets, number of children, tax burdens, etc. From these figures as well as from the earning capacity of the student, an estimate is made of the student's needs, and scholarships are granted accordingly. If, for example, Cornell finds that it has estimated the need of a student at $700 and Harvard estimates the need at $1,200 (I assume here that costs are the same), then the Cornell dean of admissions would want to know from the Harvard dean of admissions why Harvard has given this boy on their calculations $500 more than he needs.[17]

In his 1953 statement Monro said as follows:

Most of us appear to be fishing in the same suburban pools for the same young man. Here we must certainly ask ourselves if we are, individually or as a group, putting our scholarship money where it will do the most good for the country.

As the competition for enrollment and talent gets tighter, as it will, we may undercut the old fashioned idea that scholarships are intended to help the needy and deserving scholar, and that well-off families should help themselves. We will do ourselves and the country no good if we diminish the force of this fine old idea.

Obviously any program that encourages competition on a national scale (the National Merit Scholarship program, for example) should produce better choices than the more restricted types of scholarships.

THE WISDOM OF USING SCHOLARSHIPS TO DIRECT STUDENTS INTO PARTICULAR FIELDS

Many propose that scholarships should be given with a view to attracting young men and women into particular fields. In the midst of the great Sputnik crisis of 1958, for example, many expressed the view that scholarships and fellowships should be made available especially for students in the sciences. Others think that this is not the most effective approach to these problems. In fact, most of the scientists who testified before the Senate and House committees in 1958 repudiated the view that special incentives should be given in order to get more concentrators in science. Actually, as the National Merit Scholarship program showed, a very large proportion of bright young people intend to concentrate in the sciences. Of the 1957 finalists, 24 per cent intended to go into research, 23 per cent into engineering, 16 per cent into teaching, and 9 per cent into medicine.[18]

Indeed the 1958 administration bill proposed that special consideration be given to students with training in mathematics, but the administration also made it clear that successful candidates would not be required to go into the sciences. Secretary Folsom was aware of the pitfalls:[19]

I might say parenthetically that the scientists agree with us that it is better to have an across-the-board scholarship and not just have it directed towards mathematics and science, because as they say "if we get these youngsters into college, we will get our share of science and mathematics people," so the main thing to do is to get the youngster into college. We can do that in a scholarship program.

In support of the Secretary's position, Undersecretary Perkins said:[20]

Scholarships to be most helpful should not be earmarked for those who are from a particular geographical location or who will pledge themselves to pursue a particular course of study. When scholarship programs are rigid in such respects, the use of funds is inefficient—the scholarship needs in one place or field of study may not be great, and in another there may be needs but no funds. Further, the role of the scholarship can divert students from their greatest interests and potential competence to the individual's and society's detriment.

In his testimony, the representative of the American Association for the Advancement of Science said:[21]

I recommend that the emphasis on science and mathematics be stricken out of the scholarship provision entirely. Where a special need is evident, it is appropriate to give specialized fellowships at the graduate level. In the high school, it is proper now to give special attention to the teaching of science and mathematics, not because these subjects are more important than say English, but because it is important to redress some of the imbalances that we have allowed to develop.

Riesman, the Steelman report, and Wolfle are all agreed that a policy emphasizing short-term goals would be a mistake. As Riesman expresses it, "Men should not be forced by the needs of society to give more than traditional cooperation to specific short-term goals." Or as Steelman says in *Science and Public Policy,* "What we require as a nation is to extend educational opportunities to all able young people, leaving it to them to determine the field of study they desire to pursue."[22]

RELEVANT ISSUES OF TESTS AND CHOICE

Still another problem arises from the difficulty in choosing the most effective and likely candidates. In the absence of counseling, students often go into fields where their talents are wasted, and the best applicants for possible scholarships and fellowships are thereby lost. Improved testing and counseling would produce better results in the selection of winners, and one of the objectives of the legislation of 1958 was to achieve this. It would cost about $20 per student to get really effective counseling.

As Berdil has argued,[23]

A scholarship program, to be effective, must particularly aim at increasing the number of competent students attending universities. This can be done only by first identifying early in high school talented students and counselling them so as to increase their motivation for continued education. High school students and their parents, counselors and teachers must be informed of the availability and nature of scholarships while the student is in his early years of school. In addition, if competent students are to apply for the scholarships made available to them, the amount and quality of counselling guidance now provided in the high schools of the country must be increased. . . .

Tests and examinations are the second major aid in selecting and placing good students. Henry Chauncey, president of the Educational Testing Service, tells us that it is very important that the students be tested in the eighth and ninth grades, since they make very important educational decisions in those years. He also contends that we must know both the academic ability and the grades of the students. Then he adds:[24]

Aptitude tests, on the other hand, provide a comparable set of observations of pupils that are unaffected by these influences (discipline, working habits, etc.). They provide another, and an independent view of the student. There is, of course, greatest probability of success for pupils who rank high on both predictors—both grades and aptitude test scores; . . .

According to Roger W. Russell, executive secretary of the American Psychological Association, tests can identify pupils of superior potential who are handicapped, for example, by poor reading skill. Tests can help to identify the students who provide the reservoir from which our creative scientists, engineers, educators, etc., are drawn; but, Russell adds, these tests cannot measure potential creativity or inventiveness:

" . . . They will not pick out particular individuals who will make new discoveries and put them to work. Tests are not pushbutton, slot-machine devices where children go in at one end and a guaranteed list of future Einsteins come out the other. Test results give expectancies rather than biographies in advance."

Tests do not identify distinctive types of talent. We have " . . . no secure guides that distinguish aptitude for scientific research from aptitudes for the diplomatic service or military command or any other high-level responsibility."[25]

All evaluations of tests are not low.[26]

One extensive research project studied 800 men who had been identified as superior on a general mental test given at age 10. By the time these men reached the age of 40, they had published 67 books (46 of them scholarly) and more than 1400 scientific, technical and professional articles. They had more than 150 patents to their credit. Nearly all of these numbers are from 10 to 30 times as large as would be found in the general population.

According to one report, college applicants who rank in the top 20 per cent of students tested occasionally have among them a student who will fail, but for every failure there will be 32 satisfactory students, including 15 who will win honors.

Some educators express skepticism about the tests nevertheless. For example, President Headly of the South Dakota State College of Agriculture and Mechanic Arts, has this to say:[27]

. . . 5 per cent of the people who have been hitting the top 10 per cent of this group (in tests) are, when they get into college, among the low 10 per cent of the achievers in college in our institution. . . . But the fact is that those youngsters who do hit the top 5 per cent in the college aptitude test just do not perform up to what we would anticipate for them.

And Dean Douglas Brown of Princeton writes as follows:[28]

But even here, objective tests are but a minor measure of talent potential. The showing of a very high mathematical aptitude on a brief test in probably the most readily measured area of human capacity still leaves many important elements in doubt. It may indicate what a student could do in a hundred-yard dash under conditions of utmost pressure. It does not indicate the habits of study, the degree of persistence or that creative quality of mind which makes the difference between a first-rate mathematician and a person who is "good with figures." . . .

Perhaps the strongest attack on choice of students and scholarship winners through recourse to aptitude and high school grades comes from members of the National Merit Scholarship Corporation staff.[29] They conclude that the grade hunters, not the likely creative, get the scholarships. Finalists in the NMSC competition, it is held, " . . . have less potential for creativity than do students with lower grades." Teachers prefer and rate higher the intelligent than the creative. A sample of architects and scientists, nominated by experts for their creativity, generally had C or B averages in college.

Undoubtedly there is some truth in this position. I recall criticizing an otherwise excellent report of the Harvard Admissions Committee of 1960 on similar grounds. The tests proposed would, in my opinion, not allow admission of many of the later successes in the business and professional world. An examination of the most successful Harvard College graduates in general business and the professions would not reveal, I am reasonably sure, a high correlation with grades. I do not mean to imply that this means that the *magnas, summas*, and Phi Beta Kappas do not achieve success. Indeed they do. But it is also true that a substantial number of outstanding graduates are content with the Gentleman's C. With current pressures for admissions, many of these potentially able young men and women will fail of entry into the better colleges. The question not answered by the writers of this paper, nor by the Harvard Admissions Committee of 1960, is how are the Roosevelts, the Dillons, the Herters, the Kennedys, the Marquands, the Cabots, the Grosses, the Henry Adamses, the Emersons to be discovered?

Finally we have some interesting experiments of students who were checked after four years in college and whose records were compared with the recommendations of experts on admissions. For example, in one instance 10 expert admissions committees had selected unanimously three girls named Iona, Grace, and Diana. Iona was highly recommended by her principal. "Always has been an outstanding school citizen and student. Highly respected by students, mentally alert, cooperative and loyal." She impressed her interviewer as a person of seriousness with a certain force of personality. Her IQ at grade 9 was 136, at grade 11, 144. Her Standard Aptitude Test verbal score was 693, and her Standard Aptitude Test mathematical score was 706.

Diana had an IQ of 132 at Grade 11; her College Board test revealed SATV, 688 and SATM, 600; she was reported by her school as being an excellent student.

Grace's record was also very good but not up to those of the other two. What happened? Grace's standing in her college at graduation was in the 98 percentile; Iona's, in the 47th percentile; and Diana dropped out of college after her freshman year. She failed four academic courses and physical education in her freshman year. Iona had a generally poor record in her freshman year, failing the second half of the mathematics course.[30]

These failures in prediction should not, however, allow us to underestimate the over-all results; I have often heard Ivy League college admission officers and deans comment on the large proportion of students who perform in college as might be inferred from the aptitude tests, grades, and letters. The National Merit Corporation, in assessing the first year work for its first group of winners, on the basis of aptitude tests, found that their average grade in college was men, 3.13; women, 3.43 (4 = perfect). Of the entire group, 82 per cent were in the top quarter of their class— although they went to exacting institutes.[31]

IS THE SCHOLARSHIP PROGRAM COSTLY TO THE COLLEGES?

A final issue is: is the scholarship program costly to the colleges? I have already indicated elsewhere that the colleges finance the largest part of the scholarships under their own control out of free funds or out of annual gifts. In recent years, however, the largest increase of scholarships has been from the outside, that is, scholarships subject to control by outside contributors.

In one respect, the scholarship program is a financial gain for the college. Colleges can use the scholarships now as a means of making their tuition increases acceptable to their clients.

But, on the other hand, a discussion sponsored by the Carnegie Foundation among outstanding college presidents included the following:[32]

A program which places more money in the hands of students will encourage even more youngsters to go to college but will do nothing to strengthen the institutions which must receive these youngsters, thus intensifying the danger which thoughtful educators fear most: that more and more youngsters will flood into weaker and weaker institutions.

In discussing the proposed Federal program, Congressman Wainwright[33] said that:

If you take either the 10,000 figure or the 40,000 figure of total scholarships, and you add this to the existing financial burdens of the universities, you will find almost unanimity among the corporations, the Harvard Overseers, the various presidents and trustees of organizations, that additional scholars brought to them by scholarships at this time are going to create one heck of a burden.

To an economist the case does not seem as clear as it does to most of the college administrators. Certain questions must be answered. One is: does the granting of additional scholarships mean an increase in numbers? It may, for example, mean merely that the scholarship student squeezes out another student who might have come to college. In that case, there is no additional cost. There is, indeed, a gain, because the college may now either make its own scholarship money go further or use it for general purposes. For all institutions the effects will probably be a *rise* of students as the number of scholarships increase, but not to the same extent for all institutions.

Perhaps more important, the comparison should be not of tuition received for additional students with average costs but rather with additional costs per student associated with expansion.[34] Where tuition is high in relation to costs and where excess capacity exists, there is a strong possibility that the college will not lose from external scholarships. But if, as is likely for many institutions, increased enrollments are accompanied by a rise of costs in excess of tuition (and often in excess of average costs), the university should be compensated for any rise of enrollment associated with scholarship programs.

CONCLUSION

This chapter is devoted largely to showing that scholarship money is not used in the most effective manner. It is evident, for example, that only a relatively small proportion of those receiving scholarships would not have gone to college without them. This does not mean, however, that the scholarship does little good. Again, high-income groups probably receive *relatively* too many scholarships, even though a strong case can be made out for large increases in number of recipients and stipends. Frequently the value of scholarships is reduced because of restrictions put upon their use: they do not then go to the best qualified. Attempts are being made to tailor the scholarships to needs. Still another problem is the failure of tests, which contribute to the choices made, to be infallible. Again, for the college, the scholarship may often be costly rather than the reverse. These considerations raise questions not so much about the wisdom of large scholarship programs, but rather of how they might be much more effective than they are today.

FOOTNOTES

[1] J. F. Morse, "How and Why Scholarships are Awarded," *College Entrance Examination Board,* vol. 4, 1957, pp. 82–83.

[2] Rexford G. Moon, Jr., "Aid Programs—from Application to Award," *College Board of Review,* Winter, 1957, p. 17.

[3] The Council of State Governments, *Summary of Proceedings, of the Conference of State Higher Education Study Commission,* 1958, p. 22. (Mimeographed.) Note that Thackrey was considering a $1,000 scholarship program to be offered by the Federal government. *Hearings, on Scholarship and Loan Programs, House Committee on Education and Labor,* 1958, p. 221; and D. Wolfle, *America's Resources of Specialized Talents,* 1954, pp. 246–47; J. K. Little, *A State Wide Inquiry into Decisions about Education beyond High School,* 1958, p. 101.

[4] See footnote 3.

[5] R. G. King, "Financial Thresholds to College," *President's Economic Report, 1960,* p. 132; J. U. Monro, "Who Gets the Scholarships?" *Harvard Alumni Bulletin,* Dec. 10, 1955, pp. 256–59.

[6] State University of New York, *Crucial Questions about Higher Education,* p. 59.

[7] Parker and Wright, "Do Scholarships Influence College Attendance," *Journal of Higher Education,* 1956, p. 147; R. G. Moon, Jr., *op. cit.,* p. 17.

[8] R. G. Moon, Jr., *ibid.*

[9] R. G. Moon, Jr., *College Board Review,* Spring, 1958, p. 23.

[10] *Hearings, on Scholarship and Loan Programs, op. cit.,* p. 1170.

[10a] For the last few paragraphs see R. G. Moon, Jr., "The Truly Representative College Student Body," *College Board Review,* Spring, 1959, p. 23; F. H. Bowles, *Admission to College: A Perspective for the 1960's,* 1960, pp. 38–39, 110–111; HEW, *Retention and Withdrawal of Students,* 1958, pp. 69–71; W. J. Bender, "A Critical Role for the Colleges," *College Board Review,* Fall, 1959, p. 10; *Report of the CSS Subcommittee on Scholarship Practices,* 1958 (mimeographed).

[11] HEW, *Costs of Attending College,* Bulletin 9, 1957, p. 55.

[12] *The Survey of Higher Education in Michigan: Financial Assistance to Students in Michigan Institutions of Higher Learning,* Staff Study 8, May, 1948, p. 40.

[13] HEW, *Costs of Attending College, op. cit.,* p. 52.

[14] T. P. Pitre, "Administration of Financial Aid," *College Admissions, CEEB* II, 1955, p. 91.

[15] E. Hodnett, *Industry-College Relations,* 1955, pp. 80–81.

[16] *Development of Scientific Engineering and Other Professional Manpower,* 1957, p. 219.

[16a] See Table 15A-1.

[17] See College Scholarship Service, *Computation Manual, 1957,* 1958; and also the excellent statement by John U. Monro, "Helping the Student Help Himself," *College Board Review,* May, 1953, pp. 351–57.

[18] National Merit Scholarship Corporation, *Second Annual Report for the Year Ending June 30, 1957,* p. 15.

[19] *Hearings, on Scholarship and Loan Programs, op. cit.,* p. 704.

[20] *Ibid.,* p. 12.

[21] *Hearings, on Science and Education for National Defense, Senate Committee on Labor and Public Welfare,* 1958, p. 553.

[22] C. C. Cole, Jr., *Encouraging Scientific Talent,* pp. 176–177; E. West, *Background for a National Scholarship Policy,* pp. 117–119; J. Steelman, *Science and Public Policy,* vol. I, pp. 35–36; and D. Wolfle, *America's Resource of Specialized Talent,* p. 266.

[23] *Hearings, on Scholarship and Loan Programs, op. cit.,* p. 222.

[24] *Ibid.,* p. 1108.

[25] *Hearings, on Science and Education, op. cit.,* p. 759.

[26] *Ibid.,* pp. 759–760.

[27] *Hearings, on Scholarship and Loan Programs, op. cit.,* p. 316.

[28] Brown and Harbison, *High Talent Manpower for Science and Industry*, 1957, p. 36.

[29] Holland and Kent, *The Concentration of Scholarship Funds and its Implication for Education*, 1960.

[30] *An Exercise in Assessment, College Admissions 4, 1957*, pp. 90–106.

[31] National Merit Scholarship Corporation, *op. cit.*, p. 6.

[32] *Federal Programs in Higher Education; Summary of a Discussion of the Carnegie Foundation for the Advancement of Teaching*, 1957, p. 10.

[33] *Hearings, on Scholarship and Loan Programs, op. cit.*, p. 740.

[34] For example, the college would not lose on the following assumptions: Tuition = $1,000; no. students = 1,000; average costs = $1,200; total costs = $1,200,000. Add 100 students as result of scholarship program. Additional costs = $800 per student or $80,000 in all.

But additional revenue is $100,000 (100 × $1,000). Since marginal revenue ($100,000) exceeds marginal costs, the college gains, rather than loses.

APPENDIX. SCHOLARSHIPS AT HARVARD

Students who are descendants or relatives of the persons listed in Table 15A-1 may have a preference for certain scholarships, provided they qualify and are chosen for scholarship aid.

TABLE 15A-1
Scholarship Funds and Family Names and Relationships

Brief name of scholarship fund	Date founded	Terms in part
Abbot..........	1852	Descendants of Dr. Benjamin Abbot or his brothers
Borden..........	1896	Relatives of Samuel Augustus Borden
Bright............	1880	Descendants of Henry Bright, Jr., of Watertown, who bear the name of Bright
Browne..........	1687	Descendants of William Browne II
Cook............	1948	Descendants of Ebenezer W. Cook of Warsaw, New York
Coolidge.........	1917	Descendants of John Coolidge of Watertown (1630)
Downer..........	1927	Descendants of Joseph and Robert Downer, of Wiltshire, England (1650) bearing the surname of Downer, or to those of English or Anglo-Saxon stock, bearing the surname of Downer by right of birth or inheritance
Eliot.............	1926	Descendants of Charles William Eliot, A.B. 1853
Ellis Aid..........	1899	Descendants of David Ellis and Beulah Newall of Dedham, and John Ellis and Hannah Ellis of Walpole
Fisher...........	1908	The collateral heirs of Francis P. Fisher, A.B. 1848
Freiman..........	1921	The children of Mitchell Freiman, A.B. 1901
Henry............	1945	Nephews of Phineas M. Henry, Jr., class of 1936, or their descendants
Hudson...........	1928	Descendants of Alan Bedford Hudson
Huntsman.........	1947	Descendants of Jaspar Gregory Van Buskirk
Kroll.............	1945	Son of World War II veteran
Morey...........	1686	Descendants of Rev. George Morey, A.B. 1776
Mowlson.........	1643	Kinsmen of Lady Mowlson (Ann Radcliffe) of London
Pennoyer.........	1670	Descendants of Robert Pennoyer, a brother of William Pennoyer of England
Reed............	1907	Descendants of William Reed, father of Milton Reed, A.B. 1868
Saltonstall........	1730	Relatives of Mary Saltonstall (Mrs. Gordon) or Leverett Saltonstall, A.B. 1802, who are preparing for the ministry
Smith............	1903	Sons of present members of the Harvard Club of Chicago resident in Chicago or its vicinity
Troutman.........	1949	Sons of widows residing west of the Appalachians
Tyler.............	1915	Sons of former pupils of Adams Academy in Quincy, Mass.
Welles...........	1936	Descendants of Benjamin Welles of the Class of 1800
Whitaker.........	1929	Descendants of Samuel Craft Davis, A.B. 1893, or his brother, Dwight Filley Davis, A.B. 1900
Whiting..........	1874	Descendants of William Whiting, A.B. 1833, or of the Rev. Samuel Whiting

Chapter 16

DISTRIBUTION OF SCHOLARSHIPS AND FELLOWSHIPS: A STATISTICAL VIEW[1]

Many readers may find the material in this chapter dull—nevertheless necessary. They may prefer to read a summary at the end.

Before discussing the statistical aspects of scholarships and fellowships, I refer readers to Table 16-1, from *Costs of Attending College*. Most students' income comes from family and long-term savings (58.5 per cent for these two categories) and employment (26.3 per cent). Scholarships account for only 4.8 per cent (both college scholarships and those from outside sources). For 1957–58 I estimate student aid (scholarships and loans) from both inside and outside sources at only 3 per cent of student income.[1a] To the students who receive them, however, scholarships are much more important than these figures would suggest. According to the 1952–53 study, 22 per cent of all students receive scholarships;[2] on this basis, *these* students receive almost one-quarter of their income from scholarships, but the 1957–58 national figures yield only about 15 per cent. The table suggests that the scholarship student in 1952–53 received $293 from his college and $352 from outside scholarships—20 and 24 per cent respectively (cf. Table 16A1-1). Earnings account for more of total student income than scholarships, because the amounts of money obtained through jobs are larger per student employed than the average scholarship. Also, there are more working students than scholarship students. Loans make only a small contribution, and the pattern of receipts is quite different for men than for women. Women depend more on parents and savings, less on employment, scholarships, veterans' benefits, and loans. Their total income (per capita) is also 15 per cent less.

The HEW study might be compared with a survey by the Survey Research Center:

Parents' contributions equal 61 per cent (roughly equal HEW's 58.5 per cent for long-term savings and parents' contributions). Scholarships account for 8 per cent (4.8 per cent in the HEW study), students' earnings equal 23 per cent (26.3 per cent in the HEW study). The 8 per cent

224

TABLE 16-1
Major Sources of Student Income, 1952–53,* by Sex
(Number and per cent of 15,036 students receiving income from various sources)

Source of funds	Per cent item is of total income	Mean amount for all who have this source of income	Total number of students	Median family income	Male		Female	
					Per cent receiving income	Mean amount received	Per cent receiving income	Mean amount received
(1)	(2)	(3)	(4)	(5)	(6)	(7)	(8)	(9)
Long-term savings......	20.0	$ 695	419	$5,067	44.5	$ 660	39.8	$ 759
Family:								
Parents.............	38.5	765	11,139	5,349	70.1	727	80.5	817
Other..............	2.0	221	2,110	4,150	12.5	225	16.5	216
Summer earnings.......	9.3	395	5,223	4,864	38.7	389	28.3	296
Earnings, school year...	17.0	413	9,104	4,768	65.8	486	52.0	265
Scholarships:								
College...........	4.8	293	2,434	4,788	15.0	340	18.2	230
Other.............		352	994	4,208	5.8	439	7.9	247
Veterans' benefits....								
Vocational rehabilita-	4.3	1,003	883	4,079	9.4	1,002	0.1	1,112
tion..............	....	316	166	3,512	1.2	342	0.9	262
Borrowed:								
College...........		162	291	4,125	2.3	153	1.3	186
Other organizations	1.5	300	342	3,600	2.6	296	1.7	309
Elsewhere.........		358	496	3,705	4.0	375	2.1	306
Gifts from others.......	0.7	57	2,735	4,702	16.8	63	20.5	50
Funds from other sources	1.9	263	1,557	5,513	12.3	269	7.2	249
Total, school year....	100	$1,462	15,036	$5,119	....	$1,547	....	$1,324

* The money needed to adjust to 1957 living costs can be projected by using the Bureau of Labor Statistics Cost of Living Index and U.S. Office of Education studies of increases in tuition costs. The interim rise in the cost of living was 5 per cent, and tuition and fees increased by 15 per cent.
Source: HEW, *Costs of Attending College*, Bulletin 9, 1957, p. 48.

estimate for scholarships seems very high on the basis of my estimate of scholarship funds available—roughly 3 to 4 per cent of total costs to students. Where family resources are not available as indicated above, more recourse to earnings, scholarships, and loans is necessary—as a Kiplinger study shows.[3]

AVERAGE SIZE OF SCHOLARSHIPS AND FELLOWSHIPS

The total amount of scholarship money under control of IHL was $65.7 million in 1955–56 and the total number of scholarships, 237,000. Hence the average size of each scholarship, according to these national figures, was around $275. (The 1960 figure seems to be above $300.) Employment was available to 288,000, and earnings from this employment totaled $66 million, making an average of $230. (Employment figures are undoubtedly greatly understated.)

This national survey reveals much smaller relative earnings from employment than the Hollis study. In his sample of 15,288 students, Hollis found that the *median* size of scholarship awards in 1952–53 was $218 where the college controlled the funds, and $268 where it did not.[4]

Since the fellowships awarded in 1955–56 amounted to $18.2 million and the number of fellowships was almost 25,000 (roughly one-tenth of the number of scholarships), it may be concluded that the average value of a fellowship was about three times that of the average scholarship.

Why are fellowships so generous? They seem especially large when one considers the fact that the training of graduate students is much more costly to IHL than that of undergraduates. The higher costs of training graduate students is explained partly by the fact that most graduate students are trained at high-cost institutions, and partly because of the small classes and the talent used in teaching them. I believe the explanation of the high level of fellowships is the impecunious state of the graduate student who often has a wife and family to support, and also intense competition for these students. Institutions get back some of the money they spend on graduate students by obtaining relatively low-cost teachers.

REGIONAL DISTRIBUTION OF SCHOLARSHIPS AND FELLOWSHIPS

From Table 16-2 it is clear that some regions have a larger percentage of scholarships and fellowships than might be expected by their income and population. The Northeast is especially favored in its proportion of

TABLE 16-2
Percentage of Scholarships, Fellowships, Income, and Resident College Enrollment

Percentage item	Northeast	South	Central	West	Total
Scholarship dollars............	43	21	24	12	100
Scholarship numbers...........	27	29	32	12	100
Fellowship dollars.............	41	13	35	12	100
National income..............	35	20	29	17	100
Resident college enrollment.....	28	26	29	17	100

Source: Calculated from HEW, *Financial Aid for College Students, Undergraduate and Graduate; Statistics of Higher Education, Faculty, Students and Degrees, 1953–54;* and U.S. Department of Commerce, *Regional Trends of the American Economy.*

the nation's scholarships and fellowships, considering its relative income and resident college enrollment. The South is not too much out of line with its income in its share of scholarships, but its scholarships are substantially out of line with its proportion of college enrollment; and fellowships are far below what might be expected from its income or resident college enrollment. The reasons for this last fact are a smaller concentration of graduate work and the policy of state universities which provide relatively few fellowships.[5] In the Far West the amount of money available for both scholarships and fellowships is low compared to income and resident college enrollment. Here again the large part played by public institutions is relevant. The reader will note that the relative scholarship stipend is much higher in the Northeast than elsewhere. This is suggested by a comparison of the percentage of dollars and of scholarships in different regions in relation to the percentage of the total number of students. The Northeast has 43 per cent of the dollar value, but only 27 per cent of the scholarships. The South, on the other hand, has 29 per cent of the number of scholarships and only 21 per cent of the dollar value of scholarships.[6]

In 12 states the total amount of fellowship money is roughly two-thirds of the total amount available for the whole nation. These states are, in order of fellowship money available, New York, Massachusetts, Minnesota, Illinois, California, Michigan, Pennsylvania, Connecticut, Ohio, Wisconsin, Indiana, and New Jersey. The first five account for roughly one-half of the fellowship money.

FELLOWSHIPS: BREAKDOWN BY INSTITUTIONS

There is naturally a large concentration of fellowships in a limited number of institutions. Because there are more than one hundred institutions that yield Ph.D.s, there have been many complaints about this over-centralization. Eight institutions account for roughly 25 per cent of the total amount of fellowship money. These institutions, in the order of the amounts of money available in 1955–56, are the University of Chicago, Harvard, Columbia, Yale, MIT, Johns Hopkins, Princeton, and Cornell. Five state universities have $5.16 million of fellowship money available. These states, in order of their amount of such money, are Minnesota, Illinois, California, Ohio, and Wisconsin. All told, thirteen institutions account for about two-thirds of the total fellowship money.

According to Algo D. Henderson, $1,293,000 was available for scholarships in the state of Connecticut in 1949–50; but 82 per cent of the total was at five of the twenty-five colleges, and 61 per cent at only one. He presented this evidence to support his arguments on the bad distribution of scholarships.[7]

The National Defense Education Act of 1958 provides help for fellowships for IHL, with grants to the institution on the condition that the institution is expanding or that it provides a new program. This approach stems from a desire to distribute fellowship funds more widely and to encourage students to enter teaching.

As a result of the NDEA program, the distribution of fellowships will be greatly changed. Thus fifteen states which ranked 32 to 48 in the number of doctorates awarded in the years 1956–1958, obtained 180 NDEA fellowships. Three states, Idaho, Maine, and South Dakota which had awarded no Ph.D.s in these two years, received 29 fellowship grants. The average for twelve other states of number of NDEA fellowships as per cent of doctoral awards was 190 per cent. The fifteen states then receiving the smallest number of fellowships in relation to doctoral awards were ranked 1 to 16 in number of Ph.D.s awarded in 1956–1958. They received 396 grants, yielding a ratio of grants to doctorates of 6.2 per cent, or about 3 per cent as many relatively as the fifteen states with few doctorate awards in the past.[8]

BREAKDOWN OF SCHOLARSHIPS AND FELLOWSHIPS WITHIN THE INSTITUTION AND BY FIELDS

In a recent study on the future of Columbia University, the University Committee made some interesting breakdowns of the distribution of fellowship or scholarship aid in 1956–57 for the various departments and colleges at Columbia.[9] The maximum percentage of students helped by fellowship or scholarship aid was 51.3 in the undergraduate college as compared with the university average of 18. Next was international affairs with 35.9 per cent. Almost 19 per cent of the students in law received scholarships, 14 per cent in engineering, 11 per cent in business, and the minimum was general studies, nonmatriculated, 3.1 per cent. Unfortunately the total for medicine was not given, but the percentage for nursing was 20, and for dental and oral surgery, also 20. These figures seem to support the theory that those who perform the largest public service get the largest number of scholarships. (At least I assume that there is no direct relationship between a training at Columbia College, say, or in international affairs, and vocational results.) It is to be expected that business school students receive the smallest amount of aid, considering the vocational aspects of their discipline and the large earnings to be expected later.[10]

According to the National Science Foundation study, the support by IHL and outside resources reveals the large advantages to students in the natural sciences. In the academic year 1953–54,

An estimated $48 million was paid by educational institutions, the Federal government and other sources to the 37,000 graduate students surveyed—the median payment per student being under $1,300 excluding any remitted tuition and/or fees. Thirty-two million dollars went to the students in the natural sciences and engineering who constituted 32 per cent of the resident students, while the remaining 68 per cent received an estimated $15 million. Proportionately, more than three times as many students of the natural sciences and engineering as of other fields received some financial help (49 per cent as against 14 per cent), and their median stipend was also somewhat higher, $1,395 as against $1,035.

About six out of every ten graduate students of the natural sciences received support . . . twice as many as in any other major field. In engineering, psychology, the social sciences, and the humanities, roughly two to three students in ten received support.

Actually, as Table 16-3 shows, the ratio of fellowships to number of students is not greatly out of line by fields except in education, which is

TABLE 16-3
Distribution of Fellowships and Ph.D.s

Field	Tuition fellowships 1959–60, per cent	Other fellowships 1959–60, per cent	Awards 1,000 national defense fellowships 1959–60	Ph.D.s 1949–53, per cent
	(1)	(2)	(3)	(4)
Engineering...........................	9.2	13.51	6	7
Major physical sciences, inclusive of mathematics and statistics...................	23.1	24.63	28	37
Biological sciences.....................	14.0	16.46	18	6*
Social sciences........................	23.1	22.89	23	19†
Humanities............................	24.6	17.81	20	12
Education.............................	6	4.68	5	16

* Applied biology.
† Includes psychology and business and commerce.
Source: (1) and (2), HEW, *Summary of Data from Graduate School Survey*, 1960 (mimeographed); (3) *Higher Education*, September, 1959, p. 16; (4) D. Wolfle, *America's Resources of Specialized Talent*, 1954, p. 45. Since finishing this book I note the Office of Education (*Doctoral Study*, 1961) published a volume with a breakdown of fellowships by fields, sources of funds, and average stipend.

low on fellowships. The explanation of the greater availability of fellowships in relation to the number of students in the physical sciences must lie in part in a larger number of students in relation to Ph.D.s in other fields. Also of some interest is the high ratio of fellowships to Ph.D.s in the humanities.

SCHOLARSHIPS IN RELATION TO THE QUALITY OF THE STUDENT

In a survey of about one hundred colleges that use the College Scholarship Service, it was found that in general students of higher quality tend to apply for scholarships and ultimately are enrolled in a CSS college—group I in Table 16-4; group II includes those who applied but were not enrolled; and group III, those who enrolled but did not apply for aid. The median SATV score of applicants in group I receiving aid was 576, while the median for applicants in group I who were not given financial aid was 540.[11]

Institutions participating in the CSS are of unusually high quality. Yet on aptitude scores the scholarship winners under Merit Scholarships revealed an even more impressive record than the CSS students.

The average score for College Entrance Examination Board population is 500; two-thirds score from 400 to 600; scores above 700 are normally

TABLE 16-4

Group	Scholastic aptitude	
	SATV	SATM
Group I.............	562	586
Group II............	514	550
Group III..........	540	542

TABLE 16-5
Percentage of Merit Scholarship Winners Achieving an Aptitude Score

	Verbal		Mathematics	
	1956	1957	1956	1957
Above 700..............	65	46	70	69
Below 600..............	½	3	2	5

attained by 2 per cent, and scores above 750 by 0.6 per cent. "The median combined score for the Merit winners, expressed on the 200–800 scale, is 710. Two-thirds of the Merit winners scored between 680 and 750." This is far above the CSS average for scholarship winners. In fact, only three Merit winners (½ per cent) scored less than 600 in the verbal section, and only 10 in the mathematics section. But the average CSS for scholarship winners was substantially below 600.

These results are for 1956; for 1957 the record was not quite so good for Merit Scholarship holders, but still extraordinary. Perhaps a change in method of selection is relevant in 1957 (see Table 16-5). These results point to the conclusion that the CSS colleges put less emphasis on aptitude tests than the Merit Corporation and also that their reservoir is not as good.[12] (The Merit winners are indeed top students.) Relevant also is the point that the objectives of the Merit Corporation and members of the CSS vary to some extent.

A New York study also reveals that scholarships are related to the aptitude of the student. Table 16-6 shows that in general those with IQs of 120 and over receive scholarships of from $300 to $500 and over $500 in larger percentages than those with lower IQs. Those with IQs below 110 receive relatively more of the smaller scholarships.

TABLE 16-6

Number of High School Graduates Planning to Attend Any Kind of College, by Ability (IQ), and Percentage Distribution according to Amount of Scholarship, 1953

Ability (IQ)	Number of students	Percentage receiving each amount			
		Less than $100	$100–$299	$300–$500	Over $500
Below 110	320	19	41	23	17
110–119...........	475	14	42	25	19
120 and over.......	734	9	27	31	33

Source: State University of New York, *Crucial Questions about Higher Education,* 1955, p. 58.

In general, then, scholarship students are likely to be of higher quality than nonscholarship students, but since need is a factor, too, some of the best scholars in a class do not receive scholarships because they do not need them.

In a study undertaken by students at the University of Wisconsin, the following statement was made: "Many voice the opinion that the grade-point average is weighted too heavily in selecting scholarship recipients. The point is made by several that the necessity for heavy workloads results in lower grade-point average and resulting failure to qualify for scholarship aid."[13]

On most scholarship grants there are restrictions made on the basis of academic achievement or on the basis of need, or both. For example, in a careful study of the state of Michigan, the writers concluded:

"Of the total amount of scholarship money awarded, 38.4 per cent was for scholarships carrying some restriction on academic achievement, while 56 per cent carried restrictions involving both high academic achievement and financial need; only 3.6 per cent of the amount awarded was restricted to financial need only."[14]

In general, privately controlled institutions have fewer restrictions on their scholarships than publicly controlled institutions. But this conclusion is based on the Michigan experience, which may not be typical. For example, the public IHL in Michigan gave out only 1.2 per cent of their total scholarship funds with no restrictions based on financial need or academic achievement; but those privately controlled allocated 6.9 per cent of their funds without restriction. Publicly controlled schools restrict 40.7 per cent of their total funds to students of high academic achievement, whereas the privately controlled IHL restrict only 26.8 per cent in this way.[15]

From this section one can draw the following conclusions:

More able students apply for scholarships.

Standards for scholarships are much higher (and different) for National Merit than for grants by CSS colleges.

Higher awards tend to go to students with higher IQs (New York State study).

Students earning scholarships are brighter than those who do not.

Awards of scholarships are dependent on need as well as academic excellence.

But all this is still consistent with the conclusions of the last chapter, which revealed certain wastes in scholarship administration, including a tendency to award grants excessively to higher-income groups.

SCHOLARSHIPS AND INCOMES

In the Hollis sample the median family income for those with no scholarship aid was $5,260 and for those with some scholarship aid, $4,323. A Chicago study revealed median parental incomes of $9,000 for students without aid, $5,044 for students with aid, and $4,071 for unsuccessful scholarship applicants.[16] A striking observation in the Hollis study is that the amount of scholarship money does not vary greatly with family income. The extremes of scholarship grants vary from $168 for those with incomes of $1,000 to $1,999 to a maximum of $300 for those with incomes of $15,000 to $24,999. The reader will recall an earlier statement on high incomes of scholarship winners and especially applicants at Harvard.[17]

Many experts have observed that scholarships seem to be available to those with fairly high incomes or middle incomes, but not so much for those with low incomes, and least available to those with very low incomes. One expert writes as follows:[18]

We discovered another important thing, in my opinion. Many of the students now being awarded scholarships are not in the lowest income groups because it has been found, even though a student has outstanding ability, he needs more assistance than most of the scholarships provide, and as a result there is a tendency—and actually there is more than a tendency; it is going on —to avoid giving scholarships to those in the most needy groups, since such scholarships do not permit them to go to college anyway.

SCHOLARSHIPS IN RELATION TO EXPENDITURES

The CSS study for about one hundred participating colleges has revealed a relationship between scholarships and expenditures. The higher the expenditures at college by students, the larger the scholarships tend to be. This may merely suggest that colleges where expenditures were higher tended to give large scholarships, not that the same college gave larger amounts to those who spend more.

In the New York State study it was found that students who planned to attend college and who estimated expenses of under $900 obtained 17 per cent of their scholarships in the over $500 category. Those with estimated college expenses of $1,500 and over received 42 per cent of their scholarships in this category.[19]

(I noted earlier that the relation of expenditures and income is not as high as might be expected. Students from very high-income groups do not spend as much relatively as might be expected from their higher incomes.)

DISTRIBUTION OF SCHOLARSHIPS BY COLLEGE CLASSES

Many people suspect that colleges give a large number of scholarships to freshmen in order to entice them to enroll and then later do not sustain these scholarships. In the Hollis study it is shown that freshmen received 29.5 per cent of the scholarships, sophomores 29.3, juniors 21.5 and seniors 18.5. These figures would suggest that the general opinion is right. But in view of the attrition of students through the four college years, the proportion of scholarships to freshmen and sophomores does not seem excessive. A study of 14 IHL, mostly prestigious, does not reveal large differences in the proportion of freshmen and all undergraduates receiving scholarships in 1953–54. At Pomona, oddly enough, 14 per cent of freshmen and 20 per cent of all undergraduates had scholarships.[20]

There are, however, variations among institutions. In Utah, according to the president of Brigham Young University, some institutions give as few as 20 per cent of their scholarships to freshmen; one gives as many as 86 per cent, the average in the state being 60 per cent.[21]

In Michigan, freshmen receive 23 per cent of the scholarships in state-controlled institutions, other undergraduates 68 per cent, and graduates 8 per cent. But in the privately controlled institutions freshmen receive 40 per cent, other undergraduates 58 per cent, and graduates 2½ per cent. The private institutions, then, seem much more anxious to attract freshmen than the public institutions. Since more freshmen continue through the four college years in private institutions than in public ones, differences are even larger than is suggested here. The difference is more significant also because state-controlled institutions give 16 per cent of their scholarships *funds* to freshmen, whereas privately controlled institutions give 36 per cent.[22]

SCHOLARSHIPS IN PUBLIC AND PRIVATE INSTITUTIONS

It is clear that public institutions generally depend less on scholarships and fellowships than do private institutions: public institutions control only one-third of the total scholarship funds. A breakdown by regions points to that conclusion. The largest scholarships are given by institutions in the Northeast, where state institutions have made the smallest headway.

The Michigan study, however, suggests that this does not hold true in all states. In Michigan the tradition of the state university is a strong one. There were 68,910 full-time equivalent students in state-controlled institutions, and these students received 11,509 awards, 167 awards per 1,000 full-time students. In the private institutions there were 23,579 students who received 1,849 awards, or only 78 per 1,000 full-time students. The average amount of award per full-time student was $39.07 in the state-controlled institutions and only $17.78 in the privately controlled institutions. But the amount of award per recipient was roughly the same, $234 and $227, explained of course by the much larger number of awards in the state institutions.[23]

Competition between state-controlled and private institutions is of course reflected in their scholarship programs. In some respects, of course, they do not compete, because the prestige of the private institution often attracts students in spite of its higher costs. Still, the competition is likely to be especially severe over those young boys and girls who cannot afford to pay the high tuition costs of the private institutions. How do the private institutions fare under this competition?

Table 16-7 shows that private institutions defend themselves in one very effective way: they tend to give scholarships to a larger percentage of their students, and the amount of these scholarships is usually greater than the scholarships in public institutions. (Recall also the discussion of Merit Scholarships.) For example, the University of California at Berkeley bestowed scholarships on only 6 per cent of its students, while Stanford gave scholarships to 16 per cent of its students. The difference between tuition and fees for the two institutions was of the order of $660. But the Stanford scholarships averaged about $600 more than the Berkeley scholarships. For their students on scholarship, therefore, Stanford provided enough help to wipe out the difference. In a similar way the University of Chicago competes with the University of Illinois by giving scholarships to 44 per cent of its students and by providing scholarships that pay $458 more than those of the state university. This enables Chicago to offset the advantage of the lower (by $510) tuition of the University of Illinois.

Carleton College, however, competes with difficulty with the University of Minnesota, since the difference in scholarships is only $160 as compared to a difference in tuition and fees of close to $500. But 34 per cent of the Carleton College students receive scholarships as compared to only 5 per cent at the University of Minnesota. Obviously students at the University of Minnesota, especially those who live near the university, are at a great

TABLE 16-7

Comparison of Enrollment, Scholarships, Tuition, and Average Value of Scholarships, 1955–56, for Major State-controlled Institutions and Private Competitors in Eight States

Institution	Under-graduate enrollment	Number of scholarships	Scholarships, per cent of enrollment	Tuition and fees	Average value of scholarships
California:					
Stanford....................	5,176	836	16	$ 750	$757
University of California, Berkeley.	13,022	752	6	90	151
Illinois:					
University of Chicago...........	2,462	1,098	44	690	602
University of Illinois............	19,933	3,077	15	180	144
Minnesota:					
Carleton College..............	903	306	34	660	352
University of Minnesota.........	20,766	986	5	183	190
New York:					
Columbia University............	2,405	558	23	816	665
City College of New York*......	7,265				
Tennessee:					
Vanderbilt University...........	2,877	435	15	550	476
University of Tennessee.........	6,353	316	5	159	203
Massachusetts:					
Harvard.....................	4,452	1,148	26	856	723
University of Massachusetts......	3,628	258	7	139	185
Connecticut:					
Yale........................	3,923	1,112	28	1,000	697
University of Connecticut........	6,918	809	12	160	211
Pennsylvania:					
University of Pennsylvania †......	7,168	1,715	24	935	554
Pennsylvania State University....	13,613	561	4	250	315

* Free; no significant scholarships.
† Private but receives some help from the state government.
Source: Compiled and calculated from HEW, *Financial Aid for College Students: Undergraduate.*

financial advantage in going there. Naturally, Carleton College, being a small liberal arts school, attracts a particular clientele.

In its competition with the City College of New York, Columbia is at a similar disadvantage, especially since CCNY students live at home, and many of Columbia's do not. But still, 23 per cent of Columbia students, who must pay $816 in fees as against virtually no fees, receive average scholarships of $665.

Despite a large number of scholarships, Vanderbilt University is still at some disadvantage in relation to the University of Tennessee. Harvard is at a financial disadvantage to the University of Massachusetts (tuition is $717 higher, scholarships only $538 higher) but has a large advantage, as does Yale, in the amount of employment available in a large city and also in that a larger proportion of the students live at home. Even for the 24 per cent of the students who receive scholarships at the University of Pennsylvania there is a differential of about $450 in favor of Pennsylvania State University. But this disadvantage is wiped out for those students who live in the Philadelphia area.

The competition of colleges which charge no tuition is suggested by an announcement from Yeshiva University, New York City, which competes with tuitionless CCNY. According to this announcement, Yeshiva University in 1957–58 planned to spend $753,825 to provide scholarship aid for 84 per cent of its student body. This scholarship assistance program represents more than 25 per cent of the university's total maintenance budget of $3 million.[24] (The national average is only 2 to 3 per cent.)

All these facts, allow me to emphasize, relate only to the scholarship students. For the others, the public institutions retain a large advantage.

These statistics related to the situation in 1955–56. Differentials tend to rise. For example, the tuition rise was about 33 per cent, or $50, for public IHL and 33 per cent, or $150, for private IHL in four years ending 1958–59. In Massachusetts the tuition differential is about $1,000 in 1960 between Harvard and the state university. Should tuition in prestige IHL rise to $2,000 by 1970 (a realistic forecast) and in public IHL about $125 to about $300, then a differential of about $1,700 would emerge. Very large scholarships might maintain competitive advantages for these institutions, but the problem for private IHL of competing for nonscholarship students would be serious indeed.

SCHOLARSHIPS IN RELATION TO RESIDENCE OF STUDENTS

Despite the fact that living away from home is more expensive, scholarship awards do not seem to vary greatly with the distance of the student from his home. The median size of awards made from college-controlled funds is $218; for a student living at his parents' home, $208; and for one residing in a college-operated dormitory, $235.[25]

But the Moon study showed that for the CSS colleges there were substantial differences. According to that study, in men's colleges the awards for commuter students were $371, $411, and $427 for those whose yearly expenses were less than $1,500, $1,500 to $1,700, and more than $1,700, respectively. Corresponding figures for residents were $626, $675, and $940.[26] Differences were also found in women's colleges and coeducational colleges, although they were not so large.

SCHOLARSHIPS IN RELATION TO THE RISE OF TUITION

The tendency has been to increase scholarships more than tuition. Table 16-8 suggests that conclusion.

The total amount of scholarships has risen from 5 per cent of total fees to 12 per cent. The amount of student aid per student has gone up from roughly $7 to $34. This relative rise is two to three times that of the rise in average fees. Even when allowance is made for the substantial rise of numbers of scholarships relative to enrollment, the amount *per student aided* has increased more than tuition per student.[27] It does not follow, however, that stipends rose more than total costs. A very rough estimate also reveals that tuition minus scholarship aid is a smaller proportion of per capita disposable income than twenty years ago.

TABLE 16-8

Relation of Scholarships and Tuition Fees, 1939–40, 1953–54, 1955–56, and 1957–58

Year	Total fees (millions)	Scholarships (millions)	Enrollment (millions)	Tuition and fees per student
1939–40	$201	$ 10 (est.)	1.5	$133
1953–54	554	75	2.2 (nonveterans only)	250
1955–56	741	96	2.66	277
1957–58	939	109*	3.24	290

* Adjusted student aid totals for estimates of loans.

Source: HEW, *Statistics of Higher Education: Receipts, Expenditures and Property,* 1955–56; and *Memo to the Board,* 1960 Series, no. 4.

From a survey made available by (then) President Stevenson of Oberlin, I find that tuition income rose at Oberlin from $1,089,000 in 1948–49 to $2,148,000 (estimated) for 1958–59. In the same period scholarships rose from $160,000 to $524,000. The rise for the former was 97 per cent; for the latter, 226 per cent. Again the rise of scholarships has exceeded the rise of tuition fees. (These gains should be adjusted for a moderate rise in enrollment.)

For the years 1925–26, 1933–34, 1946–47, and 1956–57 scholarships at Oberlin as a percentage of tuition fees were 10.6 per cent, 25.2, 9.7, and 23.8. The high figure in the midst of the Depression is explained by unsatisfactory economic conditions, the low figure in 1946–47 by the large amounts of veterans' money available. The tendency has been distinctly upward since that period.

In a release of April 11, 1958, Harvard University announced a new scholarship and loan program and an increase of tuition from $1,000 to $1,250. Total amount of help, including loans, would rise from $1,330,000 to $1,830,000. Approximately 1,200 of Harvard's 4,300 undergraduates now receive scholarship aid, and 300 receive loan aid.

The trends are evident in the following:

Year	Student's budget	Tuition	Average scholarship
1946	$1,200	$ 400	$400–500
1958	2,600	1,250	900+

In a period when the budget rose by $1,400, tuition rose by $850 and scholarships by $400 to $500. Here the rise of the stipend was less than that of tuition, and tuition minus aid, as well as total costs, rose more than family income. I estimate gift aid at 18 per cent of tuition income in 1949–50 and 25 per cent in 1958–59. Almost 35 per cent of the rise of tuition income went to scholarships. Thus, though the average value of scholarships has not increased as much as the average of tuition at Harvard, scholarships tend to absorb an increasing share of tuition. The latter is evident from the Harvard and the national figures. As tuition rises it becomes necessary to help a larger proportion of students—20 per cent at Harvard ten years ago and close to 30 per cent today. From 1939–40 to 1957–58, an increase of scholarships of about $100 million for the nation contributed to a rise of tuition income of seven to eight times as much. But we should note that enrollment more than doubled in this period. By 1960–61 national tuition income should be at least $1¼ billion and scholarships under institutional control more than $125 million. If so, the rise of tuition income to date has been more than eight times that of scholarships, as can be seen in Table 16-9.

TABLE 16-9
Fees and Scholarships, U.S., 1940 and Later Years

Income	Millions of dollars			Rise 1940 to 1961 (dollars)
	1939–40	1958–59*	1960–61*	
Fees...............	200	1,000	1,250	1,050
Scholarships.........	10	120	135	125

* Estimated on basis of change from 1953–54 to 1955–56.

SUMMARY

1. Despite high costs of graduate study to IHL, fellowships tend to be three times as large per grant as scholarships.

2. Distribution of scholarships and fellowships is uneven among regions,

with the heaviest concentration in the Northeast and the smallest in the South. Thirteen institutions account for two-thirds of the fellowship funds.

3. The amounts given in scholarships vary directly with aptitude, but the score differences between scholarship and nonscholarship students are not so large as might be expected.

4. Though in general scholarships go to those of low economic status, variations in the amount received by each student are relatively small in relation to income. Many low-income students are excluded because needs are too great to be overcome with the available resources.

5. The amount of a scholarship varies directly with expenditures of the student. This stems from the tendency of high-cost IHL to offer relatively large stipends.

6. The evidence that a large number of scholarships are given to freshmen in order to attract them and are afterwards withdrawn is not great. But private IHL seem to use this technique more than public IHL (at least in Michigan).

7. Many private institutions competing with public ones offset their higher fees by offering many more scholarships at a level adequate to offset the tuition difference. Thus the top fifth or quarter of students can choose a private IHL without loss of funds. It remains to be seen whether this capacity of private institutions to compete with public will continue into the 1970s.

8. Scholarships do not by any means reflect the differences between costs of living at home and at college.

9. An important function of scholarships is that they make increases of tuition practical. In twenty years a rise of scholarship of $125 million is related to an increase of fees of more than $1 billion.

FOOTNOTES

[1] Unless otherwise indicated, the material upon which this study is based is HEW, *Financial Aid for College Students, Undergraduate; ibid., Graduate;* and *Costs of Attending College.*

[1a] This is based on national totals, not a sample (the 1952–53 total), and points to smaller contributions of scholarships.

[2] The 15 per cent suggested on pp. 54–55 of HEW, *Costs of Attending College* relate to scholarships under college administration only.

[3] *Ibid.,* pp. 48 and 54–55; Lansing et al., *How People Pay for College,* 1960, p. 22; and Kiplinger, *Changing Times,* September, 1960, p. 44.

[4] *Ibid.,* p. 53.

[5] A study made by the National Science Foundation for 1954 of *all* aid to graduate students reveals the South in a more favorable position. (National Science Foundation, *Graduate Student Enrollment and Support,* 1959.)

[6] The geographical distribution, according to the National Science Foundation's survey, *ibid.,* p. 34, does not reveal as large a percentage of stipends for the Northeast in relation to enrollment as my institutional statistics have suggested,

Apparently, when the distribution of fellowships and assistantships are considered together and when allowance is made for the contribution of the Federal government and outside aid, the South comes out much better than my earlier analysis seems to suggest.

Regional Distribution of Stipends and Students, April, 1954

Region	Stipend		Per cent	
	Numbers	Per cent	Resident students	Full-time students
North Central........	12,369	33.5	22.9	28.7
Northeast............	10,538	28.5	37.4	27.8
South..............	7,018	19.0	19.7	18.9
Pacific.............	4,595	12.4	13.7	16.1
West..............	2,451	6.6	6.3	8.5
Total..............	36,971	100.0	100.0	100.0

Source: National Science Foundation, *Graduate Student Enrollment and Support*, p. 34.

[7] F. J. Brown (ed.), American Council on Education, *Approaching Equality of Opportunity in Higher Education*, March, 1955, p. 16.

[8] From *Higher Education*, October, 1959, pp. 14–15.

[9] *The Report of the President's Committee on the Educational Future of the University*, Columbia University, New York, 1957, pp. 220–227.

[10] For a comparison of resources by departments, see Table 16A1-1.

[11] C. C. Cole, Jr., "Scholarship Applicants Today," *College Board Review*, Spring, 1957, pp. 17–18.

[12] Cf. *National Merit Scholarship Corporation, 1956*, p. 21; *ibid., 1957*, p. 23.

[13] S. Goodnight and P. Trump, *Student Expenses and Financial Resources of the University of Wisconsin*, 1953, p. 25. (Mimeographed.)

[14] *The Survey of Higher Education in Michigan: Financial Assistance to Students in Michigan Institutions of Higher Learning*, Staff Study 8, May, 1958, p. 49.

[15] *Ibid.*, p. 50.

[16] HEW, *Costs of Attending College*, p. 55; *College and University*, 1951–52, p. 384.

[17] R. C. King, "Financial Thresholds to College," *College Board Review*, Spring, 1957, p. 22.

[18] *Hearings, on Scholarship and Loan Programs, House Committee on Education and Labor*, 1958, p. 589.

[19] *Crucial Questions about Higher Education*, p. 57.

[20] HEW, *Costs of Attending College*, p. 57; *College Admissions*, II, p. 91.

[21] *Hearings, on Scholarship and Loan Programs, op. cit.*, p. 434.

[22] *The Survey of Higher Education in Michigan, op. cit.*, p. 22.

[23] *Ibid.*

[24] "Educational Tickertape," *School and Society*, Jan. 18, 1958.

[25] HEW, *Costs of Attending College*, p. 53.

[26] Rexford G. Moon, "Aid Programs—from Application to Award," *College Board Review*, Winter, 1957, p. 17.

[27] These figures have been compiled from HEW, *Statistics of Higher Education: Receipts, Expenditures and Property, 1953–54, 1955–56;* and *Education, Faculty, Students and Degrees, 1953–54, 1955–56.*

APPENDIX 1.

TABLE 16A1-1

Departmental Fellowship, Scholarship Rankings, Columbia University 1956–57

Departments with more than 50 students	Total registration	Total fellowships	Average fellowship	Percentage of students on fellowships	Fellowships per capita
Zoology..................	51	18	$1,062	35	$375
Geology..................	68	23	944	33	319
Chemistry.................	110	28	1,057	25	270
Sociology.................	98	23	943	23	221
Public law and government..	297	52	829	18	145
Economics.................	186	34	711	18	130
History...................	448	81	573	18	104
Mathematics..............	88	9	992	10	101
Anthropology.............	101	19	520	19	98
Physics...................	196	23	806	12	95
English...................	506	56	756	11	84
Philosophy................	132	14	660	11	70
Psychology...............	96	9	511	9	47
Romance languages.........	173	9	387	5	20

Source: *The Educational Future of Columbia University*, p. 223.

APPENDIX 2. SCHOLARSHIP FUNDS

Appendix 2 contains six tables of some importance. But first comes a summary:

Table 16A2-1. A historical survey of scholarship funds, numbers receiving and average stipend, both for scholarships and fellowships. Stipends increase, and number of stipends over a twenty-year period rise more than enrollment.

Table 16A2-2. The ratio of scholarship aid to tuition income and general and educational income rises substantially.

Table 16A2-3. But the upward trend is not so clear from Harvard material going back one hundred and thirty years.

Table 16A2-4. Over a period of forty years ending 1940–41, scholarship funds at Amherst do not rise as much as tuition income.

There follow various estimates of scholarships and fellowships not under the control of IHL.

Table 16A2-5. Sources of funds for scholarships and fellowships. (General funds tend to provide a rising share.)

Table 16A2-6. Presents for the years 1940 and 1956:

Percentage of students aided

Dollar stipend per student aided, for:

14 Ivy and other outstanding private universities

10 high-quality women's colleges

20 high-quality liberal arts colleges

40 large urban institutions

23 large Catholic institutions

This table reveals changing policies and financial problems of these groups and varying recourse to price discrimination.

TRENDS

In Table 16A2-1 are some statistics on scholarships and fellowships compiled from numerous sources. These statistics reveal that scholarships increased in numbers substantially more than enrollment in the last twenty years, in fact more than three times as much from 1940 to 1956. From 1950 to 1956, scholarships in numbers roughly doubled, while enrollment changed little. Note the substantial rise since 1940–41, though at this time military service was beginning to keep numbers aided by IHL down. In 1946–47 and 1949–50 the availability of GI benefits also tended to depress the number of students aided.

TABLE 16A2-1

Enrollment, Scholarships, and Fellowships, Numbers, Dollar Value, and Financial Sources,
1936, 1940–41, 1946–47, 1949–50, 1952–53, and 1955–56

Year	Enrollment (000s)	No. of IHL in study	Scholarships ($000)	No. receiving aid	Average stipend ($)	Sources of funds ($M)	Fellowships $000	No.	Average stipend ($)
1936	1,494[a]	674	8,863	66,708	133	....	2,577	5,797	444
1940–41		967	10,210	61,290	165	....	4,514	11,390	394
1946–47[b]	.....	?	21,229	113,425	187				
1949–50	2,659	1,198	27,000	124,223	218	....	9,266	13,659	678
1952–53	2,425[d]	c	.....	338,000[e]	218[f] 268[g]				
1953–54	2,534	....	74,789	......	...	a = 13.6[h] b = 16.8[i] c = 2.52[j] d = 45.7[k]			
1955–56	2,661	1,321	96,224	237,370	277	....	18,239	24,855	734

[a] 1939–40.
[b] Scholarships and fellowships combined.
[c] Sample 14,066 students in over 100 IHL.
[d] Interpolated.
[e] I obtain this figure by applying Hollis' result of 16.7 per cent receiving aid to total resident enrollment in 1952–53. This includes fellowships also. The 17 per cent figure seems high in part because outside aid is also included.
[f] 218 = college controlled.
[g] 268 = other.
[h] Restricted endowment.
[i] Gifts.
[j] Public.
[k] Transfers.

Source: HEW, *Scholarships and Fellowships*, Bulletin 16, 1951, (Reprint 1956); *Costs of Attending College*, Bulletin 9, 1957, pp. 53–55; *Statistics of Higher Education: Receipts, . . . 1953–54*, p. 42; 1955–56, pp. 6–7, 52–53; *Financial Aid to College Students, Undergraduate; ibid., Graduate*; R. G. Axt, *The Federal Government and the Financing of Higher Education*, 1952, pp. 229–230; The President's Commission on Higher Education, *Higher Education for American Democracy*, II, pp. 46–47.

According to the President's Commission of 1947,[1] scholarship holders numbered about 5 per cent of enrollment in 1940–41 and 1946–47.

Average value of scholarships also rose; the rise roughly paralleled the increase in the cost of living and exceeded, though not by much, that of tuition and other costs of going to college.

* * *

As tuition has risen in recent years, scholarships have tended to become a larger part of the total intake of fees. For example, Table 16A2-2 gives an indication for the country as a whole. From 1939–40 to 1949–50 the scholarship aid funds of IHL tended to decline relatively. Part of the explanation here is the large resources available under the GI Bills. From 1949–50 to 1957–58, however, scholarship funds rose from 2.3 to 10.7

TABLE 16A2-2
Relation of Student Aid to Student Fees Inclusive of Veterans' Payments
to Universities for Tuition, and Educational and General Income*

Year	Outlay on scholarships, percentage of tuition income	Scholarships, percentage of educational income
1939–40	5	2
1949–50	2.3	0.9
1953–54	12.5	3.1
1955–56	10.9	2.8
1957–58	10.7	2.7

* I assume that student aid in 1939–40 was $10 million.
There are some variations from this estimate.
Source: Computed from HEW, *Statistics of Higher Education: Receipts, Expenditures and Property, 1955–56,*
and *1957–58* (Preliminary).

per cent of tuition and from 0.9 to 2.7 per cent of general and educational income. Reductions of GI money contributed to this result. From earlier statistics, it is clear that the recent rise is associated with the increased number of scholarships as well as with a rise in average value.

Similar trends are noted in the detailed study of Yale's finances. For example, in 1940–41 aid accounted for 23 per cent of established tuition fees at Yale, and for 32 per cent in 1952–1954.[2]

A LONGER VIEW

Taking a rather longer view on the basis of available Harvard figures (Table 16A2-3), we see that the trend is not clearly upward. There was a

TABLE 16A2-3
Scholarships, Harvard

Year	Thousands of dollars	Percentage of total expense
1829–30	1	2.7
1889–90	67	8.1
1929–30	661	5.7
1956–57	3,145	3.1

Source: *Treasurer's Reports, Harvard University.*

large rise from 1829–30 to 1889–90. But from 1889–90 to 1956–57, despite the very large increase in total amounts of student aid, the percentage contribution of student aid to total expense declined greatly.

The figures in Table 16A2-4 from Amherst over a very long period are of some interest. Since the total of scholarships in 1940–41 was 6 times that of the beginning of the century and tuition income (tuition times enrollment) 8.8 times that of the year 1900–1901, we conclude that scholarships over this long period did not rise as much as tuition income. From 1930–31 to 1952–53 instructional cost per student at Amherst rose by 75 per cent and scholarships by only 31 per cent.[3]

TABLE 16A2-4
Amherst, Scholarships and Related Variables, 1900 to 1941

Year	Scholarships (thousands)	Loans (thousands)	Enrollment	Tuition
1940–41	$89.9	$3.9	851	$450
1930–31	73.3	6.3	670	400
1920–21	26.2	1.9	498	200
1910–11	17.7	0.5	494	110
1900–1901	14.6	?	393	110

In general then the evidence is that in *recent* years scholarship funds have been rising more rapidly than tuition or than total educational income or expenditures. Over the long run, however, this trend is not at all clear, and some evidence seems to suggest that scholarship funds have not risen as much as over-all instructional expenditures.

*   *   *

SCHOLARSHIPS UNDER OUTSIDE CONTROL

On the basis of the Hollis study (again I note that this is a small sample), we infer that total scholarships in 1955–56 (institution controlled and outside) amounted to $98 million or roughly $100 million. But the 1955–56 HEW study puts the total student aid *by IHL* at $96 million.

We do not know the exact amount of outside scholarships. The HEW[4] submits the following:

The estimates of the Sponsored Scholarship Service of the Educational Testing Service for the current academic year (1957–58) for the principal volume of this non-institutional scholarship assistance, that granted by business firms and corporations place a number of these grants at approximately 28,000 or a total value of approximately $18 million. The largest segment of this

TABLE 16A2-5

Sources of Scholarship and Fellowship Funds under Institutional Control, Two Years

Source	Scholarships, per cent		Fellowships, 1949–50, per cent
	1949–50	1953–54	
State funds.................	16.6 ⎫	3.3	19.3
Local funds.................	1.7 ⎭		1.4
Endowment earnings..........	25.6	17.3	19.3
Gifts......................	22.3	21.3	24.0
Unrestricted income..........	33.8	58.2	36.0
Total....................	100.0	100.0	100.0

Source: HEW, *Statistics of Higher Education: Receipts, Expenditures and Property, 1955–56*, pp. 42–43; T. V. Wilkins, *Scholarships and Fellowships Available at Institutions of Higher Learning*, Bulletin 16, 1951, p. 1.

group of scholarships are those administered by the National Merit Corporation. This year approximately 60 business firms and corporations awarded about 1,400 Merit Scholarships and their total value was almost $900,000.

These seem to be only part of the total of outside scholarships and fellowships. My estimate based on the Hollis figures is about $33 million. The President's Commission (1957) put the total of outside scholarships in 1955 at $20 million, $10 million through corporations and foundations, and $10 million in various state programs. But the estimates of both institutional scholarships and outside scholarships are low.[5]

Some indication of the external grants can be had from a study by the National Science Foundation.[6] These statistics relate to fellowships and assistantships. In 1954, of the 37,000 stipends available, 45 per cent were in teaching assistantships, 32 per cent in research, and 23 per cent in fellowships. The field which deviated most from this average was humanities, with 72 per cent in teaching, 5 per cent in research, and 23 per cent in fellowships.

Of the total awards, natural sciences and engineering received 53 per cent of the institutional stipends, 89 per cent of the Federal, and 65 per cent of the other, and 61 per cent in all.

In all, IHL provided 65 per cent of the stipends, Federal government 19 per cent, and other sources 16 per cent. Those in sciences received relatively high stipends provided by the Federal government.

The average stipend was $1,285.

These statistics might be compared with those of the HEW study, *Financial Aid for College Students, Graduate,* 1957. Total amount of money available for fellowships was $18 million, for loans $5 million, and for assistantships $5 million. The average stipend for fellowships was about $750, and for assistantships a little over $800. The National Science Foundation stipend is clearly a much higher one than that revealed by the HEW study. According to the National Science Foundation study, the average teaching assistantship yielded $1,200, while research assistantships awarded by educational institutions paid $1,300; those by the Federal government, $1,595; and by other sources, $1,435. The fellowships awarded by the educational institutions averaged $890; those by Federal government, $1,620; and those by other sources, $1,375. It is clear that since the HEW study provided information only on fellowships and assistantships provided by the institution, the difference in results between the National Science Foundation and the HEW study is partly the result of the fact that the National Science Foundation included Federal and outside stipends, which are generally higher than institutional stipends. There are also some differences in the definition of aid and in the period of time surveyed.

These grants administered outside of IHL should not be confused with the contributions of philanthropic organizations and individuals to IHL for scholarships. The Council for Financial Aid to Education reports that $33.7 million were made available to IHL for student financial aid for current use, and $25.8 million in addition for endowment for student financial aid.[7] Though it is not made clear, I suspect that these grants were made through the institutions and do not include those contributions over which the corporations or their agents have control. If these figures are accurate—and they are probably as accurate as we can get—the contributions from these sources would account for roughly half of the total amount of scholarship aid controlled by IHL, or about 40 per cent of the total amount of scholarship and fellowship aid in a year. This excludes the capital sum of $25.8 million. This sum should yield about $1 million a year, and if we assume that over recent years ten times this amount were made available for student financial aid as endowment, this might make an additional $10 million available each year. But part of this sum is undoubtedly for loans.

At this point we quote some figures from the Hollis report.[8] For all students the percentage of scholarship aid to total expenses was 4.8 per cent. But in addition 4.3 per cent are put down as a contribution of veterans' benefits and vocational rehabilitation. The average amount of aid to students, both scholarship and nonscholarship holders, was then $133; that is to say, out of an average income of $1,462, the average student in 1952–53 received $133 in aid, or roughly 9.1 per cent. From 1946 to 1959, the government provided help under Public Law 346 to 2.2 million students (maximum of 883,000 in 1948 and minimum of 47,000 in 1955), and 1.2 million students under Public Law 550 (Korea). By May,

1958, only 195 were still in IHL under Public Law 346, but 304,556 were in IHL under Public Law 550.[9]

State funds were an important outside contribution in 1949–50. Endowment earnings contribute only about one-fourth of the total of scholarships and one-fifth of the total of fellowships. The remainder under the control of the institutions apparently comes primarily from unrestricted income (about one-third), gifts (about one-fifth), and state and local funds (a little more than one-sixth).

By 1953–54 substantial changes had occurred, notably a much smaller contribution by government and endowment funds, and a much larger diversion from operating funds. From 1951–52 to 1955–56, the excess of expenditures on student aid over income received for this purpose rose from $20 million to $43 million, and to $60 million by 1957–58. Under the pressure of rising tuition, private IHL tended to increase scholarships and draw more heavily on unrestricted income.

STUDENT AID BY TYPE OF INSTITUTION, 1940 AND 1956

In Table 16A2-6 I compare the percentage of students aided and the dollar aid per student receiving aid, for 14 Ivy and other outstanding private universities, 10 high-quality women's colleges, 20 high-quality liberal arts colleges, 40 large urban universities where the enrollment exceeded 5,000 and where the university was in a community with a population of 200,000 or more, and 23 large Catholic colleges. In the first four columns a comparison is made of all institutions for which material is available for 1940 and 1956, the only years for which I could find comparable figures. Columns under *B* compare identical institutions in 1940 and 1956. In other words, in some instances figures were not available for 1940 and 1956, and in such cases they were eliminated from columns under *B* for both years.

These statistics reveal some interesting trends. First they show that in 1940 high-quality women's colleges provided the highest average dollar of aid for students. The average was roughly three times as high as for students in the liberal arts colleges, the urban universities, and the Catholic colleges, and even about 75 per cent above the average in 14 Ivy and other outstanding private universities.

In this same year the high-quality liberal arts colleges had the largest percentage of students aided, 25 per cent as compared to 14 for the Ivy, 17 for the high-quality women's colleges, and 6.4 and 3.0 for large urban and large Catholic colleges, respectively. What is of even greater interest is the change from 1940 to 1956. These changes reflect a weakening of the competitive position of high-quality women's colleges. It will be noted that the average increase of aid was only about 5 per cent per student

TABLE 16A2-6
Student Aid, Funds under Control of IHL, Groups of Institutions, 1940 and 1956

Institutions	A*				B†			
	1940		1956		1940		1956	
	Per cent of students aided	Aid per student aided	Per cent of students aided	Aid per student aided	Per cent of students aided	Aid per student aided	Per cent of students aided	Aid per student aided
14 Ivy and other outstanding private universities.	14.2	$544	20.0	$ 746	14.2	$544	20.0	$ 746
10 high-quality women's colleges.............	16.8	952(?)	21.4	1,000	16.8	952	21.4	1,000
20 high-quality liberal arts colleges.........	25.5	329	28.0	.....‡	25.5	323	28.1	556
40 large urban institutions (enrollment > 5,000)..	6.4	338	6.5	685	6.4	348	7.2	779
23 large Catholic IHL....	3.0	304	6.4	609	3.0	304	6.3	644

* A = all institutions for which information is available in each year.
† B = comparison only of institutions for which information is available for both years.
‡ Omitted for technical reasons.
Source: Compiled and calculated from materials in ACE, *American Universities and Colleges*, 1940 and 1956.

aided. In total amount of aid per student the Ivy colleges lost ground relatively to the large urban and the large Catholic colleges. Perhaps the largest relative gains were made by the large Catholic colleges. The percentage of students aided in these institutions increased by more than 100 per cent, and the average aid per student increased by about 100 per cent.

From these figures we may infer that in the last fifteen or twenty years the position of the high-quality women's colleges has deteriorated and that the position of the large Catholic colleges and, to a lesser degree, that of the large urban institutions, has improved. The high-quality liberal arts colleges also show some signs of weakness. The Ivy and other outstanding private universities fall in between.

A few other aspects of these figures should be noted. First, by 1940 the high-quality women's colleges seem to have used price discrimination in a much more effective manner than other colleges. The higher level of the average student aid suggests that they charged high basic fees and offset these by substantial scholarships for the able and needy. Second, when one considers the relatively low total expenditures per student in the Catholic and urban institutions, one may conclude that in recent years the urban and Catholic colleges are also resorting more to price discrimination. In other words, by increasing the size of their scholarships and by increasing the proportion of those receiving scholarships, IHL are able to increase their tuition fees much more effectively than they otherwise could.

FOOTNOTES TO APPENDIX 2

[1] *Higher Education for American Democracy,* 1947.

[2] E. C. Budd, *op. cit.,* p. 22.

[3] G. Kennedy (ed.), *Education at Amherst: The New Program,* 1955, pp. 176, 330.

[4] *Hearings, on Scholarship and Loan Programs, House Committee on Education and Labor,* 1958, p. 812.

[5] The President's Committee on Education Beyond the High School, *Second Report to the President,* 1957, p. 50.

[6] *Graduate Student Enrollment and Support,* 1954, especially pp. 22–30.

[7] *Voluntary Support of America's Colleges and Universities, 1956–57.*

[8] P. 48.

[9] Release of VA, *Monthly Veterans in Training, 1958;* and *Readjustment Benefits: Education and Training, etc., 1956,* pp. 22–23; and *Higher Education,* March, 1960, p. 5.

CONCLUDING REMARKS ON SCHOLARSHIPS AND FELLOWSHIPS

When measured against the total costs of going to college of about $8 billion in 1960–61, or $14 billion inclusive of income forgone, the $100 to $150 million available for scholarships and fellowships seems relatively unimportant. But the significance of scholarships and fellowships is greatly increased when consideration is given to the relation of scholarships and the salvage of able young men and women, and the contribution of scholarships to the rise of tuition fees and income—the latter rose ten times as much as the cost of additional scholarships in twenty years.

Scholarship stipends seem to have risen at least as much as tuition generally since prewar times. Where scholarships are about three-quarters of tuition—the national norm—the rise of scholarships to match higher tuition need not increase greatly in excess of the increase in tuition. The objective is to keep constant the ratio of tuition aid to per capita disposable personal or family income. But when scholarships are a small part of tuition, a much larger percentage increase of scholarships is required. Moreover, we have to consider the increase in nontuition costs. Where, as is generally true since 1940, total costs of going to college have risen substantially less than family income, there is no problem. But in many instances, when family income does not respond to rising prices and productivity, an increase of scholarship stipends to match the increase of tuition may not solve the student's problem. Moreover, as tuition rises, an increased number may be confronted with inadequate resources even if tuition rises only about one-half as much as family or per capita income —for tuition is only about one-third of student costs in private IHL and about one-tenth in public. In the last twenty years the number of scholarships in relation to enrollment has greatly increased—undoubtedly in response to the needs of those affected adversely by rising costs. The tie-in of rising stipends should be with increasing total costs, not merely with the inflation of tuition fees.

On the basis of various criteria, the additional funds needed for scholarships and fellowships range from about $400 million to more than $2 billion. My proposal is a rise of aid to about $500 million currently and $1,000 million by 1970. The higher figure by 1970 reflects rising enrollments, higher tuition, gains in family income (an offsetting item) and a larger proportion of part-time students living at home. (I assume no aid for part-time students on the theory that they are largely full-time workers.) How much will be needed for scholarships depends on tuition policy (especially at public IHL), for over-all subsidies for all through low tuition is one approach, and price discrimination through scholarships based on need and ability is another and less costly approach. In fact, the more than $4 billion now being spent for higher education are all subsidies, as I argued earlier. Also relevant is the recourse to loans and employment. The application of the British system, with stipends available to 75 per cent of the students for tuition and subsistence, would cost this country about $2½ billion.

Needs are also related to effective use. Here improvements are on the agenda. Many receive amounts in excess of need; many, amounts so small as to be wasted; the most needy are scarcely considered; the pools from which choices are made are often needlessly narrowed (e.g., the National Merit program and the many corporation programs and college scholarships restricted to Murphys or Cabots or those served by the Burlington Railroad); the distribution of stipends by colleges and regions could be improved.

Perhaps the greatest obstacle to an adequate aid program lies in the conflict of interests between private and public IHL, between Northeast and South and West, and prestige and nonprestige institutions. The Northeast wants scholarships and fellowships adjusted to costs and hence at amounts that do not discriminate against the high-cost units (the British system). Others want no large scholarship program, or at most small stipends which would discourage the trek of talent eastward. The public IHL on the whole prefer help to institutions and no substantial scholarship program. They would provide help for all through low tuition. Political pressures now point to a possible acceptance of a program which allocates scholarships by states (discriminating against high scores of the Northeast) and modest stipends. Prestige IHL will have to use substantial resources from gift income to attract large numbers of able but needy students.

PART FOUR

LOANS

Chapter 17

LOANS: VIEWS OF ECONOMISTS

SOCIAL VERSUS PRIVATE PRODUCT

On the whole, the more than two hundred economists who replied to my questionnaire preferred use of scholarships or (and) loans to wholesale subsidization through low tuitions. Price discrimination based on need and hence use of scholarships or loans appeals to economists because their use is economical. The case for low tuition as against price discrimination often rests on ideological positions. This may explain the reluctance of many economists to support indiscriminate subsidies—many prefer to stick to economics and avoid value judgments.

Where society gains, loans need not be financed to cover costs. There might be elements of forgiveness or rates of interest below the commercial rate or the cost to the lender as is provided under the NDEA.

Later I present a plan for credit finance which might be extended over periods of ten, twenty, and forty years.* The essence of the forty-year plan was published in the *College Board Review* (Winter, 1959) and presented to the Deans of Admissions late in 1958. In April, 1959 William Vickrey of Columbia University, in response to my questionnaire, presented a paper full of provocative ideas. Like Friedman and the author, Vickrey was concerned with the imperfections of the market. Inability to estimate closely incomes of college graduates, and even more of the individual college graduate, contributes to underinvestment in education, as does the unavailability of property to serve as a lien, as with a house mortgage.

In his paper Vickrey proposes loans that may even cover income forgone. The borrowers would pay a tax on the excess of income over what would have been available in the absence of the additional education. Hence a graduate student borrowing would presumably profit from a larger exemption than a sophomore. In view of the uncertainties and the difficulty of obtaining capital, the student would be required to pay 6 to 8 per cent on his loan. In this manner additional needed capital would be had, though

* Summarized in Chap. 22.

later with added experience dividends could be paid by the lender, and thus the costs would be brought down. At least the excess of earnings dividends for the debtor over the amount borrowed should be exempt from taxes, and if possible all payments should be exempt from taxation. If re-payments are on a contractual basis, exemption of all repayments would require changes in the law. Exemptions would, for example, be $4,000 for freshmen and $8,000 for those with seven years of higher education. Rates might rise from ½ per cent of the first $2,000 over exemption to 1½ per cent on the amount over exemption plus $2,000. When borrowings are large—say, $40,000 over seven years, payments might rise to 54 per cent on earnings over $10,000.

Unlike Friedman, who would require public financing, Vickrey would rely on individual institutions to raise the money, or limited-profit finance corporations representing many IHL. Neither of these economists proposes subsidies in the loan program—Friedman in part because he concentrates on private gains. I would like to see the Federal government contribute, and since there are gains to society, the government might lend at rates below cost and also offer guarantees as a means of stimulating the flow of private capital—here the experience with housing is significant. In 1960 Senator Johnson introduced a bill which was approved by the Senate Sub-committee on Education, to provide Federal guarantees of student loans.[1]

In a somewhat similar vein B. A. Rogge of Wabash College considers subsidies on higher education unjustifiable, in part because the gains are private. He concludes that the subsidy results in reduced quality of instruction, for the consumer being subsidized has little control over the product. The more numerous the sources of support, the less control over the quality of the product. Above all, he finds an *across-the-board* subsidy wasteful. But, unlike Friedman and Vickrey, he does not propose investment measures to increase the resources in education. In fact his position would lead to reduced resources.[2]

In 1956 Ernest V. Van den Haag wrote an interesting book, *Education as an Industry,* which raises similar problems, and this is as good a place as any to discuss his book. In this volume he criticizes his predecessors, sometimes rather unkindly, but also introduces some interesting ideas into his discussion. More recently there has been a brilliant review of this book by David Riesman.[3]

Van den Haag supports a loan system and even more the free market. He rejects subsidies except in special situations. His argument is roughly as follows:

In many of the professions, particularly in medicine, reward exceeds what might be expected on the basis of costs of investment. What is more, many able potential doctors are unable to go to college and get a medical degree because of financial difficulties. A loan program would enable all potential men of ability to enter the competition. The result would be lower relative rewards for these professionals, though not necessarily lower absolute rewards. In this analysis he follows (or at least does not disagree with) much of what I wrote fifteen years ago in my "How Shall We pay for Education?" and *The Market for College Graduates.*

Perhaps the unique aspects of Van den Haag's analysis lie in his emphasis on the free-market approach. Where rewards (in medicine, for example) are large compared to investment, he expects that large additional numbers will enter the profession. IHL would support those likely to succeed because obviously potential doctors would not undertake these large commitments of loans unless they expected large rewards. In teaching he would not set up such a program, because the teachers receive less than is suggested by their social contribution, and therefore should be aided by scholarships rather than be required to pay a larger part of their education through a loan program.

Van den Haag is quite correct in contending that measures should be taken to break down the monopolistic position of physicians. Yet I find some difficulties in his analysis. The writer assumes a free market, and, as more enter a particular profession, he anticipates that rewards would decline and that those best fitted would be selected for these professions. Indeed, the reservoir from which the professional schools could pick would be greatly increased. But he fails to note that the free market does not exactly operate in these areas. An increase in competition may tend to depress rewards, but this assumes that the training capacity required by the potential doctors, engineers, etc., will be available. Actually, what may happen is that the deans of admission will have a larger number from which to choose; but restrictions on entry and inadequate space and facilities may result in no reduction in rewards, although there might be a greater democratization of the process of selection and entry. This would clearly be an advantage. Should recommendations be accepted for rising doctor output of 75 per cent, such as those made by the Surgeon-General's Committee of 1960, then restrictionism may be effectively treated.

Again, it is not at all obvious to me, as it seems to be to Van den Haag, that merely because a medical student is ready to risk borrowing large sums of money, he is for this reason likely to be the better physician. Willingness to take financial risks does not necessarily improve the selective process. In fact, if loans are made available, some of the more likely prospects may be discouraged. Van den Haag is right that there would then be a larger reservoir; but we must also take into account the fact that some would be deterred, and these might well be the best men for the particular profession.

Though I agree with his general position in favor of loans, I also am fearful that to some extent greater recourse to loans as against grants would discourage some students of ability. Improved public relations might help, however.

Van den Haag also recognizes some difficulties in determining whether a particular student is going to create a social product greater than his reward, a relevant consideration in a liberal arts program. We assume that when the training is primarily vocational, the student receives his reward in future income, and *ordinarily* the public or the institution should not subsidize him. When the curriculum is primarily nonvocational (though even general education which trains students to organize, communicate, and think is not exclusively nonvocational), the case for help through loans and scholarships is much greater. It is more difficult to decide the aid to be given in liberal arts than in some other areas. The reason is, of course, that liberal arts is partly justified on social and partly on vocational grounds. How much one or how much the other in practice is very difficult to discover. Kaysen, in the symposium on *Higher Education in the United States: The Economic Problems* (1960), proposed that the professional student pay the full cost of his education and the liberal arts student pay less. In fact, he has gone further to make the interesting and provocative suggestion that, when a student borrows for a professional job, the employer who engages his service should repay the loan. This is an interesting idea, though fraught with numerous practical difficulties.

Riesman expresses some doubts that a loan program will have the effect of forcing students to pay a larger part of their educational costs. Undoubtedly there is strong resistance here. A large public relations job needs to be done. As Riesman says:

> The buy-now, pay-later pattern on which van den Haag relies has already mortgaged most families for their own consumer goods, and they are unwilling to relinquish or postpone these (as some English middle-income families do) to give their children a first-rate college and professional education. . . . With the larger and earlier families that the middle class is now having and with the desuetude of the older patterns of saving, it seems all the more unlikely to me that van den Haag's plan will prove politically feasible in the face of the powerful lobbies that will strive to continue shifting the burden on to some public or quasi-public purse.

I am hopeful that Riesman's forebodings are unjustified.

Perhaps one other aspect of Van den Haag's position should be noted. He is anxious for larger numbers in many of the professions and therefore reductions in relative compensation. In my *Market for College Graduates,* I expressed the view that in the market sense we would have a surplus of those with a college education, particularly in the professions; but I also pointed out that the medical profession was a special case. Here we have strong elements of restrictionism, in that training facilities, partly through

AMA pressures, are kept in short supply. We need more doctors. There is also a shortage of teachers. We need more money to be brought into education, but this is not merely a free-market operation and will not yield to the forces that Van den Haag stresses. Correction requires action on the part of the government, though in higher education some contribution can be made from private sources. The loan program is one approach to the problem of getting more money into higher education. The 1958 Federal program for increased loans and scholarships (the latter abandoned) is another approach to this problem. Because of its special incentives to particular kinds of training, this legislation may result in a redistribution of talent rather than an increase in the numbers. At the moment, however, numbers are increasing and demand is also rising in many professions; but as the total number of living college graduates rises from $\frac{1}{2}$ million in 1900 to 6 to 8 million currently and at least twice as many twenty years from now, it is likely that the relative position of all the professions will decline.

In short, there are many arguments for an expanded loan program. One surely is that it would make possible a democratization of higher education. But whether monopolistic positions of physicians, for example, would be corrected by loan programs would depend also on the contributions of government, for example.

VIEWS OF ECONOMISTS[4] (220 Replies)

Various financing schemes (including loan programs, which will be dealt with below) were proposed, which involve either ex ante or ex post saving. Notable among the former was a plan whereby the government would issue special high-yielding bonds to be purchased by parents or prospective parents; notable among the latter was a plan whereby private groups would set up and administer revolving funds, from which a student's college expenses would be paid and into which he would later contribute enough money to pay another student's expenses, being morally obligated to do so. This system features a built-in inflation outwitter.

Dependent upon the future of the scholarship program is the loan program, to a very large extent, for the following reason: the two represent to the student alternative methods of financing his education. The more extensive the scholarship program, the less willing will students be to assume indebtedness. In the competition for students, IHL that get far out of line in forcing loans rather than scholarships on students may experience a reduction of demand for their product. But in general competitors tend to work together in such matters, as they do in raising tuition fees. Some economists argued that a loan program would not tend to bring the best students to the best schools, that it would discriminate between students who would be forced to take loans and those who would not.

On the other hand, some economists countered that the sacrifice involved would help to separate the serious from the casual students and foster more responsible attitudes among students generally.

A more disconcerting effect would be the desertion of the liberal arts by materialistic generations of students in favor of the more liberally rewarding sciences and professions. It is admittedly more difficult to "take a flier" when one is carrying $3,000 indebtedness on one's back. Thus the loan program would strengthen the forces of conformity and conventionality and higher management, and decimate the ranks of education, social service, civil service, and general education. The extent to which this would occur would depend on the size of the debt and the extent to which students understood the relation of this financing to expected income.

Another serious criticism of the loan program, especially for undergraduates, is that it ignores, and induces the public to ignore, the public interest in higher education. One economist said that the weak assumption of the loan program is that education is a personal investment undertaken for personal ends. In fact, his argument runs, it serves society's ends and should thus be a social investment. Indeed, however, while the assumption behind the loan program is not cast-iron, neither is it entirely vaporous. Education serves two masters, the individual and the society, and should thus be sustained by both. Nor need a loan program be financed at cost. Subsidies are possible.

A loan program, in the eyes of many economists, is at bottom an intergeneration welfare problem and has implications concerning other such welfare problems. For example, should the offspring rather than the parent pay for his education, on whom does the responsibility for old-age support devolve? Some would say, "On the government, as always." But is it not likely that whatever sense of obligation remains among young Americans for the support of their aged parents would be shaken should their obligation to their parents for their education be removed? To the extent that this would occur, the loan program would be subversive of family ties.

Moreover, to increase by such numbers the people in the class of long-term debtors would be to increase thereby the popular stake in inflation.

Now we have enumerated all the objections to the concept of the expanded loan program and in so doing have probably painted a dreary picture of prevailing economic opinion. In the interests of fairness and accuracy, we must fill in the brighter values. One effect of the availability of loans would be to mitigate the influence of the scholarship board's bias in favor of well-rounded types and the random factors involved in students' secondary school records and aptitude tests. Students would be able to second-guess the board as to whether they had the "stuff" to benefit greatly from college training. This is especially important for the late bloomers. Greater recourse to credit widens the pool of potential students, and thus democratizes higher education—and especially if the funds made available cover all costs, even some income forgone. It does not really matter whether the scholarship board's opinions are usually more accurate than the students' own as much as it matters that students have the opportunity to prove their faith in themselves justified.

Most of the respondents agreed that there is more room for loans in the financing of higher education, that loan programs could and should be expanded *along with* other resource-providing programs. Some doubt that serious difficulties would develop on the supply side, and most concede that there is some potential on the demand side. Loans should be one of the supports on which higher education will rely. After all, the grubstake is an old American tradition.

Few economists, however, conceded much relevance to the magnitude of other kinds of credit. They distinguished education loans from mortgages and consumer credit by the facts that no tangible asset nor calculable future income is involved in education loans. Most economists preferred to think of the level of housing and consumption indebtedness more as a datum than as a variable inversely related to indebtedness for educational purposes. Others, however, commented on the malallocation of credit facilities, with individual debt at $265 billion and debt incurred for education at less than $100 million.

On a more specific level, the respondents contributed many practical suggestions on the implementation of the program, dealing with what they envisage as problem areas. On the supply side, they suggest the advisability of Federal or state government participation, to take the form of guarantees for all loans. This would, as in the FHA, greatly encourage the entrance of private capital. Federal participation might also take a more immediate role: one economist pointed out that by 1970, barring war, the government would be glad, indeed grateful, if it could engage in a spending program for educational services. Other suggestions emphasized the importance of foundation and business support, the advisability of some sort of risk sharing, and the necessity to investigate the legal issues, such as the obligation of minors for debts incurred.

On the demand side, which they recognized as by far the stonier row, they agreed that such a program is feasible if adequately sold and administered. Indeed, they go further and caution that only if adequately sold and administered is such a program feasible. The burden of the program on the students is substantial, the tradition behind it slight, the alternatives to it several, and the current acceptance of it not overly encouraging. The success of the program would depend on (1) the concerted action of IHL to minimize the possibility of the student's "shopping for the best deal"; (2) a large-scale "selling" job to emphasize the value of a college education and overcome the resistance of young people against indebtedness; and (3) implementation of the program in such a way as to eliminate inequities, limit the burden to what is reasonable, and facilitate repayment.

One proposal frequently advanced would serve to equalize the burden among people engaged in occupations of differing profitability, and people enjoying differing financial success. It is a contingency scheme of some sort, whereby the amounts people pay back are governed by their earnings. It could even be some sort of equity arrangement, whereby people return a certain proportion of their incomes. Thus, entrants into low-paying but valuable occupations would not be penalized or disadvantaged. A related proposal was mandatory term life insurance on the borrower.

Considerable importance was attached to the terms of repayment, particularly the repayment period. It was deemed essential that the burden should not fall until the most difficult period, the years right after graduation, had passed. On the other hand, there was some discontented murmuring over a forty-year repayment period, on the ground that no other forms of personal credit extended for that long a period and that one generation's debt should be paid before the next one's was incurred. A moratorium of three to five years after graduation and a fifteen- to twenty-five-year repayment period, possibly with a rising interest rate added as an inducement to thrift, emerged as the most favored term.

The loan program might be more equitable, and considerably more popular, if repayments should be made deductible from income for tax purposes. At present, it is anomalous that such repayments are not, while contributions made in recompense for scholarship aid, for which the obligation is moral rather than merely legal, are. Moreover, should the program be administered by government, repayment could be extracted through a "withholding" device, with less to-do and less conscious pain.

One rather shrewd objection to government administration of the program was raised, however: the more popular the program became, and the more numerous the debtors, the more political pressure would be generated, with the eventual result that all debts would be canceled. On the other hand, administration by the college directly might lead to the estrangement of large segments of the alumni body. The best administrator would probably be an impersonal third party, which asked from the debtors no allegiance and owed to the debtors no deference.

Other proposals also were designed to implement this feeling that the burden on young people should be limited. One method would be, of course, to limit the total amount of debt a student could incur. Another would be to restrict the loan program to students in graduate and professional schools. (Some economists would also include juniors and seniors in college.) Yet another would be to restrict the program to the *parents* of college students, on the ground that they normally have fifteen years of "grace" after their offsprings' graduations in which to repay the debt. To this proposal the problem of old-age assistance is obviously related.

It is apparent that few of these suggestions offered by the respondents were intended as cure-alls. Few are mutually exclusive; many are obviously complementary. Thus a synthesis might result in an outline for a workable loan program.

FOOTNOTES

[1] See *Federal Assistance to Higher Education, Hearings, Senate Committee on Labor and Public Welfare,* 1960, especially pp. 101–122 and 179–206. (My statement and responses.)

[2] B. A. Rogge, *Financing Education in the United States,* pp. 9–14.

[3] Van den Haag, *Education as an Industry,* 1956, especially pp. 37–39, 57–77, 97–100, 114–115; and D. Riesman, "Who Will and Who Should Pay for Higher Education?" *School Review,* The University of Chicago, 1958.

[4] Reginald Green, a first-rate research assistant, now an assistant Professor at Yale, and I independently studied the views of 220 economists. I am greatly indebted to him.

Chapter 18

STUDENT LOANS: BROAD ISSUES

LOANS AND OTHER AIDS

A large part of the students' resources comes from loans and employment as well as scholarships. For example, according to one HEW study, the amounts available to undergraduates from scholarships was $66 million in 1955–56; from loans, $12.4 million; and from employment, $66 million, the last undoubtedly an underestimate. But a recent study for 1957–58 gives $131 million for student aid, presumably inclusive of prizes, scholarships, and loans. For graduate students the comparative figures were: fellowships, $18.2 million; loans, $5 million; and assistantships, $35 million. Clearly, loans play the smallest part in the financing of the students. Another study by HEW shows that $49 million of funds were available to colleges for lending, and that actually only $18 million were outstanding. (Some difference is to be expected with any revolving fund.) Still another official study revealed that only 1.5 per cent of total student income was accounted for by loans, mostly from outside the universities themselves. With less than ninety thousand borrowing in 1955–56 from IHL an average of $188, only $3\frac{1}{2}$ per cent of the students were involved. All loans, inclusive of outside funds, may have reached $50 million for a year early in the 1950s.

Here we see that the dependence on borrowed funds is slight indeed, and also that in percentage terms about one-half as many women as men borrow. Scholarships, excluding veterans' payments, account in 1957–58 for about five times as much aid as loans. The largest sources of student income are long-term savings, contributions of parents, and the student's earnings.

One reason for the small recourse to loans is an increasing dependence on jobs, in part related to a prosperous economy.

More students work now than previously. In 1940 only 17 per cent of those enrolled in school aged eighteen to twenty-four were full- or part-time members in the labor force. By 1956 the total was 40 per cent.

264

Again, from 1951 to 1956 the percentage of students working increased from 25 to 34 per cent at ages eighteen to nineteen, and from 28 to 47 per cent at ages twenty to twenty-four.[1] By projecting Hollis' results into the early 1960s, I estimate the contribution of employment as approaching $1 billion or around 15 per cent of total costs to students and families.

But the largest aid to students comes from the resources of the colleges. A rough estimate suggests that the amount of aid provided by the colleges through use of capital, interest on endowment, gifts, and the appropriations of government amount roughly to $4 billion.[2] Against this sum the amount of money available from scholarships, fellowships, loans, and employment is small. The total amount had from all these sources is more than $1 billion as against the $4 billion of aid through subsidized tuition by IHL.[3] As more resources are needed, it seems to me that the most likely source, aside from contributions by government or gifts, is loans. It probably will not be necessary to reduce the subsidies. In fact they will increase. But students' contributions will grow, and loans should help make this possible. In the discussion of scholarships I proposed a $500 million program in the early 1960s and $1,000 million by 1970. Loans might well be of larger proportions and certainly in excess of the *likely* scholarship program.

THEORY IN SUPPORT OF LOANS

What is behind the growth of loans? Obviously this movement is snowballing, and it must be supported by strong arguments to offset the strong prejudice against borrowing for higher education. Let us therefore run over some of the major points made on behalf of a loan program. Our economist questionnaires dealt with these issues to some extent.

With limited funds available for scholarships, many students cannot qualify on grounds of an inadequate record. For these students a loan program may become of great importance. Generally, these students must show need.

In supporting a Federal program for loans, Philip Coombs, of the Ford Foundation, said: "Eligibility for a loan, therefore, would be much broader than eligibility for a scholarship. The loan, it seems to me, should not be limited by the kinds of performance tests which a scholarship program would require, nor should it be limited by a means test on the financial end."[4]

Loan funds would, of course, make the scholarship money go further and would restrict scholarships more completely to the able and needy students. As John Monro, former financial aid officer at Harvard, said, such a large cooperative credit program for students would release " . . . scholarship money for really impoverished students who need it the most, and enable better-off students to pay for education on time payments."[5]

Many have protested against the increased tendency for students to look on scholarships as a handout. They believe that the student himself should make a contribution and that as a result he would appreciate his education more. Here is what the chairman of the Engineering Manpower Commission had to say on this issue:[6]

It is my feeling that any enterprising, ambitious young man who desires to obtain an education can get that education if he is willing to work for it. . . .

When I was in college, I washed dishes in a restaurant and did janitor work to help myself along through school. My father was able to help very little. That was not enough. I had to borrow, and I borrowed from a student loan fund which was available to me. When I graduated from college I was $1,000 in debt. . . . I repaid that loan, and I am proud to have done so. I think I can appreciate what I have better, because I worked for it. I am better off, so to speak, than if a better education had been handed to me on a platter and I had not had to pay it back.

Perhaps a more important point on behalf of a loan program is that it can be used to make it possible for institutions to raise their tuition, enabling them to pay adequate salaries and make up for their backlog of construction needs. At least the sting of higher tuition is thus reduced. A loan program shares this advantage with scholarships, but is less costly because the money is repaid. The well-known MIT lending program, which was instituted at the beginning of the Great Depression, has been a model. It was justified on the grounds that it would enable students to finance a larger part of their own education and enable the university to give them better service by providing higher faculty salaries. For the same reason that many favor this kind of credit, those who are against higher tuition, such as many representatives of the land-grant colleges, object to it.

Gerard Swope, in the booming twenties, contended that an institution such as MIT might continue to meet its future capital needs for buildings and equipment from gifts and bequests, but it should expect students to pay a tuition fee more nearly commensurate with the cost of their education to provide for mounting operation costs, especially salaries. "But to increase tuition without at the same time making provision for students who have not sufficient means to take advantage of the education offered by the institute would be tragic."[7]

Another argument for loan finance follows: if credit were used to finance higher education, higher education would obtain a larger part of the total resources of the nation. This is another potent argument for consumer credit, or perhaps it is more appropriately called productive credit.

Under our present economic system, housing and all kinds of consumer goods are purchased in much larger quantities and absorb a much larger part of the national income because credit facilities have been made available. There has been underexploitation of these resources for higher education. If an adequate credit program were invoked, higher education would be able to obtain a larger share of the national flow of goods and services.

Many who receive higher education go on into the world of affairs and earn large incomes, frequently incomes much beyond what is justified by the increased cost and period of their training. This result suggests the need for asking the student to pay a large part of the cost of education. Loan finance helps him do this and enables more to take advantage of higher education.

LOAN PROGRAMS

That loans are on the increase, and especially in the 1950s, is attested to by the views of those who are closest to the financial needs of students. They see great possibilities here. Frank Bowles, head of the College Entrance Examination Board, wrote in his annual report:[8]

The creation of a new concept of student aid, based on appraisal of the individual student's need and assumption of responsibility through loans for at least part of the cost of his education, may be justly viewed as a major achievement, certain to bring rich results in the opening of new college opportunities. . . .

Scholarship funds have been so supported by loan funds in the formation of an enlarged pattern of school aid that the number of students who may expect to receive some form of student aid in 1960–61 can be safely estimated at twice the number who got help in 1957–58.

In a comment on the National Defense Education Act John Monro, who has contributed as much as anyone to the effective use of student aid, stressed three conditions for adequate development of loans: The first is easy conditions of interest and repayment, so that the student feels he is getting a bargain and he is confident he can repay. (The NDEA has been a great stimulus here, both in terms of the funds made available—the financial conditions—and in educating college-aid officers in pressing for more effective use of available funds. In 1960, loans to 100,000 students under the NDEA were expected, as compared to 83,000 from all IHL in 1955–56, and average loans would rise from $188 by IHL to about $600.) The second condition is to entrust the task to those who believe in the loan principle. And the third is to administer loans, scholarships, and jobs under one central office.[9]

To R. G. Moon, Jr., of the College Entrance Examination Board, loans would be a device for treating without discrimination those who saved and those who did not. Now the nonsavers get special treatment. Moon is also eloquent on the ingenious methods used to expand loan funds.[10]

Many of the leading college administrators also spoke out for greater use of loans as an effective means of facilitating the financing of students. President Charles Cole of Amherst, President A. Whitney Griswold of Yale, President Barnaby Keeney of Brown, President Grayson Kirk of Columbia, President Robert F. Goheen of Princeton—these and many others urged the greater use of loans. President Kirk wrote Senator Johnson that, whereas Columbia advanced $500,000 in loans in 1957, they would need $5 million by 1967.

Representatives of the land-grant colleges are, however, less enthusiastic. They want low tuition and help with facilities rather than large increases in scholarships and loans. Additional enrollment resulting from more aid means greater demands for funds, since tuition covers such a small part of costs.[11]

The College Life Insurance Company of America lists 88 loan funds, mostly by outside interests inclusive of a few state funds.[12] The maximum annual loan varies from $150 (Thompson Fund for Girls) to $2,000 (North Dakota Medical Center Loan Fund); maximum total loans from $300 (Iowa Congress of Parents and Teachers) to $10,000 (Bank of America); interest before graduation from 0 to 6 per cent; interest after graduation from 0 to 6 per cent. Generally repayments are required within a few years, though several allow a period of ten years. Many funds are of recent origin and hence could not report losses. But most reported no losses or losses of 1, 2, or 3 per cent, and a maximum of 5 per cent.

In November, 1960, the Prudential Life Insurance Company announced a plan for financing higher education over a period of eight to twelve years, with 45 major American banks cooperating and loans ranging from $2,000 to $12,000. Insurance would cover the father who takes out the policy. The Home Life Insurance Company enables a parent to finance the child's education over a period of twenty-five years—in part covered by insurance payments and in part by a loan.[13]

CONCLUSION

This chapter suggests that loans have not been a vital factor in the financing of students; but they are becoming a much more important force. The drive behind them stems from the limited funds available for scholarships, rising costs of higher education, and an increased awareness of the contribution of credit to the deployment of resources elsewhere and to the democratization of higher education. The NDEA has increased interest and improved administration. Failures in the past are related to outmoded views about borrowing and, as a result, ineffective administration. But public IHL are much less enthusiastic than private IHL.

FOOTNOTES

[1] I owe these figures to Harold Clark from a forthcoming study, *How Much Can the People of the U.S. Afford to Spend on Education?*

[2] See Summary: Loans, at end of Part Four.

[3] Sources of raw materials of last few paragraphs are HEW, *Financial Aid for College Students: Undergraduate; ibid.: Graduate; Statistics of Higher Education: Receipts, Expenditures and Property, 1953–54*, p. 71; and *Costs of Attending College*, p. 49.

[4] *Hearings, on Scholarship and Loan Programs, House Committee on Education and Labor*, 1958, p. 1171.

[5] For three excellent statements on these issues, see J. Monro, *Proposal for College Finance Assurance Cooperation*, Nov. 12, 1957 (mimeographed); "Untapped Resource: Loans for Student Aid," *College Board Review*, Winter, 1956; and "Helping the Student Help Himself," *College Board Review*, May, 1953.

[6] *Hearings, on Science and Education for National Defense, Senate Committee on Labor and Public Welfare*, 1958, p. 809.

[7] H. E. Lobdell, TLF Survey, *Technology Review*, February, 1952, p. 181.

[8] F. H. Bowles, *Admission to College: A Perspective for the 1960's*, 1960, pp. 35, 73.

[9] J. U. Monro, *A Preliminary Comment on the National Defense Student Loan Program*, 1958, p. 9 (mimeographed); for the NDEA loan program, see P. E. Muirhead, "National Defense Education Act: Progress at Midpoint," *Higher Education*, May, 1960, p. 8, and R. C. M. Flynt, "Major Departures in Financing College," *College Board Review*, Fall, 1958, pp. 15–16.

[10] R. G. Moon, Jr., "Who Should Pay the Bill?" *College Board Review*, Spring, 1958, pp. 21–24.

[11] C. C. Cole, G. K. Smith (ed.), *Current Issues in Higher Education*, 1958, p. 86; *Senate Subcommittee on Education: Federal Assistance to Higher Education*, 1960, pp. 102–109, 168–69; R. Thackrey, "University of Nevada Commencement Address," 1957, pp. 8–9 (mimeographed).

[12] The College Life Insurance Company of America, *Credit for College*, 1959, pp. 12–29.

[13] *The New York Times*, Nov. 18, 1960; W. P. Worthington, "Financing a College Education," *School and Society*, Mar. 11, 1961, p. 120; also see *Financing Higher Education*, Special Bulletin 276, American Bankers Association, Installment Credit Commission, August, 1960, for details on bank loan programs to students.

Chapter 19

LOANS: HISTORY AND PROPOSALS

I have already briefly discussed the issue of the amounts involved. It is clear that the students are now spending about $6 billion a year for higher education. If, as in 1952–53, roughly 1½ per cent of this money comes from loans in 1960–61, then the loans are financing less than $100 million of the total outlays of students, a surprisingly small amount. There has been some expansion since the early 1930s. Hollis estimates that in the early 1930s $10 million were available for loans from IHL, in addition, of course, to loans from private sources. Many of these private funds, as both Hollis and Russell show, were used in a very ineffective manner. Frequently private lenders used only the interest on their capital and even used repayments to increase the capital loan fund. Obviously the lenders could have increased their loans by several times if they advanced funds from capital.

In one sense the loan program has been disappointing. If we take the figures of Cavan, the percentage from loans relative to scholarships has declined since the middle 1930s. He finds, for example, that in 35 colleges the net amount of scholarships equaled 16.8 per cent of the net income from students, whereas the corresponding figures for loans was 14.2 per cent. In 1955–56, however, loans from IHL accounted for only one-fifth as much as scholarships.

For 1,026 IHL reporting (accounting for 89 per cent of enrollment) the total amount of college funds available for loans in 1955–56 was $58.5 million, or 19 per cent in excess of the 1953–54 total. But the per capita amount declined by 18 per cent. Private institutions covered, with 52 per cent of the total enrollment, accounted for 63 per cent of the funds. A Kiplinger study shows that the total amount available was $42.3 million and that the public institutions accounted for $19 million, or close to one-half. That of the $58 million principal about $34 million were inactive is explained by the restrictions placed on loans in many institutions and also the frequent use of short-term loans usually repaid before the end of the

TABLE 19-1
Loans, as Percentage of Student Charges, 1955–56

Type	Private — Undergraduate No.	Enrollment	Weighted mean per cent of student charges	Private — Graduate No.	Enrollment	Weighted mean per cent of student charges	Public — Undergraduate No.	Enrollment	Weighted mean per cent of student charges	Public — Graduate No.	Enrollment	Weighted mean per cent of student charges
Universities	87	279,139	0.997	71	58,975	3.43	101	553,023	1.15	88	59,096	6.63
Liberal arts and general colleges	563	341,813	0.77	76	5,952	1.15	122	176,603	1.86	38	7,314	1.39
Teachers colleges	7	2,939	0.62	5	399	2.29	103	108,400	0.53	20	2,446	2.25
Engineering colleges	13	21,339	2.93	11	3,255	3.77	6	20,313	0.56	6	2,051	0.91
Theological colleges	91	21,833	2.23	38	1,715	4.81						
Junior colleges	116	27,991	0.91	….	….	….	189	135,682	0.36			
Technical institutes	16	12,943	0.56	2	731	0.03	19	13,263	0.31	1	13	4.6
Medical schools	14	5,602	1.14	….	….	….	10	4,080	3.45	3	44	101.8
Law schools	10	3,770	3.18	….	….	….	2	303	0.0			
Business schools	6	3,903	0.03	….	….	….	2	2,867	0.0			
United States totals	923	721,272	0.98	203	71,027	3.24	554	1,014,534	1.085	156	70,964	5.83

Source: J. B. Levine, "Student Subsidization in American Institutions of Higher Education," honors thesis, Harvard College, 1960, pp. 5–111. (Based on materials collected for the author.)

year. Here again the private institutions made up for the difference in costs per student to some extent by making more credit available, just as they make more and higher scholarships available.[1]

In a table Julius Levine, my undergraduate tutee and also research assistant (now a Rhodes scholar), performed the herculean task of analyzing the relation of loans to student charges for tuition, room, and board for the year 1955–56. He classified the material by types of institutions and by four regions of the country. The United States totals are presented in Table 19-1. What stands out are differences among regions (see original thesis for these), higher proportions of loans to charges for public institutions,[2] great variations among types of colleges—e.g., in private undergraduate IHL the percentage varies from 0.035 for business schools to 3.18 for law schools. Also of some interest is the much higher percentage of loans for graduates than for undergraduates, a pervasive relationship. The explanation is undoubtedly both lower incomes of graduate students and greater willingness to borrow, in turn related to prospective incomes.

We may conclude that there has been some increase in the money available for loans but that the amounts available and absorbed have been disappointing and that loans still perform a very limited function. The future promises more, as we have pointed out above.

In some institutions the expansion of loans has been most satisfying. For example, Massachusetts Institute of Technology, with an enrollment of about three thousand in the early 1930s, had $1.5 million available.

WHAT IS WRONG?

Perhaps this section should better be headed "Why has there not been a greater expansion in student loans?" As Riesman has suggested, students prefer getting a gift to making commitments and sacrifices. To some extent this attitude is shared by the administrators of colleges.

For example, in the Kiplinger study a questionnaire was sent to 1,874 colleges. There were 588 replies, the responding IHL accounting for 31 per cent of the enrollment. Thirty-six per cent of the administrators were in favor of grants, sixteen per cent in favor of loans, and fifty-six per cent in favor of part-time work. Students' first preference was 82 per cent for grants, 2½ per cent for loans, and 22 per cent for part-time work.[3] (Double counting is to be noted.)

In the words of George B. Risty, director of student financial aid, University of Minnesota:

I heard that students are willing to accept a free ride, but they won't invest in themselves because they feel insecure. We have experienced this in the last 15 years. There are those who don't like to borrow even though a college education, as you mentioned, is worth $100,000. However, a large proportion of those, in answer to your question, are borrowing for cars, televisions, radios, and everything under the sun. For something material they can put their hands on they are very willing to go on an installment plan, but for their own education, which is an intangible thing, worth $100,000, no.

Risty nevertheless goes on to say that students at the University of Minnesota are more interested in borrowing than in scholarships.[4]

As suggested earlier, many mistakes of administration are made. One college administrator, confronted with a student asking for a loan of $50, immediately pointed out to the student that he could save a couple of hundred dollars if he stopped smoking and made very careful calculations to that point. In the State of Wisconsin the loan program for public institutions is (or very recently was) in the hands of the Public Welfare Administration, hardly a procedure that would tend to encourage loans. Many college administrators, in testifying before the Elliott committee in 1958, pointed out that when administration of the loan system is sound, loans tend to increase.

Still another hindrance to loans is the use of scholarships to attract students in the competition with other institutions. Administrators may fear that if loans are substituted for scholarships, they will discourage students from coming to their institutions. I hope that this particular obstacle can be removed or greatly reduced in significance as demand for colleges continues to rise. A 1958 conference of officers of CSS colleges, though responsive to the wisdom of loans, nevertheless " . . . was adamant in its resistance to the scholarship offer contingent upon the acceptance of an offered loan—the so-called 'compulsory loan.' "

In general, students in professional schools, anticipating high incomes in the near future, are more inclined to borrow than others. This is as it should be. In fact, the breakdown of loans does suggest much larger amounts available to graduate schools than to undergraduate. But it should be pointed out that there is a great deal of earning power available even if one does have to go to a graduate school later on. According to one survey with limited coverage, loans in undergraduate schools in 1955–56 amounted to $12½ million, in graduate schools $5 million. The proportion of these funds in graduate schools is a few times that available to undergraduates if allowances are made for the larger numbers in undergraduate schools. (In 1953–54, undergraduate enrollment was ten times graduate enrollment.) In the Kiplinger sample, loans are shown to expand with the level of education: loans of $176,000 were made by institutions with less than four years of curriculum, $521,000 by those giving a bachelor degree, $1,017,000 by those conferring the master's degree, and $3,399,000 by those giving the Ph.D. degree. The rise is explained in part by the fact that the largest and richest institutions give higher degrees and also that the amount of money available tends to increase greatly as the student gets nearer to an earning position.[5]

Terms of loans, the public relations job, and the quality of the financial counseling influence the result. For example, in the Kiplinger sample the question was asked: "Which of the following [see below] do you believe would be most likely to achieve more effective use of loan funds?" The answers were:

	Per cent
Low interest rates	39.0
Longer period of repayment	38.4
Larger maximum loan	23.6
More liberal rules	17.4
More publicity	44.0
Better financial counseling	76.2
Other	8.3

Another question in the Kiplinger study relates to this: "Is education an investment for which it is appropriate to borrow?" More than 95 per cent of school administrators and 67 per cent of the students replied "yes."[7]

Some are opposed to loans because they assume that there are difficulties in repaying. On the whole, history on this matter is most reassuring. The survey by the College Life Insurance Company of 88 loan funds, referred to earlier, reveals very small losses in most instances. Indeed, collections were bad on many of the loans that were made in the midst of the Great Depression and which were badly administered and faultily followed up, but the history of loan repayments generally has been most favorable. Of course, should the country experience a major depression like that of the 1930s, which is most unlikely, there would be many defaults, or at least postponements. At MIT, in the twenty-one years ending June 30, 1951, loans totaled $2,314,517; repayments, $1,811,806, or 98.2 per cent of the amount due at that time. Approximately $31,000 were maturities in arrears against $9,000 written off and interest receipts of $234,184. A survey at Wabash, a study of 100 IHL in the Middle West, and the Kiplinger study all support the conclusion of few defaults.[8]

RECENT PROPOSALS AND PROGRAMS

As is evident from the many proposals in recent years, the movement to expand loans is snowballing. The Committee on Education beyond the High School concluded in its report " . . . that private capital should be made available to make terms of interest and repayment attractive until the graduate is in a position to repay." The committee did not encourage Federal financing of a loan program. Devereux C. Josephs, head of this committee, before a congressional committee also supported a loan program but primarily through private funds. He would distinguish between those who have credit but are in a difficult position temporarily and those who are in need, that is, those who come from low-income families. He proposed that different terms be made available to these groups. Many bills reached Congress before the NDEA finally provided for a substantial loan program.

The NDEA provided $295 million in four years for loans, with $47.5 million the first year and $90 million the fourth year; maximum loans to be $1,000 per year with interest at 3 per cent to start one year after graduation; the maximum total loan $5,000. The IHL was to provide one-tenth of the sum advanced, and the limit on each institution was to be $250,000. The government would allocate funds among states on the basis of enrollment. Those intending to teach and students in science and languages were to receive special treatment. A forgiveness feature for future teachers was included in the act.

In its report, the Kiplinger group proposed a self-supporting capital fund. Under this plan large state, regional, and nationwide pools of private capital would be made available to students at low interest rates, say, at 3 per cent. Repayment periods would be long, with a suggested maximum period of fifteen years. In return for the ability to draw on these funds, colleges should try to sell this program to their students, and the funds should have the widest publicity and support.

Under its help plan (Higher Educational Loan Plan), the Massachusetts Commonwealth has also made an important contribution to the financing of student loans. The Massachusetts Higher Education Assistance Corporation through private subscriptions made available $500,000 as a guarantee for loans made to students. A student can borrow $500 in any one year and $1,000 altogether, and the Commonwealth guarantees 80 per cent of any losses. This $500,000, as a revolving fund, makes available $5 million. Several other states have already followed the Massachusetts example, and apparently more are on the way.

The Harvard Business School's program, launched in recent years, allows each student to borrow $1,000 as a formal loan. This loan carries no interest until graduation and 4½ per cent after graduation. Repayment is due six years after graduation. Awards above this sum are advanced as aid (up to $2,500 in all), the excess over $1,000 carrying a moral obligation of repayment, with no interest charge. The school expects to recover most of the loans within ten to fifteen years after graduation. In one recent year, the school advanced $500,000 to 350 students, about one-third of the student body.

The California Institute of Technology, with the help of California banking interests, offers a plan which would finance all tuition with repayments of $50 a month for ten years.

John Monro, one of the leaders in this field, has proposed a College Financial Assurance Corporation to deal with these problems. He would put upon the colleges the responsibility for making loans to individual students, and for collecting repayments, and would allow the colleges to borrow from the corporation without interest, or at low interest, to fulfill its obligations. It is not, however, too clear where the money is to be had.

In an interesting paper, Roth has also proposed a similar type of student loan: foundations would provide the subsidy which would make it possible to attract a certain amount of equity capital, possibly with a government guarantee or insurance. Particularly impressed by the failure of the colleges to enlist the support of credit as other sellers of services have, Roth, who thinks there are great possibilities in moving along these lines, points out:

> Student loans today are in a primitive state. This is as if each of hundreds of automobile dealers had his own finance plan, some lending 10 per cent of the purchase price, others 20 per cent, and so on, and as if term conditions were equally variable. One can well imagine the chaos that would exist in automobile financing under such conditions.

Roth also suggests that with adequate insurance or guarantee it might be possible to enlist the support of pension funds, endowments, and other investors.

In recent years a number of plans on a smaller scale have also emerged. For example, there are various tuition plans which apportion payments evenly over one year and frequently cover the full four years of college. Sometimes these plans go on to provide insurance, with payments over a period of six or eight years. These are becoming increasingly popular.

At Queens College in Charlotte, North Carolina, a program has been arranged with the local bank under which the student can finance his tuition and part of his other college expenditures over a period of six to eight years. The local bank allows the student to start the monthly payments while the youngster is attending high school. By paying from $50 to $65 a month, the smaller sum over eight years, the larger sum in six years, a substantial part of the total costs of going to college, namely, $4,800, can be thus financed.[9] A genuine mushrooming of plans has occurred in recent years. Some would use loans as a means of getting tuition up; others would use them as an instrument for improved instruction. The larger the loan outstanding, the greater the stake of the institution in the success of its graduates.[10] The reader should also recall the Prudential and Home Life insurance companies mentioned in the last chapter.

FOOTNOTES

[1] On the issues in the last few paragraphs, see the admirable study by the editors of the Kiplinger magazine, *Student Loans: Their Place in Student Aid,* 1956, pp.

70–71; HEW, *Financial Aid for College Students, Undergraduate; ibid.: Graduate; Statistics of Higher Education: Receipts, Expenditures and Property, 1955–56;* E. V. Hollis, *Philanthropic Foundations and Higher Education,* 1938, pp. 187, 190; J. D. Russell, *The Finance of Higher Education* (rev. ed.), 1954, pp. 235–239; and J. T. Cavan, "The Student and the Financing of the College, . . . " unpublished doctoral dissertation, The University of Chicago, 1935, pp. 129, 222–224.

² The higher percentage revealed here for public IHL is explained by the manner of presentation—since charges are much lower, the ratio of loans to charges is higher for public IHL.

³ Kiplinger, *op. cit.,* pp. 14–15.

⁴ *Hearings, on Scholarship and Loan Programs, House Committee on Education and Labor,* 1958, pp. 242–243.

⁵ Kiplinger, *op. cit.,* p. 33.

⁶ *Ibid.,* p. 20.

⁷ *Ibid.,* p. 19.

⁸ For the material in the last few paragraphs, see Kiplinger, *op. cit.,* p. 33; *Hearings, op. cit.,* I, pp. 233, 242, 261, 269, 354, 433; W. K. Bokelman, "Making Student Loans," *College and University Business,* April, 1954, pp. 22–25; F. R. Ormes, "Repayment of Student Loans," *College and University Business,* March 1957, pp. 23–26; H. E. Lobdell, TLF Survey, *Technology Review,* February, 1952, pp. 181–182.

⁹ For the details of these plans see *Hearings, op. cit.,* pp. 591, 930, 1002, 1026–27, 1210–11; *Hearings, on Science and Education for National Defense, Senate Committee on Labor and Public Welfare,* 1958, pp. 950–56, 1210–12; *National Defense Education Act of 1958,* House Committee on Education and Labor Report 2157, 1958, pp. 5, 29–33; *National Defense Education Act of 1958,* Senate Report 2242, pp. 10 and 11; *The National Defense Education Act of 1958;* M. L. Miscally, "The Banking for College Program at Queens," *College and University Business,* August, 1956, pp. 30–31; S. M. Rourke, "Why Shouldn't We Finance Careers as We Do Houses?" *ibid.,* December, 1956, pp. 24–26; J. U. Monro, *Proposal for a College Financial Assurance Corporation,* 1957 (mimeographed); Harvard press release, Apr. 11, 1958, University News Office; J. U. Monro, "Untapped Resource: Loans for Student Aid," *College Board Review,* Winter, 1956; J. M. Cahill, *Manhattan College's Proposed Insured Tuition Plan* (mimeographed); Kiplinger, *op. cit.,* pp. 3–4; R. G. Knight, *Paying Educational Expenses through the Insured Tuition Payment Plan; The Tuition Plan,* New York, N.Y.; Second Report, Committee on Education beyond the High School, 1958, pp. 48, 49, and 55.

¹⁰ See, for example, L. C. Peters, *Possible Methods of Financing College and Graduate School Educations* (mimeographed), (no date); V. C. Blum, "Financing Higher Education," *The Journal of Higher Education,* June, 1958, pp. 309–316; A. W. Homer, *Lend-lease Education,* 1957.

Chapter 20

EXPANSION OF LOANS

From the survey which has preceded this chapter it is clear that a number of issues ought to be discussed further. In conjunction with that discussion I have put together Table 21A-1. This table provides information for eleven major private institutions and four first-class public institutions. In this table I present material on scholarships, loans, and employment.

SOURCE OF FUNDS

The crucial question is: where is the loan money coming from? According to the Kiplinger study, the sources of 2,277 loans funds (total value of $24.3 million) were as follows: endowment or gifts accounted for 83 per cent of the total amount, schools' own funds for 9 per cent, foundations 4 per cent, state government 2 per cent, other sources 3 per cent. The 1955–56 HEW report shows $15.8 million of loans granted by IHL and $13.0 million repaid, or an *extension* of credit of almost $3 million. In this year additions to principal were $1.97 million by private gifts and $3.67 million in all. These minor accretions of loans by colleges should be compared for 1956 with a rise of debt of $35 *billion* for the economy, a rise of $10.8 *billion* of housing credit and $3.7 *billion* of short-term consumer credit.[1]

The large MIT fund was provided by a number of prominent alumni. Harvard College is fortunate enough to have available about $120,000 a year from a private trust fund in Boston, the Lowell Loan Fund, established in 1839 with a capital of $10,000. In a period of 116 years this fund has been used solely for the purpose of making loans to Harvard undergraduates, and its capital currently exceeds $1 million.[2] Many institutions have been able to get large funds for loans, as is suggested by the MIT and Harvard experience. Where management has been good and an understanding of the possibilities obtained, remarkable progress has been made. For example, Table 20-1 gives a brief summary of Harvard's experience. Note the large rise in numbers and amounts for loans versus scholarships: loans rose from 2 per cent of scholarship to 37 per cent. (In 1948–49 aid was low because of the GI Bill, but not in 1952–53.)

TABLE 20-1
Harvard College Long-term Student Loans and Scholarships,
1948–49, 1952–53, and 1959–60 (est.)

Year	Long-term loans		Scholarships and gift aid		Tuition fees
	No.	Amount	No.	Amount	
1948–49	50	$ 10,000	1,000	$ 480,000	$ 525
1952–53	237	76,000	1,199	675,000	600
1959–60	769	467,000	1,183	1,253,000	1,250

Source: J. U. Monro, A Preliminary Comment on the National Defense Student Loan Program, 1958, p. 8 (mimeographed); also see Harvard News Office release of Jan. 19, 1959; and Report of President of Harvard College, 1959–60 Admission and Scholarship Committee, p. 11.

But the general picture is not nearly as encouraging as the HEW statistics quoted above suggest. Even the heads of prestige institutions in their comments on the Johnson bill (S. 2710) admitted to needs of more loan funds and even asked for ceilings per year in excess of $1,000.[3] Later I suggest the possibilities of a massive loan program, with forty years allowed for repayment. The public is probably not quite ready for this. But current methods are not adequate. Loan funds are scarce indeed. Even the Federal program, with all its importance, provides only $90 million a year as a maximum, or about $30 per full-time student, and IHL funds now yield about $5 per full-time student. In all, even inclusive of the NDEA, the total amount available from all sources probably does not yield more than $150 million in 1960–61, or less than $50 per full-time student, or 2 to 3 per cent of total student costs. Even the state programs with their introduction of guarantee funds largely financed by private or semiprivate sources are not very promising. New York State in less than one year advanced $2.5 million. A similar program for all 50 states would yield about $30 million of loans per year.

I see little help other than for a Federal program. Indeed such a plan as that envisaged by Vickrey is worth exploring, but so far the techniques for channeling savings into this area are primitive, undoubtedly in part because of lack of knowledge or enthusiasm by financial institutions. In his comment on the Johnson bill, President Goheen of Princeton complained of the lack of interest on the part of financial institutions.[4] A guarantee by the Federal government, as envisaged by the Johnson bill approved by the Senate Committee on Education in 1960, might help keep rates down a little and encourage private financing. But even here the $100 million guarantee is a small amount compared to potentialities. And the rate of interest of 4¾ per cent plus guarantee fee of ½ per cent kept at a minimum still seemed too low to attract private capital. Hence, despite fairly wide opposition to Federal financing, as revealed by the Kiplinger survey,[5] I find this the only practical approach to the problem.

What students are fearful of are high rates. A twenty-year loan at 5 per cent (the total ceiling costs under the Johnson bill are 5¼ per cent) means interest payments of 50 per cent of the initial loan. Assuming that society also gains from higher education, I suggest that the Federal government might contribute through rates below costs. And I shall show that student loans are the least costly method of help. The New York State act of 1961, which reduces rates to 3 per cent, with the government paying the difference between 3 and the market rate (6 per cent maximum), is significant.

A rough calculation of what may be done follows.

ASSUMPTIONS

1. Loans per Student

Loans of $1,000 per student. The average loan at Harvard is about $650; in the New York State program, $600. I assume that Harvard's needs are less than the nation's, because family incomes in relation to student costs are higher. Here I also allow for the rising costs of higher education, inclusive of a moderate rise of tuition. (Under the 1961 legislation of New York, students may borrow $1,500 per year and $7,500 in all.)

2. Number of Loans

The Federal government should be prepared to advance 1 million loans per year at $1,000 (average, say, limits of $100 to $2,000). The 1 million was one-third of full-time enrollment in 1960–61. I also assume that in future years larger numbers of loans would not be needed despite increasing enrollment. I am counting on an expected rise of per capita income of 30 to 40 per cent to yield an even larger percentage gain of income available for education.

Many may insist that students in public institutions would not need loans of these proportions, since tuition is about $500 less than in private IHL. But according to the HEW study *Retention and Withdrawal of College Students* (page 104), average family income of students enrolled in public IHL in 1952–53 was $5,243; in privately controlled IHL, $6,570.

3. Magnitude of Loans

Investments by the government would be $1 billion the first year. (Obviously it would take several years to get a program of these dimensions in operation.) On the assumption of a ten-year repayment period, the total loans of the government (net of repayments) would be approximately $5.5 billion, and by the eleventh year repayments would equal new loans.

On the assumption of a twenty-year repayment period, total loans would come to about $10.5 billion, with repayments equaling new loans in the twenty-first year.

4. Costs to the Treasury

I assume an annual rate of 2 per cent. Since the government borrows at 4 per cent now, long-term, this means a 2 per cent subsidy, and a gain to the student of at least 3 per cent. The subsidy would decline when rates descend to their norm of the 1940s and 1950s.

For the average amount of loans outstanding over ten years ($3.25 billion) the cost to the Treasury would be $650 million;[6] for twenty years, $2.3 billion.[7]

That this is a low-cost operation for the Treasury is suggested by the following; under the ten-year plan, 10 million loans are made at a cost per $1,000 loan of $65; under the twenty-year plan, 20 million loans are made at a cost per loan of $115. Thus in relation to scholarships of $1,000 each, the cost to the Treasury is 6½ and 11½ per cent as much respectively.

The reader may ask, "What about defaults?" They should not exceed 1 per cent of loans. To assure this, the college should make the loans and provide 10 per cent of the funds advanced. A default of 1 per cent would roughly double the costs of the loan program.

On the whole, I have been optimistic concerning the dimensions of the program. The magnitude is likely to be less than here assumed, and it would require several years to launch an annual program of $1 billion. This might be our goal; but a more realistic view of what might happen is a program of about one-half of these proportions.

I believe that a program such as this, together with earlier suggestions of $500 million of scholarships in the early sixties and $1,000 million by 1970, would remove the dollar sign from the enrollment problem. It might be assumed that roughly one-third of the full-time students, coming from families with incomes in excess of $7,500,[8] would encounter no serious problems that could not be solved by prior savings and employment; that one-third would receive scholarsips; and one-third, loans. (Those who need help from families with incomes in excess of $7,500 would be offset by those with lower incomes who do not need help—e.g., scholarship winners.) This conclusion holds even if it is assumed that tuition will rise substantially; with an increase of tuition by 30 to 40 per cent by 1970

($100 to $150 average rise) roughly matching the gains of per capita income, the proposed scholarship and loan program would be adequate. Greater increases might require somewhat greater recourse to loans.

Under the proposed program, rates of interest would be lower than those now charged by most IHL. Table 21A-1 makes this clear, as does the survey of the College Life Insurance Company of America. In the latter listing the average rate after graduation for 80 funds is 3.4 per cent. The rates for 100 IHL in the prairie states are generally above those for prestige IHL listed in Table 21A-1. More than one-quarter charged 6 to 7 per cent.[9] The median charge in the Kiplinger survey was 4 per cent. Current loan programs generally set limits on loans per year or total loans much below those set under this program. A ceiling of $1,000 yearly or $5,000 in all is the exception rather than the rule. For the 100-college study, only one IHL allowed loans in excess of $1,000 in one year, and two allowed loans of $750 to $1,000.[10]

Again, the ten, twenty, or forty (later) years of repayment are much more generous than current programs allow. In most of the surveys modal periods are three to five years, with smaller institutions tending to demand payments in even shorter periods. The loan program under the NDEA is a great advance over current practices in amounts available per year per student, total loans per student, rate of interest, and subsidies involved both in rates charged and the forgiveness feature. My proposals here go much beyond those under the NDEA. For those who are skeptical of the possibilities, I can only point to the substantial increases of loan finance in recent years at Harvard and in many other CSS institutions. Nor is the general rise of both consumer and capital credit in the economy entirely irrelevant.

FOOTNOTES

[1] Kiplinger, *Student Loans: Their Place in Student Aid,* 1956, p. 30; HEW, *Statistics of Higher Education, 1955–56: Receipts, Expenditures and Property,* pp. 87–89; *Report of the President, January, 1960.*

[2] J. U. Monro, "Untapped Resource: Loans for Student Aid," *College Board Review,* Winter, 1956.

[3] *Federal Assistance to Higher Education,* Senate Subcommittee on Education, 1960, pp. 105–112.

[4] *Ibid.,* p. 109.

[5] Kiplinger, *op. cit.,* p. 24.

[6] 2 × 10 (20 per cent) × 3.25 billion = $650 million.

[7] 2 × 20 (40 per cent) × 5.75 billion = $2.30 billion.

[8] Recall that incomes at ages when sons and daughters go to college are higher than the average, and, moreover, parents of children at college have higher incomes than the average.

[9] W. R. Bokelman, "Making Student Loans," *College and University Business,* April, 1954, p. 23.

[10] *Ibid.,* p. 22.

Chapter 21

COMPETITIVE ASPECTS OF STUDENT AID

In the preceding chapter I stressed the inadequacies of the current loan programs and considered a massive program which, together with a scholarship plan previously described, would contribute greatly to the democratization of higher education. Such a plan would facilitate the financing of higher education for most students who need help. IHL would also gain, for with aid of these proportions IHL would be able to increase their tuition perhaps as much as per capita disposable income rises (30 to 40 per cent, or an average of about $150 in ten years). Larger increases might well put some pressures on students, for many may require even more aid. Before turning to an even more ambitious loan plan, in this brief chapter I discuss the competitive aspects of student aid, inclusive of scholarships and loans.

Tables 21A-1 and 21A-2 reveal certain aspects of the problem of competition. In the discussion of scholarships I pointed out that the large private institutions compete successfully with state universities by providing more scholarships with much larger average values. For *scholarship* students, then, the difference in costs between the state and many private institutions is largely eliminated. In the present study I have taken nine large private outstanding universities and four outstanding state universities. Here we find a difference in undergraduate tuition of about $650. If we consider the four state universities competitors of the nine prestige private institutions, we can conclude that by offering roughly $500 more per scholarship this difference of tuition is largely eliminated. A comparison of room and board charges does not reveal significant differences. For 37 comparisons in 37 states, room and board costs $80 more on the average in the private institution than in its public competitor. In the 1959–60 HEW *Planning and Management Data* covering most IHL, the weighted excess in private IHL is about $65. Furthermore, the nine private institutions provide many more scholarships in relation to enrollment. On an average, 28 per cent of the students in these private institutions receive scholarships, whereas only

12 per cent do so in the four public institutions, though for Michigan the percentage is high—24 per cent.

In providing loans the large private institutions in my sample of 13 IHL also reveal a marked advantage over the public institutions. The average amount advanced for all students does not vary so much, though in general the individual loans are larger in the private institutions. But in percentage of students provided with loans these 9 prestige institutions have an advantage of about 2 to 1 in relation to these 4 top-notch public institutions. (The differences between public and private IHL on a national scale are not so great as revealed by these 13 institutions.)

In offering employment to their students, private colleges and universities again are at an advantage. The comparison is not easy to make, because public institutions sometimes combine undergraduate and graduate employment figures. But from evidence available the advantage lies with the nine prestige universities against the four large public universities.

Then in all these ways, by offering more and higher scholarships, relatively more loan and more employment, the private institutions competing with the major public universities reduce the advantage that the public institutions have in low tuition. All these figures, by the way, relate to 1955–56 (except the HEW management study), and the tuition advantage in dollars of the public institutions has increased since then.

These general conclusions relate not only to ordinary undergraduate liberal arts colleges but also to undergraduate professional schools. For graduate schools it is another matter. In the private institutions the average fellowship is about $950, compared with about $1,200 in the 4 major public institutions. The latters' average graduate fellowship is almost seven times as large as their average undergraduate scholarship. In the private institutions, however, the average fellowship is only about half again as large as the scholarship. But the private institutions offset this advantage of the public institutions by offering three times as many fellowships in relation to enrollment. One reservation must be made: the state universities seem to offer larger numbers of teaching and research assistantships. For example, in the 11 major universities listed by the Columbia University study, the average of research and teaching assistantships in relation to graduate full-time enrollment is 44 per cent for the 4 major state universities and 25 per cent for 7 major private universities. This results from the fact that enrollment of undergraduates is very large relative to graduate enrollment in the 4 major public institutions compared with the 7 major private institutions.[1]

As might be expected, graduate loans tend to be larger than undergraduate loans, though this is not true at the Massachusetts Institute of Technology. The percentage of students receiving loans also tends to be larger in the graduate than in the undergraduate branches.

In Table 21A-2 I compare Columbia, Harvard, Johns Hopkins, and Yale, for which figures are available. Among these four institutions there are substantial differences in the number of undergraduates who receive scholarships, varying from 40 per cent at Johns Hopkins to 23 per cent at Columbia. In medicine the percentages are a maximum of 40 at Harvard and a minimum of 13 at Columbia. In law the respective figures are 36 per cent for Yale, 18 per cent for Harvard, and 11 per cent for Columbia. Close to 90 per cent of the students at the Harvard Divinity School receive scholarships, and 50 per cent at Yale. In graduate work the percentages vary from 71 at Johns Hopkins to 9 at Columbia, with 33 per cent for Harvard and Yale. The amount of awards varies substantially also, with Harvard a maximum for undergraduates at $723 and Johns Hopkins a minimum at $530. In medicine the maximum is $656 for Columbia, and only $414 for Yale. Against a large percentage of students getting law scholarships at Yale is the low average grant of $371 against $690 at Harvard and $549 at Columbia. In graduate instruction the largest fellowships are at Harvard and Yale with $1,090 and $1,080, and the lowest at Columbia with $515. Except at Columbia the value of the graduate fellowship exceeds those in the various professional schools as well as the undergraduate average.

The figures suggest that the professional graduate schools rely on loans more than the undergraduate colleges, both in numbers aided and in average amounts. But on the whole Columbia and Johns Hopkins are far behind Harvard and Yale in these matters. The average loan at Yale is in roughly equal amounts in all the different schools, whereas at Harvard they tend to be much larger in the professional schools and graduate schools, except in Divinity, where the tuition is low.

Aid varies greatly according to the school. At Harvard, for example, in twenty-five years tuition rose by $8.2 million, or 350 per cent, but aid rose by $5.5 million, or 1,200 per cent.

Harvard College:

1,271, or 26 per cent, received *gift* aid in 1957–58	= $1,136,140
586 received loans	= 233,882
Graduate School of Arts and Science: two-thirds received aid	= 2,000,000*
Business School: 35 per cent received aid (more than half in loans) =	658,125
Law School: one-third received aid:	
In scholarships	= 335,000
In loans	= 193,000
School of Public Health: 92 per cent received aid	= 341,134

* See footnote *n* on page 289.

FOOTNOTE

[1] Material compiled from *The Educational Future of Columbia University*, p. 230, and HEW, *Financial Aid, College Students: Graduate*, 1957.

APPENDIX

Scholarships, Loans, Employment, Several
Numbers, Average Value, Per Cent

IHL	Number of students	Scholarships			Loans			Total
		No.	%	Av. $	No.	%	Av. $	
Harvard:[a]								
Undergraduate...................	4,452	1,148	26	723	590	13	354	
Divinity.........................	100	88	88	358	18	18	211	
Law.............................	1,415	254	18	690	235	16	534	
Medical.........................	529	212	40	598	142	27	585	
Graduate[n]......................	1,196	395	33	1,090	565	28	705	
Columbia[c] (all undergraduate):	8,188				98	1	408	
Barnard.........................	1,294	252	19	399	......	...	...	
Columbia College[d]...............	2,405	558	23	665	......	...	...	
School of Eng....................	340	80	24	443				
Law.............................	738	84	11	549	......	...	...	8,415
Medical.........................	1,084	136	13	656				
Graduate........................	12,130	1,121	9	515	162	13	410	
Yale:								
College of Eng...................	3,923	1,112	28	697	639	16	313	
Divinity.........................	312	157	50	345	57	18	338	
Law.............................	436	159	36	371	159	36	381	
Medicine........................	312	83	27	414	73	23	334	
Graduate........................	1,545	505	33	1,080	86	6	315	
Massachusetts Institute of Technology:[c,e]								
Undergraduate...................	3,633	654	18	543	493	14	641	
Graduate........................	1,935	700	36	760	154	8	520	
California Institute of Technology:								
Undergraduate...................	585	188	32	664	104[f]	18	456	
Graduate........................	421	285	68	940				
Princeton:								
Undergraduate...................	2,926	805	28	663	668	23	325	
Graduate........................	628	255	41	1,425	67	11	195	
University of Chicago:								
Undergraduate...................	2,462	1,098	45	602	891	36	360[f]	
Graduate[h]......................	2,091	1,280	62	670				
Johns Hopkins:								
Faculty of Phil. & School of Engineering.	1,244	496	40	530	50	4	340[g]	
Medicine........................	286	58	20	439	15	5	624	
Graduate........................	648[i]	458	71	815	30	5	345	
Stanford:								
Undergraduate...................	5,176	836[i]	16	757	596[k]	12	214	
Graduate........................	2,425	285	12	985				
University of California, Berkeley:								
Undergraduate...................	13,022	752	6	151	1,145[l]	9	117	
Graduate, all campuses.............	9,924	284	3	1,045	2,408	24	145	

Institutions, by Colleges, 1955–56
of Enrollment of Scholarships, Employment, and Loans and Terms of Loans

Employment				Loan conditions		
No.	%	Av. $	Total	Loans	Interest rate	Repayment
1,200	27	333		Max. Ann. = $400 4 yr. = 2,000	3% after leaving school	Min. = $120 per year
7	7	215		$1000 Ann. = $800 3 yr. = $2,000–2,400	1% before & 2% after[b] 2% before & 4% after	$100 a year Within two years after graduation
98	18	500			1% before & 3 yrs. after, then 4½%	Five years after graduation
268	22	1,267		$2,400	3% to 5 yrs. after	First, five years after graduation; final ten years after
				Fresh. = 1 term tuit. Upper = 2 term tuit. Max. = $1,500 Med. = $2,000	2% before, 4% after	Not less than 10% earnings per month
178	14	65				
1,380	57	185				
38	5	8,415				
100	9	30				
66	5	1,097	72,390	$1,500	2% before, 4% after 1 year	To be determined
1,431	36	316		$2,000 Ann. = $450 All = $1,350	2% after 2% after 6% after due date or withdrawal	Five years after graduation After 25 years
36	8	112	4,018	Max. schol. loan = $900 ann.	Complicated 0–6%	Complicated—three-year, five-year loans due three and five years after
68	22	119	8,125	Ann. = $900 4 yr. = $3,600	2% to 5 yrs. after, 6% on unpaid	Five years after
286	18	477	136,570	$1,800	2% after	Five years after
1,238	34	223		Max. Ann. = $1,000 4 yrs. = $3,300 Same	1% Same	$50 semiannual; begin six months after graduation (period reduced in 1959)
		200	188,990			
				$2,000	3–5% after	
180	43	455[f]				
723	25	333	240,960	Ann. $600–800	1% before	
216	34	1,361	294,670	$1,500	4% after	
900	37	667		$460 ann.[f] Less Fresh. & Soph. $1,610—4 yrs.	3% before[f] 4% after; tuition deferment	One month after begin[f]—first ten years at monthly rate, $100 a month
265	13	1,470		$2,000 Profess.		
97	8	236	22,930	$800 (ann. & 4 yr.)	2½% before and after	
282	44	1,755	494,960	$800	Same	To be arranged
1,203	23	203	244,410	Ann. = $500 4 yr. = $1,000	4% after	Usually final—one year after
895	37	184	164,875	Max. $1,000	4% after 1 year	
1,877[f]	14	243	454,966		3% after	First = one–three months after; final = 2 years after
3,724	37	818	3,047,000	$600	Same	Same

TABLE

IHL	Number of students	Scholarships			Loans			
		No.	%	Av. $	No.	%	Av. $	Total
University of Illinois, Urbana and Chicago: Undergraduate....................	19,933	3,077	15	146	2,558	13	96	
Graduate, Urbana.................	1,928[l]	222	12	1,245	1,706[f]	?	95	
University of Michigan: Undergraduate....................	14,513	3,432	24	225	954	7	233	
Graduate[m]......................	2,541	836	33	840	777	31	310	
University of Minnesota: Undergraduate....................	20,766	986	5	190	840	4	153	
Graduate.......................	3,230	284	9	1,584	150	5	170	

[a] Dollar loans to gift aid, Harvard.

Year	Per cent
1949–50	6
1954–55	21
1957–58	21
1958–59 (est.)	28

Source:[a] Harvard Press Release, Apr. 11, 1958.
[b] After or before means after or before graduation.
[c] Includes all undergraduate for loans.
[d] Columbia rated second in loans funds available among 11 large universities but 10th in loans made. Of these 11 universities, Columbia is last in number of research and teaching scholarships (67 yielding 73,618) and Yale second; and Columbia is last in total compensation ($351 000 as compared to average of $1,120,000 and a maximum in excess of $3 million for California and Illinois and a maximum of $1,356,000 for private universities). The Educational Future of Columbia University, 1958, pp. 229–230.
[e] MIT loans = $3.7 million since 1930. 98–99 per cent collected on time. Only $9,651 written off as against $265,000 collected in interest.
[f] Undergraduate and graduate; no freshmen.
[g] No freshmen.
[h] 384 part-time.
[i] 334 part-time.
[j] Includes law and medicine.
[k] Some inconsistencies in figures for loans

21A-1 *(Continued)*

Employment				Loan conditions		
No.	%	Av. $	Total	Loans	Interest rate	Repayment
3,438	17	266	915,667	$300–500 (Sophs to Seniors Ann. max. rise) 4 yr. & Profess. = $1,000	3% before and after	First = four months after; final = 4 years after
1,573	?	1,433		$1,000 = max.	Same	Same
3,443ᶠ	24	280		Ann. & max. = $600 Profess. max. = $1,800	3% when current; 6% otherwise	First payment one to four–six months; final four–six years
1,251	49	1,010			Same	
				Ann. max. $400 4 yr. max. $1,000 Prof. max. $1,500	2% before; 5% after	Final, not later than ten years after
1,078	33	1,405		Max. $750	2–4% immediately; 5% after	First, by one month after; final one–ten years

Berkeley: loans (undergradute and graduate enrollment) given
as 1,145 at average of $117;
all campuses—undergraduate and graduate loans, 2,408 at $145;
but note especially *employment*:
Berkeley undergraduate and graduate
887 Teaching & Research = $158 average
990 Others   at $318
All campuses undergraduate and graduate
1,524 undergraduate and graduate Teaching & Research = $1,525 average
2,200 others at $320.

ˡ 1,261 part-time.
ᵐ 3,235 part-time.
ⁿ The Harvard authorities put the number of fellowships and loans substantially below these figures. (Harvard fellowships at only 23 per cent.) (Letter from Dean R. H. Phelps of March 19, 1962).
Source: HEW, *Financial Aid for College Students: Graduate and Undergraduate*, J. U. Monro, "Untapped Resource Loans for Student Aid," *College Board Review*, Winter, 1956.

IHL	Loans	Scholarships
MIT.........................	$350,000	$300,000
Yale........................	200,000	700,000
Rensselaer Polytechnic Institute.....	190,000	365,000
Union College.................	50,000	157,000
Stanford.....................	71,000	315,000
Princeton....................	110,000	543,000
Brown.......................	55,000	370,000
Wellesley....................	31,000	280,000
Harvard Business School.........	320,000 (loans) 180,000 (aid)	

TABLE 21A-2
Percentage and Amounts, Scholarships and Loans, Four Private Universities, 1955–56

IHL	Per cent of students receiving scholarships					Scholarships, dollar awards					Loans, per cent					Loans, dollars				
	U-G*	Med.	Law	Div.	Grad.	U-G	Med.	Law	Div.	Grad.	U-G	Med.	Law	Div.	Grad.	U-G	Med.	Law	Div.	Grad.
Columbia.........	23	13	11	...	9	665	656	549	...	515	1	...	...	...	13	408	...	...	...	410
Harvard..........	26	40	18	88	33†	723	598	690	358	1,090	13	27	16	18	28†	354	585	534	211	705
Johns Hopkins....	40	20	...	...	71	530	439	...	...	815	4	5	...	...	...	340	624	...	...	315
Yale.............	28	27	36	50	33	697	414	371	345	1,080	16	23	36	18	6	313	334	381	338	315

* U-G = undergraduates.
† See footnote n, on p. 289.
Source: HEW, *Financial Aid to College Students: Graduates; Undergraduates*, 1957.

Chapter 22

A PROGRAM FOR STUDENT CREDIT

At this point it would be well to summarize briefly the central theme of the book. America's institutions of higher learning are in difficult financial straits, and this condition can only be expected to worsen as college enrollment doubles in the next ten years, unless some way can be found to improve their position. For reasons which I have already given, two of the principal sources of funds—philanthropy and state government—are not likely to satisfy the enormous need, though large additional sums will come from these sources. And the third source usually mentioned, the Federal government, has growing needs in other areas; furthermore, many believe that aid of the magnitude required coming from this source could not be given without compromising the independence of private institutions and the autonomy of state educational systems.

This argument, in my view, is rather overdone. And though a case can be made for substantial Federal aid, at least in 1960–61, it does not seem that this will be made available in the immediate future, though a large loan program, since it is the most economical approach, is the most likely one.

Yet the need is there, an estimated additional $6 to $7 billion a year by 1970. Because of their plight, colleges and universities may have to raise their tuition fees substantially in the near future; the students themselves are the only remaining source from which the required funds can be obtained. By tapping the growing incomes of students and their families, IHL can make up at least a substantial part of the actual and concealed deficits which they now run and can provide educational services without a deterioration in quality for the growing volume of students. Without the necessary funds, either enrollment must be restricted, or there will be a considerable deterioration in the quality of education which our colleges offer. Again I repeat what I said earlier, namely, that a large rise of tuition is not the most acceptable solution; but on the basis of the current outlook, this is a likely way of obtaining additional resources. I would like to see the contributions of government, state and Federal, greatly increase, but this is not going to be easy to achieve.

A college education is an expensive item for a student and his parents, and it has steadily become more expensive. On the average, four undergraduate years now cost the student and his family about $7,000 in actual expenses, not to mention the income which the student must forgo while at college. As we have seen in Chapter 16, one survey revealed that in 1952–53, 40.5 per cent of a college student's expenses were contributed by his parents, and another 26.3 per cent came from his own earnings.[1] Clearly it would be better for students to work less and study more while in college, and better for both students and parents if payment of college expenses could be spread over a longer period than the four years.

The proposal which I have in mind—loans to students on a vastly expanded scale—will contribute toward solving both these problems: (1) it will enable IHL to raise their tuition to some extent and help them do a good job; (2) it will enable the student to spread the direct cost of his education over a much longer period.

In the *College Board Review,* (Winter, 1959) I published an article ("Student Credit Could End Colleges' Financial Plight") which I had previously presented to Deans of Admissions. Here I proposed a loan program which might allow repayments over the working life of the student, and also a prefinancing program. What follows is a summary (with some revisions) of the treatment in that article.

Here again the plan was a loan averaging about $1,000 for students in private institutions, but only $500 for those in public IHL, the explanation of the difference being the much larger tuition expected in private IHL.

COSTS TO BORROWERS

Costs to borrowers would not be large and would depend on the rates of interest charged and the duration of the loans. For a 2 per cent loan for fifty years, for example, the *annual* costs would be 60 per cent less than those of a loan at 5 per cent for twenty years. Costs might be reduced by perhaps one-third or more if repayment of the loans were made a moral obligation, so that amounts repaid could be deducted from gross income reported for taxes. Even with a formal loan contract, the interest charges could be so deducted.

The kind of loan I propose is a counterpart to a house-mortgage loan, only here the earning power of the college graduate rather than a house is mortgaged. The current college graduate may look forward to a lifetime income of about $600,000 ($750,000 if we assume, realistically, some inflation); his total payments on a loan of $4,000 would be $5,882 under a twenty-year, 4 per cent loan, or $6,920 under a forty-year, 3 per cent loan. Hence the cost would be merely 1 per cent of the student's future income. Insurance on the life of the borrower, or a five-year interval after graduation before repayment begins, would increase the costs somewhat but not greatly.[2]

A variant of this is the plan of Vickrey, discussed earlier, under which the borrower pays only on the excess of income over what it would have been without the additional education. Obviously, rates would have to be higher on the excess.

It is absurd to concentrate the costs of higher education in a period of four years when they can be spread over twenty or forty or (if combined with a precollege savings plan) even sixty years. With a family income of $7,500 to $8,000 (my estimate of average income of families with students at college in 1960), the costs per student are about 30 per cent of family income per year during the four years at college. But spread over forty years the costs average only a fraction of that amount.[3]

Loan financing enables the parent to shift some of the financial burden of his education to the child, and the latter in turn reduces this burden by distributing it over the years and diverting payment to a later economic period when, presumably, incomes will be rising. This rise of per capita income—the result of both increased productivity and inflationary forces —enables the college student to exploit the growth of the economy and inflation.

In the field of medicine, especially, inequities arise. A physician graduating in 1961 can look forward to a lifetime income about $1.5 million (allowing for some inflation). Is it fair to ask the community to subsidize him over eight years to the extent of about $11,000?[4]

I find it difficult to understand the position of the parent who unhesitatingly borrows to buy a car or a home and yet would be most reluctant to allow his child to mortgage 1 per cent of future income for a college education. What makes it morally acceptable for the parent to commit himself to a payment of over $1,000 a year on his car and about $1,500 a year on his home and morally unacceptable for his child to commit himself to the payment of $100 to $200 a year on a college education? Yet one of the toughest problems in instituting an extensive loan program arises in overcoming objections of just this sort. Whatever the merits of the program, it cannot succeed without a wide degree of acceptance by the American public. An extensive public relations program conducted by college leaders and other influential persons would, I am sure, successfully convince the public of the need for a very large college loan program. How can we justify $160 billion ($3,000 to $3,500 per family) in relatively nonproductive loans for homes, television sets, and the like, and only some $150 million dollars in college student loans, inclusive of those under the NDEA? The total debt allocated over the nation's families in 1959 was $15,000; of private debt, $10,000; of short-term consumer debt, $1,000; of housing debt, $2,500—compare these with average debt per full-time college student of about $50. It is up to college administrators to alert financial institutions to the underexploitation of this field.

One possible objection to wider use of loans might be the special problems they presumably pose for women students. A girl might be afraid to borrow for her education and offer her future husband a debt instead of a dowry. But this argument can be overdone. The amounts involved are not large; a college education increases the contribution of the wife to the family; and women college graduates remain in the labor market in greater proportion than do all women (women make up one-third of all college graduates, and half of them stay in the labor market). Increasingly reports from the women's colleges confirm the wider use of loans by women.

Time and again another argument is raised against a program of this type; and the argument has both relevance and substance. John Morse, the able vice president of RPI, has put it well in a letter to the author. In this letter he proposes a three-pronged attack: scholarships, loans, and Federal construction.

The scholarship would have sufficient range—say 0–$1,200—to cover full costs at some institutions, but leave a gap at high cost institutions. This gap would be filled by summer work, term-time work, and loans. Since, however, the scholarships would vary according to need, the gap would remain fairly stable for all, and the least and most needy would tend to graduate with about the same amount of debt. . . . I cannot see selling—I am not sure I'd want to—a full credit program, which would place the largest debt on the neediest student.

A program of this type might be more acceptable or workable than mine. A large debt seems most forbidding to those in greatest need. Though I must add that loans for housing, automobiles, television sets, and even travel are surprisingly large for low-income groups. In fact, most of the loans for housing and consumer durable goods are contracted by the income groups that send children to college. Only for the very low incomes does one find reluctance to getting into debt.[5] And something can be said against penalizing the very poor with the heaviest debt. But we should also take into account the fact that the poor *in college* are much more highly motivated, and this ultimately will be reflected in higher incomes. But to treat excessive fears of debt requires an educational program.

It may well be that a program which, say, provides $500 in loans, $500 from scholarships, and $500 from employment for the neediest each year and (say) $500 in loans for the less needy is the most practical approach for the time being. Obviously the high-cost institutions may have to provide $2,500 in all for the neediest, and for others as little as $1,000.

Here is a rough estimate of a program based on the Morse suggestion. I assume a college cost of $2,300. (The excess over the current $1,800 is the result of additional tuition to cover higher salaries, construction needs, etc. $500 × 3 million = $1.5 billion additional income currently.)

I assume 50 per cent of the students need $1,000 additional per year. (In my discussion of the ten- to twenty-year repayment plan the assumption was a somewhat larger proportion in need.)

Average	Number (millions)	Costs
Loans $400..............	1.5	$600 million
Scholarship $300..........	1.5	450 million
Work $300..............	1.5	450 million
Total................	...	$1.5 billion

Up to needs of $400, the student would receive loans; beyond that, an equal amount from scholarships and work.

This is a possible transitional program. I would prefer a greater relative dependence on loans.

From the viewpoint of colleges, loans are a means of balancing the books, ending the exploitation of teachers, and obtaining the needed physical plant. (Incidentally, fair pay to teachers would also bring improved education and still higher productivity and income for the college graduate and the nation.)

In my *College Board Review* article, I estimated that a loan program of these proportions would require almost $1.5 billion in the early years and about $2½ billion annually by 1970. The latter would be reduced substantially by repayments. On the basis of estimated enrollment and smaller needs for students in public IHL, the students in public IHL might need about 45 per cent of the total in 1970 and those in private IHL about 55 per cent.

Should tuition payments rise to $4 billion by 1970, then under this program a ceiling of loans might be set by tuition payments. The total amount of loans by 1970 would be $2.6 billion. But if the rise of tuition could be kept down to 50 per cent in ten years, a much slower rate than in the years 1954–55 to 1958–59, then the total loans limited to tuition payments would be about $1.5 billion.[6]

Student loans totaling $1½ billion a few years from now and $2½ billion in ten years may seem excessive. Undoubtedly an extensive public relations program justifying loan finance would be required before we could attain loans of these proportions. But in relation to total savings and loans now in the economy and expected in the future, the total of these highly productive loans can easily be justified.

In 1957 gross savings in the nation amounted to $65 billion. By 1970 they should reach $100 billion on the basis of past trends, since in 1947 savings amounted to $37 billion. In the ten years ending 1970, GNP should rise by at least $200 billion, or 40 per cent. Hence in stable prices, on the reasonable assumption that savings will rise proportionately to GNP, the total should increase to $100 billion. In the ten years ending in 1957, consumer credit rose an average of $3⅓ billion yearly and mortgage indebtedness about $11 billion per year.

Against these figures an increase of debts for higher education of $1½ to $2½ billion yearly (gross) does not seem out of line by any means. Actually, in the case of forty-year loans, repayments within fifteen years would amount to about $600 million per year, and in the case of twenty-year loans to $1⅕ billion, net borrowing thus being reduced from $2½ billion to less than $2 billion in the first case and to about $1½ billion in the second.

BOON TO THE ECONOMY

How would such a large-scale student loan program influence the economy and the various interests involved? Undoubtedly one result would be that a greater share of the national income would be channeled into education. This is all to the good, because we underspend for education and we need more educated men and women. Educational spending contributes disproportionately to high employment rates, since in education machine processes cannot be substituted for employees as they can in industry and business. Therefore this kind of spending is an effective way to keep buying on an even keel with production. More important, the rise of output over the years three times as great as input of resources, capital, labor, and management is explained in substantial part by the heavy investments in education.

Is the rise of educational debt dangerous? If the average annual increase of $38 billion of all debt and $32 billion of private debt in the 1950s did not damage our economy (in fact, it did contribute to economic health), a rise of $1 to $2 billion per year for college loans is not going to destroy it. In fact, it is likely to make the economy more robust.

Moreover, a billion-dollar expansion of college loan programs is not expected immediately because of the time that would be required to launch the program and to overcome public resistance to student loans. It will in fact take several years of intensive activity to get loans up to $1½ billion per year. How much they will rise and how rapidly will depend upon the manner in which the financing is done and the way in which public relations are handled. The lower the rate of interest and the longer the financing period offered, the greater the expansion that may be expected. High money rates and dear money policies since 1955 have been an obstacle to the advances of loan financing.

In the first years, loans outstanding would tend to rise—both because new loans would exceed repayments and because the number of students taking loans would rise. College costs per student would also rise.

Furthermore, one must allow for the rise of national income and savings as factors that would tend to offset the increase of loans as college enrollments increase. In the 1950s the dollar value of GNP almost doubled, and gross savings more than doubled. There is an element of inflation in these figures, and I have assumed unrealistically no inflation in the future. Nevertheless, the growth of the economy (in stable dollars) that has been estimated at 40 per cent in ten years is a relevant factor.

So much for the economy. What of the effects of college loans on IHL? In so far as a massive loan program makes possible a moderate rise of tuition, to this extent the college would gain. Current tuition is now (1960–61) about $1.2 billion. In my original budget I estimated that unless heroic efforts were made to increase the contributions of government and philanthropy, tuition might have to rise to about $4 billion by 1970. Roughly one-half of the rise would be associated with an increase of enrollment. The proportions of the increase of the tuition charge are large indeed.

But the following may interest the reader: Should tuition charges rise in the years 1960 to 1970 at the rate of the years 1953–54 to 1957–58, then tuition *fees* would increase by 116 per cent. With an increase of enrollment of 75 per cent in the 1960s, the total *income* from tuition would increase by about 275 per cent, or almost as much as is assumed in my budget. But it is to be hoped that a realization of the importance of higher education to the nation will result in small rises of tuition and larger contributions by government and philanthropy. Whatever the rise of tuition— and it seems most unlikely that the increase will be less than 50 per cent —a substantial loan system (and scholarships) will make possible increases without serious effects on the structure of the student body.

What of the student? He would gain, since the financial burden of a college education would be distributed over many years for him. He would also gain in that, on the basis of past experience, per capita incomes should be four times as high at the time of his retirement, and more than twice as high during most of his working life (average) as they will be at the time of his graduation from college.[7] In other words, with growth the burden of a given debt is greatly reduced.

How much a loan would cost depends on the rate of interest and the number of years it takes to mature. At 2 per cent for fifty years, the annual cost per $1,000 is $31.80; at 5 per cent for twenty years, the cost is $80.20, or about 2½ times as great.*

Costs per student for $1,000 per year or three years in all (the average stay in college) would be 2.28 per cent of anticipated income over twenty years for a twenty-year, 4 per cent loan; for a forty-year loan at 3 per cent, the average cost of a $3,000 loan would be less than 1 per cent of income over forty years. For a forty-year 4 per cent loan the costs would be in excess of 1 per cent. Since we compare with graduates' incomes, this is the more significant calculation.

BURDEN ON BORROWER

In assessing the burden to present students over the years, the following considerations are relevant:

First, incomes will rise as productivity increases and even more as inflation continues. That means for a forty-year loan the costs of payments relative to income would probably decline by about 60 per cent.[8] For I assume that payments would be made over forty years. With a 3 per cent rise of productivity and a modest 1 per cent inflation, the average income would be 250 over these forty years (100 at time of undertaking debt obligation). Then the burden would be reduced by more than 70 per cent. (100 = 28 per cent of 350.)

Second, if the obligation to repay were a moral one, the debtor would receive relief of perhaps one-third (marginal rate) through deductions from gross income reported for taxes. In any case, interest is deductible.

But there should be a small offset. We might increase the costs by 10 to 20 per cent in order to cover administrative costs and defaults or deaths. (An insurance policy might also cover deaths.)

The loan burden might be reduced for those graduates with low incomes through an assessment on the basis of a percentage of income, with a ceiling for very high incomes, rather than an ordinary loan contract. In other words, for a given debt, payments might vary with incomes earned after graduation. Thus, possibly the borrower might pay from ½ to 2 per cent of income for long-term loans, the exact amount to vary with the duration of the loan and the rate of interest charged on the loan. In this manner, the low-paid preacher or teacher might be spared heavy charges.

But this kind of financing might arouse more opposition that one based on repayments of amounts borrowed plus financing charges. Other approaches to differential treatment are to forgive loans for those going into low-paying professions which are currently short of manpower. The Na-

* See Appendix at end of chapter.

tional Defense Education Act of 1958 provides that full-time teachers will be relieved of repayments of educational loans by 10 per cent for every year of teaching with 50 per cent as maximum.

It is possible to reduce the burden of loans by giving borrowers alternatives in making payments. For example, one could provide for no payments while at college and in graduate schools, smaller percentages generally in the first ten years out of college, and the largest percentages in the ten- to twenty-year and thirty- to forty-year periods after graduation. (The twenty- to thirty-year period after graduation is likely to be a troublesome one, since the graduate's children are then at college.)

How does this proposal compare with measures for financing higher education that have either been urged upon or adopted by the Federal government? Considering first the major proposed plans, there are at present great pressures on the government to provide Federal scholarships or various income tax devices to help the nation's youth to secure a college education.

Scholarships, as we point out earlier, should make much larger contributions, perhaps as much as an additional $800 million to $900 million by 1970. Scholarship funds can be used to help the able and impecunious, with an assist from loans. But if the most effective use is to be made of scholarships, they should be disbursed on the basis of need as well as quality of student. It is scarcely necessary to add here that, dollar for dollar, scholarships are much more costly than loans. A combination of the two, say $1 of scholarships to $2 of loans by 1970, would be an economical and effective program for increasing the tuition income of IHL and yet easing the financing problems of students and their parents.

Tax credit or increased tax-exemption plans, which have also been urged on the government, would be costly and wasteful, because they would be available to parents irrespective of need. Here I need only say that these are the most costly approach to aid for students, and in many ways inequitable. In a later chapter I shall discuss these issues more fully.

Perhaps the least costly program for the government would be a guarantee of college loans; this would reduce loan rates as it did under the Federal financing of home mortgages. In the six years ending in 1958, government loans and guarantees rose by $46 billion, or $7⅗ billion annually, with the major rise in guarantees. There were about $85 billion in loans and guarantees outstanding (estimated for June, 1958).[9]

In an economic sense, the Federal program of educational loans is especially significant. In the postwar period, partly as a result of Federal policy but also because of the development of private credit, the growth of credit plans for housing, durable consumer goods, and the like has been enormous. The national spending structure has thus been modified in favor of these commodities. Greater provision of savings and credit for higher education would put education, a highly productive form of spending, on a more competitive footing with them.

PREFINANCING

Thus far I have discussed only loan financing, or what might be called postfinancing, of a college education. As I mentioned in Chapter 10, however, prefinancing through savings is also possible and should be encouraged. Parents financially able to do so should take out insurance when a child is one year old and assume that the direct annual costs of a college education will not be $1,800—the average at present—but at least $3,600 by the time the child is ready for college.

(One complication should be introduced at this point: Assume a parent begins paying for his child in 1960. In 1980, the child of 1960 begins paying a substantial part of his own college credit bill. This makes it more difficult for him to finance through savings the college education of his child in (say) 1985 and later. To this extent the pressure to put the burden on postfinancing, and hence on the child, after the lapse of a generation of postfinancing would grow. But if the total charge is not too heavy this is not a very serious matter and a parent might then at the same time indulge in pre- and postfinancing.)

In his paper Eckstein has given some illustrative costs of prepayments required for $1,000 annual tuition for four years, shown in Table 22-1.

TABLE 22-1

Number of years	Interest rate	Without life insurance	With life insurance on parent
10	3%	$365	$383
15	4%	212	228
20	5%	130	143

A treasurer of Michigan State University estimated that prepayments of $15 per month at birth ($180 per year) would yield $1,200 per year during four college years.

One approach to prefinancing is through equity investments; Merrill, Lynch, Pierce, Fenner & Smith advertise a monthly investment plan that could finance an $8,000 to $10,000 college education. On the basis of performance in the 1950s, the advertisement reads:

At $50 a month in the 10-year period you would have put $6,000 of your own money, plus the dividends you received. . . .

After deducting all your commission costs and a maximum capital gains tax . . . the stock you owned now would be worth $13,059—more than enough to take care of college.

Eckstein reveals that postpayment is much more costly: "For example, 20 years of post-payment, after a 5-year moratorium, at an interest rate of 4 per cent requires an annual charge of $425 per $4,000 of tuition; 20 years of pre-payment would cost only $155."

In all instances, the charge should be reduced by at least one-third, since the payments would presumably be deductible for income tax.

Adequate insurance of the prefinancing type could solve all the financial problems of a college education. But in many instances the parents will not take these measures, and in many other cases they will not be able to do so. Precollege financing is especially effective in that the interest augments funds set aside for college.

To summarize, the techniques for financing higher education could be greatly improved. The most promising approach is through loan finance. With the spreading of costs over a longer period of time, the burden on the student would be greatly reduced, both because of reduced costs per year and because of his rising potential income. The financial gains to institutions of higher learning would be great because in so far as other alternatives are not available, IHL will be able to raise tuition fees without serious effects on low-income groups. In so far as government aid for higher education is needed, student loans or guarantees of loans would be the most economical approach.

Through loan finance, higher education would become a more strenuous bidder for the resources of the nation via-à-vis housing, automobiles, television sets, travel, and so forth. I would especially stress this point.

Both prefinancing and postfinancing of a college education have certain advantages in common: the reduction of an immediate financial burden on parents and students, the exploitation of inflationary and growth processes in the national economy by institutions of higher learning, the contribution toward higher fees and more revenue for colleges, the provision of an equitable method for financing college education, and the democratization of higher education. But note inflation erodes savings under prefinancing.

Of the two methods, postfinancing through loans seems the more feasible way to channel into higher education the very large sums that it urgently needs. Exploitation of credit appears to be necessary to assure a fair share of the consumer's and the investment dollar and of the nation's resources for higher education.

Earlier I considered a loan program with repayments in ten or twenty years. Here I have developed the program further, even suggesting the possibility of a sixty-year plan of savings and credit. But it will take much time to get wide acceptance of such long period financing. Nevertheless one should not keep quiet because institutional blocks are apparent. Over the years these may be broken down. In the meanwhile we should give serious consideration to a massive loan program providing repayment in ten to twenty years.

FOOTNOTES

[1] See Table 16-1.

[2] Cf. O. Eckstein, "The Problem of Higher College Tuition," in *Higher Education in the United States: The Economic Problems,* 1960, pp. 66–68.

[3] Even if the student borrowed *all* the money he needed for four years at college, say, $8,000 in all, the annual payment on a 3 per cent, forty-year loan would be just $345.60, or about 5 per cent of lifetime income.

[4] $3,000 during his undergraduate work and $8,000 while at medical school.

[5] Cf. S. E. Harris, *The Incidence of Inflation: Who Gets Hurt?,* Joint Economic Committee of Congress of the United States, Study Paper 7, 1959, pp. 80–82.

[6] The $2.6 billion figure is obtained as follows:

	Total loans, 1970
Private enrollment—2 million; loans to one-half —average tuition = $1,300	$1.3 billion
Public enrollment —4 million; loans to two-thirds—average tuition = 500	1.3 billion

[7] On the basis of past trends, I assume a 3 per cent gain of productivity per year. Any inflationary trends would increase the rise of incomes further.

[8] Cf. the Vickrey proposal given earlier.

[9] For a proposal of a billion-dollar insurance program (total outstanding) see *Senate Committee on Government Operations, 1958, Science and Technology Act of 1958,* pp. 50–51; also see *Federal Assistance to Higher Education, Senate Subcommittee on Education,* 1960, pp. 101–123 and 179–248.

APPENDIX

TABLE 22A-1
Costs per $1,000 (Amortization and Interest)

Rates of interest	Years to maturity			
	Twenty	Thirty	Forty	Fifty
2%	$61.20	$44.60	$36.60	$31.80
3%[1]	67.20	51.00	43.20	38.80
3½%	70.40	54.50	46.80	42.60
4%	73.60	57.80	50.60	46.60
4½%	76.80	61.40	54.40	50.60
5%	80.20	65.00	58.20	54.80

A rough calculation yields the following:

Lifetime incomes of college graduates at 1949 incomes...... $268,000
At 1958 incomes... 400,000
Annual income (forty-five-year working life)............... 8,900

This average is appropriate for college graduates out fifteen years. (This is the weighted average years out of college for living college graduates.)

For a twenty-year loan at 4 per cent the costs would be as follows:

Average income, first twenty years out of college (assuming no further growth of economy) = $7,500 (average of $5,000 and $10,000).*

But we add 30 per cent to $7,500 for estimated rise of per capita income in ten years, associated with growth of the economy, or in all an average of $9,750 for the first twenty years.

Hence the annual costs would be $73.60/$9,750 = 0.76 per cent for a loan of $1,000, or 2.28 per cent for a loan of $3,000,† and 3.04 per cent for a loan of four years. ($73.60 = interest and amortization for a 4 per cent $1,000 twenty-year loan.)

In the first year of payment the cost would be 1.47 ($73.60/$5,000) per cent × 3, or 4.41 per cent (or 5.88 per cent for four years): in the twentieth year = 0.57 per cent of income per $1,000 loan, or 1.71 per cent for three years, (or 2.28 for four years) ($73.60/$13,000).‡ (These payments could be equalized as a percentage of income by reducing payments in early years and increasing them later.)

* Adjust $8,900, fifteenth year income, upward.

† The average student stays in college less than three years. I assume three years.

‡ Add 30 per cent for growth for ten years to $10,000 (the $10,000 already reflects growth for the first ten years out of college).

SUMMARY: LOANS

At present, loans account for only a small part of students' resources—even less than scholarships and employment. All three of these are small compared to the contribution of $4 billion by the institutions themselves through subsidized tuition.*

The arguments for a large loan program are as follows:

1. It will remove some of the unfortunate effects of higher tuition.

2. It will make scholarship money go further.

3. It will require the student to contribute to his own education, and not to depend too much on subsidies (I am afraid this is a moral judgment and perhaps does not belong here).

4. It will divert larger sums of money to higher education, in the same way that consumer credit has increased sales of automobiles and houses.

5. It will enable higher education to obtain added resources through its exploitation of the growth of the economy. The burden of loans will decrease as per capita incomes rise, both because of the inflation process and rising productivity.

6. It will enable larger numbers to enter programs such as medicine, where both training cost and financial rewards are high.

7. It will provide help for deserving students who are not quite good enough to merit scholarships.

8. It will aid the students whose value to society is greater than their pay, teachers, for example, although such people represent the best use for scholarship money.†

Over the years the growth of loans has been disappointing. There is even some evidence that loans in the 1950s were less important than they were in the middle thirties when measured against scholarships. The interest in loans as a means of financing higher education seems to have increased recently, however.

The reason for the disappointing performance in loans is simple. Most students prefer a grant to a loan, and it is natural that they should. Other obstacles have been poor counseling and administration, and harsh terms for the loans themselves. Yet where loan funds have been established and applied with vigor, the results have been excellent. The loan program at MIT over the last twenty-one years shows a collection of interest

---

* Obtained as follows: Educational and general income = $4 billion; capital costs ($20 billion replacement value, fifty-year life and 4 per cent interest = $1.2 billion); deduct tuition = $1.2 billion (4 + 1.2 − 1.2 = 4).

† In the forthcoming volume of the HEW (Miss Mushkin, ed.) Prof. William Vickrey (*A Proposal for Student Loans*) presents an ingenious plan for loans related to students' future earning power.

twenty-five times the amount of loans written off, and repayments equal to 98 per cent of amount due.

Many present loan funds are ineffective because the individual loan is too small. A loan of $100 or $200 may be useful to the student in a tactical sense, tiding him over a difficult month, but it does not help the student greatly to support himself for a whole school year. An adequate loan program must greatly increase the ceiling on the amount borrowed, reduce interest rates, and extend the date of the loan's maturity. Properly managed, the loan program would provide flexible terms to meet varying needs. Increasingly the ceiling on loans is being realistically put at $1,000 per year and $4,000 to $5,000 in all, and repayment over a period of ten years or longer.

If a substantial program is to be created, it must be accompanied by a change in the public attitude toward borrowing. It is unfortunate that the American consumer, who buys his house, his car, and his bedroom furniture on credit, shrinks from the thought of borrowing to increase his own future income through education, and to achieve the even greater nonmaterial benefits of education. Yet such a state of mind does exist, and it will take a sound public relations program to change it.

At present, private institutions provide more money relatively for loans than do public institutions. The private schools have used this money to offset in part the advantage which the public institutions have in their lower tuition.

In recent years, many proposals, both public and private, have been made to increase the amount of loan money available. The 1958 Federal program provides about $300 million over a four-year period, aside from allowances for graduate study and military service. Proposals for nonpublic aid generally center on the creation of a private corporation which would make loans guaranteed by the government and coinsurance by the educational institution itself. Under such a program, the individual college would have the responsibility for administering the loans. This private program would meet the objections of those who fear that Federal aid means Federal control.

But on the basis of present trends, I see little hope for a massive loan program without the Federal government's primarily providing its financing. A ten-, twenty-, or even forty-year repayment program, supplemented by savings, could revolutionize college financing as it has the financing of consumer durables. Then an adequate scholarship, loan, and saving plan, even with moderate rises of tuition—say, 50 per cent in ten years as compared to a 40 per cent rise of per capita income—would largely equalize opportunities for higher education and contribute toward the solution of the financial problems of IHL.

PART FIVE

GOVERNMENT CONTRIBUTIONS

Chapter 23

FEDERAL AID TO HIGHER EDUCATION

INTRODUCTORY

The country is demanding a larger participation by the Federal government in the financing of higher education. Among the reasons is the difficult financial position of state and local governments: they increased their indebtedness by 300 per cent in the ten years ending 1959, or $3¾ billion a year, and are spending a few billion dollars more each year. Their fear of competitive losses to other states makes them hesitate to raise taxes sufficiently to meet their increased demands. Secondly, the Federal government itself has the most productive forms of revenue. It obtains its major revenue through direct taxes based on ability to pay, while state and local governments raise only a small part of their revenues in this way, relying instead upon taxes that burden the low-income groups. Thirdly, the burden of higher education varies greatly among states. Because some states have per capita income three times as large as the poorest states and because the cost of higher education to states is five times larger (in relation to income) for some of the poorer states than for the richer ones,[1] pressure for Federal equalization increases. Finally, competition with the Russians, and the cold war in general, have quickened interest in Federal leadership.

In 1957–58, according to a preliminary survey, of the total educational and general income of $3,762 million, the Federal government provided $16 million for veterans' education, $534 million for research, $84 million for land-grant colleges, and $89 million for other purposes, or $723 million in all; this was 19 per cent of the total. But it should be noted that this was not all genuine direct aid. Payments were made to veterans themselves, not to schools, for one thing; moreover, the money for research was often given specifically for those projects undertaken primarily at the instigation of the Federal government. Only a relatively small part was genuine aid, though some provisions of the National Defense Education Act of 1958 qualify as such.

Federal aid might be easier to obtain if the accounting system of the government were improved. There is little reason, for instance, why capital outlays should be included as operating expenditures, as they now are. Considering, for example, an increase in housing loans or loans for college students as an operating expense, and therefore as an expenditure from the budget, makes it more difficult to achieve adequate expenditures of this type.

The pressure for Federal aid which had been growing for years finally culminated in the 1958 National Defense Education Act.

VIEWS ON FEDERAL AID

Perhaps the most advanced position on the issue of Federal aid to education was taken by President Truman's Commission on Higher Education (1947). It urged a strong Federal program and a budget in 1947 dollars for 1960 of about $2,600 million. The Federal government was to provide $848 million of the money for operating expenses and $1 billion for scholarships and fellowships. In addition, it was to provide one-third of the $8 billion required in eight to twelve years for capital outlays for instructional purposes. But the government accepted very little of what was recommended in this report.

The Josephs Committee under President Eisenhower issued a report which was not quite so enthusiastic about Federal help. It did propose a program for grants-in-aid for construction which would have made an important contribution, but Congress never gave the matter very serious consideration, in part because of the fear of a large deficit in the budget. A change in ideology was reflected in these proposals of the Josephs Committee, so much more restrained than those of President Truman's Committee. Federal aid had become a residual matter for the Josephs Committee.[2]

In the *Pursuit of Excellence in Education and the Future of America,* the Rockefeller brothers urged considerable Federal aid for education. Basing their proposals on an expected national income of $600 billion in 1967, the writers of the report foresaw no great difficulty in providing additional educational aid out of higher income. They anticipated a rise of total expenditures on education of more than 100 per cent in ten years. The additional public services were to be financed out of additional income. These proposals to some extent followed the earlier suggestions of Governor Stevenson which had been reproduced in a program paper, "Where Does the Money Come From?"[3]

The trustees of the Carnegie Foundation for the Advancement of Teaching also recently discussed this problem. The Carnegie group pointed out the dangers of control that go with budgetary grants. They were fearful that Federal aid might result in a reduction in state and local government effort. But they " . . . simply believe that these dangers can be kept in check and they are smaller than the dangers of deterioration if higher education is not adequately supported."

The conclusion of their study is as follows:

It is not necessary to take a strong entrenched position on either side of this doctrinal battle. A clear grasp of the issues leaves one to expect certain items from both sides. American higher education *is* in desperate straits with respect to its financial future. This *is* a matter of national importance. . . . A healthy pattern of financing will involve contributions from many sources—students, alumni, states, Federal Government, business corporations, philanthropic sources.

This group favored subsidies for construction, but was wary of operating subsidies; they would not support tax revision favoring those families sending children to college, on the ground that the parents could afford to pay the charges.

Another important and powerful group, the land-grant colleges, favored Federal aid to a considerable degree. They were not enthusiastic about scholarship aid, because, they argued, operating expenditures for increased faculty pay and construction help were more important.

Finally, the Commission on Financing Higher Education, which issued an excellent report in 1952, opposed Federal aid on the whole. It was fearful of government intervention, for " . . . independence will be threatened if higher education is subjected to further influence from the Federal Government." For a detailed treatment of numerous proposals for, and discussion of, Federal aid, the reader should consult the 1960 volume of the Legislative Reference Service.[4]

TAX EXEMPTION

One important contribution of the government, particularly of state and local governments, is tax exemption. I estimate the value of capital plant of IHL at $20 billion in replacement value. The property taxes on this plant would amount to about $300 million a year. This relief is given by local government primarily, not Federal. In addition, the $4 billion of endowment yield about $150 million in income; if this were subject to usual taxation, perhaps $50 million additional taxes would be paid, mostly to the Federal government.

Indeed at times the colleges exploit their tax exemption, operating businesses and putting up little of their own money. Colleges have gone into the macaroni business, purchased a property (at 61 Broadway) largely with borrowed funds, owned Allied Stores, operated a large publishing company, etc.

Legislation since 1950, however, has greatly reduced abuses arising from tax exemption. The Internal Revenue Code now distinguishes between true portfolio investment and going into business with the protection of tax exemption.

MORE FEDERAL AID?

Should there be more Federal aid to education? This is not an easy question to answer. Governments have great responsibilities, with about $133 billion of cash payments in the calendar year 1959 (72 per cent by the Federal government) compared to a GNP of $479 billion.* In other words, 28 per cent of the GNP was being used by government although only 21 per cent of goods and services, when allowances are made for transfer payments such as social security. In 1959, cash payments of the Federal government were $96 billion; budgetary expenditures, which exclude certain trust fund payments, were $81 billion.

Yet in some respects this situation is not too serious. From 1947 to 1959 the increase in budgetary expenditures was $42 billion as compared to a rise of GNP of $244 billion, or a rise of 17 per cent of the increased GNP. This suggests that Federal expenditures have not been growing faster than the national income. In fact, from 1952 to 1959 Federal budgetary expenditures declined from 20 to 14 per cent of GNP. But when we allow for the large rise of state and local expenditures, the reduction is substantially less. State and local government *cash payments* in these years rose from 6 to 8 per cent of GNP.

In this connection it is of some interest that, had Federal expenditures in relation to GNP remained unchanged from 1952 to 1959, $20 billion more of spending by the Federal government would have been achieved. This is in addition to the amounts expected from the rising GNP from 1959 to 1970. Again, had the rate of growth of the years 1947 to 1952 been maintained from 1952 to 1959, approximately $70 billion additional GNP per year would have been available, and this amount would have yielded about $10 billion additional to the Federal government. All these statistics suggest possibilities.

But let us mortgage only $12 billion of the gains of Federal revenue— of the $36 billion additional expected from our growing economy by 1970 —at current rates. We disregard the stunted rate of growth in the 1950s and the relative decline of Federal spending in the years 1952 to 1960. Priorities are a matter of value judgment, and here are mine: I would allocate $4 billion of the $12 billion to education, and at least $1 billion of the $4 billion to higher education. I estimate the rise of educational needs from $18 billion currently to $35 billion in 1970, about two-thirds

* This comparison is subject to some reservations.

for public schools and one-third for higher education. State and local governments are likely to have to carry most of this additional burden in local public school education—especially until real progress is made with the integration and church issues. In higher education some relief may be had if tuition is increased substantially. But if such relief is not had, then the problem of financing public higher education is aggravated.

At any rate, in Table 23-1 are my projected increases of welfare outlays. I need not add that, should disarmament even on a 50 per cent basis become a reality, $25 billion more would be available, of which half might go to welfare. It is even possible and not unreasonable to multiply these figures by 2 for the rises by 1970.

TABLE 23-1

Actual Expenditures and Suggested Minimum Rise (Federal), 1954–1961, Fiscal Years
(In millions of dollars)

Expenditure	1954	Maximum 1954–61	Budget 1961	Proposed rise (one-half as soon as possible—remainder, say, by 1967)
Housing and community development..	$ 506*	$1,291 (1959)	$ 430	$ 1,000
Public assistance...................	1,439	2,087 (1961)	2,087	1,000
Public health.....................	290	904 (1961)	904	1,000
Education........................	274	565 (1961)	565	4,000
Science, research, etc..............	33	221 (1960)	220	500
Natural resources.................	1,316	1,938 (1961)	1,961	1,000
Depressed areas..................	......	....	......	500
Old age, survivors, and disability insurance...........................	......	....	....	2,000
Miscellaneous, e.g., REA, public works, rehabilitation, school lunches......	......	....	......	1,000
Total.........................	......	....	.....	$12,000

* Receipts through sales of mortgages, etc., exceeded outlay.

Much depends on the competing demands on the Federal government and particularly those related to the cold war. With an anticipated rise of GNP of at least $200 billion or more in the next ten years, government under the present tax structure could raise an additional $55 billion of which $36 billion might go to the Federal government. Under these circumstances, and barring war, it might be possible for the Federal government to contribute $1 to 2 billion more annually to higher education. Perhaps one half could go to scholarships and loans and the other half to construction under some matching grant program. The 1958 act provides about $200 million per year. But most of the funds under this act do not go directly to IHL. (This estimate was made before the rise of security outlays following the Berlin crisis of 1961.)

ALTERNATIVES UNDER FEDERAL AID

What are the alternative approaches? An effective and relatively inexpensive one could be loans to private and public institutions at a very low rate of interest.

Another would be matching grants in the manner of the Hill-Burton act for the hospitals. In view of the fact that IHL require about $1½ billion a year for the next ten years for construction purposes, construction grants would be a very helpful form of aid.

Still another approach is through aid to students. Though this may not seem as helpful to the colleges as direct operating grants or construction loans or grants, an adequate loan or scholarship program which enables colleges to increase their tuition substantially can help them enormously, even if the money does not come directly to them. A loan program such as the one outlined in a previous chapter providing $1 to 2 billion a year within a period of ten years, would be very helpful.

If loans on a large scale are not forthcoming, then there is an even stronger case for a large scholarship program. A program to provide, say, an average of less than $1,000 a year for 20 per cent of the students, or about $500 million, would be adequate now, though this amount should increase with rising enrollments and higher costs of education.

One of the most controversial issues is that of the government's compensation for research. Many college administrators hold strongly to the view that the Federal government (and notably the National Institute of Health and the National Science Foundation) do not pay the full cost of research undertaken for the Federal government. This position has been put effectively by President Furnas and Vice President Ewell of the University of Buffalo in their essay in the McGraw-Hill anniversary volume, *Financing Higher Education, 1960–70.*

Their contention is that the Federal government pays much less than full costs. With research for many institutions accounting for 25 per cent or more of the budget, it is their contention that research should contribute fairly to the total direct and overhead costs—this is not merely an incremental cost. (In fact in 1955–56, 25 per cent of *university* income was spent on organized research.) Furnas and Ewell note that out of Federal payments of almost $500 million for organized research by IHL in 1958–59, the university contributes $95 million of their own funds for Federal projects (and $160 million of their own funds in all in relation to $830 million of outlays on organized research). The contribution of institutional funds is especially large to the National Health Institute

(NHI) ($40 million) and the National Science Foundation ($25 million).

In a typical example they show that compensation of the National Health Institute is $10,350 for a project for which compensation should be $16,250. The NHI refuses compensation of one-quarter time for the research director and, instead of paying 50 per cent of salaries to cover overhead, provides only 15 per cent. Even the armed services, dedicated to full compensation under the blue book, pay only 63 per cent of direct salaries as wages, instead of actual costs of 82 per cent, to the University of Buffalo. The writers are critical of the richly endowed universities for not pressing harder for full compensation.

It is conceivable that if IHL were treated as well as business they might get as much as $25 to 50 million or even more additionally, and perhaps twice as much additionally by 1970. But it should also be noted that many of these projects are undertaken at the initiative of the college and faculty, and sometimes these research outlays even contribute to the instructional budget (e.g., in some medical schools). Such outlays also provide faculty with research projects which are part of the psychic income required to hold them. But even allowing for this, a case could certainly be made for additional compensation of, say, $50 million for research undertaken by IHL. This is not a large sum, but of great importance to perhaps 50 IHL.

The struggle to obtain coverage of full costs from the government continues. Especially crucial is the determination of IHL to obtain compensation for instructional as well as research outlays on the theory that these are indistinguishable and related. By 1960 the Budget Bureau seems to have yielded on this point, though it is not clear that all Federal agencies have followed. The Defense Department is especially reluctant to cover all costs. Grants by the HEW, and notably for medical research, are costly to IHL, since there is a statutory limit of 15 per cent for coverage of all indirect expenses. The medical schools estimate their indirect costs at 25 per cent. These schools seem to suffer losses on this item alone of about $7 million, and estimates are $25 million additionally by 1970.[5]

Each year Congress is flooded with bills urging help for higher education through Federal aid to students. One report, *Federal Aid to Students for Higher Education, 1956,* says: "Over 50 bills proposing legislation to provide some direct and indirect Federal aid to students for higher education were introduced in the last session of the 84th Congress."

A controversy has raged as to whether the Federal aid should take the form of direct subsidies or tax concession to parents of college students. The argument for direct subsidies is that the problem is in the open and can be controlled; those who favor tax concessions contend that the increase of bureaucratic control over education likely with a direct subsidy program would be avoided. So far the tendency has been to provide direct subsidies rather than tax relief.

One method of increased tax relief for parents who send their children to college would be to double the exemption per student, at present $600. The cost for 3 million students would be roughly $400 million, assuming that the average tax is about 20 per cent and that all students or their families are subject to it. This is probably not too far out of line with the actual cost. The major objection to this plan is that, aside from the issue of further erosion of the tax base, the well-to-do taxpayer would get a larger dollar advantage.

Partly to contend with this problem a tax-credit program has been proposed by the American Council on Education, and ably presented by Vice President John Meck of Dartmouth.[6] The council's proposal is that every parent who sends a child to college should receive a tax credit of 30 per cent of the amount of tuition to a limit of $450 (meaning that for tuition in excess of $1,500 there would be no additional tax credit). Hence any parent, regardless of income, would receive the same dollar credit. The American Council on Education estimated the cost rather modestly at $150 million. My own estimate today is substantially higher. Tuition at the present time for 3.2 million students would amount to roughly $1.2 billion, or $1.1 billion after deduction of scholarships. Thirty per cent of this sum would leave a net cost of about $330 million, with a modest further reduction for children with parents not paying taxes.

The major objection to this proposal is that such concessions are wasted on students of well-to-do parents. Probably one-quarter to one-half of the students do not need this help, or do not need so much of it. Other objections are that the result may be higher tuition charges and hence no net gain to parents—to some this is an advantage; and the gains to the parents may be inadequate to induce attendance at college.

Another proposal is one supported by the American Association for the Advancement of Science (AAAS) and others. Its objective is to equalize the net cost after taxes for all contributors to philanthropic programs. Thus a high-income taxpayer saves 80 or 90 cents on the dollar for a contribution. The net cost to him is (say) 20 cents per dollar donated. The low-income taxpayer is to be given a similar saving. An estimated loss of revenue to the Treasury is $4½ billion; at current income, my estimate is $5½ billion, probably too large a sum for any congressional finance committee to consider at present.

A serious objection to this program is that it would abandon tax receipts now available. To this extent the proposal is wasteful. If we assume $6 billion are now contributed in philanthropy, this proposal would involve large losses to the government of taxes now paid on the $6 billion, losses quite unnecessary to induce *this* sum into charitable activity. For example, consider a taxpayer with a tax rate of 20 per cent. He gives his college $100. He gets $20 tax relief. Under the proposal of the AAAS the donor would get tax relief of $90 and contribute net $10; the Treasury would lose $70. One objection already made by the chairman of the Ways and Means Committee is that such a proposal would mean that individuals would receive the right to spend government money at their discretion. The attitude of competitors for the donated dollar is also relevant here. The tax concessions would spread to other fields.[7] Additional incentives would be offered where they are not now needed.

Perhaps a crucial issue is how much of this $5½ billion in taxes which the Federal government would lose would be ultimately diverted into contributions. I doubt that a very large proportion of these tax gains would then be donated, and certainly not a multiple. First, the percentage of contribution to income was remarkably stable from 1922 to 1943 despite great variations in the rate of taxation. This suggests that a large tax saving per dollar contributed does not have any great effect. Again, for incomes from $5,000 to $50,000 the proportion of income contributed to philanthropy remains remarkably stable, yet the $50,000-income recipient gets a much larger tax concession for a given contribution than a person with a low income does. At present, for example, if a person with a $10,000 adjusted gross income contributes $365, he gets a tax relief of $90. Under the proposed program the relief would rise to $335—the taxpayer would profit to the extent of $245. The crucial issue is what part of these $245 would be put into contributions. My guess is that considerably less than all of it would be.

FRINGE BENEFITS

One final point on help from the Federal government. If fringe benefits[8] were 15 per cent of total faculty pay by 1970, this would amount to about $500 million on the basis of estimated payrolls. Most of the $500 million would be tax-free for the faculty. In other words, for about $500 million of payments by the college, faculty members might gain about $700 million of income before taxes. This would be an important contribution by the Federal government.

FEDERAL AID: QUANTITY AND QUALITY

In my early presentation I estimated that Federal expenditures would rise from $733 million in 1957–58 to $1,800 million in 1969–70, or an increase of less than $1,100 million. The major part of this increase would be in research—$766 million. This is not a very optimistic projection for future Federal aid. In a study made in 1959, Musgrave would have the Federal government's share *rise* $2,700 million, a figure obtained on the basis of the likely returns from other sources of income in relation to needs. And of this total $2,200 million would be for purposes other than research. This would be a large contribution by the Federal government. Musgrave supports his projection on the theory that more expenditures on higher education are an *investment* in America's future, not merely a diversion from private to public consumption, and hence merit a very high priority.

Whether such large sums will be forthcoming from the Federal government depends on many factors. The case for contributions of this magnitude by the Federal government is strong. On the assumption of adequate management, economists estimate that GNP should rise by $200 to $300 billion by 1970. Surely an investment of $2 to 3 billion more in higher education could be supported out of the $30 to 40 billion of additional revenue of the Federal government to be expected with this increase of GNP—unless other claims—e.g., intensification of the cold war, urbanization—become much more pressing. The rise to (say) $2½ billion by 1970 could be paced carefully. Much will depend on the party in power—the Democrats are more likely to be amenable to such a program than the Republicans. The kind of aid is also relevant. The Congress is more inclined to favor scholarship aid or construction aid than help for operating expenses—e.g., salaries. Musgrave strongly supports the last. Most representatives of the public IHL—and even to some extent private IHL—prefer direct aid to IHL rather than help for students, which in their opinion aggravates the financial problems of IHL. They receive more students as aid rises, and hence their deficits increase correspondingly. A final issue of some relevance is the manner of providing aid. John Perkins has put effectively the great contribution that could be made by adopting the British Grant System for our use, a system that allows wide discretion to the IHL, minimum government control, and planning ahead for five years.[9]

I would strongly support a program of $2 to 3 billion additional Federal aid, largely for nonresearch purposes. IHL could use these funds for construction, salaries, and even for scholarships. With this contribution, the pressures to raise tuition to a high level would be contained to a substantial degree. A large Federal subsidy and increases of state aid above the amounts anticipated earlier in this book could keep the rise of tuition to a reasonable level.

In this connection, Elliot Richardson, the (then) able Assistant Secretary of HEW, could envisage relatively small Federal contributions. He stressed especially the responsibility of state and local government; but his estimate of additional needs seemed lower than mine.[10]

How much Federal aid is made available will depend to some extent upon the decisions concerning aid to private IHL. In the *Report of the President's Commission of 1947* (the Zook Committee), though the writers stressed the important public contributions of the private IHL, they would subsidize only public IHL. The reasons were not entirely clear, though the Committee stressed the responsibility of the Federal government to public IHL and any help to private IHL would be at the expense of public IHL; and the Committee held that Federal aid would mean Federal control of private IHL. Two members of the Committee strongly dissented. In this connection it should be noted that no questions have been raised concerning Federal aid to denominational hospitals or for aid to students in church-related IHL for scholarships or Federal fellowships. The view of most authorities is that the issue of separation of church and state involved in Federal aid to IHL should be resolved in the courts. But obviously if the IHL with 25 per cent of enrollment with religious affiliations are excluded, or the 40 per cent in independent IHL, then the possibilities of serious Federal aid would be greatly reduced. Private IHL would then oppose aid.[11]

A widespread fear of Federal control of higher education contributes toward the reluctance of Congress to appropriate funds for higher education and also to some extent determines the kind of aid—e.g., preference for scholarships, loans or construction over operating subsidies. Yet there is little evidence of Federal control of education even though expenditures have been as high as $2 billion annually. The Hoover Commission in the late 1940s published numerous letters from heads of public IHL which showed clearly that there were no serious complaints on this score. Perkins has commented on the inconsistent behavior of private institutions that accept research funds from the Federal government and issue philosophic pronouncements against Federal aid; again, private IHL that want to appeal for private funds and wish to ingratiate themselves with private donors make much of the evils of Federal handouts and controls.[12]

The more economically Federal funds are spent, the greater the contribution of the Federal government would be to higher education. In other parts of the book we have discussed the possibilities of economies by IHL. But serious problems stem from the hundreds of Federal programs, for which numerous departments and agencies are responsible. Despite discussions of the lack of integration over many years, little has been done to coordinate these programs. Even in 1947, the President's Commission estimated total Federal outlays for higher education at $1,772 million: grants-in-aid, $35; direct education, $74; contracts, $84; housing and facilities, $422; individual aid, $1,157—the Commission listed 11 departments or agencies that were responsible for these funds and urged some coordination through the Office of Education.

An expert for the Hoover Commission wrote: " . . . it is often impossible to arrive at even a crude estimate of that portion of total funds for an activity or group of activities which eventually reaches higher institutions. . . . " Since those days, and especially with the passage of the National Defense Education Act, Federal activities in higher education have multiplied, and the case is greatly strengthened for an organization in education like the President's Economic Council. Most recently (1960) Gardner, in the government's report to President Eisenhower, has urged an Educational Council.[13]

WHAT KIND OF AID?

According to the American Assembly, there are four kinds of Federal participation in higher education:

1. Services purchased—e.g., technical assistance projects overseas, ROTC

2. Federal programs to meet specific national needs—e.g., Federal encouragement for training of scientists

3. Research support by grants or aids

4. Direct support of higher education—e.g., contributions of operating expenses of land-grant colleges[14]

Under services purchased, the major attack of administrators is that the government does not pay full costs—under the ROTC program, for example, the government does not contribute to plant expenses.

The college administrators are also frequently not enthusiastic over Federal grants for scholarships and loans, and even criticize any tax concessions to parents. On the latter it is of some interest that the representative of the American Council of Education, which speaks for most IHL, pressed strongly for a tax-credit program for parents. But the representatives of the land-grant colleges dissented: this was not a program, as is generally claimed, that would in their view help IHL. According to the land-grant colleges, any help meant for the IHL should be given to them directly. (The implication had been that with tax credits, colleges could then raise tuition.)

Nor, as has been said before, were all groups of institutions enthusiastic about scholarships. The private institutions were much more favorable than the public. Undoubtedly the opposition of public IHL stemmed in part from the fear that increased scholarships would mean a reduction in tuition payments and hence a loss of competitive position vis-à-vis private IHL. In addition, of course, there was the problem of increased numbers and deficits. Speaking on behalf of public universities, President David Henry of the University of Illinois put it as follows:[15]

The more students our colleges and universities get without the means to pay faculties or provide buildings, the higher the charge must be to students.

And the higher the charge to students, the more demand for scholarships, loans and fellowships . . . we will either have to have a scholarship so fantastically large . . . and so administratively complex and costly as to be frightening; or shift the burden of paying for this education from this generation to the next through loans; or deny educational opportunity to large numbers of qualified young people.

On the whole, the conservatives favored tax relief for parents or scholarships and loans rather than direct aid to IHL. In general this was the thrust of the Josephs Committee. The land-grant colleges, however, preferred direct aid for operating expenses, a position endorsed by the 1947 Commission, Ordway Tead, and others.

In the late 1950s and in 1960–61 the major debate was around help on construction. The housing loans were universally approved; but tussles with the government developed in the late 1950s, first, because the government wanted to taper off the program and, second, because they wanted higher rates of interest. The opponents of the government's policy objected to the proposed higher rates on the following grounds:

1. The government should not charge on the basis of costs for new money for long periods of time. Housing loans were paid off year by year, and hence they were partly short-term loans.

2. The government was paying substantially lower rates on trust funds held than it proposed to charge the public IHL.

3. A rise in rates would greatly reduce the demand for these loans. Even at the then rates (1959) the cost of a forty-year loan was $160 per resident per year. One authority pointed out that in 1955 when rates were reduced from $3\frac{1}{4}$ to $2\frac{3}{4}$ per cent, applications rose from $98 million to $430 million for the year after the reduction of rates. A proposed increase from $2\frac{7}{8}$ to 4 per cent would drastically reduce applications.

One of the suggestions of the President's Committee on Education beyond the High School had been construction grants for higher education. Educators also urged strongly that the Federal government should lend for academic facilities as well as provide grants. Indeed some feared that loans for academic plant would not be very helpful, because many universities were not allowed to borrow, and also there was a widespread fear that loans for academic buildings might require increases of tuition for financing the loans.

At any rate, the government was slow to respond to these pressures. In 1960, the government proposed a $2 billion loan program for IHL to be repaid in twenty years, with a provision that the Federal government would finance the repayment of $500 million of these loans. College presidents objected to the program for various reasons: first, because of the pauper's oath required (i.e., a requirement of proof that access to the private markets was not available) and, second, because of the large financing charges. The government seemed to be relaxing on some of these provisions in 1960; but little progress was made on this legislation, or on proposals to finance construction for junior colleges, guarantees of loans for buildings, loans on all kinds of facilities, guarantees of student loans, scholarship programs, etc.

In general, the Federal government progressed very little once the National Defense Education Act became law. Despite the fact that the needs for construction and grounds were estimated from $12 billion to as much as $33 billion for the 1960s and only $700 million was being spent per year, the government was unable to push through its modest program. Legislation to cover operating expenses was still farther from realization: no serious proposals were forthcoming from the Executive or the Congress. On another issue, adequate compensation for research, the government conceded a little in 1959; but there was still much dissatisfaction. One authority wanted to know why private enterprise should be allowed to write off its plant in ten years whereas IHL have to take fifty years, and also why businessmen should receive full coverage of indirect expenses and fees in contrast to payments to IHL, which do not cover all indirect costs.[16]

In early 1961, President Kennedy, partly using a task-force report as a basis, asked for an expansion of the existing college housing program for a five-year period at $250 million per year. He would also provide $300 million of loans for five years for academic purposes, as well as a modest scholarship program yielding four-year scholarships to 212,000 students over five years. A month earlier a serious obstacle to Federal aid arose as the Civil Rights Commission urged no Federal aid to states where IHL were segregated.[17] In 1962 President Kennedy presses again for his program.

CONCLUSION

The Federal government has a greater responsibility for higher education than might be inferred from the current contributions of the government. But any suggestions for Federal aid should be related to competing demands on government and the current burdens. It is clear that substantial resources are likely to become available as the economy continues to grow and especially if management improves. Disarmament would further increase resources for welfare. Any help from the Federal government for higher education would facilitate the financing of about $11 billion additional needed by 1970 for the public schools, a burden now falling on state and local government.

Additional contributions by the Federal government are not likely to require increases in taxes. In fact there is a good chance that in the next ten years larger diversions to welfare fields may be accompanied by tax cuts. (I assume no hot war.)

Federal aid, should it be forthcoming, should not come in the form of further erosion of the tax base.* (Colleges already are favored by substantial tax exemptions.) The Federal government can make its largest contributions (and least costly) through scholarships, loans to students, loans to colleges for construction (possibly also matched grants), and guarantees for loans to students and colleges. The government could also be more generous in its payments for research and ROTC.†

* Cf. an ingenious proposal of Richard Goode (in HEW forthcoming volume, S. Mushkin, ed.) where he would allow depreciation deductions for income subject to taxes on investments in education, as on other investments.

† Cf. A. M. Rivlin, *The Role of the Federal Government in Financing Higher Education*, 1961, an able presentation of issues relevant to Federal aid of all kinds. This book and another promising volume (Babbidge and Rosenzweig) will appear too late to be discussed in this volume.

FOOTNOTES

[1] For example, 0.47 per cent of income in Mississippi versus 0.09 per cent in New York.

[2] *The President's Committee on Education beyond the High School, Summary Report*, July, 1957, pp. 21–22.

[3] Republished in his volume *The New America*, Harris, Martin, and Schlesinger (eds.).

[4] C. A. Quattlebaum, *Federal Educational Policies, Programs and Proposals.*

[5] See G. F. Baughman, "Formula for Determining Indirect Cost in Research," *College and University Business*, March, 1961, pp. 32–34; Executive Office of the President, Bureau of the Budget, *Circular No. A-21 Revised*, Jan. 7, 1961; on Education, *Recommendations Concerning Budget Circular A-21* and *Joint Letter No. 41 of the Army, Navy and Air Force*, September, 1960; *School and Society*, Dec. 3, 1960, pp. 456–57.

[6] See, for example, S. E. Harris (ed.), *Higher Education in the United States: The Economic Problems*, pp. 76, 93–95.

[7] Surveys and Research Corporation, *Stimulating Voluntary Giving to Higher Education and Other Programs*, April, 1958; *Federal Educational Policies, Programs and Proposals*, pp. 169–170.

[8] See Chap. 24 for further discussion.

[9] On these issues, see Dexter M. Keezer (ed.), *Financing Higher Education: 1960–70*, McGraw-Hill, New York, 1959, chap. 3 by S. E. Harris; R. A. Musgrave, "Higher Education and the Federal Budget," in *Higher Education in the United States*, 1960, pp. 96–101; Perkins and Wood, "Issues in Federal Aid to Higher Education," in *The Federal Government and Higher Education*, 1960, pp. 169–171.

[10] E. L. Richardson, "Towards a National Policy for Higher Education," in *Higher Education*, September, 1959, pp. 3–6; cf. R. G. Axt, "The Josephs Report: Toward a Federal Policy in Higher Education," *The Educational Record*, October, 1957, pp. 295–97.

[11] Perkins and Wood, *op. cit.*, p. 164; R. G. Axt, *The Federal Government and Financing Higher Education*, 1952, pp. 198–204; The President's Commission on Higher Education, *Higher Education for American Democracy*, V, pp. 57–68.

[12] See H. K. Allen, *The Federal Government and Education,* study for the Hoover Commission, 1950, pp. 141–160 and chap. 13; A. T. Hill, *The Small College Meets Its Challenge,* 1959, pp. 127–129; *The Federal Government and Higher Education,* p. 159.

[13] H. K. Allen, *op. cit.,* p. 249; *Higher Education for American Democracy,* III, pp. 38–50; *Federal Funds for Education, 1956–57; Education,* Democratic Advisory Council paper, 1959; American Council on Education, *Higher Education in the United States,* 1956, chap. 6; HEW, *Federal Funds for 1956–57 and 1957–58; Goals for America: The Report of the President's Commission on National Goals,* 1960, pp. 98–99.

[14] *The Federal Government and Higher Education,* pp. 194–95.

[15] *Hearings, Senate Subcommittee on Education, Federal Assistance to Higher Education,* 1960, pp. 163, 169, and *Proceedings of American Association of Land-Grant Colleges and State Universities,* 1957, pp. 98–103; Legislative Reference Service, *Federal Aid to Students for Higher Education,* 1956.

[16] For the discussion of the last few paragraphs, see especially *Senate Banking and Currency Committee, Hearings on the Housing Act of 1959,* especially pp. 389, 473–530; *Hearings, ibid., President's Message Disapproving S-57,* pp. 384, 389, 428; *Hearings, Senate Subcommittee on Education, on Federal Assistance to Higher Education,* 1960, especially pp. 1–39, 147–210; *The Federal Government and Higher Education,* pp. 111–118; D. D. Henry, "The Role of the Federal Government in Higher Education," *The Educational Record,* July, 1959, pp. 197–200.

[17] See *Congressional Quarterly,* Feb. 24, 1961, p. 308; *The New York Times,* Jan. 16, 1961; also see *House Committee on Agriculture Hearings on Increased Funds for Land-grant Colleges,* May, 1960, pp. 3–8. These colleges ask for additional Federal aid to compensate for increased prices and population since 1935.

Chapter 24

STATE EXPENDITURES ON HIGHER EDUCATION

TRENDS IN STATE PUBLIC EXPENDITURES FOR HIGHER EDUCATION AND IN COMPETITIVE FIELDS

This is another chapter with some weighty statistics that may bore some. The summary at the end may therefore be adequate for many. The main problems treated here are the relative demands of higher education and the varying capacities and achievements of low- and high-income states, a factor of relevance in assessing the need of Federal aid.

TABLE 24-1

Expenditures and Percentage of State Expenditures, by Categories, 1902, 1922, 1938, 1953, 1957, and 1958

Expenditure	1902	1922	1938	1953	1957	1958
			Millions of Dollars			
Total expenditures..........	188	1,397	4,598	16,850	24,234	28,080
			Percentage			
Higher education............	7	10	5	8	9	8
Education—payments to local government..............	24	14	14	16	17	16
Highways..................	3	27	25	22	20	20
Public welfare.............	5	3	10	9	7	7
Hospitals.................	15	7	5	6	6	6

Source: U.S. Census, *Historical Statistics of the State and Local Government Finances, 1902–1953; ibid., 1902–1957; ibid., Governmental Finances in 1958.*

In Table 24-1 I indicate the percentage of state expenditures by categories for several selected years. The proportion of state expenditures on higher education rose from 1902 to 1922, declined from 1922 to 1938

325

and rose from 1938 to 1953, and then stabilized to 1957–58. In the years 1902 to 1922 total state expenditures rose by more than six times. This made it possible to increase expenditures greatly in important categories. In these years both relative expenditures on education (direct payments to local government) and those on public welfare and hospitals declined greatly. Against this there was a very large rise in the percentage of expenditures for highways. On the whole, this was a prosperous era, and therefore, despite the increased needs for highways, higher education was able to attract a larger part of state budgets. Enrollments were rising rapidly during this period, as well.

From 1922 to 1938, however, the share of higher education dropped by about 50 per cent. The other important relative change was public welfare, an increase from 3 to 10 per cent. Here, with governmental expenditures up a little more than two times and with a serious depression to contend with, it might be expected that higher education would not do so well. This became a government outlay of lower priority than it had been in 1922, partly because of the growth of highway demands and partly because of the Depression, which increased pressure to spend for public welfare.

From 1938 to 1953 relative changes were not large except for a substantial rise for higher education from 5 to 8 per cent. Other educational payments also rose substantially. This was a period in which education was attracting much more attention and the number of students in public schools and colleges rose greatly. In view of the prosperity, public welfare put a somewhat smaller relative burden on the economy than in 1938. Total outlays of all states rose from $4½ billion to almost $17 billion, or about 300 per cent. By 1957 higher education had further increased its share of state expenditures and had almost reestablished its relative position of 1922. Highways, public welfare, and hospitals lost ground from 1953, and higher education experienced a relative loss in 1958.

Of some interest also is the relative rise of expenditures on higher education in relation to state outlays on public school education: 25 per cent in 1902, 46 per cent in 1922, 41 per cent in 1938, 48 per cent in 1957, and 52 per cent in 1958.

Table 24-2 gives state government expenditures for 1950, 1957, and 1959. This table also reveals large absolute and even relative gains for higher education. With continued prosperity the increased demands of public welfare rose considerably less than the increase of all expenditures. Highways, education, and intergovernmental expenditures were putting the *relatively* heaviest demands upon the economy. Health and hospitals, however, also increased their total receipts by 124 per cent, a factor related to the increased contributions of the Federal government to be matched by state outlays.

From these trends we can draw certain conclusions. It is not too helpful to say that higher education obtained a smaller percentage of state outlays in 1953 or 1957 than in 1922. One has to consider the changing pattern of state expenditures and, what is also relevant, the changing values of our society. In 1902 highways were relatively unimportant, but their total share of state outlays rose from 3 to 22 per cent in a period of fifty years. Public welfare also became a much more important factor, especially after the beginnings of the Depression. In other words, highways have a much higher relative priority than education these days, compared with fifty years ago, and public welfare has also a higher priority, especially since 1933. With the increased number seeking education both in the schools and colleges, and the greater relevance of education for security, the

TABLE 24-2
State Government, Total Expenditures and Categories, 1950, 1957, and 1959

Expenditure	1950 (millions)	1957 (millions)	1959 (millions)	Rise, 1950–1959 (per cent)
All expenditures..........................	$15,082	$24,234	$31,124	+106
Public welfare...........................	2,358	2,770	3,217	+ 37
Education................................	3,413	6,553	8,050	+136
Higher education, exclusive of commercial....	791	1,644	2,237	+183
Intergovernmental........................	2,054	4,094	8,539	+319
Highways................................	2,668	5,956	7,621	+186
Hospitals and health.....................	1,042	1,905	2,327	+124

Source: U.S. Census, State Government Finance, 1952, 1957, and 1959.

relative priority of education has increased since the end of the war. These governments have not, however, neglected higher education since the early part of the century. In 1902 the state expenditures for higher education were $13 million. They rose to $143 million in 1922, $268 million in 1938, and $1,277 million in 1953. The figure for 1957 was $1,958 million, and in 1958 it reached $2,305 million, of which $598 million was for capital expenditures. Part of course was for auxiliary expenditures— e.g., $314 million, or about one-sixth, in 1957.

State expenditures on higher education are high, in part because of the heavy capital outlays. The explanation of these substantial outlays lies in the large backlog in construction as a result of the Great Depression and the war with its large restrictions on capital outlays, and in the increased needs associated with rising college population. From 1930 to 1956, the college population had risen by about 140 per cent, or 1.5 million. Whereas total (public and private) capital outlays were 25 per cent of current expenditures ($125 million) in 1929–30, they declined to $84 million or 12 per cent in 1939–40 (and less in earlier years) and to $71 million or 7 per cent in 1945–46 (with much larger cuts during the war), and rose from 7 to 19 per cent (19 in 1949–50 and 1955–56) for 1950 to 1956. Total plant outlays were $686 million in 1955–56, compared with receipts for this purpose of $826 million in 1955–56. Total state expenditures for physical facilities were, it will be recalled, $600 million, or 27 per cent of current expenditures, in 1958. From 1930 to 1956, value of plant per resident student rose from $1,880 to $3,560, and total value from $2.1 to $9.5 billion. These increases are primarily from increased outlays; that is to say, plant is carried at cost, not replacement value. Many college treasurers have informed me that replacement value is about three times original cost or book value. But there seems to have been some marking up as prices and costs rose. From 1948 to 1956, plant and plant funds rose in value by $5.5 billion; but expenditures increased only by $3.9 billion, and the excess of receipts of plant funds over expenditures on plant only about $300 million. Hence about $1.3 billion of the rise may be ascribed to a writing up of plant.

In considering expenditures for higher education we should also take account of the fact that the state tax systems are hardly progressive. In Table 24-4 I present the estimated effective rates of taxes for 1954, for which Musgrave is responsible. This table shows very clearly that neither the Federal nor the state and local tax systems are as progressive as is generally assumed. The Federal tax rates rise from 13.7 per cent of income for incomes up to $2,000 to 31.8 per cent for incomes over $10,000. For the very high incomes, despite the paper maximum rate of 92 per cent, average rates seldom go above 40 per cent. All kinds of tax avoidance are used.

But what is crucial here is that under state and local taxes the tax burden tends to be heavier on the low-income than on the high-income groups. Note the 9.8 per cent rate for incomes up to $2,000 as against 7.4 per cent for those with incomes over $10,000. Of course a burden of, say, 10 per cent imposed on low incomes is much greater in welfare terms than 10 per cent levied on an income above, say, $10,000. Yet instead of tax rates rising with rising incomes, they fall. In determining the source of funds for higher education in public institutions, this is a matter that should receive serious attention, for on the whole the college-trained population has much higher incomes than the people who pay a large part of the taxes.

In 1959, excluding social security taxes, which are paid for a special purpose, 83 per cent of revenues of the Federal government were direct taxes on personal income and corporations; for state and local governments the corresponding percentage was only 17. These figures suggest that if additional burdens of education are to be put upon government, there is a case for putting them on Federal rather than on state government, for these direct taxes are the most productive and the most equitable. But this of course has to be interpreted in terms of all the other burdens on Federal government.

Furthermore, the position of state and local finance has become much more precarious even than Federal finance. Table 24-3 makes this clear.

TABLE 24-3
Federal, State and Local Governments—Financial Trends

Trend	1947 (billions)	1957 (billions)	1959 (billions)	Percentage change, 1947–1959
Federal:				
Cash receipts..........	$ 44.3	$ 84.5	$ 87.6	+ 98
Cash payments........	38.6	83.3	95.6	+148
Debt (net)............	222.6	219.8	237.3	+ 7
State and local:				
Cash receipts..........	13.1	32.3	36.7	+170
Cash payments........	12.1	32.2	37.8	+212
Debt................	14.4	46.7	55.6	+286

Source: *Economic Report of the President, January, 1960.*

The cash receipts and cash payments of state and local governments have increased about 70 and 40 per cent, respectively, more than those of Federal government in the years 1947 to 1959. The rise of Federal debt in these twelve years was 7 per cent, but for state and local governments the increase was 286 per cent.

Yet we can overdo the precarious condition of state finances. In an article in *College and University Business* (September, 1960) M. M. Chambers shows that from 1958–59 to 1960–61 the weighted increase of appropriations for 16 states was 30 per cent—a minimum of 8¼ per cent for Vermont and a maximum of 70 per cent for Nevada. Should this rate of rise be applied over ten years for the 50 states, the growth would be close to 300 per cent. Then state appropriations would rise from about $1,200 million in 1959–60 to about $4,800 million by 1969–70. Can this rate of increase be continued for ten years? If it can, many problems will be solved. Appropriations rising by 30 per cent for all states in the 1960s would solve many problems. Another approach is to assume that state and local revenues will rise with GNP as in the past. Then subsidies to higher education could rise from $1 billion in 1960 to $2 billion in 1970 and $2.6 billion in 1975.

TABLE 24-4
Estimated Effective Rates of Taxes for 1954
(Tax as per cent of income)

Taxes	Spending-unit income brackets ($1,000)							
	$0–2,000	$2,000–3,000	$3,000–4,000	$4,000–5,000	$5,000–7,500	$7,500–10,000	$10,000	Total
Federal taxes..........	13.7	16.1	17.3	18.0	20.5	22.6	31.8	22.0
State and local taxes....	9.8	9.4	8.9	8.8	8.4	8.2	7.4	8.4

Source: *Joint Committee on the Economic Report: Federal Tax Policy for Economic Growth and Stability*, 1955, p. 98.

DETAILS: RATIO OF EXPENDITURES ON HIGHER EDUCATION TO INCOME

In 1950 the expenditures by state governments for higher education, exclusive of commercial operations, amounted to $791 million. By 1959 the total had risen to $2,237 million (Table 24-2). The rise was from 0.33 per cent to 0.56 per cent of national income. These totals do not, however, include the total amount of money made available to state-controlled institutions. The report of the Council of State Governments of 1952 *Higher Education in the Forty-eight States* shows that *parts* of nonveteran student fees, Federal payments for veterans' fees, local government contributions, earmarked state taxes, Federal funds, and endowment earnings and auxiliary-enterprise income are not included in the above figures. They include 40 per cent of private gifts and grants and up to 100 per cent of the budget appropriations of state funds.[1]

The total given by the U.S. Census for state expenditures for higher education of $1,958 million for 1957 should be compared with expenditures reported by IHL for 1956 of $2,789 million. But the explanation of the lower figure reported by the Census Bureau is largely the inclusion of local expenditures in the HEW totals and the exclusion of some categories by the Census Bureau.

As might be expected, the state governments in the Northeast contributed the lowest percentage of personal income, only 0.21 per cent as compared to 0.71 to 0.76 for the other three regions of the nation. New England's record is better than that of the Middle Atlantic states, 0.29 as against 0.19. The West North Central states provide more relatively than the East North Central states, and the West South Central much more than other parts of the South. The Mountain states with 1.27 per cent of personal income in 1957 contributed for state institutions provide twice as much as the Pacific states with 0.63 per cent.

The expansion of state expenditures for higher education (Table 24-2) is surprisingly large. The only serious competition, aside from intergovernmental expenditures, is highways with an increase from 1950 to 1959 of 186 per cent as compared with 183 per cent for higher education. It is of some interest that, should expenditures in the next nine years rise percentagewise as much as in the nine years 1950 to 1959, the state outlays would increase by more than $4 billion. Since my projection called for an increase of state outlays of but $800 million for the twelve years from 1958 to 1970, the rise yielded on the basis of the *percentage* rise from 1950 to 1959 is large indeed. But we cannot of course count on a continuance of the rapid rate of expansion of the 1950s—in part because of the large backlogs of capital expenditures in the 1950s, in part because an inflation of about 25 per cent should be corrected. Once we do this, we find a gain of only 124 per cent in state outlays on higher education in these nine years and hence of less than $2,800 million for the nine years of the 1960s.

SOME BROAD COMPARISONS FOR HIGH AND LOW PER CAPITA STATES

Here I treat a more limited category of state aid than above, state contribution to operating expenditures of state IHL.

In Table 24-5 note that the 10 states with the highest per capita income in 1950 had 45.6 million population as against 27.7 million for the 10 states with the lowest per capita income. But despite about 1⅔ times as much population, the 10 rich states had only about 1¼ times as large a college-age population as the 10 poorest states. This comparison suggests a heavier burden of education imposed on the low-income states. As compared with roughly 5 per cent of total population in the college-age group for the high-income states, the percentage for the low income states was 6.5.

But the rich states spent roughly twice as much in support of higher education as the poor states. Hence, even allowing for differences in costs, the affluent states had a great advantage in total outlays and in outlay per member of *population of college age*. This is subject to one reservation of some importance. The high-income states tend to be those with large outlays for organized research and public services. Should these be excluded, the advantage of higher expenditures by high-income states would be reduced to some extent.

The burden for rich states was not nearly so great as that of the low-income states. The ratio of state support of higher education to total income payments was 0.190 per cent for the high per capita income states (and despite heavy research outlays) and 0.293 for the low-income states, or roughly 50 per cent more for the latter. In short, the burden of higher education was much greater for the low per capita income states. This despite the fact that they tended to educate a smaller proportion of their college-age population.

Resident enrollment as a percentage of college-age population was 35 for the rich and 18 for the poor states. The rich states, with only about 70 per cent as many people of college age relative to total population as the poor states, had a resident enrollment in relation to college-age population almost twice as great. Indeed the wealthy states had a great advantage in higher education.

TABLE 24-5

Comparison of 10 High and 10 Low Per Capita Income States with Regard to Population, Enrollment, Income Payments to Individuals, and Expenditures of IHL, Total and per Resident Student

All Institutions, State Support, 20 States, 1950

Item	10 high per capita income states	10 low per capita income states
Total population...	45,640,201	27,699,294
Total college-age population................................	2,265,000	1,804,000
College-age population as percentage of total population...........	4.96	6.51
Total state support of higher education (thousands)................	$154,435	$74,633
Total income payments to individuals of the state (millions)...........	$81,054	$25,439
State support of higher education as percentage of total income payments for individuals.......................................	0.190	0.293
Total resident enrollment....................................	792,473	326,865
Resident enrollment as percentage of college-age population.........	35.0	18.1
Total educational and general expense (thousands)................	$616,257	$207,906
Educational and general expense per member of total population.....	$13.50	$7.51
Educational and general expense per member of college-age population...	$272.08	$115.25
Educational and general expense per resident student	$777.61	$635.98

Source: All data computed from Council of State Governments, *Higher Education in the Forty-eight States,* 1952, pp. 86–87, 170–72, 191, 194–95, 209–57. (Our computations.)

These conclusions are further confirmed by the expenditures for education and general expenses in IHL in relation to the population: the per capita expenditures in this category were $13.50 for the 10 rich and $7.51 for the poor states. On the basis of college-age population, the expenditures were $272 as against $115. (Again, I remind the reader of the greater importance of research in the high-income states.)

An examination of the ratio for individual states shows that geographically small states like New Jersey and Delaware have low percentages of expenditures for higher education in relation to personal income, in part because of the size of the state. From these states there are large migrations of students to other states. In general, large migrations to other states tend to keep outlays of IHL down—e.g., New Jersey; a lack of tradition of public higher education keeps outlays down for some states though private outlays may be adequate to offset these low outlays—e.g., Massachusetts. Where population is small and territory large, costs are likely to be high—e.g., Wyoming.

It should be noted that within the two groups of rich and poor states there are large variations. New Jersey, with resident enrollment of 3.4 per cent of college-age population in *public* institutions, should be compared with Connecticut with 10 per cent. Even within the Western states the proportions vary from 19 to 28 per cent. Southern states tend to fall in between, partly because they have large public facilities, but also their percentages are not so high because of the relatively impoverished condition of these states.

As might be expected for *private* institutions, the advantages lie largely with the rich states. For example, 19.7 per cent is the figure for resident students in relation to college-age population for the high-income states and only 6.6 per cent for the low-income states.

Rich states stand out especially in their greater resources in private institutions. The affluent states show a ratio of resident enrollment to college-age population about one-third larger than that for the poor states in public institutions but three times as large in private institutions. The respective ratios of rich to poor states for educational expense per member of the college-age population was 1½ for public institutions and 4 to 1 for private institutions.

The following comparison is of some interest:

State Expenditures, Higher Education, Per Cent of Personal Income

10 richest states, 1950.............. 0.190	10 poorest states, 1950.............. 0.293
12 richest states, 1957.............. 0.373	12 poorest states, 1957.............. 0.800
12 states with largest population, 1957. 0.453	12 states with smallest population, 1957. 1.139

In general, the state contribution in relation to personal income increased greatly over seven years, especially for the poor states. The relative outlays on the basis of population rather than per capita income are much larger, especially for the poor states. Here again the high cost of higher education for the sparsely populated states is evident.

I present in Table 24-6 a comparison of the 12 largest and the 12 smallest states by population. Here again the large states seem to show much larger personal incomes but spend a much smaller percentage of their income for state IHL. The 12 largest states by population and the 12 richest states by per capita income generally reveal much larger expenditures but a smaller percentage of their personal income for state IHL.

TABLE 24-6

Comparison of the 12 Largest and Smallest States by Population and the 12 Richest and Poorest
States by Per Capita Income, with Respect to Total and Relative Expenditures
of State Institutions of Higher Learning, for Selected Years

Item	12 largest states by population	12 smallest states by population	12 richest states by per capita income	12 poorest states by per capita income
Total expenditures, state IHL, 1952 (millions)....	$580.4	$81.6	$378.2	$259.1
Personal income of residents, 1951 (millions)....	$157,742	$9,553	$122,728	$32,382
Total expenditures, state IHL, 1952, percentage of personal income, 1951.................	0.368	0.854	0.308	0.800
Total expenditures, state IHL, 1957 (millions)....	$962.3	$140.5	$618.7	$340.1
Personal income of residents, 1956 (millions)....	$212,497	$12,332	$165,942	$49,909
Total expenditures, state IHL, 1957, percentage of personal income, 1956.................	0.453	1.139	0.373	0.682
Ratio of total expenditures, 1957, as percentage of personal income, 1956, to total expenditures, 1952, as percentage of personal income, 1951............................	1.231	1.334	1.210	0.805

Source: Data from a *Compendium of State Government Finance in 1952* and a *Compendium of State Government Finance in 1957.*

* * *

Trends vary greatly over the years, even among states that are of
similar economic conditions. Compare, for example, the trends of Illinois,
Michigan, and Wisconsin.

TABLE 24-7

State Support for Higher Education in Relation to Personal Income
in Six Midwestern States, 1939 and 1957, Per Cent

	1939–40	1957–58
Illinois...............	0.13	0.30
Indiana..............	0.30	0.41
Iowa................	0.41	0.57
Michigan............	0.26	0.54
Minnesota...........	0.38	0.50
Wisconsin...........	0.33	0.36

Source: *Coordinating Commission for Higher Education in Wisconsin, Informational Item*
No. 6, December, 1960, p. 2.

SUMMARY

Competing increasingly with roads and welfare, higher education lost ground relatively in its claim on state resources in the interwar generation. But the colleges retrieved lost ground and even gained in the post–World War II years. Moreover, over the years since 1900, higher education has become a much larger factor vis-à-vis public school education: 30 per cent as large at the beginning of the century and about one-half now ($2 billion against $4 billion roughly). By 1970 the respective totals may well be $3–4 billion for higher and $8 billion for lower education.

Heavy incidence of higher education on state finances is especially troublesome because, given the tax systems of most states, the beneficiaries of higher education on the average come from higher-income classes than the taxpayers. As one of my colleagues once said: "Why should the impoverished farmer in Northern Michigan subsidize the sons of the vice-president of General Motors?" At any rate, the case for large subsidies becomes stronger as the tax system becomes more progressive.

An examination of costs of higher education to state governments reveals that costs per student tend to be high in states with much territory and sparse population. Higher education is costly when enrollments are small. Costs to the taxpayers are smaller where, as in the East, the tradition of public higher education is weak, though large variations even in the Northeast are to be found. Some states (e.g., New Jersey) keep outlays down by exporting large numbers of students to other states.

An important area of exploration is the relative position of low- and high-income states. The high-income states, frequently without much interest in public higher education, spend much more per student in private higher education than the low-income states. In general, the high-income states have a smaller proportion of the population in the college-age group, spend much more on higher education, and yet spend a much smaller percentage of personal income (one-third less) and educate twice as large a proportion of the college-age population. The excess of expenditures of the 10 high-income states is reduced to some extent, however, if allowance is made for their heavier outlays on organized research.

One additional point is worth making: the heavy outlays for higher education in the late 1950s reflect in part underspending for capital in the 1930s and 1940s.

FOOTNOTE

[1] There is more on this problem in later chapters on individual states.

Chapter 25

SOME ASPECTS OF DIFFERENTIALS IN HIGHER EDUCATION AMONG STATES

DIFFICULTIES INVOLVED IN INTERSTATE COMPARISONS

In the McGraw-Hill volume *Financing Higher Education: 1960–70* I published a table, "Higher Education and State Finance: Various Indices, 1957."[1] This table in turn was based on an earlier table which was never published but which was submitted to experts in the (then) 48 states. Any table which compares variables for 48 states is subject to all kinds of reservations. For this reason, many would prefer to omit such tables. Yet in my work on this study I have found hundreds of comparisons in rather crude form of indices of expenditures, enrollments, costs per student, and of general indices of effort, capacity, and achievement. I am particularly anxious that no one, least of all governors or budget officers, should use this table without a realization of the pitfalls. These comparisons are always made, and therefore it is important to have them as free of error as is possible. I hope that further studies will be made.[2] Administrators in public IHL are especially sensitive to any comparisons that show relatively large outlays per student.

After publishing my McGraw-Hill table, I sent a copy to the heads of major public universities in the 48 states, to the 48 budget officers, and the higher-education boards, or similar organizations. I asked for criticisms of my table and also put specific questions to these experts. Since one of the criticisms made was incomparability of accounting methods, I asked each expert to check whether such items as endowment income, tuition, contributions of local governments, research gifts, and the like, were or were not excluded from the state budget, and also to designate the amounts involved. Note that exclusion or inclusion of these items is relevant only for the totals for state expenditures, not for *IHL* expenditures—the latter include all these items.

The replies to my plea were generous indeed and helped remove some of the confusion. Yet some obscurities remained. Despite the replies and examination of each state budget, we are not entirely satisfied with the results. In some instances, we had inconsistent replies from the state universities and the budget bureau; in others, e.g., Georgia, there was scarcely a higher-education budget to study. Again, one of our problems is that in some states the university is treated more generously than other state IHL, e.g., state colleges. Revenues other than state appropriations are often not included in the state budget for universities but are included for others.

My McGraw-Hill table raised some general issues. For example, I included organized research as part of the educational expenditures. Representatives of land-grant colleges urged that organized research should be eliminated from the rubric, educational expenditures. Obviously, if organized research is included, the costs per student are higher than they otherwise would be. Moreover, the rankings of states on the level of expenditures per student are affected. Organized research, as a factor in total expenditures, varies among states. In 16 states accounting for about 70 per cent of expenditures for student higher education, organized research accounted for a minimum of 8.6 per cent of educational and general expenditures in Ohio, and a maximum of 41.3 per cent in California. Obviously the inclusion of organized research tends to inflate California's outlays vis-à-vis Ohio's.

In an examination of 1955–56 statistics, I found an average for organized research and extension and public services of 25 per cent of total general and educational outlays in *public* IHL. For the purposes of this calculation I deduct these from general and educational expenditures. When the percentage greatly deviates from 25, it may be assumed that per student expenditures vary according to whether these items are included or excluded. Their exclusion is especially important for California with 40 per cent spent for these items. Their exclusion reduces per unit outlays for instruction. In the following states, the exclusion of these items tends greatly to increase their *ranking* for per student costs: New Jersey (2 per cent); New York (6 per cent); Ohio (10 per cent); West Virginia, Florida (13 per cent); Massachusetts, Colorado (14 per cent).

But it is not at all clear that organized research should be excluded. The Association of American Universities seems to have taken the position that instruction and research are tied in such a manner that they should not be separated. President DuBridge of California Institute of Technology took a similar position in a conversation with the author. Research is a necessary ingredient of instruction, and without it the first-class teacher cannot be held and the student is deprived of a laboratory for learning how to do research. Indeed a project such as Los Alamos (for California) or Lincoln (for MIT) may not be tied closely to instruction.

In my revised table I reluctantly excluded organized research, and also extension and other public services, the assumption being that they are

Master Table: Various Measures Relevant for Higher Education, and Rankings by States, 1957–58

State	College-age (18–21) population 1957^a (1)	Enrollment, Public IHL 1957^b (2)	(2)/(1), % (3)	Rank	Full-time undergraduate enrollment, Public IHL 1957 (4)	(4)/(11), % (5)	Rank	State resident enrollment, Public IHL 1958^c (6)	(6)/(11), % (7)	Rank	Total enrollment, all IHL Fall, 1958 (8)	Public IHL enrollment Fall, 1958 (9)	(9)/(8), % (10)	Rank
Alabama	193,884	24,902	12.9	39–40	22,697	11.7	33–34	28,368	14.6	29	42,852	32,028	74.8	17
Arizona	50,505	22,979	45.5	1	15,548	30.8	1	22,278	44.1	1	28,024	27,377	97.7	3
Arkansas	101,548	17,009	16.7	26	14,205	14.0	24	15,503	15.3	25	21,782	16,989	78.8	10
California	663,234	230,626	42.3	2	149,272	22.5	8–9	235,522^d	35.5	2	328,731^d	258,486^d	78.6	11
Colorado	83,579	25,702	29.0	7	22,317	25.2	6	19,175	21.6	14	38,640	29,464	76.3	13–14
Connecticut	93,757	15,059	16.1	27–28	10,626	11.3	35	13,414	14.3	30	39,109	14,642	37.4	44–45
Delaware	17,411	3,380	19.4	20	2,388	13.7	26	2,647	15.2	26	4,584	3,789	82.7	7
Florida	175,767	27,813	15.8	29	20,844	11.9	31	27,936	15.9	24	55,266	31,203	56.5	33
Georgia	234,259	30,243	12.9	39–40	21,345	9.1	40	25,120	10.7	41	44,355	29,564	66.8	24
Idaho	39,704	7,644	19.3	21	6,758	17.0	18	5,416	13.6	34	8,943	6,762	75.7	15
Illinois	452,706	64,809	14.3	34	44,751	9.9	38	67,652	14.9	28	160,503^d	72,168	45.0	43
Indiana	230,155	35,352	15.4	30	28,811	12.5	29	42,036	18.3	21	85,890	51,662	60.1	29
Iowa	152,176	26,291	17.3	25	22,371	14.7	23	21,236	14.0	31–32	47,675	36,415	55.4	35–36
Kansas	100,023	35,782	35.8	4	28,057	28.1	3	31,429	31.4	3	45,371	36,830	81.2	8
Kentucky	190,607	24,434	12.8	41	17,249	9.0	41	23,668	12.4	38	42,231	26,914	63.7	27
Louisiana	182,235	33,176	18.2	24	28,451	15.6	21–22	34,325	18.8	18–19	51,852	36,905	71.2	21
Maine	51,326	5,644	11.0	43	5,471	10.7	36	4,708	9.2	42	9,781	5,539	56.6	32
Maryland	132,761	25,416	19.1	22	16,243	12.2	30	20,023^d	15.1	27	51,151^d	30,549^d	59.7	30
Massachusetts	234,089	14,162	6.0	48	12,962	5.5	47–48	14,462^d	6.2	48	115,182^d	14,997^d	13.0	48
Michigan	356,752	96,697	27.1	9–10	64,957	18.2	14–15	97,397	27.3	5	144,732	112,426	77.7	12
Minnesota	173,683	36,040	20.8	19	30,350	17.5	16	34,288	19.7	17	58,721	38,531	65.6	26
Mississippi	166,042	22,118	13.3	37	19,576	11.8	32	20,846^d	12.6	36	29,214^d	23,511^d	80.5	9
Missouri	203,790	30,678	15.1	31	25,615	12.6	28	26,153^d	12.8	35	63,806^d	29,788	46.7	41
Montana	34,945	8,829	25.3	13	7,854	22.5	8–9	8,042	23.0	10–11	10,971	9,606	87.6	6

Nebraska	67,691	17,865	26.4	11	13,676	20.2	11	16,517	24.4	12	27,069	18,950	70.0	23
Nevada	9,503	2,779	29.2	5	1,838	19.3	13	2,110	22.2	13	2,446	2,446	100.0	1-2
New Hampshire	30,052	4,443	14.8	32	4,148	13.8	25	3,753	12.5	37	9,846	4,852	49.3	39
New Jersey	216,893	30,189	13.9	35	14,945	6.9	45-46	30,402	14.0	31-32	70,008	31,684	45.3	42
New Mexico	53,092	12,944	24.4	15	8,483	16.0	19	11,223	21.1	15	15,094	14,244	94.4	5
New York	701,514	95,180	13.6	36	51,806	7.4	44	116,344	16.6	22	323.872d	121,118	37.4	44-45
N. Carolina	299,295	29,303	9.8	44	25,561	8.5	42	26,882	9.0	43	59,490	31,115	52.3	38
North Dakota	36,049	10,507	29.1	6	9,755	27.1	4	10,091	28.0	4	12,857	12,351	96.1	4
Ohio	420,188	76,758	18.3	23	53,838	12.8	27	67,144	16.0	23	140,572	76,887	54.7	37
Oklahoma	138,438	37,568	27.1	9-10	31,326	22.6	7	34,985	25.3	7	52,462	40,016	76.3	13-14
Oregon	86,099	21,101	24.5	14	18,982	22.0	10	19,269	22.4	12	32,134	22,965	71.5	20
Pennsylvania	539,652	32,937	6.1	47	29,750	5.5	47-48	33,895d	6.3	47	166,980d	36,522d	21.9	47
Rhode Island	45,959	3,469	7.5	46	3,173	6.9	45-46	3,385	7.4	45	13,043	3,839	29.4	46
S. Carolina	148,864	14,054	9.4	45	12,551	8.4	43	12,221	8.2	44	26,992d	15,207	56.3	34
South Dakota	35,292	9,770	27.7	8	9,063	25.7	5	8,106	23.0	10-11	13,571	10,132	74.7	18
Tennessee	217,936	28,642	13.1	38	22,834	10.5	37	25,608	11.8	39	53,550	29,686	55.4	35-36
Texas	540,347	118,085	21.9	17	85,748	15.9	20	111,431	20.6	16	166,565d	117,903	70.8	22
Utah	47,765	17,513	36.7	3	14,100	29.5	2	12,953	27.1	6	26,829	16,454	61.3	28
Vermont	22,482	3,623	16.1	27-28	3,504	15.6	21-22	2,451	10.9	40	8,364	3,954	47.3	40
Virginia	229,541	26,620	11.6	42	21,058	9.2	39	16,001e	7.0	46	36,418e	21,647	59.4	31
Washington	143,419	34,811	24.3	16	27,823	19.4	12	33,148	23.1	9	51,177	36,849	72.0	19
W. Virginia	130,690	18,920	14.5	33	15,307	11.7	33-34	17,940	13.7	33	26,989	20,363	75.4	16
Wisconsin	184,427	38,775	21.0	18	32,040	17.4	17	34,763	18.8	18-19	60,897	40,446	66.4	25
Wyoming	21,293	5,546	26.0	12	3,870	18.2	14-15	3,924	18.4	20	4,710	4,710	100.0	1-2
48-state total	8,686,519	1,606,187	18.5	.....	1,153,902	13.3	.....	1,496,190d	17.2	.....	2,931,301	1,700,485d	58.0	.....

a While recent studies, e.g., Max Wise, They Come for the Best of Reasons, American Council on Education, Washington, 1959, show that a substantial proportion of college students are twenty-two to thirty, they do not suggest that using an eighteen-to-twenty-one population base—best available for 1957—introduces systematic bias in rankings.

b Resident, degree credit, full and part time, undergraduate, and graduate.

c Residents of state X attending state, municipal, or district IHL in state X.

dAdjusted for institutions not replying to survey.

e Apparently Virginia institutions listed only full-time students in answering this survey; other estimates yield total enrollment of up to 50,000.

f Includes general administration and general expense, instruction and departmental research, libraries, plant maintenance, educational department's organized activities, and student aid only (items 24, 25, 27, 28, 30d, & G of "Financial Statistics of Institutions of Higher Education, 1957-1958" questionnaire of Office of Education, HEW).

g Virginia's results are heavily influenced by nearly $12,000,000 in department-related medical activity, by far the highest per capita or as a per cent of total expenditure in the United States. In other areas its expenditure pattern puts it near average on expenditure per student and far below on expenditure per college-age individual.

Master Table: Various Measures Relevant for Higher Education, and Rankings by States, 1957–58 (Continued)

State	Public IHL educational, general plus student-aid expenditures 1957–58 ($000) (11)	Public IHL adjusted, educational plus student-aid expenditures 1957–58/ ($000) (12)	(12)/(11), $/college-age individual 1957 (13)	Rank	(12)/(2), $/student 1957–58 (14)	Rank	State and local tax revenues 1957 ($000) (15)	Net state local support, public IHL (current expenditures) 1957^h ($000) (16)	(15)/(11) (17)	Rank	(15)/(12) (18)	Rank	State and local support, public IHL (capital expenditures) 1957 ($000) (19)	(12)/(11) (20)	Rank
Alabama	34,230	24,305	125	35–36	976	22	319,974	13,259	1,650	47	12,849	33	3,777	19	44
Arizona	17,171	12,917	256	9–10	562	48	183,081	8,376	3,625	13	7,967	47	10,546	209	2
Arkansas	21,070	14,535	143	32	855	36	178,579	8,355	1,759	42	10,499	42	3,558	35	37–39
California	368,155	205,484	310	4	732	43	3,311,173	247,649	4,992	3	11,800	35	87,970	133	7
Colorado	34,480	27,821	314	3	1,082	14	314,372	15,150	3,549	16	12,231	34	13,471	152	5
Connecticut	14,929	12,682	135	33	842	37	461,968	8,843	4,927	4	30,677	6	4,848	52	27–28
Delaware	5,773	4,140	238	17	1,225	6	58,781	2,145	3,376	19	17,391	21	1,781	102	9–10
Florida	38,850	27,310	155	31	982	18–19	666,780	20,996	3,794	11	23,974	9	15,118	86	13
Georgia	35,717	23,754	101	41	785	39	469,978	12,686	2,006	40	15,540	25	3,719	16	45–46
Idaho	9,585	6,943	175	26	908	31	100,314	4,628	2,527	35	13,123	32	2,826	71	16
Illinois	100,225	75,386	166	29	1,163	11	1,731,535	63,036	3,825	10	26,718	7	22,547	50	31
Indiana	65,651	49,485	215	19	1,400	4	638,502	21,066	2,774	31	18,061	17	40,140	174	3
Iowa	51,775	37,304	245	15	1,419	2	489,636	26,835	3,218	22	18,624	12	9,359	62	22
Kansas	41,048	32,540	325	2	909	30	368,640	22,653	3,686	12	10,302	43	8,697	87	12
Kentucky	24,843	17,398	91	45	712	46	324,975	14,109	1,705	43	13,300	31	12,168	64	20–21
Louisiana	41,280	32,523	178	24	980	20	498,233	23,906	2,732	33	15,018	26	10,165	56	24
Maine	7,164	5,542	108	39	982	18–19	140,695	3,218	2,741	32	24,884	8	1,267	25	41
Maryland	34,900	28,416	214	20	1,118	13	461,207	13,975	3,474	17	18,146	16	6,398	48	32
Massachusetts	14,564	12,321	53	48	870	35	1,017,840	8,465	4,348	6	71,871	1	3,755	16	45–46
Michigan	151,730	117,074	328	1	1,211	8	1,396,320	93,720	3,914	8	14,440	28	58,717	165	4
Minnesota	59,767	44,191	254	11	1,226	5	600,087	28,614	3,455	18	16,651	23	11,733	68	19
Mississippi	21,967	15,491	93	43	700	47	234,341	10,054	1,411	48	10,595	41	3,576	22	42
Missouri	30,574	23,341	114	37	761	40	553,531	14,052	2,716	34	18,043	18	7,082	35	37–39
Montana	12,831	9,545	273	8	1,081	15	125,992	5,715	3,600	14	14,270	29	4,883	140	6

Nebraska	22,782	16,873	249	13	944	25	201,259	12,422	2,973	25	11,266	38	5,757	85	14
Nevada	3,774	2,666	281	7	959	23	60,262	1,913	6,341	1	21,685	10	2,240	236	1
New Hampshire	6,738	5,305	177	25	1,194	9	87,086	2,912	2,898	26	19,601	11	1,539	51	29–30
New Jersey	29,639	22,944	106	40	760	41	990,616	15,842	4,567	5	32,814	5	9,345	43	33
New Mexico	16,414	11,332	213	21	875	34	128,107	10,461	2,413	37	9,897	45	2,817	53	25–26
New York	92,246	87,886	125	35–36	923	28	3,723,393	78,040	5,308	2	39,119	3	25,360	36	36
N. Carolina	47,259	33,810	113	38	1,154	12	503,209	19,130	1,681	45	17,173	22	4,224	14	47–48
North Dakota	11,420	9,230	256	9–10	878	33	107,799	6,065	2,990	24	10,260	44	2,488	69	17–18
Ohio	81,282	71,062	169	28	926	27	1,404,084	45,450	3,343	20	18,292	14	22,078	53	25–26
Oklahoma	34,715	27,368	198	23	728	44	346,518	16,986	2,503	36	9,224	46	9,571	69	17–18
Oregon	33,986	24,618	286	6	1,167	10	349,584	14,774	4,060	7	16,567	24	9,858	114	8
Pennsylvania	47,315	33,342	62	47	1,012	17	1,776,853	21,458	3,293	21	53,947	2	10,808	20	43
Rhode Island	5,510	4,225	92	44	1,218	7	130,134	3,101	2,832	30	37,513	4	1,792	39	35
S. Carolina	18,235	12,914	87	46	919	29	245,708	9,775	1,651	46	17,483	20	2,105	14	47–48
South Dakota	11,618	8,626	244	16	883	32	112,801	5,430	3,196	23	11,546	37	2,822	80	15
Tennessee	29,045	21,074	97	42	736	42	404,291	13,560	1,855	41	14,115	30	7,255	33	40
Texas	111,141	84,420	156	30	715	45	1,258,768	66,929	2,330	38	10,660	40	28,212	52	27–28
Utah	20,383	14,261	299	5	814	38	136,779	10,530	2,864	28	7,810	48	2,749	58	23
Vermont	6,500	5,110	227	18	1,410	3	64,872	2,685	2,886	27	17,906	19	1,439	64	20–21
Virginia	49,490a	39,290a	171a	27a	1,476a	1a	491,620	17,828	2,142	39	18,468	13	7,946	35	37–39
Washington	50,783	36,091	252	12	1,037	16	513,947	32,021	3,584	15	14,764	27	14,565	102	9–10
W. Virginia	20,644	17,550	134	34	928	26	220,205	8,607	1,685	44	11,639	36	6,691	51	29–30
Wisconsin	54,947	37,947	206	22	979	21	708,906	25,878	3,844	9	18,283	15	7,709	42	34
Wyoming	7,159	5,277	248	14	951	24	60,645	4,019	2,848	29	10,935	39	1,909	90	11
48-state total	2,051,304	1,493,669	171	…	930	…	28,673,980	1,137,321	3,301	…	17,852	…	539,380	62	…

a This column is derived by subtracting state IHL noncommercial budget revenues from budget expenditures, adding public IHL student aid (not included in IHL by Census Bureau), and adding noncommercial expenditures of local public IHL. Thus the figure approximates net use of general revenues (or tax revenues) for public IHL. The total is slightly biased upward, because data for correcting local IHL expenditures from gross to net (by subtracting noncommercial revenues) was lacking, but since these revenues are very small and since the total local IHL share is 10 per cent of state, the error should not exceed 2 per cent at the outside.

Sources:

Column 1: Ronald B. Thompson, Projected College Enrollments 1950–1975, College Blue Book, 1959, pp. 921–932.

Columns 6, 8, 9: Home State and Migration of American College Students, Fall 1958, Association of Collegiate Registrars and Admissions Officers, 1959, pp. 8–9.

Columns 2, 4, 11, 12: Office of Education, HEW, draft 1957–58 data supplied from worksheets.

Column 15: 1957 Census of Government: Compendium of Government Finances, vol. III, no. 5, Bureau of the Census, 1959, p. 28.

Column 16: ibid., pp. 31, 50; worksheet; Office of Education, op. cit., item G; Expenditure of IHL, Operated by Local Governments: Fiscal 1958, Bureau of the Census 1960.

Column 19: 1957 Census of Government: op. cit., p. 48, and Expenditure of IHL operated . . . , op. cit.

irrelevant for the major instructional tasks of IHL. The reader can, however, compare the McGraw-Hill table where organized research is not excluded. But I did not exclude related activities in my Master Table, as it seemed to me that these are part of the instruction bill—e.g., hospitals for medical students. The NPA, however, excluded the last. Incidentally, in 1957–58 organized research, extension and public services, and related activities accounted for 20, 5, and 10 per cent, respectively, of total educational and general expenditures.[3]

For public IHL in the nation (1957) the adjusted total of expenditures was 72.7 per cent of the unadjusted. The use of adjusted figures greatly would reduce unit costs for California with a ratio of 56 per cent of adjusted to total expenditures. But this adjustment would greatly increase relative unit costs for others, with ratios of 95 (New York), 87 (Ohio), 85 (West Virginia, Connecticut, and Massachusetts), and 81 (North Dakota and Colorado).

A few other general issues arise. In the McGraw-Hill volume I concentrated on state expenditures. Obviously where local governments contribute substantial sums to higher education, these sums should be included. In the fiscal year 1958, local governments contributed $277 million for higher education, $28 million for commercial activities, $55 million for capital outlay, and $194 million for other (educational and general).[4]

For the year 1957–58 the HEW's estimate of local government expenditures is only $129 million. The NPA estimate is $110 million for *student higher education*—this category, it will be recalled, accounts for 16 states with 70 per cent of outlays on student higher education.

Inclusion of local government expenditures, exclusive of capital and auxiliary, as given by the Census Bureau, raises public educational expenditures (adjusted as given in column 12 of Master Table) substantially more than the average of 12 per cent only in the following states:

	Per cent		Per cent
California	34	New York	50
Kentucky	32	Ohio	20
Mississippi	20	Texas	21

Indeed the inclusion of local expenditures affects the other states in varying degrees. In the NPA study, the local expenditures for 16 states of $110 million are estimated at 13.4 per cent of state and local funds for student higher education. Of the 16 states those with relatively large local contributions for 1957–58 are the following—note these relate to all IHL though local contributions are almost wholly for public IHL.[5]

	Per cent
California	26.7
New York	32.3

In response to my request for criticism of the McGraw-Hill table, several respondents raised the issue of incomparability resulting from varying practices of excluding or including in the state budget items not financed by tax receipts. For this reason, comparison of *state* expenditures for IHL may to some extent be misleading. But this criticism applies only to the state expenditures, not to income or outlays of IHL. I shall discuss the resulting reservations state by state later. But for public IHL state and local government contributions are the major source of income, especially if organized research is omitted. Thus in 1955–56, educational and general income of public IHL contributed by state and local government was $612 million, or 53 per cent of total income. Should we deduct $145 million of income from the Federal government for organized research, then the share of state and local government contributions would rise to 61 per cent.

In my questionnaire I asked authorities in state IHL and state governments for information on the following items: tuition, endowment earnings, private gifts, *net* income from auxiliary services, earmarked taxes, contributions of local government, income for organized research not included under private gifts, and any other. (The last would include a substantial item of $99 million in 1955–56 from related activities, e.g., income from hospitals, farms.)

TABLE 25-1
Miscellaneous Sources of Income, Public IHL, 1955–56

Source of income	Amount (millions)	Per cent of general and educational income minus Federal contributions of organized research
Student fees.................	$135	13.4
Endowment earnings...........	14	1.4
Private gifts and grants........	44	4.4
Related activities..............	99	9.8
Other......................	30	3.0

Source: HEW, *Statistics of Higher Education, 1955–56; Receipts, Expenditures and Property,* p. 10.

COMPARISON: CAPACITY, EFFORT, AND ACHIEVEMENTS

A column-by-column discussion of the McGraw-Hill table will reveal some of the issues raised by this table.

In column 1, per capita income for 1957 was presented. In general, it is clear (columns 1 and 2) that states with high per capita income (capacity) spend a relatively small percentage of their income on public higher education (effort); and those with low per capita income spend a relatively large part of personal income on public higher education. In the preceding chapter comparisons limited to 20 states yielded similar results. Some exceptions are to be noted. California is 4th in capacity and 14th to 15th in effort; Kentucky is 43d and 40th. Material in the last chapter further elaborates this point. Hungate found association of outlays with per capita incomes lower for high- than for low-income states.[6]

In an earlier study, Table 25-2, I compared the average *rankings* (1st

TABLE 25-2
Rankings, 24 States, Several Variables, Higher Education, 1957

Variable	Rankings of 12 states with highest per capita income (highest ranking among 48 states in each variable = number 1)	Rankings of 12 states with lowest per capita income
State expenditures on higher education as a percentage of personal income......................	33.7	23.0
Total expenditures per member of the college-age population................................	15.1	39.4
Higher education as percentage of tax revenues.....	30.6	29.0
College-age population as percentage of total population...................................	39.4	8.7
Enrollment as percentage of college-age population..	17.7	39.3

to 48th) for several variables for 12 states with highest per capita income and 12 states with lowest per capita income. This table shows that the wealthy states spend much less on public higher education relative to their income. (A high rating, 33.7, means lower relative expenditures than a lower rating, 23.0.) Yet the rich states spend much more per member of the college-age population (average ranking of 15th versus 39th for poor), a fact explained by high incomes and low college-age population (ranking of 39th for the latter for rich states and 9th for the poor). Despite the relatively small outlays in relation to personal income, the rich states' enrollment vis-à-vis college-age population is much higher (18th versus 39th). There is little difference in the proportion of tax revenues to higher education.

ONE YEAR AN ADEQUATE GUIDE?

One criticism to be made of column 2 (and of some others) is that it covers but one year. It would be better to study several years. What is more, the situation has changed since 1957. The relatively larger rise for the ratio of outlays on higher education to personal income occurred for poor rather than for rich states from 1950 to 1957—see the preceding chapter.

The California master plan estimates the percentage of personal income of states spent for public higher education for the years 1952–1958. This is a much more comprehensive treatment of outlays for public higher education than my results for 1957. Yet in 10 instances the rankings were identical. In only 10 instances did the rankings in the California study deviate more than five places (see Table 25-3).

TABLE 25-3

Rankings, State Outlays on Higher Education as Percentage
of Personal Income, 1952–1958 and 1957

State	Ranking, California 1952–1958	Ranking, S. E. H., 1957
Montana................	8	17
Arizona.................	10	19
Arkansas................	11	18
Indiana.................	15	22
Michigan...............	16	6
Idaho..................	21	28
West Virginia...........	24	33
Delaware...............	27	36
California..............	34	14–15
Vermont................	40	5

Source: S. E. H. table, col. 2, in Dexter M. Keezer (ed.), *Financing Higher Education: 1960–70*, McGraw-Hill, New York, 1959; and *A Master Plan for Higher Education in California*, 1960, p. 213.

Of some interest is the fact that of the top five (Master Plan ranking for 1952–1958 of state expenditures for higher education in relation to personal income) only one deviates more than one rank from the S. E. H. rankings for 1957; and of the last nine the deviations average only one-third of one rank. Another interesting point is that the largest state expenditures in relation to personal income from 1952–1958 fall mainly to states where territory is large, population sparse, per capita incomes below average, and traditions of higher education strong. The rankings in order from 1st to 10th are: New Mexico, Utah, North Dakota, Oklahoma, South Dakota, Colorado, Minnesota, Montana, Wyoming, and Arizona. Of these 10 states only Minnesota does not fit this general description. In the sparsely settled states, unit costs tend to be high. These are also states with incomes below average—per capita incomes are 15 per cent below average; the average population is only one-third that of the average state, and the territory is very large. I conclude that the 1957 statistics on the ratio of state expenditures on public higher education to personal income do not deviate greatly from those for 1952–1958.

For the 12 states in the Southeast average ranking for 1952–1958 is 24th. Their low incomes tend to depress their tax payments for higher education. Moreover, their tradition of higher education is not so strong as for the 10 states listed above. But they do not suffer from the disability of these 10 states associated with low and scattered population and hence high unit costs. Average population is only about 15 per cent less than the 48-state average. In comparing state contributions to higher education, the analyst should keep in mind the relevance of population and population concentration—not only in considering the ratio of state expenditures to the state personal income, but also in considering expenditures per student.

A ranking of 40th to 48th belongs primarily to high-income states and those with heavy concentrations of population. But they are also the states having generally weak traditions of public higher education. Their low position stems in part from high personal income, in part from large concentrations of population (a factor tending to reduce unit costs), and in part from heavy reliance on private institutions. The states ranking from 40th to 48th are: Illinois, Ohio, Rhode Island, Missouri, Connecticut, New Jersey, Pennsylvania, New York, and Massachusetts. These generalizations apply especially to the last six. Their average per capita income is 17 per cent above the national level.[7]

TABLE 25-4

State Tax Revenues as Percentage of Personal Income, Six States, 1955–1958 and 1957

State	1955–1958	1957
Oregon............	19	10
California...........	21	27
Rhode Island..........	26	38
Pennsylvania..........	37	31
Virginia..............	38	20
Texas................	40	34

Critics have also commented on columns 3 and 4 of the McGraw-Hill table. The former is total state tax revenue per capita; the latter, state tax revenues in relation to personal income. Of the former, the criticism was that state tax revenues are not a good measure of capacity to support higher education. The appropriate variable is state and local tax revenues. I shall return to this item.

It would be better to consider first the point raised earlier: is a one-year comparison adequate? I have, therefore, compared the ratio of state tax revenue to personal income in 1957 with a similar series for 1955–1958.[8]

Rankings vary surprisingly little in 1955–1958 from 1957. The average variation in rank for the 48 states is 2.6. Only 6 states varied more than five places (Table 25-4).

INCLUDE LOCAL EXPENDITURES?

Is the tax revenue per capita an unacceptable variable for our purposes? I am not certain that this is so. Public IHL are supported primarily by state revenue, and hence the relevance of state taxes. But in one respect it would be better to include local as well as state tax revenues. For the heavier local taxes are, the more difficult it becomes to increase state taxes. And the proportion of state and local taxes varies greatly. In 1957 state taxes were 50.5 per cent of state and local taxes. But the minimum was 25.9 per cent in New Jersey and the maximum, 78.9 per cent in New Mexico. In seven states the state contribution was more than 70 per cent and in five, less than 40 per cent.[9]

State taxes per capita do not necessarily measure the capacity of states to levy taxes. Some states at a given economic status are much less inclined to tax than others. Of the 12 states in 1957 with highest per capita income, 6 also were among the highest 12 in taxes per capita (California, Connecticut, Delaware, Michigan, Nevada, and Washington). But note the 6 in Table 25-5.

TABLE 25-5
Rank Per Capita Income and State Taxes Per Capita, Six States, 1957

State	Rank per capita income	Rank state taxes per capita
Louisiana............	37	3
New Mexico..........	31	4
Oklahoma............	36	8
Oregon..............	20	6
Wyoming.............	14	7
Arizona..............	29	12

Source: My calculations from *Survey of Current Business* and U.S. Census, *State Government Finances in 1957.*

States with heavy state taxes per capita are often sparsely populated states—with large unit costs for services. Their efforts relative to income are large.

The 12 states with highest state taxes per capita had average ranking of 17th in per capita income.

What does a study of the association of per capita income and state *and local* tax revenues as a percentage of state's personal income reveal?

348 Government Contributions

Here the 12 states with the highest state and local tax revenues vis-à-vis personal income revealed an average rank of 31st in per capita income. In other words, the correlation of state *and local* taxes with per capita income is much less than that of state taxes alone. The 11 states with heaviest state and local taxes vis-à-vis personal incomes are, in order: North Dakota, Mississippi, South Dakota, Louisiana, Vermont, Montana, Minnesota, Oregon, Kansas, Idaho, and Wisconsin. Only Montana, Minnesota, Oregon, and Wisconsin rank lower than 24th in per capita income, that is, have relatively high per capita income. A majority of these 11 states are low in population and low in income. For these states, additional revenue is likely to prove more difficult than for others.

EFFECT OF INCLUDING LOCAL EXPENDITURES

In Table 25-6 I compare state tax revenues as a percentage of state's personal income and rankings of this variable by states (McGraw-Hill table, column 4) and state *and local* taxes as a percentage of personal income.

Where rankings increase in column 4 over column 2, this is an indication that local taxes tend relatively to be less heavy than state taxes. Where the rankings decline, the inference is heavier local taxes.

In *order* the *rise* of rankings, and hence an indication of the extent to which low local taxes tend to depress relative state and local tax revenues, is as follows:[10] West Virginia (a rise of ranking of 24); South Carolina, North Carolina, Alabama (all 22); Arkansas (20); Georgia, Tennessee (19); New Mexico (17); Washington (16); Viriginia (13); Oklahoma (12); Delaware (11); Kentucky (10). These are mainly low-income states in the South, where local taxes yield relatively little in relation to income.

Thirteen states with large reductions in rankings—that is, states with local revenues that tend to improve rankings in state and local tax receipts, are: South Dakota (reduction of 33); Montana (25); Kansas (23); New York (20); Minnesota (18); Massachusetts (16); New Hampshire (14); California, Colorado, Wisconsin, Iowa (all 13); Idaho (12); North Dakota (11).

RELEVANCE OF TAX STRUCTURE

One other aspect of taxes deserves comment. A state that depends on excise, sales, and similar taxes tends to put the tax burden on low-income groups and siphon off income from this group for the benefit of higher-income groups, the college-student group. A greater dependence on direct taxes, e.g., corporation and income taxes, tends to increase the yield of tax programs and to provide a more equitable system. In 1957, 14 states

TABLE 25-6
State Taxes and State and Local Taxes in Relation to Personal Income, 1957

State	State tax revenues		State and local taxes	
	As per cent of personal income	Ranking	As per cent of personal income	Ranking
Alabama................	5.51	14	7.67	36
Arizona................	5.38	16	9.21	19
Arkansas...............	6.16	7	8.77	27
California..............	4.66	27	9.42	14
Colorado..............	4.59	29	9.41	16
Connecticut............	3.58	40	7.27	42
Delaware..............	3.72	37	4.90	48
Florida................	4.99	21	8.86	25
Georgia...............	5.82	9	8.69	28
Idaho.................	4.86	23	9.62	11
Illinois................	2.93	46	7.34	41
Indiana...............	3.27	42	7.01	45
Iowa..................	4.90	22	9.68	9
Kansas................	4.14	33	9.66	10
Kentucky..............	4.82	24	7.79	34
Louisiana..............	7.76	1	10.37	4
Maine.................	4.50	30	8.97	22
Maryland..............	4.02	35	7.39	40
Massachusetts..........	3.64	39	8.96	23
Michigan..............	4.62	28	8.36	31
Minnesota.............	4.76	26	9.76	8
Mississippi.............	7.67	2	11.20	2
Missouri...............	3.22	44	6.70	47
Montana..............	4.17	32	9.98	7
Nebraska..............	2.79	47	7.62	37
Nevada...............	5.45	15	9.21	18
New Hampshire.........	3.12	45	8.18	31
New Jersey............	1.99	48	7.03	44
New Mexico...........	6.94	3	9.16	20
New York.............	3.52	41	9.09	21
North Carolina.........	6.24	6	8.49	28
North Dakota..........	5.60	12	11.67	1
Ohio..................	3.26	43	6.77	46
Oklahoma.............	6.39	5	9.40	17
Oregon...............	5.73	10	10.33	6
Pennsylvania...........	4.22	31	7.62	38
Rhode Island...........	3.65	38	7.59	39
South Carolina.........	6.59	4	8.79	26
South Dakota..........	3.97	36	10.49	3
Tennessee.............	5.61	11	8.44	30
Texas.................	4.03	34	7.69	35
Utah..................	5.32	17	9.48	13
Vermont...............	5.58	13	10.36	5
Virginia...............	5.01	20	7.80	33
Washington............	6.13	8	8.87	24
West Virginia..........	5.05	19	7.17	43
Wisconsin..............	4.80	25	9.56	12
Wyoming..............	5.20	18	9.42	15

Source: Dexter M. Keezer (ed.), *Financing Higher Education 1960–70*, McGraw-Hill, New York, 1959, p. 63 (by S. E. H.); and U.S. Census, *Compendium of Government Finances, 1957 Census of Governments*, p. 61.

had neither corporation nor income taxes.[11] Twenty-one other states collected less than 20 per cent of tax revenue from these taxes.[12] Greater recourse to these direct taxes would increase revenues and facilitate financing of higher education.

EFFECT ON RANKINGS OF EXCLUDING NONINSTRUCTIONAL EXPENDITURES ON HIGHER EDUCATION AND INCLUDING LOCAL OUTLAYS

Column 14 of the Master Table gives the adjusted educational and general expenditures per resident student for public IHL. This column varies from an earlier study in that:

1. Outlays for organized research and extension and public services are excluded.

2. State *and local* expenditures are included.

3. The year covered is 1957–58 rather than 1957.

4. The estimates are by HEW (the earlier estimates were by the Census Bureau), and coverage of expenditures, aside from inclusion of local government by HEW, varies to some extent.

TABLE 25-7

Expenditures for Public Higher Education, Local, and Local as Percentage
of State and Local, Six States, 1957

State	Fiscal 1958 expenditures, local IHL (millions)	Local as percentage of state and local, 1957*
California..................	$69	28
New York..................	44	55
Texas.....................	17	25
Ohio......................	14	31
Illinois....................	11	18
Washington................	4	11

* This comparison is not exactly the appropriate one, for the
figures for the local government are expenditures by local *IHL*, not
the *contributions by local government*. The former is a smaller
figure, though with virtually no tuition charged in California and
little in New York, the difference made is not great in these states.
Source: Bureau of the Census, *Expenditures of Institutions of
Higher Education Operated by Local Governments,
Fiscal Year 1958;* and column 16 of Master Table.

Where local expenditures for public higher education are large, the ranking for outlays tends to rise; that is, outlays per student tend to fall, the explanation being that inclusion of both expenditures of local IHL and enrollment in these IHL tends to reduce unit costs—thus in California the local IHL are community colleges, with low unit costs. The states where local expenditures are especially important are listed in Table 25-7. These six states account for more than 80 per cent of the total expenditures of IHL by local government.

Once we exclude organized research and public services, include expenditures of local IHL, and recall that the U.S. Census coverage is somewhat different from the HEW, then we find large differences in the rankings of states in expenditures per student. California's per capita outlays drop from 1st in the earlier McGraw-Hill table to 43d, a fact explained both by large local outlays and the very large expenditures for organized research. Texas drops from 17th to 45th, and New York from 2d to 28th. These are all states with large local outlays. Kansas, South Carolina, Wyoming, and New Mexico also experience large increases in rankings, that is, relatively reduced expenditures per student. The largest declines in rankings (increased relative expenditures) occurred for Delaware, Rhode Island, Minnesota, Virginia, West Virginia, and Alabama.

COMPARISON OF STATES WITH LOWEST AND HIGHEST EXPENDITURES PER PERSON OF COLLEGE AGE AND PER ENROLLEE IN PUBLIC IHL

In Table 25-8 I compare the 10 states with the lowest expenditures (adjusted)[13] per member of college-age population (highest rankings) and the 10 states with the highest expenditures (lowest rankings).

States with the smallest contribution to public IHL are divided between the Northeast and the South, five from the former and five from the latter. The contribution of the South, or lack of it, is largely related to the low economic status. These states average 44th in ranking for per capita income; the five states in the Northeast average 16th. Their failure to provide more is related both to the absence of a strong tradition of public higher education and the entrenchment of private IHL. It will be recalled from earlier discussion (Chapter 24) that the low-income states spend more on education relatively than the high-income states. On the basis of tax revenues as a percentage of personal income, the average ranking in 1957 of these five Southern states was 10th; of the five Northeastern states, 36th.[14]

The last column of Table 25-8 further confirms this thesis. The average of state and local tax revenues spent on public IHL in 1957 was 3.74 per cent of their tax revenues as compared to 1.66 for the five Northeastern states. It is interesting that five states with per capita incomes two-thirds in excess of the five Southern states contribute less than half as large a percentage of their tax revenues to public higher education. The importance of the contribution of the private IHL in the five Northeastern states is suggested by the fact that rankings based on current expenditures

TABLE 25-8

Twenty States: Tax Resources, Expenditures, Public IHL in Relation
to College-age Population and Enrollment, 1957
(Rankings, 1957, except last column)

State	Rank of col. 13* public IHL exp. (adj.) divided by college-age population	Rank of col. 14* ibid. divided by enrollment public IHL	Total enrollment divided by college-age population	Rank of col. 17* net state and local tax revenues IHL divided by college-age population	Rank of col. 18* ibid. divided by enrollment public IHL	Columns 16/15,* per cent net state and local exp. on public IHL of state & local taxes
	(1)	(2)	(3)	(4)	(5)	(6)
Ten states with smallest expenditures of public IHL per member of college-age population:						
Georgia.................	41	39	45	40	25	2.7
Kentucky................	45	46	38	43	31	4.3
Maine..................	39	19	44	32	8	2.3
Massachusetts..........	48	35	4	6	1	0.8
Mississippi.............	43	47	47	48	41	4.3
New Jersey.............	40	41	24	5	5	1.6
Pennsylvania...........	47	17	29	21	2	1.2
Rhode Island...........	44	7	31–33	30	4	2.4
South Carolina.........	46	29	46	46	20	4.0
Tennessee..............	42	42	36	41	30	3.4
Average..............	43.5	32.1	34.5	31.2	16.7	2.7
Ten states with largest expenditures of public IHL per member of college-age population:						
Arizona................	9–10	48	2	13	47	4.6
California..............	4	43	3	3	35	7.4
Colorado...............	3	14	7	16	34	4.8
Kansas.................	2	30	6	12	43	6.2
Michigan...............	1	8	9	8	28	6.7
Montana................	8	15	25½	14	29	4.5
Nevada.................	7	23	35	1	10	3.2
North Dakota...........	9–10	33	17½	24	44	5.6
Oregon.................	6	10	14½	7	24	4.2
Utah...................	5	38	1	28	48	7.7
Average..............	5.5	26.2	12.0	12.6	34.2	5.5

* Of Master Table.

Source: Master Table and Dexter M. Keezer (ed.), *Financing Higher Education: 1960–70*, McGraw-Hill, New York, 1959, p. 63, table 5; column 3 from other sources.

for all IHL per student are 24th for the five Northern states and 33d for the five Southern states—with outlays per student 11 per cent higher in the Northeastern states.[15]

What of the expenditures *per student* enrolled in public IHL? Here the Southern states continue their high rankings, i.e., small outlays. But the five Northeastern states experience a large drop in rankings, that is, a large increase in expenditures. The respective average rankings are 41st and 24th (column 2 of Table 25-8).

Despite the large recourse to taxes and use of these resources for public higher education, the five Southern states experience a much less impressive achievement as measured by the ratio of total enrollment to college-age population (column 3 of Table 25-8).

Another interesting feature of this table is revealed by column 4 which ties local and state tax resources to college-age population. The five Northeastern states have the resources for financing public higher education. Their average rank is 19th for this variable, as compared to 44th for the five Southern states. Since the enrollment in public IHL is low, the rankings for these states of revenue in relation to enrollment in public IHL is low indeed, and hence revenue available per enrollee is large—an average rank of 4th for the five Northeastern states compared to 44th for the five Southern states. In the Northeast large resources are available and little is spent; in the South small resources are available and much is spent.

The 10 states with the largest ratio of expenditures of public IHL (adjusted) to college-age population are in the West. These are states with strong traditions of higher education—their average ranking in enrollment to college-age population is 12th (column 3 of Table 25-8). But the results are not nearly so favorable when we measure the relation of enrollment to expenditures of public IHL (column 2). The average ranking is 26.2, the reduction of resources being explained by the large numbers attending public IHL. Similar trends are to be noted from columns 4 and 5 where state and local tax revenues are compared with college-age population and enrollment in public IHL. The respective rankings average 13th and 34th. These are states which on the whole take their responsibilities in higher education seriously. Their average of state and local tax revenues spent on public higher education was 5.5 per cent as compared to a national average of 4 per cent, and an average for the 10 states in the upper part of the table of 2.7 per cent. These states are not predominantly rich or poor. They average 21st in per capita income rankings, with 4 states below the average on rankings.

Average rankings of states by regions in the percentage of enrollment in public IHL to total enrollments were:

Average ranking

West, 11 states..................... 11
South, 16 states.................... 22
North Central, 12 states............ 25
Northeast, 9 states................. 42

In a recent provocative study, Hungate estimates the support of higher education (public *and* private) by states on what would be expected on the

TABLE 25-9
Measures of Public Burdens of Education, 1958

State	Total state and local government expenditures for education ($ million) (1)	Personal income ($ million) (2)	Cols. (1)/(2), % (3)	Rank	State and local government expenditures on public IHL ($ million) (4)	Cols. (4)/(2), % (5)	Rank	Public IHL adjusted expenditures per student, 1958 $ (6)	Per capita personal income, 1958 $ (7)	Cols. (6)/(7), % (8)	Rank
Alabama........	204.4	4,379	4.7	26–27	34.4	0.8	24–30	976	1,355	72.0	6
Arizona........	147.0	2,202	6.7	3	26.1	1.2	7–9	562	1,893	29.7	47
Arkansas.......	109.6	2,152	5.1	18–21	23.3	1.1	10–15	855	1,200	71.3	7
California......	1,876.3	37,131	5.1	18–21	345.6	0.9	19–23	732	2,493	29.4	48
Colorado.......	202.4	3,508	5.8	7–8	45.9	1.3	3–6	1,082	2,034	53.2	21
Connecticut....	224.3	6,506	3.4	46–47	23.6	0.4	41–44	842	2,716	31.0	45
Delaware.......	62.2	1,248	5.0	22–23	10.5	0.8	24–30	1,225	2,856	42.9	37
Florida........	375.9	8,367	4.5	28–31	44.5	0.5	38–40	982	1,882	52.2	24
Georgia........	283.9	5,672	5.0	22–23	33.5	0.6	34–37	785	1,471	53.4	19–20
Idaho.........	53.1	1,127	4.7	26–27	10.0	0.9	19–23	908	1,723	52.7	22
Illinois........	834.4	24,230	3.4	46–47	106.0	0.4	41–44	1,163	2,501	46.5	33
Indiana........	451.1	9,122	4.9	24–25	104.8	1.1	10–15	1,400	2,006	69.8	8
Iowa..........	272.6	5,256	5.2	16–17	50.2	1.0	16–18	1,419	1,918	74.0	4
Kansas........	215.5	4,214	5.1	18–21	41.2	1.0	16–18	909	1,983	45.8	35
Kentucky.......	184.2	4,336	4.2	36	25.5	0.6	34–37	712	1,456	48.9	29
Louisiana......	315.8	4,933	6.4	4	57.9	1.2	7–9	980	1,537	63.8	10
Maine.........	64.5	1,642	3.9	40–41	8.9	0.5	38–40	982	1,707	57.5	16
Maryland......	259.5	6,661	3.9	40–41	32.0	0.5	38–40	1,118	2,248	49.7	27

State										
Massachusetts	345.0	11,677	3.0	48	22.8	0.2	45–48	870	2,335	37.3	42
Michigan	908.0	16,581	5.5	11–12	216.5	1.3	3–6	1,211	2,166	55.9	17
Minnesota	369.2	6,486	5.7	9–10	73.4	1.1	10–15	1,226	1,942	63.1	12
Mississippi	122.1	2,298	5.3	14–15	21.5	0.9	19–23	700	1,070	65.4	9
Missouri	317.1	8,644	3.7	42–43	37.3	0.4	41–44	761	2,021	37.7	41
Montana	60.9	1,342	4.5	28–31	16.2	1.2	7–9	1,081	2,024	53.4	19–20
Nebraska	119.0	2,759	4.3	33–35	21.2	0.8	24–30	944	1,979	47.7	30–31
Nevada	30.6	685	4.5	28–31	4.6	0.7	31–33	959	2,575	37.2	43
New Hampshire	45.2	1,105	4.1	37–38	9.5	0.9	19–23	1,194	1,886	63.3	11
New Jersey	540.0	14,442	3.7	42–43	33.8	0.2	45–48	760	2,496	30.4	46
New Mexico	105.2	1,554	6.8	2	24.0	1.5	2	875	1,748	50.1	26
New York	1,718.3	42,157	4.1	37–38	82.3	0.2	45–48	923	2,586	35.7	44
North Carolina	331.1	6,318	5.2	16–17	53.1	0.8	24–30	1,154	1,406	82.1	3
North Dakota	54.4	1,063	5.1	18–21	12.2	1.1	10–15	878	1,677	52.4	23
Ohio	812.8	20,527	4.0	39	90.5	0.4	41–44	926	2,206	42.0	39
Oklahoma	216.4	3,954	5.5	11–12	49.9	1.3	3–6	728	1,728	42.1	38
Oregon	200.8	3,528	5.7	9–10	39.8	1.1	10–15	1,167	2,017	57.9	15
Pennsylvania	830.4	23,589	3.5	45	57.9	0.2	45–48	1,012	2,142	47.2	32
Rhode Island	61.8	1,726	3.6	44	10.9	0.6	34–37	1,218	2,045	59.6	13
South Carolina	155.5	2,924	5.3	14–15	24.8	0.8	24–30	919	1,247	73.7	5
South Dakota	68.5	1,132	6.1	5–6	15.2	1.3	3–6	883	1,648	53.6	18
Tennessee	228.0	5,028	4.5	28–31	31.1	0.6	34–37	736	1,441	51.1	25
Texas	835.0	17,129	4.9	24–25	111.4	0.7	31–33	715	1,847	38.7	40
Utah	109.1	1,516	7.2	1	24.1	1.6	1	814	1,767	46.1	34
Vermont	39.2	645	6.1	5–6	7.0	1.1	10–15	1,410	1,671	84.4	1–2
Virginia	287.4	6,660	4.3	33–35	47.6	0.7	31–33	1,476	1,748	84.4	1–2

TABLE 25-9 (Continued)

State	Total state and local government expenditures for education ($ million) (1)	Personal income ($ million) (2)	Cols. (1)/(2), % (3)	Rank	State and local government expenditures on public IHL ($ million) (4)	Cols. (4)/(2), % (5)	Rank	Public IHL adjusted expenditures per student, 1958 $ (6)	Per capita personal income, 1958 $ (7)	Cols. (6)/(7), % (8)	Rank
Washington.........	323.8	5,977	5.4	13	54.1	0.9	19–23	1,037	2,173	47.7	30–31
West Virginia.......	129.2	2,960	4.4	32	23.1	0.8	24–30	928	1,576	58.9	14
Wisconsin..........	329.6	7,648	4.3	33–35	58.2	0.8	24–30	979	1,993	49.1	28
Wyoming...........	39.4	676	5.8	7–8	6.7	1.0	16–18	951	2,086	45.6	36
Total U.S.........	15,877.8*	355,416	4.5	.....	2,304.6	0.6	.....	930	2,069†	44.9	

* Because of rounding in the source, details do not add up to totals.

† Personal income per capita is an average for the whole nation including District of Columbia, Alaska, Hawaii.

Sources: Columns 1, 4: U.S. Department of Commerce, Government Finances in 1958; columns 2, 7: U.S. Department of Commerce, Survey of Current Business, August, 1960; column 6: HEW, adapted by S. E. H.

basis of per capita income. The highest support comes in Colorado, Massachusetts, Utah, and Connecticut in that order, and the lowest in Pennsylvania (48th), Maryland, Maine, and Georgia. But one reservation is necessary here: no allowance is made for support from outside of the state—e.g., gifts and endowment. He also estimates the contribution by fees in each state.[16]

RESIDENT VERSUS NONRESIDENT STUDENTS

A few more points on the Master Table: a comparison of columns 2 and 6 yields an indication of the extent to which public outlays on higher education are spent on resident (i.e., from the state) and nonresident students. I shall deal with this later in a state-by-state analysis.[17]

Where rankings are lower in column 5 of the Master Table than in column 3, the inference is that undergraduate enrollment is a large part of total enrollment. Since the remainder is graduate enrollment (relatively expensive though probably less full-time than undergraduate) and extension and summer school (relatively inexpensive per student), it is not clear that a larger percentage of undergraduates necessarily means higher unit costs. The proportion of undergraduates is especially large in Maine, New Hampshire, Vermont, and Alabama, and small in California, Connecticut, Delaware, Maryland, Nevada, New Jersey, and New York.

Where part-time students are a large part of the total, enrollment statistics tend to underestimate costs per full-time student. An NPA study for 16 states shows an average of 82 per cent of total enrollment for *full-time*-student equivalent, undergraduate. The major deviations are New York (76), New Jersey (79), California (79)—allowance for this would raise unit costs. For the following states, the proportion of *full-time* undergraduates was especially high, and hence allowance would reduce *relative* unit costs: Iowa, Missouri (86); North Carolina, Pennsylvania, Wisconsin (85); and Massachusetts (84).

Graduate work is expensive. IHL with relatively large graduate enrollment to this extent should be expected to have high unit costs. Against a national average of 9.5 per cent of graduate students, New York had 19.5 per cent; Connecticut, 17 per cent; New Jersey, 13 per cent; and Michigan, 12 per cent. Below average we note especially North Carolina (5), Texas (6), Missouri (6), Minnesota (7).[18]

THE HIGH COST OF HIGHER EDUCATION IN THE SOUTH

For the year 1957–58, per capita income in the 12 Southeastern states was 71 per cent of the national level. But expenditures (adjusted) per student in public IHL in these states was 95 per cent of the national average.[19] It is difficult to understand why higher education should be so expensive in these states. I can think of two possible explanations: the national market for faculty, with the result that faculty pay is tied more to national levels than to lower income and cost-of-living standards in the South; and the large number of relatively low-enrollment IHL and hence high unit costs. The high cost in the South is all the more surprising in view of a standard that is probably below the national level.[20]

EDUCATIONAL EXPENDITURES IN RELATION TO INCOME AND STANDARDS OF LIVING

Table 25-9 will be useful for the analysis of Chapter 26. It gives rankings of public educational outlays, all and higher, in relation to personal income, and also the burden of expenditures per student in relation to per capita income.

SUMMARY

Details state by state follow in the next chapter. Here are several points for special emphasis:

Any interstate comparison suffers from elements of incomparability. One example is the effect of varying percentages of full-time students to total enrollment, or the percentage of graduate students. Obviously a unit cost of $1,000 for a state where full-time students and costly graduate students are relatively numerous does not necessarily mean higher unit costs in any meaningful way as compared to another state where unit costs are $800 but enrollment is heavily part-time undergraduates. This is aside from varying standards.

Another example is the inclusion or exclusion of organized research as a relevant expenditure in estimating instructional costs. Much can be said on both sides. My McGraw-Hill table includes it; the current table excludes it.

Should local government expenditures be included in comparing government outlays on higher education? Yes, if we are to compare all public expenditures. But since state governments are the main support of public IHL, a case can also be made for comparison of state outlays. Inclusion of local outlays makes a difference, especially in California and New York, and to some extent in several other states. Since state tax revenues, as a percentage of state and local, varied in 1957 from 26 to 79 per cent, the inclusion of local taxes necessarily has some effect.

As was noted earlier, the material in this chapter reveals high grades for effort for the less affluent states, and low grades for achievement. In general, states with sparse population, high traditions of public higher education, and low incomes spend the largest percentage of their personal income and tax revenues on public higher education. The rich states with heavy concentration of population and high incomes devote relatively small parts of their income to this purpose.

Capacity to finance public higher education is not given merely by per capita tax revenues. Of 10 states with high per capita tax revenues, 5 are states with very high per capita incomes and 5 with very low incomes. In general, inclusion of local taxes tends to reduce the correlation of taxes and income per capita.

Much depends also on tax structure. States without corporate or (and) income taxes tend to subsidize students at the expense of lower income groups.

A group of five relatively low-income states provide about 3.74 per cent of tax revenue for public higher education, but five Northeastern states provide only 1.66 per cent. Yet in the South per capita income is 28 per cent less than the national average, and higher education is very costly, for unit costs in public higher education are but 5 per cent below the national average. Again, whereas in the affluent Northeast tax resources are very high in relation to enrollment, they are low in the South, where enrollment is much larger in public IHL. The largest ratio of expenditures on public higher education to college-age population is in Western states; but the high enrollment in public IHL greatly reduces this advantage when measured in outlays per enrollee. These states spend 5.5 per cent of tax revenues on public higher education as compared to a national average of but 4 per cent.

FOOTNOTES

[1] Dexter M. Keezer (ed.), *Financing Higher Education: 1960–70*, McGraw-Hill, New York, 1959, pp. 63, 77–78.

[2] A very helpful study was issued in 1960 by the Heald committee, National Planning Associations: S. H. Mushkin and E. P. McLoone, *Student Higher Education*, March, 1960 (hereafter referred to as NPA).

[3] *Ibid.*, p. 15.

[4] Bureau of the Census, *Supplementary Data to Table 18, Governmental Finance, in 1958.*

[5] NPA, *op. cit.*, p. 59.

[6] T. L. Hungate, *Financing the Future of Higher Education*, 1946, pp. 55–60. Current expenditures of state IHL exclude commercial activities and capital outlays. For the purposes of this column, this is adequate. I assume here that state IHL perform important research and other public service activities as well as instructional, and to some extent these are related.

[7] Income and population statistics from *Survey of Current Business*, August, 1959, p. 15. (My calculations.)

[8] The 1955–1958 series is to be found in *A Master Plan for Higher Education in California, 1960,* p. 212.

[9] U.S. Census, *Compendium of State Government Finances in 1957*, p. 58.

[10] Thirteen states with increases of 10 or more.

[11] New Jersey, Illinois, Nevada, Ohio, Michigan, Washington, Wyoming, Indiana, Florida, Nebraska, Texas, Maine, Virginia, West Virginia.

[12] Connecticut, California, Pennsylvania, Colorado, Rhode Island, Missouri, Montana, New Hampshire, Iowa, Kansas, Arizona, Oklahoma, Louisiana, South Dakota, North Dakota, Georgia, Tennessee, Alabama, South Carolina, Arkansas, and Mississippi.

[13] Exclusive of organized research and public services.

[14] Keezer, *op. cit.*, p. 63, table 5, col. 4.

[15] *Ibid.*, cols. 4, 8.

[16] T. L. Hungate, *A New Basis of Support for Higher Education*, 1957, pp. 29–36.

[17] The results are subject to reservations, for coverage is for 1957 (col. 2) and 1958 (col. 6). And the sources vary. An NPA study (p. 27) of 16 states for *all* enrollment reveals especially large *net* in-migrants to Indiana (25 per cent); Massachusetts (24 per cent); North Carolina (11 per cent); and smaller ones for Michigan, Minnesota, Missouri, Ohio, Pennsylvania, Texas, and Wisconsin. Largest exports are from New Jersey (35 per cent); Connecticut (15 per cent); Illinois (7 per cent); New York (4 per cent).

[18] NPA, *op. cit.*, pp. 16, 21.

[19] A study for 1952–53 for *all* IHL puts the cost per student at 10 per cent below the national level. NPA, *op. cit.*, p. 40.

[20] Column 14 of Master Table; and *Survey of Current Business*, August, 1959.

Chapter 26

HIGHER EDUCATION: BURDEN, CAPACITY TO FINANCE, EFFORT, AND ACHIEVEMENTS, STATE BY STATE

THE APPROACH

I am hopeful that this chapter will help university administrators, commissions on higher education, budget officers, governors, taxpayers, and the general public to understand relative burdens of, capacity to finance, efforts for, and achievements in higher education. The results are to be interpreted with caution, and wherever possible I have noted reservations.

The results are derived from my original table in the McGraw-Hill volume *Financing Higher Education: 1960–70*, not reproduced here,[1] the Master Table (Chapter 25), which is based partly on the McGraw-Hill table, and finally a table derived in turn from these two tables (Table 26-1) and some additional material. The years covered vary from 1957 to 1959.

In the last, I have ranked each state (1 to 48) on the basis of 12 variables. The advantage of doing so is that the impact of statistical weaknesses is thus reduced. Results need not be so precise. The grades are as follows:

Rank of State

1–5 = A+, 6–10 = A = Very high
11–15 = B+, 16–20 = B = High
21–25 = C+, 26–30 = C = Average
31–35 = D+, 36–40 = D = Low
41–44 = E+, 45–48 = E = Very low

A word about the interpretation of Table 26-1. For example: New York State is very low in column 1 (E+). This means that the proportion of college-age population to total population is very low, and here the burden is low (42d of the 48 states). But two measures of capacity to pay reveal grades of A+ and A+, or a ranking among the first 5 states. These measures are (1) per capita income and (2) net state and local tax revenues

TABLE 26-1

Twelve Crucial Variables

(1957 unless otherwise indicated)

State	Burden	Capacity		Effort				Achievements				Supplementary
	College-age population (CAP) as per cent of total population (M-11)* (1)	Per capita income (M-1) (2)	Net state and local tax revenues per member CAP† (C-17) (3)	State and local taxes per $1,000 personal income,ª 1958 (4)	Total state tax revenue per capita (M-3)ᵇ (5)	Educational expenditures, state and local government, per cent personal income, 1958ª (6)	Higher-educational expenditures, state and local government, per cent personal income, 1958ᵇ (7)	Total IHL enrollment as per cent of CAP (M-9) (8)	Enrollment in public IHL as per cent of total IHL enrollment, 1958 (C-10) (9)	Adjusted dollar expenditures, public IHL per enrollee public IHL (C-14)ᶜ (10)	Net state and local taxes per enrollee, public IHL (C-18) (11)	Percentage expenditures adjusted per student, public IHL, to per capita income,‡ 1957–58ᵇ (12)
Ala.......	A+	E+	E	D	D	C	C	E+	B	C+	D+	A
Ariz......	B+	C	B+	C+	B+	A+	A	A	A+	B	E	E
Ark.......	A+	E	E+	C+	E+	B	B+	E	A	D	E+	A
Calif.....	E+	A+	A+	B+	A+	B	C+	A+	A	E+	D+	E
Colo......	E	B	B	A	B+	A	A+	A+	B+	B+	D+	C+
Conn.....	E+	A+	A+	E+	A	E	E+	A	E+	D	A	E
Del.......	E	A+	B	E	A	C+	C	C+	A	A	C+	D
Fla.......	E	C+	B+	C+	B	C	C	D	D+	B	A	B+
Ga.......	A	E+	D	C	C+	C+	D	E+	C+	D	C+	B
Idaho.....	B+	D+	D+	B	C	C	C+	D	B+	D+	D+	C+
Ill........	D	A	A	D	D	E	E+	B	E+	B+	A	D+
Ind.......	C	B+	D+	D+	E+	C+	B+	C+	C	A+	B	A
Iowa.....	C+	C	C+	B	B	C	B	C+	D	A+	B+	A+
Kan......	D	C	B+	B+	D+	C	B	A+	C	C	E+	D+
Ky.......	A	E+	E+	D	E+	D	D	D	C	E	D+	C
La........	B+	D	D+	A+	A+	A+	A	D+	C+	B	C	B
Maine....	B	D+	D+	B+	B+	E+	D	E+	E	B	A	B
Md.......	D	A	B	B+	C+	E+	D	C	C	B+	B	C
Mass.....	D	A	A	C+	C	E	E	A+	B+	D+	A+	E+
Mich.....	D+	B+	A	C+	B+	B+	A+	B	B+	A	C	B
Minn.....	C	C+	B	A	C+	A	B+	A	C	A+	C+	B+
Miss......	A+	E	E	A+	D	B+	C+	E+	E	E	E+	A
Mo.......	C	B	D+	E	E+	E+	E+	C+	E+	D	B	E+
Mont.....	C	C+	B+	A	C	A	A	D+	A	B+	C	B
Neb......	D+	C+	C+	D	E	D+	C	B+	C+	C+	D	D
Nev......	E	A	A+	B	A+	C	D+	D	A+	C+	A	E+
N.H......	D+	C+	C	D+	E	D	C+	B+	A	B+	B+	B+
N.J......	D+	A+	A+	E+	E	E+	E	D+	E+	E+	A+	E
N.M.....	A	D+	D	C	A+	A+	A+	D+	A+	D+	E	C
N.Y.....	E+	A+	A+	B	B	B	E	A	E	C	A+	E+
N.C.....	A	E	E	D+	C+	B	C	E+	E	B+	C+	A+
N.D.....	B	D	C+	A+	C	D	B+	C	C	D+	E+	C+
Ohio.....	D	A	B	E+	C	B	E+	C+	D	C	B+	D
Okla.....	B+	A	D	B	A	B+	A+	B+	B+	E+	E	D
Ore......	C+	B	A	A	A	B+	A+	B+	B+	A	C+	B+
Pa.......	C+	B+	C+	E	B	E	E	D+	E	A	A+	D+
R.I......	E+	B	C	C	D+	E+	D	D	E	A	A+	B+
S.C......	A+	E	E	C	D+	B+	B+	E	D+	D+	B	A+
S.D......	B	D	C+	A+	E	A	A+	B	B	D+	D	A+
Tenn.....	A	E+	E+	C	D+	A+	D	D	D	E+	C	C+
Texas.....	C+	C	D	D	D	C+	D+	B	C+	E	D	D
Utah.....	B	C	C	B+	B	A+	A+	A+	D	D	E	D+
Vt........	B+	D+	D+	A+	B+	A+	B+	A+	D	A+	B	D+
Va.......	C+	D+	D	E	C	D+	D+	D	D+	A+	B+	A+
Wash.....	D+	B+	B+	C	A+	B+	C+	B+	B	B	C	D+
W. Va.....	A+	D	E+	D+	C	D+	C	E	B	C	D	B+
Wis......	C	B	A	B+	B+	D+	C	C	C+	C+	B+	A
Wyo.....	B	B+	C	A	A	A	B	C	A+	C+	D	D

* See key to sources below.
† College-age population.
‡ This relationship reflects the burden of unit expenditures for public higher education in relation to per capita income.
Sources: M = McGraw-Hill table, in Financing Higher Education: 1960–70, 1959; C = current Master Table in Chap. 25; e.g., C-18 = column 18 of Master Table.
ª U.S. Census, Governmental Finances in 1958, p. 24.
ᵇ Calculated from ibid. and Survey of Current Business.
ᶜ General and educational exclusive of organized research and public services.

in relation to the college-age population. The latter may of course also be a measure of effort. Again, two measures of effort give New York a grade of B (high). These measures are (1) state and local taxes per $1,000 personal income and (2) total state tax revenue per capita. Finally, there is one measure of achievement where New York obtains a grade of A —e.g., the ratio of enrollment to college-age population, and one, an E, the proportion of public to total enrollment. The last column can be interpreted as a measure of burden or achievement: the ratio of adjusted (exclusive of organized research and public services) expenditures per enrollee in public IHL to per capita income. Burden is high when the ratio is high, say, 75 per cent, and low when it is low, say, 25 per cent.

In the discussions of each state I summarize the net results and also point out any adjustments or reservations that might be made. For example, where public expenditures for IHL may be misleading because of exclusion of items actually spent by IHL, this is noted; also, where costs per unit may be inflated because of large numbers of graduate and medical students, expensive types of instruction; and where local government expenditures are relatively large, the reservations to the use of state figures are generally noted.

These tables are based primarily on 1957 or 1957–58 figures. Statistics for state taxes and spending are available for 1959.

MATERIAL BASED ON AN NPA STUDY

In addition, I have availed myself of the results of a study by the National Planning Association, prepared for the Heald committee in New York.[2] The NPA presented a study for 16 states which account for about 70 per cent of the expenditures for student higher education, for more than two-thirds of the enrollments in 1957–58, 60 per cent of the college-age population, and more than 70 per cent of the personal income in the nation. Note that per state these 16 states account for four to five times as much enrollment as the other 32 states. In Table 26-2 compiled from materials in the NPA study I compare the 16 states on the basis of the following:

Column 1: *Expenditures on student higher education as per cent of educational and general expenditures.*[3]

Columns 2 and 3: *Estimated expenditures on student higher education (SHE) per full-time-student equivalent (FTSE) as percentage of United States average.* This item is helpful, for it is based on full-time-student equivalent. (A similar comparison is to be had by comparing columns 2 and 3 with columns 4 and 5 of my Master Table. But note these items in my table relate to enrollment in *public* IHL, and the NPA to all enrollment.)

Columns 4 and 5: *Graduate students as percentage of total resident degree-credit enrollment,* and *medical school budget as percentage of total higher education expenditures.* Where these are large, one would expect to this extent high unit costs. I comment in the state-by-state analysis on those states which are much out of line in the proportion of graduate or medical students.

Column 6: *Percentage of migration: imports* (−) *and exports* (+). Where in-migrants are large, the resources are used to that extent in supporting nonresident students, and hence given resources yield less for resident students.[4]

Columns 7 and 8: *Per capita state and local government funds, current and capital, for SHE and scholarships.*

Column 9: *Local funds for SHE as percentage of state and local expenditures for higher education.* This column indicates the contribution of local to state and local outlays.

Columns 10 and 11: *State and local funds for SHE and scholarship expenditures as a percentage of personal income.*

Columns 12 and 13: *Expenditures all higher-education functions, current and capital, as percentage of personal income.* This approach is helpful in that current and capital funds are put together in relation to personal income.[5]

Columns 14 and 15: *SHE financed from all sources as percentage of personal income.*

Column 3 is a helpful index of achievement.

Columns 8, 11, 13, and 15 are indices of effort.

In the state-by-state analysis I discuss the adapted NPA table where it throws additional light.

In this detailed analysis I also consider such factors as the following:

Exclusion of items from state expenditures. (These are based on studies of state budgets, and correspondence with university presidents, higher education commissions, and similar organizations, and budget officers in 48 states. Virtually all the 150 questionnaires sent out were returned. They often included criticism of my McGraw-Hill table, which was sent with my questionnaire.[6]) The object of this adjustment is to make state expenditures comparable. One state may exclude from *state expenditures* such items as tuition, gifts, endowment income, etc., and another may include such. *But these corrections are not germane for the expenditures by IHL—for these are all inclusive.*[7]

PROBLEMS OF ANALYSIS

The McGraw-Hill table was submitted for criticism to 48 presidents of state universities, 48 state budget directors, and board of higher education or similar organization in every state. Replies were returned by more than 90 per cent of those receiving questionnaires. The respondents were most helpful, and I appreciate their contributions. The answers and further consideration by the author resulted in the new Master Table and the summary tables.

Some of the respondents wrote that interstate comparisons were futile. But a much larger number held that, properly interpreted, they shed a helpful light on the issues. The reader will have to judge whether this large effort adds to or detracts from our understanding of the issues.

At the outset I should explain my approach. Primarily I dealt with public IHL, the reason for this being partly that I had the strongest reactions from representatives of the public IHL. Where a table shows large resources for a public IHL under a national scale, the fear immediately arises that such results may militate against continued fair treatment by the taxpayer and his representatives. *In advice to governors and in correspondence with them I was acutely aware of the danger of using this kind of material without an understanding of the reservations involved. I urge all public officials to keep this in mind.*

A second and more important reason for concentrating largely on the public IHL is that their growth is the crucial item in higher education. They account for 60 per cent of current resources and 80 per cent of growth in recent years. Here the measures of relative burden, capacity, effort and achievement are especially important.[8]

In my questionnaire I pointed to substantial discrepancies between income and expenditures as given by the Census Bureau and the HEW. The explanation in part is the inclusion of expenditures by local government in the HEW totals and also the exclusion of some items by the Census Bureau, e.g., outlays on hospital and experiment stations. It was also almost the unanimous view of the authorities that the HEW statistics were more reliable—the reason being largely that the educational outlays are just one of many categories of interest to the Census Bureau, which according to many depends largely on contacts with the state governments and not primarily on contacts with IHL.* This is not meant in any sense to reflect on the Census Bureau, a highly efficient organization. Rather, it has a different job to do.

This discussion leads me then to a frequent criticism made of the McGraw-Hill table—the use of state expenditures as a guide to effort or achievement. Many respondents pointed out that several items are excluded from appropriations and yet are part of state expenditures for IHL. In my questionnaire, therefore, I asked the president of one state univer-

---

* A. B. Manvel of the Census Bureau wrote me (December 12, 1958) that their information comes from correspondence with IHL. Surprisingly, many officials do not seem to realize this.

sity in each state, the state budget officer, and the higher-education board
to indicate what items are included or excluded, and amounts involved,
among the following: tuition, endowment earnings, private gifts, net income from auxiliary services, earmarked taxes, contributions of local government, income for organized research, and other exclusions.

In so far as these items are not included in the budget, to this extent
state expenditures give a misleading indication of expenditures of public
IHL. I have, therefore, in the state-by-state discussion briefly given the
results of this questionnaire. In some states the exclusion makes a large
difference—e.g., New York. But in general the difference is not likely to
be large. Note that in a recent year, student fees were only 13 per cent of
general and educational expenditures of public IHL, endowment income
1 per cent, private gifts 3 per cent.

The exclusion of local government expenditures on higher education
also detracts from the usefulness of the total for state expenditures. In a
recent year they accounted for 6 to 7 per cent of general and educational
activities. But the 16-state study put local funds for *Student Higher Education* as 13.2 per cent of state and local expenditures for current and
capital purposes. Most of the states receive little or no funds from local
government for higher education. But among the 16 states the following
are especially out of line on the high side: California, 23.1 per cent; New
York, 35.2. The others among the 16 with substantial local contributions
are Texas, Michigan, and Ohio.[9]

In my Master Table and Table 26-1, I have used state and local totals
wherever this seemed appropriate (see, for example, columns 3, 4, 6, 7,
and 11 of Table 26-1). I do not, however, agree that the state figures are
of no significance. The criticism generally made is that a measure of
burden or effort should include both state and local figures. Some states
depend largely on state and some largely on local revenue and expenditures. My respondents in the state of Washington were especially concerned on this point. There the state government restricts the yield of the
property taxes, and, therefore, the state collects large revenues to be disbursed for the benefit of local government. (In fact, Washington was second to Louisiana in taxes per capita in 1959.) A concentration on state
revenues or expenditures, therefore, exaggerates the resources available
for state purposes. In fiscal year 1958, state tax revenue as a percentage
of state and local tax revenues was 49.1 per cent, with a maximum of
77.6 per cent in Delaware and a minimum of 27.1 per cent in New
Jersey. State expenditures in seven states exceeded 70 per cent of the
total, and in six states accounted for less than 40 per cent.[10]

Despite these reservations, I do not go all the way with those who
would exclude studies based on state figures alone. The point is that public higher education is financed primarily by state government. Therefore,

TABLE 26-2

Fifteen Variables Relevant for a Study of Higher Education in 16 States, 1957–58

State	Expenditures on SHE* as percentage of educational and gen'l expenditures (1)	Estimated expenditures on SHE per FTSE† as percentage of U.S. average (2)	Rank (3)	Graduate students as percentage of total resident degree-credit enrollment (4)	Medical school budget as percentage of higher-education expenditures (5)	Percentage migration: imports (−) and exports (+) (6)	Per capita state and local government funds (current and capital) for SHE and scholarships (7)	Rank (8)	Local funds for SHE as percentage of state and local expenditures for higher education (9)	State and local funds for SHE and scholarship expenditures as percentage of personal income (10)	Rank (11)	Expenditures all higher-education functions, current and capital, as percentage of personal income (12)	Rank (13)	SHE expenditures financed from all sources as percentage of personal income (14)	Rank (15)
United States	65.0	100	...	9.5	6.7	−0.8	.....	...	.....	...	...	1.6	...	0.6	...
16 States	64.1	104	...	10.9	6.6	−0.7	10.43	...	13.2	0.5	...	1.5	...	0.6	...
California	48.3	94	10	8.5	4.9	−3.7	25.16	1	23.1	1.0	1	1.8	6	0.6	7
Connecticut	79.4	140	1	17.0	4.8	1.5	11.39	4	1.0	0.4	10	1.3	11	0.7	9
Illinois	58.0	122	4	11.4	6.5	6.5	10.93	7	2.5	0.4	9	1.4	9	0.6	11
Indiana	72.4	105	6	10.4	3.3	−25.0	11.07	6	1.3	0.5	7	1.9	3	0.7	5
Iowa	58.3	91	13	7.3	6.9	−4.3	10.60	8	1.3	0.6	5	1.9	4	0.8	4
Massachusetts	54.9	127	2	11.6	4.8	−24.0	3.79	15	1.6	0.2	16	2.4	1	1.0	1
Michigan	71.1	118	5	12.2	4.7	−5.1	13.99	2	8.8	0.7	3	1.8	7	0.7	6
Minnesota	64.4	91	12	7.2	7.3	−3.5	13.53	3	1.9	0.6	2	1.9	5	0.8	3
Missouri	72.2	91	14	6.3	10.6	−7.2	6.92	13	4.8	0.3	12	1.3	12	0.3	10
New Jersey	68.2	103	9	13.5	1.7	35.0	4.57	14	4.0	0.2	14	0.7	16	0.3	16
New York	73.7	91	11	19.5	9.1	3.9	7.49	12	35.2	0.3	13	1.3	13	0.8	8
North Carolina	63.4	92	8	5.1	8.9	−11.0	7.74	11	0.9	0.6	6	1.9	2	0.8	2
Ohio	84.4	104	7	7.7	7.2	−3.0	8.22	10	8.3	0.4	11	1.1	15	0.6	15
Pennsylvania	69.6	104	3	10.6	9.1	−1.8	3.58	16	0.4	0.2	15	1.1	14	0.6	14
Texas	69.3	73	16	6.4	5.7	−2.5	8.70	9	10.3	0.5	8	1.4	10	0.6	12
Wisconsin	63.0	86	15	7.1	5.7	−3.5	11.12	5	2.4	0.6	4	1.5	8	0.6	13
Page of original material of NPA	16	18	18	21	22	27	53	55	58	63	63	71	71	76	76

* Student higher education.
† Full-time-student equivalent.
Source: NPA, *Student Higher Education*, March, 1961, Mimeograph, adapted by author.

the amount of state revenues and their proportion of personal income are significant measures for an understanding of the financing of public higher education.

Perhaps the most important point to be made in any discussion of these issues is that these qualifications apply only to the support or expenditures of government for higher education. *They do not apply to expenditures of the institutions.* These include all state and local government contributions.

Some other criticisms have been made of the questionnaire which I do not hold to be very important. Some hold that burdens are not measured by taxes paid but by the incidence of these taxes. In a paper before the Senate Banking and Currency Committee several years ago, I dealt fully with issues of this kind. Musgrave and others have also considered these problems. But for our purposes the issues are not very important. They arise especially for Federal taxes—e.g., automobiles in Michigan, tobacco in North Carolina, where incidence deviates greatly from that suggested by initial payments. In state revenues the issue is of some significance in corporate income taxes; but these account for only 6 per cent of total state tax revenues.

Some of the most troublesome measures are those that depend on enrollment statistics. The reason for this is that enrollment figures include full-time and part-time, candidates for degrees, and others. Compilation methods vary even within the same state. What is especially troublesome is that the proportion of part-time students varies greatly from state to state. One state many have almost 100 per cent full-time students—the latter is roughly the proportion for Vermont. Crude enrollment figures for 100,000 students in one state may then mean almost 100,000 full-time students, and in another, 67,000. (I assume part time is on the average one-third.)

Columns 8, 9, 10, 11, and 12 of Table 26-1 relate variables to enrollment and are, therefore, subject to some reservations. In the Master Table, enrollment figures or their derivatives appear in various columns. But note that column 4 (full-time undergraduate enrollment, public IHL) can be compared with column 2 (enrollment in public IHL). For the United States the ratio of full-time undergraduate public enrollment to total public enrollment is 72 per cent. By comparing these variables state by state, the reader can discover where states are substantially out of line. In the state-by-state comparison, I list a number of states much out of line. Where a state, for example, New York, has a large proportion of part-time students, it may be assumed that the unit costs per full-time equivalent are substantially larger in a national rating than is suggested by the crude figures. Where the enrollment is primarily full-time, a state which, for example, is 30th in unit costs might well fall to 35th to 40th once the state's position is corrected for the out-of-lineness in the proportion of full-time students.

This observation is subject to one reservation. States that have a large proportion of graduate or medical students tend to have somewhat higher unit costs, for unit costs are two to three times as high for these as for other curricula. The 16-state study reveals an average of 9.5 per cent of graduate students in the country, and medical school budgets of 6.7 per cent of higher-education expenditures. The states with a large percentage of graduate students are Connecticut (17), New York (19.5), New Jersey (13.5). (These figures apply to both public and private IHL.) Medical expenditures are especially high in Missouri (10.6 per cent), New York (9.1 per cent), and Pennsylvania (9.1 per cent).

Where junior college enrollments are large, unit costs are in fact higher than they seem to be once allowance is made for this factor; for a junior college education is less costly than a four-year education. In 1959 junior college enrollment was 12.1 per cent for the nation. The states with large percentages were Delaware (13.2), Illinois (13.8), Florida (19.9), Georgia (14.8), Mississippi (24.1), Arizona (18.1), Texas (16.6), Idaho (30.0), Wyoming (29.0), California (47.5), Washington (16.5).*[11]

Despite all these reservations, the unit costs give a rough idea of the relative expenditures per student in public IHL. In the public IHL the difference between enrollment and resident undergraduate is only 450,000, or 28 per cent of enrollment. Graduate enrollment may be estimated at 160,000, or almost 100,000 full-time equivalent. Hence at the undergraduate level only 350,000, or about 20 per cent, is the difference between enrollment and full-time resident undergraduate enrollment. I should point out here that for some purposes total enrollment may be as significant a figure as full-time equivalent—e.g., for measuring achievement, why not compare *all* enrollees in relation to college-age population?

In general, one finds about what one expects in a study of unit expenditures. Unit costs are low in the South and tend to be low also in poor agricultural states. But the unit outlays are high in states with high per capita income and strong traditions of higher education. Deviations are often explained by special issues—e.g., high unit costs in small states like Delaware, Vermont, and Rhode Island. Louisiana, in part as a result of the Long regime, shows unusually high unit costs for a Southern state. Iowa is also out of line. California unit expenditures are surprisingly low, explained in part by large junior college enrollment and many large state colleges making for low unit costs.

To get an acceptable measure, we also have to adjust for expenditures not closely tied to instruction. Many of my respondents were highly criti-

* The 16-state study uses full-time-student equivalents. To the full-time undergraduate enrollment is added part time for the undergraduates (estimated at two-sevenths of full time), and also an estimate is made for graduate students part time (32.8 per cent = full time) working at four-tenths of full-time graduate load. NPA, *op. cit.,* pp. 16, 81–83.

cal of my McGraw-Hill table because outlays for organized research and public services were included. I am not convinced that organized research should be entirely eliminated. Many contend that it is part of the instructional program. But I have yielded to pressure here with many reservations. I do not exclude activities related to instruction, an exclusion made in the 16-state study. Of one thing we may be sure—the elimination of the two categories, organized research and public services, greatly changes the ranking of states' unit costs—a comparison of column 7 of the McGraw-Hill table and column 14 of the Master Table will reveal large differences.

Whereas public IHL educational expenditures were $2,051 million in 1957–58, the adjusted figure was $1,494 million, or about 27 per cent less. The effects of excluding organized research, public services and related activities are suggested by the fact that only 48 per cent of general and educational expenditures then finance student higher education in California, and 84 per cent in Ohio.[12]

At best, the rankings of states on unit outlays should be considered as rough ones, and for this reason the A, B, C, D, E ratings are much to be preferred to the 1, 2 . . . to 48 rankings.

Still another problem harasses the student. The figures relate to enrollment in the state, not to the resident students at institutions. Many states export students net, and others import them net (Table 26-3). Hence where a state exports heavily (e.g., New Jersey) the burden of higher education is put substantially upon other states. Thus New Jersey exports net 37,400 of its students, and, at a conservative estimate of $1,000 subsidy per student (inclusive of capital costs), this means that New Jersey puts $37 million yearly upon other states for providing higher education for its residents. Indeed some of these funds also come from residents of other states—e.g., Chicago alumni of Princeton University. Massachusetts imports net close to 22,000, or pays a bill of about $22 million for students from other states.[13]

The NPA study is devoted primarily to all IHL, *both public and private,* and generally relates results to full-time-student equivalent and also for some purposes to expenditures on student higher education. This variable is even more restricted than my *adjusted* expenditures, because some overhead items are excluded as are also organized activities related to education. I am doubtful that the last should be excluded, and though for the purpose of this analysis I have also excluded organized research, I am not at all certain that this is appropriate procedure. Among educators, there is disagreement on this point, for many hold that research is tied to instruction.

Since the NPA study is devoted to 16 states (accounting for about 70 per cent of expenditures and more than two-thirds of enrollments), the figures in column 1 of Table 26-4 should be substantially inflated for the purpose of comparing with columns 2 and 3. (Column 1a is devoted to a prewar year.)

In 10 of the 16 states the agreement is not too far out of line once adjustments are made for the variations in numbers ranked—16 and 48 for the variables in columns 1 and 2. Moreover, the figures in column 1 are based on full-time-student equivalent. Organized research, public services, and related activities are excluded. Since these items account for one-third

TABLE 26-3
The Major Exporting and Importing States,* 1958

State	Net exports (number)†	Net exports as percentage of students residing in state	State	Net imports (number)†	Net imports as percentage of students residing in state
New Jersey.........	37,400	35	Vermont.........	3,500	70
Nevada...........	1,200	33	Utah.............	7,600	40
Idaho.............	2,900	24	Colorado........	9,500	32
Wyoming.........	1,400	23	New Hampshire....	2,000	26
Delaware.........	1,000	18	Rhode Island......	2,600	25
Connecticut........	7,000	14	Indiana..........	16,900	25
Arkansas..........	2,300	10	Massachusetts.....	21,700	24
Maryland.........	3,500	10	Tennessee........	7,700	17
Montana..........	1,300	10	North Carolina.....	6,200	11
Virginia...........	3,300	8	Arizona..........	2,200	8
Florida...........	4,200	7	Michigan.........	7,000	7
Illinois............	11,400	7	Missouri..........	3,800	7
			Louisiana........	2,900	6

* 5 per cent or more.
† Nearest 100.
Source: Calculated from *Home State and Migration of American College Students, 1958.*

of the total general and educational expenditures and their proportion varies greatly from state to state, their exclusion greatly changes the ranking. The 16-state study, for example, shows that expenditures for *student higher education* vary from 48.3 per cent (California) to 84.4 per cent (Ohio) of general and educational expenditures.

Another factor that makes for variations in ranking is the adjustment for full-time-student equivalent in column 1. Such an adjustment would be reflected in higher ratings for states where part-time enrollment is especially high—this accounts in part for the high unit costs per full-time student in New York (3d) as compared to the rating of 34th in column 2 based on crude enrollment figures. (Adjustments to full-time equivalent in New York would reduce relative enrollment and raise unit expenditures.)

Table 26-4 is of interest for another reason. The contrast of rankings in columns 1 and 3 reflects several factors, but especially the difference made by assessing *all* IHL (column 1) and *public* IHL (column 3). The major difference between columns 1 and 3 comes from coverage of *all* IHL in column 1 and only *public* IHL in column 3.

TABLE 26-4
Comparison of 16-State Study by NPA and S. E. H.

State	Estimated student higher-education expenditures (SHEE) full-time-student equivalent, per cent United States (column 1)	Ranking, 48 states, current expenditures in public and private IHL per capita of population aged eighteen to twenty-one (column 1a)	Current expenditures all IHL per student, 1957 (column 2)	Public IHL adjusted educational expenditures plus student-aid expenditures per enrollee, 1957–58 (column 3)
	Ranking, 16 states	Ranking, 48 states*	Ranking, 48 states	Ranking, 48 states
	(1)	(1a)	(2)	(3)
California..............	10	(6)	42	43
Connecticut.............	1	(4)	14	37
Illinois.................	4	(13)	15	11
Indiana................	6	(16)	18	4
Iowa..................	13	(8)	5	2
Massachusetts...........	2	(2)	10	35
Michigan...............	5	(19)	7½	8
Minnesota..............	12	(12)	11	5
Missouri................	14	(25)	33	40
New Jersey.............	9	(40)	38	41
New York..............	3	(7)	34	28
North Carolina..........	11	(37)	3	12
Ohio..................	8	(25)	41	27
Pennsylvania............	7	(34)	31	17
Texas.................	16	(37)	46	45
Wisconsin..............	15	(18)	24	21

* Figures for 1939–40, educational expenditures, both public and private.
Source: Column 1: NPA, *Student Higher Education*, March, 1960, p. 18; column 1a: T. Hungate, *Financing the Future of Higher Education*, 1946, p. 41; column 2: McGraw-Hill table, col. 8, in *Financing Higher Education: 1960–70*; column 3: Master Table, column 14.

The following states show much higher relative unit costs for *all* IHL than for public: California, Connecticut, Massachusetts, New Jersey, New York, Ohio, and Pennsylvania. In these states a low achievement as measured by unit costs in public IHL gives a misleading impression of the total picture. Thus Connecticut is 37th on the basis of public IHL, but 1st for *all* IHL. In these states it may be assumed that the independent IHL tend to raise the general average. In most of these states independent IHL count heavily. But again I warn the reader that the figures need to be adjusted—thus the difference for California is not 10th as against 43d, but something like 30th against 43d.

In these states, it may be held that the over-all picture is much more favorable than for public IHL. The great private IHL in Massachusetts or Connecticut, for example, more than make up for lack of support of public IHL. But the fact remains that in many of the states an inadequate effort is made by government, and therefore many students are denied access to IHL, for without public IHL costs may be $500 to $1,000 more than if they are available.

The higher unit costs in independent IHL, it should be added, may reflect not only higher standards but also small and inefficient units. The public IHL may incur low unit costs in part because of the economies of scale, though large agglomerations may also mean low standards.[14]

In some states, the public IHL set the pace as evidenced in unit costs: Indiana, Iowa, Michigan, Minnesota, and Wisconsin—among the 16 states.

A word about the burdens of education. In the state-by-state analysis I comment on the trends in state taxes, outlays on total education and on IHL. The general trend from 1950 to 1959 is a rise of 100 per cent in taxes, and 133 per cent in education, and a similar total for outlays on higher education. Where the trends in individual states vary greatly from the general average, I note those facts in the state-by-state study. The failure of tax receipts to rise may of course reflect the relative slow growth of particular economies. Relative gains in outlays for IHL vis-à-vis tax receipts show a tendency to treat the difficult problems of inadequate finance in higher education.

In 1959, state expenditures on IHL (recall that these are less than public outlays on IHL) were roughly one-third of all state outlays on education. But there were large deviations from these averages: the following spent 50 per cent or more of educational funds on higher education: Alabama, Colorado, Indiana, Iowa, Montana, New Hampshire (a maximum of 71), North Dakota, South Dakota, and Wisconsin. Of these states all but Alabama, Indiana, and New Hampshire revealed high efforts in my Master Table.

The following states spent less than 25 per cent of educational outlays on IHL in 1959: Arkansas, Delaware, Florida, Georgia, New York, Pennsylvania, South Carolina, Tennessee. But a large proportion of state outlays on education or on higher education does not necessarily reflect vigorous efforts. Much depends on the proportion of tax funds (both state and local) to personal income. In my tables I relate taxes to income and educational outlays to taxes.

The states (inclusive of local government) that devote a large percentage of their tax income to state and local outlays on education (in excess of 6 per cent against an average of 4½ per cent) are Arizona, Louisiana, New Mexico, South Dakota, Utah, Vermont—these are states with small population and high unit costs and low per capita income. Those with less than 4 per cent were Connecticut, Maine, Maryland, Massachusetts, Missouri, New Jersey, Pennsylvania, Rhode Island—mostly affluent states.

State and local government expenditures on higher education averaged 0.6 per cent of personal income in 1958. Those states that spent 0.4 per cent or less were Connecticut, Illinois, Massachusetts, Missouri, New Jersey, New York, Ohio, Pennsylvania. States with expenditures in excess of 1 per cent were Arizona, Arkansas, Colorado, Indiana, Iowa, Kansas, Louisiana, Michigan, Minnesota, Montana, New Mexico, North Dakota, Oklahoma, Oregon, Utah, Vermont, Wyoming. These are states with strong traditions of higher education.[15]

A comparison of a few states in columns 13, 14, 17, and 18 in the Master Table is of some interest (see Table 26-5). Column 13 is public

TABLE 26-5
Rankings, Four States, per CAP and per Enrollee

State	Column 13, expenditures, public IHL, per CAP	Column 14, expenditures, per public IHL, enroll.	Column 17, state and local taxes, per CAP	Column 18, state and local taxes, per enroll.
California...........	4	43	3	35
Kansas..............	2	30	12	43
Massachusetts........	48	35	6	1
Pennsylvania.........	47	17	21	2

Source: Master Table.

IHL adjusted expenditures, 1957–58, per member of college-age population (CAP), Column 14 is public IHL adjusted expenditures, 1957–58, per enrollee in public IHL. Column 17 is state and local tax revenue per CAP. Column 18 is state and local tax revenue per enrollee.

On the basis of CAP, the record of states with strong traditions of public higher education (e.g., California and Kansas) is impressive. Their rankings in columns 13 and 17 are high. Column 13 might be a measure of achievement and column 17 of capacity. But when the measure is not CAP but enrollment (columns 14 and 18), these states experience a large decline in ranking, the explanation being the large enrollments. For states without strong traditions of public higher education the rankings are low per member of CAP, that is small expenditures per CAP in public IHL (e.g. Pennsylvania), and relatively higher per enrollee, that is small expenditures per enrollee: small resources in states without traditions in *public higher* education for public higher education depress the indices per CAP, but small enrollments tend to raise them per enrollee. But these states perform better on the basis of total taxes (columns 17 and 18).

FOOTNOTES

[1] Dexter M. Keezer (ed.), *Financing Higher Education, 1960–70,* McGraw-Hill, New York, 1959, p. 63. In col. 10 there is one serious mistake: California should be 73.36, not 32.36, and the rank 6, not 42; col. 2 heading should read "Current Expenditures *State* IHL vs. Personal Income."

[2] NPA: S. H. Mushkin and E. P. McLoone, *Student Higher Education: Expenditures and Sources of Income in 16 Selected States,* 1960. (Mimeographed.)

[3] Excludes " . . . expenditures for organized research and overhead connected with research, *expenditures related to organized activities* and sales services of educational departments, expenditures of auxiliary enterprises and expenditures for student aid." (I would *not* exclude the item italicized, for this is part of the educational process.)

[4] Cf. columns 2 and 3 and 6 and 7 of my Master Table.

[5] Cf. columns 16, 17 and 19, 20 of my Master Table.

[6] I am especially indebted to Daniel Khazzoom for summarizing the results of this questionnaire and the relevant state budgets.

[7] Many struggles have persisted on the control of special income, e.g., gifts, endowment income, tuition. The public IHL want control in order to perform functions for which the Legislatures provide inadequately. The government is fearful of assumption of programs not approved. In general, state universities are frequently under less control in these matters than other public IHL. Even when the public IHL presumably control tuition, the government exercises pressures through the threat of reduction of appropriations if tuition is not increased. See L. A. Glenny, *Autonomy of Public Colleges,* 1959, chap. 5; and Moos and Rourke, *The Campus and the States,* 1959, pp. 93–95, 188–191.

[8] Cf. H. K. Allen, *The Federal Government and Financing Education,* 1950, p. 137, where it is estimated that in the last 2 decades (1930s and 1940s) about four-fifths of the plant of public IHL were added and only one-third of the value of the privately controlled plant.

[9] The complications of state versus local finance are revealed by the conditions in California. In 1953–54 the state provided 33 per cent for junior colleges, 72 per cent for state colleges, 68 per cent for the University of California, and 59 per cent for all public IHL. The county provided 18 per cent of the income of junior colleges; the district, 44 per cent of income of junior colleges. *A Study of The Need for Additional Centers of Public Higher Education in California,* 1957, p. 32.

[10] U.S. Census, *Compendium of State Government Finances in 1959,* pp. 49–50, 58.

[11] HEW, *Opening (Fall) Enrollment in Higher Education, 1959: Analytic Report,* p. 32 .

[12] My comparisons are subject to a few other reservations. One series is for 1957 and for *state* expenditures; the other series is for 1957–58 and includes adjusted expenditures for *all public* IHL.

[13] Material from American Association of Collegiate Registrars and Admissions Officers, *Home State and Migration of American College Students, Fall 1958,* 1959.

[14] It may be of some interest to compare Table 26-4 with some crude measurements of state level support (*both* public and private) for 1939–40 by Hungate, a pioneer in these areas of research. The highest expenditures per capita in 1939–40 were in New Hampshire, Massachusetts, Vermont, and Connecticut, clearly not states with large public support. In the twenty years since 1940 approximately, the following states substantially improved their ranking (note an adjustment is made for the fact that the ranking is for 16 states in column 1 and 48 states in column 1*a*) and experienced a substantial deterioration; but I warn the reader that these are very crude comparisons.

Improvement	*Deterioration*
New Jersey	California
Pennsylvania	Iowa
	Minnesota
	Missouri
	Wisconsin

[15] Cf. NPA, *op. cit.,* p. 75.

Chapter 27

DIFFERENCES AMONG STATES: DETAILS FOR 48 STATES

INTRODUCTION

The reader should consult the last chapter for reservations to be kept in mind. Only those interested in the burdens, capacity, efforts, and achievements of individual states in higher education should consult this present chapter.

In the state-by-state analysis, I took special pains to discover the inclusions and exclusions of certain items of revenue that are not ordinarily considered tax revenue and frequently are not appropriated and hence not included in the state expenditures for IHL. Appropriations by state government for IHL are one thing; total expenditures of public IHL are another. Accounting practice varies state by state, and often within the same state; and in the 150 questionnaires sent to university presidents, state boards, and state budget officers, I frequently found state officers' replies to be at variance with those of university presidents, and in some instances replies of university officials were not in agreement. In an effort to get at the facts I also inspected the budgets of all but a few states.

In this chapter I have generally put this information in footnotes. The results may not be worth the efforts made. But for comparisons of the state expenditures (not for those of IHL), the exclusions and inclusions help to understand the statistics.

My questionnaires asked administrators whether the following items were excluded or included in the state budget, and what were the amounts involved:

1. Tuition paid by students
2. Endowment earnings
3. Private gifts for operations
4. Net income from auxiliary services
5. Earmarked taxes
6. Contributions of local government
7. Income for organized research, exclusive of item 3
8. Other

The reader will find that disagreements in replies stem partly from the fact that the state university frequently bypasses the Legislature (e.g., tuition does not go through the budget) whereas in other public IHL all or most of these items have to be appropriated.

ALABAMA

Alabama is typical of the low-income states of the South. Its burden of higher education as measured by the relationship between college-age and total population is very heavy. In its capacity to finance higher education it is very low, for both net state and local tax revenue per member of college-age population and state and local taxes per $1,000 of personal income reflect very low capacity to pay indeed. Effort, as measured by four different variables, points to a low rating on the basis of two of these, and average on the basis of the two others. Hence the ranking for state and local taxes per $1,000 of personal income is a D; total state tax revenue per capita, also a D; educational expenditures, state and local, as a percentage of personal income, C; and educational expenditures, state and local, for higher education, also a C. It will be recalled that C is an average and D is low; A is very high and B is high.

In the light of the heavy burden, very low capacity, and less than average effort, what is finally achieved? The proportion of enrollment in IHL in relation to college-age population is low indeed—very low. But as is true in many states with low income and adequate public facilities, the achievement as measured by the relationship of public enrollment to total enrollment is high.

Adjusted unit expenditures—that is, expenditures per student adjusted for the elimination of organized research and public services—show that Alabama's achievement is a little better than average, and on the basis of expenditures by state and local governments per enrollee is a little less than average.

Perhaps one of the striking aspects of the Alabama situation is the high cost per student in the public institutions as compared to the average per capita income—a state with relatively low incomes and fairly high unit costs tends to have a high ratio of expenditures per student to per capita personal income. In this category Alabama ranks 6th in the nation, and its adjusted expenditures per student are 72 per cent of per capita personal income. The extremes are 84 per cent in Vermont and Virginia and only 29 per cent in California. It is interesting that a student in a public institution costs, in relation to per capita income, about 2½ times as much in Alabama as in California. In other words, the cost of higher education, or the expenditures of the public institution per student, tends to be very high in states with low income. The explanation of this may very well be partly that unit costs tend to be high in poorer states because of the small number of students educated and partly that the market for personnel is national. In other words, the cost per professor tends to be set by national standards and not by the local level of income.

Alabama also seems to have a lower rating in state and local taxes per member of the college-age population than per enrollee in public institutions. This is explained partly by the substantial contribution the public institution plays in states such as Alabama.

In conclusion, Alabama is a state with heavy burden, very low capacity, efforts greater than might be expected in view of her low capacity, and modest achievements. A greater effort could perhaps be expected from this state than is currently being made in the field of higher education. From 1950 to 1959 there has been some tendency to increase state tax receipts more than in the nation generally, but expenditures on education, and especially expenditures on higher education, have risen much less than the increase in tax receipts. In other words, in this period of nine years, despite the rising trends in higher education, the increase of expenditures has been surprisingly small in the state institutions. (I have not reproduced the table of state expenditures 1950 to 1959.)

ARIZONA

The burden of higher education is high; capacity, average and high on two variables; effort as measured by four criteria is average, high, very high, and very high. In particular, note that Arizona ranks 3d in total state and local government expenditures for education as a percentage of personal income and 8th in the percentage of state and local government expenditures on public IHL in relation to personal income. This is a remarkably good record, explained to some extent by the small population and, therefore, high unit costs.

Achievements are both high and low. When measured in relation to the proportion of enrollment to college-age population the achievement is high; when measured in relation of the enrollment in public institutions of higher learning to the total enrollment, Arizona is virtually at the top. But in adjusted expenditures per enrollee in public IHL, the state is very low. In ratio of adjusted expenditures per student to per capita personal income the state ranks 47th. That means that the expenditures per student in public IHL are relatively small as compared to the per capita personal income.

It should be said, however, in support of the state, that there has been substantial improvement since 1957—these figures are largely for 1957 or 1957–58. The 1950–1959 taxes, expenditures on education, and expenditures on higher education have increased much more than the national average; but this is related in part to the large increase of population.

The expenditures of the state government should be increased to some extent because of the exclusion from the state expenditures of the land-grant endowment, which in one year yielded $125,000, and also of private gifts in one year of $833,000. Against current operations, exclusive of commercial activities, of $16 million in 1959, the excluded amount is significant. It does not necessarily mean that Arizona's relative place would be changed greatly, because we would also have to take into account, as we do later, the exclusions in other states.[1]

Perhaps one more word should be said about the Arizona situation. Whereas the 48 states raise about 17½ per cent of their income from corporate and personal income taxes, Arizona raises only 11 per cent. This might be expected in view of the structure of the economy. But it is also significant that in 1959 Arizona was one of 16 states without a general sales tax. Indeed, in the state taxes per capita she ranked 23d, and therefore her taxes were moderately heavy. But it is possible for her to raise substantially larger sums through the introduction of a general sales tax.

ARKANSAS

Arkansas has one of the highest burdens of any state, and low capacity. Like so many relatively low-income states its efforts are to be commended, for they are substantially above average. But from 1950 to 1959 taxes rose much less than the national average, and the same can be said for expenditures on education and on public institutions of higher learning.

Its achievements are not high. Enrollment as a percentage of college-age population is very low, but public enrollment as a percentage of total is very high. As is generally true of states with this structure of achievements, the unit cost, measured by adjusted dollar expenditures for public IHL per enrollee or net state and local support per enrollee, tends to be low. With limited resources, large dependence on public institutions tends to reduce the unit expenditures per student.

It is not easy to get a clear picture of the efforts made by the state. On the basis of state and local taxes per $1,000 of personal income, the effort is better than average, but on the basis of state tax revenue per capita it is very low. That is explained in part by the low general per capita income. But on the basis of educational expenditures or expenditures for IHL by state and local government in relation to personal income, the efforts are high.

Against per capita personal income of $1,200 the adjusted expenditure per student was $855, a relationship that gave Arkansas a ranking of 7th in the burden of expenditures per student in public institutions as against per capita personal income.

These remarks apply primarily to operating expenditures. It should also be noted that Arkansas was relatively low in its contribution for construction expenditures in 1957.[2]

CALIFORNIA

Very high burden—very high capacity—high effort—and very high achievement as evidenced in the proportion of students in IHL in relation to college-age population, and a high achievement as measured by the relationship of enrollment in public to all IHL.

With such large enrollment, however, the unit cost as given by adjusted dollar expenditures for public IHL or by the net state and local support per enrollee in public IHL is respectively very low and low. Here the large enrollments in the public institutions tend to depress the unit expenditures. Perhaps another factor is the low unit cost that comes with large enrollment per institution. California's efforts are especially strong when measured against its tax receipts, either per capita or in relation to personal income, but the expenditures on education and higher education in relation to personal income are not quite so satisfactory.

One of the striking aspects of the California situation is the small percentage of adjusted expenditures per student in 1958 for public institutions in relation to per capita personal income. The percentage is 29.4, and this makes California the 48th state in the percentage of adjusted expenditures per student in relation to personal income per capita. This is all the more surprising in view of the remarkable higher-education program in the State of California.

Since California is one of the states considered in the study by the NPA of the 16 relatively high-income states, I shall comment on this study.

In the category "estimated student higher education expenditures full-time-student equivalent," California ranks 10th of the 16 states. This in general corroborates my own estimate of the unit costs. In per capita expenditures of state and local government for all purposes in higher education, that is, current and capital, California is in the lead with expenditures of $25.16 as compared to a $10.43 average for the 16 states. For all state and local funds for student expenditures on higher education as the percentage of personal income for both current and capital accounts, again California is first. For all expenditures for higher education, current and capital, as a percentage of personal income, and the same for student higher education, she ranks in the middle —6th and 7th respectively.[3]

In short, California stands out for its high burden, very large capacity,

382   Government Contributions

strong efforts, and remarkable achievements. These achievements do not seem to be so great, however, when the unit expenditures are considered. And despite all these efforts, and the high standards and the great achievements, California is the 48th state in the proportion of adjusted expenditures per public enrollee in relation to per capita income.

A few other comments on California: as is well known, reducing the expenditures by the outlays for organized research and public services greatly reduces California's total expenditures and therefore brings down unit costs very much. Whereas for all states the percentage was 73, for California the percentage of the adjusted expenditures in relation to total was only 56 per cent. Again, California has a very low percentage of full-time undergraduate in relation to total enrollment in public IHL, roughly 53 per cent. The over-all figure is about 70 per cent. This suggests a larger proportion of part-time students in California public institutions and to this extent suggests that unit costs are somewhat higher than they seem to be. Also capital expenditures were very heavy in this one year.

But state and local government take a relatively large proportion of tax revenues for higher education, namely, 7½ per cent in one year against a national average of 4 per cent. And from 1950 to 1959 state taxes rose more than twice as much as in the nation generally. The relative percentages were 2.2 times rise for taxes, 3.3 for education, and 4.8 for higher education. Clearly California is putting a heavy stake in higher education. Moreover, California's local governments contribute an unusually large percentage of total state and local expenditures on higher education, 23 per cent as compared to a 16-state average of 13.2 per cent.

Finally, a large proportion of total expenditures are not revealed in the state budgets. In 1957–58, for example, the total current expenditures were $277 million, of which state funds provided $155 million. For capital outlay the respective figures were $157 million and $132 million.[4]*

In his analysis Chambers compares appropriations out of tax funds exclusively. The importance of state appropriations varies greatly. In states like California, the state appropriations are large indeed.

Hence, almost $150 million of the University of California budget did not appear in the state expenditures in the year 1958–59. We should, however, leave out of account $142 million of income for organized research, because this is not generally considered part of the instructional budget. But even if we include only tuition, endowment earnings, private gifts, and income from auxiliary services, this total of about $21 million is a substantial factor in raising the $89.5 million available to the University of California from state funds in 1957–58.

* For these two items, 122 million and 157 million —132 million = 25 million, or 147 million in all.

Bruce F. Austin, administrative planning officer of the State of California Department of Education, wrote me as follows on April 20, 1960:

For the California state colleges (as well as for the University of California) the estimated income from tuition and fees paid by students is included in state's budgets, in the sense that such reimbursements are subtracted from the total proposed expenditures so that a net appropriation for support is made. Most of the other categories [that is, the categories mentioned in my questionnaire] are not applicable to the state colleges.

One final point on the California situation: in the 16-state comparison California is first in per capita expenditures for current and capital purposes by the state and local governments for IHL. This, of course, stems from the large appropriations for public higher education. In contrast the expenditures of public IHL in California per enrollee are very low, a fact explained in part by the very large enrollments in California in public institutions, and perhaps also by the structure of the enrollments. Enrollment in state colleges is very high, and the large enrollments prevail in the junior colleges. As against an enrollment in junior colleges of 12 per cent for the nation, the figure for California is 47.5 per cent, by far the largest in the nation. On the whole the junior colleges are less costly than others.

COLORADO

Colorado is a state with a very high burden, high capacity, high to very high efforts (and more nearly very high than high), and unusual achievements.

From 1950 to 1959 state taxes rose much less than for the 48 states. Expenditures on higher education rose considerably more than taxes, suggesting that these categories were tending to take a larger part of tax revenue. Colorado especially stands out for its efforts, as indicated by the proportion of state and local government expenditures for education and for public IHL in relation to personal income. Its rankings in these two categories are 7th to 8th and 4th to 5th.

An interesting aspect of the Colorado situation is the large in-migration of students. Whereas total enrollment in 1958 was 38,640, the residents of Colorado accounted for 24,235, or 60 per cent. This means, of course, that a large part of resources for higher education went not to residents of Colorado but to residents of other states, and in this sense the state was making a large contribution toward the education of the rest of the nation.[5]

One final point about Colorado. In the particular years studied construction was very high, coming to about 90 per cent of the current operating expenditures; the average for the nation was less than 50 per cent.

In conclusion, Colorado has a record in higher education of which it should be very proud. In particular in relation to personal income, expenditure for both education and for higher education is very high. Achievements are much greater than might be expected from the very high burdens incurred and the capacity to finance these burdens.[6]

CONNECTICUT

Connecticut is typical of the rich state with an absence of tradition of public higher education. Burden is very low; capacity very high; and effort very low. Achievement varies according to the measures. Its enrollment in IHL is very high in relation to college-age population, a fact explained in part by its excellent private institutions. As might be expected, its percentage of enrollment in public institutions to total enrollment is very low. Its adjusted dollar expenditures for public IHL per enrollee instructed is low, but for net state and local support per enrollee in public IHL its record is very high, a fact explained by its relatively low enrollment in public institutions. State and local taxes per $1,000 of personal income are very low, as are educational expenditures and higher educational outlays of state and local government in relation to personal income.

Since personal income per capita is very high ($2,716) and adjusted expenses per student in public institutions only $842, Connecticut is 45th in the relationship of expenditures per student in public IHL to per capita personal income.

The 16-state study throws further light on Connecticut. Estimated student-higher-education expenditure per full-time-student equivalent is 40 per cent above the national average and puts Connecticut first among the 16 rich states. Here the high-quality *private* IHL are relevant. Expenditure for student higher education in relation to general and educational expenditures was also very high—79.4 as against a national average of 65. Unit expenditures are lower than they seem to be, in part because of the very high proportion of graduate enrollment, a proportion almost twice as large as for the nation.

The 16-state study also shows that Connecticut has a relatively low rating for state and local support per student as a percentage of personal income, and similarly for all expenditures for higher education, both current and capital, as a percentage of personal income. Here it ranks 11th out of 16 states. When the last variable is reduced to student-higher-education expenditures, its position improves to 9th, and this is explained partly by the large proportion of expenditure for student higher education.

Connecticut's relatively small effort is also explained by its tax structure, for it raised only 12½ per cent of income by corporate income taxes, and it has no personal tax. Connecticut is one of 18 states with no income tax.[7]

Connecticut, like many other states, exports a large percentage of its students. Whereas 46,000 reside in the state, IHL provide for only 39,000, a net exportation often occurring in small states.

DELAWARE

Delaware is a small state, and we would therefore expect high unit costs. The burden is very low, capacity to pay is high, state and local taxes as a percentage of personal income are very low, but, in part because of the high per capita income, taxes per capita are very high. Measuring effort on the basis of state and local government expenditures for education as a percentage of personal income, and similarly for expenditures for public IHL, Delaware's rank is average. Unit costs per student in public institutions are relatively low as compared with per capita personal income.

For an Eastern state its public enrollment is very high in relation to total enrollment. And unit expenditures are very high on the basis of expenditures of the state institutions, but average for state and local taxes per enrollee in public institutions. In this one year expenditures on capital were very high. Since 1950 its taxes have risen more than in the nation, and educational expenditures more than twice as rapidly as taxes, and higher education outlays more rapidly than taxes. But higher education accounts for a relatively small part of the total expenditures on education, as compared with the national figures.

A case could be made out for heavier taxes in the state. The state collects 47 per cent of its taxes through corporate income and income taxes, which is a very high percentage compared to an over-all average of 17 per cent. But the state has no general sales tax.

It should be noted that the actual appropriations of the state government do not give an adequate idea of the expenditures for comparative purposes. For the state budget excludes tuition paid by students, endowment earnings, private gifts, net income from auxiliary services, and income for organized research not included in private gifts.

In 1958 there were 4,605 students enrolled in Delaware IHL and 5,607 residents of the state in IHL in the nation. In other words, Delaware to a considerable extent depends on other states. Provision for students is much better than might be indicated by the enrollment in the state.[8]

FLORIDA

As in most Southern states, the burden is very high, but relatively speaking, and I suppose in part because of the large immigration of northerners, capacity to pay is better than average. Achievements are about average. Construction expenditures are relatively high, in part because of the rise of population.

Taxes and educational expenditures have tended to rise much more than the national average since 1950.

When effort is measured by comparing state and local expenditures on education or higher education in relation to personal income, Florida's record is average and less than average, respectively. In general a larger effort might be expected of Florida, especially since it has no state income and no corporate income law, and depends wholly on sales and similar taxes for state revenue.

The budget director of the state of Florida, Harry G. Smith, writes as follows:[9]

I believe that development and use of this type of information in relation to higher education is an excellent step forward. . . . However, any publication of these tables and indices should be accompanied by warnings as to their misuse and misinterpretation. . . . State expenditures for higher education are, in part at least, determined by what private facilities exist. Since the states you mention contain large private institutions [these are New York, Connecticut, Pennsylvania, and New Jersey] which receive large research grants and care for a large percentage of the students, the state is not required to support higher education at the same level as is necessary in Florida, for example, to produce a comparative product. . . .

GEORGIA

Georgia is a typical low-income Southern state with a very high burden, very low capacity to pay, efforts in excess of the capacity, and only a very modest achievement. Since 1950, however, taxes and expenditures on education have risen much more than the national average. Outlays for higher education in relation to total tax revenue is about 3 per cent, which is less than the average. Adjusted expenditures per student in public higher education is somewhat more than one-half of the per capita personal income, a fairly substantial burden.

IDAHO

The burden is high, the capacity low, effort somewhat better than average. Achievements are rather low except that enrollment in public as against all institutions of higher learning is high. In spite of the low achievements the state spends about 4½ per cent of its tax revenues on higher education, which is more than average. Idaho takes care of only about 76 per cent of its students in its own state. There is a large exportation. This suggests that the state's achievements are greater than heretofore indicated, merely because it depends upon other states for higher education.

In the years 1950–1959, tax receipts rose less than the average in the nation; education expenditures, less than taxes; and expenditures on IHL rose only 16 per cent, a very low figure compared to the national average of around 133 per cent. The state depends heavily on corporate income and personal income taxes. For a relatively low per capita income state it has high per capita state taxes, the 17th in the nation.[10]

ILLINOIS

Illinois' burden is low, capacity very high, and effort low. Its efforts are especially low when measured by state and local expenditures on education or on higher education as a percentage of personal income. Its achievements are high when measured as the percentage of enrollment to college-age population, and also for adjusted dollar expenditures for public IHL per enrollee. But its position is very low vis-à-vis the ratio of public enrollment to total enrollment in IHL.

The 16-state study also confirms the fact that expenditures per student are very high. This study presents the student-higher-education expenditures per full-time-student equivalent as a percentage of the United States figure. For the variables that give an indication of effort, Illinois again is not high. Various categories place it 7th, 9th, 9th, and 11th among the 16 states. These categories do not reveal as low effort as my own studies. But it must be recognized that in general the 16 states are high-income states and generally their efforts tend to be low.

Since the undergraduate full-time enrollment is 30 per cent less than the total enrollment, the inference is that the state has a large number of part-time students and therefore unit costs on a national basis are somewhat higher than they seem to be. Since 1950 the rise of state taxes has been less than the national average, and expenditures on higher education have risen less than the average for the 48 states, though higher education is a relatively high percentage of total state expenditures on education.

Unit expenditures (adjusted) of public institutions are high.

The Illinois tax system is surprisingly inadequate. The state has neither a corporation income tax nor an income tax nor a general sales tax. In spite of its high income, state taxes per capita are 40th in the nation. Certainly a case could be made for much stronger taxation and hence greater support for public education.

The Illinois situation is not so bad as it seems so far, because there is a net migration of 11,411 or 6 to 7 per cent of the students residing in this state. In other words, other states carry the burden of Illinois to some extent.[11]

INDIANA

Burden is average, capacity is high when measured by per capita income but rather low on the basis of net state and local taxes per member of college-age population. Effort is low, and very low on the basis of two tax criteria. In other words, this is a low-tax state, but the relationship of state and local expenditures on education to personal income is better than average and even higher for the same variables in relation to higher education.

Achievements are high on the basis of enrollment in relation to college-age population, and average on public enrollment as percentage of total. For unit costs, the achievements are very high on the basis of public IHL expenditures per enrollee and high on the same basis for net state and local support per enrollee in public institutions. Adjusted expenditures per student in public institutions are very high in relation to per capita income, the percentage being 69.8 and the ranking 8th in the nation; in other words, adjusted expenditures per student in public IHL are very high in Indiana in relation to per capita income.

In the 16-state table we obtained the following (for both public and private IHL): student-higher-education expenditures are relatively high as compared to general education expenditures. Estimated student-higher-education expenditures per full-time-student equivalent are relatively high. For per capita state and local funds for current and capital purposes, Indiana is again a little above average and tends to be above average for state and local funds for student higher education as a percentage of personal income, and the same for expenditures on all higher education, current and capital, as a percentage of personal income, where it is very high, being 3d among 16, and 5th when this is reduced to student-higher-education expenditures as a percentage of personal income. In this one year capital expenditures were very large, being 3d relatively in the nation.

From 1950 to 1959 taxes rose less than in the nation. Educational expenditures rose relatively more than taxes, and expenditures for IHL rose very much more than taxes. Moreover, IHL take about half of the state's total expenditures on education, a relatively high figure. The explanation may be low state taxes, a proportion in relation to personal income substantially below the national average, but state outlays on education in relation to total outlays are above average.

Indiana has neither a corporation tax nor a state income tax, and therefore a larger effort and greater achievements could be had if Indiana, like most states, had such taxes. Furthermore, this kind of taxation would more easily justify higher expenditures for higher education. The absence of these taxes in part explains the relatively low per capita state taxes, 20 to 25 per cent below the national average.

Imports of students are very large. In 1958 there were 69,000 students residing in the state. Student enrollment in the state was 86,000; in other words, net importation accounted for 20 per cent of enrollment. These figures point to the fact that the contribution of Indiana toward higher education is much greater in relation to the total student body than to Indiana residents. The state financed higher education for other states.

State budgetary figures for Indiana tend to underestimate the total contributions, since many items are excluded from the state budget. For example, Indiana University tuition paid by students, endowment earnings, private gifts, proceeds from auxiliary services, earmarked taxes, contributions of local governments, and income for organized research not included in private gifts are all excluded.[12]

IOWA

Burden is less than average, effort and achievement high.

But the 16-state study shows that for Iowa the student-higher education expenditures per full-time-student equivalent is only 13th among the 16 states. This suggests a somewhat lower achievement than my indices show. This is, of course, in comparison with 15 relatively rich states. This 16-state study in general confirms my own studies on effort. The indices for the four measures of effort in the 16-state study put Iowa 8th, 5th, 4th, and 4th.

From 1950 to 1959 taxes rose substantially less than in the nation, and expenditures on higher education rose a little more than taxes. But higher education received more than half of the total state educational expenditures, a relatively high figure. But total educational expenditures relative to all are low.

Particularly striking is the high achievement as measured by unit (per student) expenditures, whether on the basis of the expenditures of all IHL or by state and local government. Iowa rates fourth in cost of public higher education per student in relation to the per capita personal income; that is to say, higher education is costly relative to economic standards.

In short, Iowa has performed well in higher education, for with average capacity effort has been better and achievement high indeed. Its record here seems to be especially strong when we consider *all* higher institutions, because the achievement measured by the proportion of public to total enrollment is not high; in fact it is low.

President Virgil Hancher of the State University of Iowa wrote me that all items listed in my questionnaire are either inapplicable or included in the budget.[13]

KANSAS

Burden is low, capacity is above average, effort tends to be above average except that per capita taxes are relatively low. Achievement as measured by the percentage of students in relation to college-age population and the proportion of public school attendance in relation to total enrollment is very high but on the basis of unit cost, especially as measured by state and local expenditures per enrollee in public institutions, is rather low.

An indication of the strong efforts is suggested by the fact that 6 per cent of the state tax revenue is spent on IHL. But from 1950 on taxes tended to rise less than in the nation, partly because of the rate of growth of this state, though outlays on education and higher education tended to increase more rapidly than total tax revenues.

According to the budget analyst for the state of Kansas, tuition paid by students, private gifts, earmarked taxes, and income for organized research are included in the budget, but endowment earnings and contributions by local governments are excluded.

KENTUCKY

This state achieves a low score or a very low score on almost every criterion. Burdens are very high, however, capacity very low; effort low to very low, achievement low or very low. This is a pattern which is unusual in a low-income state, where generally efforts are relatively high. It should be said, however, that since 1950 educational expenditures and expenditures for IHL have tended to rise substantially more than taxes. The state is dependent much more than the average on corporate income and income taxes, the percentage obtained through these sources being 29. But there is no general sales tax in Kentucky. Capital expenditures are much above the average in this one year.[14]

LOUISIANA

Louisiana is almost unique: in relation to a very heavy burden and low capacity, the efforts are very high and achievements are also high. As measured by total expenditures in relation to college-age population, the achievements are not really high, but they are high for adjusted expenditures per enrollee in public IHL.

Taxes have not risen as much as in the nation, as might be expected from the economy of the state, but educational expenditures since 1950 have risen about two-thirds more than taxes.

The state might improve its position by depending more heavily on corporate and income taxes because these yield only 7 per cent of the total revenue of the state, and yet the per capita state taxes are very high, third in the nation.

The controller of the state of Louisiana wrote me that the only items excluded from the state budget are net income from auxiliary services and contract research and restricted gifts, the former $465,000, the latter $1,771,000.

MAINE

Burden is high, capacity low, effort varies according to the measure: high on the basis of state and local taxes per $1,000 of personal income, low on the basis of state per capita taxes, and low on the basis of expenditures on education or higher education in relation to personal income. On the whole, the net is a rather low effort. On the basis of enrollment, achievement is low. On the basis of adjusted expenditures per student enrolled in public institutions, and similarly for state and local outlays on higher education in relation to enrollment, achievement is high. But this is partly explained by high unit costs associated with low population states.

The tendency since 1950 is below average rise of taxes and expenditures on education and higher education. Perhaps one explanation of the low rate of taxes per capita on the state level, and therefore one explanation of low effort, is the absence of either a corporation income or personal income tax.[15]

MARYLAND

Burden is low, capacity is high to very high, effort is high on the basis of state and local taxes in relation to personal income and also high, or above average at least, for per capita state taxes, but very low and low when the measure is the proportion of personal income spent by state and local government on education and on higher education.

Higher education expenditures for the last nine years have not risen nearly as much as taxes. The percentage of tax revenue spent on higher education is 3, or about three-fourths of the national level. Corporation income taxes yielded 36 per cent of total tax revenue in 1959, roughly twice as much as the national average.

On the whole, achievements are high when measured by the adjusted expenditures of public IHL per enrollee and also state and local expenditures per enrollee in public institutions.

Exports of students were very large, roughly 10 per cent of the total, and to this extent it may be said that the support is higher than it seems to be since a substantial part of the burden is put on other states.[16]

MASSACHUSETTS

Massachusetts is most unusual. Burden is low, capacity very high, effort average, achievement very low as measured by public higher education funds available in relation to college-age population, and similarly for state and local taxes in relation to enrollment in public institutions.

Other evidence of low effort is the ⅔ per cent of tax revenue that goes to higher education, or about one-seventh of the national average. It could be said, however, that its educational expenditures have risen 150 per cent from 1950 to 1959, higher education by 200 per cent, and taxes by 100 per cent, suggesting some attempts to make up for deficiencies.

The 16-state study also shows Massachusetts very low in effort. Its per capita state and local expenditures for student higher education are only about one-third that of the nation, and it ranks here 15th among the 16 states. The 16-state study also shows a very high expenditure per student in higher education. Here the excellent record in private IHL is relevant. In student expenditures per full-time-student equivalent, Massachusetts is 27 per cent above the national average and second among the 16 states.

The 16-state study also shows Massachusetts as the 16th, or last, in state and local expenditures for student higher education as a percentage of personal income for current and capital expenditures. But for *all* students and *all* expenditures for higher education for *all* purposes, Massachusetts ranks first, as does the student-higher-education expenditure from all sources in relation to personal income. Here, indeed, the very large contribution of private institutions plays a decisive part and offsets the very low contribution for public higher education in Massachusetts. Here Massachusetts is last on a 16- or 48-state level.

Expenditures for public institutions per student are low in relation to the per capita income—42d in the nation.

In one respect, young men and women of Massachusetts in public *and* private IHL do not achieve the high level that has been suggested so far. The point is that total enrollment in Massachusetts institutions is 113,000 as compared to 91,000 students residing in the state going to IHL. In other words, roughly 22,000, or 20 per cent of the students, are net from outside, that is the state's imports of students exceed its exports.

In public higher education, Massachusetts might make a larger contribution by introducing a general sales tax. Its net income and corporate income taxes are very heavy, accounting for 51 per cent of the total state tax revenue, by far the highest in the nation except for Oregon with 55 per cent.[17]

MICHIGAN

Michigan is a relatively rich state. Its burden is low, capacity from high to very high, effort above average. Its achievements on the whole have been high to very high. Effort is substantially above average, unusual for a rich state, and this in part explains the high achievement. Effort is especially high when measured by the expenditures on education or higher education in relation to personal income. The only exception to a high standing for achievement is the taxes of state and local governments per unit enrolled in public IHL where the achievement is average. This is a likely pattern for states that have large resources or large enrollments in public institutions.

The 16-state study confirms this general pattern. For achievement in the estimated student-higher-education expenditures per full-time-student equivalent, Michigan ranks 5th among the 16 states. The other four criteria which can largely be classified as effort give Michigan ratings of 2d, 3d, 7th, and 6th, all confirming the fact that Michigan's efforts are on the whole high.

Since 1950 the taxes at the state level have risen more than for the 48 states, in part reflecting prosperous economic conditions, and what is more the rise of expenditures on higher education has been more than of taxes. Another indication of strong measures is the 6⅔ per cent of tax revenues going to higher education against a national level of about 4 per cent. Michigan could make an even larger contribution if it would introduce a corporate income and income tax. But the state has neither of these taxes, and this partly explains some financial difficulties in recent years. Public capital expenditures in relation to college-age population was unusually high, 4th in the nation.

Aside from the strong support of higher education in Michigan, the state also, to some extent, subsidizes students from abroad or outside of Michigan, for its enrollment exceeds by 5½ per cent, or 7,000 students, the net number residing in the state and going to IHL in the nation.[18]

MINNESOTA

Burden is average, capacity rather high, effort high to very high, and achievements on the whole high, ranging from average to very high. Public expenditures in relation to number of college-age population are very high, but as is often true in states of this kind, the record in relation to enrollment of the same variable is only a little better than average.

In general the 16-state study confirms these results. The achievement index as given by the estimated student-higher-education expenditures per full-time-student equivalent as the percentage of the United States puts Minnesota rather low, with a ranking of 12th among the 16 states. Again these are of course the high-income states. The four measures of effort for *all* IHL given in the 16-state study put Minnesota 3d, 2d, 5th, and 3d, a very high effort, which in part accounts for the unusual achievements. The state expenditures in this year on capital have been relatively low, and its expenditures in relation to tax revenue for higher education are 4⅔ per cent against the national average of 4 per cent.

Minnesota depends heavily on a state personal income tax and corporate income tax. These together account for 33 per cent of tax revenues as compared to a national average of 17 per cent. The state, however, does not have a general sales tax.

In the years 1950 to 1959 taxes rose much more than the national level, but education and higher education expenditures did not rise as much as taxes. However, on the whole higher education takes a larger percentage of the educational budget than in most states.

According to the assistant controller of the University of Minnesota, the items such as tuition for the University of Minnesota are excluded from the budget. The only item in my questionnaire included is earmarked taxes. Aside from $13.7 million of gross income from auxiliary services and $11,500,000 income from organized research, the amounts excluded are $6.3 million for tuition, $768,000 for endowment earnings, $4.8 million for private gifts. Obviously, outlays are larger than suggested by budget appropriations. For state colleges tuition is included.

Florence Reber, state budget officer, also indicates that whereas most of the items for the University of Minnesota are excluded, they are all included for the state colleges except net income from auxiliary services and some gifts.[19]

MISSISSIPPI

This is the lowest-income state in the nation, a state with a very high burden and very low capacity. Efforts range from very high to average. Indeed per capita state taxes are rather low, a fact explained by the low per capita income. Despite the effort, achievements are very low as measured by the expenditures in public IHL per enrollee and public outlays vis-à-vis college-age population.

From 1950 to 1959 taxes increased much more relatively than outlays on higher education; higher education expenditures in relation to taxes were $4\frac{1}{2}$ per cent. Note again that, as compared to the effort, achievements are low or very low on all counts, a fact explained by the very low capacity and very high burdens.[20]

MISSOURI

Missouri is a relatively high-income state. Its burden of higher education is average, capacity as given by state and local support per member of college-age population is high, although per capita state taxes are low. The last also reflects low effort—very low on all counts, in fact on five different measures. Expenditures on public higher education in relation to state and local taxes are only $2\frac{1}{2}$ per cent. Moreover, expenditures on higher education since 1950 have not risen nearly so much as tax receipts. On most counts achievement has been low as well.

The 16-state study in general supports these conclusions. One index of achievement puts Missouri in 14th place. Four other measures of effort put Missouri 13th, 12th, 12th, and 10th among the 16 states. These figures suggest that, when allowance is made for the private institutions and adjustments are made on the basis of full-time-student equivalent, the record is not greatly changed. On the whole, Missouri is one of the most disappointing states. Despite the high capacity, a very low effort and heavy burden account for the relatively low achievements.

As unsatisfactory as Missouri's place in public higher education is, it is even less satisfactory when allowance is made for the fact that the state imports (net) about 3,800 students, or 7 per cent of its students. In other words, it makes a substantial contribution to the higher education of students from other states.

The state budget in Missouri finances its program by two kinds of funds, state funds and funds other than state. This method is followed for the University of Missouri, for state colleges, for Lincoln University. The various activities of these institutions are supported by state-funds appropriations whenever expenditures for these activities exceed the amount coming from sources other than state funds.

MONTANA

The burden is average, capacity above average, effort high. The achievements are especially high when measured by the relation of public to total enrollment. But on the basis of total enrollment the achievement is below average.

Since 1950 expenditures on IHL have risen only about one-third as much as total tax receipts. The state also suffers from a very low rate of rise of per capita income.

Approximately 10 per cent of the students residing in this state (net) go to IHL elsewhere, and therefore to that extent Montana is living on other states.

Montana has no general sales tax. For this one year capital expenditures were very high, being about 85 per cent of current expenditures.[21]

NEBRASKA

Burden is low, capacity is somewhat above average, effort as measured by four criteria is low. But the state spends $6\frac{1}{2}$ per cent of its tax revenue on higher education, and on this score the effort is much above average. On the basis of total enrollment in relation to college-age population the achievement is high, but not so on the basis of public in relation to total enrollment.

From 1950 to 1959 taxes rose about 200 per cent, but for higher education the increase was only 71 per cent, a trend suggesting underspending for higher education, although it should be noted that higher education was 61 per cent of the total educational budget, a large part of the state educational budget.

Nebraska's record could be improved greatly if she had a corporation income, personal income, and general sales tax. It is not surprising, therefore, that the state ranks low in the per capita state tax revenue.[22]

NEVADA

Burden is very low, capacity very high, effort as measured by state and local taxes in relation to personal income is high and on the basis of state per capita taxes is very high. The effort, however, when measured by the percentage of tax revenue spent on education, is average, and on higher education is less than average. In view of the high resources and the efforts, it might be expected that the achievements would be large, but Nevada stands low in the proportion of those of college age at college. Nevada, however, tops the nation in the adjusted dollar expenditures in public IHL per enrollee, and in the proportion of public enrollment to total enrollment. It ranks very high in net state and local support per enrollee in public IHL. The high unit costs are undoubtedly explained in large part by the small population; hence low enrollment, and hence costly scale of operations.

In the years 1950 to 1959 taxes rose about five times, but higher education outlays rose only by about 100 per cent, suggesting large relative losses for higher education.

Nevada also puts a heavy burden on the rest of the country, for it exports (net) about one-third of its students; to that extent achievements are greater than they seem to be. In this particular year capital expenditures were very high and even exceeded current expenditures.

With no corporate income or personal income tax, Nevada's potential contribution is much larger than its current contribution. Yet despite these gaps, Nevada is 18th in per capita state taxes.[23]

NEW HAMPSHIRE

Burden is low, the capacity average, the effort low or even very low. The achievements are high on the basis of enrollment in relation to college-age population but low on the basis of public enrollment in relation to total enrollment. On the basis of adjusted dollar expenditures for public institutions and public expenditures per student the achievements are high and very high. But this is explained in part by the small population of the state, with resultant high unit costs.

In the years 1950 to 1959, whereas taxes rose less than in the nation generally—in part explained by the slow rate of growth of the state, educational expenditures inclusive of higher education rose substantially more than the rise of taxes. With low enrollment in public institutions, achievements as measured by expenditures of public institutions or net state and local support of public institutions per enrollee are high.

New Hampshire supports net imports of students equal to 23 per cent of the residents of New Hampshire in attendance at New Hampshire IHL. This means that a substantial part of the expenditures in the state go to support those coming from other states. This applies particularly, of course, to the private institutions, of which Dartmouth is the most important. But we should allow for the inflow of gifts from outside to finance IHL.

New Hampshire obtains only 4 per cent of its tax revenues from corporate and income taxes, a very low percentage. The state also has no general sales tax, a fact in part explaining the very low yield of per capita taxes on the state level.[24] In his *Report for 1959–60* the President of the University of New Hampshire asks for a rise in the millage rate on property as a means of getting adequate financing of the university.

NEW JERSEY

New Jersey has one of the worst records for higher education in the whole nation. The burden is low, capacity very high, and effort low to very low. In the proportion of expenditures on education or on higher education in relation to personal income the record is very bad, nor does it have a good record on achievements, being low in the proportion of students in IHL in relation to college-age population, and very low in the proportion in public institutions. The adjusted dollar expenditures for public institutions of higher learning per college-age population is also very low, but because of the very low enrollment in public institutions, the adjusted dollar expenditure for state and local governments per enrollee in public institutions is very high.

Its burden is also very low on another count, since New Jersey is the 46th state in the proportion of adjusted expenditures per student in public institutions in relation to per capita personal income, the ratio being 30.4 per cent.

The 16-state study in general confirms these results, although on the basis of estimated student-higher-education expenditures per full-time-student equivalent, both public and private, New Jersey ranks 9th among the 16 states, spending about 3 per cent more than the average in the nation. This is still an unsatisfactory record for a state as rich as New Jersey. The improvement here compared to my results stems in part from the upgrading related to high standards of private IHL.

In the effort categories covered by the 16-state study, again New Jersey comes out very low, ranking 14th, 14th, 16th, and 16th.

As might be expected, New Jersey spends very little of its state and local tax revenue on public IHL, namely, 1.6 per cent.

In public institutions the undergraduate full-time enrollment is relatively low in relation to total enrollment. This fact points to somewhat higher unit costs than has so far been assumed.

New Jersey's bad record in education is explained partly by the fact that it has no income tax and no general sales tax, and the corporate net income tax yields only 5 per cent of total state revenue. It ranks 41st, despite high income, in the state tax revenues per capita, yet is 5th in per capita income.

One of the striking aspects of New Jersey higher education is that 107,000 of its students are educated in IHL, but there are only 70,000 educated in New Jersey in all. Hence net exports of students number 37,000, or about 35 per cent of its students, the highest net migration in the country. In other words, New Jersey puts a considerable part of the burden of educating her students on other states.

According to Kenneth R. Fer, vice president and treasurer of the State University (Rutgers) all the additional items like tuition and endowment earnings are excluded from the budget of the state university. Tuition, endowment earnings, private gifts and income for organized research and Federal appropriations come to $11.6 million. Fer also points out their variations in the manner of dealing with these matters; for example, some of the Federal accounts are included as Federal appropriation and are also part of the university income. There is a netting in the state-university accounting as compared with state colleges, where income is picked up by the state. "The State appropriation bill shows university expenditures of approximately one-half of actual since the end figure is just the State appropriation." There are also inconsistencies in enrollment versus college-age population. Incidentally, President Johnson pointed out that only about 56 per cent of the college population comes in the age group from eighteen to twenty-one.[25]

NEW MEXICO

New Mexico is a unique state: its burden is very high, capacity low, effort on the whole very high. State and local taxes as a percentage of personal income are average, but the per capita state taxes are very high, as are the expenditures on education or on higher education in relation to personal income. That the state spends 8 per cent of state and local tax revenue on higher education, as compared to an average of 4 per cent in the nation, suggests large efforts as well as high unit costs for a small state. Despite the unusual efforts, the achievements are not high: low on the relationship of enrollment to college-age population, but very high on public enrollment in relation to total enrollment, and low and very low on relationship between state and local support of college-age population, and per enrollee.

On the whole, higher-education expenditures since 1950 have risen much more than the increase of taxes, suggesting strong efforts to improve standards. Capital expenditures in this one year were relatively low as a percentage of operating expenditures. New Mexico obtains only 6 per cent of its income from corporation income and personal income taxes, a relatively small percentage, a fact explained by the nature of the economy.[26]

NEW YORK

New York is of course unique. Its burden is very low, capacity very high, effort high when measured on the basis of state and local taxes in relation to personal income or per capita state taxes but low when measured on the basis of expenditures on education in relation to personal income, and very low for expenditures on higher education in relation to personal income. Burden is low as measured by the percentage of adjusted expenses per student in public IHL to per capita income: 36 per cent, or 44th in the nation. Yet despite the unsatisfactory efforts, especially in the public domain, the state has a remarkable record in the proportion of college-age population at college. Of course, public enrollment in relation to total enrollment is low. (But compare the Cowen statement below.)

One feature of the New York situation should be emphasized; namely, that only 55 per cent of the total enrollment is undergraduate full time. This suggests a large part-time enrollment, and to that extent it must be assumed that unit costs or expenses are much higher for full-time students than is revealed by our measures. But there is a partial offset here: enrollment in graduate schools and medical schools is very high, and this is highly expensive education. It appears to that extent that the student equivalent in other areas is relatively low for unit costs.

New York State is also one of the states with a heavy contribution by local government, roughly about 35 per cent of the total state and local expenditures for student higher education.

The 16-state study in general confirms these results. For the estimated student-higher-education expenditures per full-time-student equivalent, New York ranks 3d with 123 per cent of the national average, a result that reflects the large contribution of private institutions, so important in the state of New York.

The four categories in the 16-state study which reflect effort do not give New York State a very high rating, the rankings being 12th, 13th, 13th, and 8th. The relatively high ranking (8th) for student-higher-education expenditures from all sources in relation to personal income is explained partly by the high relative outlays for student higher education vis-à-vis all expenditures for higher education.

Capital expenditures are also low, since they are only about one-third of operating expenditures in this one year. As might be expected, the contribution to higher education of state and local revenue is only a little more than 2 per cent as against a national average of 4 per cent. Net exports of students are roughly 13,000 or 14,000, or 4 per cent of the total, this indicating some exploitation of other states.

New York State has a very high percentage yield of corporate income and personal income tax, 52 per cent of the total, but it has no general sales tax. Despite that fact it ranks 19th in the state taxes per capita. It should be noted, however, that the city of New York has a large sales tax.

The U.S. Office of Education enrollment figures include both part-time and full-time students and exclude most of the students in community colleges who are enrolled in terminal programs. Our rough calculation looks as if total state expenditures for institutions of higher learning were divided by an enrollment figure which omits students enrolled in terminal programs but for whom state expenditure is made. Moreover, there are state expenditures of around $10 million going to the municipal colleges of New York City, but I doubt if any of the students there are counted as state students. In the case of community colleges, the state pays one-third of current expense for all students—both terminal and continuing—but only the continuing, or degree-credit, students would be included in the U.S. Office of Education enrollment.*

* Paraphrased from letter of P. Cowen, division of research in higher education in New York State.

Of the seven items in my questionnaire, only research appears in the budget. Research includes outlays for overhead not specifically included under research.

The data included in my original table apparently does not include support by New York State to the State Retirement System on behalf of state-university and contract-college employees, estimated at $3,631,000; state scholarship grants of $5,105,000; state assistance to City College of New York of $6.5 million; and $1.8 million for assistance to community colleges' operating expense. Of the state appropriation expenditures of $36.5 million, $9.3 million were for organized research and extension, community services, and the like. Another estimated $2.2 million were expended to support elementary and secondary public schools operating in conjunction with 11 colleges of education for demonstration and practice-teaching purposes. The excluded items from the state budget for tuition, endowment earnings, and private gifts amounted to $3.8 million. In all, $27 million in 1956–57 and $54 million in 1960–61 were excluded from state figures for higher education. Hence state, not IHL, totals substantially underestimate public funds for higher education.*

NORTH CAROLINA

The burden for the state is very high, both on the basis of the number of students to be educated in relation to the population, and on the basis of the cost per student in public institutions in relation to per capita personal income. In the latter category North Carolina is third in the nation, with the adjusted expenditures per student 82 per cent of the per capita income. Like most Southern states, the capacity to pay is very low and effort much higher. State and local taxes in relation to personal income are somewhat below average. State per capita taxes are somewhat above average, and expenditures on education in relation to personal income are high, though for higher education they are just average. Achievement is low, but high in relation to burdens and capacity.

That undergraduate full-time resident enrollment is only 11 per cent less than total enrollment means a large proportion of full-time students, and to that extent, on a national scale, expenditures per unit are less than otherwise might be assumed. Capital expenditures are also relatively low, ranking last in the ratio of state and local support of public institutions of higher learning to college-age population.

The 16-state study reveals that North Carolina is 11th in the per capita expenditures for students of higher learning by state and local governments; it does much better when the expenditures are related to personal

* I owe this paragraph to President Thomas H. Hamilton of the State University of New York and C. H. Foster, controller of the State University.

income, with rankings of 6th, 2d, and 2d. In other words, among the 16 high-income states North Carolina's record looks much better than when compared to the 48 states. This is especially true because the criterion for the 16 states is expenditures on *all* higher education rather than on public higher education in relation to personal incomes, for here the ratings are 2d and 2d among the 16 states. The influence of the private institutions is great.

In the years 1950 to 1959, taxes did not rise as much as in the nation, and higher education expenditures rose considerably less than taxes. North Carolina obtains 26 per cent of its income from corporate income and personal income taxes, a proportion substantially above the average. Nevertheless, its tax receipts per capita in the state rank it only 32d.

The net import of students into the state is about 6,200, or 12 per cent. This, of course, suggests a substantial amount of subsidizing of students from out of state, and therefore somewhat lower resources available for the students within the state.[27]

NORTH DAKOTA

North Dakota is a state with large area and small population. Like most agricultural states, the burden is high, capacity rather low, and the effort runs from high to very high. In fact, in the relationship of state and local taxes per $1,000 of personal income, North Dakota is one of the top states in the nation. Its expenditures for education and higher education in relation to personal income are also high. Enrollment in relation to college-age population is average, but public enrollment in relation to total enrollment is among the highest in the nation. With this high enrollment in public IHL the adjusted dollar expenditure per enrollee tends to be low.

In part because of the slow economic developments in the state, taxes have not risen even half as much as the national average; but expenditures on education have risen somewhat more than taxes, and higher education takes a very large part of the total educational budget, in fact more than half. Another indication of the unusual efforts is that 6 per cent of the tax revenue, both state and local, is taken for public higher education, with full-time undergraduate enrollment as much as 93 per cent of the total, an indication that the national rating per student is lower than it at first sight seems to be. The state exports, net, about 6 per cent of its students. Despite reliance on corporate income and personal income taxes for only 10 per cent of its revenue, the state ranks 5th in the state tax revenues in the nation. This is explained in no small part by the high unit costs of carrying on state services in sparsely populated states.

The report of the state auditor and the North Dakota Budget Bureau reveals that state appropriations represent excess of expenditures over income. Income is deducted from expenses to get the state's appropriation to the university and other state colleges. President George W. Starcher of the University of North Dakota writes me that tuition, earmarked taxes, and income for organized research are included in the budget but endowment earnings, private gifts, and net income from auxiliary services are excluded. These are not large items.[28]

OHIO

Burden is low, capacity very high to high, effort low to very low, and the achievements are about average, reflecting low efforts and high capacity. A record somewhat better than average for enrollment in relation to college-age population is partly explained by the large contributions of the private institutions; but public in relation to total enrollment is low. On the basis of adjusted dollar expenditures for public institutions per enrollee the record is somewhat better than average.

The 16-state study shows a moderate achievement—8th among the 16 large states; but on effort the general position agrees with my own study, for the ratings are 10th, 11th, 15th, and 15th for the four measures of effort. It must be recalled that for the 16 high-income states efforts generally tend to be less than in the poorer states, and these ratings therefore put Ohio fairly low. Of the state and local tax revenues only 3⅕ per cent go for higher education.

Ohio is another state with no corporate income or personal income tax. It is not surprising, therefore, that it ranks 43d in state taxes per capita.[29]

In one respect the Ohio record is remarkable. In an advertisement in *The New York Times* (November 13, 1960) the authorities boast that more than 97 per cent of the state's residents are within 25 miles of a college.

OKLAHOMA

Oklahoma is a low-income state. Burden is high, capacity low, effort from high to very high. Achievement measured by the percentage of college-age students in IHL is high, as is the proportion of public enrollment to total enrollment. In the public institutions adjusted dollar expenditures per enrollee are low and similarly for state and local expenditures. The latter two, of course, reflect the large public enrollment.

On the whole, taxes rose much less than in the nation, again reflecting the state of the economy. And outlays on higher education rose even less than taxes in the years 1950 to 1959. A strong effort is suggested by 5 per cent of expenditures on public higher education in relation to state and local tax revenue.

Oklahoma's corporation income and personal income taxes provide only 10 per cent of the total state revenue, a fact explained in part by the nature of the economy. Oklahoma ranks 20th, however, in per capita state taxes, a relatively high figure for a state of relatively low per capita income.[30]

OREGON

The burden is average; the capacity, high to very high; effort, high to very high; achievements, high on the average and very high for enrollment in relation to college-age population. This state is a high-income state. Unlike many high-income states it also makes a large effort on the basis of all relevant variables.

That 95 per cent of the enrollment is undergraduate full-time resident suggests that the unit expenditures are lower in relation to other states than would otherwise be indicated.

From 1950 to 1959 state taxes did not rise as much as might be expected, and less than the national average. But higher education expenditures rose twice as much as taxes in the nine years, and take a relatively large part of total educational expenditures. Also capital expenditures were large in this year, being almost two-thirds of operating expenditures. On the basis of expenditures in public institutions per student, the burden is relatively high in relation to per capita income.[31]

Oregon's tax system, it may be said, is relatively progressive, for the state raises 55 per cent, the highest in the nation, from personal income and corporation income tax but does not have a general sales tax. Nevertheless its per capita state taxes put it 8th in the nation.

PENNSYLVANIA

Pennsylvania is a rich state. The burden of higher education as measured by the percentage of college-age population to total population is average, but when measured by public expenditures per student in relation to personal per capita income the rating is low. Capacity is above average and effort is very low, except that it is high on the basis of total state tax revenue per capita. In the other three categories the effort is very low.

Achievements also tend to be low for total enrollment in relation to college-age population, and very low for enrollment in public institutions in relation to college-age population. As is often true for states with relatively small public and higher education enrollments, achievements on adjusted dollar expenditures for public IHL per enrollee are very high, and similarly for state and local expenditures per enrollee are high.

The 16-state study shows Pennsylvania's achievement as 7th among the

16 states on the basis of estimated student-higher-education expenditure per full-time-student equivalent as a percentage of the United States— 4 per cent above the national average. But the four measures of effort in the 16 states do not reveal a high standing for Pennsylvania; in fact, its ratings are 16th, 15th, 14th, and 14th, again suggesting very low effort, even in comparison with the rich states, which generally show low effort.

In the years 1950 to 1959 taxes rose about as much as the average over the country, but higher education rose only about 80 per cent as much as taxes. It is not surprising that of the total state and local tax revenue only 1.2 per cent went to higher education, a very low percentage compared to a national average of 4 per cent. With no income tax, Pennsylvania raises 14 per cent of its state tax revenue from corporate income taxes. It is not surprising, therefore, that it ranks 45th in the per capita tax burden. It is also very low in state and local support of capital expenditures in relation to college-age population for the one year under consideration.[32]

RHODE ISLAND

The burden as measured by the relationship of college-age population to population is very low, but when measured by the expenditures (adjusted for public IHL per enrollee to per capita income, it is high [above average]). Effort is decidedly below average on all four counts. In 1950 to 1959 taxes rose about 100 per cent; but expenditures on higher education rose twice as much relatively. Undergraduate enrollment, full time, is 91 per cent of total enrollment, suggesting *relatively* lower unit costs than would otherwise seem likely. Low effort is also suggested by the 2.4 per cent of state and local revenue going to higher education. Achievement is high. Rhode Island is without an income tax, and its corporate income tax yields only 10 per cent of state tax revenue. Though the state was 17th in per capita income, in per capita state taxes it ranked only 33d. Though its expenditures on capital in relation to total operating expenditures were not much out of line with the others, public capital outlays were low in relation to college-age population.

Since about 2,600 students are (net) imported from other states and abroad, Rhode Island to a considerable extent finances higher education of students from elsewhere.[33]

SOUTH CAROLINA

South Carolina is typical of the very poor Southern states: the burden is very high. The percentage of adjusted expenditures per student in 1958, as compared to per capita personal income, puts South Carolina 5th in the nation, with a ratio of 73.7 per cent: in other words, higher education is relatively very expensive. Capacity is very low; effort is about average and therefore high compared to capacity. And what is more, in total expenditures for education in relation to state and local taxes the effort is high.

The poverty of the state, despite the relatively high effort, accounted for very low enrollment in higher education in relation to college-age population. Enrollment in public institutions is also relatively low. But adjusted dollar expenditures in relation to enrollee is relatively high for public institutions. Since undergraduate enrollment is 85 per cent of total enrollment and therefore part-time students a relatively small proportion, the national rating of unit costs is somewhat reduced.

Moreover, capital expenditures are very low.

The questionnaire returned by the University of South Carolina suggests that, except for tuition, all applicable categories under section 3 are excluded from the budget. The budget gives a similar picture for all IHL. Tuition fees are directed to the General Revenue fund, from which appropriations are made to supplement income obtained by IHL.

SOUTH DAKOTA

South Dakota's burden is high; capacity varies from low to average; effort as measured by state and local taxes in relation to personal incomes is very high; but, in part because of the low per capita income, taxes per capita are very low. Educational expenditures, both general and higher, in relation to personal income are very high. In general, then, the effort is high. Achievement as measured by enrollment in relation to college-age population and enrollment in public institutions in relation to total enrollment is high. But as is true so often in states of this kind, adjusted dollar expenditures in public IHL per enrollee on the basis of state and local expenditures are low.

The full-time undergraduate enrollment is 94 per cent of the total, suggesting perhaps a somewhat lower unit expenditure than otherwise would be the case.

From 1950 to 1959 taxes rose less than one-third, much less than the average of $1\frac{1}{3}$ for the nation; educational expenses rose by $1\frac{1}{3}$, and higher education by $1\frac{1}{2}$, suggesting strong efforts to improve the program of public higher education. What is more, public higher education accounted for 70 per cent of educational expenditures.

A striking feature of the South Dakota situation is that the state raises only 1 per cent of its total income from corporate and personal income taxes. In fact, it has no personal income tax. Yet it rates 2d in the nation in per capita taxes at the state level. Explanation of this in no small part is the high unit cost of government in a state with low population, and also substantial efforts to expand the governmental function. Public expenditures on construction are above the average in relation to college-age population.

Of the items under section 3 only tuition is relevant, $800,000 of which is excluded. The other items are small.

TENNESSEE

Tennessee is a poor state. Burden is very high, capacity very low, effort is slightly below average but in relation to capacity is high.

Taxes and expenditures on higher education on the whole rose less than in the nation in the 1950s. Achievements are low or very low, except that the adjusted dollar expenditures for public IHL on the basis of enrollment is average.

The yield of personal income and net corporation income taxes was only 8 per cent of the total state taxes, and this partly explains the low per capita yield of the state taxes, though this yield is high compared to the rating in per capita income.[34]

Tennessee is also a state that has large imports of students, net imports numbering 9,650, or 21 per cent, and therefore it heavily subsidizes other states, a factor that perhaps should be weighted heavily in view of the low status of higher education.

TEXAS

The burden is a little higher than average on one criterion and low on another. Capacity is average and low. Effort on the whole is low, though somewhat higher when measured by the expenditures for education or for higher education in relation to personal income. Achievements are high on the basis of enrollment in relation to college-age population, and a little better than average for public enrollment in relation to total enrollment. But adjusted dollar expenditures on public IHL per enrollee rating is very low; in relation to state and local outlays, low.

Among the 16 states Texas comes out last in the achievement measure, and for effort, 9th, 8th, 10th, and 12th, ratings not really out of line with ours for effort. The state is, however, rather low on graduate students, a fact tending to depress its record to some extent when compared with other states.

It should be noted, however, that 5¼ per cent of state and local tax revenues go to higher education, a relatively high percentage.

The tax structure to some extent explains the position of 36th in per capita state taxes, a ratio substantially below its position in per capita income. It has no corporate or personal income tax or general sales tax.[35]

UTAH

Burden is high on one criterion and low on the other. Capacity is average, but effort is unusually high, ranging from high to high plus, and especially high on the basis of state and local educational or higher educational expenditures in relation to personal income. In view of these strong efforts it is not surprising that Utah is second in the nation in college attendance in relation to college-age population. Unit expenditures for public IHL are, however, low and very low.

One important reason for this low unit expenditure is undoubtedly the very large imports of students, amounting to 40 per cent of the residents of Utah in IHL in Utah, a fact explained undoubtedly by the great appeal of the location of the mother church of the Latter-day Saints.

The large efforts are also suggested by $7\frac{1}{2}$ per cent of state and local tax revenue that are spent on higher education, a proportion almost twice as much as the national average.[36]

VERMONT

The burden is high, capacity a little below average, and effort unusually high, two measures for the last giving a high rating and two others a very high rating. Ratio of enrollment to those of college age is high, but enrollment in public institutions is low. As is often true with states with low public enrollment, unit expenditures are high or very high on the basis of state and local expenditures or on the basis of expenditures of public IHL.

There are two striking aspects to Vermont's situation: One is that though taxes from 1950 to 1959 rose less than 100 per cent, expenditures on higher education rose in excess of seven times. Second, the high unit cost in part is related to the size of the state.

Another interesting feature of the Vermont situation is the very large in-migration. Total enrollments are almost 3,500 more than Vermont residents in Vermont IHL—a net in-migration of 70 per cent. Hence institutions in Vermont to a considerable extent subsidize students from the outside. (But we should allow for the source of funds financing such institutions as Bennington and Middlebury.)

Again, Vermont is the first state in the nation in the per capita state taxes, again related to size. High taxes are related to its raising 30 per cent of tax revenue through personal income tax and corporate net income tax. There is no general sales tax.[37]

These large efforts are reflected in high enrollment in relation to college-age population, and also high unit costs or expenditures per enrollee in public institutions. The ratio of public enrollment to total is, however, low.

It should be noted that almost all students are full time and undergraduate. To that extent in the national rating the position of Vermont is not quite so high as it otherwise seems to be.

Vermont is at the head of the nation in the percentage of adjusted expenditures per student in state universities in relation to per capita personal income, with a percentage of 84.4 per cent. This is indeed a heavy burden and a high unit cost, especially in a state with relatively low income.

VIRGINIA

Virginia's burden is a little higher than average as measured by the relation of college-age population to total population, and shares with Vermont a very high burden as measured by public expenditures per enrollee in relation to total per capita personal income. Capacity is low, and efforts very low or low except average for total state tax revenue per capita.

As might be expected from this capacity and effort, ranking is low for both the ratio of enrollment to total college-age population and public enrollment in relation to total enrollment. In such situations the unit expenditures tend to be high or very high per enrollee.

The state tends to export students (net) by 7 to 8 per cent, thus putting part of the burden of higher education on other states or the District of Columbia.

Since 1950 higher education expenditures have risen more than twice as fast as taxes of state government. Public expenditures for capital purposes is low in relation to the national standard for this one year.

Despite the fact that Virginia raises 35 per cent of its income through personal income and net corporate taxes, it is 40th in the tax revenue per capita and has no general sales tax.[38]

WASHINGTON

The burden is low, capacity high; effort varies from average for two indices to high and very high for the other two. Achievements on the whole are high. The high effort is also suggested by the 6 per cent state and local taxes spent on higher education. From 1950 to 1959 expenditures on higher education did not, however, rise as much as tax receipts. With no corporate income or personal income tax the state's per capita state revenues in 1959 were just about average.[39]

WEST VIRGINIA

The burden is very high; capacity, low to very low; efforts, average to low but higher than capacity; achievements, in general low, particularly low or very low for the relationship of enrollment to college-age population but high for public enrollment in relation to total enrollment. Its low per capita state tax revenue is explained partly by the absence of a corporate or personal income tax.

WISCONSIN

Burden is average, capacity high to very high, efforts high and average minus on two criteria. Achievements also tend to be around average.

Capital expenditures are relatively low in comparison with operating, and also in the proportion of public capital expenditures per member of college-age population.

Wisconsin depends heavily on corporate income and personal income taxes, for these yield 45 per cent of the state revenue. This partly explains the fact that Wisconsin is 12th in state tax revenues per capita. Higher-education expenditures had tended to rise more than taxes from 1950 to 1959, and higher-education expenditures at 55 per cent of total education expenditures were high.

The 16-state study shows that in achievements among the 16 states Wisconsin was low, namely, 15th. The effort indices indicate ranks of 5th, 4th, 8th, and 13th. These check reasonably well with the first two indices of effort in my study, namely, for total tax in relation to personal income and state per capita taxes.

William H. Young, assistant to the president of the University of Wisconsin, provided me with the following: he says quite rightly that the expenditures of state IHL should not be compared with state tax revenue because these expenditures generally include large sums that are not from state tax revenue.[40]

WYOMING

The burden is high on one measure and low on another. Capacity is a little above average, efforts are very high on all counts except high on the ratio of public expenditures on higher education to state and local tax revenue. Achievements are average on enrollment in relation to college-age population, very high on public enrollment in relation to total enrollment, and a little below average for unit expenditures (public).

This is a typical state with very small population and high unit costs, and with higher education expenditures in relation to state and local tax revenues high, from 6 to 7 per cent. For 1950 to 1959, however, the efforts were indeed rather weak as measured by a rise of taxes of more than 100 per cent against that of higher education by only 15 per cent.

Net exports of students are very large, numbering 1,420, or roughly 23 per cent of residents in IHL.

Despite the fact that there is no personal income or corporation income tax, partly explained by the economy of the state, Wyoming ranks 9th in state taxes per capita, again a fact related to high unit costs.[41]

* * *

This detailed examination does not lend itself to a summary. But I should add that by 1970, burdens will rise, and at a very uneven rate. Where per capita incomes rise greatly, as well as population, the additional costs may not be a great obstacle. But even a state like California may have its problems. Its relative growth has been in numbers, not in per capita income. Of the 16 states studied by Chambers, the largest increases in appropriations were for Nevada, Hawaii, Colorado, and Kentucky, in that order; the smallest, for Vermont, Kansas, Mississippi, New Jersey, and Maryland. New York and California were in the middle. But estimates of enrollment increases are also significant—compare 290 and 230 per cent rises for Florida and California, respectively, and 79 per cent for Kansas, and 164 per cent for the country from 1950 to 1970.[42]

FOOTNOTES

[1] I appreciate very much some help I have had from President Richard A. Harvill, University of Arizona, on these matters, as well as a report from the state Office of Education, on the university and two state colleges. The latter suggests that the state government controls only student fees and state and local government contributions and does not control endowment, Federal government contributions, private benefactions, sales and services, and miscellaneous sources. To this extent expenditures are larger than suggested by the state expenditures as usually presented.

[2] On the basis of a letter from Marcus Halbrook, director of the State of Arkansas Legislative Council, of Apr. 21, 1960, and accompanying documents, e.g., the *Budget Manual*, it is clear " . . . that the State-appropriated funds are considered in the State budget for each institution of higher learning. All other income from tuition, endowment, gifts, auxiliary services, etc., is considered cash funds of the individual institution." In other words, the total expenditures of the IHL are higher than indicated by state-appropriated funds. Unfortunately, the precise amount is not available.

[3] This is an adjusted figure of expenditures for instruction.

[4] *A Master Plan for Higher Education in California, 1960–1975,* p. 179.

According to a letter from President Kerr of the University of California, the following items were not included in the California state budget but were no doubt income available to the University of California:

	Millions
Tuition paid by students	$ 13.2
Endowment earnings	3.3
Private gifts	4.9
Net income from auxiliary services	.8
Income for organized research not included in private gifts	142.0
Sales and service departments	12.2
United States government grants	12.8

[5] These figures are taken from the American Association of Collegiate Registrars and Admissions Officers, *Home State and Migration of American College Students, Fall, 1958,* 1959. Compare also my Master Table, columns 2 and 6, for migration into and out of public institutions.

[6] I am indebted to T. R. Mason, assistant director of budget and planning, The University of Colorado for bringing to my attention Colorado's documentation and analysis, i.e. the 1960–61 Request Budget. The budget shows for the University of Colorado and for all other IHL under a separate section called "Institutions of Higher Learning: Two Major Resources Financing IHL Expenditure, General Fund and Cash Fund." "Cash Fund" covers apparently all university revenue except for state appropriation from the "General Fund."

[7] Apparently in Connecticut all receipts are included in the budget. We have been unable to get any reply from the state university, but the state budget for 1959–1961 shows expenditures of $34.7 million and receipts of a similar amount. General funds in the budget provide $17.1 million, special funds not appropriated (e.g., auxiliary) $15,645,000, Federal funds $1,162,000, and a few smaller funds bring a total of $34,680,000 in all. This of course does not give us the facts concerning all the other public institutions in the state.

[8] I am indebted to the budget commissioner of the state of Delaware, Mrs. Lillian Martin, chief accountant, and President John A. Perkins of the University of Delaware for some help.

[9] The budget director writes that the following items are included in the budget: tuition paid by students, endowment earnings, private gifts, net income from auxiliary services, earmarked taxes, contributions of local governments, income for organized research not included in private gifts; but excluded are student activity fees ($3.35 million) and a medical enrichment fund, amount not available. But J. W. Bailey of the State Board of Control of Florida writes that net income from auxiliary services, earmarked taxes and income for organized research are excluded.

[10] The questionnaire answered by the University of Idaho suggests that categories such as tuition, endowment, gifts, etc., are excluded from the state budget; therefore in a sense the state expenditures give an inadequate idea of the total expenditures. However, the percentage of the students in junior colleges was 30, a rather high percentage as compared with the national average of 12 per cent, and therefore suggests somewhat higher unit costs than otherwise would be the case.

[11] Letter from T. R. Lath, assistant to the director, superintendent of the budget, state of Illinois, Apr. 7, 1960. Lath brings out the difficulties of comparing unit costs or expenditures. Even in the state of Illinois the enrollments are not always reported in the same manner. Moreover, the Census Bureau differences with HEW result partly from the manner of compilation, for the Census Bureau deals with all kinds of activities as well as education. Included in the budget in Illinois is tuition paid by students, but excluded are University of Illinois endowment earnings, private gifts, and income for organized research not included in private gifts. Net income from auxiliary services is excluded by Teachers College, Southern Illinois University, and the University of Illinois.

H. O. Farber, vice president and comptroller of the University of Illinois, in a letter of Apr. 12, 1960, writes as follows: " . . . the data in the Census Bureau reports were not assembled for the purpose of showing state support of higher education, but the category 'institutions of higher education' is included as one of the functional classifications in total expenditure of state governments, and the Census Bureau is not interested in relating specific income to specific expenditures. Nowhere do the *state appropriations* to the education institutions appear." Farber is also dubious that you can isolate strictly instructional costs on a comparable and meaningful basis. Differences beween the Census Bureau and those of education are explained partly by the fact that "Census Bureau excludes agricultural research and extension and medical school hospitals. For the University of Illinois, these amounted to $11,733,000 in 1957. . . . "

The university deposits tuition and all other income available for the general budget of the university in its separate university income fund in the state treasury. This money is reserved for the exclusive use of the university but not in excess of the amount appropriated by the Legislature. All other income is retained in the university's own treasury. These include endowment, $3,690,000; auxiliary enterprises, $9,000,000; Federal funds, $11,632,000; and sales, $2,166,000.

The budget seems to indicate that university income is included in special funds. Reappropriation from those funds, together with appropriation of general funds, make total state appropriations.

The state budget for higher education excludes the following:

Endowment..................	$ 238,000
Gifts.......................	3,691,000
Auxiliary enterprises..........	9,088,000
Federal funds................	11,632,000
Sales.....................	2,166,000

The top two items suggest some understatement of public funds for instruction.

[12] From Joseph A. Franklin, vice president of the University of Indiana, I find that all items in my list (tuition, endowment income, private gifts, etc.), are excluded. The total is $23 million. But $18 million are for organized research and gross income from auxiliary services, irrelevant for our purposes.

Philip L. Conklin, director of the budget, confirms these exclusions for the state.

[13] President Hancher also warns of distortions in rankings caused by varying amounts of gifts and grants, and also by use of crude enrollment figures rather than full-time-student equivalent. I have tried to contend with these difficulties.

[14] President Frank Dickey of the University of Kentucky writes me that tuition paid by students, endowment earnings, net income from auxiliary services, earmarked taxes, are all included in the budget, but private gifts ($347,000) and income for organized research ($489,000) are excluded. James L. Peel, director of the budget division of Kentucky writes that for all public IHL endowment earnings, private gifts, earmarked taxes, contributions from local government, and income for organized research are excluded.

The detailed budget of the State gives expenditures and receipts. The budget table for each institution gives what is available from appropriations, from general fund and the road fund, adds to this receipts by institutions, and balances the total against total expenditures. Receipts by agencies differ with different schools.

[15] I am indebted to President Floyd H. Elliott of the University of Maine and Chester T. Booth, supervisor of administrator services, Maine State Department of Education for the following: According to President Elliott, all items on my check list are excluded from budget—these are large items in the budget. Tuition, endowment earnings, and private gifts amount to $2.6 million. The state teachers colleges' revenues are available for appropriation to the state for any purpose whatsoever.

[16] Comer S. Coppie, budget analyst of the state of Maryland, said that all the extraneous items like tuition, etc., are included in the budget. H. D. Fisher, controller of the University of Maryland has a somewhat different picture for the

University of Maryland. Parts of tuition are included and excluded; similarly with endowment earnings; private gifts, contributions from local governments are included; income from organized research is excluded.

[17] According to Kenneth W. Johnson, treasurer of the University of Massachusetts, tuition paid by students, endowment earnings, private gifts, net income from auxiliary services, and income for organized research are all excluded from the budget of the University of Massachusetts. The first three items amount to more than $1.2 million. Hence public funds are larger than they seem.

[18] In the state of Michigan the state budget does not include any of such items as organized research, tuition paid by students, private gifts, earmarked taxes, etc. In a letter to the author of Apr. 11, 1960, Robert L. Williams, administrative dean of the University of Michigan, writes that such items as organized contract research and auxiliary enterprises should of course be excluded. These amount to $45 million to the University of Michigan, and since they are self-supporting activities not financed by the State, " . . . we seriously question the charge of such expenditures in institutions of higher learning as if they were state appropriations. . . . all funds of the kind listed are regarded as earnings or income to the University which are not part of the state support budget."

Frank M. Landers, director of the budget division, in a letter of Apr. 15, 1960, also raises some issues about comparability of these various measures. He says, however, that $26.5 million tuition paid by students in the state are included in the state budget and all other items on my questionnaire are excluded. Hence public contributions are larger than so far indicated.

[19] In the budget, revenue from IHL inclusive of the University of Minnesota is recorded in the dedicated receipts, part of the General Fund only, the source of these receipts being different for the University of Minnesota than for the state colleges. For 1960–61 there is an entry for state colleges of $2.2 million under tuition and fees. This was reappropriated, together with additional appropriation of nondedicated receipts of General Fund of $6.8 million to finance the expenditures of all state colleges. The University of Minnesota has two entries in dedicated receipts of the General Fund, both also reappropriated, one originating from the hospital for $3.9 million, the other, labeled "maintenance," for $11.1 million.

University maintenance, 1958–59	Thousands
Reappropriated balance	$ 374
General revenues	23,084
Student course fees	6,262
Receipts, special income	3,820
Total	33,540

[20] The executive secretary of the board of trustees of IHL in Mississippi, E. R. Jobe, in a letter of May 10, 1960, wrote that, except for private gifts and income for organized research not included in gifts, all the other categories are included in the budget. The budget (1960–62, pp. 57 and 62) gives the budgets of the state institutions; revenue includes student fees, government appropriation, endowment income, organized activities, and other income. Private gifts amount to $850,000 and organized research $1,560,000. Enrollment in junior colleges is roughly about twice as large as for the nation generally, and this suggests that the unit expenditures on a national ranking are really somewhat higher than are suggested by over-all categories.

[21] According to President H. K. Newburn of Montana State University, all categories, e.g., tuition, gifts, are included in the state budget. From the state budget it

appears that revenues of IHL are credited to special funds from which they are reappropriated.

[22] The state's budget shows appropriations to state teachers colleges and the university by funds. There are the General Fund, License Fee and Cash funds, Federal funds, Institution of Military Building Fund. Whether revenue of the IHL passes through these funds for reappropriation is not clear from the budget.

Joseph Soshnik, comptroller of the University, notes that financing of IHL includes (1) "funds designated in Nebraska budgeting as 'Cash Funds' (e.g., tuition and fees, income from organized activities, cash reimbursements, etc.), (2) Federal funds in support of teaching programs; (3) endowment earnings." (These are not from the usual state revenues.)

[23] Charles J. Armstrong, President of the University of Nevada, writes me that one reason for the high unit costs in Nevada is " . . . that it is required by law to provide a number of regulatory services for the State government." President Armstrong also reveals that expenditures are larger than suggested by appropriations from state funds. Excluded are $489,000 of tuition, endowment earnings and private gifts—especially relevant for our purposes.

The state budget shows the resources for the university originating from two budgeted sources: (1) General Fund and (2) All Other Funds and Revenues. The latter includes Fees and General, Special Grants, Federal Subventions, County Subventions and Sales, etc.

[24] President Eldon Johnson of the University of New Hampshire, in a letter of Apr. 25, 1960, writes that the only special item of all these special items included in the state budget is tuition paid by students, $261,000. This is not clear from the budget. Probably President Johnson had in mind the deduction of tuition from the amount requested for appropriation. Appropriation consists of Expenditures, minus Restricted Revenue, and balances the difference, giving "Net Appropriation." There is nothing in the report of the university indicating that restricted revenue and balances be subtracted from the expenditures.

[25] Three questionnaires were returned; the one filled by the State University of New Jersey suggests all categories are excluded; the one filled by the Commissioner for Higher Education for the State Colleges puts income from auxiliary services as included and marks the rest as either "does not apply" or "excluded." The state budget director, on the other hand, marks everything as included.

From the budget of the state of New Jersey it appears that two procedures are followed: One is for the state colleges, in which *part* of the revenue of the state colleges is poured into the General Treasury Funds—this part of income including regular tuition, miscellaneous cafeteria and boarding-hall fees, summer, extension, field, graduate fees; all expenditures of the state colleges appearing in the budget are covered on the other side by State Appropriations. Another part of the state's colleges revenue is credited to "Revenues Dedicated and Not Budgeted." This part of the income includes student service fees, student teaching fees, clinical service charges, room and board excess receipts, etc. In addition some Federal aid to state colleges is also not budgeted.

For the State University of New Jersey the procedure is different. Expenditures are scheduled and totaled; out of this total are deducted "General Services Income," "Auxiliary Service and Special Fund Income," and "State University Scholarship." The balance, roughly one-half of the total, is the state appropriation to the State University.

[26] I am indebted to John Perovich, comptroller of the University of New Mexico, and the Department of Financial Administration for the State for making it clear

that all the categories under consideration are included in the budget. The state budget shows that appropriations to IHL that enter into the Over-all Budget are appropriations to meet the excess of expenditures over income of IHL. There is no apparent indication in the budget that any IHL revenue is included. Resources of IHL are shown as "State Appropriations" and other income.

[27] I am indebted to President William Friday of the University of North Carolina and Charles Holloman, budget analyst for education in the state of North Carolina, for the statement that all items are included among the items earlier mentioned except that endowment earnings, $199,000 for 1956–57, were excluded, and also about $175,000 for retirement of state employees. The budget gives for the University of North Carolina total expenditures, out of which estimated receipts have been deducted to get the amount of appropriation. Deductions include tuition, student fees, endowment and trust funds, distributive education receipts from extension and public services, receipts from maintenance and operation of buildings, etc.

[28] President Starcher is critical of the use of per capita tax revenues because they ignore variations in per capita income. (Indeed this should be kept in mind.) He also points out that the tax burden can be misinterpreted, because to some extent, of course, the burden is passed on to residents of other states. This is particularly true for corporation taxes and perhaps even to some extent for some of the other taxes.

[29] I am indebted to Gordon B. Carson, vice president of business and finance at the Ohio State University, letter of Apr. 19, 1960, for the following: We should allow for " . . . those states which are largely agrarian in makeup and thus have less incentive to provide higher education for a large number of young people than do those states where the competition of industry forces an interest in learning. The expenditures of the state government in supporting farming and secondary education should also be noted. In some states these expenditures constitute an extremely high percentage of the total budget and make it difficult for higher education to get adequate support. . . . "

Carson also notes that if capital expenditures are included, this is misleading, because many states have crash programs. Where population tends to rise, there is an increased awareness of the need for additional expenditures for higher education.

According to Carson and the state budget analyst, endowment earnings, private gifts, and net income from auxiliary services ($3.1 million in all) are excluded, and all nontax and nonappropriated funds. Hence outlays are somewhat larger than suggested by *state* figures. The budget analyst agrees with the preceding analysis except that *for the state* he includes $8.9 million for organized research as being excluded. The budget analyst is also skeptical of comparisons because of the peculiar relations of public and private higher education.

The General Fund Revenue side of the budget includes student fees of state colleges, Ohio University, and Ohio State University. No other revenue of IHL seems to be included in the budget. The budget shows only that part of the expenditures covered by General Fund appropriations.

[30] According to Burton Logan, budget director of the state of Oklahoma, only net income from auxiliary services is excluded from the state budget. For the University of Oklahoma, Q. M. Spradling, the controller, suggests the excluded items for *the state* are endowment earnings, $224,000; private gifts, $1,120,000; net income from auxiliary services, $577,000.

The state budget shows that allocations come from appropriated and dedicated funds. For the years 1959–1961 the state's system of higher education was allocated

$50 million, all from appropriated funds. Total operation budget of IHL for the fiscal biennium 1959–1961 was $73 million. This is offset by $50 million of state funds, $23 million from other funds. It is not clear whether other funds are simply deducted from expenditures before budget request is made.

President George L. Cross and Vice President Horace B. Brown are critical of the U.S. Census for an underestimation of population which in turn affects other variables, such as tax burdens, per cent of college-age population, etc.

[31] I am indebted to Leon D. Margosian, administrator, Management Division of the State Government for the following: all items are included in the budget of 1959–1961. The budget of the Board of Higher Education amounts to $54.8 million general funds and $34.1 million dedicated funds. The dedicated fund is balanced against receipts to the dedicated fund of roughly equal amounts—e.g., instructional and general purposes, receipts = $15.2 million; expenditures = $15.4 million; auxiliary, receipts = $12.5 million; expenditures = $12.1 million.

[32] I owe the following to David R. Baldwin, budget secretary and deputy secretary of administration, state of Pennsylvania. Except for tuition, all categories of expenditures under my listing are excluded from the state budget.

The state budget itself does not suggest any items of higher education revenue as being included in the budget. In the budget two categories are to be distinguished: (1) state teachers colleges, 14 in number; expenses of those colleges, as is shown in the budget, are financed by general-fund appropriation, by student fees, board, and lodging; (2) for universities, colleges, and other institutions; the budget shows only state aid, and this consists of general-fund appropriations; hence no category in my questionnaire is included in the budget.

[33] I am indebted to President Francis H. Horne and Edmund H. Hallenbeck, Office of Institutional Research, University of Rhode Island, for the following: all items are included in the state budget. They point out, quite correctly, that assessing her ability as measured by per capita income Rhode Island rates fairly high, and on a basis of state financial support, they rank very low. They also point out that the *Compendium on State Government Finance* lists Rhode Island's current operating expenditures, less commercial, at $3,945,000 for 1957, while their state budget data lists state appropriation for IHL in 1957 at $2,955,000. I was also criticized for failing to deal with the difference made by the varying treatment of sponsored research, extension, reapportioned tuition fees and other income. I have taken account of these comments.

[34] According to E. B. Heilman, coordinator of higher education and special schools in the state of Tennessee, all items in my questionnaire are included. But according to the chief budget analyst of the state, Roy S. Nicks, private gifts are excluded. But the budget gives a different picture. For every IHL "programmed expenditures" are given, from which amounts are deducted the expendable receipts to give the state's appropriation. No indication is given of inclusion of "expendable receipts" in the budget.

[35] The items for the University of Texas under section 3 that are excluded, according to former President Logan Wilson of the University of Texas, are endowment earnings, private gifts, net income from auxiliary services. This applies only to the University of Texas.

The state budget reveals that some IHL revenue is included in the budget. For the University of Texas, total resources are (1) appropriations from the General Fund (2) Local Funds, and (3) Available University Funds (less than 2 per cent in 1961). For other state colleges all sources are included in the budget.

[36] Unfortunately the matter of inclusion and exclusion of income for the State

University of Utah is not clearly made by the two respondents. They both agree that private gifts of $1,015,000 are excluded. The vice president for business includes tuition, and the office manager excludes it. The former includes endowment earnings; the latter excludes it ($55,000). Private gifts ($1.016 million) are excluded by both. There is serious disagreement on net income from auxiliary services. Income for organized research of over $4 million is excluded by both. Also excluded are $92,000 of other income by the vice president and $632,000 by the other respondent.

The state budget for 1959–1961 shows appropriations to IHL coming only from General Fund Revenue. Possibly the disagreement of the two officials of the university may be explained by the fact that the vice president classified as included in budget categories those subtracted from total expenditures.

[37] I owe the following to President John T. Fey of the University of Vermont and Dean L. S. Rowell: all items are excluded. These amount to $1.9 million for tuition paid by students; $270,000 for endowment earnings; $228,000 private gifts; $6,822 net income from auxiliary services; $15,200 contributions by local governments; $1,108,000 income for organized research; and $500,000 for other items.

The budget gives no indication that IHL revenue is included except for a very small item.

[38] I owe the following to the director of the budget, state of Virginia, and the comptroller of the University of Virginia. Excluded from the budget are endowment earnings of $878,000, private gifts of $1,578,000, income for organized research of $2,021,000. These latter figures are all for the University of Virginia. These exclusions also apply to the state. On the state basis it is said that net income from auxiliary services are sometimes included and sometimes excluded; and there were other exclusions for the state such as student activities and organized athletics. For fiscal year 1962, $28.9 million of IHL revenue are included in special funds paid into the state budget (apparently tuition is included). Appropriations include funds from General Fund and from Special Funds *paid* into the treasury. For the University of Virginia, $9.9 million are appropriated from the General Fund and $7.9 million from the Special Fund.

[39] I owe the following to President Charles Odegaard, University of Washington: The biennial budget for 1959–1961—$45.4 million come from state appropriations, $30 million from local receipts, that is from receipts of the university. This total includes only operating expenses and excludes trust funds and other items like university and intercollegiate athletic programs. Of the $30 million from local receipts, $14 million are grants and contracts, $6.6 self-sustaining services, $3.3 million from hospital, almost $1 million health science division, $5.2 million university proper.

According to the university, all items in my questionnaire are excluded, but the state budget director says they are all included. The difference may well be explained by varying accounting methods for the Univeristy of Washington vis-à-vis others. The budget director writes me that under the Accounting Act of 1959 public funds (inclusive of IHL) should be included in budget, even if not subject to legislative appropriation.

The state budget director also warns me that the relatively low rank in current expenditures for state IHL in relation to state tax revenues is a reflection of the state's high rank in total tax revenues per capita. The latter in part reflects the low per capita tax revenues by local government in relation to personal income. With serious limitations on the local property tax, a heavier burden on state government results.

Philip Cartwight, associate dean of the university, in a letter to President Odegaard of Apr. 14, 1960, sent along to me, criticizes comparisons based on state tax revenues. For state tax revenues are unusually high in Washington, and local tax revenues are low, and therefore concentration on state revenues gives a distorted picture of the ranking of Washington. Hence the high per capita state tax revenues yield much higher effort than a current study based on state and local taxes.

[40] For the University of Wisconsin the state budget excludes endowment earnings, private gifts, income for organized research, operating, and income from auxiliary services, gross. Amounts involved are $350,000, $4,836,000, $5,327,000, and $7,430,000. Also excluded is hospital, $3.3 million.

The following is from the 1956 Wisconsin budget: The budget presents a General Fund and Segregated Funds (which are financed in part from the General Fund). In addition to financing some of the Segregated Funds, the General Fund finances the Executive Budget and the Revolving Budget. The latter is financed in addition from certain receipts which are reappropriated for purposes prescribed by Wisconsin law: institutional industries, dormitories, cafeteria, student fees, Federal aid, and certain fee and licensing activities form this category.

[41] According to the acting director of finance and budget of the University of Wyoming, tuition and endowment earnings are included in the state budget; other items are excluded. The president of the university writes that all items are included. The state budget includes General Funds, from which appropriations are made, and Federal Funds and other income. The last two pass through the budget for reappropriation.

[42] Figures from Educational Number of the *Saturday Review of Literature,* Jan. 21, 1961, and M. M. Chambers, *The Campus and the People,* 1960, p. 58.

PART SIX

MANAGEMENT OF PRODUCTIVE FUNDS

Chapter 28

MANAGEMENT: VIEWS AND HISTORY

At the outset let me say that current gifts and income from endowment contribute a relatively small part of the total resources of institutions of higher learning. This is especially true for public institutions. In 1958–59, according to the 1958–59 survey of the *Council for Financial Aid,* state-controlled institutions received only $140 million from gifts, and a large part (39 per cent) was from government. But gifts for public IHL are becoming more important and in the years 1955 to 1959 rose by 131 per cent as compared to 94 per cent for all IHL.

I shall say little here on investment policies of public institutions, since their endowment, except for a relatively few institutions, is so small. Their problems are also somewhat different from those of the private schools. Either because of restrictions on investments or reliance on government appropriations, public institutions often avoid equities and invest primarily in fixed-interest-bearing assets: they invest rather heavily in real estate and (in so far as they invest in equities) in domestic corporations. But under pressure of local interests they are forced to divest themselves of real estate which pays no taxes and gradually to seek investments on a national market. However, of late the investment policies of public institutions have tended to become less restrictive. For example, oil was discovered on 2.1 million acres of land given to the University of Texas in 1933. This land, once considered an oilman's graveyard, now produces 41 million barrels of oil each year. Under 1956 constitutional amendments 50 per cent of the permanent fund may be invested in corporate securities and guaranteed real estate mortgages.[1]

There is a fairly heavy concentration of endowment funds among a limited number of private institutions, and endowment income has been losing ground relative to the total income of IHL. In 1957–58, 16 IHL accounted for 56 per cent of the $4.83 billion of endowment funds. From 1929–30 to 1956–57 endowment income fell from 12 per cent to 5 per cent of educational and general income, or by about 60 per cent. Current gifts, however, rose from 5 to 9 per cent, and the total amount of gifts relative to endowment income each year steadily increases. In 1957–58 the total of private gifts and grants, according to the Office of Education, was $325 million. For 1958–59 the Council for Financial Aid to Education estimated gifts at $413 million for current operations and $339 million for capital purposes, or $752 million in all.[2]

On the whole the history suggests that the management of endowments has been rather conservative. Arnett, one of the leaders in this field, described an investment fund as " . . . a fund which shall be maintained inviolate, income of which shall alone be used." Or again, "Safety of principal is the first consideration; otherwise the financing of the income may be in danger. Size of the income, though important, is secondary."[3]

A famous investment house, Wood, Struthers, and Co., had this to say during the Great Depression: "The average board of trustees is concerned, not mainly with eliminating risk, but primarily with reaching a wise decision as to the amount of risk that may be properly accepted in order to expand income." This is a judicious statement which suggests that it was impossible to invest without taking some risks. Yet this company recommended that colleges should hold no more than 10 per cent of their investments in common stocks, and also said: "Trustees who have put so much of their productive funds into railroad securities need not feel unduly apprehensive about the future of the best railroad securities." There were not many who at that time foresaw the future of the railroad industry.

By the late 1940s the principles of investment of college funds had changed considerably. One observer, N. F. Willoughby, insisted that income requirements should be reasonable and a proper balance of capital risk and income should be assured. The writer proceeded as follows:[4]

A properly constituted endowment fund should have investments in high grade bonds and common stocks. . . . Common stocks are the best means of gaining capital appreciation, and it therefore follows that a college's relative holding of stocks and bonds should vary according to the state of the market, a greater proportion being held in stocks in bull markets, and defensive bonds in bear markets.

Stocks first began to appear as substantial investments in the financial holdings of colleges in the 1830s. Until that time almost all investments were in notes, mortgages, advances, and real estate. Bonds began to play an important part after the Civil War, with the large issues of government securities and railroad bonds. In the latter part of the nineteenth century, bonds became more important and stocks less so. The large increase in stock investments began only after 1929. Harvard University's general investments as shown in Table 28-1 is a good example of this tendency.

College financial officers seem much more inclined now than in the past

TABLE 28-1
Harvard University—General Investments

Period	Total general investment	Bonds[a]	All stocks	Stocks,[b] per cent of total		Real estate[c]	Notes,[d] mortgages, and advances
				Common	Preferred		
1956–1957	$500,962,260.00	37.17	61.67	58.67	3.00	0.11	0.44
1949–1950	245,119,149.56	46.64	46.38	37.95	8.43	1.51	5.47[e]
1939–1940	124,918,616.96	50.08[f]	44.31	33.68	10.63	3.40	2.21[f]
1929–1930	101,811,043.48	54.16	26.77	20.63	6.14	12.22	6.85
1919–1920	37,048,275.14	56.64	17.16	11.53[g]	5.63[g]	14.52	11.68
1909–1910	19,060,268.55	56.28	19.34	17.35[g]	1.99[g]	15.46	8.92
1899–1900	9,934,284.67	55.94	8.88[h]	.....	.....	25.69	9.49
1889–1890	5,503,693.06	48.69	9.23	4.77	4.46	31.14	10.94
1879–1880	2,918,952.38	30.78	6.79[h]	.....	.....	31.03[i]	31.40
1869–1870	2,228,659.74	25.60	11.99	.....	.....	32.58[i]	29.83
1859–1860[j]	975,222.27	1.23	20.45	.....	.....	21.75	56.57
1849–1850	727,780.86	.....	16.65	.....	.....	20.59	62.76
1839–1840	515,809.49	.....	15.53	.....	.....	21.23	63.24
1830–1831[k]	398,906.70	.....	3.84	.....	.....	18.95	77.21

[a] Bonds include United States government bonds.

[b] Stocks have been separated into common and preferred when possible.

[c] Real estate excludes investment in college buildings in accordance with procedure followed by all the treasurers.

[d] Current practice of the treasurer is to include notes with bonds rather than with mortgages.

[e] Includes $8 million in short-term loans and $3 million in cash listed by treasurer as investment funds.

[f] Notes are included with bonds in this year.

[g] Treasurer includes 1,337 shares of preferred stock with common.

[h] Treasurer does not specify common or preferred.

[i] Excludes unoccupied lands listed separately by treasurer.

[j] Prior to 1867, the corporation does not distinguish between special and general investments. Therefore, totals from this period back represent total investment rather than general investment.

[k] List of general investments was not published in 1829–1830. 1830–1831 has been substituted.

Source: Based upon summaries of investment compiled from the published reports of the treasurers for the years indicated. Book value has been used except for the years 1939–40, 1949–50 and 1956–57, when estimates of market value were given by the treasurer. Totals above are lower than actual because of the exclusion of cash, which was necessary because of the impossibility of separating cash available for investment from cash for current use.

to adopt common investment policies. For example, in 1900 Harvard had 9 per cent of its investments in mortgages, Yale 38 per cent. Harvard had 26 per cent of its investments in real estate, Yale 5 per cent. Even in 1930 Harvard had 27 per cent of its investments in common and preferred stocks and Yale 50 per cent, whereas a large number of independent liberal arts colleges had only 10 per cent in common stocks. In this same period 27 per cent of Yale's investments were in bonds, 54 per cent of Harvard's, and for the independent colleges, 50 per cent. Such large differences in investment policy among major universities are not likely now.[5]

By the 1930s it became increasingly clear that it was difficult to play safe. For example, a trustee of Lehigh University said: "A great criticism against trust companies and trustees charged with the investment of funds is that they have been actuated more by an effort to play safe and according to certain formulas, rather than to exercise personal vigilance and watchful care over not only the preservation, but also the enhancements of funds for which they are held responsible."

It was Oliver Wendell Holmes who said: "Every year, if not every day, we have to wager our salvation upon some prophesy based upon imperfect knowledge."[6]

Looking back, it is easy to see that many mistakes were made. For example, from 1938 to 1947, 12 institutions increased their holdings of bonds from $166 million to $228 million, and the percentages of bonds to total investment from 38.7 to 42.9. By this time the probability and fact of inflation was clearly evident, and this might seem like poor policy. However, this increase is explained in part by the need of supporting the government-bond market in the midst of war, although the sacrifice of income to patriotic impulse varied from college to college. By 1947 Dartmouth had put 13.5 per cent of its total investments in government bonds, and Columbia 14 per cent, whereas Oberlin had 41.5 per cent and Harvard 35 per cent. Even by 1947 these 12 institutions had increased their proportion of investments in common stocks (book value) from 22 to 29 per cent, a relatively small rise in view of the economic conditions. Those with the highest proportion in stocks were Mount Holyoke with 41 per cent, and Harvard with 38: and the lowest proportion, Carnegie with 14 and Columbia with 17 per cent.[7]

FOOTNOTES

[1] See the excellent statement of the treasurer of the University of California, R. M. Underhill, "Investment Problems of the Large State University," *Second Annual Boston Forum on Open-end Investment Companies,* 1945, pp. 9–18; R. M. Underhill, in S. E. Harris (ed.), *Higher Education in the United States: The Economic Problems,* 1960, pp. 245–247; HEW, *College and University Endowment Investments: A Survey as of June 30, 1958,* 1959, p. 3; Council for Financial Aid to Education, *1958–59 Voluntary Support of America's Colleges and Universities,* 1959, pp. 8, 11, 13, 66.

[2] Council for Financial Aid to Education, *1958–1959 Voluntary Support of America's Colleges and Universities,* 1959; HEW, *Statistics of Higher Education, 1955–56: Receipts, Expenditures and Property,* 1959; *Higher Education,* March, 1960; HEW, *College and University Endowment Investments . . . 1957–58,* 1959, pp. 46–48.

[3] J. L. Kirkpatrick, "A Study of University Endowment Fund Investment," unpublished master's thesis, New York University, 1949, p. 24.

⁴ N. F. Willoughby, "Management of Endowment Funds Is a Heavy Responsibility for the College Treasurer and Investment Committee," *College and University Business*, May, 1949.

⁵ *Treasurers' Reports*, Harvard and Yale; *Bulletin of the Association of American Colleges*, 1932, p. 74; cf. Boston Fund, *A Comprehensive Study of Colleges and University Endowment Funds*, 1960.

⁶ S. D. Warriner, "Care and Investment of Endowment Funds with Special Reference to the Budgetary Needs of the Institution," *Proceedings of a Conference of Trustees of Colleges and Universities on the Responsibilities and Problems of Governing Boards of Educational Institutions*, Easton, Pa., Apr. 26, 1935, pp. 67–68.

⁷ J. L. Kirkpatrick, *op. cit.*, pp. 40–49.

Chapter 29

THE CASE FOR COMMON STOCKS

Inflation will probably be with us for many years to come. With trade unions tending to send wages up beyond the amounts justified by increased productivity, with many businesses in semimonopolistic conditions, with farmers guaranteed prices or incomes, with government entrusted with heavy responsibilities which cannot always be financed through taxes, and with our financial institutions not always able to control the inflationary pressures, we may expect continued inflation. It would be a rash economist who would predict less than 2 per cent inflation a year on the average in the next ten years. In such periods there is a strong case for investment in common stocks.

In this connection I introduce a table which reveals that colleges have largely abandoned their earlier policies. By 1950 they held about 40 per cent of their investments in common stocks. In so far as they depend upon investment income, they are likely to suffer if they do not invest much of their funds in equities; bonds pay a fixed return and, therefore, do not offset inflationary pressures. As inflation proceeds, colleges must pay higher prices for services, construction, and supplies, and therefore they need a rising income as prices rise.

At an early date Bump, treasurer of Mount Holyoke College, found that endowment return on X dollars yielded 152.8 in 1932 and only 80.5 in 1943 in relation to commodities (1926 = 100), and 102.3 and 74.9 respectively in relation to educational services. A slight decline in yield at first was offset by a large reduction of prices, and hence the position of IHL really improved. Excessive concern with book values obscured that picture.[1] Later, the rise of prices was costly (e.g., 1943). Unlike insurance companies and banks, IHL are not in a position to meet inflationary pressures by incurring obligations to pay back a *fixed* number of dollars.

One would not expect insurance companies, casualty companies, savings banks, and loan associations to hold as large a proportion of their funds in common stocks as colleges and universities. But in fact investment trusts

428

in 1950 had about 83 per cent of their investments in common stocks—a much larger proportion than colleges and universities with 40 to 45 per cent (Table 29-1). By 1958, however, IHL had increased their investments in common stocks to 48 per cent, investment trusts had reduced theirs to 80 per cent, and 277 common trust funds also had 48 per cent in common stocks.

One important reason for investing in common stocks is the probability of inflationary pressures. In determining his investment policy the average college treasurer or investment officer should require an excess return on bonds of 2 per cent (say) over common stocks in order to recoup the probable losses associated with a rise of prices. In addition, he should expect a rise of returns on bonds over stocks of about 2 to 3 per cent to make up for the growth element (net of risks) which is available to holders of equity investments. In fact, the owners of common stocks are in a strong position to obtain more than what is suggested by average growth; for the corporation is run on behalf of the stockholder, and therefore one might expect the stockholder to gain more than the average given by national growth.

The possibilities of growth are suggested by average corporate profits after taxes of $1.7 billion in the 1930s, $12.2 billion in 1940, and $19 billion from 1950 to 1958, or the rise of GNP in stable dollars from $175 billion in the 1930s to $227 billion in 1940 and $412 billion in 1950–1958. By 1960 the GNP was $503 billion. For the 1960s the range of expected increase at present prices is from $200 billion to $290 billion. Since the price level for the 1950s was about twice that in the 1930s, one can see that the *real* rise in profits and GNP was still of large proportions. To some extent of course the improvements in profits should be associated with the large cyclic decline in the thirties. But the total was substantially higher in the 1950s even than the peak corporate profits after taxes in 1929. All these reasons, then—the inflationary pressures, the operation of the corporation on behalf of the stockholder, and the fact that the normal redemption price of bonds is the same as the amount lent— all these suggest strongly that IHL should hold stocks. I would say they have not moved enough in this direction. This does not mean that stocks are not at some times temporarily overvalued.

Of course the financial officer must weigh present needs against future needs in determining his investment policy. A heavy investment in growth stocks may result in very low current income and much larger incomes later on. If resources of the college are inadequate at the present time, this may not be a wise policy. The university would be sacrificing the interests of its present students and faculty in order to get larger gains, say, a generation later. Some faculty members, aware of excessive investments in growth stocks by their institutions and of their own inadequate

TABLE 29-1

Estimated Holdings of Perpetuity Portfolios and the Estimate of Available Investments, December 31, 1950

(In billions of dollars)

Investors	Total investments (1)	U.S. govt. bonds (2)	Municipal bonds (3)	Corporate bonds (4)	Mortgage debt (5)	Consumer debt (6)	Pfd. stocks (7)	Common stocks (8)	Real estate (9)	Estimated annual growth* (10)
Life insurance companies..........	$ 60.2	$ 13.7	$ 1.1	$23.4	$16.1	$ 2.5	$1.6	$ 0.4	$ 1.4	$ 4.0
Fire and casualty companies........	12.0	5.2	0.7	.8	0.2	....	0.8	3.4	0.9	0.5
Mutual savings banks..............	22.4	10.9	0.2	3.3	8.0	....	....	....	....	1.0
Savings and loan associations......	16.6	1.6	....	1.2	13.8	....	1.0	....	....	1.5
Pension trusts.....................	13.5	4.2	....	5.2	1.0	....	0.2	2.1	....	2.0
Investment trusts..................	3.5	0.2	....	0.1	....	....	0.3	3.0	....	0.2
Colleges and universities..........	3.5	0.7	....	0.5	0.1	....	1.5	1.5	0.4	0.3
Churches and charitable trusts.....	12.0	3.0	0.1	1.0	0.7	....	....	3.7	2.0	0.5
Federal agencies and trusts........	11.9	5.5	0.4	0.6	1.5	3.9	....	....	....	1.5
State and local trusts..............	7.8	7.8	....	....	....	....	0.5	....	....	0.5
Commercial banks..................	104.9	62.0	8.2	3.5	15.0	15.2	....	....	0.5	3.0
Private trusts......................	‡									
Total investments held.............	$268.3	$114.8	$10.7	$39.6	$56.4	$21.6	$5.9	$14.1	$ 5.2	$15.0
Total of all investments available...	$628.8	$186.6	$20.4	$50.7	$74.3	$33.3	$150.0		$113.5	$ 5.0§
Percentage of total held...........	42.7%	61.5%	52.5%	77.6%	75.9%	64.9%	13.3%		4.6%	
Percentage and amount of total available to these funds†......	57.6%	70.0%	60.0%	80.0%	80.0%	64.9%	50.0%		20.0%	
	$362.2	$130.6	$12.3	$40.6	$59.4	$21.6	$ 75.0		$ 22.7	
Balance of potential available.....	$ 93.9	$ 15.8	$ 1.6	$ 1.0	$ 3.0	....	$ 55.0		$ 17.5	$20.0

* Annual increment.
† Includes funds not thus invested.
‡ Unknown.
§ Funds available for reinvestment because of maturities, prepayments, and calls.
Source: H. L. Wells, *Higher Education Is Serious Business*, Harper, 1953, p. 208.

salaries, sense injustices. On the other hand, some growth stocks also yield a substantial current income.[2]

In 1945 Bump emphasized the importance of concentrating on income rather than capital:

> While I believe that investment policies which curb income substantially or for any appreciable length of time are educationally and philosophically un-justifiable, I would not apply the conclusion to similar policies, adopted for such short periods that income is not sacrificed to any considerable degree. In other words, the basis of evaluating investment philosophies should always be income—the dollar medium for procurement of educational services.

The major objective of investment policy is, according to Bump, to obtain maximum income:[3]

> This statement does not specifically refer to security labels, to market values or to book values. It puts the first emphasis on maximum income, where it belongs. If that income is continuous, permanence of principal is implied, but the basis for judgment is to be found in capacity to produce income. As endowment need never be liquidated, hence market values attached to principal can be rated as of secondary importance. . . .

Obviously one can justify investment in growth stocks on the theory that such investments will grow in value, and on the basis of capital gains and dividends the yield would exceed that on other investments. But a decision must be made to sell these stocks if additional income for meeting bills is to be had. If the investors believe in steady growth, then the college holds on to the growth stocks ad infinitum. Income does not become available for use, and current students and faculty are exploited.

In a discussion at my seminar on higher education[4] a vigorous disagreement emerged on the use of capital gains. Investment in growth stocks is supported on the theory that the income derived exceeds that from alternative investments. A growth stock may yield (say) 2 per cent in dividends and 4 per cent on capital appreciation; an alternative investment, only 4 per cent. But the penchant for growth stocks would be greatly reduced if the treasurer were not allowed to consider the capital gain as income and therefore disbursable. Several members of the seminar held that endowment is inviolate and hence any capital gains resulting from investment of endowment are inviolate. I do not agree. The task of the trustee of endowments is to achieve the highest income, and income is normally to be used. Accumulation of capital gains without right of disbursement would be a deterrent to the use of the most effective investment policy.

A comparison of the yield of Aaa bonds with common stocks suggests that in 1929 further investment in common stocks was unwise. This is, of course, using hindsight. Yield on bonds was 4.73 and on common stocks, 3.41 per cent. Furthermore, at this time there was little fear of inflation, although with the coming of the New Deal and rising Federal deficits, some authorities expressed increasing concern over it.[5] Beginning in 1932 and until 1958, the yield on common stocks greatly exceeded that on bonds, for example, in 1932 by 2.3 per cent, 1938 by 1.2 per cent, in 1947 by 1.4 per cent, in 1956 by 0.7 per cent, and in December, 1957, by 0.9 per cent. By early 1959 the yield on bonds exceeded that on stocks. The combination of higher yield on common stocks and the threat of inflation throughout most of these years beginning in the 1940s suggests an investment policy largely dependent on common stocks.

I am not even convinced that when, as late in 1958 and in 1959–60, the yield on common stocks fell below the yield on bonds it necessarily follows that investment managers should turn to bonds. They would do so in so far as they exploit short-run changes in average returns. If my analysis is correct, it would be unwise for investors to shift from stocks to bonds at this point except to exploit short-run swings. The *long-run* trend of common stocks should certainly be upward. The favorable price of common stocks may result in their increased issue and, therefore, a tendency for prices of common stocks to fall. But I do not think this would be a very important factor, especially because of the large tax advantages of issuing bonds.

*   *   *

Policy of course depends upon the importance of endowment income in the budget of the particular institution. There are large variations. In the 60-college study for 1953–54, endowment income accounted for 18 per cent, and gifts and grants for 13 per cent of total educational and general income; but the maximum for endowment was 72 and the minimum 2 per cent.[6] If an institution depends almost wholly upon endowment income, it might seem risky to invest heavily in common stocks. Losses on the value of bonds as interest rises are also possible; but if income is our major objective, then we need not be overly concerned about declines in prices of bonds.

There are very few institutions where the yield of investment accounts for a large proportion of total income. Even at Harvard, which had an endowment at market value in excess of $600 million in 1959, endowment income accounted for only about one-third of the total, exclusive of organized research. Just before the war the contribution of endowment income was about two-fifths. Yet in the meanwhile endowment income has increased roughly from $5 to $20 million. In a sample of 57 private universities as of June 30, 1950, 23 IHL each with endowments of over $10 million accounted for about 90 per cent of the total for these 57 institutions.

But even when endowment is as much as 25 per cent of the income of the institution, the problems are not serious. Large investments can still be made in common stock. Even in the 1930s dividend payments in the nation declined only from $5.8 billion in 1929 to an average of about $3.5 billion in the next four years. This was a decline of less than half. Against this we should put of course the gains through falling prices and hence costs. Once we allow for this, the "real" loss on dividends was only 20 per cent.

Because corporations paid out only about 40 to 50 per cent of their profits as dividends in the postwar period, they have accumulated very large reserves, and, therefore, even with a substantial decline in economic conditions, dividends would likely be stabilized for a great many years. In the recession of the fourth quarter of 1957 and the first quarter of 1958 dividends were as high as in the corresponding quarters a year earlier.

Furthermore, each institution can build up a reserve of its own—and a reserve of one year's income from endowment under the economic conditions we are likely to have in the coming years would be more than adequate to protect against large losses of endowment income. Because endowment is a small part of the income of most institutions, there is no great risk; and in fact risks are reduced by investing heavily in common stocks.

Our economic history also suggests similar conclusions. From 1871 to 1937 the Cowles Commission found that investment in common stocks yielded an average of 8.8 per cent per year, and Sedgwick estimates a return (exclusive of utility issues) at 12 per cent average from 1938 to 1951. According to the latter's calculation, an investment of $1,000 with dividends reinvested would have risen to $248,360 from 1871 to 1938. These results are subject to some reservations.[7]

Because it is not necessary for a college to liquidate its investments in the manner of a bank or an insurance company, the risk of a sharp but temporary fall in market values is not so serious. Moreover, capital gains are much more profitable, for the IHL is exempt from taxation. However, the institutions should be liquid to some extent in order to capitalize on changes in the investment market. An investment officer should be able to play the swings in the market. If a bond decline has been overdone, a smart investment officer may purchase bonds for later resale. Nonetheless, many investment officers are inclined to take the long view.

At times IHL may take risks in buying equities—e.g., in purchasing growth stocks at values based on incomes far from attained. When dependence on such income is great and large commitments relatively fixed, treasurers may have to be cautious.

Of course, investments in common stocks can be carried too far. Increased interest in stocks may reduce the yield to, say, 2 per cent or even less. Lack of interest in bonds, especially in the face of government deficits, may raise bond rates to 5 or 6 per cent or even higher. According to Wells, the various perpetual funds (colleges, insurance companies, etc.) in 1950 had about $15 billion to invest, and IHL alone had about $500 million. But new issues of common stock *averaged* only about $2½ billion even in the prosperous years 1955 to 1957. The tax advantage lies with issues of bonds. It is obvious that if a large part of the $15 billion sought an outlet in common stocks—and with inflationary fears this trend is strengthened—a large inflation of common stock prices was bound to occur. In the absence of substantial inflation and growth, the trend toward common stocks may be contained as yields on stocks decline and those on bonds increase. (In part the reaction of stock prices in 1959–60 and in 1962 may be traced to reduced rates of growth and containment [at least temporary] of inflationary forces.)

There is no doubt that serious differences in policy prevail among institutions. This is evident from the differences in returns as well as in the structure of investments. The difference in return may be not so much a difference in the type of assets held as in the particular assets purchased.

In 1940, 20 institutions with the poorest yield record averaged 2.98 per cent return on investment, and 20 with the best records averaged 4.93. The explanation of the difference is not primarily size or distribution of securities between bonds and stocks. Institutions with the best records held 29.5 per cent of their investment in stocks, preferred and common, whereas those with the poorest record held 20.2 per cent. The difference is not nearly large enough to explain the variations in return. Obviously the major factor was the quality of the asset purchased, whether a bond, a mortgage, or a common stock. Varying propensities to take risks are also relevant. Yet as late as 1949 differences in portfolio are striking, even though major universities not restricted by special regulations pursue investment policies more nearly alike than a generation or two ago. Among 10 private universities in 1949 the range of investment in bonds was from 15 to 47 per cent, in preferred stocks 12 to 35 per cent, in common stocks 26 to 44 per cent, and in real estate 4 to 29 per cent.

* * *

In summary, I have argued here for an aggressive equity investment policy. In this manner, the IHL is protected to some extent against inflationary forces. The *long-run* policy should be along these lines though there might be temporary shifts from equities. That endowment income is generally a small part of income strengthens the case for taking these risks— in fact larger risks are involved in purchasing bonds in large quantities. As a facet of this policy the financial officer should have the privilege of spending capital gains as well as dividends.

Chart 3[8] expresses well the issues discussed in this chapter. From 1940

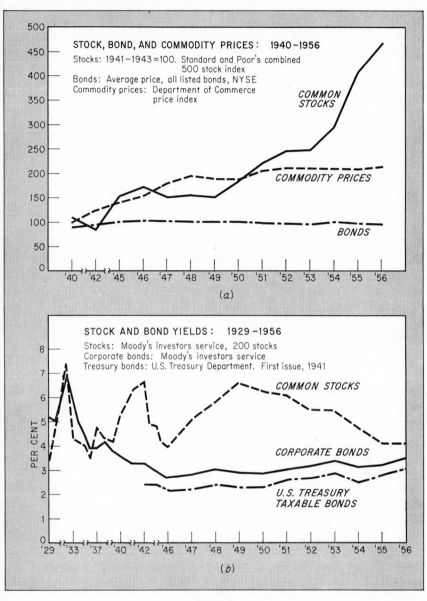

Chart 3

to 1956 the return on common stocks generally exceeded that on bonds, and at times by close to 4 per cent. Furthermore, the price of common stocks rose by 350 per cent, against a gain of only 100 per cent in commodity prices. Obviously, a treasurer who had invested 50 per cent of his institution's endowment in common stocks much more than offset the losses from rising prices. In a recent period of 10 years, the yield of assets in 5 investment trusts (largely invested in common stocks) was 8 per cent against a 3 per cent yield for bonds.

In the 1960s the experience may not be so fortunate: yields on common stocks are already below those on bonds. But note that with commodity prices rising by 20 per cent, a gain of common stock prices of only 40 per cent (3 per cent a year) in the 1960s would (with equities equal to 50 per cent) protect against rising prices.

The record of book and market values as of June 30, 1958, does not suggest as large gains from investment in common stocks as adumbrated above. Market value of all investments is but 27 per cent, and for common stocks 89 per cent, above book value. The rise in the value of common stocks is less than that in prices, and since stocks are but one-half of investments, the offset is less than one-half. Part of the explanation is that investment in common stocks was much less in 1940 than in 1956; part is that to some extent book values are inflated as a result of revaluations and sales of stocks and reinvestment in others, and hence the difference in book and market value does not reflect fully the rise of stock prices. A final point is that in the years 1940 to 1958, the yield on common stocks exceeded that on Aaa bonds by 41 per cent. This is an important contribution to the neutralization of inflationary forces.

FOOTNOTES

[1] B. Bump, "Philosophical Aspects of Endowment Management in the Small Colleges," *Second Annual Boston Forum on Open-end Investment Companies,* 1945, p. 22.

[2] Tripp, treasurer of Rochester University, showed that growth stocks yielded not only large capital gains but also higher income than other stocks in the 1950s; cf. RES, *Higher Education in the United States,* Supplement, August, 1960.

[3] B. Bump, *op. cit.,* pp. 24, 29.

[4] *Higher Education in the United States: The Economic Problems,* Harvard University Press, 1960, part VII.

[5] See, for example, E. W. Kemmerer, *The Outlook of Our College Endowments,* 1939, pp. 8–12.

[6] *A Study of Income and Expenditures in 60 Colleges,* pp. 26–27.

[7] See R. H. Sedgwick, "A New Pension Plan," *Harvard Business Review,* January–February, 1953, pp. 73–74; *The Boston Fund,* 106th Quarterly Report, July 31, 1958; and J. D. Millett, *Financing Higher Education in the United States,* 1952, pp. 317–318; cf. G. Bates in *Higher Education in the United States, op. cit.,* p. 217.

[8] For this chart I am indebted to my former research assistant, now at the University of California, Saul Hymans.

Chapter 30

FORMULA INVESTMENT POLICIES

Investment managers should not hold on to their securities without substitutions as conditions change. In general, financial managers tend to be cautious. The reason may be that they underestimate the long-run growth of the economy and the entrenched institutional factors making for inflation. They often assume few risks, since risk taking might be interpreted as a breach of faith with the donor who wished his endowment to be a permanent fund. This does not make much sense, because the risk of erosion through inflation is greater than the risk of loss through the purchase of diversified equity securities.

After the debacles of 1929 and 1937 (i.e., large deflations of stock values) those responsible for financial management relied excessively on formulas. In the 1930s one survey revealed that a large proportion of IHL depended on them. It was thought that formulas would prevent losses and would provide continued control of investments and assure a larger income. On the whole, the case for investment policy based on formulas does not seem to be strong. There is no substitute for judgment.

Formulas are not all equally bad. In 1938 Yale introduced a formula which, while on the whole unsuccessful, has been better than most. This was labeled the "Thermostatic Theory of Investment." Under this formula the normal investment mixture was to be 30 per cent in stocks and 70 per cent in bonds. The guide to investment behavior was the *Standard Statistics* index of 90 common stocks. As the price of stocks rose, the value of the stocks would rise as a proportion of the total value of the portfolio. When it once reached 40 per cent, sales would follow automatically until the proportion was down to 35 per cent. In a declining market no purchases would be made until the common stock had fallen to 20 per cent of the portfolio. Then purchases would be made to raise the total to 25 per cent.

Vassar had a more flexible formula, and many other institutions used formulas of various kinds. But institutions that adhered to a formula would not reap the benefits of markets that have prevailed for many years; and the institutions which sold stocks automatically when the proportion of common stock rose from 30 to 40 or from 40 to 50 per cent would obviously not be able to capitalize on a steadily rising market. Consider, for example, the rise in stock-market prices from 1939 at 100 to 442 in 1959. The institution that put itself in such a strait jacket was bound to lose in such a period. Of course much of the rise reflected inflation rather than speculative influences.

The formula approach was not even dead in the 1950s. H. L. Wells, financial officer of Northwestern, referred to a formula at Northwestern in the early 1950s: one-third in bonds, one-third in common stocks, and one-third in real estate. According to a vote in 1955 of the trustees of a men's college with endowments in excess of $50 million, when equities exceed 70 per cent of the portfolio, the committee on investments is to report back to the trustees.[1]

Perhaps the most important reason for the failures under the formula approach is that the underlying theory of this procedure is that cyclic fluctuations explain the movements in value and yield. But this leaves out of account the long-run (secular) movements.

FOOTNOTE

[1] On this issue, see S. E. Harris, *How Shall We Pay for Education?*, pp. 157–158; J. D. Millett, *Financing Higher Education in the United States,* 1952, pp. 315–317; N. F. Willoughby, "Management of Endowment Funds Is a Heavy Responsibility for the College Treasurer and Investment Committee," *College and University Business,* May, 1949; J. L. Kirkpatrick, *A Study of University Endowment Fund Investment,* 1949, pp. 31–37; Council for Financial Aid to Education, *Voluntary Support of America's Colleges and Universities,* 1956–57; *Federal Reserve Bulletin,* July, 1958; *College and University Endowment Investments: A Survey, 1958,* p. 241; H. L. Wells, *Higher Education Is a Serious Business,* 1953, *passim.*

Chapter 31

HOW TO MANAGE ENDOWMENT?

In the large universities investments are generally handled by an investment committee consisting of several members of the board of trustees well versed in investments. In addition, the college would have an investment officer or treasurer to carry out the policies dictated by the investment committee. There are indeed exceptions as, for example, at Harvard, where the manager of a noted open-end investment trust also invests the Harvard funds as part of the operations of the trust. In the smaller colleges, particularly those with endowments of less than $5 or $10 million, the problem is more serious. It is not ordinarily practical for institutions with small funds to set up their own investment agency. It is often wiser to hire outside counsel.

One sample suggests (Table 31-1) that the highest earnings are realized when the enterprise is in charge of corporate trustees, or a committee of

TABLE 31-1

Rates of Income on the Invested Funds of Colleges Having Various Types of Fund Management

Type of management	Number of colleges	Rates of income,* per cent		
		Average	Highest	Lowest
Completely in charge of a corporate trustee........	6	5.3	6.0	4.8
Committee of the board plus an investment counsel...	1	5.3		
Financial officer of the college....................	3	5.2	6.5	3.2
Committee of the board plus large assistance from the financial officer of the college..................	3	4.8	6.0	3.4
Partially in charge of a corporate trustee, remainder with committee of board........................	5	4.1	5.1	2.6
Committee of the board in full charge.............	15	3.9	6.1	0.0

* For the year 1928–29 for some institutions, and the year 1929–30 for the remainder.

Source: Reeves, Russell, Gregg, Brumbaugh, and Blauch, *The Liberal Arts College*, University of Chicago Press, Chicago, 1932.

the board plus an investment counsel, or a finance officer of the college. In 1958–59, out of 200 IHL, 68 relied on outside investment counsel, 64 on a committee of the governing board, 49 on a trust company, and 19 on their own institutional investment staff. The trend was toward expert advice. The least satisfactory results seem to occur when a committee of the board is in full charge. The sample is small, however, and the year of the study quite some time ago, and hence the results are acceptable only with reservations.

For many years it has been suggested that a central organization should be created to handle the investment funds of small colleges. This is a very sensible idea and might result in better investment advice at lower cost. It is clear from past performance that the small institutions do not earn as much as the large institutions in the management of their investments. But a recent study of HEW reveals small variations by size of fund, with the range from 3.62 per cent ($15 to 30 million and $3 to 4 million) and the maximum 3.82 per cent ($2 to 3 million). The return for the largest funds ($50 million or over) was 3.65 per cent. As we suggest elsewhere, accounting differences impair comparisons to some extent.

The proposal of a central investment organization was at one time made to the Carnegie Corporation; but they turned it down on the grounds that actual judgment must rest on those who are legally responsible, namely, the trustees of each particular institution. Others feared that a concerted management policy might have unfortunate effects on the stability of investment markets.

It is of some interest that trustees of many IHL have been able to shift this responsibility in recent years to investment trusts that sell shares to their institutions. Apparently one of the largest investment trusts reported that 110 colleges and schools owned nearly $2 million of its outstanding stock; another reported 28 educational institutions among its 1,374 fiduciary holders of its shares.[1]

FOOTNOTE

[1] C. P. Bassett, "Report of the Committee," *Second Annual Conference of Trustees of Colleges and Universities on the Responsibilities and Problems of Governing Boards of Educational Institutions,* April, 1936, pp. 42–45 (mimeographed); J. L. Kirkpatrick, *A Study of University Endowment Fund Investment,* 1949, p. 23; *College and University Endowment Investments: A Survey, 1958–59,* pp. 13, 20; L. Tomlinson, "How About Investment Company Shares and Endowment Holdings," *College and University Business,* August, 1948; HEW, *College and University Endowment Investments as of June 30, 1958,* 1959, p. 7.

Chapter 32

THE EFFECTIVE USE OF ENDOWMENT FUNDS

Educational values change. Paleontology may not be as important vis-à-vis theoretical physics as it was fifty years ago. What seemed a fruitful use of university or college funds in 1900 may not be particularly effective in 1960. Funds that have been made available for a restricted purpose in earlier years may not yield the most beneficial results currently or in the future. Many institutions try to get around this problem by entering their funds at book value rather than at market value.[1]

In general, with inflation and growth, market values are likely to exceed book values of endowment funds. Of course, in a great depression the reverse is likely to be true, though even in the 1930s the difference between market and book values was not as great as in current years.

Assume that the book value of an endowment fund is $20 million and the market value $30 million, a proportion not too far out of line with conditions in 1959. Assume that a gift of $1 million is made available. Obviously if the income is $1 million for the $20 million of book value (30 million of market value) and if the $1 million are entered in relation to book rather than to market value, the current donor receives a great advantage. Instead of getting one thirty-first of the total amount of the college's fund income, the new fund receives one twenty-first of the total income.

This is a technique which is fairly widely used, though there are many universities, for example, Chicago and Dartmouth, that are strongly opposed to this practice on ethical grounds. Their treasurers will contend that the book-value rather than the investment-trust (market-value) type of entry is unfair to the dead, who cannot protest. Under Pennsylvania law, entry and removal of funds into or out of nonprofit organizations must be on the basis of market value.[2]

J. Parker Hall, treasurer of the University of Chicago, pointed out to me that under their method (market value) $100,000 obtained the following returns in 1959:

Invested in 1936.................. $7,508
Invested in 1947–48.............. 7,064
Invested in 1952–53.............. 5,454
Invested in 1957.................. 3,383

Perhaps the strongest case which can be made for this allocation of income on the basis of book value is that it enables the university to put its funds to the most effective use given current educational values. On moral grounds possibly something may be said against this practice, for in periods of rising values the older funds receive back relatively less than they earned. It should be noted, however, that as values continue to rise, under book-value entry current donors will suffer by comparison with future donors. In so far as endowment funds are for unrestricted purposes, though, it makes little difference whether the money is entered on book or market value. John Meck, the treasurer of Dartmouth College, revealed that unrestricted funds are the exception: 4, 4, 7, 15, 19, and 23 per cent respectively for Princeton, Amherst, Yale, Dartmouth, Wellesley, and Wesleyan. But for 10 colleges in the 60-college study, unrestricted income was ten times as large as restricted income. Another factor that reduces the significance of choice of bookkeeping is the capacity of the college administrator to reallocate operating funds. If endowment income is a small part of total income, as is usually true, the college administrator can reallocate resources to a greater extent than through the entry of new endowment funds at book value.[3]

Other ways of reallocating funds are also available. For example, one famous institution uses part of the income on endowment funds for general purposes. If the return on pooled funds is, say, 4 per cent, 3½ per cent is allocated to participating funds in the pooled fund on the basis of their stake in the common fund. The remainder, ½ per cent, is allocated for the general purposes of the university as the administrators direct its use.

Another example of this approach was given in the 1930s at a meeting of the Conference of Trustees of Colleges and Universities on the Responsibilities and Problems of Governing Boards of Educational Institutions.[4] At this meeting a treasurer said:

Some years ago the Finance Committee acted favorably upon the suggestion of my predecessor that it was just as necessary to provide insurance for the protection of an endowment fund against loss of principal as it was to buy insurance for the reconstruction of the physical plant in face of disaster. . . .

By December 1928 that fund amounted to $5 million and $1 million was used to provide additional facilities on. . . . [a] Campus where the College for Men was then in the course of construction. . . . The income from the reserve fund is used to meet the general administrative expenses of the university. The costs of conducting the offices of the president, the treasurer, the bursar and the superintendent of buildings and grounds and so on are not included in our operating budget. All income from endowment and from fees is used for educational purposes.

These paragraphs show clearly that endowment funds or income from endowment has been siphoned off for purposes other than those intended for the original grant. If this had not been done, the reserve fund would have been allocated to all the various funds in proportion to their interest. In my discussions with college administrators I soon discovered that some outstanding institutions which were ready to deny the propriety of entering new endowment funds at book value nevertheless, in the distribution of these funds, either through the use of reserve funds or simply by special allocation, tended to favor funds that were in great need of additions. For example, one university president frankly admitted that in their distribution they made specially favorable allocations for scholarships.

Finally, colleges can avail themselves of the cy pres doctrine. This allows a university administrator to go to court where the gift is eccentric and the deeds cannot be carried through. Such procedure, however, is time-consuming and often takes many years before adjustments are made. In the struggle over the McKay millions, when Harvard and MIT wanted to combine for an engineering curriculum, the courts, though not relying on an interpretation of the cy pres doctrine, refused to allow this merger. They held that, although it would be beneficial indeed for the country and those interested, the conditions of the gift could be fulfilled.

An example of the difficulties of applying the cy pres doctrine is suggested in a particular case where a will was set up in 1851 providing an income of one-third of the testator's estate " . . . to furnish relief to all poor immigrants and travelers coming to St. Louis on their way *bona fide* to settle the West." By 1902 litigation was under way to have the cy pres doctrine apply. Over a period of almost forty years the trustees had collected $848,000, out of which they had expended $211,000 for relief of poor immigrants and travelers, and the rest was consumed in expensive administration. It was not until 1934 that cy pres was actually applied.[5]

An example of the manner in which universities are confronted with difficult decisions is suggested by the professorships made available in the eighteenth century. These obviously would yield only a few hundred dollars of income today, whereas the average professor might be earning, say, $15,000. Obviously the courts could not force a college to continue to pay $15,000 when the endowed chair yields only, say, $500. One solution is to drop the professorship, and this has been done by some universities. Others, however, insist on maintaining the chair, although to some extent the definition of the job to be done may be changed, or other funds may be reallocated to provide for the rising salary of the professor. Where the university still maintains a substantial interest in the teaching of such subjects as classics or history, no serious problems arise. The university merely adds part of its regular budget to these departments to make up for the deficiency of funds for a particular chair. But where the subject to be taught has little interest for current administrators, more serious problems arise.

A related problem is the following: at what price should an IHL agree to set up an endowed chair? If a high-priced professor receives $20,000, then at 4 per cent $500,000 would be needed. But a university may accept less—say, $250,000—where the chair is badly needed and on the assumption that the agreement can be made in such a manner that it will not spoil the market; that is, others will not be deterred from offering much more. But there is another aspect. Twenty-five years from now the $20,000 professorship may cost $40,000. Should not this be taken into account in setting a price for a professorship—in a generation a deficit of $20,000 per year may emerge. In part this would be offset by investments in growth stocks resulting in a rise of income, though not likely equal to the increased costs of the chair. Obviously where the chair seems to offer a large contribution for the foreseeable future—e.g., science—the administration need not be deterred too much by the need of an additional, say, $20,000 per year to finance the chair by 1985.

FOOTNOTES

¹ Here I am not discussing the problem of how much attention generally should be paid to book values. My view is that too much attention is paid to book values, especially in periods of economic decline. The emphasis should be on income, and treasurers should not be excessively concerned over declines in book values. Original value is more significant than book value, especially since book values are occasionally modified. But, unfortunately, book, not original value, is usually available.

² According to the 1959 HEW study, *College and University Endowment Investments,* 140 of 200 IHL accounting for the larger part of endowment use the book value approach; also see *Higher Education in the United States: The Economic Problems,* 1960, pp. 208–211, and *Senate Bill No. 254, Session of 1947, The General Assembly of Pennsylvania.*

³ R. S. Johns, "Preferred Method of Pooled Investments," *College and University Business,* July 1, 1953, p. 27; C. H. Foster, "Applying Investment Trust Accounting to the Pooled Funds of the College," *ibid.,* November, 1956, pp. 47, 48; R. G. Funkhouser, "Applying Investment Fund Accounting to Consolidated Endowment Funds," *ibid.,* June, 1954, pp. 21–23, and July, 1954, pp. 44–47; J. D. Russell, *The Finance of Higher Education* (rev. ed.), chap. 11; *A Second Look at the Sixty College Study,* 1960, exhibit XI.

⁴ R. L. Thompson, *The Care and Administration of Endowment Funds,* pp. 19, 20, 22–23.

⁵ See especially L. M. Simms, *Public Policy in the Dead Hand,* 1955, pp. 119–131, and T. E. Blackwell, "Who Has the Power to Modify Charitable Trusts?" *College and University Business,* June, 1953, pp. 30, 31.

Chapter 33

THE DECLINE OF ENDOWMENT

According to the Office of Education, endowment in 1957–58 amounted to $4.65 billion. The Council for Financial Aid to Education, in its 1958–59 report, puts the total at $4.61 billion for that year. These figures are for book value; market value early in 1960 was substantially higher. In fact a special survey (*College and University Endowment Investments, 1958*), gave a total of $4.83 billion market value for an 85 per cent sample, or $5.56 billion in all. For some institutions endowment is a very important matter—e.g., for the 48 major private institutions that account for more than 40 per cent of the endowment of 1,042 IHL studied by the Council. Where endowment is around $5,000 per student (book value), the contribution is roughly $250 per year per student. Major private universities, private men's and women's colleges, and professional and specialized schools come under this category.

Nevertheless, we may be sure of one thing: endowment is much less important than it used to be. In 1900 it accounted for 25 per cent of educational income. But by the late 1950s its relative contribution was only about one-fifth as large, or 5 per cent. The decline of endowment income, in relation to total income, results in part from the large rise of current gifts. In 1957–58, $325 million became available for current operations out of gifts, *the equivalent of income from $8 to $9 billion of endowment,* over twice the value of endowment in that year. By 1958–59 the Council for Financial Aid to Education estimated grants for *all* purposes at $751 million, or four to five times the endowment income of 1957–58. Another indication of the reduced significance of endowment is the large relative rise of physical property. In 1889–90 and 1929–30 the endowment was roughly 80 per cent of the value of physical property. By 1957–58 it was only 40 per cent of this value. The trend toward a declining percentage of gifts to general educational income is reflected in a declining significance of endowment.[1]

Why the reduced importance of endowment? One explanation of course is inflation. Since before the war endowments have lost up to one-third of their total value as a result of inflation; but this does not allow for any excess of capital gains in the postwar period over losses in the 1930s. Most institutions reduced the loss due to inflationary process by putting more of their funds into common stocks. Endowment also becomes relatively less important as per capita income at stable prices rises. Obviously the income from $4 billion of endowment accounts for less in an economy where the per capita income has doubled than it did when the per capita income was only half as large.

Another factor that may have reduced the significance of endowment is the increase of taxes on high-income groups. Previously many gifts to the universities came from these high-income groups. A high-income recipient ($200,000 unmarried, $400,000 married), subject to a marginal tax rate of 92 per cent, may hesitate about making gifts to IHL. The reason is that he has so little left after he pays these heavy taxes. On the other hand, many contend that, since a gift would cost only 8 cents for every dollar given because the tax collector would pay the other 92, this stimulates giving by high-income groups. The fact is that these high-income groups have actually increased their gifts in relation to their income, although the reduction in their numbers has more than offset this advantage. Despite the large rise of tax rates since the 1920s, gifts are roughly the same percentage of income in the 1950s as in the 1920s. It has been proposed that low-income groups would increase their contributions if they had the same advantage as the large-income groups, namely, that a gift of $1,000 would cost the donors only 8 per cent, or $80. Undoubtedly this would stimulate giving, but the net effect would be a heavy cost to the government. For this reason this proposal is not practical.[2]

Still another factor is of some relevance. At the present time gifts are given for endowment to a much smaller degree than in the past. Thus of private gifts, endowment received 76, 51, and 34 per cent in 1919–20, 1939–40, and 1955–56, respectively. At Harvard the decline was from 38 per cent in 1930 to 24 per cent in 1950; at MIT, from 51 to 6 per cent for these two years.

Even for institutions where endowment funds are large and increasing, they are a declining factor in the economy of the college. For example, Yale's endowment fund at market value in 1934–35 was $66 million; in 1952–53 it had risen to $153 million, an increase larger than would be suggested by the rise of prices. Yet from the 1930s to 1956–57 the contribution of endowment to Yale's educational income has fallen from 55 to 33 per cent. A large rise in enrollment also helps explain the reduction in endowment per student. The more students, the more thinly endowment is spread. In this connection, Harvard's decline of investment income over a period of thirty years was relatively (percentage of educational income) only half as great as for the country. A rise of enrollment only 20 per cent that of the nation contributed to this result.[3] In my discussions with college presidents I discovered that where endowment was relatively important, the administrators tended to be reluctant toward rises of enrollment.[4]

Another reason for the decline of endowment has been the abuse of endowment funds. Many years ago President Eliot of Harvard stated " . . . that the problem of annual deficits is becoming a greater problem year by year." He contended " . . . that the using up of unrestricted funds bearing the name of a benefactor by charging annual deficits to these funds was highly objectionable. Such a practice would in time discourage the giving of such funds. . . . "[5]

In the 1930s other authorities were as pessimistic as President Eliot had been in the 1880s. In 1936 one authority had this to say: ". . . correct college accounting was conspicuous by its absence, and where one was found, it was based on wishful thinking and was for the most part ignored. Endowment was treated as capital of a commercial company to be drawn on for deficits or needs of any other purchase. . . . " Many institutions use endowment funds as loans to meet current expenses and then experience losses when they are unable to raise funds to repay them.[6] Even in 1958 I consulted with a college president who was rather annoyed that the board of trustees had not allowed him to use funds belonging to endowment in order to pay off debts.

Reeves and others have found that fewer than half the college boards investigated a generation ago had a clear record with regard to violation of trusts through hypothecation and endowment security. Goodwin found a tendency to disregard trust provisions of endowment gifts and warned trustees to seek legal advice and pay attention to their trust obligations. Blackwell also made some interesting studies along these lines. One of the leaders in this field wrote as follows in the 1930s:[7]

> Special attention was given to the subject of endowment, about which very hazy ideas then prevailed. The nature of endowment was defined, and attention was called to many unsuitable practices then in use. Examples were given where institutions had pledged endowment funds for loans for current expenses, then had lost them because they were unable to raise the funds to pay the loans. Instances were cited where loans were made by denominational colleges on denominational properties, which tied the hands of the college trustees in enforcing collections of delinquent income and principal. The same difficulties were pointed out in cases where loans had been made to trustees, officers and others connected with the college. . . . Reference was made to the plan which some institutions had followed in writing up the value of endowment asset to offset the use of endowment cash for nonendowment purposes.

Many are critical of the use of endowment funds for capital purposes of the institution. I do not, however, see any objection where the investment is carefully assessed. At current conditions, for example, where funds are not easily procurable for the purpose, the use of unrestricted endowment funds for the construction of a dormitory may easily be supported—and especially in view of the expected rise of enrollment. But rents should be set high enough to amortize the building over a period of thirty years (say), and a return should be had equal to that available from alternative investments.

But the reduction of endowment through steady rises of deficits is another matter. One of the best small liberal arts colleges in the Middle West accumulated a deficit of $620,000 over a period of twenty years which made serious inroads on its endowment. In one period of eleven years (1946 to 1957) endowment had almost doubled. Yet the amount available for investment had increased only by about 50 per cent.

In more recent years complaints of abuse of endowment funds have been much less frequent. Authorities are better informed on their legal and moral responsibilities, and the pressures toward abuse emanating from a great depression are no more.

Many believe that a large endowment is a protection for a college or a university. Protected by endowment income, the university need not depend upon donors or yield to current pressures to change educational practices. A certain amount of freedom of this kind is certainly essential for an IHL; colleges should not be subject to all the pressures of the day. But it is also true that the availability of endowment income may make the institution altogether *too* independent of current social values.

In this connection, Adam Smith's views in 1776 are of some interest:

> Have those public endowments contributed in general to promote the end of their institution? Have they contributed to increase their diligence and to improve the ability of the teachers? Have they directed the costs of education toward objects more useful both to the individual and to the public than those to which it would naturally have gone of its own accord. . . ?
>
> In every profession, the exertion of the greater part of those that exercise it is always in proportion to the necessity they are under in making that exertion. This necessity is greatest to those to whom the emoluments of their profession are the only source from which they expect their portion or even their ordinary revenue or subsistence. . . .

A more vigorous attack on the right of the dead to dictate to the living was made by Sir Arthur Hobhouse in 1880:[8]

> Having then endeavored to define and to illustrate the essential character of a Charity, I want you to ask yourselves this question: How comes it that people are allowed thus to devote property according to their caprices for ever? To me it seems the most extravagant of propositions to say that, because a man has been fortunate enough to enjoy a large share of this world's goods

in this life, he shall therefore and for no other cause, when he must quit this life and can enjoy his goods no longer, be entitled to speak from his grave *for ever* and dictate *for ever* to living men how that portion of the earth's produce shall be spent. . . .

Will any contemporary of mine at Eton assert that the then state of the College was useful or edifying? Will any contemporary of mine at Oxford say that the Foundations of Merton or Wayneflete or Chichele were then playing their part in the world? There may be times of awakened conscience and active exertion, but the question is whether rich Foundations derived from private origin do not invariably gravitate towards sloth and indolence? It is difficult to point to one instance of a private endowment for learning achieving great results by itself alone. Where such results have been achieved, whether on a small scale or a great, whether in a rural school or in Eton or Trinity College, it has been by superadding a voluntary or unendowed department, rising and falling with public estimation, and lying open to all the influences which excite hope or fear, which animate the zealous or rouse the apathetic.

In the 1930s the General Education Board (Rockefeller) abandoned its policies of providing endowment and began to give for a definite period of years. The board even allowed beneficiaries to use up endowment that had been provided in earlier years.[9] Writing in *The Atlantic Monthly,* Julius Rosenwald had this to say in 1929:[10]

I am not in sympathy with this policy of perpetuating endowment and believe that more good can be accomplished by expending funds as trustees find opportunities for constructive work than by storing up large sums of money for long periods of time. By adopting a policy of using the funds within this generation we may avoid those tendencies towards bureaucracy and a formal or perfunctory attitude toward the work which almost inevitably developed in organizations which prolonged their existence indefinitely. Coming generations can be relied upon to provide for their own needs as they arise. . . .

I am not opposed to endowment for colleges or other institutions which require some continuity of support, provided permission is given to use part of the principal from time to time as needs arise. . . .

In 1934 Alfred Sloan, another great philanthropist, wrote:

Let's cut out gifts to endowments. . . . I do not believe that relying on endowments is the most effective use of your money. You need capital now, not only money for expansion and development, but money to take care of the deficits you are facing. I feel that you would be better off to get as much money as you can now, use it up in ten years and then trust to your confidence and your efforts, and work with those who are helping you to carry this institution along at the end of the ten year period.

Amos Jones, President of the University of Technology of Los Angeles, California, has an interesting plan to solve financial problems and free the world of crime. He would spend $10,000 of endowment per student, 35 per cent of which would be used to insure the student for $6,000. When the student dies, the college would be reimbursed. But Jones does not realize that this means an erosion of endowment. The college would lose the returns on the $6,000 for forty years or so.

One aspect of endowments should not go unnoticed. When a college borrows to build a dormitory (say), in a sense this means a reduction of capital funds. Yet a strong case can be made for recourse to borrowing when the funds can be had at lower rates than the income yield on endowment funds. Why not limit demands for funds in large campaigns to those categories where loan financing is not practical? Where a college houses most students, for example, and does not charge for capital, then such a college, by borrowing for dormitories and allocating the financing charges among *all* students in dormitories, can by an increase of rents of about $50 per year avoid appeals for millions in fund drives.[11]

In conclusion let me say that as a result of certain past abuses in the use of endowment funds, as a result of inflation, rising productivity, and increase of enrollment, and because endowment funds are often not effectively adapted to current educational values—for all these reasons endowment funds have become less important. The growth of other sources of revenue, including governmental grants and student fees, also tends to make endowment funds less important. In order to alert the faculty, Adam Smith undoubtedly was excessively hostile to endowment funds; but it is nevertheless true that universities and colleges should be sensitive to the needs of the community to some extent and that if they are excessively endowed, they are less likely to achieve even this minimum degree of sensitivity.

Nevertheless we should not minimize the importance of endowments. They assure some continuity of policies and a minimum of freedom from outside pressures. Even public IHL, with very little endowment income, are finding in rising endowment a degree of freedom which is especially welcome to institutions too much under the control of legislators and state budget officers.

But the major reason for shift from endowment to current gifts is that gifts are the most effective way to get necessary revenue when needed.[12] Another point on behalf of current gifts is that a dollar spent today is likely to yield more plant, equipment, and services than a dollar spent tomorrow.

FOOTNOTES

[1] T. Arnett, "Address before the Association of University and College Business Officers of the Eastern States," *Minutes of the 17th Annual Meeting,* 1936, p. 62; HEW, *Summary of 1953–54 Financial Statistics of Institutions of Higher Education,* p. 5; Commission on Financing Higher Education, *National Needs of Higher Educa-*

tion, p. 139; S. E. Harris, *The Economics of Higher Education*, 1957, p. 24 (mimeographed); *Where's the Money Coming From?*, p. 11; T. L. Hungate, *Financing the Future of Higher Education*, 1946, p. 117; *Higher Education*, March, 1960; Council for Financial Aid to Education, *Voluntary Support of America's Colleges and Universities, 1958–59*, p. 9.

² Cf. discussion in Chap. 23.

³ A similar explanation is relevant for Princeton. Endowment income declined only from 31 per cent of all income in 1934 to 28 per cent in 1957. But gifts rose from 6 to 18 per cent. From *Princeton University Financial Reports*.

⁴ E. C. Budd, *Trends in Yale's Finances*, p. 2; R. A. Mestres, "The Changing Role of Endowments," *Meetings of the Eastern Association of Colleges and Universities*, Dec. 11, 1955, p. 62; S. E. Harris, "The Economics of Harvard," *Harvard Alumni Bulletin*, Feb. 20, 1960, pp. 383–384.

⁵ E. L. Hawthorne, *Fund Raising for the Small College*, 1950, p. 191; HEW, *College and University Endowment Investments*, p. 4.

⁶ T. Arnett, *op. cit.*, pp. 62–65.

⁷ *Ibid.*, p. 55; also *Encyclopedia of Educational Research*, (rev. ed.), 1950, pp. 251–252.

⁸ Adam Smith, *The Wealth of Nations*, Modern Library ed., pp. 716–717; Sir A. Hobhouse, *The Dead Hand*, 1880, pp. 9, 43.

⁹ E. L. Hawthorne, *op. cit.*, pp. 42–43; E. V. Hollis, *Philanthropic Foundations and Higher Education*, 1938, p. 203; *Philanthropic Giving*, pp. 198–199.

¹⁰ Julius Rosenwald, "Principles of Public Giving," *The Atlantic Monthly*, May, 1929, p. 606.

¹¹ I quietly argued this case in the midst of the recent Harvard drive. For details see S. E. Harris (ed.), *Higher Education in the United States: The Economic Problems*, 1960, pp. 211–213, 239–242.

¹² E. T. Stewart, Jr., "Alumni Support and Annual Giving," *The Annals, Higher Education under Stress*, September, 1955, p. 135; and A. P. Sloan, Jr., "Operation Expansion," *College and University Business*, April, 1956, p. 21.

Chapter 34

CORPORATE AND OTHER BUSINESS GIFTS

Discussion of the decline of endowment leads naturally to a consideration of business gifts to IHL. Erosion of endowments and increased demands on IHL have attracted attention to current giving and especially to gifts from business.

In 1958–59 corporate and business gifts amounted to more than $98 million, about 13 per cent of all gifts to IHL. Current tax policy has tended to increase the contribution of business. With a corporation income tax of 52 per cent, plus income taxes on individuals, plus state taxes, it is clear that every dollar given by a corporation costs the corporation and its owners about 25 cents.

A legal decision based on a gift of the A. P. Smith Manufacturing Company in 1951 to a Princeton University fund clarified the issues. A small stockholder protested the contribution as being beyond the charter powers of the corporation. The Smith company relied on legislation enacted in 1950 by the New Jersey Legislature which

. . . declares that it shall be the public policy of this state that encouragement shall be given to the creation and maintenance of institutions or organizations engaged in community fund, hospital, charitable, philanthropic, educational, scientific, or benevolent activities, or patriotic or civic activities conducive to the betterment of social and economic conditions . . . and to the end that the public policy herein declared may be supported . . . [corporations] shall have power . . . to appropriate, spend or contribute to such purposes such reasonable sums of money as they may determine. . . .

Judge Stein said that the corporations " . . . have not only used those powers expressly conferred upon them by charter franchise or articles of association, but also all incidental powers reasonably designed or required to give fuller or greater effect to the expressed powers." In fact, when one corporation with 118,000 stockholders donated a large sum of money to 75 liberal arts colleges and after six months received not a single

452

protest, the corporation heads decided that the " . . . stockholders are way ahead of us."[1]

Among the recent reasons for help to colleges by business leaders were the following:[2]

1. Unless business comes to the aid of IHL, the Government will. This would end the freedom of the colleges.

2. IHL provide the college graduates that business must have. They provide three-quarters of the leaders of our biggest industrial and commercial enterprises, and nearly seven-eighths of our rising business executives nowadays have college or university origins.

In determining its gifts the General Electric Company emphasized the development of new knowledge through research and inspired teaching; the provision of an adequate supply of educated manpower for the company, industry, and the economy generally; the maintenance and improvement of the economic, social, and political climate necessary for the continued existence and progress of competitive free enterprise.[3]

Corporations, under the 1935 Internal Revenue Act, were allowed to deduct up to 5 per cent of net income for philanthropic contributions, including gifts to higher education. In 1936 the total philanthropic donations were $30 million, a little more than $\frac{1}{3}$ per cent of corporate net income in that year. In 1954 the amount was $314 million, and the contribution amounted to 0.85 per cent of net income. Five per cent of total corporate income before taxes would yield about $2\frac{1}{2}$ billion in 1959.

It is not at all unlikely that the corporations might contribute 2 per cent of their net income, and with IHL obtaining 25 per cent of this total the amount made available by corporations to IHL might increase to $250 million, and perhaps $350 million by 1970.

College presidents are well aware that donors may try to set conditions in making gifts to universities. A few years ago a number of the presidents of the Ivy colleges issued a statement warning potential givers on this issue.[4]

Early in this century a very interesting case arose. The will of Anna T. Geanes provided as follows:

I condition to give and bequeath to Swarthmore College my coal lands and mineral rights in the State of Pennsylvania together with my five eighths ownership in the Rebecca Steadman tract (Hazel Brook Colliery) on the condition that the management of the aforesaid Swarthmore College shall discontinue and abandon all participation in collegiate athletic sports and games, but should the managers of Swarthmore College fail to accept these conditions I will direct that the aforesaid coal lands and mineral rights shall be sold and the proceeds thereof . . . in the amount realized shall be included and merged in assets of my estate.

The board of managers of Swarthmore College were unhappy about this gift and asked for opinions from various university experts. They even seemed prepared to accept the gift if they could use the income so long as they abided by the deeds of the gift. But they wanted the freedom to reconsider. College presidents, however, were skeptical and warned the managers of Swarthmore College that it would be unwise for them to bind the hands of their successors.

President Eliot of Harvard wrote as follows:

I am not a lawyer and do not know whether under the statutes of Pennsylvania and the decision of its courts the present trustees of Swarthmore College have the right to bind the college for all time to go without forms . . . of athletic sports. I am clear, however, that it is inexpedient for the present trustees to undertake so to bind the trustees of 50 or 100 or 200 years hence, having seen during my lifetime all methods of teaching the oldest subjects in the American college fundamentally change, many entirely new subjects of instruction produced, and having personally witnessed the introduction of all the present athletic sports in our colleges, and being unable to discover any single industry in the country which is now conducted as it was 50 years ago, I think it is imprudent for any existing body of college trustees to attempt to foresee the conditions of any American college, and of American society in general 50 years from now. . . .

According to President Schurman of Cornell it would be unwise to accept the gift. "On general principle, I am convinced that our colleges and universities should be centers of unrestricted freedom. I see no reason why a board of trustees which limits the freedom in one direction should not by parity of reason be justly expected to limit it in another." He pointed out, though, that intercollegiate football is "a game which is a battle not a sport, one which invites by its very nature . . . brutality, one that is planned throughout not by players but by high priced professional coaches who cannot [support] academic ideals. . . . " He was sympathetic with the objective but not the approach.

President Jordan of Leland Stanford said: "A university (or a healthy American college which is a young university) must be free to work out its own career. Any dead hand tying it up to anything no matter how good is a burden and a danger."[5]

* * *

Corporation gifts are becoming more important. From 1954–55 to 1958–59 they rose from $39 million to $98 million, or from 11.7 to 13.1 per cent of all gifts. In 1958–59 *all* gifts were for the following purposes: unrestricted, 26 per cent; buildings, grounds, etc., 24 per cent; basic research, 21 per cent; student financial aid, 13 per cent; faculty and staff compensation, 6 per cent; other, 9 per cent. In this connection it is of some interest that 75 presidents from the 100 largest corporations expressed the following educational problems of first importance: increased teachers' salaries, 57 per cent; improved curriculum, 43 per cent; additional plant facilities, 17 per cent (some voted for two). Yet they preferred to give their money for the following purposes: scholarships, 28 per cent; research, 17 per cent; increased salaries, 17 per cent; better buildings and facilities, 7 per cent.

A study by the Council for Financial Aid to Education of 275 companies which contributed $28.7 million to education in 1956, or 34 per cent of their total contributions, showed large variations in contributions by industries and companies. The over-all contribution was 0.76 per cent of net income before taxes (total gifts). Companies with foundations for giving were more generous, as were small corporations. Whereas the 275 corporations gave 0.26 per cent of net income for education, the range was 0.05 per cent for telecommunications to 0.53 per cent for textiles. The maximum rate for one company was 4.18 per cent. In 1958–59 corporation and business gifts were 13 per cent of all gifts to IHL. Professional and specialized schools (19.6 per cent), state-controlled (15.2 per cent), and private coeducational (14.8 per cent) depended disproportionately on business.[6] In 1961, 21 Cleveland companies pledged to give at least 1 per cent of profits before taxes to higher education, or $2 million on the basis of the preceding year's profits. It was hoped that this would set an example for others.[7]

FOOTNOTES

[1] T. E. Blackwell, "Stockholders and Corporate Gifts to Colleges," *College and University Business,* September, 1953, pp. 41 and 42; W. M. Compton, "Financial Support Will Follow and Not Precede Public Confidence," *College and University Business,* May, 1954, pp. 17 and 18; also see *Summary Report of Conference on Corporate Contributions to Higher Education,* Harriman, N.Y., March and April, 1955.

[2] W. M. Compton, "Corporation Support," *The Annals, Higher Education under Stress,* September, 1955, pp. 140–142.

[3] "One Viewpoint on Corporate Aid to Education," advertisement in *The Atlantic Monthly; The Development of Scientific, Engineering and Other Professional Manpower,* Joint Congressional Committee on Atomic Energy, 1957, p. 123; F. W. Abrams, "Growth of Corporate Giving to Education," *School and Society,* Jan. 18, 1958, p. 30. For thoughtful programs of large corporations see Standard Oil Company of California, *A Program of Aid to Education, 1961,* and United States Steel Corporation release of May 5, 1960.

[4] The seven presidents urged *inter alia* unrestricted gifts, coverage of overhead or supplementary outlays, gifts that would not restrict the freedom of the university or involve large overhead charges. *The New York Times,* June 25, 1956.

[5] See "Minutes of the Forty-fourth Annual Meeting of the Stockholders of Swarthmore College," *Swarthmore College Bulletin,* Dec. 3, 1907, especially pp. 50–65;

and also "Papers on the Bequest of the late Anna T. Geanes," *Swarthmore College Bulletin*, 1907.

[6] *1958–1959, Voluntary Support of American Colleges and Universities*, pp. 9, 13, 66; *The Public Pulse*, September, 1958, a report from 75 presidents; Council for Financial Aid to Education, *The Trend Is Up*, 1958; J. A. Pollard, "Emerging Pattern in Corporate Giving," *Harvard Business Review*, May–June, 1960, p. 106; cf. *Development of Scientific, Engineering and Other Professional Manpower*, p. 116.

[7] *Business Week*, Feb. 4, 1961, p. 68.

Chapter 35

HIGHER EDUCATION'S SHARE IN THE PHILANTHROPIC DOLLAR

We have already noted that endowment income has become less important in higher education. But the trend has also been down for the proportion of income from productive funds *plus* benefactions to total income. In 1872 these accounted for almost two-thirds of the total of higher-education income, by 1915 only 24 per cent, and by 1958 about 13 per cent. (Because of accounting difficulties, these figures are indicative of trends only.)

One estimate early in the Depression showed that the property and endowment of nonprofit organizations amounted to roughly $9 billion. Higher education accounted for $2.8 billion, or roughly 30 per cent, but higher education received only 13 per cent of the total yearly gifts. These figures point to a declining proportion for IHL.[1] From 1893 to 1916, according to one estimate, education was receiving from 16 to 79 per cent of gifts annually, with a median of 49 per cent to 1916—these are for gifts in excess of $5,000. Again, a study by the Department of Commerce shows that in 1929 IHL had 8.6 per cent of the gifts and bequests, in 1933 only 6.2 per cent, and in 1942 only 4.9 per cent.[2] During the Depression and the war the competing agencies and institutions had improved their organization for raising funds much more than colleges and universities. In more recent years the balance has been swinging back, because of the development of the alumni-gift program, large endowment-fund drives, development programs, and parent drives. Thus, according to Miss Mushkin's forthcoming book, the share of corporate gifts to education rose from 13 per cent in 1947 to 39 per cent in 1959.

An indication of the trends is suggested by Table 35-1, which shows that the large IHL have experienced substantial declines in the proportion of national income which they receive as gifts. Another classification, under *B,* of smaller institutions does not show the same general trend. Nonetheless, there has been a decline for all institutions, since on the whole

457

large institutions account for the major part of gifts. The experience since 1953–54, however, points to an improvement in the position of IHL.

A recent survey of business leaders showed that 74 per cent favored help to IHL; 75 per cent, to community chests; 67 per cent, for hospitals and health organizations; 49 per cent, for welfare organizations; and 33 per cent, for churches and religions. A Yale University release suggested a distribution of 30, 30, 30, 10 for religion, education, community services,

TABLE 35-1
Gifts, Higher Education in Relation to National Income, 1920 to 1956–57

Year	Gifts (millions)	National income (billions)	Gifts as per cent of national income
A. Fifty-one large IHL, average:			
1920s	$551*	$ 70	0.079
1930s	421*	60	0.070
1940s	622*	167	0.037
1951–52	91	284	0.032
1953–54	88	296	0.030
B. Private IHL:			
1930	22	76	0.030
1940	35	82	0.043
1950	104	240	0.043
C. Public and private IHL:			
1953–54 (728 IHL)	336	300	0.112
1956–57 incl. Ford (910 IHL)	833	351	0.238
1956–57 excl. Ford (910 IHL)	623	351	0.178

* Divide by 10 for single year.

Source: Collected and computed from J. P. Jones Company, *Three Decades of Philanthropy for Higher Education,* 1951; J. D. Millett, *Financing Higher Education in the United States,* 1952, pp. 335–338; *College and University Business,* April, 1953 and April, 1954; Council for Financial Aid to Higher Education, *Voluntary Support of America's Colleges and Universities,* 1958.

and world services. The head of the Ford Foundation could boast that of $1 billion of gifts, education in a general sense had received 80 to 90 per cent of Ford gifts. The spectacular salary-endowment gift served also as a catalytic agent: a survey of 275 business corporations revealed that they contributed 34 per cent of their gifts to education in 1956.[3]

FOOTNOTES

[1] J. B. Sears, *Philanthropy in the History of American Higher Education,* Department of Interior, Bureau of Education Bulletin, 26, 1922, pp. 55–61.

² *Survey of Current Business,* June, 1944, p. 12; R. P. Ludlum, "How High Should Tuition Go?" *The Educational Record,* October, 1958, p. 307.

³ Cf. J. A. Pollard "Fund Raising for Higher Education," p. 107; Council for Financial Aid to Education, *The Trend Is Up,* August, 1958, p. 1; H. T. Heald, "Higher Education and the Philanthropic Foundation," *The Educational Record,* January, 1957, p. 14; R. K. Mellon, "Business Has a Duty towards Public Causes," *College and University Business,* June, 1954; and *Corporate Contributions to Higher Education,* p. 7.

Chapter 36

TRENDS OF ENDOWMENTS AND GIFTS

In Table 36-1 it will be noted that the increase of endowment of the Ivy colleges (both total and per student) greatly exceeded that of all colleges and each of the other groups listed: for example, a rise of 180 per cent from 1928 to 1956 as against one of only 26 per cent for 6 other large private universities and 71 per cent for 10 women's institutions. The best summary of current gifts is the study by the Council for

TABLE 36-1

Endowment

(In millions of dollars)

College groups	Average of all cases					
	1928	1940	1956	Percentage rise		
				1928–1940	1940–1956	1928–1956
Total U.S...........	1,372*	1,764	3,837	29	118	181
8 Ivy League........	21.5	52.6	95.4	147	82	345
6 other private......	24.9	35.4	51.6	44	45	107
10 women's.........	4.4	5.1	10.2	16	98	132
20 liberal arts.......	3.5	5.6	9.4	61	66	170
40 large urban......	9.8	15.5	22.6	57	47	130
23 large Catholic....	1.6	1.3	2.7	...	111	68
	Endowment per Student					
Total U.S...........	1,245*	1,180	1,442	−5	22	16
8 Ivy League........	4,326	8,334	12,103	93	45	180
6 other private......	6,168	9,397	7,738	52	...	26
10 women's.........	4,501	4,864	7,704	8	60	71
20 liberal arts.......	6,247	7,500	9,765	21	30	56
40 large urban......	1,590	2,080	2,050	31	...	29
23 large Catholic....	606	490	542	...	11	−11

* This figure is for the year 1930.

Source: *American Universities and Colleges,* 1928, 1940, 1956. (Compiled and calculated by S. E. Harris.)

TABLE 36-2
Proportion of Total Enrollment, Alumni, and Gifts, etc. by Categories of Institutions, 1956–57
(Per cent)

IHL	Enroll-ment	Living alumni	Living graduates	Per cent of effectiveness (alumni donors as per cent of alumni solicited)	Total gifts	Gifts of corpora-tions and business	Total alumni gift support	Gifts of welfare founda-tions	Gifts of govern-ments	Bequests
Major private universities.........	24	23	18	23	47	43	44	60	42	56
State universities and land-grant colleges..............	39	36	39	11	10	13	14	3.8	33	12
Private men's colleges..............	4.1	3.6	4.2	25	5.3	4.0	7.8	5.2	0.3	5.0
Private women's colleges..........	4.1	5.4	6.6	34	7.7	4.7	8.2	7.4	0.7	5.0
Private coeducational.............	18	23	20	19	23	25	19	19	15	14
Professional and technical.........	3.1	3.7	6.0	22	5.2	9.2	4.8	4.6	5.2	6.0
Municipal and urban..............	2.9	2.0	4.3	13	0.3	0.5	0.9	0.06	3.4	0.8
Junior colleges..................	4.9	3.3	3.1	14	1.3	0.8	1.3	0.07	1.7	0.7
All......................	100.0	100.0	100.0		100.0	100.0	100.0	100.0	100.0	100.0

Source: Computed from *Voluntary Support of America's Colleges and Universities, 1956–1957.* Figures do not add exactly to 100.0 because of rounding and slight inaccuracies in original figures.

Financial Aid to Education for 1956–57 and for 1958–59. The coverage by enrollment is not exactly like the national sample, and for this reason these results are subject to some reservations. For example, in 1956–57 public institutions were underrepresented, as were private men's colleges and private women's colleges.

It is appropriate to compare the gifts to each group of colleges as a percentage of total gifts with its percentage of total enrollment and percentage of total alumni. The percentage of enrollment suggests the needs of the college; the percentage of the alumni may suggest the reservoir of gifts. For example, it is significant that for state universities and land-grant colleges, private men's colleges, municipal and urban universities, and junior colleges the proportion of alumni is less than that of enrollment. This is a financial disadvantage. When we compare the effectiveness of the request for funds, that is, the proportion of alumni solicited who became donors, we find that private women's colleges had the greatest success, followed by private men's colleges, major private universities, professional and technical schools, private coeducational schools, junior colleges, municipal and urban universities, and state universities and land-grant colleges, in that order.

Which institutions receive the largest gifts in relation to their enrollment? The order is as follows (I indicate the proportion of gifts to the proportion of enrollment):

> Major private universities.................... 1.95
> Private women's colleges.................... 1.9
> Professional and technical.................. 1.7
> Private men's colleges....................... 1.3
> Private coeducational....................... 1.3
> State universities and land-grant colleges....... 0.25
> Junior colleges............................. 0.25
> Municipal and urban universities.............. 0.10

Of course different types of institutions experience varying results in the categories of their gifts. Thus private men's colleges have a substantially better record in the proportion of all alumni gifts than for gifts generally. Private coeducational institutions and professional and technical schools, however, receive a smaller proportion of total alumni gifts than of all gifts. Professional and technical schools are more successful in obtaining help from business: 9 per cent of the total, and of all gifts only 5 per cent. Major private universities have had a very profitable experience with foundation grants, and state universities have a substantially inferior record in this category compared to gifts generally. The share of private universities in both these categories greatly exceeds their relative enrollment, and the reverse holds for public IHL.

Studies of the Council for Financial Aid to Education throw some light on the gifts to higher education (Table 36-3).

TABLE 36-3
Amounts Contributed by the Various Groups of Donors

Donor	1954-55	1956-57	1958-59	Changes from 1954-55 to 1958-59, per cent
Corporations, business concerns.........	$ 39,432,625 (11.7%)	$ 76,897,762 (9.4%)	$ 98,456,255 (13.1%)	+149.7
Religious denominations.............	42,853,747* (12.7%)	78,100,606* (9.6%)	64,214,314 (8.5%)	+ 49.8
Governing board............	9,651,036 (2.9%)	29,400,237† (3.6%)	24,422,178‡ (3.2%)	+153.1
Alumni(ae).........	52,100,093 (15.6%)	101,123,447§ (12.4%)	152,582,763 (20.3%)	+192.9
Other individuals and/or families.......	30,938,033 (9.2%)	52,507,574 (6.4%)	129,349,375 (17.2%)	+318.1
Bequests.........	35,699,311 (10.6%)	74,274,211† (9.1%)	Credited to donors	
Trusts.........	6,631,650 (2.0%)	16,068,775† (2.0%)	Credited to donors	
Annuities and life contracts.........	4,668,304 (1.4%)		Credited to donors	
General welfare foundations.........	50,247,321 (14.9%)	319,085,152¶ (39.0%)	88,337,037 (11.8%)	+ 75.8
Nonalumni(ae), nonchurch groups.........	18,681,898 (5.6%)	37,497,821 (4.6%)	52,351,448 (7.0%)	+180.2
Governments.........	29,855,030 (8.9%)	53,691,505 (6.6%)	124,822,028 (16.6%)	+318.1
Other sources.........	15,271,058 (4.5%)	17,199,691 (2.1%)	16,870,192 (2.3%)	+ 10.5
Total.........	$336,030,106 (100%)	$817,378,017¶ (100%)	$751,405,590 (100%)	+123.6
	728 institutions	(net total)	1,071 institutions	+ 47.1
		904 institutions		

* Includes estimated value of "contributed services" of Catholic clergy and religious: $16,633,557 in 1954–55, and $25,568,407 in 1956–57.
† Includes giving by alumni for these categories.
‡ Does not include $11,348,783 from alumni members.
§ Includes all alumni giving—annual fund ($62,654,683, or 7.6% of grand total), through governing board ($9,392,133), or in form of bequests ($23,730,810), and trusts, annuities, and life contracts ($5,345,821).
¶ Includes $199,522,710 in faculty-salary-endowment grants from the Ford Foundation.

Source: *1958–59, Voluntary Support of America's Colleges and Universities*, p. 9.

463

TABLE 36-4
Summary

Group and number of institutions	Volume of support			Sources of support				
	Grand total of support (1)	Current operations (2)	Capital purposes (3)	Corporations & business (4)	Religious denominations (5)	Governing board (6) Exclusive of alumni	Governing board (6) Alumni members*	Total alumni support (7)
Major private universities (49).........	$280,680,201 (100%)	$154,722,544 (55.1%)	$125,957,657 (44.9%)	$30,563,794 (10.9%)	$12,591,550 (4.5%)	$ 2,856,375 (1.0%)	$ 2,410,476 (0.9%)	$ 70,690,523 (25.2%)
Public institutions, state-controlled (165)..	140,004,802 (100%)	103,408,147 (73.9%)	36,596,655 (26.1%)	21,241,970 (15.2%)	55,266 (N.S.)	1,833,038 (1.3%)	148,697 (0.1%)	11,843,348 (8.5%)
Private men's colleges (64).............	44,673,848 (100%)	13,312,501 (29.8%)	31,361,347 (70.2%)	4,186,918 (9.4%)	2,135,211 (4.8%)	1,583,365 (3.5%)	1,963,474 (4.4%)	17,476,151 (39.1%)
Private women's colleges (142)..........	34,687,442 (100%)	14,457,201 (41.7%)	20,230,241 (58.3%)	3,011,027 (8.7%)	2,905,841 (8.4%)	1,507,945 (4.3%)	692,248 (2.0%)	14,143,619 (40.8%)
Private coeducational institutions (366)...	163,085,511 (100%)	70,256,855 (43.1%)	92,828,656 (56.9%)	24,136,917 (14.8%)	30,556,217 (18.7%)	11,217,636 (6.9%)	4,925,626 (3.1%)	29,531,574 (18.1%)
Professional & specialized schools (108)..	67,869,595 (100%)	42,705,829 (62.9%)	25,163,766 (37.1%)	13,306,923 (19.6%)	10,804,881 (15.9%)	4,588,364 (6.7%)	1,168,900 (1.7%)	7,626,591 (11.2%)
Municipal colleges and universities (11)..	8,473,698 (100%)	7,382,259 (87.1%)	1,091,439 (12.9%)	831,169 (9.8%)	15,300 (0.2%)	300 (N.S.)	0	502,864 (5.9%)
Junior colleges (166)...................	11,930,493 (100%)	6,633,025 (55.6%)	5,297,468 (44.4%)	1,177,537 (9.9%)	5,150,048 (43.2%)	835,155 (7.0%)	39,362 (0.3%)	768,093 (6.4%)
Grand total (1,071)...................	$751,405,590 (100%)	$412,878,361 (54.9%)	$338,527,229 (45.1%)	$98,456,255 (13.1%)	$64,214,314 (8.5%)	$24,422,178 (3.2%)	$11,348,783 (1.5%)	$152,582,763 (20.3%)

* Figures in this column represent gifts from alumni members of the governing board and should be added to the dollar figures to the left of them to get total governing-board support.

Group and number of institutions	Sources of support†					Forms of giving			
	Other individuals	Welfare foundations	Other groups	Governments	Other sources	Current immediate gifts	Bequests	Trusts, annuities, life contracts	Other forms or methods
	(8)	(9)	(10)	(11)	(12)	(13)	(14)	(15)	(16)
Major private universities (49)......	$ 53,613,299 (19.1%)	$40,426,370 (14.4%)	$18,463,054 (6.5%)	$ 48,817,125 (17.4%)	$ 2,658,111 (1.0%)	$220,464,232 (78.5%)	$43,484,674 (15.5%)	$14,449,187 (5.2%)	$ 2,282,108 (0.8%)
Public institutions, state-controlled (165)	14,522,269 (10.4%)	17,609,122 (12.6%)	14,075,935 (10.0%)	54,498,920 (38.9%)	4,324,934 (3.1%)	126,266,773 (90.2%)	4,135,985 (2.9%)	5,577,354 (4.0%)	4,064,690 (2.9%)
Private men's colleges (64)........	5,682,833 (12.7%)	3,892,020 (8.7%)	7,050,264 (15.8%)	2,332,472 (5.2%)	334,614 (0.8%)	36,880,216 (82.6%)	4,760,166 (10.6%)	2,513,806 (5.6%)	519,660 (1.2%)
Private women's colleges (142)....	7,777,034 (22.4%)	2,697,053 (7.8%)	799,307 (2.3%)	1,167,060 (3.4%)	678,556 (1.9%)	27,036,375 (77.9%)	6,236,583 (18.0%)	1,038,131 (3.0%)	376,353 (1.1%)
Private coeducational institutions (366)	38,390,935 (23.5%)	14,206,991 (8.7%)	4,977,629 (3.1%)	5,782,704 (3.6%)	4,284,908 (2.6%)	131,862,721 (80.9%)	19,655,904 (12.0%)	8,788,526 (5.4%)	2,778,360 (1.7%)
Professional and specialized schools (108)	6,489,159 (9.6%)	9,077,707 (13.4%)	5,607,029 (8.3%)	7,798,180 (11.5%)	2,570,761 (3.8%)	61,503,476 (90.6%)	4,237,930 (6.2%)	1,960,824 (2.9%)	167,365 (0.3%)
Municipal colleges and universities (11)	865,880 (10.2%)	191,881 (2.3%)	695,637 (8.2%)	3,665,078 (43.3%)	1,705,589 (20.1%)	7,747,864 (91.4%)	250,244 (3.0%)	89,067 (1.0%)	386,523 (4.6%)
Junior colleges (166).............	2,007,966 (16.9%)	235,893 (2.0%)	682,593 (5.7%)	760,489 (6.3%)	312,719 (2.6%)	10,539,216 (88.3%)	546,746 (4.6%)	641,614 (5.4%)	202,917 (1.7%)
Grand total (1,071).............	$129,349,375 (17.2%)	$88,337,037 (11.8%)	$52,351,448 (7.0%)	$124,822,028 (16.6%)	$16,870,192 (2.3%)	$622,260,873 (82.8%)	$83,308,232 (11.1%)	$35,058,509 (4.7%)	$10,777,976 (1.4%)

† Per cent gives relation to grand total. Thus 19.1% for individual gifts to major private universities means that these gifts accounted for 19.1% of total support of these IHL ($53.6 million = 19.1% of $280.68 million).

Source: Council for Financial Aid to Education, Voluntary Support of America's Colleges and Universities, 1958–1959, pp. 66–67.

First, note the trend is clearly upward—the 1956–57 total is inflated by the large faculty-salary-endowment grant from the Ford Foundation. Second, a striking increase is to be noted for government grants, related in large part to research. Third, religious denominations are losing ground,

TABLE 36-5
Support for All IHL

IHL	Much in excess of average*	Much less
Major private universities............	Alumni Foundations Bequests	Corporations Religious
Public institutions—state-controlled......	Corporations Governments	Religious Alumni Other individuals Bequests
Private men's colleges...............	Alumni	Corporations Religious Other individuals Foundations Governments
Private women's colleges............	Alumni Other individuals Bequests	Corporations Foundations Governments
Private coeducational...............	Corporations Religious Other individuals	Foundations Governments
Professional and specialized..........	Corporations Religious	Alumni Professional and specialized Governments Bequests

* This means that, for example, corporations and business provide 13.1 per cent of all grants to all IHL. But professional schools receive 19.6 per cent of their $68 million from corporations. Hence they receive support much in excess of average.
Source: Council for Financial Aid to Education, Voluntary Support of America's Colleges and Universities, 1956–57, and 1958–59, Voluntary Support of America's Colleges and Universities.

as might be expected. Fourth, business donations are advancing more rapidly than all gifts. Fifth, the relatively large gains of individuals, alumni, etc., may be associated in part with numerous large programs, and in part with the merging of bequests with these totals. Sixth, the gains of other groups are reflected in a relative decline for foundations. Seventh, the increase in these four years suggests that the total may well rise from ½ to 1 billion dollars in addition by 1970.

A comparison of the 1956–57 and 1958–59 gift receipts by types of institutions is of some interest. Whereas private universities' share dropped from 47 to 37 per cent, state IHL's share increased from 10 to 18½ per cent. There was also a large relative decline for private women's colleges (7.7 to 4.6 per cent) and a substantial improvement for professional and specialized schools (5.2 to 9.0 per cent).

Public institutions are without a doubt seeking private gifts more aggressively. But the gains of public and the decline of major private IHL are explained partly by the reduced coverage of private (65 to 49 IHL covered) and also by the $200 million Ford grant made in 1956–57. Foundation grants for private universities were $192 million in 1956–57 and only $40 million in 1958–59. With foundation grants excluded, these IHL would experience a gain of $46 million instead of a decline of $105 million.[1]

The general picture for 1958–59 is given in Table 36-4.

One other aspect of the trends should be noted: gifts do not come in proportion to the structure of spending by IHL. On the whole, the gifts for instruction are relatively much less than their importance in the budget, and gifts for student aid much larger. But the 26 per cent for unrestricted or general purposes might of course to some extent be used for instructional purposes. Table 36-6 presents some rough comparisons:

TABLE 36-6

Purpose	Per cent of gifts, three years, 1954–55, 1956–57, 1958–59	Per cent of budget, three years, 1953–54, 1955–56, 1957–58
Faculty and staff compensation.......	17	41 (instruction)
Basic research....................	16	19
Student aid......................	10	3½
Receipts for plant expansion.........	21	24*

* 1953–54, 1955–56 only.

Source: *1958–59, Voluntary Support of America's Colleges and Universities*, p. 15; and various issues of HEW, *Statistics of Higher Education: Receipts, Expenditures and Property, 1957–58* (Preliminary).

FOOTNOTE

[1] All figures in the last few paragraphs from Council for Financial Aid to Education, *Voluntary Support of America's Colleges and Universities, 1956–57*, and *1958–59, Voluntary Support of America's Colleges and Universities.*

Chapter 37

TECHNIQUES FOR RAISING MONEY

Before World War I leading colleges depended heavily upon very rich donors for required funds. This was the approach of both President Lowell of Harvard and President Butler of Columbia before World War I. A handful of rich men made gifts exceeding $1 million to Columbia, and the university noted seven bequests exceeding $1 million from 1881–1945.

Beginning with the end of World War I, the large colleges started to undertake systematic programs for raising money. In part the explanation is the beginning of higher tax rates. It is interesting to note that, although the tax rate at incomes from $6,000 to $50,000 varies tremendously, the fraction which contributions take of income is roughly unchanged. This certainly points to the conclusion that the taxpayer does not give more merely because the government shares a larger part of total costs.

Beginning in the early part of the twentieth century, when Bishop William Lawrence in one year raised $2,400,000 from 2,000 Harvard alumni, the concentrated drive has increased in popularity.

In the years soon after World War I, the record shows 65 IHL with endowment drives. These institutions had $171 million of endowment in 1918. They sought $114 million, or about two-thirds of their endowment: they obtained $90 million, or 77 per cent of the amount sought. The larger drives were less successful than the smaller ones in achieving their goals. In 1919 Harvard launched a new program in which it set its mark at $15 million. Actually it obtained only $13.8 million. In 1926, 68 colleges obtained almost $150 million from a half million donors. Finally, there were the $21 million campaign of Yale in 1927 and the $82.5 million Harvard campaign in 1957–1959.

The last depended on a model of organization, with mobilization of Harvard's best writers, public relations, radio, press, and television, and the cooperation of some 10,000 other alumni. Careful estimates were made of the potential gifts of groups and individuals: the goal was one-third from gifts in excess of $1 million, one-third from those in excess of $100,-

000, and one-third from the remaining 99+ per cent of the alumni. The alumni provided close to two-thirds of the funds, a proportion far beyond the national average. (See *Harvard Alumni Bulletin,* March, 1960.)

More recently a movement toward development programs has gained momentum. These programs are based on a longer period and are not concentrated campaigns. Careful plans are laid for raising money. In the later 1950s we have had announcements of a $100 million campaign at New York University, a $76 million program at Johns Hopkins, and a recommended program for more than $100 million at Yale (more recently reduced to $69 million)—these sums to be raised over a number of years. The development fund is a more or less continuous campaign, often including alumni funds and special capital drives. An over-all investigation of needs and sources of funds is the base of the development approach.

The alumni fund is a relatively new development. In 1870 William Graham Sumner, a famous Yale sociologist and economist, pointed out that many alumni would " . . . give according to their ability in order that the college might hold the same relative position to future generations which it held to their own. The sense of gratitude, the sense of responsibility, and light and interest in the cost of education, which are felt by these men, constitute a source which has never yet been [used] but which would yield richly."

Late in the nineteenth century a Yale Alumni Fund was established. By 1930 there were 46 such funds and by 1946, 142; and approximately 26 per cent of the alumni were participating in them. By the middle 1950s the total amounts received were $21, $25, and $36 million, respectively, in three years, and the alumni fund was contributing about one-third of the total amount of money made available by alumni. One estimate puts the alumni-fund yield at $60 million in 1959. For 1958–59 the Council for Financial Aid to Education estimated *all* alumni gifts at $153 million.

Potentialities of the alumni fund have not been exhausted by any means. Out of 5.5 million alumni solicited, 1.1 million contributed toward these funds in 1956–57. Actually a completely successful drive among all alumni with contributions at $35 per capita might yield several hundred million dollars a year. This is clearly a realistic goal, although the probabilities are that no more than $100 or $200 million could be had in the years immediately ahead. Within ten years there might very well be 20 million alumni, including nongraduates, and an average contribution of $35 would provide $700 million, an income four to five times the current income from endowment.

In view of the large contributions made by a relatively small percentage of donors in many IHL, some may question the wisdom of alumni drives. At Harvard, in a period of twenty years, a very small part of 1 per cent accounted for 90 per cent of the new capital. But there is a case for widespread appeals; often, for example, they uncover large potential donors.

President Eliot of Harvard once said:

It is of course largely by the extent of the support accorded to a college by its own graduates the world judges of the right of that college to seek co-operation from others in planning the future. An institution that cannot rally to its finance the assistance of the men who have taken its degree and whose diploma is their passport to the world is in a poor position to ask assistance from others. It is not merely what the alumni give, it is the fact that they do give that is of supreme importance.

The proportion of alumni gifts to total contribution by various categories of colleges, 1956–57, is given in Table 37-1. (These ratios vary from year to year. For example, the 1958–59 report of the Council for Financial Aid to Education reveals alumni gifts as a proportion of the total as 60 per cent for Harvard, 36 per cent for Princeton, 20 per cent for Northwestern, 26 per cent for Cornell, and 20 per cent for Pennsylvania.)

TABLE 37-1

Proportion of Alumni Gifts to Total Contributions,
by Various Categories of Colleges, 1956–57

IHL	Per cent	IHL	Per cent
Private universities:		Private universities (cont.):	
Dartmouth	48	Pittsburgh	1
Harvard	41	Rochester	1
Princeton	34	Men's colleges:	
Northwestern	34	Williams	58
Buffalo	27	Amherst	37
Yale	24	Colgate	30
Cornell	23	Bowdoin	26
Pennsylvania	19	Haverford	25
MIT	18	Wesleyan	12
Brown	16	Women's colleges:	
Stanford	8	Wellesley	60
Columbia	7	Vassar	41
Chicago	6	Radcliffe	23
Johns Hopkins	2	Barnard	17
New York University	2	Bryn Mawr	10

Source: Computed from Voluntary Support of America's Colleges and Universities, 1956–57.

Other techniques are also popular. For example, IHL seek aggressively to provide lifetime income to a donor in exchange for gifts. The donor receives tax advantages and the IHL a gift, the difference between the value of the gift and the income paid out to the donor (or even his heir). A release by Mills College of February, 1959, urged friends of the college to transfer assets to the college in return for a lifetime income. The donor gains because the college pays no capital gains tax and because a substantial proportion of the gift is tax deductible. Annuities and life contracts do not account for a large part of total gifts; but of a sample of 120 colleges and 32 universities, 56 and 59 per cent, respectively, solicited life income trusts as a means of obtaining funds. An excellent presentation of the possibilities is given in *Americans Like to Give*.

Then there is a technique developing widely among new IHL: the sponsors shop around seeking the largest donation from local interests as a return for establishing a college in a particular locality. A Presbyterian college selected St. Petersburg, Florida, among 20 competitors because the authorities offered a site valued at $2 million and help in raising $2.5 million. Another Presbyterian college in a competition among 18 towns in North Carolina accepted an offer from Laurinburg of $3 million and a pledge of $1.6 million from the Synod of North Carolina.

As the proportion of college-age population at college increases, the importance of alumni gifts is likely to become of increasing importance. The average year of graduation of the large donors examined in the next chapter was 1900. At that time but 4 per cent of the college-age population was at college: the figure now is 36 per cent. For this reason the gifts from alumni through annual drives or the big drive are likely to become more important. Thus in 1946 annual giving at Harvard and Yale yielded $328,000 and $368,000, respectively. By 1960 the totals had risen to $1,238,000 and $2,313,000. But it is also well to note a contrary trend related to the increasing significance of governments, business corporations, and welfare foundations. These three categories accounted for more than 40 per cent of all gifts in 1958–59.[1]

FOOTNOTE

[1] For material in this chapter see E. T. Stewart, Jr., "Alumni Support and Annual Giving," *The Annals, Higher Education under Stress,* September, 1955, pp. 126–139; Johns Hopkins University, release of the office of public relations, Dec. 17, 1957; Marts and Lundy, *Fund Raising Survey Report Made for Kenyon College,* 1956; A. V. McClain, "Colleges Can Raise the Money They Need," *College and University Business,* August, 1954, pp. 27–29; C. H. Diefendorf, address, University of Buffalo Convocation Dinner, Jan. 8, 1958 (mimeographed); A. O. Davidson, "A Concept of Development for Iowa Colleges," *Association of American Colleges Bulletin,* December, 1957, pp. 609–615; Council for Financial Aid to Education, *Voluntary Support of America's Colleges and Universities;* E. L. Hawthorne, *Fund Raising for the Small College,* 1950, pp. 58–61, 67–68, 159–162, and 153; the 1956 fund survey of the American Alumni Council, "Educational Fund Raising," *College and University Business,* May, 1953; J. E. Armstrong, "Alumni Support Can Be Substantial," *College and University Business,* July, 1954, and May, 1955; F. W. Abrams, "Growth of Corporate Giving to Education," *School and Society,* Jan. 18, 1958; W. M. Compton, *Eastern Association of Colleges and Universities,* December, 1955, p. 55; C. T. Bissell, "The Business of the University," *School and Society,* Mar. 29, 1958;

J. A. Pollard, "Fund-raising for Higher Education," *Fortune*, February, 1948, pp. 104, 105, 140–45; H. J. Dudley, "Renaissance in Higher Education," *The Educational Record*, April, 1957, p. 116; Hugh Long & Co., "Investment Practices," *College and University Business*, May, 1960, p. 61; John Price Jones, "Reports: 300th Anniversary Report," *Harvard Archives*; R. F. Duncan, *College Trustees and the Raising of Money*, March, 1960; *The New York Times*, Oct. 5, 1957, and Sept. 21, 1958; Council for Financial Aid to Education, *Americans Like to Give*, 1961; and various issues of *Harvard To-Day*, 1960.

Chapter 38

A SURVEY OF LEADING DONORS OF HIGHLY ENDOWED COLLEGES AND UNIVERSITIES[1]

THE ISSUE

Very little is known about the philanthropists who have given close to $5 billion at book value to endowment funds, and recently as much as $750 million per year in current gifts. Occupations? Are they graduates of the colleges to which they contribute? Were they good students?

At the outset I should point out that alumni account for a small part of the contribution to IHL. From the national figures of the Council for Financial Aid to Education, alumni contributed 15.6, 12.4, and 20.3 per cent in the years 1954–55, 1956–57, and 1958–59; governing boards, 2.9, 3.6, and 3.2 per cent; and other individuals and/or families, 9.2, 6.4, and 17.2 per cent. In addition, bequests accounted for 10.6 and 9.1 per cent in the first two of these three years. (Bequests are included in the other totals for the third year.) In all, private giving, inclusive of these four items, accounts for one-third to two-fifths of the total.[2] But without question alumni have contributed a much larger part of the $5 billion or so of endowment funds.

For many colleges alumni giving counts for much more than 20 per cent of total gifts. In the Harvard $82.5 million campaign, for example, more than 60 per cent came from alumni. Alumni support was especially important for the following:[3]

Percentage of Support from Alumni, 1958–59
Private women's colleges................ 40.8
Private men's colleges.................. 39.1
Major private universities.............. 25.2

THE SAMPLE

In exploring this problem, I sought information from 77 IHL listed in 1958 as having endowments exceeding $10 million (book value). These institutions would account for close to 90 per cent of total endowment, though not nearly so large a part of current gifts. (Harvard is not included, in part because its endowment is out of line with the others, and partly because it seemed useful to analyze the Harvard episode separately.)

Of the 77, we had useful responses from 23 IHL (24 inclusive of Harvard) with endowments having market values of about $1 billion. Since only 19 (plus 1) provided information on the 24 top donors, we analyzed the returns of these 19 IHL (plus Harvard). We have no reason for believing that the occupational and scholastic performance of the sample would vary greatly from that of the universe. In all we had 456 donors to analyze (19 × 24).

COLLEGE ATTENDANCE AND ACADEMIC PERFORMANCE

Table 38-1 reveals the academic history of the 456 donors.

More than 80 per cent of the top 24 donors of the 19 IHL who attended college were alumni of the college to which they contributed. In the higher-degree category, the percentage of donors at the beneficiary institution was less than 40 per cent.

TABLE 38-1

Data relating to College and University Attendance and Completion
for the Leading 24 Donors of Each of 19 Institutions

College and university attendance and completion	Donor group		
	Top 24	Top 10	Top 5
College attendance:			
Known to have attended college..............................	342	137	67
Known not to have attended college...........................	32	18	9
No information...	82	35	19
Known to have attended "beneficiary" college..................	276	106	56
College completion:			
Known to have attended and received a college degree...........	303	119	57
Known to have attended without receiving college degree..........	39	18	10
Completion of a higher degree:			
Known to have completed a higher degree.....................	115	45	22
Known to have completed higher degree at "beneficiary" institution..	64	19	7
Total number of donors..	456	190	95

Another interesting feature of this table is the large percentage of higher professional degrees vis-à-vis first degrees, a percentage much higher (and particularly for the earlier years involved) than in the nation generally. Even today higher degrees are only a little more than 20 per cent of total degrees; in 1900, a year that might be suggested as the average year of graduation of major philanthropists considered here, graduate degrees were 8 per cent of first degrees. In this sample of 456 donors the figure was close to 40 per cent. Moreover, the percentage of higher degrees seems to increase with the rise in the ranking of donors (from top 24 to top 5).

The scholastic achievement of the donors is surprisingly high. I have been concerned that excessive emphasis on grades in school, aptitude tests, and the like might exclude from first-class colleges many who are late bloomers and contribute so much to maintaining the high quality of IHL through their gifts. For those numerous IHL which depend for as much as 50 per cent of their income on endowment and current gifts from alumni and other private sources, this becomes a matter of importance. Would men of the quality of Eisenhower, Lodge, Roosevelt, Dillon, McElroy, Herter, Joseph Clark, Lourie, Ford, etc., get into first-class colleges if attention were paid mainly to aptitude tests, which will tell little about motivation, genius, and other important qualities not tested in this manner?

The information available on class standing was scant; only 4 IHL (exclusive of Harvard) could furnish adequate information on the class standing of their leading donors. But these show that for the 74 who completed college, 34 fell in the first quarter, and 25 in the second quarter, a ranking much better than the average 18 and 18 for the first two quarters.

TABLE 38-2
Class Standing

Donor-group ranking	1st quarter	2d quarter	Lower half	Total
Top 5...............	7	5	2	14
Second 5............	7	6	2	15
Last 14.............	20	14	11	45
Total.............	34	25	15	74

OCCUPATIONAL DISTRIBUTION OF MAJOR DONORS[4]

Table 38-3 reveals, as might be expected, the predominance of the businessman as the most important source of *large* gifts. Since businessmen (managers, officials, and proprietors, except farm) account for about 10 per cent of the employed, and professional, technical, and kindred an equal percentage, and since the former have the highest incomes, the business contribution would be expected to be the largest.[5]

Of particular interest is the contribution of businessmen in relation to the subtotal (the remainder belongs to categories that might well largely

TABLE 38-3

The Occupational Distribution of the 24 Leading Donors of 19 Institutions

Occupation	Top 24		Top 10		Top 5	
	Number	Mean percentage for 19 IHL	Number	Mean percentage for 19 IHL	Number	Mean percentage for 19 IHL
Business.....................	222	48.9	109	57.4	62	65.2
Lawyer.....................	44	9.6	15	7.8	11	11.3
Engineer....................	33	7.2	10	5.2	3	3.1
Physician...................	26	5.7	10	5.2		
Educator....................	20	4.4	3	1.6	2	2.1
Government.................	4	0.9	1	0.5		
Dentist.....................	1	0.2	1	0.5		
Subtotal..................	350	76.7	149	77.5	77	81.2
Other......................	31	6.8	9	4.7	3	3.1
Women (not otherwise classified)	17	3.7	8	4.2	3	3.1
Retired (not otherwise classified).	6	1.3	1	0.5	1	1.1
No occupation...............	10	2.2	6	3.1	4	4.1
No information..............	42	9.2	17	8.8	7	7.2
Total....................	456	100.1	190	100.1	95	99.8

be allocated to other groups). The donations of the business group increase as the size of contribution increases.

Per Cent Subtotal for 19 IHL

Top 24................. 64

Top 10................. 74

Top 5................. 80

THE HARVARD STUDY

1. Year of A.B. or B.S.

The average year of graduation for the 24 largest donors with an A.B. or B.S. was 1900[6] (but the average for the 9 largest was 1890).

2. Degrees

Of the top 30 donors, 25 received an A.B. or B.S. Of those not with degrees 4 were women who had left estates to Harvard, inclusive of the Nieman estate.

3. Non-Harvard Degrees

The largest gift of all came from the estate of Edward Harkness (Yale, 1897, $9.7 million). Here the genius of President Lowell in being ready for Harkness with a house plan was decisive. The only other large donors with college degrees other than from Harvard were: John D. Rockefeller ($6.1 million, Brown, 1897, fifth largest donor) and S. S. Kresge Foundation ($2.1 million, Albion College, 1923, and fourteenth largest donor).

4. Highest Professional Degrees

Of the 25 Harvard donors with college A.B. or B.S., 9 received higher professional degrees, a proportion much above that for the average college population:

Harvard L.L.B.	4
Harvard M.D.	1
Harvard M.A.	2
Harvard M.B.A.	1
St. Lawrence M.A.	1

5. Honorary Degrees of 30 Donors

Harvard	1
Cornell	1
Brown	1

Apparently the reward of an honorary degree to a large donor is the exception rather than the rule.

6. Occupation

Business	15
Lawyer	5
Physician	1
Government	1
No occupation	6
Not given	2
Total	30

The dominance of business is again revealed.

7. Class Standing

Plain A.B.	10
Honors	7
First in class of 96	1
Tenth in class of 111	1

As in the sample discussed above, class standing is much above the average for all students. In the years of graduation of these donors, an average of 25 per cent with honors was high. Yet 47 per cent of the large donors received honors grades.

* * *

In summary, the 24 top donors in 19 IHL (456 in all or 486 inclusive of Harvard) were relatively good students, were generally graduates of the

IHL receiving their benefactions, graduated in larger proportions and went on to graduate work in larger numbers than all students. Business dominated the interests of these donors.

It is of some importance for IHL greatly dependent upon gifts from alumni to consider carefully their admission policies from this angle. This study suggests at least that the potential donors are also likely to be good students. To this extent we may be assured that they will not be excluded from first-class colleges. But increasing emphasis on aptitude tests and school grades in the years of rising competition for openings at college may well exclude many of those who, for example, through their benefactions provide about two-thirds of the income of a $3,500 education at Harvard for which the student pays only $1,200. We need improved techniques for discovering the future philanthropists and other men of eminence.

FOOTNOTES

[1] Paul David processed the answers to this questionnaire and also made many helpful suggestions for the statistical treatment.

[2] Council for Financial Aid to Education, *1958–59, Voluntary Support of America's Colleges and Universities*, p. 9.

[3] See U.S. Census, *Income of Families and Persons in the United States*, 1958, p. 51; *Fact Book on Manpower*, BLSM Bulletin 1171, September, 1954, p. 54; S. E. Harris, "Who Gets Paid What," *The Atlantic Monthly*, May, 1958, pp. 35–38.

[4] We had many difficulties in classifying the donors—e.g., business engineers were classified as engineers, women were not classified by the occupation of husband who acquired the funds, "retired" is a difficult category, and we had no information for 9 per cent of the sample.

[5] Cf. the admirable report, Harvard Faculty of Arts and Sciences, *Admissions to Harvard College*, 1960, especially pp. 32–35, 46–50.

[6] In one instance the gift was from a mother and in another from the father. (The son's class was used.)

Chapter 39

THE STRUCTURE OF INVESTMENTS

In Table 39-1 I present the history of investments from 1926 to 1958. It is clear from this table that investment patterns are related to the samples chosen. In particular, any sample of large institutions gives a different result from one based on many small institutions or from a more comprehensive group including both large and small institutions.

One thing is clear: by 1940 IHL (particularly the larger institutions) had cut down their relative investments in bonds and increased their relative holdings of common stocks. In 1935, 25 large universities had 28.7 per cent of new issues, in 1935 they were 2¼ times as large as new issues colleges had 17.5 per cent invested in this way.[1] But in general they were slow to adapt themselves to a greater interest in equity investments. In order to maintain their income, they bought the common-stock investments which were available at low prices during Depression years.

Refunding bond issues at lower rates in the Depression further increased interest in common stock. Whereas in 1929 refunding issues were only 14 per cent of new issues, in 1935 they were 2¼ times as large as new issues and 2¼ times as high in value as in 1929.[2]

In the thirties the large institutions tended to dispose of real estate and mortgages, although this was not a universal rule. Smaller institutions still held relatively large stakes in property.

In the years 1938–1947 the large institutions expanded their investments in common stock, especially at the expense of mortgages and real estate. In the ten postwar years IHL greatly expanded their equity investments.

Since 1950 for the first time there has been a substantial decline in the proportion of bonds as well as of mortgages and real estate, and a very large relative increase in common stocks. But this increase in common stocks could be explained completely by the rise in values of common stocks without any shifting of purchases. I assume of course that purchases would increase with the rise in the total endowment fund. It was during

TABLE 39-1

Structure of Investment, Colleges and Universities, 1926 to 1957

Source of data	Year	Dollar value (millions)	No. of IHL	Per cent							
				Bonds	Stock		Mortgage	Real estate	Plant	Other
					Preferred	Common				
1. Cain	1926	All in excess $15 million	8	59.7	9.0	9.2	10.1	5.3	5.5	1.2
	1929			62.0	5.4	9.9	12.7	4.6	4.5	0.9
	1933			59.0	5.5	12.7	11.6	7.2	3.2	0.8
	1940			42.2	8.2	29.3	4.3	9.7	1.9	4.6
2. Teachers College	1929	549	45	45.2	5.8	12.6	12.2	18.4	1.4	4.4
	1940	686	45	39.5	9.0	20.6	9.3	16.3	2.0	3.4
3. Wood, Struthers	1931	537	29	49.8	7.8	10.0	13.5	13.1	....	5.8
4. Association of American Colleges	1931	614	143 indep. colleges	49.3	5.1	5.1	21.7	10.4	....	6.0
5. Cain	1940	1,263	120	40.3	10.3	21.8	7.7	15.3	....	4.6
6. Kirkpatrick	1938	428	12	38.7	10.7	22.5	7.9	15.7	....	4.5
	1947	532	12	42.9	9.2	29.5	4.0	11.4	....	3.0
7. Scudder, Stevens and Clark	1946	1,300	59	42.0	11.0	30.0	5.5	8.0	Cash = 2½	0.5
8. Cain	1950	1,466	29	45.3	8.0	28.7*		16.2	....	1.8
	1951	1,566	29	43.9	7.7	29.5*		16.6	....	2.3

9. Barron's								
10. Boston Fund								
1952	783	15	39.2	8.5	52.3‡	6.0	1.5	1.0
1956	2,770	56	30.4†	4.6	56.5			
1957	2,490	42	32.0†	3.3	56.1	8.4	1.2	
11. Boston Fund								
1958	2,535	54	33.2	3.6	51.7	4.4	2.4	2.2	2.5
12. HEW								
1958 {	3,781§	200	44.1	4.8	32.5	6.7	3.6	3.4	4.8
	4,857¶	200	33.7	3.7	47.4	5.2	2.8	4.8	3.8

* The low level of common stocks is explained by the fact that they are valued at book and hence by 1950 common stocks are substantially undervalued.

† Includes cash.

‡ $143 million, or more than one-third of common stock value, is at book value, and hence common stocks are undervalued. But this breakdown excludes nonsecurity investments. If included, the 52 per cent would be reduced to about 42 per cent. Hence total given is only roughly accurate.

§ Book Value.

¶ Market Value. Book value of common stocks = $1,229 million; market = $2,324 million.

Sources: 1. J. H. Cain, What is Happening to College and University Investments and Income?, American Council on Education Studies, June, 1941, p. 30.
2. The Administration of College and University Endowments, p. 44.
3. Wood, Struthers & Co., Trusteeship of American Endowments, 1932, table 1.
4. Bulletin of the Association of American Colleges, 1932, p. 74. Totals do not add to 100 per cent.
5. Cain, op. cit., p. 37.
6. J. I. Kirkpatrick, A Study of University Endowment Funds, 1947, p. 41.
7. Scudder, Stevens, and Clark, Survey of University and College Endowment Funds, 1947, p. 17.
8. J. H. Cain, "College Investment Funds and How They Grow," College and University Business, July, 1952, p. 25.
9. Barron's, Mar. 16, 1953.
10. Boston Fund, A Study of College and University Endowment Funds at June 30, 1956; Vance, Sanders & Company, Brevits, vol. N, no. 21; and Barron's, June 17, 1957.
11. Boston Fund, A Comprehensive Study of College and University Endowment Funds, 1958.
12. HEW, College and University Endowment Investments: A Survey as of June 30, 1958, p. 12.

the war and afterward that the growing fears of inflation, large profits, and a substantial decline in the return on bonds created this tendency for investments in equities to rise relatively. Because of these developments, investment managers watched with equanimity the proportion of common stocks rise *pari passu* with the increase of equity prices.

In the Great Depression there was no consistent investment policy among institutions. At the bottom of the Depression the larger funds tended to hold relatively large amounts in bonds; the small funds, a larger proportion in bonds and a smaller proportion in common and preferred stocks, and a relatively large proportion in mortgages and real estate. There were large variations among institutions. For example, the proportion of bonds varied from 0.7 per cent for a very small fund to 81.6 per cent for a $16 million fund; common stocks from 0 for one fund to 24.4 per cent for a $30 million fund; mortgages from 0 to 93.6 per cent for a $5 million fund. There were 6 funds out of 143 with more than 15 per cent in common stocks, and 12 with less than 5 per cent.[3]

In general the larger institutions seem to have a relatively large proportion of *productive* funds[4] to total capital assets. Institutions with 800 to 999 students in 1930 had productive funds per student equal to 51 per cent of total capital assets; for institutions with less than 200 the proportion was 28 per cent.

That IHL were slow to adopt the equity approach is suggested by Table 39-2. This table shows that the most successful fire insurance companies, national-bank trust departments, trust funds, trust institutions, and four large foundations all had much larger proportions of their investments in common stocks in years around 1940.

By 1946, however, there were important changes: common stocks had increased from 11½ per cent to 30 per cent for a large number of IHL. United States government bonds had increased from 2½ to 27 per cent, reflecting in part the unavailability of other investments and in part the need for support for war finance. Investment in real estate, mortgages or mortgage bonds, and real estate equities had declined from 27 to 14 per cent.

How investment policies may vary at different institutions in the same general class is suggested by Table 39-3. In 1921 Harvard had 20 per cent of its investments in stocks, Yale 13, Columbia 19; in 1930 the respective figures were 27, 43, and 5; and in 1947, 47, 43, and 19. The low percentage for Columbia is the result of heavy investments in real estate.

By 1956 common stocks accounted for more than half the value of investments. The rise of stock prices accounted for this gain. From 1949 to 1957 stock prices rose by 158 per cent. With other prices unchanged and with no increase in purchases of any assets, a rise of stock prices of these proportions could easily explain the rise in the proportion of equities to

TABLE 39-2

Percentage Distribution of Endowment Funds of 120 Institutions, according to Class
of Investment, Compared with Other Types of Institutions*

Distribution of investments	120 Institutions in this study	Wood, Struthers study of 30 institutions in 1932	Most successful fire insurance companies	49 legal reserve life insurance companies	National-bank trust departments	16 common trust funds reported to Congress	Trust institutions	Four large foundations	Several church boards of education
	(1)	(2)	(3)	(4)	(5)	(6)	(7)	(8)	(9)
Bonds..................	40.3	49.8	33.5	56.3	48.6	33.9	50.4	55.0	34.8
Preferred stocks..........	10.3	7.8	11.1	1.5	.....	19.7	24.1	4.5	3.6
Common stocks..........	21.8	10.0	39.0	0.4	32.1	32.6	25.5	40.0	21.0
Mortgages..............	7.7	13.5	0.6	19.0	7.1	11.5	.....	0.5	15.8
Real estate..............	15.3	13.1	0.5	7.1	7.4	0.3	.....	.....	8.2
Other..................	4.6	5.8	15.3	15.7	4.8	2.0	.....	.....	16.6
Total................	100.0	100.0	100.0	100.0	100.0	100.0	100.0	100.0	100.0

* Except for column 2, around 1940.

Source: J. Harvey Cain, *What is Happening to College and University Investments and Income?*,
American Council on Education Studies, June, 1941, p. 37. Data in columns 1 through 9 as
follows:

1. *The total endowment funds of 120 institutions as compiled for this bulletin, $1,263,653,056.*
2. *Trusteeship of American Endowments*, Wood, Struthers and Company, 1933, a study of endowment funds of 30 institutions holding $536,000,000 in funds.
3. Breakdown of assets of the most successful fire insurance companies, as of December, 1939, furnished by Dwight C. Rose of the Investment Counsel Association, New York. Total funds, $18,350,000,000.
4. Proceedings of the 33d annual convention of the Association of Life Insurance Presidents, December, 1940. $26,800,000,000 in funds.
5. Annual report of the Comptroller of the Currency, October, 1938. Total funds, $8,059,-393,406.
6. Report of Securities and Exchange Commission, *Investment Trusts and Investment Companies*, August, 1939.
7. Symposium on Common Trust Funds, *Trust Bulletin*, American Bankers Association, March, 1941.
8. Composite funds of four large foundations, from latest published reports.
9. Composite unpublished figures of several church boards of education.

total investments in the years 1949 to 1957. These figures point to one
conclusion: a large relative rise of percentage of common stocks to all investments (fixed total) is possible with no purchases of common stocks
whatever.

By the 1950s the colleges had more uniform policies. At 42 IHL, 31
had more than 50 per cent of their funds in common stocks, and 11 had

TABLE 39-3
Comparison of Diversification of Investments of Three Universities,
1921, 1930, 1938, and 1947, per cent

University and year	Bonds	Stocks	Real estate	Mortgages	Miscellaneous
Harvard:					
1921	69	20	...	11	
1930	53	27	12	8	
1938	56	37	6	1	
1947	51	47	1	1	
Yale:					
1921	63	13	12	8	4
1930	32	43	10	11	4
1938	22	51	5	7	15
1947	39	43	6	2	10
Columbia:					
1921	45	19	...	36	
1930	17	5	57	21	
1938	8	11	61	20	
1947	15	19	52	14	

Source: Adapted from G. I. Kirkpatrick, "A Study of University Endowment Funds," unpublished
master's thesis, New York University, 1949; the 1921 and 1930 percentages are from
John H. Prime, A Study of University Endowment, New York University, 1933.

more than 60 per cent. The maximum was Wesleyan with 81 per cent and
Delaware with 85. Only 2 had less than 40 per cent in common stocks.

By June 30, 1958 (Table 39-1), 200 IHL with 85 per cent of the total
endowment funds had investments of $3,781 million at book value and
$4,857 million at market value (128 per cent of book); market value of
common stocks was 189 per cent of book. Common stocks were 32.5 per
cent of book and 47 per cent of market; bonds, 44 and 34 per cent
respectively; and other investments (college plant, mortgages, real estate,
etc.), 18 and 16 per cent respectively.

FOOTNOTES

[1] American Council on Education, *Current Investment Practices of Colleges and
Universities*, 1936, p. 16; also see E. L. Hawthorne, *Fund Raising for the Small
College*, pp. 132–137, esp. chaps. 6–8.

[2] *Ibid.*, p. 6.

[3] *Ibid.*, p. 16.

[4] Yielding income.

Chapter 40

RETURN ON INVESTMENTS

The yield on investment funds depends upon the proportion of investments in various categories: common stocks, bonds, preferred stocks, real estate, etc. But these proportions alone do not tell the whole story. Much depends, for instance, upon whether short-term or long-term bonds are purchased. Short-term issues are generally less risky and give the investor the convenience of quick conversion into cash, so they generally yield lower income. Another factor of great importance is, of course, the quality of the particular issue, whether it is common stock, bonds, etc. The investor who put too much money into railroad stocks or even bonds in the 1930s did not do nearly so well as the man who bought real estate or industrial securities. It also makes a great deal of difference whether a security in a particular class is sound or unsound. For example, the purchaser who bought Lackawanna Railroad stock or bonds is much better off than the one who bought New York, New Haven & Hartford. The evidence available seems to suggest that the large investors had a better record than the small ones. They purchased common stock in larger quantities when such purchases seemed profitable and also preferred real estate to mortgages. They also seemed to have less interest in railroad securities and more in industrial issues. This is perhaps explained by the more expert advice available to the large institutions. But a survey for 1958 by the HEW (*College and University Endowment Investments*) does not reveal that the IHL with large investments earn more than the others.

In the Great Depression income of IHL tended to decline with the large reduction of output and the fall of prices. Yet one can exaggerate the significance of this. According to a study by Cain, dollar income on endowment funds for 45 IHL was $25.1 million in 1929, $28.3 million in 1930, $30.2 million in 1931, $29.2 million in 1932. Only in 1933 and 1935 did total dollar income fall below the level of 1929; the fall in prices greatly increased the purchasing power of each dollar received. By 1940 it was once more up to $28.9 million. Of course, the colleges received new funds,

485

which partly offset the decline in the average rate of return.[1] This record is much better than is suggested by corporate profits. Relatively small investments by IHL in common stocks before 1930 partly explain this fact. The figures above are more favorable than those given earlier, which are based upon the return from a *given* value of assets.

Fortunately for colleges, they are not much restricted in the types of investment they can undertake. They have a much greater degree of freedom than insurance companies or banks or ordinary trustees. This freedom stems from a case in November, 1823, when John McLean left $50,000 to his trustees to be held and invested by them according to their best judgment and discretion. Upon the death of his wife, who received the income during her lifetime, the trustees delivered one-half of the trust fund to the president and fellows of Harvard College to create an endowment for a professorship of ancient and modern history. The other half of the trust fund was turned over to the trustees of the Massachusetts General Hospital for the general charitable objects of that institution. When the surviving trustee filed his final account with the probate court, the judge approved, but counsel for the college objected that the money had not been invested in "safe and prudent stock"—that is, in public funds, bank shares, or other stocks—but had been invested " . . . in greater part thereof in trading companies whereby the principal sum was exposed and still continued to be exposed to great loss." In March, 1830, the Supreme Judicial Court of Massachusetts delivered its opinion, a landmark in the history of trusts in this country.[2]

All that can be required of a trustee to invest is that he shall conduct himself faithfully and exercise the soundest discretion. He is to observe how men of prudence, discretion and intelligence manage their own affairs not in regard to speculation but in regard to the permanent disposition of their funds, concerning the probable income, as well as the probable safety of the capital to be invested.

Trustees are justly and uniformly considered favorably and it is of great importance to bereaved families and orphans that they should not be held to make good losses in the depreciation of stocks or the failure of the capital itself which they held in trust, providing they conduct themselves honestly and discreetly and carefully, according to the existing circumstances in discharge of their trusts. If this were held otherwise, no prudent man would run the hazard of losses which might happen without any neglect or breach of good faith.

In this chapter we discuss the trends of return on endowment and also differences in return at the same time. But, unfortunately, varying accounting methods reduce the significance of these comparisons, especially among IHL. Thus when a stock dividend is paid, some IHL include this as income and others do not. Gains and losses are made on securities; the income will reflect often the extent to which the gains and losses are realized. Even where realized, differences in practice prevail: some IHL put the gains and losses in segregated accounts. Again, some IHL give historical book values; others correct for gains and losses on investments. Treasurers will quote return of all kinds, e.g., average net return from all investments, earned rates on pooled investments, yield on book or market value, return on endowment funds only. Often differences arise because the income is not related accurately to the capital which is supposed to yield the income. Some IHL depreciate real estate; others do not: a majority amortize bond premiums. Real estate is listed on the basis of book value of total equity held by the college, but also on the basis of the total value of the real estate.[3]

The return on endowment depends on a number of factors. We have already mentioned the structure of the investments, that is the percentage in bonds, stocks, etc. The tendency to buy well-known securities, for example, railroad bonds in the 1920s and early 1930s, is not always the wisest policy. The blue chips of one period do not always remain the blue chips of the next.

In 1925 *Barron's* compiled a list of the 12 most mentioned stocks. Had one invested equally in these dozen favorites, his list would have depreciated 33½ per cent in the following four years. Meanwhile the Dow Jones industrial average gained 7½ per cent. Young growing companies like General Electric, General Motors, and Du Pont, favorites today, were not held to be safe for investment then. Purchasers bought New York Central instead, which dropped from 116 to 15⅛. In 1939 *Barron's* compiled a list of 26 stocks most frequently mentioned. At the end of a ten-year period this group of favorites advanced only 19 per cent as compared to 24.7 per cent for industrials as a whole.

Barron's wrote in 1939: "I believe the age-old theory of the favorite well known stocks being the only investments for widows and orphans is all wrong. Hindsight in statistics shows that investing in the popular favorites for a long pull is the surest way towards a never increasing income and a diminishing capital. . . . "

Finally there is the problem of diversification. To reduce risks it is important to diversify by regions, types of securities, industries, companies, and the like. Sometimes, however, IHL reduce their returns by excessive diversification. If high-return securities are ignored because of a great desire for diversity, the net result may well be a reduction in yield.

It is reasonably clear that the trend of returns on endowment funds has been downward since the 1920s, although there was some improvement in the 1950s. Unfortunately, varying methods of accounting suggest that figures indicating this improvement must be taken with some reservations (Table 40-1).

Generally colleges keep their endowment funds at book value, that is, at the price of purchase. Sometimes they revalue, but not very often. However, in the last ten years, and increasingly, colleges reveal both book and market value. For example, in 1958–59 market value exceeded book value for 200 institutions with 85 per cent of all funds, by 28 per cent. The market value of common stocks exceeded book value by 89 per cent.

In a period of rising values a return based on original value is relatively high, and returns based on market value are correspondingly low. If readjustments are not made on book value, the usual case, then of course in rising markets the yield on book value is exaggerated.

An interesting case is the following: Columbia's Upper Estate (Rockefeller Center) was received from the state of New York in 1814 in exchange for land granted to the Province of New York in 1767 and 1774 and later ceded to New Hampshire. As a result of effective lobbying by the provost of the university, the state conveyed the botanic gardens, which had been given to the state, to Columbia. The Legislature estimated the value at $75,000, but Columbia claimed it was worth not more than $6,000. But in 1928 this land, the Upper Estate, was leased to the Rockefellers, and in 1946–47 the annual net income from rentals was $3,752,000. This asset has generally been undervalued on the books. (The yield on original value of $6,000 was 62,500 per cent.)

On special investments returns may be unusually large. Livingston Houston, chairman of the board of trustees of Rensselaer Polytechnic Institute (RPI), presented at my seminar the fascinating experience with 61 Broadway. With an initial investment of $100,000 and a bank loan of $1,035,000 in 1950, RPI by 1959 had obtained a return of 5.8 per cent per year on total investments of $2,225,000. By 1970 the expectation is $3,895,000 of ordinary income and a special reserve income of $2,500,000 (13½ per cent of income). In addition the college will have paid off $7,555,000 in loans, the equivalent of 15.9 per cent per year. By 1971, income should amount to $855,000 a year, or 39 per cent of original investment.

The University of Chicago has also indulged in unorthodox investments which have proved profitable.

The HEW study on college and university investment describes a program of a large university (undoubtedly Stanford) which is developing about 6,000 acres for shopping centers, light industry, etc. Since the university is not allowed to dispose of this property, the land is made available on lease, with minimum charges plus sharing in profits from sales.[4]

To some extent returns are affected by restrictions put upon investment policy. A donor may require an institution to keep a particular stock as, for instance, a gift of United States Steel stock made to Rensselaer Polytechnic Institute. Again, it is not easy for the University of Rochester to dispose of Eastman Kodak stock, although investment in Eastman Kodak stock has been highly profitable over the years. Oberlin College has large investments in the Aluminum Company, for its largest contributor was a high official in the Aluminum Company of America. Here again the net results seem to have been good. Trinity College, in a great insurance center, holds large quantities of insurance stocks. It apparently is not diplomatic for Trinity College to dispose of these stocks even though other investments might yield higher returns. Many other similar cases are to be found.

Unfavorable yields have sometimes been the result of unwise annuity practices. Colleges sometimes underestimate the life probability of the annuitant. A study of 25 colleges a generation ago showed that 26 per cent of total gifts were raised by the sale of annuity contracts. At present these contracts are relatively unimportant compared to the total endowment income. At least one institution *now* offers annuities at book value to new investments, thus giving the annuitant an advantage over other claims to investment income. Thus, though market value may be 50 per cent above book, the share of income given to new investors is based on the lower book value.[5]

Exemption from taxation inflates the income of IHL. If all the real property held by colleges were taxed at a rate of 1½ per cent of replacement cost, the average rate in the nation, it would be subject to taxes of about $300 million. (Replacement value is at least $20 billion.) In addition, the colleges and universities receive about $150 to $200 million of income from endowment and other investable funds. At an average rate, the colleges would be subject to additional taxes of around $50 to $75 million. In other words, the tax exemption is worth roughly about 7 per cent of the total current income of IHL.

Special tax exemptions also favor incomes of IHL. In many instances colleges receive property and compete with commercial enterprise, with the advantage of tax exemption. For example, Harvard received the rights to penny slot machines in New York subways through an inheritance. Obviously the university disposed of these properties as soon as possible. In the forties Yale purchased an eight-story building and warehouse in Kansas City and leased it back for one hundred years.[6]

Abuse of tax-exemption privileges has finally resulted in the government's cracking down on the colleges which compete with commercial enterprise. Investments are distinguished from commercial operations. Investments in business enterprise, in competition with private enterprise, and abuse of tax-exempt privilege is the exception rather than the rule. According to the 1958 survey of HEW, investments in business enterprises were only $10 million, or ⅕ per cent of all investments. (This figure seems rather low.)

An indication of the yield on investments of colleges is given in Table 40-1. The trend is downward.[7] It will be recalled that one study showed that 20 institutions earned an average of 2.98 per cent against 20 institutions with the best records earning 4.93 per cent. Those with the best

TABLE 40-1
Returns on Investment

Year	Number of IHL	Total yield (based on book value unless designated market)
1926[a,d]	45	5.14
	59	4.99
1929[a,b]	45	5.08
	22	5.69
1930[a,c]	45	5.16
	19–20	4.97 market
1933[a,b]	45	4.58
	22	4.15
1936[b,d]	22	4.15
	59	4.25
1940[a,c]	45	4.42
	19–20	4.50 market
1946[d]	59	3.90
	59	3.33 market
1950[c]	19–20	4.37 market
1953[e]	26	4.75
	21	4.00 market
1956[f,g]	39	3.36 market
	904	4.12
1958[h]	200	3.84 market
	200	4.91

Source: [a] J. H. Cain, *What Is Happening to College and University Invest-ments and Income?*, 1941, p. 29.

[b] *The Administration of College and University Endowments*, p. 54.

[c] "College Investments," *Barron's*, June 25, 1951. (Based on market value.)

[d] Scudder, Stevens and Clark, *Survey of University and College Endowment Funds*, p. 21.

[e] S. H. F. Goldstein, "Investing Returns by Endowment Funds," *The Commercial and Financial Chronicle*, no. 5224, 1953. (Includes some foundations.)

[f] Boston Fund, *A Study of College and University Endowment Funds*, 1956, p. 24.

[g] Adjusted 1956 market figures by ratio of market to book values, given in *Voluntary Support of America's Colleges and Universities, 1956–1957*, pp. 38–39.

[h] HEW, *College and University Endowment Investments: A Survey*, as of June 30, 1958, p. 12.

records had a smaller percentage in bonds and real estate and larger proportions in common stocks and mortgages. But this does not seem to be the most important explanation of the differences. Earlier studies in the Depression period showed that those with the highest returns tended to invest their funds in more risky enterprises.

In the postwar years, on the whole, the return on common stocks exceeded that on bonds, although by late 1958 this was no longer true. In 1958 the return on book value was 4.91 per cent, and on market value 3.84 per cent. The yields on market value were as follows: real estate, 5.91; business enterprises, 5.64; preferred stocks, 4.87; mortgages, 4.64; common stocks, 3.70; bonds, 3.65; college plant, 3.04 per cent.

The financial officer of a college naturally takes into account not only the current yield but also the possibility of capital appreciation. In concentrating on growth stocks he may sacrifice the current return on investments. This, as I have suggested earlier, raises questions about the distribution of resources between current and future needs. Those who are particularly interested in the current situation, the present faculty or students, may feel that they are being sacrificed to the future. A college administrator must take these issues into account in deciding the structure of his investments, particularly the choice between bonds and common stocks, or defense and growth common stocks.

In a similar vein H. Wells, formerly financial officer of Northwestern University, showed how difficult it was to select the growing industries and the profitable firms in the new industries: in the 1930s artificial refrigeration destroyed the natural ice business; in the late 1930s, aviation was on the way, but it was impossible to select the companies that would survive; and in the early 1950s the difficult choice was to pick the companies that would grow with television and decide on the future of the cinema. " . . . we must be alert at all times to the progress of science, invention, and promotion which may be influencing our investment holdings."

The extent to which a college will go in finding outlets for its money is suggested by a piece written by the treasurer of the University of Chicago:[8]

At the University of Chicago we not infrequently lent stock to a dealer who for one reason or another may have gone short and wishes to borrow shares in order to deliver. In such a case the dealer deposits with us cash equal to 100 per cent of the market value of the stock. All dividends of the stock come to us as usual and of course we can invest the cash and make additional income from that. Finally the borrower usually pays a fee of 25¢ or 50¢ a share on the stock borrowed.

. . . Commercial banks and life insurance companies are prohibited from owning or lending on vacant lots, and yet as all of us know, parking lots are frequently very remunerative. The University had a number of attractive investments as an owner of or as a holder of a real estate mortgage on a parking lot. Because of the lack of competition, these afford a higher rate of return with relatively little risk.

We have pioneered in the development of equipment trusts covering cars and trucks leased to companies of high credit standing in much the same way freight cars are leased to the railroads. Just recently we started leasing 8-ft. in diameter neoprene containers, suitable for the transportation or storage of liquids or flowable solids, to a major chemical company at an attractive rate. Again, not being hemmed in by legal restrictions, we have been able to place real estate mortgages up to 100 per cent of the value of the property. Of course we do this only when the credit of the lender is of top quality. . . .

Oil payments, ship financing, lease-backs, private placements, and numerous other unusual transactions are available to the enterprising endowment fund manager if he will keep an open mind in looking for sound and profitable deals. The nice thing about these investments is that they usually produce a fixed return higher than that available from bonds and provide a reasonably rapid amortization so that funds are flowing back all the time for use as other opportunities open up. . . .

The University of Chicago has also profited greatly from its interest in the *Encyclopaedia Britannica,* a gift of Sears, Roebuck and Company. Senator Benton provided working capital of $100,000, for which he received common stock, and the university received preferred stock and royalties on copies sold. Apparently, after the Rockefellers, the *Encyclopaedia Britannica* has been the largest contributor to the income of the university.[9]

FOOTNOTES

[1] J. H. Cain, *What Is Happening to College and University Investment and Income?,* American Council on Education Studies, 1941, p. 29.

[2] I owe this to T. E. Blackwell, "The Prudent Man Investment Rule in College Endowments," *College and University Business,* May, 1955, pp. 45–46.

[3] C. R. Sattgast, *Administration of College and University Endowments,* 1940, p. 88; and J. L. Kirkpatrick, "Accounting for Investment Income," *Proceedings College and University Business Officers,* 1947, pp. 54–60.

[4] See, for example, E. L. Hawthorne, *Fund Raising for the Small College,* p. 126; also on the issue of accounting, see Ralph S. Jones, "Accounting for Endowment Funds," *College and University Business,* March, 1951, pp. 25–28; and J. L. Kirkpatrick, *op. cit.,* pp. 92–98; S. E. Harris (ed.), *Higher Education in the United States: The Economic Problems,* pp. 232–34; *College and University Endowment Investments,* p. 26.

[5] See earlier discussion of market versus book value. Annuity contracts involve an exchange of a capital sum given to the college for designated annual payments, generally for life.

[6] *Wall Street Journal,* Apr. 12, 1947.

[7] Since the IHL studied are not identical, the results can be held to be rough only.

[8] J. P. Hall, "Don't Be Afraid of Unorthodox Investments," *College and University Business,* December, 1955, pp. 23–24.

[9] H. Kogan, *The Story of the Encyclopaedia Britannica,* pp. 253–279.

Chapter 41

SOME DETAILS OF HISTORY[1]

In general the major IHL with substantial endowment were greatly embarrassed by the collapse of our economy in 1929–1933. They frequently held large investments in real estate, return from which soon reflected the state of the economy. Dartmouth, Chicago, Harvard, and especially Wesleyan were hit by heavy investments in real estate and mortgages. Harvard had to write down substantial losses and has consistently avoided real estate investments ever since.

Another embarrassment resulted from large losses on railroads, affected not only by the Depression but by a secular decline which was not widely recognized at that time. The University of Chicago in 1939–40 carried railroad equities at book value at 12.7 per cent of the total; at market their value was only 2.9 per cent of the total. Whereas railroad bonds were 32 per cent of all bonds at market value in 1929–30, they had fallen to 3.8 per cent by 1944–45, and for railroad common stocks the decline was from 27 per cent to zero. The university lost about $7 million on railroad stocks held before the late 1930s. In the midst of the Depression, MIT continued to invest in railroads.

Many IHL reacted to the large decline of capital values by insisting, as did the comptroller of the University of Chicago in his 1944–45 report, that " . . . market fluctuations are relatively unimportant where investments are selected and held primarily with reference to their productivity and stability of income and ultimate capital realization."

Indeed in the 1930s the low capital values stimulated purchases of common stocks then available at low prices and hence high yields, which compensated for losses on bonds and stocks especially hard hit by the Depression. What is remarkable about a period when national income fell by about 45 per cent and dividends by 47 per cent is that investment income stayed up remarkably well. One explanation is, of course, a decline of interest income of only 15 per cent. Another is the continued influx of gifts, though at a much reduced rate. At Brown, for example, investments yielded

$463,000 in 1929 and ranged from $516,000 in 1931 (maximum) to $461,000 in 1933 (minimum) from 1930 through 1937.

Institutions varied in their enthusiasm for equities. Dartmouth, for example, was caught with a large percentage of equities at the time of the 1929 crash and hence had to be slower than many other IHL in purchasing equities in the 1930s. But in the period 1937–1943, Dartmouth plunged. Harvard, Princeton, and Brown all moved with some dispatch into equities. Those IHL that purchased industrials heavily profited greatly, for they tended to rise much more than other equities.

The trend toward equities resulted in gains of investment income much in excess of the rise of commodity prices. In part the explanation was, of course, a rise of new gifts as well as the excess of the increase of prices of equities over commodity prices.

At MIT investment income rose by 186 per cent from 1946 to 1956, and commodity prices rose but 39 per cent.

How much income rises depends also upon the relative stress put upon current income against capital gains. When the latter is weighted heavily, the rise of income is contained to some extent, for part of the gain is then to be expected in capital gains. For example, from 1946 to 1953, investment income of the University of Chicago rose only 55 per cent, the lowest among Chicago, Princeton, MIT, and Harvard. Princeton's gain was 109 per cent. A greater emphasis on growth stocks explains in part Chicago's record. At Wesleyan market values of common stocks rose in excess of 400 per cent from 1946 to 1958; investment income, in excess of 200 per cent.

In the 1930s IHL had to take substantial losses on capital. Book values had to be reduced as officers sold securities at prices below book value. In the later years they were able to realize profits as they sold securities at prices above the book value. Thus Brown realized losses of $2.4 million from 1934 to 1939 and realized gains of $5.5 million from 1956 to 1958.

As purchases of equities were made in the 1930s, book value did not rise greatly, partly because of the low prices of stocks purchased and partly because of sales of assets below book value. But as security prices rose after the Depression, market value tended to rise above book. At Harvard market was 93.6 per cent of book in 1939–40 and 111.4 per cent in 1944–45. In 1950–51 common stocks accounted for 46 per cent of investments at Harvard, but 67 per cent of investment income. Rising prices of equities raised the proportion of common stocks to all investments to 59 per cent in 1956–57; but the yield of these stocks was down to 61.6 per cent of investment income—a reflection of rising prices of equities. Again, Dartmouth's ratio of market to book value was 82 per cent in 1937 and 128 per cent in 1946.

One other interesting point emerges from a comparison of investment policies of seven IHL. As we said elsewhere, the distribution among large categories—e.g., stocks, bonds, real estate—does not vary nearly so much as in the earlier part of the century. But striking contrasts are to be found in the distribution among industries. Thus a comparison of MIT and Harvard, both in Cambridge,[2] is given in Table 41-1.

TABLE 41-1
Per Cent Investments in Common Stocks

Stock	1956 MIT	1955 Harvard
Oils........................	20	23
Chemicals...................	16	6
Automobiles.................	17	3
Public utilities...............	8	29
Banks and insurance...........	8	15

FOOTNOTES

[1] The analysis in this chapter was prepared by Saul Hymans, now of the University of California and formerly my research assistant, and is based on studies of investments since 1929 in the following IHL: Brown, Chicago, Dartmouth, Harvard, MIT, Princeton, Wesleyan.

[2] Material in this chapter comes from treasurers' and comptrollers' financial reports of the seven IHL.

SUMMARY: MANAGEMENT OF PRODUCTIVE FUNDS

In general IHL suffered a reduction in their share of the philanthropic dollar during the last generation, although new techniques developed in the 1950s are beginning to be reflected in a larger share for IHL. Effective exploitation of alumni and business may indeed result in annual returns of $500 million to $1,000 million a year, on the assumption that each alumnus would contribute $35 per year. This amounts to $1,050 each over thirty years, a sum less than the four-year subsidy generally provided by IHL.* Such contributions would be several times larger than those available today from these sources, and would roughly double the total philanthropic intake. It is conceivable that out of the $6 to 7 billion more required per year in ten years, philanthropy might provide $1 billion, and for private IHL these sources might well yield one-third to one-half of added funds required. But this is an optimistic projection, the fulfillment of which will require much intelligence and energy.

Endowment is certain to become less important. With increased taxes and a rise of competing demands, hard money (endowment) is more difficult to get and soft money (current funds) easier. The influx of soft money reflects the erosion of endowment as a result of inflation, increased enrollment, mismanagement occasionally (before World War II), and losses associated with funds so restricted that their use cannot be adapted to changing values of our society.

But endowment continues to be an important asset for a relatively small number of institutions. For many institutions, endowment offers protection against excessive sensitivity to public pressures. Endowments can yield more income if investment policy is adapted even more to the inflationary and growth trends of our economy, which especially favor equities against the *rentier* interests. They can be more effective as accounting practices favor current contributions. Preservation of capital values is not nearly so important as maximizing income, although the two are related. Since IHL, unlike banks and insurance companies, do not have to be liquid, they need be less concerned over capital values and less exposed to risks which accompany purchases of common stocks.

One of the toughest problems is the distribution of capital income between present and future. Excessive recourse to growth stocks may unduly burden the present generation of students and faculty, though it is not at all clear that this happened in the 1950s.

* Note $1,050 available in 1962–1991 is worth much less than $1,050 available in 1962.

496

APPENDIX

Distribution of Investments and Rate of Return for Institutions Having the Best Earning
Records and Those Having the Poorest Earning Records, Year Ended June 30, 1940
(In thousands)

Distribution of investments	Poorest records		Best records	
	20 Institutions earning 2.30 to 3.19%	Per cent	20 Institutions earning 4.43 to 5.86%	Per cent
Bonds...............................	$ 62,793	48.08	$ 39,166	33.92
Preferred stocks........................	11,925	9.13	13,967	12.10
Common stocks.........................	14,500	11.10	20,147	17.45
Mortgages (including real estate bonds and stocks).............................	5,857	4.48	13,739	11.90
Real estate............................	24,772	18.98	15,044	13.03
Investment in institutional property..........	3,571	2.73	5,713	4.95
Personal loans and notes.................	331	0.25	499	0.43
Endowment funds loaned to other funds.....	2,472	1.89	748	0.66
Other.................................	573	0.44	4,205	3.64
Uninvested cash........................	3,806	2.91	2,219	1.92
Total principal of endowment investments..	$130,600	100.00	$115,477	100.00
Total income received for year..........	$ 3,895	......	$ 5,697	
Average rate of return.................	....	2.98	....	4.93

Source: T. Harvey Cain, *What Is Happening to College and University Investments and Income?*,
American Council on Education Studies, June, 1941, p. 34.

PART SEVEN

COSTS AND ECONOMIES

Chapter 42

THE PROBLEM OF COSTS

INTRODUCTORY

On the whole, colleges and universities, unlike industry, have neglected cost studies. There is one obvious reason for this: industry relates its prices to costs and therefore tries to discover costs. This does not mean that industry always charges at cost; prices may be much above costs, or under pressure of excess supplies industry may sell at a loss. But cost accounting remains a principal source of guidance for management.

Industry also examines costs to find means of recording and reducing them. Surely IHL are also interested in reducing costs where the loss of educational value is not a serious restraining factor. And it is not true that colleges pay no attention to costs in setting prices. To be sure, the college is less interested in tying prices to costs than is industry, but we have already seen that college authorities do pay some attention to costs. For example, the tuition in public medical schools relative to private ones is much higher than in other fields of instruction. Higher costs are one reason for charging more in medical schools. Where the major benefits of education accrue to individuals rather than to society at large, the case for tying prices to costs is strengthened.

Although cost studies are rather neglected by IHL, there has been a long history of cost accounting for IHL. As early as 1932 the National Committee on Standard Reports for Institutions of Higher Education analyzed 45 unit-cost studies in higher education in which such issues as (1) the item to be measured, e.g., student credit hour, (2) coverage of cost items, (3) treatment of overhead, etc., were examined. In more recent years, the recourse to cost studies, especially in public IHL, has increased greatly. In Oklahoma, California, Georgia, New Mexico, Texas, and Indiana, for example, the authorities use cost studies to explain and justify budgetary demands. In some instances the formulas used are quite primitive (e.g., Texas), with comparisons made per student or per student credit hour, with inadequate allowance for differences in standards, enrollment, location, objectives, and the like; in others (California) the attack is more advanced.[1]

From my questionnaire addressed to more than 200 IHL, I find that out of 115 private IHL answering a question on use of cost studies, only 38 per cent claimed that they made a serious cost study. Among 43 public IHL the corresponding percentage was 56 per cent. Generally larger IHL were more disposed to make such studies than small ones.

CAN WE MEASURE COSTS?

Part of the failure to pay more attention to college costs is due to a widespread view that the measurement of these costs is impossible. One of the leading university educators informs me that costs vary according to the investigator chosen and hence little faith can be put in the results. This position is understandable where the college or university turns out a joint product, as in the medical school where the teacher instructs undergraduates, graduate students, and doctors taking refresher courses. He also does a great deal of research which has very little to do with his teaching, serves the patient in the hospital, and performs other public services. Obviously it is not easy to relate the relevant costs of the university and the hospital to instructional costs for medical students. The doctor at a medical school who is treating patients in a hospital is at the same time instructing the student observers.

Consider, for example, research. I asked President Lee DuBridge of California Institute of Technology whether he included research in his instructional costs. His reply was yes except for two large organized research projects. To estimate unit costs he would divide the $10 million budget by the number of students, even though a large part was research. His view was that research is a necessary operation to hold faculty and to train students, 70 per cent of whom were to do research later. In a discussion with some state-university presidents, however, the position taken was that the inclusion of organized research unnecessarily inflated the costs of instruction. These were held to be irrelevant.

In a study of the cost of medical education at Emory University in Georgia, the following sensible conclusion appeared:[2]

Cost analysis, no matter what system is used, is not an exact science but, rather like medicine, an art based upon a science. It is an art in the same sense that judgment is an important part of the process. Judgment must be used in such matters as determining how to distribute each overhead cost most equitably and develop the best estimates for the distribution of personnel time, determining where the exceptions to the established rules are justified, or perhaps in considering the relationship of the purpose of an expenditure to the method of distribution. Obviously, these judgments must be based upon a familiarity with the general philosophy of the enterprise under study. These judgments should be supported by reason, and reason, of course, is frequently debatable.

WHY MEASURE COSTS?

Purposes of unit-cost studies in higher education had been noted in a study a generation ago as follows:[3]

Secure information concerning the financial status of institutions for comparative purposes. (Mentioned in 12 cases.)

To report information concerning the financial status of institutions, no comparisons being made. (7)

To present information to legislatures, alumni, taxpayers, boards of trustees, etc. (6)

To evaluate financial standards employed by accrediting agencies. (5)

To show trends in the financial status of individual institutions over a period of years. (4)

To analyze the cost of instruction, to evaluate the different methods of instruction. (3)

To improve business management and secure economies in business administration. (2)

To secure information to be used in developing the budget. (1)

To develop techniques to be employed in unit cost studies. (1)

Five other purposes were listed (1 instance in each).[3]

One reason for measuring costs has already been suggested, namely, that although colleges do not base prices on costs, there is frequently some relationship between the two. A second reason is that knowledge of costs is helpful in budgeting, For example, it may be found that the cost of turning out a student in classics may be a hundred times greater than turning out a student in history. This certainly does not mean that the classics department should be abolished, but it might suggest the wisdom of some cost-reducing measures, such as alternating courses. The differences of unit costs between two different programs may be so great *relative to their educational value* that the authorities will decide to eliminate or reduce the cost of a particular program. A third reason for measuring cost is to suggest to the student whose fee is much less than cost that he is being subsidized. This is important when he is asked, later on, to make contributions to his college. In making such estimates the college administrator would be wise to include capital costs which are almost never included in a study of student costs. At Harvard, for example, a very rough estimate suggests that if construction costs were allocated in businesslike fashion, they would amount to about $800 per student per year. These are capital, not operating costs. For all IHL, on the basis of replacement costs, forty-year life, and 4 per cent interest, capital costs are about $300 to $400 per resident student.

One authority who supported cost investigations noted the following trends:[4]

(1) The gradual breaking down of the philosophy that higher education is in a class by itself and not subject to the application of norms in carrying on its activities in respect to procedures in cost; (2) the increase in tendency to substitute rational analysis in decision making for trial and error methods; (3) demands for knowledge as to educational costs by state legislatures and the general public. . . . ; (4) the general advances made in the last few decades toward the development of costing techniques and the realization of the importance of resultant data as an aid in decision making.

One reason for studying costs is the continued rise per unit. Ever since the nineteenth century, despite the large increase in the number of students per institution, the cost of higher education per student (in stable prices) has continued to rise.[5] This surprising result might suggest great inefficiency in the operation of colleges and universities, but this is not the only possible explanation. Higher education has become more costly with the increase of services, the rising cost of laboratories, and the accumulation of knowledge. It is difficult to measure the product of higher education, and for this reason among others we cannot explain rising unit costs with certainty. Finally, rising costs associated with the increased productivity of the whole economy are gradually felt by colleges and universities, which compete for services, capital goods, and supplies. Unlike industry, IHL are unable to match rising costs of services (about 5 per cent per annum) by a substantial increase of productivity. The shortage of funds caused by this inability to increase productivity *pari passu* with the profit economy keeps college salary scales from rising with those of business.

In discussing the problems of his university, President Millis of Western Reserve in his report of 1955–56[6] stressed the factors accounting for rising costs in higher education.

Thirty years ago, an early edition of a well-known college textbook contained approximately 400 pages which roughly defined the quantity of material to be covered within a nine-month period with three recitation or lecture hours per week plus two three-hour laboratory periods. This task required diligence on the part of both teacher and student and a really rapid pace. Today, the same textbook in its twelfth edition is used in many colleges but it now has nearly 800 pages. . . .

President Millis also refers to the change in medical school education. Fifty years ago a student went to medical school from high school, and in four years he achieved his education. Now approximately nine to thirteen years are required to consummate the training beyond high school. Another aspect of the problem is the increased flood of recorded knowledge pouring from the printing presses of the world.

There are to date 20,000 journals being published in the field of biology including the health sciences. Picture if you can the dilemma of the scholar, the student or the practising specialist in the field when he is faced with this flood of records.

THE UNIT OF MEASUREMENT

What is the unit for which cost is to be measured? Some authorities prefer to measure the costs per full-time student; others stress the costs *per clock hour* of the student; and still others the student credit hour. It is possible for the college to study, for example, the costs accounting for instruction, for buildings and grounds department, or for the operation of the service department and auxiliary services, each per student.

The total cost of a department can be obtained, for example, by taking the credit hours of each teacher, the number of students of each teacher, the total school-credit-hours equivalent, and then the salaries of the teachers. That is, three teachers in one department may have 41 credit hours, 250 students, a total school-credit-hours equivalent of 785 (that is, the number of credit hours in the department by the 250 students), and a semester's salary of $6,100. Other instruction items cost $900, and therefore the gross semestral expense of the department is $7,000 divided over these three teachers. Hence unit cost per student is $28—$7,000 divided by 250 (students). Unit cost per credit hour offered is $170.73—$7,000 divided by 41 (credit hours taught by faculty). Unit cost per student credit hour equivalent is $8.92—$7,000 divided by 785 (school-credit-hours equivalent). At Purdue an attempt is made to estimate the unit cost of each course. Hence the time distribution of each faculty member is required, the salaries paid, and all other relevant instructional costs and allocation of plant costs and other overhead.[7]

In order to estimate costs one must include overhead. Costs of administration have to be allocated over departments and courses. Library costs may be allocated on the basis of the number of students in each college or department, or by estimates of the use of the library per student in different departments of the college. Physical plant cost may be allocated on the basis of the number of square feet used by each department or college.

Alternate methods of allocation are available. For example, in allocating general administrative expenditures for dental schools, 12 different methods were used, but the most frequent (9 of 28 schools) was the ratio of direct expenditures of dental school to total university expenditures, and the second most frequent method (6 of 28) was the ratio of full-time dental students to all full-time students of the university. For the allocation of expenses for operation and maintenance of the physical plant 13 different methods were used, with the largest number using the ratio of the number of dental students to the total number of students in the university, and the second largest based on the square foot area of space used by dental schools in relation to space for total students. For allocating instructional expenditures of the schools, seven institutions used faculty hours of instruction, and six used credit hours of work of students.[8]

In these dental schools *direct* expenditures were 78 per cent of the *total* expenditures, and *allocated* expenditures 22 per cent. Allocated expenditures of administration were 48 per cent, of the library 44 per cent, of plant operation and maintenance 45 per cent, and of instruction 11 per cent.

One of the most important reasons for studying costs is the ever-increasing importance of the research contracts, particularly with the government. In trying to obtain a fair compensation for the college, we require estimates of direct personnel costs and indirect or overhead costs.

In an attempt to deal with this problem, 47 colleges studied their overhead costs in relation to instructional costs. Overhead costs in relation to teaching salaries varied from 167.42 per cent of teaching salaries for a school with 170 enrollment to 105 per cent for the group of schools with enrollment of more than 3,000. In general the groups with the smallest enrollment had the largest overhead ratio to teaching salaries, though this relationship was not a consistent one.[9]

In determining payments to be made to colleges under the GI legislation, many colleges had to estimate costs of instruction. They were to receive (Public Law 268) " . . . such fair and reasonable compensation as will not exceed the estimated cost of teaching personnel and supplies for instruction. . . . "[10]

From my questionnaire I find that from 1948 to 1958 administrative costs in relation to total costs tend to decline more frequently the greater the size of the IHL. But changes in accounting methods to some extent detract from the usefulness of the result. Administration, moreover, has different meanings, college by college. For example, for enrollments from 10,000 to 30,000 in public IHL, administrative costs range from 1.0 per cent to 13.7 per cent, and for enrollments of 900 to 10,000, from 3.8 to 38.7 per cent. For 37 private IHL below the median enrollment, there was a rise in the ratio of administrative to total costs from 1948 to 1958 for 51 per cent; of the 51 IHL above the median, only 31 per cent reported such a rise.

There is some evidence that at a given size of IHL administrative costs tend to decline relatively the larger the increase of enrollment. But this is subject to some reservation, and notably when a large rise means great expansion of plant and services.

SIGNIFICANCE AND DANGERS

In the late 1930s the National Committee on Standard Reports for Institutions of Higher Education published the financial reports of the colleges and universities which contained necessary information on accounting methods and instruction for making allocations of overhead and general expense. In their view it was necessary to divide the charge for an instructor's time among his various activities, though of course the allocation might not be as accurate as with factory employees. All overhead costs should also be included. The calculations should be based on reasonable assumptions, and if they remain reasonable, the trends would be of some significance.[11]

Unit costs should be used with great discretion. A higher cost per graduate student for one college or department does not necessarily mean inefficiency. It may mean broader counseling programs, better paid faculty, and more fully equipped laboratories. The higher-cost institutions as a rule are also generally the better institutions, with a few reservations.[12] One writer goes so far as to say that the provision of unit instructional costs is dangerous. Misuse of these statistics is especially costly to state universities. The accreditation procedures put emphasis on the unit costs and tend to favor those colleges that have high unit costs. As this book goes to press, President Logan Wilson of the University of Texas discusses ably the need of more cost studies, the manner of making them, and the dangers of confusing low costs with high efficiency and attainments.[13]

In 1920 the president of the University of Toledo fired several faculty members. He found that the unit costs varied from 25 to 77 cents per unit, and he wrote: "It is not by accident that four of the men whose student-hour costs were above 40 cents are no longer in the service of the University. A college is not a factory into one end of which is fed all green freshmen, where professors pull various levers called lectures, and where knowledge is automatically injected into students' skulls. . . . "

One writer said: "In other words, there are dangers in U.I.C.'s [unit instructional costs], educationally speaking. They *are* interesting but, like dynamite, they are likely to go off. If you seek high U.I.C.'s you are likely to be accused of wastefulness. If you seek low U.I.C.'s you are underpaying your professors or overloading your professors. . . . "[14]

According to one writer, cost accounting relates unit costs to the expenses of the department and to the number of students carried by the department. In this manner, we can compare departments, colleges, etc., improve institutional planning, and help with budgets. This information is also used by accrediting agencies, but these statistics do not solve administrative problems, nor are they the sole guide for policy. Lower costs do not necessarily mean greater efficiency. According to Lloyd Morey, unit costs shift with price levels, salaries, and enrollment. Even if the comparisons are based on the same formulas, they should be used with caution. Comparisons with outside institutions are limited in significance. Studies of similar departments for the same year, and the same department for different years, are especially useful. "No institution should be without figures of unit expense for instruction; but they should be used only with due regard for their uncertainty and complexity."

Even Harry Wells, one of the most articulate critics of IHL, warns that comparisons of costs *among* IHL are likely to lead to dubious results. But he sees some value in observing costs for such items as physical plant. instruction, administration. He is critical of those faculty members who insist on going beyond classroom hours in estimating instructional costs.

In some public IHL, e.g., California state colleges, studies of unit costs have helped in assessing programs for development. But comparisons among these institutions which do not take into account variations in tasks, enrollment, location, etc., are not very helpful. For example, a cost comparison of Mills College, a small liberal arts college, and Berkeley would be meaningless. In 1953–54 general administration as a percentage of educational and general expenditures varied from 11.23 per cent for one branch of the University of California to 26.98 per cent in another, and from 9.88 per cent in one state college to 16.30 in another. It would take a great deal of investigation to prove that San Jose (9.88 per cent), a very large institution, was run much more efficiently than Humboldt (16.30 per cent), a small IHL.[15]

COST COMPARISONS

We have had all kinds of comparisons of unit costs. Here are a few examples. The University of Nevada compares its unit costs with 17 other Western institutions and finds that its costs are much above the minimum but not much above the average for the 17 Western states. In view of the small population of Nevada, this might well suggest inadequate expenditures for higher education per student there. In administration and general expenses, the costs per unit are high in Nevada, compared to the average, in fact the highest among these colleges. These figures suggest high costs where enrollment is small. Resident instruction cost per student is also low, implying perhaps that salaries are low and classes are large. Actually the student-faculty ratio is about the same as the average for all 17 institutions.[16] A study of costs of higher education in public IHL by states reveals relatively large outlays in relation to income of the state residents in Nevada. The explanation is in large part high unit costs in sparsely populated states.

Another study for 1955 to 1957 gives the instruction costs per student credit hour as well as the total costs per student credit hour by departments of the university. These statistics relate to a better-than-average university in the Northeast. For 12 different departments of the university, the college costs per student credit hour vary from $13.48 for a school of public administration to $38.64 for an engineering school, and $55.04, the maximum, for library science. Obviously the high costs in library science must be related to the small enrollment. Trends are also evident and are of some importance: in library science the costs rose from $28.41 to $55.04 in two years, but in home economics there was actually a decline.

A study of Methodist colleges in the Great Depression showed that administrative costs rose steadily with the reduction of enrollment. Educational expenditures also rose, though not nearly so much in relation to enrollment. Moreover, the percentage of expenditures on instruction was highest for the largest institutions and smallest institutions. Administration tended to take a larger percentage of total costs for the small institutions.[17]

In a study of medical colleges one writer found that one private college had a budget of $3,356,000 ("College C"), while another college ("College D") had a budget of $991,250.

With relation to College C, we note that physical plant is fully developed and in full operation; that facilities are better than average; that teaching and research programs are fully developed in most areas; that leadership and quality of teaching is the primary college goal; that the college supports pioneering and research in medical education; that the college provides basic support for permanent research by the faculty; that the college assumes a heavier than average loss on medical service responsibilities in hospitals and clinics; that the M.D. candidate enrollment is high (above 400); that the college has fully developed full-time departments in most areas; that the college is located in a high-salary and high-expense area; that the basic sciences faculty is paid for a 12-month rather than a 10-month year.

By comparison we see for College D, that physical plant and facilities are inadequate or outdated; that facilities are overcrowded; all full-time departments are not fully developed; the value of volunteer faculty services is high; the college does relatively little pioneering in research or medical education; instructional budgets are inadequate; the college has desirable affiliations with psychiatric and other specialty hospitals which provide faculty, teaching facilities and teaching patients at minimum costs; the college is handicapped by limited financial support; the college benefits from sponsorship by a religious organization; the supporting staff salaries are low.

Teaching expense per student credit hour in California varied from $21.13 to $71.94 in the lower division, $23.22 to $183.89 in the higher division, and

$34.83 to $205.84 for graduate work. But variations could not be explained merely by varying size.[18]

Finally, I refer briefly to a study of the law schools, treated in the discussion of faculty status. The direct teaching costs per full-time student in schools of varying enrollment ranged from $221 for the largest institutions to $1,253 for the smallest institutions. The faculty-student ratio on a full-time basis ranged from 1 to 56 for the schools with large enrollments to 1 to 10 for those with enrollments of less than 100. It is quite clear that the size of the school makes considerable difference in its unit costs.[19]

In a similar analysis we find that as we go from large to small institutions, the receipts from each student tend to fall. For 193 independent colleges of liberal arts in 1930 those with enrollment in excess of 1,000 obtained receipts of $453 per student. The smallest groups with enrollments of less than 200 had receipts of only $345. Capital outlay also varied in the same manner. We also find that the proportion of expenditures on buildings and grounds was only about two-thirds as large for the group with the highest enrollment as for that with the lowest enrollment. The large institutions also tended to have a large percentage of their funds in productive use. Again, those with enrollments of less than 200 had a median salary of $3,500, whereas those with enrollments of 500 or more had a median salary of $6,850.[20]

*   *   *

Running our IHL has become big business. The expenditures now are beginning to approach $4 billion, and in ten or twelve years the total amount may well be $10 to 11 billion. Yet surprisingly little concern is shown for measuring our costs and how the job can be done more efficiently. The business manager may have virtually complete control over plant operations and maintenance, though this is limited by scheduling of classes and other items over which the faculty maintains control. Plant operation and maintenance, however, accounts for only about 10 or 12 per cent of total educational and general expenditures. In the operation of auxiliary services, which may well account for one-fifth of total current expenditures, the business manager has considerable control. In this area of operation he can suggest a mechanical leaf-raking machine, increased use of IBM machines, the substitution of student care of room as against care by maids with the resultant reduction in room and board, central purchasing, and the like. But he has little control over the educational practices which are the most important determinant of total costs.

This does not mean that academic authorities take no interest in costs; they also have to balance their budgets. In introducing a new program most good administrators today would estimate the increased costs involved and suggest the resources that are required to finance it. They would also estimate alternative ways of achieving an objective—e.g., improve instruction by spending X dollars by introducing Y new seminars, or by increasing salaries.

John Dale Russell suggested that there ought to be a program of cost accounting as a restraint on introducing new programs. That is, when a new program is to be introduced, the authorities should estimate the minimum amount of money required to run this program, regardless of the number of students. Then costs should be estimated on the basis of varying enrollment under this particular program. This, he wrote, would provide a check on the introduction of new programs.[21]

What is disturbing is that the colleges as a rule are not inclined to estimate their unit costs for services already being given. For example, the major universities do not estimate the cost of, say, the freshman curriculum every few years, or the cost of running a particular department or, more important, the cost of turning out a student in one department rather than in another. Generally no attempt is made to estimate the cost of giving a particular course. These unit costs change greatly from year to year without inspection, as a rule, by the authorities. It would be helpful, for example, to know how much it would cost to turn out a student in paleontology, say, twenty-five years ago and today, and to measure this against the value to society and to the student of a paleontologist today as against twenty-five years ago. Similar remarks may be made regarding other fields. What may have been a justifiable expenditure, given educational objectives twenty-five years ago or even ten years ago, is not necessarily justifiable today. Therefore, if it is at all possible, it is wise to inspect the costs of a course, of departments, of curricula, etc., every few years. It is not easy to transfer resources from one department to another or from one course to another, but gradually adjustments can be made—especially through allocations of new money.

The business manager of Northwestern University may have exaggerated when he wrote the following, but his position has some substance:

Educational administrators have been chosen largely from the field of scholars and they have not been trained in the economic understanding of their assignments. The correlation of the myriad activities in an institution must be doubly watched when a change of educational authority is in process. Scholars rarely approach an administrative appointment in education with an understanding of the intricacies of fund accounting, educational costs, budget control, centralized purchasing, and investment management. As a result, good business management is evident in successful institutions and weak business managements have foredoomed many colleges to extinction. It is a rigorous assignment, for men in these business positions are supposed to be wise enough in education to win the confidence of the educator and sufficiently proficient in executive management to meet the test of trustees who are successful in business management.

In his new interesting volume (*Governance of Colleges and Universities*) John Corson stresses the need of limitation of authority of faculty over educational policies, and even more over other matters related to educational policies. Among the reasons given are faculty objections to change, absence of adequate materials for determination of policy, lack of interest of faculty in educational policies, concentration of faculty on their own teaching assignments.[22]

A word of caution is necessary here: IHL are run largely by faculty. The relations of administrators, trustees (boards), and faculty are not like those between management and labor in the economy generally. This kind of government is necessary to assure freedom of investigation and thought. Faculty control, as great as it is, is much less than in European universities. But the important point is that these relationships increase the difficulty of operating a college like a business. Yet I do believe that education of faculty in the economics of the problem can and does yield favorable results. College faculties are not unlike members of other professions. Like doctors, for example, they resent advice or interference from their clientele or from the public generally. Medicine is held to be the province of doctors, and education, of the teachers. But both groups would profit greatly from a greater willingness to listen to the consumers of their products and others.

* * *

On the whole, administrators of IHL have not been as much interested in cost accounting as they ought to be. Their aversion can be justified only in part by the danger of misuse of cost figures and the practice of not tying charges to costs as in the profit economy. Cost studies are helpful in making decisions on educational policies; these cannot and should not be determined irrespective of costs, for resources are limited. It is, however, not always easy to agree on the relevance of various items and to estimate costs.

That cost accounting can be helpful is suggested by the experience in Indiana where the presidents of the two major public universities have found that cost comparisons facilitate budget decisions in the legislature. That cost accounting can lead to unfortunate results is attested by the Texas experience, where for all public institutions the same sum is provided for allocations per credit hour, administration per student, grounds upkeep per student, etc. The result of course is that all public IHL tend to be at the same level of mediocrity. Fortunately for the University of Texas, higher allocations for M.A. and Ph.D. programs and special endowment funds enable that university to rise to a point of distinction and above the level of the other public IHL. In contrast, in California, Berkeley boasts of its higher unit costs than UCLA, and UCLA in turn presents unit costs higher than the other branches of the University of California. Though salary scales for all branches of the university are similar, Berkeley and Los Angeles are allowed to pay above the maximum of $13,000 to $14,000 (1959). Moreover, general unit costs tend to be higher in the universities than in the four-year colleges, and higher in the latter than in the junior colleges. Teaching burdens also vary.

* * *

A committee of the American Council on Education (President Pusey, chairman) wisely pointed to the wastes of unnecessary duplication of programs associated with institutional imperialism and special-interest pressures. President Charles Odegaard of the University of Washington and the president of the Land-Grant Colleges in 1955 also had some judicious remarks. But the Pusey committee also wisely warns against oversimplified use of unit cost studies. " . . . Society, however, must challenge those who refuse, in the name of economy, to face the implications of such facts as the urgent need for first-rate teachers and the present scarcity of good libraries and laboratories required to futher the expansion of knowledge."[23]

FOOTNOTES

[1] See for example Moos and Rourke, *The Campus and the State*, 1959, pp. 84–88; *A Study of Methods Used in Unit-cost Studies in Higher Education*, National Committee on Standard Reports for Institutions of Higher Education Bulletin 3, 1932; California State Department of Education, *A Restudy of the Needs of California in Higher Education*, 1955, chap. 7; *A Report of a Survey of the University System in Georgia*, 1949, chap. 7; Board of Educational Finance, State of New Mexico, *Class Size, Teaching Loads . . . 1957–58*.

[2] Emory University, *Pilot Study: Analysis of Expenditures, Medical Education Program, 1954–55*, December, 1956, p. 14. (Mimeographed.)

[3] *A Study of Methods Used in Unit-cost Studies in Higher Education, op cit.*, p. 2.

[4] J. M. Evans, "Total Cost of Educational Program," *College and University Business*, September, 1954, p. 41; also cf. E. R. Rand, "If Unit Cost Calculations Are to be Valid," *ibid.*, August, 1955, p. 25.

[5] See Chap. 1.

[6] *Warning: Floods Ahead!*

[7] P. K. Nance, "Unit Cost Analysis," *College and University Business*, March, 1952, pp. 24–25; *Purdue University Cost Studies for Legislative Requests*, 1956–57 (mimeographed).

[8] Van Dyke and Levine, "Allocating Indirect Expenditures," *College and University Business*, May, 1953, pp. 22–25.

[9] H. R. Patton and G. E. Gere (of Carnegie Institute of Technology), *Final Report: Study of Educational Costs for the Annual Meeting of the Eastern Association of College and University Business Officers*, December, 1951. (Mimeographed.)

[10] *Readjusted Benefits: A Report by the President's Commission on Veterans' Pensions*, 1956, Staff Report IX, Part B, p. 77.

[11] See E. R. Rand, pp. 25–26; and W. E. Elmore, "Cost Accounting," *College and University Business*, August, 1955, pp. 45–48.

[12] Cf. R. W. Kettler, "What's Wrong with the Unit Cost Idea," *ibid.*, May, 1953, p. 17.

[13] H. Scherer, "U.I.C.'s Are Dangerous," *ibid.*, February, 1955, pp. 39–40; L. Wilson, "Analyzing and Evaluating Costs in Higher Education," *The Educational Journal*, April, 1961, pp. 99–105.

[14] *Ibid.*

[15] C. Scheps, *Accounting for Colleges and Universities*, 1949, pp. 293–94; *A Restudy of the Needs of California in Higher Education*, 1955, pp. 409 *et seq.*; L. A. Glenny, *Autonomy of Public Colleges*, 1959, pp. 65–67; H. L. Wells, "Standards of Service in University Management," *The Annals, Higher Education under Stress*, September, 1955, pp. 175–182.

[16] See *The University of Nevada: An Appraisal*, 1956, pp. 181–182.

[17] Reeves, Russell, Gregg, Brumbaugh, and Blauch, *The Liberal Arts College*, 1932, pp. 486–87.

[18] A. J. Carroll, *A Study of Medical College Costs*, 1958, pp. 24–25; Technical Committee on Costs . . . , *The Costs of Higher Education in California 1960–1975*, p. 40.

[19] See Chap. 53.

[20] *Bulletin of the Association of American Colleges*, vol. 18, 1932.

[21] See J. D. Russell, "Early Notes on Experience in Coordination of State Higher Education," *Current Issues in Higher Education*, 1952, pp. 83–85.

[22] H. L. Wells, *Higher Education Is Serious Business*, 1953, p. 24; J. J. Corson, *Governance of Colleges and Universities*, 1960, pp. 104–106, 113–115.

[23] American Council on Education, *The Price of Excellence*, October, 1960; *Presidential Address of Dr. Jones to Association of Land-Grant Colleges and Universities, at East Lansing, Michigan*, Nov. 15, 1955; and C. E. Odegaard, *Report to the Faculty*, Oct. 5, 1959.

Chapter 43
CASE STUDIES ON COSTS

In the preceding chapter I tried to shed light on the general use of cost studies, their relevance and dangers. Here I develop some of the points further and list some of the important by-products of cost studies. The literature is voluminous, and I do believe greater use could be made of cost studies, as I said above.

Cost studies are helpful. But I repeat, they must be used with caution. That a medical school curriculum costs $4,000 per student and one in liberal arts $1,000 does not mean that the medical school is inefficient. Nor can one draw any conclusions merely by comparing a unit cost per student credit hour of $100 for Latin and $14 for biology. Berkeley may spend four times as much per student credit hour as, say, Riverside (a branch of the University of California) and yet be as efficient. Still it would be unwise to say that information of this kind is useless.

Indications of profit from cost studies are to be had, for example, from a study of unit costs at Bard which revealed that financial salvation lay in rising enrollment; from a study at Hiram College that revealed a rise of enrollment from 550 to 1,000 would reduce excess capacity, improve financial status and the educational product; from a University of Texas study that shows administration costs decline from $65 per student at an enrollment of 1,500 to $40 at enrollments in excess of 6,000; from the University of Oklahoma study which suggests that with the first 6,800 students the base faculty would be 453 (15 to 1), but for each additional 25 students one additional faculty member would be required, and hence an enrollment of 11,000 would need a faculty of 621 (a student-teacher ratio of 17.7 to 1); from a California study revealing that cost per Average Daily Attendance (two-thirds of costs of full-time student) *for a campus* in seven California junior colleges varied from $4,006 for a capacity of 3,500 to $2,355 for a capacity of 3,000, and $2,881 for one of 800; that for state colleges the cost per full-time student was $3,889 for a campus with a capacity of 8,276 and $6,224 for one with a capacity of 3,562, that the minimum, optimum, and maximum enrollment for junior colleges should be 400, 3,500, and 6,000 respectively and for state colleges in densely populated areas in metropolitan centers 5,000, 10,000, and 20,000, respectively, and in other places, 3,000, 8,000, and 12,000, and that in University of California campuses the minimum, optimum, and maximum should be 5,000, 12,500, and 27,500. In Louisiana a projected cost study concluded that the net cost to the state of 1970–71 would be $74 million if present policies were continued but only $44.5 million if suggested economies of staff, improved planning, and coordination were achieved.

Again, studies reveal that costs of lower division, higher division, and graduate instruction vary greatly (Table 43-1). A cost study reveals large

TABLE 43-1
Direct Instructional Costs for One Semester Hour

Institution	Freshmen-sophomores	Juniors-seniors	Grad.*-prof.	Ratio
In California:				
Institution A..................	$ 9.03	$13.64	$53.66	1:1.6:6
Institution B..................	9.04	18.11	53.32	1:2:6
Institution C..................	11.34	23.13	42.51	1:2:4
In New Mexico.................	9.10	17.22	39.33	1:1.9:4.3
At Michigan University............	......	......	......	1:2:4
At Purdue University.............	Net student cost 1956–57 = freshmen, $539; sophomores, $610; juniors, $708; seniors, $803; graduates, $1,020.			
At Louisiana State University.......	Undergraduate, $773.49; graduate work: in general, $1,600; law, $1,625; medicine, $3,700.			
At University of Chicago...........	During the Depression, instructional costs per student were $61, with a maximum of $94 for biological sciences and a minimum of $45 for social sciences. In the professional area, the average was $40, with graduate library costing $170 and law a minimum of $15. Here the graduates are all professional, and costs are low except for medicine and library.			

* For some comments on the small numbers and hence high costs for the student in graduate programs, see B. Berelson's fascinating book, *Graduate Education in the United States*, 1960.

differences in the costs per credit hour. For example, in a recent year the teaching costs per credit hour in the University of New Mexico varied from $6.50 in music to $13 in Latin and Greek, and for chemistry the range was from $8.90 to $15.30 among seven public IHL in New Mexico. Class size ranged in 1956–57 from 14.1 to 23.3 for the seven public IHL in this state, and the average size seemed to rise by about one-third in a period of five years—evidence of the pressure of large numbers.

Some explanation of the higher costs with academic advance is revealed by the data in Table 43-2.

TABLE 43-2

Division	Per cent of classes of		1957–58 salary cost per student credit hour
	4 or less	9 or less	
Lower division.........	1.1	3.9	$ 9.09
Upper division........	12.8	22.9	15.54
Graduate............	65.9	81.8	45.97

The high cost of graduate instruction is reflected by the following:

University of New Mexico, Average Student Credit Hours
per Full-time-equivalent Faculty Member

Biology
Lower division, undergraduate........... 723
Upper division, undergraduate........... 455
Graduate.......................... 62

From 1951–52 to 1957–58, average instructional-salary cost per student credit hour in New Mexico changed but ½ per cent, suggesting that the increase of pay rates was offset by heavier teaching loads, that is, number of student credit hours per member of faculty. The number of courses dropped by a few per cent, and the weighted average of class size rose by more than 40 per cent.

In Georgia a careful study of 15 public IHL for the year 1949 was also revealing. Instructional cost per credit hour was $2.42 in business administration, $4.66 in arts and science, and $12.50 in home economics. Budgetary officers might want to know to what extent the nature of the subject, the size of enrollment, the curriculum requirements, or inefficiency accounts for the high unit costs in home economics. Student/faculty ratio was only 6.5 to 1 in home economics as compared to an average of 19.8 for the university, and enrollment only 117 against 2,867 in arts and science and 1,035 in business administration. Despite average salaries in home economics 10 per cent below the average, unit costs were high.

At the University of Georgia in Athens the cost per full-time-student equivalent was $370, but in the Atlanta branch, only $195. What is the explanation? One is clear at once. The Atlanta branch used large numbers of part-time instructors who were paid (on a full-time basis) less than two-thirds as much as full-time faculty. Furthermore, classes were larger and teaching loads probably heavier in Atlanta. The average class size was 29 in Athens and 39 in Atlanta. Clearly these statistics point to the need of upgrading in Athens.

At Williams College, the faculty estimated the need of faculty members on the basis of the total student-teacher–contact hours required in relation to the number of teachers available. The load to be carried by the average teacher, on the basis of these variables, was an average of 180 student-contact hours. The faculty committee found this a precise measure of requirements for the average teacher. But the working load per teacher is another matter. Here differences in subject matter taught, time required for preparation, size of class, committee work, number of different courses are all relevant. At any rate the faculty committee concluded that there were too many small classes (119, or almost half, with 1 to 17 students) and that a shortage of faculty, as suggested by the above calculations, could be met by enlisting undergraduate assistants, an innovation which has proved to be highly productive.

An administrative dean of the University of Michigan, Dean Williams, after many years of experience, comments on the many cost studies introduced " . . . with a view toward maintaining high quality at minimum cost." Instructional costs, in his view, are based on faculty salaries, number of hours taught by faculty members, number of students enrolled, and cost of maintaining plant, library, administration, and other supporting services. From twenty-five years of experience, Williams finds that costs rise with advance in class level and specialization and with the reduction of enrollment in a curriculum and that costs vary with the proportions of enrollment in the lower, upper, and graduate levels, and he concludes that low instructional costs are not necessarily correlated with high quality or with instructional efficiency.

Such considerations may explain why in a 1937 study instructional expenditures per student credit hour (inclusive of overhead) for nine universities varied from $4.96 to $11.55 and cost of a full-time student, from $148.75 to $346.67. Each of these universities might well be interested in discovering to what extent the quality of instruction (e.g., high-priced and able faculty and first-class library), the class structure of the university (e.g., proportion of graduate students), the teaching load, the number of small classes, variation in enrollment, excess capacity, and (related) efficiency or lack of it explains the differences—as well as dissimilar accounting methods.

Accounting methods vary greatly, and for this reason alone it is necessary to be cautious in comparing unit costs among institutions. The authorities in Texas compare their unit costs with those of other states and find that they are low. But the Texas commission warns that care is needed in making comparisons—for example, the selection of a student-teacher ratio for each program of study must be appropriate to the needs of the program and should recognize the differences in teacher work loads which depend on the character of the instructional program.

To some extent the level of costs will depend upon attitudes toward capital charges for amortization and interest. This question is seldom raised vis-à-vis academic buildings but is increasingly mentioned vis-à-vis auxiliary services—dormitories, dining halls, etc. Should these charges be included in costs, the assessments on students may become high enough to deter many from using the facilities or going to the institution. Nevertheless, an increasing proportion of auxiliary facilities are financed through loans and hence through charges to the student. But whether the charge is passed on to the student or not, a case can be made out for estimating the costs.

*   *   *

Some authorities, in discovering that prices charged are much less than cost, contend that the result is wastage of resources. In his interesting discussion Dean Rogge of Wabash College has stressed the point that, so long as the student does not pay full costs, the faculty tends to exploit him by offering a deteriorated product.

In a report to the alumni of Yale University (1957–58) President Griswold also points to the contrast between business—where the consumer is required to cover costs and the consumer is forced to choose among alternative expenditures—and higher education—where costs are concealed from the student as a result of tax and gift income, which seems to rain like manna from heaven. Charges much below cost, in President Griswold's view, seem to bring waste.

An interesting formula which takes into account all cost factors in teaching emanates from a faculty member of the L. C. Smith College of Engineering at Syracuse University. From a consideration of the relevant variables he draws a no-loss formula where costs and income are equated.

$$\text{Number of full-time faculty for teaching} = \frac{NL}{CF} \tag{1}$$

$$\text{Costs of instruction} = \frac{NL}{CF} S(1 + O) \tag{2}$$

$$\text{Income} = NT(1 + E)$$

For no loss, equate (1) and (2). Then

$$S = \frac{F}{L} CT \frac{1 + E}{1 + O}$$

where N = number of equivalent full-time students

C = average class size

L = average full-time-student credit-hour load

F = average full-time-faculty credit-hour load

S = average academic-year salary

T = academic-year tuition

O = teaching overhead rate on teaching salary

E = endowment gift, tuition income, and other than tuition income

Obviously costs will rise with increased students, reduced size of classes, reduced teaching loads, and a rise of average faculty salary and of overhead; and income will rise with increases in tuition and other income.

Unfortunately IHL still do not keep their accounts in a uniform manner, although work of the National Committee on Standard Reports for Institutions of Higher Education since the Depression has helped greatly to improve the situation. But even today colleges differ on the unit to be measured, though the trend is toward the student credit hour. IHL also tend to study the costs per student credit hour for instruction, administration, and fixed charges. This approach is much to be preferred to an alternative—study of salaries, wages, materials, and the like. The latter should supplement cost studies by functions, not supplant them.

Perhaps the greatest difficulty arises from the manner of allocating overhead to each function. One difference arises from the expenditures allocated —e.g., all, administration, library, operation and maintenance of plant. Where operation and maintenance were allocated in one study, four used square feet of physical space, and four used square foot-hours of space. But in the last chapter, alternatives were discussed more fully.

IHL are increasingly interested in cost studies, though the enthusiasm, partly induced, is greater among public IHL. Such studies can clarify many issues: if graduate instruction is four times as expensive as undergraduate, college administrators may wish to modify the proportion of graduate and undergraduate students. If a course in botany costs six to seven times as much as one in chemistry per student credit hour or if the cost in chemistry per student credit hour is eight times as large in one IHL as in another, some examination of the differences may be helpful. Again, the relation of unit costs and the size of enrollment in schools and departments are relevant. One medical school may cost fifty times as much as the law school per student in the same university. This ratio may be worth investigating, and in relation to similar ratios in other universities, as well. Where administrative costs relative to total costs vary as much as they do among similar IHL, the problem may be worth further study.

But I end this chapter with a warning from one educator.[1]

If this university accepts the responsibility for rounded curricula, islands of these high-cost courses may be numerous. Cost accounting can disclose which courses, departments or divisions are high cost per student hour, but cost accounting cannot decide whether the courses should be offered or abandoned. . . . The decision to offer such a marginal course needs to consider cost, but it should not be influenced or determined by the vague feeling that high student-hour courses are somehow reprehensible in themselves and should be discouraged.

FOOTNOTE

[1] A great deal of material is available for the study of costs. I found particularly helpful in writing this section the following:

A Study of Methods Used in Unit-cost Studies in Higher Education, National

Committee on Standard Reports for Institutions of Higher Education Bulletin 3, 1932.

University Unit Costs, U.S. Department of the Interior, Office of Education Bulletin 21, 1937.

Reeves, Henry, and Russell, *Class Size and University Costs: University of Chicago Survey,* vol. IX, 1933.

R. L. Williams, "Instructional Cost Studies in Perspective," *College and University Business,* March, 1959, pp. 28–29.

Moos and Rourke, *The Campus and the State,* 1959, pp. 84–88.

California State Department of Education, *A Restudy of Needs of California in Higher Education,* 1955, chap. 7.

A Master Plan for Higher Education in California, 1960–1975, 1960, chap. 9.

A Report of a Survey of the University System of Georgia, 1949, chap. 7.

Board of Educational Finance, State of New Mexico, *Class Size, Teaching Loads . . . 1957–58.*

Biennial Report of Louisiana State University and Agricultural and Mechanical College, 1954–56.

Purdue University Cost Studies for Legislative Requests, 1956–57. (Mimeographed.)

Financial Report 1956–57: Letter from President, Hiram College Bulletin, 1957.

Louisiana Commission on Higher Education, *A Summary of Report of the Commission, 1954–55.*

"State-supported Higher Education in North Carolina," *The Report of the Commission on Higher Education,* 1955, esp. pp. 68–73.

Texas Commission on Higher Education, *Report,* 1954, esp. pp. 10–25.

Williams College, *Report of the Committee on Teaching Resources,* 1957.

The President's Report to the Alumni of Yale University, 1957–58, Bulletin of Yale University, ser. 54, no. 20, Oct. 15, 1958, pp. 29–30.

American Council on Education, *College and University Business Administration,* vol. 2, 1955.

Chapter 44

ECONOMIES THROUGH THE CURRICULUM AND INSTRUCTIONAL METHODS

INTRODUCTORY

Beardsley Ruml has popularized the idea that salaries could be doubled if the student/faculty ratio was doubled. He proposes a substantial number of large lectures and many very small groups but would eliminate "recitation classes," as he calls them.

It is possible to make substantial savings through the elimination and alternation of courses and the increase in the size of classes, as well as through the greater use of assistants. A movement was announced to substitute machines for teachers. Some of the suggested improvements are intended to make teaching more effective, others to find substitutes for that scarce commodity, the teacher.

I estimate at first glance that if we increase the student/faculty ratio from 13 to 1 to 20 to 1 we might save $2 billion a year or more, about one-third of the estimated additional $6 billion per year required within ten years. But the problem is not as simple as that. First, the economies are likely to be largely at the expense of the young, low-paid members of the faculty. Furthermore, economies will come primarily through replacements as faculty members leave. Also, the college, and even more so the university, feels impelled to "cover fields." Hence difficulties in increasing the student/faculty ratio. Therefore fields will often be covered even when the number of students is small in relation to the number of faculty. And at a university the faculty member is hired not only to teach but also to do research. Yet even allowing for all these factors, it may very well be that we could save substantial sums of money annually within ten years.

With the expected rise of enrollment, there will undoubtedly be a serious shortage of teachers as well as financial resources. The question of the small versus the large class is really not before us. There *must* be larger classes, and possibly even larger teaching loads. The experience of New

522

TABLE 44-1
Enrollment, Faculty, and Courses, Eleven Institutions and Total, 1901–02, 1926–27, and 1956–57

Item	Year	Harvard	Mt. Holyoke	Princeton	Smith	Swarth-more	Vassar	Williams	Wiscon-sin	Yale	Columbia	Brown	Total
Enrollment:													
Undergraduate.........	1901–02	1,983	608	1,237	1,038	207	789	370	2,137	1,915	777	778	11,839
	1926–27	2,825	1,004	2,309	2,071	560	1,149	744	7,804	3,140	3,182	1,833	26,621
	1956–57	4,431	1,293	2,927	2,276	920	1,462	1,057	13,878	3,942	4,158	2,970	39,314
Graduate arts and science	1901–02	861	3	117	10	...	10	33	831	338	2,219e	94	4,516
	1926–27	796	28	217	66	...	...	7	1,032	1,120	5,300	276	8,842
	1956–57	1,468	44	628	83	5	8	8	2,583	1,198	15,263	394	21,682
Faculty total.........	1901–02	483	61	112	75	19	84	32	180	354	323	79	1,802
	1926–27	1,088	130	299	227	60	143	78	1,178	825	1,210	137	5,375
	1956–57	3,195	199	877a	263	108	218	137	1,868	1,698	1,850	260	10,673
Semester courses:													
Undergraduate.........	1901–02	84	220	292	296	166	...	...	561	278	...	164	
	1926–27	77.5	416	331	643	335	...	...	508	581	815b	186	
	1956–57	146.5	268	640	675	330	...	...	391c	1,125	1,313	276	
Graduate.........	1901–02	132.5	...	66	...	...	...	...	126	174	...	23	
	1926–27	184	43	409	...	...	...	...	650	835	792	103	
	1956–57	574	82	643	200	...	...	...	533	1,561	1,512	330	
Undergraduate and graduate.........	1901–02	148.5	...	56	...	...	...	...	...	...	...	40	
	1926–27	162.5	...	75	...	...	...	...	...	...	944	262	
	1956–57	254.5	202	...	...	134	...	...	1,028	...	...	368	
Total courses.........	1901–02	365	220	414	296	166	224d	206	787	452	715	227	4,072
	1926–27	424	459	815	643	335	506	191	1,158	1,416	2,551	551	9,049
	1956–57	975	1,206	1,283	875	464	563	367	1,952	2,686	2,825	974	14,100f

a 290 = research faculty.
b Including teachers colleges.
c Letters and arts only.
d Varying credits per course.
e Graduate and professional.
f Totals in last column should be interpreted carefully since there are gaps in figures. But this reservation does not apply to the total numbers of courses. For undergraduates, the rise is from 1,500 to 3,460 courses for seven IHL where comparable figures are available in 1902 and 1957; for graduates, with five IHL (comparable), the increase is from 521 to 3,641 courses.
Source: Catalogues of institutions listed, for the relevant years.

Mexico and projections in Louisiana discussed earlier point in this direction. The real issue is how to do the most effective job in the larger classes. In my visits to IHL, I find many are planning a rise in the student/faculty ratio. The alternative may often be a serious deterioration in the quality of the faculty. The proliferation of courses is suggested by Table 44-1, where I list the number of courses, students, and faculty members by individual institutions[1] in the last half century.

This table reveals that there has been a serious rise in the number of courses, especially at the graduate level. The totals for courses should be accepted with reservations, since there are gaps, some elements of incomparability, and also problems of interpretation of the materials in catalogues upon which the author relied.

These figures suggest the following conclusions:

1. Since 1902, the relative rise in faculty has greatly exceeded that in enrollment, a conclusion strengthened when one allows for the relatively small percentage of students in graduate arts and science. This of course means a reduced teaching burden for faculty and a decline in the student/faculty ratio. But when allowance is made for the increase in research, the gains for teachers are reduced to some extent. Relief for teachers would have been much greater had not courses in graduate areas skyrocketed.

2. Once comparison is made of undergraduate and graduate courses, available in both 1902 and 1957 on a comparable basis, we find that undergraduate courses have increased by $1\frac{1}{3}$ times, and graduate courses by 6 times. The rise for all courses for this limited sample was $2\frac{1}{2}$ times. Whereas graduate instruction accounted for one-quarter of all courses in 1902, it accounted for 52 per cent by 1957. Since enrollment in graduate arts and science in the nation is of the order of 10 per cent and roughly one-third for the institutions here considered, the graduate students in these IHL have about two times as many courses in relation to enrollment as undergraduates have. Once allowance is made for a large percentage of students on part time in the graduate schools of these IHL, the disparity is even greater. Furthermore, even the two do not give an adequate notion of the higher costs of graduate vis-à-vis undergraduate instruction, for the higher-priced faculty tends to gravitate to graduate work.

3. The rise of graduate enrollment and courses has been especially large, absolutely and relatively, since the 1920s (Table 44-2). Earl McGrath finds both educational and financial reasons against the use of highly specialized courses in liberal arts colleges. Why should one college with 1,117 students offer only 45 hours of English instruction and another with 916 students offer 113 hours? The author shows how much more expensive instruction is in the college with more courses and hence more small classes.

Ruth Eckert notes[2] that despite all the talk about general education, it was found

TABLE 44-2
Rise in Enrollment, Faculty, and Courses, 1902–1957

Item	1902 to 1957	1927 to 1957
Enrollment:		
Undergraduate......................	2½ times	½ times
Graduate..........................	4 times	1½ times
Faculty..............................	5 times	1 time
Courses:		
Undergraduate for 7 IHL................	1⅓ times	
Graduate for 5 IHL.....................	6 times	
All (7 undergraduate and 5 graduate).....	2½ times	

Source: See Table 44-1.

. . . at Minnesota that 1,304 different courses have been added in a recent five-year period, while only 412 have been dropped. These figures reach astronomical proportions when the increase continues decade after decade. And this multiplication has occurred in practically every field on the level of higher education—in the areas of general education, in fields of specialization at the baccalaureate level, in the addition of entirely new varieties of undergraduate programs, and in the continued lengthening and diversification of professional and graduate education. . . .

Too many courses and the resultant small classes have become a disease of higher education. The Commission on Financing of Higher Education put the issue well when its members wrote:[3]

The greatest extravagance in almost every type of institution from the smallest to the largest lies in the curriculum. This situation usually arises from the absence of even a broad general conception of purpose by which course offerings can be assessed. Partly to meet overrefined needs, partly to attract students, partly to meet competition, real or imagined, institutions have permitted their course offerings to grow more and more numerous, to proliferate far beyond real needs. Too many of our institutions have been victimized by the cult of coverage. Since the complete offering of every conceivable course is impossible, it follows that the selection should be guided by some broad educational principles. . . .

. . . and many courses, once started, continue a life of their own until they become gnarled branches of the past, left unpruned while new branches of learning grow all around them. . . . Many faculty members and department heads would do well to remember the aphorism of a distinguished British educator, Sir Richard Livingstone, who said that a great teacher "is known by the number of valuable subjects that he declines to teach."

Time and again authorities stress the economies that can be made in this area of operation; " . . . reduction in the number of small classes;

reexamination of the relative amounts of laboratory and non-laboratory instruction in the various subject fields. . . . "[4]

In the words of former President Wriston of Brown University:[5]

As governments have debased their currency to meet deficits so have many colleges debased their education for the same purpose. By offering courses in everything, they seek to attract enough students to help balance the budget. Scandalous sophistries have been propagated to make these devices appear to have an educational, rather than a fiscal, basis. Liberal arts colleges give courses in business administration (including stenography, typing and filing), home economics (one college gives a course in "draping") and many other subjects alien to their history and purpose. None of these additions was really designed to contribute to the pursuit of happiness, one of the basic objectives in the American tradition. Such inflationary courses were concerned with the pursuit of the dollar. . . .

Again, President Herman Wells of Indiana University, one of the most knowledgeable of all university presidents, proposes that by 1970 the ratio of students to faculty should be increased from 13 to 1 to 17 to 1. He suggests that this can only be done by improving and increasing faculty productivity by use of supplementary written materials, more imaginative use of audio-visual aids, and more independent work by students.[6]

Even those who strongly adhere to the view that the best teaching is in small classes find that we must abandon this approach in the current situation. For example, E. H. Cherrington, Jr., is impressed by the fact that the best teaching is done with small classes, but suggests that the emphasis will have to be modified from the teacher prodding the student to the student learning more by himself. The student is not supposed to be treated the way a car is treated when it comes into the garage:

Students remove the cap from their minds and expect the instructor to pump in 45 minutes work and information loaded with wisdom. . . . What we need are more adaptable methods of instruction—methods based upon the assumption that since the student is an adult he should be able to direct his own efforts so as to make full use of the opportunity to learn.

SMALL VERSUS LARGE CLASSES

Numerous small classes are the rule in IHL, and the smaller the college and the more advanced the curriculum, the larger the proportion of small classes is likely to be. At the University of Chicago in the late 1920s, 10 per cent of classes and class sections at the 100 level (lower division) had 10 or less enrolled; at the 200, 300, and 400 levels, the percentages were 19, 38, and 78 respectively. These facts largely explain instructional costs of $25, $50, $87, and $144 at the respective levels.

Similar conditions are to be found in numerous studies of this problem in recent years. In 1956–57, one study revealed the data in Table 44-3 for 25 state universities.

Data for the University of New Mexico for 1957–58 is presented in Table 44-4. The high cost of advanced instruction is explained largely by facts such as those revealed in this table. At the upper division, the percentage of classes with enrollment of less than 10 varied from 0 in several

TABLE 44-3

Cumulative Percentages in Class Enrollments,
25 State Universities, 1956–57

Class enrollment	Lower division	Upper division	Graduate division	Total
5 or less.............	4.0%	16.2%	51.9%	13.7%
10 or less............	9.6	33.4	74.7	24.9
15 or less............	19.5	49.0	85.7	36.77
25 or less............	50.6	72.0	93.4	62.37
35 or less............	76.6	84.9	96.0	82.03

Source: W. E. Green, "A Study in Class Sizes in Major State Universities," University of Mississippi, in *Summary, Abstracts and Bibliography of Studies of Class Size*, prepared by the Division of Academic Research and Services, Pennsylvania State University, June, 1958, p. 35. (Mimeographed.)

TABLE 44-4

Percentage of Credit Hours Taught in Classes, 1957–58

Class size	Lower division	Upper division	Graduate
Less than 5 students..............	1.1	12.8	65.9*
Less than 10 students.............	3.9	22.9	81.8

* In 27 Indiana IHL, the percentage of classes with enrollments of 0 to 9 ranged from 4 per cent for lower division, to 18 per cent for upper division, and 35 per cent for graduate.

Source: Board of Educational Finance, State of New Mexico, *Class Size, Teaching Loads and Instructional Salary Costs, Data for Regular Academic Year, 1957–58*, New Mexico.

departments to 100 per cent in Greek or Latin and nursing, and 71 per cent in German. Demand for some kinds of instruction is so low that once the IHL decides to provide a broad offering, classes necessarily are small, and the unit costs become high. In other instances the explanation is the need of small classes for effective teaching—e.g., nursing.

To a considerable extent the explanation of small classes rests on the size of the institution. For example, in 1953, average class size was 18 in

Santa Barbara and Davis, units of the University of California, and 25 and 29 in the Berkeley and Los Angeles units. At the state colleges the numbers ran from 29 in San Jose (a very large institution) to 15 for Humboldt. For 19 independent institutions the range was from 7.3 to 30.3.

We should warn the reader that the size of the course does not yield adequate information. A report from Amherst College notes that large enrollments in a course may be of little significance when the course is broken up into many sections. Of the courses at Amherst with enrollment of 125 or more, all were broken up into sections. In the humanities course, for example, 13 faculty members participated.

In a study of the University of Chicago for the late 1920s, Reeves and others found that there were 829 sections in all in a semester. Had all sections been as large as the largest for each course, 40 sections would have been eliminated. Had all sections been increased to 30, 45, 60, and 100, the savings in sections would have been 82, 211, 320, and 449 respectively. (The average of all courses taught in 2 or more sections was 28.)

In general, as we show elsewhere, experiments reveal that achievements are not greater in small than in large classes. Indeed, it is not always clear what is meant by a large class—50, 100, 200? Nor are all the experiments sufficiently controlled. For example, an experiment at Duke University might suggest that the large classes yielded at least as good results as the small classes. But the explanation of the favorable results in the large classes might well have been the visual aids introduced and the preparation of other helpful materials. In summarizing the results of experiments in class size for six IHL, a Ford study concludes:

> The different experiments were tried in several subject fields and in student groups ranging from 14 to approximately 400. The conclusion was that the competence of the professor is much more important in affecting student learning than class size or variations in the method of instruction. When the same instructor taught sections of different size, there were negligible differences in student performance; when small sections of a given course were taught by different instructors, there were significant differences in student performance on the same examination.

An interesting experiment in statics and strength of materials at Rensselaer Polytechnic Institute revealed that the students who were instructed in a program that required 20 contact hours performed much better than those who had 54 and 88 contact hours. The first of these groups, denied discussions, profited, however, from specially prepared materials.

Some reservations should be made in the case of larger sections. First, the tests, even as noted in the 1930s, are not adequate. They are generally objective tests and, despite some advance (e.g., at Ohio University), do not ordinarily measure any gains obtained from the give and take of small groups as reflected in increased ability to analyze, to form mature judgments, and to communicate.

Second, as has been noted elsewhere, irrespective of the case for the large class—not only economic, but also the fact that a large class is more likely to hold some superior students who may set the pace—the requirements of the curriculum, for example, in graduate work, frequently determine the size of the class.

Third, physical limitations often determine the size of classes. For example, in a statement favoring the large class, the writers of the New York University Self-study wrote:

The current practice at New York University seems to revolve around "middle-sized" classes of 30, 40, or 50 students . . . Existing courses . . . average about 45 students . . . only three or four rooms for classes of 150 or more [are available]. . . . As a matter of fact an average class of 40, while it has certain merit, is neither large enough to be economical, nor small enough to permit truly individualized instruction. . . . Television provides one way out since one lecturer can speak to several groups in class-rooms of varying size.

But those who seek the larger classes as an economy measure must consider the limitations put upon larger classes by the present physical setup— though longer day and year sessions and future construction of larger classrooms may help solve this problem.

At Dartmouth, which has been one of the leaders in this effort to study class size, it was noted that one-half of the teaching effort went to the intermediate sized groups (20 to 75), too large for seminar methods and too small to profit from lectures.

The former dean of the school of general studies at Columbia University, Louis M. Hacker, has been particularly critical of the Columbia system of small classes. He would introduce large lectures by able teachers in all introductory classes and thus economize on great talents. "A running debate between three or four students and the instructor (not necessarily among the students themselves) in a class of twenty or thirty is time-consuming, usually uninforming and a bore to the rest." Hacker realizes that there is a problem of physical plant. Hence he would use closed circuit television to reach students in small classrooms.

Fourth, since the case for larger classes rests in large part on savings of resources, many colleges support small classes simply because they can get by without these large classes and they seem to find genuine advantages in small groups. Swarthmore, a first-class liberal arts college which attracts excellent students, is an example of such an institution. The stress on the honors program is reflected also in instruction for small groups. Again, at

Sarah Lawrence College the size of the average class in a recent year was 11. And much emphasis was put upon small group discussions.

Another example is Case Institute, where the support for relatively small classes is to be found partly in the special requirements of a good engineering school. In a study of the institution, it was said: "Case Institute has operated under a policy of instruction in small classes. As a general rule, an effort is made to limit freshman classes to 25 or 26 students and classes in the other years to 18 or 20 students. . . . Nearly two thirds of the 518 laboratory classes have 15 or fewer students and more than 40 per cent have 10 or less."

A feature of the Case program is that, where a course has 1 or 2 students, it counts for only 0.33 or 0.67 of a course in estimating teacher loads, and where classes run from 35 to 44 and 45 or over, the weight is 1.33 and 1.67 of a course, respectively. This estimation of teaching loads may to some extent turn the scales in favor of larger classes.

Fifth, the appropriate size of a class depends on the subject matter to some extent. Where the material is largely factual, the student is not likely to be helped much by enrolling in a small group. Even in such a subject as English composition, large lectures are effective so long as they are supplemented by small groups for work on themes.

Yet even in such a subject as mathematics, an experiment at Kentucky University revealed excellent results from lecture sections of 150 to 200 students instead of the customary 25 to 40. The students had access also to two study rooms accommodating about 25, open thirty to forty hours a week, with a faculty member present. On the basis of performance and subjective judgments of students, teachers, and visitors, the radical change seemed a great success.[7]

EXPERIMENTS IN SIZE OF CLASS

Over the years we have had hundreds of experiments testing the effectiveness of teaching in small and large classes. Despite the fact that in the vast majority of instances these tests show either that the advantage (as shown by tests) lies with the large class or that there is no significant difference, the folklore of the small class still persists. Interested in this problem, Eurich of the Ford Foundation looked into the historical origins of the notion that one teacher is needed for every 25 students. With the aid of an eminent Talmudic scholar, President Samuel Belkin of the Yeshiva University, he found that the answer goes back to at least the middle of the third century. In Babylonian Talmud, Baba Bathra 21A, the rule was established by Rabbi Rabba, an authoritative sage of his era: "Twenty five students are to be enrolled in one class. If there are from 25 to 40 an assistant must be obtained. Above 40 two teachers are to be engaged."[8]

In the discussion before the American Council on Education the point was made that there was no difference between large and small classes. Eurich wanted to know why a first-class university in Europe could take care of 6,000 students with 90 professors, or a ratio of 60 to 70 students per faculty member. On the other hand, Wolfle came back from Europe with the observation that administrators of European institutions are fearful that they allow the students too much independence, and perhaps some movement toward our system might be desirable. At the Chicago Junior College enthusiastic teachers could perform well with a ratio of 40 to 1. But Ruth Eckert suggests that there ought to be different sizes for different functions. And Barzun comments on the fact that teaching a large class is exhausting.[9]

But what do these tests show? In a thorough discussion and examination of the issues, Otto concluded:[10]

On the basis of criteria used in the experimental studies published to date and under typical group teaching procedures, mere size of class has little significant influence on educational efficiency as measured by achievement in the academic subjects.

Although experimental evidence does not provide a clear-cut answer to the class size issue, the general trend of the evidence places the burden of proof squarely upon the proponents of small classes.

The most thorough and extensive series of experimental studies were those undertaken under Earl Hudelson of the University of Minnesota from 1924 to 1927. The studies included 59 experiments and 108 classes, distributed among 11 departments in four colleges and involving 6,059 students—4,205 in large classes and 1,288 in small classes. The size of classes studied varied from 12 to 159 students. His conclusion was:[11]

In the light of all of the available evidence class size seems to be a relatively minor factor in educational efficiency measured in terms of student achievement. . . .

All these results suggest that the techniques of instruction may have less influence upon student achievement than is generally ascribed to it, that the value of student participation may be over-rated.

In 46 of the experiments (78 per cent) a more or less decided advantage accrued to the paired students in the large sections. Only in the remaining 13 or 22 per cent was there any advantage in favor of the smaller classes. . . .

In one of the studies conducted by Hudelson the cost for a quarter for a group of 150 in physics was $4.34 per student and that for a group of 12, $36.27 per student; for another section of the same course in physics the relative costs were $2.83 for a group of 145 and $16.84 for a group of 12.[12]

After going over a vast number of experiments of this kind the Pennsylvania State Division of Academic Research in Services concluded as follows:[13]

1. Under prevailing methods—class size bears no significant relationship to educational efficiency as measured in terms either of student achievement or of any other measurable outcomes.

2. The only other instructional procedures that have appreciably and certainly increased student accomplishment in small college classes are prohibitively expensive and costly in time and labor to be used in large classes and are of doubtful justification in any size of class.

3. Most of the advantages of the small classes and materialistic methods of instruction accrue to the weaker students.

4. The only assured effect of frequent and intimate teacher-pupil contacts is personal satisfaction.

5. If pupil differentiation is a commendable aim it appears to be more attainable in large classes.

6. There is no evidence to show that, native ability equal, students learn less under modern college conditions than they did when classes were small, methods personal and relationships intimate.

A study at the University of Chicago in a course in education also reveals similar results. This study concludes:

The differences in the rankings between the large and the small class groups are all numerically small and non-statistically significant; although in the case of the comparison of classes A and B on the factor of interest taken in and the comparison of A and C on the factor of benefit derived, the differences approach statistical significance. The former differences favor the large class; the latter, the small class.

TABLE 44-5

Ratings Given the Course at the End of Unit I, on Time Required, Intellectual Challenge, Interest Taken, and Benefit Derived

Class groups	Time required	Intellectual challenge	Interest taken	Benefit derived
Average for class A (large).....	1.88	1.61	1.74	1.57
Average for class B (small)......	2.07	1.62	2.02	1.47
Average for class C (small).....	1.95	1.50	1.80	1.25

Source: Reeves, Peik, and Russell, *Instructional Problems*, 1933, pp. 163–164.

In a more recent study at the University of Miami (Ohio), the emphasis was put on studying " . . . the effectiveness of certain types of large group instruction to demonstrate the feasibility of these procedures at the college level." The techniques used were television courses, courses taught primarily by lecture method, courses taught by problem or case method, and courses with multiple sections taught by graduate assistants supervised by regular faculty members. The experiment involved 23 separate courses, many of them taught in multiple sections, 20 different departments in the university, and the approximate student enrollment of 4,457. The results were as follows:

Achievement. Performance on the course examinations administered for the purpose of assigning final grades (subject matter knowledge). Further intangible achievements such as synthesis, problem-solving, critical thinking were measured in some classes by essay tests (these were scored independently by 2 persons); in 3 courses on the matter of change in course-related attitudes were measured by pre and post tests.

Evaluation of Achievement. Of 27 comparisons between large and small classes conducted over two semesters there was only one that produced a significant difference in terms of scores in objective tests of course content.

Comparative Scores on Tests of Problem-Solving and Synthesis. Thirteen comparisons were made between large and small classes on tests selected to measure critical thinking, reasoning, ability to integrate materials and solve problems. On only one of these thirteen comparisons was a significant difference obtained.

The conclusion was that the worth of the class did not seem to be a function of class size. "Other factors, including course content and the ability of the instructor to handle larger groups of students, interact with class size to affect these attitudes."

Generally the students rate the instructors higher or more effective when they teach conventional or small sections than when they teach TV or large sections. But the writers conclude: "Some of the specific *intangible benefits* often associated with a low student-instructor ratio need *not* be sacrificed as a result of large group instruction."

NUMBER OF COURSES

So far we have quoted some authorities on the evils of excessive numbers of courses and have given a few examples of the abuse of the curriculum. But the problem is so important, both from an educational and economic viewpoint, that it should receive further attention. Even among faculty members there is a widespread awareness of this disease in the academic community—as was gleaned from the replies of a few hundred economists to a questionnaire sent by the author. But there is not an adequate grasp of the economics of the problem among faculty, and a quasi-senatorial courtesy prevails which results in each member of the faculty's being allowed to preserve his empire so long as he (she) does not trespass on the province of others.

I repeat what I said elsewhere: the gains from reducing the number of courses are not in proportion to the reduction of courses, for both in the college and university the faculty member has other tasks. Woodburne in his *Principles of College and University Administration* shows that courses and their preparation account for only about one-half the time of the faculty members, and a Minnesota University study revealed a similar distribution of time. A rise in the student/faculty ratio from 15 to 1 to 22½ to 1 suggested by reductions in courses and course requirements would in fact mean a saving, not of one-third, but more likely of one-sixth of instructional expenditures. But even this may yield $500 million currently and as much as $1 billion annually by 1970.

In a talk before the American Association of Collegiate Schools of Business, President Kirk of Columbia quoted approvingly from a faculty-committee report. Admitting that with the growth of knowledge there is an understandable emphasis on the acquisition of knowledge, the committee and President Kirk lamented the expansion of courses and curriculum in response to increasing knowledge which may soon become outmoded and dangerous.

It is impossible for any man to master all of it, even within a single university department . . . . The wiser course of action . . . is to recognize . . . that the race of the curriculum committee with knowledge is a losing one . . . each student . . . must be a searcher after truth . . . and must be aided to develop a capacity which can be utilized throughout his life.

President Kirk goes on to say that at Columbia, where there is much emphasis on graduate and professional work, the University might reduce courses by one-third to one-fourth without any impairment in the quality of work done for students or in the training of research scholars.

Similar views are expressed everywhere. President Wriston complains of the vast expansion of undergraduate curricula: " . . . the overexpansion of offerings has advanced costs beyond all reason, and immense savings could come from reform." At every institution he finds large lectures and numerous small classes with far too few students to justify the expense. " . . . Departmental satrapies, personal prepossessions and antipathies, logrolling, petty politics—these and a dozen others of the less admirable aspects of academic life account for the complicated hodgepodge that goes by the name of curriculum. . . . "

In his able study *Liberal Education in the Professions,* McGrath writes: " . . . The catalogues of University-connected liberal arts colleges now display hundreds of courses, many of which have nothing in common. When students randomly assemble these varied courses in a curriculum, the members of graduating classes have little more in common educationally than the title of their degrees."

Impressed by the factors making for a flowering of the curriculum—e.g., expansion of established fields, development and addition of new ones, the formation of new combination groupings, effects of wars, outside pressures to serve the community—President Stokes of Queens College nevertheless sees genuine dangers. "The overexpansion of curricula can result in the inclusion of the trivial with the important, and can also create the danger that there will be no distinction made between them."

One additional factor deserves mention: different colleges or departments in the same IHL often duplicate their offerings. One university may have six different courses in statistics and parts of a medical curriculum may be offered both in the college and the medical school.

A president of the Land-Grant College Association warned: "We must clear our catalogs of courses in Alligator Farm Management, Free Form Fly Fishing, and the Social Significance of Midgets in 13th Century Siam. We must eliminate overlapping and outdated courses and give careful scrutiny to those courses which draw an expensively low number of students. . . . "

Earlier I presented some statistics on the trend of courses, for a selected group of colleges. But the evil is much more widespread. Even in the Great Depression, authorities in Ohio State University " . . . had personal knowledge of many duplications, of many excessive subdivisions of subject matter, and of many courses that appeared to be unessential and even in some cases not even decorative." The university eliminated or changed to biennial offerings 450 courses.

A Carnegie Foundation study of 1933 was also concerned over the wastes, both educational and financial, of course creations. They found more than one hundred different departments within agricultural units of land-grant colleges, a rise of courses from 373 to 1,095 in arts and science at Stanford, and from 434 to 1,143 in arts and science at the University of Wisconsin.

In California the president of the public colleges controls the curriculum. The specialist in state college curricula makes his annual visitation for checking applications for staff in relation to new courses proposed. But even if disallowed, the college can include the course merely by using existing staff. A California commission complained of the excessive number of courses. At one state college at least 60 units of art are offered in one year, and another offers 200 courses and 600 units of credit in English.

A North Carolina commission is similarly critical. Each IHL in the state tends to develop a program conforming to the aspirations of its executive head and trustees. At one women's college it would take about seven years of full-time work to take all the English courses offered. French is offered as a major in six state IHL. But the six colleges produce only 23 graduates in French. Why, it is asked, would not one good French department bring 94 majors in the same period?

Sounding a warning of the dangers of proliferation of courses, a

Columbia committee quotes Charles W. Eliot's forecasts in 1869: "It will be generations before American institutions of education will get growth enough to bear pruning." In the view of the committee the time has arrived. Undue multiplication of courses has resulted, in the view of the committee, in excessive numbers of courses with small registration. In the university in 1956–57, there were 293 courses with zero registration. Of 2,020 courses offered on an advanced level, 404 had a registration of 10 or less, and 36 had a registration of more than 100.

An excessive number of courses is a great evil in higher education. Many college administrators are trying to deal with the problem, though they are often confronted with opposition by faculties. As a minimum, the knowledgeable and courageous administrator demands that a course be dropped when a new one is added; and he insists that small courses be alternated and, if not easily justifiable, be dropped. In the upper division and graduate curricula, a minimum number of courses with small enrollment is a price that has to be paid for necessary specialization. But the rise of courses has greatly exceeded the requirements of specialization. Clarence Faust relates an experience of a department anxious to add three members to its staff. The dean asked each member of the department to list courses considered essential for graduate preparation. The total of courses listed was 11, but the department offered 67 courses.

In view of the abuses of the system, it is not surprising that almost every experimental college proposes to limit the number of courses—by restricting the courses given by each faculty member, by reducing course requirements of students, (related) by requiring more independent work, by abandoning the three-times-a-week, fifteen- to twenty-week coverage of a course.[14]

EXPERIMENTS SUPPORTED BY FORD[15]

Recently the Fund for the Advancement of Education gave $500,000 to encourage experiments in teaching. The effect has been a tremendous outburst of new experiments, unparalleled in educational history. Impressed by the need of improved teaching and the shortage of teachers and resources, the fund provided this stimulation to increase experimentation in order to improve educational practice and save resources. These experiments were not limited to ascertaining the most effective size of classes. They were also directed toward making more effective use of assistants, large lectures (made possible by more effective use of assistants and machines), and of TV and machines generally, in order to exploit the effective teachers and to make instruction of large groups possible, despite the lack of large classrooms. Emphasis was also put upon reduction in number of courses and increasing independent study.[16]

Among the experiments were the following: Antioch arranged for teaching of five courses to one group of students by usual classroom methods and the second group of students through specialized reading programs, an approach to more independent study. One of the commentators on the programs suggested that independent study should be introduced at a slow rate. The student expects a certain amount of supervision, and if he does not get it, he rebels. Antioch apparently rushed into independent study too quickly, and the unprepared students protested vigorously. There was also a good deal of discussion of the problem of what kind of student is especially fitted for independent study. We need much more information on problems of this kind.

Grinnell also introduced a program aimed at better use of teaching resources by revision of the curriculum and an increase in more creative and independent study. This program was more gradual than the Antioch program, and by increasing the credit from three to four for each course, provided for a reduction in the number of classes per student from 12 to 9.

Determined to increase the amount of independent study, Marquette University[17]

. . . started an experiment with a group (150) composed of a cross-section of freshmen who were being given a special course, meeting for a double period laboratory session daily for one semester, designed to develop reading-expression skills. Reading comprehension, analysis, and economy of time as well as clearness of expression and ability to synthesize will be stressed. . . .

Perhaps the most interesting program which in a sense deprives the student of faculty in some classes and saves the faculty considerable time was one undertaken by Montana State College. The objective of this experiment was to keep the influence of the good teachers in the beginning classes but at the same time free them to work also with advanced science students by providing assistants and mechanical aids to do some of the work. The student is provided with a study room equipped with recordings and other audio-visual aids as well as biological materials. In this case there is a synchronization of slides and recordings. Mechanical self-testing devices permit students to check their own work as they proceed. Most of the experts who have analyzed this experiment were very much impressed.

A comprehensive attack was made by Wabash College. Wabash wished to adjust its course offerings and methods of instruction in the upper divisions in order to accommodate a larger number of students without a proportionate increase in teaching and without impairing its quality. It is now studying[18]

. . . a number of ways of increasing efficiency, including possible rescheduling of classes and laboratories, consolidation of offerings between and among departments, combining multi-section courses into single-section large courses, offering some courses every other year, reducing the number of class meetings per week with greater use of independent study, making more effective use of the library staff in instruction, using senior students as assistants to faculty members in handling quiz sections, reading papers and performing other non-teaching duties, and making greater use of the services of counselors to relieve the faculty members of some of their non-teaching duties.

The greater use of assistants is another approach to the problem of economizing resources. The young, inexperienced teacher assumes a substantial part of the burden, helping with small groups and saving the older members of the faculty for larger tasks. Many experiments in the present programs are directed toward making more effective use of assistants in larger numbers, obtaining part-time assistants, and training the assistants to do a better teaching job. In this context a program of the department of economics of the University of Colorado seems to have been especially successful.

In many ways the most intriguing programs are those that provide machine aids for the faculty. These include not only television but other mechanical aids as well, such as those used in the Montana experiment.

At Harvard, Skinner[19] is constructing self-teaching devices

. . . which go beyond existing audio-visual aids in giving the student an immediate report of the correctness of his own work not only on multiple-choice questions but on problems which require him to compose an answer. A set of frames of verbal and pictorial material printed on a disk is inserted in the machine. One frame is exposed at a time. The student writes his responses to each frame on a paper tape which passes out of reach before the correct response is revealed. The judgment of correctness is recorded. Each frame is presented in order until the question has been answered correctly twice. In setting up the device, plans are made to minimize rote learning; the emphasis is on encouraging plausible, logical steps in learning. The student spends part of his time in the course working in a room equipped with such devices. The instructor is thus relieved of the routine class instruction and can spend more time on material appropriate to advanced instruction. During the current year, ten such devices will be especially adapted for college teaching of beginning French and beginning physics.

APPRAISALS OF EXPERIMENTS

In discussing the Skinner machine one authority wrote:

The innate excitement of the learning process can be evoked by the proper attack, by leading the learner in the right direction, and by arranging the successive steps so that they are neither too long nor too short. It is not the *machine* but the teacher that is responsible for this; but once the teacher has thought out what should be learned and how, the chief responsibility is placed where it properly belongs—on the learner. . . .

Of the experiments, 10 used mechanical electronic aids to teaching: 3 used tape recorders, 3 used instructional films, 3 used closed-circuit TV, and 1 used a mechanical device to assist in the learning process.

In discussing the listening rooms and language labs a commentator said of an experiment at Stanford:

Here it is a question of conditioning the ear to make sense out of sounds as one does out of the mother tongue during the first two or three years of life and conditioning the tongue to reproduce sounds in a way to make sense, without embarrassment (which for the mother tongue requires but the first four years of life). In this process the ear is the vital organ, for the tongue cannot pronounce what the ear cannot receive accurately, hence the importance of the listening room. . . .

The same commentator writes:

There is no reason, in theory, that the various ideas used in the experimental program should not enable experienced college instructors to teach a much greater number of students than they ever have, and just as effectively. This *should* be the result of larger classes, the use of assistance, improved methods, the use of machines and audio-visual aids, independent study and streamlined curricula.

Again, he says:

It seems clear that the problem of numbers will be solved most easily if it is related to other basic and persistent problems of American education such as for example: helping to provide real equality of educational opportunity, helping to provide effective motivation for students, trying to arrange a proper balance between freeing students to do independent study and providing guidance when needed, trying to fit the subject to the learner by a precise analysis of the learning process and programming courses of study suitably, seeking ways to overcome the compartmentalization of education (1) vertically: elementary, secondary, higher, teacher training; (2) horizontally: between subject matter fields; and (3) between school and community.

This writer goes on to say that of the three components of the academic community, the administration is most willing to make changes, then the students; the faculty is least willing to experiment.[20]

Another expert, after examining all these experiments, many of which tend to increase the size of classes, concludes:

Given the necessity of handling a large number of students with limited staff, is it better to have large sections (or lectures) with good teachers, or small groups with the inclusion of poor or incompetent teachers? On the basis of personal experience with lecture and section methods and on the basis of the experience cited in the experiments, I am satisfied that without recourse to Chi-Square (analysis of questionable data) that it is better to have large groups with better teachers.

He goes on to say that the lecture can generate much interest on the part of the student.

The real problem is to retain some mechanism for eliciting intellectual effort from the student to get him to deal with problems, articulate ideas and lines of reasoning, perceive relations through the insights he gets through questioning and arguing (rather than by direct revelation by the teacher). This kind of commitment in learning by the student is not obtained by any amount of clear lecturing or objective testing. . . .

One observer contends that the teaching of large groups by experienced teachers is preferable to teaching small groups by less skilled teachers and inexperienced graduate assistants. In such subjects as mathematics "there is more chance that the student will participate in the learning process, because of the problems he has to work outside of class; in economics the problems he works outside of class are the more likely to be papers where he simply parrots back the lectures and the textbook. . . . "

Several experts raised the question of the validity of the tests. For example:

Ideally an experiment involving greater autonomy on the part of students should involve evaluation not only of short-term mastery of the course materials, but also the durability of this competence, and especially of the development of the desire and capacity for continued intellectual growth.

Some observers believe that the experiments do not yield large economies.

Their primary justification will probably have to rest on their larger yield in student learning per unit of faculty time invested. To effect important economies, the present system of course taking and credit collecting will probably have to be scrapped in favor of one that will recognize more directly the actual accomplishment, regardless of how much—or little—exposure the student had to formal instruction.

It is easy to exaggerate the importance of the contribution of independent study.

Independent study, in other words, is not a substitute for careful review of the program of studies to determine whether the course actually merits teaching or whether it currently makes full use of the instructor's talents. It is important that faculties develop programs of independent study related to their own philosophies of education and their abilities and interests. Since some faculty members are bound to feel threatened by any departure from conventional practices, sufficient time should be allowed for them to become accustomed to the idea and to get some real sense of involvement in its local use.

Independent study also requires a wider variety of resource materials than is needed by conventional methods. After studying many programs one observer noted:

The program has helped to alert faculties throughout the country to mounting staff shortages and to the need to meet this problem realistically, rather than to cling stubbornly to conventional concepts of class size and teaching methods. . . .

When tests are based almost entirely on text materials, as is true in some places, students might do fully as well if they stayed away from class altogether. . . .

Instead of trying to find out how students might be put through the same paces more efficiently, college staffs probably should re-question the whole course and credit structure of American higher education. . . .

This same observer notes in relation to small classes,

. . . while none provides the rigorous test of the hypothesis that class size has little influence on student learning, the similarity in measured outcome should provoke advocates of small classes to produce more tangible support of their position. . . .

In many studies the variable of class size was compounded with other variables such as the instructor's skill in using the method. As one study showed, the instructor is held by students to be a more important reason for selecting a section than the particular teaching method or the size of the group.

Still another observer writes:

The use of assistance, of whatever sort, is of course closely related to the problem of class size and teaching method. My impression is that very little is known about optimum class size for particular subjects and under various teaching methods. It is clear that some institutions which have managed to resist any great increase in class size are nevertheless utilizing instructors as lecturers rather than teachers by discussion. It seems apparent also that differences in subject matter, level, teaching method and availability of teaching assistance make it impossible to be dogmatic about the most desirable class size throughout a college or a curriculum.

Another observer:

The Skinner machine seems to me full of promise, as does the ingenious tape and slide system developed at Montana State. The dangers of the use of such gadgets are so obvious I think there is small chance of their being greatly abused. And we should not be afraid to make the discovery, if the evidence points to it, that some human teachers who will be employed during the critical part of the teacher shortage have not much more humanity than a machine. One thing about a machine. It never gets bored with its subject, so no matter how efficient it is it can never communicate actively that ennui which exudes from some bad teachers.

On the issue of size of class, another observer writes:

There is in American higher education no dogma more firmly believed and less securely supported by actual evidence than the conviction that small class instruction is always superior to large class instruction.

But we must . . . distinguish as fully as possible the effects of section size
from other factors such as skill of the lecturer, the articulation between lecturer and discussion groups, the adequacy of the training of the discussion
leaders, and the use made of problems, projects, study guides and other learning aids. . . .

The most important objection that will be raised is that the evaluation procedures are not adequate measures of the educational objectives appropriate
to the course. Evaluation methods should be used that are convincing to the
most incredulous (not to say dubious!) of the doubting Thomases. . . .

This same critic points out the greatest untapped source is assistance
from the upperclass undergraduate student. But he adds:

The use and misuse—of graduate assistance as a means of relieving faculty
members of routine tasks, as a source of additional assistance of students, and
as a method of diluting the quality of instruction, has an established place in
American higher education. . . .

Still another observer writes as follows:

None of the experiments in class size involved a massive lecture of, say,
more than 200. Theoretically this number could be pushed higher, even larger
numbers might be accommodated through the use of television. One could
visualize the situation in which a senior professor with four or five relatively
senior assistants might take the responsibility for say 1,000 students. The
massive lecture might be divided among the senior men with each contributing
from his particular area of specialization. They could divide responsibility for
supervising section leaders. Once this process were established it would not
require much of the time of the senior staff and it might well result in the improvement and teaching quality at the freshman and sophomore level, even
with the reduction in the formal education levels of the instructors in charge
of the sections.

One expert wants to know whether the abler students can benefit from
independent studies, what the relationship of the independent study is to the
honors program, and what is the possibility that independent study will
provide an opportunity for students " . . . to rationalize their knowledge
and values and compensate for the coming avalanche of facts." Will
independent study improve the student's opportunity for meaningful learning? Can graduate students and others be used in supervising independent
study effectively?

In a discussion of class size one authority writes:

The fundamental problem is not whether facts can be spewed out in an objective test given shortly after the course work has been completed. Instead it
is whether the student learns to think critically, to use data and evidence, to
know how to approach unfamiliar problems, to exercise responsible citizen-
ship or, to paraphrase William James, "to know a good man when he sees
one. . . . "

This writer finds that evaluative instruments which go beyond the measurement of factual knowledge and probe ability, critical thinking and other such qualities have not yet been perfected nor used extensively.

Can instructors eliminate themselves from the classroom? The Skinner machine is one contribution toward this. And in the Montana State experiment in an elementary botany course, " . . . the instructors hope to achieve a factual background in taxonomy plus some familiarity with plants and other materials. These limited objectives can be accomplished satisfactorily by lecture, by television, or by the use of a tape recorder and slide viewer."

One observer notes: "Ray Lyman Wilbur once said that it was harder to change a curriculum than to move a graveyard. I would bring this up to date by saying it is harder to eliminate a course or series of courses than to raise faculty salaries."

A leading scientist has this to say:

We have had a great many comparisons between the amount of learning in large and small classes. The standard expectation of such a study is that there will be no significant difference between the two classes in the scores made on final examinations. This, I suspect will continue to be the case, for a great many factors (the student's own ability, the previous courses he has taken, his own work habits, the textbook, the quality of the teacher, etc., etc.) are involved in determining final student grades. Among these factors the number of students who happen to be sitting in the same room during a given hour carries comparatively little weight in determining the grades made by individual students.

This fact, for I think it is a statistically valid fact, seems to me to be the most important criticism of the usual experiment on class size. It is not, however, the most significantly voiced criticism. The more frequently expressed one is that the standard examination forms do not measure all of the desirable outcomes of college courses and that the students in small classes gain more of the intangible benefits that are not measured by examinations than do students in large classes. Until and unless we have better measures of these intangible benefits, about the only thing we can do with this criticism is to say, "maybe so."

This writer goes on to say that there are just not enough good teachers to permit the general use of small classes. Hence the real problem is not whether we ought to have small or large classes but how to provide the best teaching in large ones.

STUDENT/FACULTY RATIOS

President Gallagher of the City College of New York once said that the student/teacher ratio is sacred. It is indeed difficult to increase this ratio.

My study of 11 colleges shows a downward trend. Over-all figures for the United States also show a tendency for the ratio to decline, that is, for this reason a tendency for instructional costs to increase. Thus from 1919–20 to 1955–56, faculty increased by 5.4 times, and students by only 3.4 times.[21]

Student/faculty ratios (SFR) depend on all kinds of factors: the kind of curriculum—a 3 to 1 ratio in medical schools is not uncommon, nor a 40 to 1 ratio in law schools; the course requirements for students—at fifteen hours per week, the SFR, *ceteris paribus,* will be lower than at nine hours; the teaching load—the greater, the higher the SFR; the number and size of classes—the more numerous the courses and the smaller the classes (at given teaching loads), the lower will be the SFR; the greater the use of assistants, undergraduate or graduate, the higher the SFR will be.

What is the SFR? According to a study of the National Education Association, the current figure is 13 to 1 and the projected ratio in 1969–70, 15.75 to 1. But the writers point out that large variations prevail, with high ratios for junior colleges and low ones for complex universities with many professional schools. At the University of Pennsylvania it is 10 to 1; and at Columbia, Cornell, and Yale, 9 to 1, 8 to 1, and 6 to 1. Moreover, variations are related to differences in items included or excluded—e.g., graduate assistants or administrative personnel.

In his brilliant study *Memo to a College Trustee,* Beardsley Ruml sought to raise the SFR to 20 to 1 through reducing the number of intermediate-sized classes and increasing the number of seminars and large lectures. In this way he hoped to finance a doubling of faculty salaries. At Dartmouth, where Ruml was a trustee, some of the most interesting work on this subject emerged. It was pointed out that Dartmouth could increase its enrollment from 2,624 to 3,000 and yet reduce its faculty from 203 to 177, or a 17 to 1 SFR. By reducing course registrations from fifteen hours weekly to nine hours, this could be done. Incidentally, an official report from the state of Pennsylvania projects a rise from 12.4 to 1 now to a maximum of 21 to 1 in 1970. A California report (*A Restudy of 1955*) envisages a 20 to 1 ratio eventually as not being undesirable.

In the colleges there is a growing awareness of the need of increasing the SFR. Difficulties of obtaining well-trained and competent teachers and lack of finance underline the need of attacking this problem. Hence the efforts to curb the inflation of courses, to eliminate or alternate small classes, to reduce course requirements for students, to impose more independent work, and to utilize more assistance, thus freeing senior faculty for teaching and research.

A word should be added on the problems of independent work and assistants. All kinds of attempts have been made to stress independent work, that is, focusing on *learning* as against *teaching.* In some kinds of independent work, e.g., honors work, the cost of instruction per student may be increased rather than reduced. From numerous experiments it is concluded that independent work will prove a failure unless preparation is made for it, that it tends to be more productive if started in the freshman year and continued throughout. On the whole, putting a student on his own for a whole semester without any preparation or guidance is likely to be disastrous. Reducing classes from three to two per week or putting aside a few weeks each semester (the Harvard reading period) for independent work seems to bring better results than a long spell of independent work. Yet the largest economies are to be had by sending the student away for one quarter, thus through a four-quarter system doubling the capacity of the plant (the Oberlin plan.) Careful preparation and guidance (e.g., abroad) may yield a successful quarter-away plan.

In my experience as a tutor for forty years I found this work rewarding and most productive for the students' development, though very costly to the tutor. Presently I am giving a seminar to 10 freshmen on public policy. Each student meets with me and a colleague at lunch once weekly and ultimately writes two papers based on source materials. This is one of my most satisfying teaching experiences in over forty years of teaching, but it is not saving of time or resources.

Use of assistants may be very productive. It is uneconomic for a $20,000, or even a $10,000, faculty member to grade papers, take attendance, go over readings with students, or supervise laboratory work. The large universities tend to utilize graduate students effectively for this purpose. I once estimated that 15 to 20 per cent of the classroom hours at Harvard (arts and science) is done by teaching fellows (graduate students), generally with two years of graduate work behind them. Where graduate students are not available, good results can be obtained with undergraduates if the position is given prestige and their contribution is well integrated—as the Williams experience showed.

Obstacles to increasing the SFR are numerous. A penchant for course proliferation has already been discussed. Faculties are always anxious to increase the size of their departments but reluctant to abandon a subject or not replace a retired or deceased member even where the need no longer exists. In their *Academic Marketplace,* Caplow and McGee showed that " . . . according to respondents' reports, 33 per cent of the actual replacements made were unnecessary in terms of continuing the functions of a predecessor."[22]

I recall that, when I was chairman of the economics department at Harvard, we averaged three leaves a year. I generally asked the dean to replace only one, and hence saved the university $25,000 to $30,000 a year. I asked for replacements only when the courses of members on leave could not be bracketed [omitted] for a year or if essential teaching assignments could not be rearranged within the department. At least some of my colleagues resented this policy, partly on the ground that any savings made became available for others not equally saving. Perhaps the solution lay in a policy adopted at Stanford where at least one department was allowed to raise its salary scale substantially and thus increase holding power of its faculty by adopting an economical curriculum and being allowed to use the resultant savings to increase salaries.

Related to the reluctance of teachers to increase the SFR is a fear that prevails everywhere—unemployment. Obviously if Dartmouth should reduce its faculty by 26 (13 per cent) in order to achieve a 17 to 1 ratio, the program would be blocked. But this would not be necessary. A slowing up of replacements would solve the problem. One estimate puts replacements at 6 per cent of staff per year.

Another obstacle to a rise in the SFR is the strong view held, and especially in small IHL, that a ratio of 5 to 1 or 10 to 1 is absolutely essential to preserve the close student-faculty relations that induce the best kind of education. The excellent results shown by the students in the small colleges in the West in scientific achievements, reported by Knapp and Goodrich, strengthen this position.

A trustee of the University of Rochester puts well a view widely held on the issues under discussion. An increase in the SFR is the opposite of what is needed, for in his view what we require is more faculty time for each student. Students see too little, not too much, of faculty. (This position might still be consistent with elimination of intermediate-sized courses.) The trustee stresses the need of courses in Greek and in Persian history even though enrollment is small, and urges as a solution that the businessman continue to dig deep. Others also have been concerned that greater use of large lectures, as under the Ruml plan, would mean fewer conferences, papers to be criticized, and the like.

" . . . Would not a fixed numerical ratio really operate to change the character of a liberal arts college so that it would become something quite different from the kind of place it was always intended to be? Is there not a real danger that we may end up with an institution in which everything is off balance except the balance sheet?"[23]

CONCLUSION

The evidence fails to support the case for the small class. The tests may not be adequate to measure all the results of the teaching process, but they show enough to suggest that the burden of proof rests on those who favor the small class.

Whatever our views, we are likely to be confronted with a rise of students greatly in excess of the increased supply of teachers at current standards. Hence the only alternative to a serious deterioration of teaching quality is a more effective use of available talent. In numerous state studies there is already evidence of a rising student/faculty ratio induced in part by elimination of small classes and increase of large classes.

Larger classes, greater use of visual aids, reductions in course requirements, more independent work, more careful scrutiny of courses and small classes, and a more receptive attitude toward machines, both to supplement the teacher or even replace him to some extent—all these are on the agenda. We can also anticipate that IHL, like industry, will increasingly try to raise productivity by conserving the energies of the most effective teachers for the most vital tasks. They will lecture to large groups and will have increased assistance for secretarial work, preparation of materials and grading of papers.

I do not draw the conclusion from all this that there is no place for the tutorial or small discussion groups. Students profit greatly from the give and take of these meetings, where they write papers, defend them, and generally are forced to think and communicate. But these meetings are expensive, especially in periods when personnel and finance are likely to be scarce. The continuation of the tutorial or groups, say, of less than 10 or 15 as well as the small classes that are needed in upper division and graduate classes are to be had only if the wastage in classes of, say, 30 to 75 can be reduced through large lectures by able and inspirational lecturers. Here I can reassure the many economists who replied to my questionnaire that the proposals for elimination of the medium-sized class where lecturing is costly and often of low quality and the proposals for savings of finance and manpower do not mean the end of the small group.

As Sir Geoffrey Crowther wrote in *The Atlantic Monthly* in April, 1960, in defense of the British system of specialization: " . . . the process of education is not to be compared to that of filling up an empty pot, but rather to that of lighting a fire. The proper test of education is whether it teaches the pupil to think and whether it awakens his interest in applying his brain to the various problems and opportunities that life presents." The tutorial and small discussion groups contribute to the achievement of this goal.

Yet the trend is likely to be toward the large class. Many may doubt that the large class is as effective as the small. Difficulties with testing point in the direction of uncertainty. But a practical issue is that good teachers are limited and the large class is a condition for exploiting them; and another issue is that, given limited resources, we shall have to have more large classes. We shall have to learn how to make them more effective.*

* In the last year or so, the Office of Education (*New Dimensions,* 1960 and 1961, especially nos. 7, 8, 9) has listed various programs in IHL directed toward increasing productivity, e.g. studies of methods of learning, greater and more effective use of independent study, substitution of tests for credits on the basis of time devoted to a study.

FOOTNOTES

[1] Cf. E. K. Graham, *Professors, Presidents, and Mounting Admission Requirements in CEEB: Planning College Policy for the Critical Decade Ahead*, 1958, p. 75.

[2] *Addresses and Discussions of the Carnegie Conference on Higher Education*, 1957, p. 60.

[3] *Nature and Needs of Higher Education*, pp. 106–107.

[4] *A Study of the Need for Additional Centers of Public Higher Education in California*, 1957, p. 110.

[5] H. M. Wriston, "How Colleges Can Handle the Throng," *Life, passim*, 1958.

[6] Lewis, Pinnell and Wells, "Needs, Resources and Priorities in Higher Educational Planning," *American Association of University Professors Bulletin*, September, 1957, p. 437.

[7] "How Many Can We Teach?" *Journal of Higher Education*, 1955, pp. 90 *et seq.* For the materials in the last few pages, see especially The Fund for the Advancement of Education, *Better Utilization of College Teaching Resources* . . . : *A Summary Report*, May, 1959; also an earlier version (mimeographed), 1957; *A Restudy of the Needs of California in Higher Education*, 1955, pp. 448–449; Rensselaer Polytechnic Institute, *Towards More Effective Teaching at Rensselaer*, 1957; *School of General Studies: Report of the Dean*, Columbia University Bulletin, 1957–58, pp. 10–14; J. Millett, "Colleges Must and Can Be More Efficient," in *College Admissions*, 5, 1958, pp. 54–56; W. B. Nelson, "An Experiment with Class Size in the Teaching of Elementary Economics," *The Educational Record*, October, 1959, pp. 330–341; *A Report to the Indiana Conference of Higher Education*, November, 1957, pp. 46–47; Reeves, Henry, and Russell, *Class Size and University Costs: University of Chicago Survey*, vol. XI, 1933, pp. 39, 66, 136; *New York University Self-study: Final Report*, 1956, p. 267; Hill and Kelly, *Economies in Higher Education*, 1933, p. 78; Amherst College, *Report of the Committee on the Future Size of the College and Related Subjects*, 1959, p. 12; E. J. McGrath, "The Future of the Protestant College," *Liberal Education*, March, 1961, pp. 52–53.

[8] A. C. Eurich, *Better Instruction with Fewer Teachers*, 1956, pp. 7–8.

[9] American Council on Education, *Expanding Resources in College Teaching*, 1956, pp. 93, 118–123.

[10] *Encyclopedia of Educational Research* (rev. ed.), 1950, p. 215; also see Long and Perry, "Effect of Increasing Class Size in College," *School and Society*, Feb. 11, 1961.

[11] Pennsylvania State University, *Summary, Abstracts and Bibliography of the Studies of Class Size*, pp. 1, 4, 7, and 20; cf. Cammarosano and Santopolo, "Teaching Efficiency and Class Size," *School and Society*, Sept. 27, 1958, pp. 338–341.

[12] Pennsylvania State University, *op. cit.*, p. 8.

[13] *Ibid.*, p. 27.

[14] *Ibid.*, pp. 28–31. I have especially depended on the following for the material in this section: E. J. McGrath, *Liberal Education in the Professions*, 1959, chap. 2 and p. 62; E. Hodnett, *Industry-College Relations*, 1955, pp. 118–121; C. H. Faust, "Rising Enrollments and Effective Use of Faculty Resources," *Association of American Colleges Bulletin*, May, 1957, p. 263; *A Restudy of the Needs of California Higher Education*, 1955, pp. 264–66; *The Educational Future of Columbia*, 1957, pp. 117–118; H. W. Stoke, *The American College President*, 1958, p. 112; L. S. Woodburne, *Principles of College and University Administration*, 1958, chap. 6; H. M. Wriston, *Academic Procession*, 1959, pp. 38–39; Hofstra College Student Committee, "A Proposal for the Establishment of an Experimental College," *Liberal Education*, May, 1959, pp. 205–215; H. W. Stoke, "The Flowering Curricula of

American Higher Education," *The Annals, Higher Education under Stress,* September, 1955, pp. 58–64; American Association of Collegiate Schools of Business, *Faculty Requirements and Standards in Collegiate Schools of Business,* 1955, pp. 25–27; *Proceedings of the American Association of Land-Grant Colleges and State Universities,* Nov. 11–14, 1957, p. 25; Hill and Kelly, *Economy and Higher Education,* Carnegie Foundation, 1933, pp. 57–72; *New York University Self-study: Final Report,* 1956, pp. 33–34; *State-supported Higher Education in North Carolina: The Report of the Commission on Higher Education,* 1955, pp. 35–41; C. E. Odegaard, *Report to the Faculty October 5, 1959.*

[15] Material in this section is based largely on preliminary reports (mimeographed) to the Ford Foundation. More recently a published version, *Better Utilization of College Teaching Resources: A Report by the Committee on Utilization of College Teaching Resources,* May, 1959, has been issued by the Ford Foundation. I take account of this at various places.

[16] See *ibid.,* October, 1956, for a description of some of these plans and programs.

[17] *Ibid.,* p. 29.

[18] *Ibid.,* p. 40.

[19] *Ibid.,* p. 23; also see B. F. Skinner, "Teaching Machines," *Higher Educaton in the United States: The Economic Problems,* S. E. Harris (ed.), 1960, pp. 83–87.

[20] These and later quotations are from mimeographed memoranda of the Fund for the Advancement of Education; also see B. F. Skinner, "Teaching Machines," *Science,* Oct. 24, 1958, pp. 969–977.

[21] These figures should be accepted as giving trends, because the percentage of part-time teachers and students probably increased at different rates.

[22] Based on all professional vacancies and replacements in nine universities in two recent years.

[23] For material in this section see especially HEW, *Statistics of Higher Education: 1955–56, Faculty, Students, and Degrees,* pp. 6–7; Ruml and Morrison, *Memo to a College Trustee,* 1959, esp. parts 2 and 3; S. E. Harris, "The Economic Aspects of 'Memo to a College Trustee,'" *Journal of Higher Education,* November, 1959, pp. 441–46; Caplow and McGee, *The Academic Marketplace,* 1958, pp. 139–144; National Education Association, *Teacher Supply and Demand in Universities, Colleges and Junior Colleges, 1957–58 and 1958–59,* pp. 50–52; N. Rogoff, *Board Member Colleges: A Comparative Analysis,* May, 1957, pp. 76–86; McEwen and Synakowski, "Planning College Enrollment for Academic Efficiency," *Journal of Higher Education,* June, 1954, p. 301–307; R. H. Shyrock, *The University of Pennsylvania Faculty: A Study in Higher Education,* 1959, pp. 225–228; L. S. Nicholson, *The Law Schools of the United States*; Commonwealth of Pennsylvania, Joint State Government Commission, 1959, *Higher Education in Pennsylvania,* pp. 36–39; S. M. Linowitz, "A Liberal Arts College Is Not a Railroad," *School and Society,* Nov. 23, 1957, pp. 351–52; *Better Utilization of College Teaching Resources,* 1959, pp. 13–23 and 44–51; P. Lauter, "Memo from a College Teacher," *New Leader,* Nov. 16, 1959.

Chapter 45

SOME GENERAL ASPECTS OF ECONOMIES

I have discussed the number of courses, the greater use of assistants, machines, more independent work, and the like. Now I will continue with some general aspects of economy, as well as some issues that are not adequately dealt with in earlier chapters.

Above all, productivity is an important problem for IHL. Over a period of fifty or sixty years unit (i.e., per resident student) costs have continued to increase even when corrected for the rise in price level—all the more surprising since the size of the average college has increased about six times during this period. Ordinarily with such a rise in numbers we would expect a lower cost per student. This may be explained by the reduction of teachers' work loads, higher real pay (over the whole period) with interruptions, increased costs of laboratories, proliferation of courses, large increase in plant requiring substantial operating costs, and the increased services outside the classroom.

An industrialist may be particularly surprised that with this growth the cost per student has steadily risen. Even stranger to him, in a period when demand for the product doubles, the colleges are confronted with serious financial problems. What would appear as a boom to the businessman is in fact a threat. Colleges do not generally gain from rising enrollments, since they usually sell their product below cost. Under these circumstances, as their enrollments increase, their deficits rise. This generalization holds unless the increase in cost for the additional enrollment is less than the additional tuition revenue. In economic parlance, if marginal revenue exceeds marginal cost, the situation is improved; but if marginal revenue is less than marginal cost, the situation deteriorates.[1] In public institutions, where tuition is generally a small part of average or marginal cost, a rise of enrollment inevitably means an increase in deficits or subsidies.

Why, it may be asked, in a period of fifty years when the average output per man rose about 2.2 per cent per year, has the real cost of higher education increased? The answer lies in part in factors mentioned above and in the difficulty of applying the advances of technology to IHL. To some extent teaching is a personal matter; it is difficult to mass-produce it. Relevant also is the fact that colleges, and particularly their faculties, have resisted change and new methods of teaching. Some fear that the introduction of machinery may bring about technological unemployment. Many are determined to maintain old teaching methods at all costs. It is difficult for administrations to force change upon teachers who are not employees, as industry can do when confronted with increased competition and falling prices.

In some respects colleges face the same problem as other sellers of services. In the highly mechanized industries, unit costs tend to fall rapidly with the great developments of technology and management. The result is that these industries are able to pay much higher wages out of the increased productivity. But other employments, not equally favored by these advances, must nevertheless meet the competition of the more productive employments for labor and materials. Colleges must pay higher prices for all that they purchase, even though these higher prices are not offset by corresponding gains in productivity. This is a most serious aspect of the economics of higher education.

ATTITUDE TOWARD ECONOMICAL MANAGEMENT

As costs of higher education rise, the public, confronted with higher charges, is increasingly critical of the management of our colleges.

From a large number of items of this kind I quote from just two or three. Kiplinger has spent a great deal of time studying the problems of higher education.[2] He asked the following questions: Why don't colleges make more efficient use of their space and facilities? One college, for instance, was found to be using only 25 per cent of its classroom capacity. Second, why do not colleges share facilities? This is particularly important for small colleges. Third, why do not colleges help their teachers with mechanical aids? The survey shows that one school boasts that 88 per cent of all its classes have fewer than 30 students, and 40 per cent have fewer than 10. Fourth, why not get rid of superfluous courses? The president of Rutgers said, "It has almost reached the point where no one expects to know anything, from how to manage the school wastepaper basket to how to deal with one's relatives, without taking a special course in it and getting a certificate." Fifth, why do not students do more independent work? We spoon-feed our students too much. Finally, why is there such a large attrition between freshman year and graduation? We lose 40 per cent of our students.

A knowledgeable writer, Peter B. Bard in the *Wall Street Journal*, reported on April 24, 1958, after a serious survey of the problem, about the management of IHL. On the issue of willingness to experiment with new devices and techniques, one of the deans in the Northeast said, according to Bard, "It is ironical that we academicians who have talked so much about creative thinking, have been so spectacularly uncreative in the vast majority of cases in dealing with our own problems."

"All too often a small discussion in class becomes a dialogue between the professor and one or two noisy students," says one Harvard University Business School professor, according to Bard.

One top college administrator told Bard, "The faculty remains opposed to this sort of thing [that is, use of mechanical devices]. The reason is obvious enough—they feared being laid off just like the worker fears automation. This fear has been reinforced by the fact that many big universities have recently been overstaffed." According to Bard, as a result of a study by Cresap, McCormick, and Paget, Stephens College saved $460,000 annually by releasing maids, janitors, and even a few professors from its roster. Stephens installed new machines in its kitchen and mail room, built a warehouse to permit greater stockpiling of materials, tightened the control over purchasing, and revised accounting procedures.

One college put up a building on behalf of a retiring dean. Instead of being vacant just 30 per cent of the working day like most other buildings, it was vacant all day long.

Bard quotes Ivey, executive vice president of New York University: "All the colleges now are raising money; but some day they are going to be embarrassed when people stop and ask, 'How well are you using the money you have already got?' "

In a paper before the Conference on Moral Standards in September, 1953, President Hancher of Iowa University, one of the leading educators in the country, had some profound things to say about these issues. One question raised by President Hancher is:

What educational program is the institution qualified to offer? The question, carefully considered, calls for an accurate, honest, complete appraisal of the institution—its staff, its facilities, its finances, its complete resources—to determine whether or not it possesses the competence and quality essential for the conduct of the program or program which it offers. It is designed to bring institutions back to a *functional integrity* which is sadly lacking in our system.

President Hancher complains, "Few institutions hesitate to rush into new and presumably popular programs which they were not organized to offer, for which they possess no special competence, and for which the demand has been created by them rather than by the public. . . . " Institutions without the requisite scientists or resources should not apply for government research contracts in order to attract staff and acquire facilities. Unrestrained and unintelligent competition reduces standards, and low standards tend to drive out high ones. Another waste that President Hancher refers to is that of recruiting new students. He is all for expensive recruiting in order to save the able students who are now left out. What concerns him is that the institution " . . . actively intervenes to affect the choice of the prospective student on grounds other than the true educational worth and attractiveness of the institution." He wants to know whether the information given is fair and accurate. Are students recruited who in their own best interests should go elsewhere? Apparently there are even solicitors who receive a commission or bonus on the basis of students signed up and matriculated. The expenditure of funds for the diversion of students from one institution to another cannot largely be justified.

And President Hancher wants to know whether the student gets the education that he is promised. "This does not preclude the giving of a trade or vocational training but it is not satisfied by such training. The educated man is more than a technician. He not only knows how a thing works but why it works. . . . "

As early as June, 1955, Alvin Eurich, in a speech before College and University Business Officers in Estes Park, Colorado, indicted IHL for their failure to present a balance sheet of their educational achievements, or an informative one on their financial statement; for their costly methods of purchasing and plant maintenance; and for their reluctance to exploit new teaching methods. College administrators, in his view, did not seem to realize that a doubling of enrollment does not necessarily mean a doubling of costs.

* * *

Under strain and stress of costs colleges will take strong measures to cut costs. In the midst of the Great Depression, for example, one survey showed that the following methods were used to reduce expenditures at college:

1. Elimination of miscellaneous expenses which do not concern directly the instruction of students. (110 cases)
2. Reduction in the cost of maintaining and operating buildings and grounds. (113)
3. Increase in the load of faculty by not making appointments to vacancies. (81)
4. Rearranging courses so as to enlarge the size of classes or so as to give courses in alternative years of semesters. (68)
5. Postponing the purchase of library books. (61)
6. Reducing expenditures for travel. (80)
7. Reducing clerical help and office expense. (78)
8. Undertaking no new construction except where special funds are provided. (92)

Numerous other economies were made: reducing expenditures for publicity bureaus and university press publications, postponing or denying all leaves of absence with pay, and so on.

In the Great Depression, President Hutchins of the University of Chicago presented two alternatives: a reduction of courses and staff and maintenance of pay structure, or an unchanged staff and pay cuts. The solution chosen was the former. In some instances the choice was the latter. In North Dakota the salaries of all university teachers, of all normal school teachers, and of teachers in all other state-supported schools were fixed at $1,290 a year.[3]

In a similar vein the president of the University of Pennsylvania in his 1956 report writes:[4].

We must be prepared also to adjust existing academic practices in the interests of efficiency in teaching. For example, without sacrifice of quality, it might be possible to re-deploy the most competent teachers so that a greater percentage of them are assigned to the larger classes; to extend the use of assistance so as to relieve the teaching staff of routine administrative duties; to expand the application of audio-visual aids. At the same time the individual student must be encouarged to assume greater responsibility in the educational process, toward the end that the teacher will be relieved of much of his present duties to transmit hourly fundamental information which is really available in textual form.

In his 1955 report he said that the university would determine which programs are (1) the most central and essential or traditionally the strongest; (2) more peripheral, specialized, or currently less developed at the university; (3) relatively narrowed or highly specialized academic activities making smaller contributions to general education; (4) inappropriate to the general educational objectives of the institution.

He was furthermore prepared to consider trends in income and allocation of resources over the last thirty years and would develop cost information per student by departments and schools, identify the areas in which the major increases have occurred since 1924, and would indicate where possible the services associated with such increases.[5]

One approach to increased economies is improved use of capacity. In various parts of this book I deal with some aspects of this problem—e.g., coordination, location of plant. But here I present several instances of relevance:

All year operation of plant involves large savings. The able presentation of President Kirk in *The Saturday Evening Post* has alerted the nation to the possibilities. The academic vice president of Tulane University, Fred Cole, estimates that twelve-month operation would provide for 50 to 75 per cent additional students without a significant rise of capacity. Another expert found that a year-round schedule for the nation's IHL would increase degrees by 56 per cent a year, provide 30 per cent more instructional facilities, and make possible a 30 per cent rise of faculty salaries. At the University of Pennsylvania, a modernization of curriculum and facilities increased the capacity for engineering students by 50 per cent. Through a lengthening of the school year and reduction of duplication—e.g., largely concentrating chemistry in the medical schools—the Johns Hopkins Medical School expects to save the student two years, and of course utilize the capacity much more effectively. Western Reserve University has also experimented in its medical school to avoid duplication, increase independent work, and further integration of staff and materials. At Kenyon College it was estimated that an increased use of capacity by increasing enrollment by 80 would reduce the average deficit over several years from $56,000 to $23,000 to $32,000. A widespread practice of upgrading teachers colleges to liberal arts or even to complex colleges also increases capacity. Though in 1921 only 42 per cent of the 165 accredited degree-granting teachers colleges operated at the baccalaureate level, by 1959 only 38 per cent of 180 institutions primarily prepared teachers.

Many other examples of moves toward fuller use of capacity are available: the Hofstra experiment for saturating the student with a full day's work (four to five days a week); the Oberlin four-quarter system, unhappily turned down by the faculty; experiments at Dartmouth; and serious consideration at Amherst, where students gave many good reasons pro and con for full-year operation.

But the Coordinating Committee on Higher Education in Wisconsin is cautious about the three-semester or four-quarter system. Student unfriendly sentiment, additional costs, underestimation of current use of campuses in the summer quarter, and loss of employment income of students are among the points raised.[6]

FOOTNOTES

[1] See the interesting article by President C. Davidson, "Industrial Techniques for Higher Education," *Journal of Higher Education,* November, 1955, pp. 408–413.

[2] *Changing Times,* November, 1958.

[3] *Bulletin of the Association of American Colleges,* vol. 18, 1932, p. 261; W. S. Gray (ed.), *Needed Readjustments in Higher Education,* V. 1933, *passim* and pp. 6-7.

[4] *Designed for Excellence,* the President's Report, University of Pennsylvania, 1956, p. 12.

[5] *Tradition and Transition, ibid.,* 1955, pp. 11 and 12.

[6] *Designed for Excellence, op. cit.,* p. 28; Hofstra College, *A Proposal for the Establishment of an Experimental College,* 1958; Amherst College, *Report of the Committee on the Future Size of the College and Related Subjects,* May, 1959, pp. 28–29; T. B. Turner, "The Liberal Arts in Medical Education," *Association of*

American Colleges Bulletin, March, 1958, pp. 73–74; E. G. Easton, *Year-around Operation of Colleges,* Engineering Research Bulletin 41, 1958, p. 36; F. Cole, *The Impending Wave of Opportunity,* address, Winston-Salem, Nov. 7, 1957; K. W. Meyer, "The Passing of the Teachers College," *School and Society,* Oct. 24, 1959, p. 416; *Kenyon College, Survey of Operations,* 1958; *Western Reserve University: President's Report, 1955–56;* Joint Staff of the Coordinating Committee for Higher Education, . . . *Feasibility of a Longer School Year for Wisconsin's Public Colleges and Universities,* part IV, October, 1960.

Chapter 46
THE BROADER ISSUES

THE ISSUE OF PRODUCTIVITY

Any economist who raises the issue of productivity or economies is likely to be met with the criticism that he stresses problems of finance more than those of education. He is also likely to be told—and the author has been confronted with this charge by a number of college presidents—that he is undermining the programs for raising funds for IHL. It is held that a businessman who hears from an academic man that colleges operate inefficiently will refuse to open his pocketbook. Yet the only answer can be that in these problems, as in others, the academician must seek truth where he finds it. Many college presidents have complained of inefficiencies in administration and serious wastes—some are quoted in this book. They can also contend that inefficiencies prevail in all large enterprises—business, governments, educational institutions. Their defense is important also. The peculiar form of government of IHL, related in turn to problems of tenure and academic freedom, tends to reduce the productivity of IHL. Without tenure, it might well be somewhat more difficult for this writer to discuss these issues as he sees them. College administrators should not, of course, blame faculty for all inefficiencies—administrators, politicians, bureaucrats share the blame. But it is my considered opinion that the largest responsibility rests on faculty, generally most reluctant to cut down on wastes and modify curricula, teaching hours, and teaching methods.

In my questionnaire to hundreds of economists likely to be knowledgeable in this field, I found a widespread grasp of the economic problems of higher education. They are aware of the costs of excessive courses and small classes; of wasteful use of plant; of the heavy costs involved in teaching poor students; and of the relation of reform to their own economic status. They are also aware of the blocks placed by faculty in the way of needed advances in curriculum—a point treated eloquently by Corson in the book mentioned earlier. Many of these economists want both more lectures and more small groups to teach; they frequently propose large classes for average or below-average students, and possibly for most in the first two years, but they seek greater personal contact for the able students. Many also want greater use of visual aids, though a minority are skeptical. Though most of these few hundred economists seek a more efficient operation, they also are aware of the danger of treating a college like a business. "Do not allow the efficiency expert to take over!" is a frequent warning.

Businessmen writing about higher education demand increased productivity. Dean Rusk (then head of the Rockefeller Foundation, not to be classed as a businessman) also warned the colleges to study costs and keep them down. An expert quoted one businessman as follows: " . . . The private liberal arts college is an inefficient operation, desperately inefficient, and this inefficiency results in low salaries, high tuition cost, shrinking enrollment, and inadequate teaching facilities. . . . "[1]

Some educational leaders do not accept the view that large savings are possible. Thus two of the most knowledgeable and able college presidents tend to discount the presumed inefficiencies. Though President Carter Davidson of Union College envisages many economies—e.g., operating dormitories at break-even point—he concludes that most decisions have to be made on the basis of educational policy, not finance. President Howard Bowen of Grinnell College believes that potential economies are often exaggerated. The difficulty of measuring output beclouds the issue. On the assumption of continued improvement of quality, he estimates that exploration of various proposals for increasing efficiency would yield economies of $100,000 per year to Grinnell, an amount equal to about 10 per cent of faculty salaries, in turn equivalent to the annual rise of pay.[2] (But if we allow for the improvements, the gains would be larger.)

Productivity is related to many, many issues, some of which have already been discussed. For example, a working paper of the Office of Education listed the following:[3]

Objectives:
A. Maximum performance—by student and faculty—in undergraduate colleges, with special attention to:
   1. Independent study and honors programs
   2. Early entrance
   3. Advanced placement
   4. Credit by examination
   5. Comprehensive examinations
   6. Better use of time and space
   7. Audio-visual aids
   8. External examiners
   9. More educative study assignments
   10. Replacements for the credit system

B. Improving the product: How to measure, profile, increase and prolong the impact of undergraduate colleges, including:
   1. Critical review of the instruments used to measure impact
   2. Institutional characteristics
   3. Student characteristics
   4. Impact of colleges: (*a*) on student attitudes and values, (*b*) on intellectual skills: critical thinking, creativity, (*c*) on undergraduate stereotypes, (*d*) on numbers of students entering professional and graduate schools
   5. Faculty sensitivity to impact of the learning experience on the student
C. Improved teaching methods and curricular patterns in undergraduate colleges—study, describe, and evaluate:
   1. Integrative concepts and processes
   2. Common or other experimental curricula
   3. Problem, case, Socratic and other methods appropriate to *A* and *B* above
   4. Emphasis on competencies rather than courses
D. Exploring application of the above techniques and concepts for undergraduate instruction in specific disciplines and subject areas
E. Exploring application of the above to undergraduate programs in liberal arts, land-grant, teachers colleges, public and private universities
F. New approaches to teacher education, especially those that feature:
   1. Clarification of objectives
   2. The Master-teacher principle in pre-professional courses
   3. Extensive clinical experience
   4. Emphasis on quality
G. Moving the mountain: applying the above techniques and concepts to graduate education for:
   1. Better utilization of talent and time (e.g., through early entrance and full-year study)
   2. Study of the undergraduate origins, characteristics, and achievements of graduate students
   3. Evaluation of assistantship, internship, and other programs for improving recruitment and preparation of college teachers; programs to improve and increase opportunities for more graduate training of all teachers
   4. Action outcome: (*a*) establishing better rapport between graduate education and its clientele, (*b*) fitting advanced techniques to requirements of specific subject areas and professions, (*c*) improving the graduate product

An examination of this list reveals many possible genuine economies, that is, saving of resources, and many that with given resources would improve the product. The net result would be a better product with a given input or a given product with reduced input.

Yet even this list does not exhaust the issues. Perhaps above all the college administrator needs to know what the objectives of his college are. One university president is impressed by the fact that heads of colleges are " . . . so occupied raising money that they allow development and public relations officers, ignorant of the true goals, to formulate their own ideas . . . and then proceed to sell what often is the equivalent of a false product." President Odegaard of the University of Washington well stressed the point that treatment of the proliferation of courses requires a clear statement of educational objectives.

Again, the Hofstra experiment is based on the premise that a job needs to be done for the average student, and in a manner to free him from excessive ties to parents and the automobile. At California Institute of Technology, the objective is to turn out first-class research scientists.

LIMITATION OF RESOURCES

Resources are limited, and no college administrator can be allowed to forget this. The prestige colleges are inclined to stress the need of turning out a first-class student. Hence, with limited resources, they tend to restrict enrollment and generally refuse to assume responsibility for contributing toward finding space for the increased student body of the next 10 to 20 years. Where a first-class institution incurs a deficit of (say) $1,500 per additional student on operating expenses and would require approximately $1,000 to $1,500[4] per additional student for housing and academic plant, and would have to spread endowment over a larger number of students and hence the endowment contribution per student would be reduced by (say) one-quarter, the governing board may refrain from accepting more students. That would clearly be its position unless the authorities can raise large additional resources, or introduce substantial economies—e.g., large classes, improved use of plant—or if they are prepared to accept some cut in quality in exchange for large numbers. A product rated at 100 may, for example, be deteriorated to 90 with a rise of enrollment of 25 per cent. Is the contribution of the college less if the quality of product is reduced by 10 per cent and its numbers raised by 25 per cent?

A college confronted with issues of this kind, unable to obtain additional resources from government or philanthropy, might conceivably increase its tuition substantially. But this raises serious problems, discussed elsewhere. A private IHL may then, as suggested above, restrict numbers. A public IHL might also restrict numbers, but there are political difficulties here, unless alternative institutions are provided. On the assumption of in-adequate resources and continued rise of demand, the way out for the public IHL may well be a general deterioration of the product. But prefer-able would be two differentiated products, as suggested above—one for the top 25 per cent and the other for the remaining 75 per cent.[5]

OBJECTIVES

A university's objectives will not be those of the small liberal arts college. The university requires of its faculty not only teaching but also research and public services. Hence some economies—e.g., larger classes, fewer courses—are not likely to reduce costs or increase productivity as much as in the liberal arts college or even in many professional schools. An increase in teaching loads or a reduction may be absorbed by inverse changes in research contributions. But this does not by any means suggest that teaching economies should therefore be abandoned by universities.[6]

Once the objectives of the institution are clarified, the optimum use of resources is facilitated. IHL are not run for profit. As an able business officer remarks, " . . . there must be a real acceptance on the part of business administration of the fact that finance and business are not the end purposes for which the educational organization exists. Instruction, research, and public service are the primary functions of the institutions of higher learning."[7]

ALLOCATION OF RESOURCES

Much is said of the application of business principles to higher education. The layman board of trustees often strives to impose maximum efficiency of operation, for it has the ultimate responsibility. At a meeting of trustees, the board's responsibilities were defined as follows:[8]

> The Board of Trustees should oversee and guide the basic financial policies of the institution, resist pressures for expenditures beyond the resources of the institution, and assure itself that budgetary decisions have been thoroughly considered. In addition, trustees should initiate and review long-range planning in educational programs and physical facilities and see that the planning is carried forward sufficiently to reveal limitations on long-run commitments or to establish the size of new resources that must be acquired within that period.

Faculties are disposed to expand courses, and commitments generally, without adequate consideration of the costs. Trustees seek to restrain faculties in their quest for empire building. In between are the president and his immediate assistants whose function it is to reconcile the faculty's emphasis on educational values and the trustees' emphasis on finance.

In general, the decisions are likely to revolve around how additional resources should be spent. Neither trustees nor faculty, nor administration, tend to examine the allocation of funds in the existing budget. Once $250,000 is allocated to paleontology, or $1 million to intercollegiate athletics, these outlays are sacred, and no cut is likely except in the midst of a great depression. Even budget officers of state governments tend to accept past budgets and only raise questions concerning additional funds requested. In a conference of Western states, the point was made that budgetary procedure is unsatisfactory, because no genuine attempt is made to examine existing budgets to discover the possibilities of cuts on past budgets.[9]

It is not even clear that the allocation of additional funds is generally the optimum. Having apprised themselves of the objectives, the authorities then may have to decide how to spend an additional million dollars of income (say) expected per year in the next few years. Unless a capital outlay is selected, they can be reasonably certain they are assuming a relatively fixed and *recurring* charge. Then they have to decide whether the million dollars is to be put into one project, say general education, or a three-year capital budget to renovate classrooms or build new dormitories, or whether the funds are to be allocated over several enterprises with the objective of allocating dollars where they yield the largest returns. Without a profit measure, the returns unfortunately are not easily measured. Will $1 million yielding $50,000 a year provide a larger product if invested in three first-class lecturers in English or in five good tutors—on the assumption that English instruction needs to be improved—or in a chemical laboratory, an area in which the college is already distinguished? The president or dean is subject to all kinds of pressures for expansion or improvement of quality, and in preparing his budget he necessarily weighs one project against another. He will also have to set up priorities and to estimate costs of alternative paths toward achieving a particular objective.[10]

MEASURES OF QUALITY

How productive an institution is depends in no small part upon the use to which it is put. If a third-rate college through modern public relations attracts first-class students, the losses to the student and the nation are serious. It is important that the college and the student be matched in a manner to maximize the product. The difficulty is partly that it is not easy to measure the product, nor is it easy to estimate the output in relation to input—a much easier problem when the product is estimated on the basis of number of cars produced or profits per car. Indeed, many measures are available:

1. The number of Ph.D.s on the faculty.
2. Number of books in the library.
3. Number of graduates in *Who's Who*. Arthur Traxter, in a paper before the AAAS, showed that over a number of years 1 of 186 college graduates (male) were in *Who's Who,* and 1 in 1,000 of the general population. The number was 1 out of 48 for 7 Ivy League institutions, 1 of 145 for state universities, and 1 of 450 for state teachers' colleges.[11]
4. Number of outstanding books published by graduates of the institu-

tion. Harvard took some pride in discovering that of a list of 250 outstanding books published in a recent year, 31 were by Harvard alumni.

5. Number of Nobel prize winners—note the success of the University of California in 1960.

6. Number of men of science graduated from the college.

7. Number of students winning a Wilson (graduate) fellowship or gaining access to outstanding graduate or professional schools.

An official California report comments on the University of California: "The eminence . . . attested . . . six Nobel Prize laureates on their faculties . . . Membership in the National Academy of Science . . . the University of California was second . . . with 44, Harvard led with 59; . . . Guggenheim . . . awards were given to 184 members of the staff; . . . Harvard was second with 94."[12]

All these are matters of importance; but they do not tell us too much about the quality of the product turned out; and what is more, they leave out of account variations of input, e.g., the quality of students entering the college. Athletic prowess, snob appeal, family ties to an institution are likely to be more decisive than considerations of choice based on matching boy (or girl) and college to yield the largest product, and, related, to quality features, e.g., ability of faculty.[13] This is aside from the wastes estimated at $75 million per year of parisitic institutions that provide virtually no product—the diploma mills.[14]

Hence even when the IHL gives an honest appraisal of its product to the parent or the potential student, the choice of the proper college is a most difficult task. But when the authorities give dishonest descriptions, the losses are greatly increased. President William Fels of Bennington pokes much fun at the descriptions of colleges given in their catalogues and similar documents. A college of 2,700 is described thus: " . . . has held itself to such a size as to maintain those small college conditions which have persisted since the days when faculty and students literally built the college together. . . . "[15]

Perhaps most important is the quality of faculty. Here at least the experts are informed, though the average parent is not. Many attempts have been made to measure the quality of faculties. A recent study, based largely on appraisals of chairmen of departments with faculty and Ph.D. programs of scholarly quality, revealed the following order of the first ten universities in 1957: Harvard, California, Columbia, Yale, Michigan, Chicago, Princeton, Wisconsin, Cornell, and Illinois. In 1925 Chicago, Harvard and Columbia led.[16]

A related problem is the reduced significance of the top IHL, that is, their reduced proportion of enrollment. This is not only true of total enrollment, as indicated in an earlier chapter, but also of graduate instruction, as Bernard Berelson makes clear.[17]

Colleges are less productive than they might be, in part because they do not obtain the best possible faculties nor the best possible students. In the discussion of faculty we have commented on some of the faculty problems. Here we should remind the reader only of the imperfections of the market which result in inferior men and women often obtaining the better positions, of the many weaknesses in the appointment procedures to which Caplow and McGee have directed our attention—for example, the excessive interest in appointments that add prestige rather than in those which promise the largest genuine contribution.[18]

ADMISSIONS AND RELATED PROBLEMS

Since there are only a limited number of places, and especially in the better institutions, it is important that those most likely to profit should obtain entry. The admission procedure is not the best. Uncertainty is excessive; ignorance among students, parents, teachers and counselors prevails. It would be most helpful if the applicants and their advisers knew what the criteria of selection of each institution were—e.g., emphasis on type of school, geographical origins, academic standing of student, preference for alumni, number of acceptances relative to applications, manner of dealing with late bloomers, financial aid available.

One expert, seeing chaos ahead, suggests five alternatives not necessarily mutually exclusive.[19]

1. A return to more rigid curriculum requirements—a means of eliminating those without adequate preparation;

2. An end to early admission and rolling admissions;

3. Widespread adoption of preliminary screening of applications—involving double decision making on many applicants;

4. Mechanistic control of the college admission process—requiring a clearing-house approach;

5. Earlier and earlier communication, with earlier decisions.

Failure to educate the best material is not due wholly to faulty admission procedures. One difficulty is the economic one, about which we said much in our discussion of pricing. One expert estimates our annual loss because of financial disabilities at 100,000 high school graduates with ability to do good work at college; another estimate is 150,000. In a 1955 study of the top 10 per cent of high school graduates in Indiana not going to college, 34.7 per cent of the youths reported finance was a factor in excluding higher education; the estimate of parents was 46.6 per cent, and of school officials 49.5 per cent. We are aware of the fact that noneconomic factors are also relevant.[20]

Perhaps another waste is to be found in the large numbers who go to IHL and who probably should not go. On this issue at one end we have views as expressed by Russell Thackrey, executive director of the Land-

Grant College Association, who would open college doors to all who want to go and meet minimum standards lest some of the late bloomers be lost. In this connection it is of some interest that in independent IHL the numbers graduating are 50 per cent higher in relation to entries than in public IHL. President de Kiewiet of the University of Rochester has expressed this view effectively, with the approval of the head of the State University of Iowa, President Hancher. "The true greatness of American education is held aloft by the two pillars of quality and quantity. What is sometimes referred to disparagingly as 'mass education' has been compatible with the emergence of graduate, professional and technical schools that are brilliant in any company. . . . "

A somewhat different appraisal is made by President Newsom of New York University. Aware that students with an IQ below 110 " . . . have great difficulty with college work that demands a high standard of achievement," President Newsom is concerned that a study of 11 New York universities in 1953 showed that 45 per cent of those with IQs of less than 110 expected to take a four-year course. In a similar vein, an official Pennsylvania study urged the discouragement of students of second-rate ability who wished to go to four-year colleges and would not profit thereby. Below we present some figures which reveal large attrition for less able students entering college. A June, 1957, survey showed that one-third of those interested in higher education had IQs of less than 110.[21]

A statement before the Western Interstate Commission for Higher Education reflected some concern with the widespread access to college:

"There is in this country a distressing overemphasis on college education as a guarantee of economic success, social acceptability, and general human worth. . . . College should be regarded as one kind of education beyond high school, suitable for those whose aptitudes and motivations fit them for that kind of further education."[22]

Higher education for the elite is the theme of a paper by former Chancellor Kimpton of the University of Chicago. His position is that " . . . private education at any rate should train the intellectual elite who have proved they are worthy of this training. The charge should be high. The private university should be flexible, experimental and not responsible to public pressures." Thus he would appeal to snobbism at the highest level.[23]

Another waste results from the large numbers who enter but do not graduate, though one should not assume that no product is derived by an attendance of one, two, or three years. Even when allowance is made for transfers, the attrition is about 50 per cent. Where the losses are of students who cannot profit greatly from higher education, the large number of dropouts is all to the good. Dael Wolfle estimated that 43 per cent of the top (81st-to-100th) percentile rank of the high school graduating class also graduated from college, but only 30, 19, 10, and 4 in the 61st-to-80th, 41st-to-60th, 21st-to-40th, and 1st-to-20th percentiles respectively. Obviously the better students survive in larger numbers. Again, of the top 0.1 per cent in ability, 69 per cent graduated from college; of the top 1 per cent, 59 per cent graduated, and 49, 42, and 34 per cent graduated of the top 5, 10, and 20 per cent, respectively. What is more, the percentages of freshmen graduating from college increased from 37.9 per cent in 1931 to 44.4 per cent in 1950. These figures are subject to some reservations, however, in view of the depressed conditions in 1931.[24]

CONCLUSION

IHL are not as efficient or productive as they might be for many reasons: the nature of the organization and hence excessive blocks by faculty; the difficulties of measuring productivity; the unavailability of facts and analysis; the concentration of attention on *additions* to budgets, not on the *existing* budgets; a failure to keep objectives in mind; institutional obstacles to the choice of the best students and faculties; inadequate contributions of trustees; misleading publicity of IHL.

FOOTNOTES

[1] "Current Issues in Higher Education," *Proceedings of the Eighth Annual National Conference on Higher Education,* March, 1953, p. 92; cf. E. Hodnett, *Industry-College Relations,* 1955, chap. 20.

[2] H. R. Bowen, "Is the Self-contained College Economically Feasible?" *Liberal Education,* March, 1960, p. 65; C. Davidson, "Painless Economies," *34th Annual Meeting of Eastern Association of College and University Business Officers,* December, 1953, pp. 67–77.

[3] HEW, *Design for Cooperative Action: A Branch Working Paper,* 1959; P. C. Reinert, "What Charges Must Be Made . . . : Current Issues in Education," *Proceedings of the Eighth Annual National Conference on Higher Education,* 1953, p. 17.

[4] On the basis of business accounting practices.

[5] Cf. B. R. Morris, "Faculty Salaries, Class Size and Sound Education," *AAUP Bulletin,* June, 1959, pp. 195–202.

[6] Cf. R. H. Simonds, "To Increase Man-Hour Output in Higher Education," *The Educational Record,* October, 1958, pp. 332–39.

[7] C. Scheps, "The Business Officer's Place in the Hierarchy of Administration," *College and University Business,* June, 1960, p. 31.

[8] *A Statement by a Select Group of College and University Trustees on the Responsibilities of Trustees for Educational Objectives and Curriculum,* 1960, p. 3 (mimeographed); cf. P. H. Davis, *Putting Trustees and Volunteers to Work,* February, 1960 (mimeographed).

[9] *Proceedings of the Legislative Workshop on Financing Higher Education,* Apr. 27–29, 1958. Cosponsored by the Western Governors' Conference, The Western

Regional Conference of the Council of State Governments, and the Western Interstate Commission for Higher Education, p. 27.

[10] On these issues see the able presentation of my student, at that time a Junior at Harvard College, K. Deitch, "Some Observations on the Allocation of Resources in Higher Education," in S. E. Harris (ed.), *Higher Education in the United States: The Economic Problems*, 1960, pp. 192–198.

[11] Paper for *Annual Meeting of American Association for Advancement of Science*, December, 1957, table 2. (Mimeographed.)

[12] *A Study of the Need for Additional Centers of Public Higher Education in California*, 1957, p. 24; cf. *The Educational Future of Columbia University*, 1957, pp. 13–14.

[13] See essays by Hughes, Caplow, and Riesman in S. E. Harris (ed.), *Higher Education in the United States: The Economic Problems*, 1960; and R. Brandes, "A College Teacher Looks to the Future," *Journal of Higher Education*, April, 1957, p. 190.

[14] R. H. Reed, "American Degree Mills," *The Educational Record*, October, 1959, pp. 294–300; and F. Hechinger, "Diploma Mills," *The New York Times*, Apr. 17, 1960.

[15] W. C. Fels, "The College Describes Itself," *College Board Review*, Spring, 1959, pp. 30–32.

[16] H. Keniston, *Graduate Study and Research in the Arts and Sciences at The University of Pennsylvania*, 1959, p. 119.

[17] *Graduate Education in the United States*, 1960, pp. 96–109.

[18] Caplow and McGee, *The Academic Marketplace*, 1958; also John W. Gardner, National Goals in Education in Goals for Americans, 1960; esp. pp. 90–91.

[19] See especially G. H. Hanford, "Free Enterprise in College Admissions," *College Board Review*, Winter, 1959, pp. 8–11; F. D. Ashburn, "Three-Wave Selection of Admission," *ibid.*, Spring, 1957, pp. 14–15; "Which Ones Would You Admit to College?" *ibid.*, Winter, 1957, pp. 11–13; J. M. Duggan, "Accepted Class Descriptions Multiply," *ibid.*, Spring, 1958, pp. 9–13.

[20] C. C. Cole, "Higher Education: Strengthening Quality in the Satellite Age," *Current Issues in Higher Education*, 1958, p. 89; "A Special Report: American Higher Education, 1958," *The Johns Hopkins Magazine*, April, 1958, pp. 11–12; Wright and Jung, "Why Capable High School Students Do Not Continue Their Schooling," *Bulletin of the School of Education, Indiana University*, January, 1959, p. 58.

[21] *Higher Education and the Future of Youth in Greater Philadelphia: A Report . . . by the Committee on Higher Education Opportunities in Philadelphia*, December, 1957, pp. 16–17; *The New York University Self-study: Final Report*, 1956, p. 18; V. M. Hancher, *The Challenge We Face*, paper for American Council on Education, 1958, p. 5 (mimeographed); R. I. Thackrey, "Some Responsibilities of the State University," *The Educational Record*, July, 1960, pp. 199–200; HEW, *Retention and Withdrawal of College Students*, 1957, p. 17.

[22] *Issues in State Supported Higher Education*, Western Interstate Commission for Higher Education, Western Governors' Conference, Colorado Springs, Colo., February, 1958, p. 2.

[23] *The Public and Private University*, an address by L. A. Kimpton, Nov. 11, 1959, pp. 5–6.

[24] W. M. Wise, *They Come for the Best of Reasons: College Students Today*, 1958, pp. 14–17; D. Wolfle, *America's Resources of Specialized Talent*, 1954, pp. 149–150; HEW, *Retention and Withdrawal of College Students*, 1958, pp. 16, 18.

Chapter 47

DETAILS ON ECONOMIES

New colleges are formed without adequate consideration of the need of resources and the job to be done. Recently I made a study of the vocational professional schools in the standard metropolitan districts of the United States. I found that there were large numbers of professional and graduate schools in the metropolitan centers, but not as a rule in other parts of the states. In Massachusetts, for example, Greater Boston, which has approximately one-half of the state's population, contained 6 of the 7 law schools of the state, all 3 medical schools, both dental schools, and 9 of the 13 graduate schools. Massachusetts is monocentric and Pennsylvania is duo-centric. Pittsburgh and Philadelphia, with more than half of the state's population, include 5 of its 6 law schools, its 7 medical schools (six in Philadelphia), 3 dental schools, and 7 of the 10 graduate schools. In a state like Texas, where there is not quite that concentration of population, the schools tend to be distributed differently. From low-income states there are large migrations to graduate professional schools elsewhere. This kind of distribution greatly increases the cost of graduate education for a substantial part of the population.[1]

The poorer states are heavily endowed with law schools, but have relatively few graduate schools. There seems to be considerable excess capacity in the law schools in low-income states. These schools often operate at 50 to 60 per cent of their capacity, whereas in the richer states the law schools may be 80 to 85 per cent full. It would be very helpful to have a study of the optimum location of these professional and graduate schools. How can we eliminate excess capacity without increasing greatly the costs of travel and living away from home?

Where unit costs are high and the required talent scarce, the case for averting duplication is especially strong. This consideration weighs more heavily than the additional costs of travel for students. In the Ph.D. program, for example, the unit costs are likely to be very high, and where there are not heavy concentrations of population, it would be a mistake to duplicate a Ph.D. program. Thus Tucson, Arizona (University of Arizona), has a Ph.D. program. But with Arizona's population and location, it would be unwise to introduce another Ph.D. program in Phoenix. Yet much pressure is exerted to achieve this objective. Similarly, Ph.D. programs in the four-year state colleges in California would bring an unjustifiable increase in costs and seriously dilute available talent.

In medicine, experts estimate that a population in the state of 2 million is required to support a medical school. Yet there are several states with smaller populations supporting medical schools.

Is the individualistic development and multiplicity of institutions of higher education justified? A 1938 study by the American Council on Education discussed this.

Sectional bargaining (politics, etc.) and other influences within the state account in part for the malallocation of universities, the distribution of normal schools, teachers colleges, etc. "These processes and influences have resulted in what under present conditions is an amazingly unintelligent and wasteful distribution of higher educational resources."[2] Where the state pays a large part of the bill, every population center is disposed to seek a state college or a junior college, irrespective of need. Perhaps the solution lies in requiring a large contribution by the local government.

Colleges tend to cluster, and clusters often mean duplication of facilities and courses and misallocation of resources.

In some states there are too many different publicly supported institutions. "Such multiplication of publicly supported institutions within single states inevitably creates the demand of informed members of the general public and politicians and statesmen who seek public favor through economy and tax reduction campaigns that these conditions be justified or changed." In Wisconsin a Coordinating Committee requires its approval for the introduction of new graduate or professional schools.[3]

Often local social and business interests win out over educational intelligence. "No national government authority has existed and no state government agency has been able or willing to control the demands of local political and economic forces in such a way to secure the development of public and private higher education so articulated as to serve public needs efficiently and economically."[4]

It seems logical to examine the social need for trained men and women in the professions and to relate educational opportunities to present and probable future demands for these services.[5]

"In the judgment of a very large number of the officers of scholarly and professional organizations and of administrative and faculty members of higher education institutions from whom comments were received, the major obstacle to greater cooperation is narrow institutionalism." Devotion and loyalty to a single school often spring from some cause other than excellence in the performance of educational functions. Another major obstacle is ignorance—ignorance on the part of controlling boards, administrative officers, faculties, educational organizations, the constituency of these institutions and the general public.[6]

Most states have placed a "coordinating board" over the separate governing boards of the several state institutions within a state. There are four distinct types of boards:

1. A single board which controls the entire state educational system
2. A single board which controls all public IHL in the state
3. A board which has general control of state teacher-training institutions and general supervision of the public school system
4. A board which supervises only teacher-training institutions

It is generally claimed that centralizing governing control has resulted in greater economy and efficiency.

* * *

In a discussion sponsored by General Electric, Chancellor Branscomb of Vanderbilt University predicted that the four-year liberal arts college would have to reduce its program to fewer years. Increased costs, the pressure of military service, the large percentage of students going into graduate instruction, and higher motivation at professional schools led Chancellor Branscomb to conclude that " . . . by keeping our young people four years in general studies, under delightful conditions, we are unnecessarily extending the educational process, adding to the cost, and continuing the immaturity which is such an obvious characteristic of many undergraduate students."[7] In March, 1960, President Kirk of Columbia also trenchantly supported a three-year college career.

Another approach to increased efficiency in the use of resources is suggested by Coombs of the Fund for the Advancement of Education. He suggests the elimination of " . . . wasteful gaps and duplications, particularly as he (the student) moves from one institutional stage to the next. . . . " Coombs commends the study, *General Education in School and College,* for suggesting that we integrate the work of the school and college in the area of general education and " . . . plan the last two years of secondary school and the first two years of college as a continuous process. . . ." Coombs is especially disturbed by the extent of duplication of courses taken in good schools which were repeated in college. The study also found important gaps in training and in intellectual experiences. At Reed College the Fund attempted to improve the articulation between schools and colleges, particularly for the gifted students. Any attempts to deal with gifted students, either through earlier college entry or skipping one year at college, eliminates a certain amount of waste. Advanced standing raises serious problems but is receiving a considerable amount of attention.[8]

One of the greatest wastes in higher education is the failure to train teachers well and to make the best use of them after they are trained. In general, it can be said that the leading graduate schools of arts and science make no attempt to train teachers. The colleges that hire the graduate students plead time and again that the Ph.D. training should include teacher training, but the graduate schools of the large universities are not inclined to take these demands seriously. One Ford Foundation study carried out at Yale University showed the need for different kinds of programs for different types of graduate students, the research man as against the teacher, or the combination research man and teacher. But graduate schools continue to insist on the same curriculum for all students.

Goucher College has instituted a teacher-orientation program in which incoming teachers take part in an internship program which includes seminar meetings devoted to the orientation of the intern to the total program of the college, followed by a departmental project in which the intern is a resident. All incoming members of the faculty participate in this program.[9]

What is perhaps even more disturbing is the failure of the college to allocate the teacher's time according to his abilities. Teachers and members of faculties are not all equally able as undergraduate teachers, graduate teachers, administrators, or researchers. The college should allocate assignments more on the basis of abilities. A member of the faculty who is exceptional in research should have a relatively small teaching load, and an outstanding lecturer of average scholarly ability should devote most of his time to lecturing. But the average college administrator sets, say, a teaching load of nine hours, and it is up to the teacher whether he does research or not. Increasingly colleges do allow time off for research, but as a general rule the tendency to give the teacher the task he does best is still in a primitive stage. A teacher in an outstanding university might, for example, do no research over a period of twenty years, yet he will have the same teaching load as another who devotes two-thirds of his time to research.

In this connection a language program at Cornell should be noted.[10] It cuts down the amount of time required of the teacher of a foreign language and it especially stresses speaking during early stages of instruction and reading more heavily later on. There was a " . . . need to economize and the desire to experiment with the reduction of time spent with native speakers to three sessions per week. . . . The program now operates on the theory that a Ph.D. *is not a necessary prerequisite* to successful elementary language teaching, but that any native of lively personality can do the job if he is adequately trained and supervised." After surveying the results of the five-year experiment, Cornell concluded that this system produced better readers and speakers than former methods.

FOOTNOTES

[1] On the issues of numbers of institutions and the wisdom of introducing graduate programs in sparsely populated areas, see I. D. Weeks, "Can We Afford Higher Education?" *College and University Business,* August, 1954, pp. 46–47.

[2] American Council on Education, *Cooperation and Coordination in Higher Education,* American Council on Education Studies Series I, II, no. 5, 1938, p. 5.

[3] *Ibid.,* p. 20; also see Coordinating Committees for Higher Education, Wisconsin, *Cooperative Long Range Planning for Education Beyond the High School,* March, 1959.

[4] American Council on Education, *op. cit.,* p. 20.

[5] *Ibid.*

[6] *Ibid.,* p. 37.

[7] General Electric, *Higher Education: A 20-Year Look Ahead,* 1957, esp. p. 25.

[8] *Current Issues in Higher Education,* 1953, pp. 54–60; P. H. Coombs, "Advancing Education—from School to College," *Proceedings of the Eighth National Conference on Higher Education,* 1953; also see University of Kansas, "A Program for Gifted Freshmen and Sophomores," *Case Book: Education beyond the High School,* vol. 1, case no. 34, June, 1958; and for a further description of the admission to colleges of advanced studies, see "Admission to College with Advanced Standing," *ibid.,* case no. 21, April, 1958, and also *They Went to College Early,* Fund for the Advancement of Education Evaluation Report 2.

[9] See "College Teacher Orientation Program, Goucher College," *Case Book: Education beyond the High School,* June, 1958.

[10] "The Language Program, Cornell University," *Case Book: Education beyond the High School,* June, 1958.

Chapter 48

THE OPTIMUM SIZE OF THE INSTITUTION*

It is generally known that costs per unit vary with size. In general the larger the size, the smaller the unit cost; but this is likely to be true only up to a certain level.

A 1957 study of California higher education raises some relevant problems.

With no attempt at this time to specify optimum sizes for particular departments, colleges or schools, it may safely be assumed that a minimum of 2,000 students is sufficient to operate an undergraduate program of university calibre, serving primarily to prepare students for graduate work and professional training.

In an earlier study, the experts opposed a college enrolling more than 5,000. Enlargements of administration, plant, etc., are likely to be so costly that one may as well start a new unit. By 1960, the master plan in California supported optimum enrollments in state colleges of 8,000 to 10,000 and a maximum of 12,000 to 20,000.[1]

It may further be assumed that enrollment of 10,000 full-time students is sufficient for a campus with full-scale university functions, including those of unlimited graduate research in education toward professions (characteristic function which the university emphasizes). On the other hand, it can be assumed that a full-time enrollment on a single existing campus of the University of California that substantially exceeds 25,000 students would tax campus facilities to a point of requiring expansion of a magnitude equal to that of establishing a new campus.

In support of this assumption, a study committee composed of faculty members of various campuses of the university pointed out:

. . . that there are important qualifications as to the number of courses that may be dropped from a university curriculum; that there are limits to the expansion of class sizes and room utilization; that growth in size can result in

* Includes breakdown of unit costs.

growth in complexity to the extent that the proper functioning of a campus is hampered; that in time physical limitations become crucial; and that "when a campus grows beyond a certain point, sheer size produces a number of psychological problems," which it is suggested affect the "process of educational and social growth." Further regarding this assumption, it is observable that the existing major campuses of the University are already so built up that expansion to provide for enrollment of more than half again the present number of students will almost surely require substantially more ground for additional buildings and necessary facilities.

In discussing this problem with the head of one of the largest state university systems, I was told that one factor limiting the size of a campus is the time required to move from one class to another. Once this time reaches ten minutes, it is necessary either to build vertically—and there are difficulties here, as the famous case of the Pittsburgh cathedral of learning showed—or else a new site must be found, or special transportation must be provided—as at Duke University.

In his excellent study of building needs at the University of Minnesota, William Middlebrook showed that spacing of buildings in a manner that might require fifteen minutes for movement from one class to another would raise serious problems. The alternatives would be a loss of five minutes per hour (one-tenth of time in classrooms), the number of class periods reduced by one each day, or the teaching day lengthened.[2]

In the discussion of the Michigan situation, Russell presented various arguments for establishing branches rather than new institutions. Obviously there are important noneconomic questions here, and the issues cannot be decided purely on grounds of minimizing costs. A particular city, for example, may wish to have the independence that goes with a separate university. On the other hand, as was indicated by the conversion of the Santa Barbara College into a branch of the University of California, the prestige of the main center of the university may make a great difference in the attractiveness of the institution.

Many institutions want to remain small. They feel that there are important educational advantages involved. An institution, for example, that stabilizes at 400 or 500 will undoubtedly have large unit costs. If this expensive type of education is to be justified, it must be on educational grounds, and the costs should be recognized.

In this connection I quote from the *Haverford College Bulletin* a statement of (then) President Gilbert White of Haverford:[3]

In the College program of 1947 it was proposed that the undergraduate enrollment should be reduced to 400. This number was reached by a series of approximations, and while it was not regarded as having particular virtue in itself it seemed to offer the best solution to the problem of maintaining essential qualitative standards without undue financial sacrifice. Since then we have reduced the enrollment each year so that during the current year it will average 450. It has seemed wise to level off at this size.

The decision to hold enrollment at 450 now is subject to two questions. First, why should we not reduce this further to 400? Second, is it desirable to remain so small in the face of an impending increase in number of possible applicants to colleges and universities? Some answers may be suggested without attempting a comprehensive analysis of the question of size of other colleges.

To the first question the answer seems relatively simple.

In recent years, as we approach 450, we have concluded in our budgeting that to reduce tuition income below that figure would require cutting expenditures which appear to be essential for serving student needs. As much as we might like to have the smaller college, it would be more expensive than present endowment resources would permit. However, we need not give up the hope for further slow reduction below 450.

The answer to the second question is more complex. . . .

In the light of that prospect [higher enrollment in the nation], we may reexamine the reasoning behind our decisions to avoid further expansion. The primary consideration was a size which would permit the development of a genuine community of faculty and students. Experience with enrollments ranging from 100 to 600 had convinced the Haverford faculty that somewhere between 400 and 500 the College passed the point at which every member of the student body might hope to know the others, and at which faculty members might expect to know all the students by sight. At present all members of each class do know each other. It does not follow that all persons in the College who might expect such acquaintance in fact achieve it, but so long as the possibility and expectancy exist, many are likely to strive for it, and some may arrive at it. A larger enrollment makes such a relationship impossible.

From it may come, with proper cultivation, a number of benefits in the educational process. Students may develop personal acquaintance with a substantial proportion of the faculty. Students are obliged to live, outside as well as within the classroom, with others having quite different vocational interests, skills and family backgrounds: the group is too small to permit large and lasting cliques of students having special interests. Heavy responsibility for management of student government and the honor system can be placed upon a student body in which each member has a clear identity for the others. There can be a regular period of common worship and meditation. Intellectual discussion of problems of broad interests, such as those posed in Collection, as well as in classes, can be widely shared. In the whole atmosphere of the College there can be, given the right people, a joining of respect for each individual's development with a sense of common aims and responsibility.

Secondary considerations in arriving at this decision are related to finances, admissions and diversity in college life. To enlarge enrollment beyond 400 or 450 would require in the long run an expansion in the dining hall, the Meeting House, the library and the laboratories. Our present program for dormitories and field house is necessary for the lower enrollment and would have to be expanded if additional students were to live on the campus. So also would scholarship funds. It is believed that a reduction in proportion of residential and scholarship students would be undesirable. Any funds which might be available for expanded facilities would be better used for faculty salaries, scholarships and books.

Moreover, a larger enrollment would impose difficulties in selecting a competent and well-balanced entering class. The process would become less personal and selectivity would be reduced. On the other hand, to admit a much smaller class would seem to make for an undesirable reduction in the diversity of outlook and background of the students that would influence both class discussion and extra-curricular life. . . .

Placing all of these considerations in the balance, we have felt that the college of 400 to 450 comes closest to providing the environment which we feel is conducive to sound education. But can this position be sustained in the face of the tidal wave of students who are moving toward the colleges? Some colleges feel they have a public responsibility to expand their facilities as best they can. Our position is that we may be of greatest service in the long run by not so expanding. To expand would clearly, but to an undetermined degree, detract from the quality of our present work. It seems important to bend our efforts to improving rather than debasing those standards in a period when the pressures of expansion will be heavily in the other direction.

The argument here is largely noneconomic, though some economic considerations are introduced. But nothing is said about the relative unit costs of an enrollment of 400 as against, say, 700 or 800.

Another interesting case is that of Marlboro College in Vermont. This is a college with about 40 students. I had a letter from the dean in which he said that when enrollment once increased to 100, they hoped to balance their budget. Here the students contribute to the running of the college, and there are certain distinct educational advantages in such a small enterprise. Everyone knows everyone else by first name, even the faculty of eight full-time teachers and a few more part-time instructors. But, as the *Harvard Crimson*[4] points out,

Some rather serious gaps are present in the catalog of courses. Almost nothing is offered in the way of philosophy, chemistry, classics, political science, economics and Asian and Russian history and literature. There are, as Marlboro administrators admit, serious omissions for a college which offers a Bachelor of Arts Degree.

There are clearly some educational disadvantages to colleges which are too small. A small college may have just one member in each department, and this member may have to give eight or ten different courses over the years. Obviously a high level of instruction cannot be given, and a student may be denied essential courses. In one small college and a very good one—Bard College—many courses are given and with the notice that " . . . this course will be given at least once in every four years."

In determining the size of a college, administrators are naturally interested in the relationship between increased enrollments and the rise of costs. They want to know how much unit costs will rise if, for example, the college enrollment expands from 600 to 800, or to 1,000. They also should estimate how much revenues will rise.

In this connection, President Wells warns that the introduction of new institutions, necessarily small, is economically inefficient. He would, therefore, be inclined to expand existing institutions.[5]

They [new institutions] would offer none of the opportunities for the economies of scale that must be sought in operating budgets. On the capital side they would be enormously costly. They would tend to accelerate the rise in the college-attendance ratio and to lower average national admissions standards at precisely the time when moderate adjustments in the opposite direction are indicated, and they would offer a smaller promise of gains in faculty productivity than exists in the established institutions.

President Wells also warns against the development of the small, uneconomic unit as paralleled in the history of the secondary schools.

Where additional students mean more dormitories, the added costs may be a serious barrier and particularly where standards are high. For example, Yale University announced the need of $15 million to house 500 students in their college program. At forty years life and a charge of 4 per cent on capital, the *real* costs are close to $2,000 per student per year for housing, plus the incidental educational advantages attached to the house or college unit.

Concerned over the failure to attract more good undergraduates, the President of Johns Hopkins writes:[6]

Indeed I am convinced that we could admit from 75 to 100 more new students each year without appreciably adding to cost, if qualified applicants entered the right program. Such an increase would strengthen the academic areas involved and provide a substantial additional tuition income which could be used to improve faculty salaries on the Homewood campus.

Along the same lines is the Oberlin proposal for a four-quarter system with students away one quarter on academic pursuits and with a vacation of one quarter, the result being a doubling in the numbers that could be educated with the present plant. This program is based on the theory that unit costs could be greatly reduced by doubling the number of students without a corresponding increase of faculty or plant.

Again, the president of Case Institute told me that a rise of enrollment from 1,200 to 1,500 would be an economical addition, i.e., would reduce unit costs.

In an able paper, Dean Vernon Alden of the Harvard Business School makes some interesting comments on the appropriate size of a college.

Is size really the basic question; isn't the ability of an institution to carry out its objectives actually determined by the organizational structure of its faculty? . . . Would you rather have your son sit in a classroom 100 feet away from a world-renowned professor, or ten feet away from a mediocre one? . . . With a student-centered curriculum, a well-stocked library and well-equipped laboratories, are small size classes run on a conventional academic calendar essential?

Dean Alden also suggests that colleges that limit their enrollment to improve their quality will encounter special difficulties in raising necessary funds. Success in raising funds is related to expansion.[7]

An interesting case that throws light on size is given by the founding of a new Presbyterian college in St. Petersburg, Florida,[7a] an episode discussed elsewhere. It was estimated that 600 students would require a plant of $6.2 million; for 1,200 students a plant only 50 per cent larger would be required. Hence the substantial saving in unit capital costs of a larger enrollment. There obviously would be substantial economies of plant. But the total cost, including salaries, would be about $600,000 for 600 students, or $1,000 per student, and for 1,200 students $1,100,000, or about $900 per student.

In a study of the 1930s Russell and Reeves showed that there was a high correlation between the size of the institution and various elements of excellence.[8] Twenty-one IHL with enrollments in excess of 750 had a correlation with four criteria of excellence twice as high as for forty-four IHL in the entire sample. The excellence undoubtedly resulted in part from higher expenditures per student.

In this same study it was shown that the dollars of expenditure per student range from $205 for institutions with enrollments of over 1,050 to $1,296 for those with enrollments of 16 to 20, with a steady rise in between. It is also suggested that excellence varies with the weighted income per student from student fees. The higher the tuition, apparently the better the faculty.

It is not easy to decide upon the optimum size of a college or university. Much depends upon the number of units within the university. Thus at Columbia the point is made that, though the university is large, the individual colleges are not. A study of architectural schools suggests that enrollment in excess of 200 brings no significant advantage. On economic grounds, a minimum size is necessary if a college is to be operated efficiently. A college with less than 1,000 is likely to be a high-cost operation. At California the minimum is set much higher. A generation ago Reeves estimated that a college of 300 would cost 50 per cent more per student than a college with 850 students. Though much is said for the value of 50 small colleges with enrollments averaging 300, it is also said that a rise of 100 or less would put many in the black. Twenty of these IHL with an average enrollment of 302 were in the red, and an equal number with 371 average were in the black.

Appropriate size depends not only on economic but also on educational considerations. An interesting approach is that of Hamilton College:

A survey of the business management of the College was made by professional consultants who estimated an optimal enrollment in terms of plant and budgetary considerations. A faculty committee on student activities was asked to discuss the relation of enrollment to student-student and student-faculty acquaintance and friendship, the sense of corporate unity, and the extra-curricular life of the student. The Committee on Studies of the faculty undertook the most difficult task of studying the general question in relation to the central academic task of the college.

On the basis of these reports a decision was made to increase enrollment to 750. A further elaboration of the issue involved is suggested by a large excerpt from a Haverford College report quoted earlier in this chapter. At Bowdoin the president expresses strong opposition to rising enrollment with which " . . . many of the internal advantages of a small college would be lost." Moreover, rising enrollment would require additional endowment and plant if the product is not to be deteriorated.

A case for the large IHL has been made in California. President John Millett points out that growth is necessary in order to obtain adequate resources. President Asa Knowles of Northeastern concludes that small IHL will find increasing obstacles in competing with larger IHL for faculty and programs, and enrollment might increase much more than costs. In part the case for rising enrollment per IHL is based on the extent of excess capacity. In 1956, in Missouri, public colleges enrolled almost 95 per cent of their stated capacity, the universities over 80 per cent, and private liberal arts colleges over 78 per cent. Availability of resources largely determines the size of an institution. Thus a study in the mid-fifties of 515 IHL with liberal arts courses revealed a projected rise of enrollment by 1970 of 45 per cent with current resources and expected increases; and on the basis of expansion of resources commensurate with the rise of enrollment, they would expand their enrollment by 72 per cent.

At New York University, where enrollments are at a record level, there is no disposition to set a ceiling.[9]

Perhaps the best plan for New York University is an elastic one that sets up standards in terms not only of the product of Metropolitan high schools, but also of the ability of the University financially to support its programs. There is a diminishing return to great size. At one point the larger student body will call for new physical facilities and perhaps for a quality of staff that is rare and expensive. . . . Here it is not necessary to freeze enrollment at either a high or a low point with respect to any division within New York

University, but rather to decide limits in terms of the facilities and staff that may be secured. . . .

BREAKDOWN OF UNIT COSTS BY TYPES OF INSTITUTIONS AND SIZE

Table 48-1 suggests some interesting aspects of the relationship between size and cost.

In general costs are higher in public than in private institutions.

Once we eliminate research, extension, and public services, unit costs drop substantially, roughly by 20 per cent.

Unit costs are particularly high in "other professional schools." It need hardly be said that costs vary by schools in this category; for example, unit costs are especially high in medicine. The costs in public "other professional schools" are roughly about three times as large as in the private schools. Undoubtedly the large enrollments in private urban universities with large professional schools is part of the explanation.

Technological schools also have high unit costs. This is explained by the expensive laboratories and the large number of classes which students are required to attend.

Low-cost operations are especially prevalent in theological schools and in junior colleges. In the former this undoubtedly is due to the low pay of faculty and persists despite the low enrollment per institution, which should bring high unit costs. In the junior colleges an explanation is low pay and less costly forms of instruction, as suggested by the high student/faculty ratio.

The average cost per student in the liberal arts college is roughly two-thirds of that in the universities. Why should this be so? The answer seems to be that the university is made up of an arts and science college, a graduate school of arts and science, which is an expensive operation, and professional schools. Indeed the average size of a university is much larger than that of a liberal arts college, and undoubtedly many liberal arts colleges are too small to be efficient. But the major factor seems to be the structure of the university and its higher level of pay.

Some light is shed by the 60-college study on the relation between size and cost. It is clear that the relative costs of general administration and of outlays for public services and information fall with rise of enrollment. But as the size of the institution rises, there is some offset in the increase of the percentage of costs and in the relative rise of outlays for student services. The trend of outlays on instruction, departmental research and specialized educational activities is not clear. Surprisingly, the highest relative cost for operation and maintenance of physical plant is to be found in the largest institutions. This may well be explained by the greater plant available in these institutions.

TABLE 48-1

Average Enrollment, 1955–56; Average Educational and General Expenditures, 1953–54 per Resident College Student Enrolled in November, 1953, by Control and Type of Institution; and Student/Faculty Ratio, 1955–56

Type of institution	Average enrollment, 1955–56			All educational and general expenditures per resident student			Educational and general expenditures except research and extension and public services, per student			Student/faculty ratio, 1955–56
	All institutions	Publicly controlled institutions	Privately controlled institutions	All institutions	Publicly controlled institutions	Privately controlled institutions	All institutions	Publicly controlled institutions	Privately controlled institutions	
All institutions, average............	1,432	2,247	989	$1,032	$1,106	$948	$811	$841	$777	
Universities........................	8,544	8,799	8,199	1,334	1,494	1,130	951	1,023	860	16.6
Liberal arts colleges..............	973	2,597	768	699	799	661	663	695	651	17.0
Teachers colleges.................	1,202	1,318	390	725	727	691	712	713	676	19.2
Technological schools.............	1,963	1,508	2,417	1,692	1,394	1,988	1,043	1,057	1,029	14.3
Theological schools...............	259	.....	259	698	.....	698	681	.....	681	16.4
Other professional schools........	483	870	448	1,538	3,194	1,095	1,407	2,741	1,032	11.6
Junior colleges*..................	668	967	258	469	420	678	457	408	669	25.5

* Includes community colleges, normal schools, technical institutes, and other institutions of higher education restricted to less than four years of work on the undergraduate or terminal-occupational level.

Source: HEW, Office of Education, Statistics of Higher Education: Receipts, Expenditures and Property, 1953–54, chap. 4, sec. 2, of Biennial Survey of Education in the United States, 1952–54, p. 61; HEW, Statistics of Higher Education, 1955–56, pp. 6–7.

TABLE 48-2
Educational and General Expenditures*

Size of enrollment	General administration	Student services	Public services and information	Instruction, departmental research, and specialized educational activities	Operation and maintenance of physical plant
200–600	10.5	8.8	5.4	48.4	15.6
601–1,000	9.7	8.6	6.1	51.2	16.5
1,001–1,400	7.9	9.8	6.3	49.6	14.7
1,401 and more	6.0	10.0	4.1	52.1	18.8

* All figures are median percentage of total educational and general expenditures.
Source: The National Federation of College and University Business Officers Associations, *A Study of Income and Expenditures in 60 Colleges: A Summary Report, 1953–1954,* pp. 38–39

FOOTNOTES

[1] California State Department of Education, *The Study of the Need for Additional Centers of Public Higher Education in California,* 1957, pp. 83–84; *ibid., A Report of a Survey of the Needs of California in Higher Education,* 1948, p. 19; and *ibid., A Master Plan for Higher Education in California, 1960–1975,* p. 13.

[2] *Ibid.,* W. T. Middlebrook, *How to Estimate the Building Needs of a College or University,* 1958, p. 9.

[3] *Haverford College Bulletin,* vol. 53, no. 2, October, 1954, pp. 6–10.

[4] *Harvard Crimson,* Oct. 10, 1957.

[5] Reference lost—unable to check.

[6] *Johns Hopkins University, Report of the President,* 1957, pp. 7–8.

[7] See V. R. Alden, "College Administration in a Rapidly Changing Economy," *Association of American Colleges Bulletin,* December, 1957, pp. 9–11.

[7a] *The New York Times,* Sept. 21, 1958.

[8] *The Evaluation of Higher Institutions,* part VII, *Finance,* 1935, pp. 13 and 15.

[9] *Ibid.,* pp. 26–28 and 63, 64; A. T. Hill, *The Small College Meets the Challenge,* 1959; McEwen and Synakowski, "Planning for College Enrollment for Academic Efficiency," *Journal of Higher Education,* June, 1954, p. 304; *The New York University Self-study: Final Report,* 1956, appendix B, pp. 23–24; *Future Size of Small Liberal Arts College: President's Report, Bowdoin College,* 1953–54, p. 24; T. C. Bannister (ed.), *The Architect at Mid-Century,* I, 1954, p. 317; G. F. Zook, "Standards of Accrediting Agencies," in W. S. Gray (ed.), *Needed Readjustments in Higher Education,* V; A. S. Knowles, "Emerging Features of Higher Education," *The Educational Record,* October, 1957, pp. 329–335; A. O. Pfinister, "Missouri Undertakes a State Wide Study," *ibid.,* pp. 341–343; D. A. Lockmiller, "Enrollment Trends and the Independent and Church-related Colleges of Tennessee," *ibid.,* pp. 343–351; A. T. Hill, "What Is a Non-accredited College?" *ibid.,* p. 350; *A Report of a Survey of the Needs of California in Higher Education,* 1948, pp. 19–20; *Business Week,* June 8, 1957, on Swarthmore College; J. A. Perkins, "Government Support of Public Universities and Colleges," *The Annals, Higher Education Under Stress,* September, 1955, pp. 109–110; *The Educational Future of Columbia University,* 1957, p. 17.

Chapter 49

PLANNING

Never have colleges and universities spent so much time and resources on planning as in the 1950s. Yet one observer who visited 42 institutions of higher learning, 10 of which had enrollments of less than 5,000, found that only half of them had plans. Those with plans considered the possibility of making more efficient use of facilities through study of class schedules, courses offered, student/faculty ratio, teaching loads, and curricular problems generally. In a few institutions there were cost studies under way to determine the maximum number of students that could be accommodated without increasing the present budget.[1]

In an able article, T. R. McConnell also deals with the problem of planning and the waste involved in not planning.[2] He is troubled by the large attrition between entry and graduation, and he wants to know what can be done to cut it down. He suggests higher admissions requirements for some institutions, particularly state universities. Clearly, the failure of more than half of the students entering college to graduate represents a serious loss of resources both for the institutions and the students. (Losses are somewhat less when allowance is made for the transfer of student from junior colleges to four-year colleges or from one four-year institution to another.)

Another issue raised by McConnell is that of the diversity of institutions. They have different standards, and some may do a relatively better job for low-quality students than some of the better institutions do for good students. "Measured against purposes which are consistent with the characteristics and potentialities of the students and the needs of its community, and evaluated in terms of the success with which its goals are attained (the personal lives and the civic responsiveness of its graduates), the second college may be a 'good' institution." (The second college is a college that is poor as compared to, say, the academic standards of Swarthmore or Haverford.)[3] I recall a president of a small church-related college in Pennsylvania boasting of the fact that his students were of inferior quality but that his institution sought these students and gave them a good education. He said that someone had to assume this responsibility.

The plans the colleges make depend partly upon their philosophy of education. Some administrators believe that the first responsibility is to " . . . eliminate those who are unfit for advanced college or university work." Others believe that it is the responsibility of higher institutions to " . . . adapt their educational processes to students whose abilities, interests, and goals require different kinds and levels of formal schooling."[4]

John Gardner, president of the Carnegie Corporation, pointed out the need for training in depth to improve the strength and vitality of American technology. In this connection, the University of California was assigned responsibility for more theoretical curricula stressing design, research, and development, and state colleges were given more practical educational programs. An engineering school, for example, might be graded according to the level, that is, a two- or four-year course; according to academic standards; and finally according to functions which the engineers performed.

The problem also arises of avoiding unnecessary duplication. McConnell contends that there should be some duplication of aims in programs, because the resources should be widely available, but he adds:

Professional and other forms of specialized education increasingly depend on relatively advanced work in fundamental disciplines. This means that it is probably impossible to provide all the basic disciplines among institutions at the undergraduate level, or even at the graduate level. To attempt to do so would be *educationally uneconomical,* even if on superficial grounds it seemed *financially economical.* But it should be possible to allocate occupational, professional, highly specialized and extremely costly programs among institutions to the benefit of the entire state.

McConnell does not find economy a vital reason for differentiation of aims in programs and for coordination of institutions. The real aim is to assure the youth and the citizens of the state a range of educational opportunities comprehensive enough to meet the justifiable goals of individuals and the demonstrated needs of a democratic and industrial society whose specialized requirements, though changing in character from time to time, are seemingly insatiable.[5]

We must have quantity, quality, variety, and accessibility, in the words of the President's Committee on Education beyond the High School. Or, as McConnell says, we have to have adequate diversity, appropriate designation and maintenance of different functions among types and systems of educational systems, appropriate allocation of resources to types and systems of educational institutions, maximum utilization of both public and private colleges and universities.

It is scarcely necessary to add that many states are planning. They are trying to find out how many students will be needed, and for what curricula, and who is to provide the resources for the additional enrollment.

For state IHL the problem of coordination and generally economizing on resources is especially important. As the number of public IHL has steadily increased, duplication of services has become more and more costly. In the depths of the Great Depression both Oregon and Georgia drastically cut facilities and introduced an element of central control. In Georgia the government eliminated 10 two-year and four-year colleges, and remaining colleges and departments were merged and functions more logically apportioned. M. M. Chambers points out that from 1896 to 1948 thirteen states established consolidated boards for all public IHL, but none has since done so.

An official report in Michigan urged a coordinating board which would make recommendations on the budget, advise on new schools and curricula, and generally be a source of information for the budget officer and legislature, and also advise on matters of policy.

The objectives of most programs of coordination are to reduce duplication, to propose priorities on the basis of most effective use of resources in the light of functional and geographical considerations. This means, in part, establishing new IHL near population centers and taking account of the effect of any new plant upon existing services given by private IHL.

Various alternatives are open: in a study of the problem a Commission on Higher Education in North Carolina considered three alternatives:

1. Abolition of all local constitutional boards of trustees, and substitution of a central board of control *without* an executive officer. Arizona, Iowa, Kansas, and South Dakota have such an arrangement.

2. A similar method with an executive officer—as in Georgia, Mississippi, Montana, North Dakota, Oregon, Florida, New Jersey, and Rhode Island —the last two with variations.

3. A central coordinating board, without abolishing the trustees of each institution, with powers limited to developing a unified state program of higher education and coordinating offerings through budgetary control—as in Oklahoma, New Mexico, and New York.

Another alternative, not mentioned by the North Carolina commission, is a purely voluntary cooperation among the public IHL, such as prevails in Indiana and Ohio. Each of these systems has advantages. A careful survey by Glenny suggests some advantages for the governing board and others for the coordinating board. But on the whole he seems dubious of the usefulness of voluntary boards: they favor the *status quo* and do not reflect the interests of the public. For a contrary view see Chambers's book, in which he emphasizes widespread shift to permissiveness and voluntary boards.

In general, the trustees of the individual IHL have retained a stronger position than central coordinating boards. The major explanation of this fact is the large political influence of each institution and the area in which it is located. These interests resent any interference from a central board, and the board in turn is very sensitive to these pressures. Excessive influence by these boards results in standardization, lack of flexibility and of experimentation, and uniform standards for all institutions. The effective division of labor such as prevails in California is also discouraged by central control. The high standards in California, for example, are held to be related to the freedom of the university from such controls. Indeed the university is subject to some controls of the budget officer, for its budget must be integrated with the general fiscal position of the state. More than once the university fiscal officers have been told that salary scales should be tied to those in the department of roads, not to those in prestige IHL in the East. Where political influences are great, the resistance to central control directed to the most economical use of resources is great—Texas is a good example. Yet through budgetary control a degree of standardization is imposed on public IHL—in Texas beyond what is desirable. In Oklahoma the complaint is that four state colleges are provided with identical sums despite substantial variations in enrollment and curriculum. In Iowa it is said that the state government tends to favor Iowa State over Iowa University because of its greater sympathy with agriculture than with liberal arts education. Where the boards have some authority, their influence tends to be limited largely to prevention of further uneconomic duplication rather than in any general cutbacks. In Oklahoma also there is an awareness of waste, but political opposition prevents any action.

Where the state budget officer allocates funds among the public IHL in order to tailor their expenditures to the state's fiscal position, resentment frequently follows. Hence the often expressed view that the budgetary proposals of IHL should be integrated by educational experts, not by the state finance officer—e.g., the Indiana system.

I shall say little here of the planning done by individual institutions. A good example is the collection and analysis of data, past and projected, for enrollment, class size, inventory of space use, etc., by the Bureau of Institutional Research of the University of Illinois.[6]

* * *

Heneman, a partner in the firm of Cressap, McCormick and Paget, raises some interesting problems of planning. This particular firm has done a great deal of work of an advisory nature for colleges and universities. Heneman says that colleges should be able to assure potential donors (1) that the objectives of the institution have been examined realistically, (2) that the curriculum has been tailored to serve these objectives and the faculty is being used effectively, (3) that proliferation of course offerings which add substantially to instructional expense is being curbed, (4) that over-all enrollment objectives have been fixed, (5) that enrollments by school and college are projected for each year to 1970 with provision for annual revisions, (6) that the intensity of use of present classrooms and laboratories is known as a result of a study of student station (i.e., seats) utilization, (7) that new building needs have been determined on the basis of equating present and later use of existing facilities with enrollment projections, (8) that priorities on new buildings have been established both on the basis of kind and date when buildings will be available, (9) that requirements for capital funds have been made on the basis of these estimates of building and enrollment, (10) that operating-fund requirements have been projected, (11) that projections of income have been made in order to determine various financial arrangements, and (12) that present funds are being used effectively.[7]

Sidney Tickton of the Ford Foundation has contributed greatly to an increased awareness of the need of budgeting and planning.

Hundreds of institutions are planning for the next ten or fifteen years and are particularly concerned about their enrollments. This is not universally true, and there are many institutions that deal with the problem on an *ad hoc* basis. Each year they face the problem of admission pressure and decide how many additional students will be taken. Policies vary greatly. Recall Haverford objectives and enrollment plans. (These are now being reconsidered.) The University of Pennsylvania is impressed by the large numbers seeking admission to the colleges of the country. To maintain the role of independent private colleges and universities without impairment of the American tradition, " . . . these institutions must be sensitive to the social pressures incident to the rise in applications and sympathetic to the adaptation of their facilities to the needs of society." The solution of the University of Pennsylvania must be in the best interests of the society which the university serves. " . . . [Our] objective should be to adjust the balance of requirements in personnel, plant and other facilities upwards to the extent necessary, in order that artificial limitations or bottlenecks may be removed and the University operated so as to extend advantages as widely as we may to properly qualified students."

How far the university will go depends upon certain factors. For example, larger enrollment of women will be possible as residential facilities are made available. The engineering division of the university can increase its enrollment by 100 per cent without any substantial rise of faculty or facility.[8]

In a discussion sponsored by General Electric, the president of Hamilton

College said that Hamilton would continue to expand slightly but not in relation to the total enrollment bulge; the president of Dickinson College would try to improve quality rather than increase numbers; President Cole of Amherst would have the private colleges do what they could to meet the problem, but the bulk of the increase would have to be taken by public institutions; the president of Centre College would increase enrollment from 450 in 1956 to 750 by the fall of 1970; for the president of Franklin and Marshall College the enrollment would have to stay at 1,200, twice the prewar figure, and could not be increased, because of the limitations of buildings and finance; according to the president of the University of Redlands, by 1970 private institutions would probably account for only one-sixth to one-seventh of our college students; President Havrill of Arizona also stressed the point that the public institutions would have to take the major part of the increase, for the private institutions would have to keep their enrollment at a level consistent with available resources. President Elkins of Maryland had similar views. Chancellor Hardin of the University of Nebraska accepted a view in between those who would adopt very high standards of known scholastic performance as a means of keeping students out and those who contend that the more students you have who can be exposed to college life, the better.

One of the most interesting bits of planning was undertaken by the state of New York in March, 1956. First they examined the number of student spaces. College executives were asked to reply on such matters as " . . . current and projected geographical destination of students; anticipated shifts in enrollment by sex; anticipated changes in curriculum, admission policy, costs, student aid, admission policy for junior college transfer students . . . , current physical capacity of the institution . . . at five year intervals from 1955 through 1970. . . . "

Then demand was estimated by the Bureau of Examinations and Testing. The authorities questioned 50,000 prospective graduating seniors. The conclusions were that IHL on a decentralized basis should be established when demand was adequate; when demand was small (e.g., graduate), centralization would be necessary. And the contribution of private IHL should not be reduced by these measures.[9]

Another program of planning is that undertaken by the 10 colleges included in the Associated Colleges of the Midwest. These colleges are trying to find ways of coordinating their programs, planning for enrollment, planning possible economies by cooperating in courses and the sharing of facilities. They also intend to identify and reexamine their objectives, provide long-range plans, establish budget priorities for each college, and improve their college management.[10]

In a study[11] that has attracted a great deal of attention, Marietta College authorities tried to estimate how much space they were using and how much space was being wasted. They studied the problem in terms of expected enrollment and in terms of needed faculty for this enrollment. With an increase of enrollment of 172 per cent, the college estimated that a rise of faculty of 95 per cent would be adequate. Whereas the college was now using only 25 per cent of its classroom-hour capacity, enrollment of these proportions by 1970 would still utilize only 63 per cent of present capacity in terms of classroom hours available for instruction. The conclusion was that no additional classroom space need be provided. Some present facilities which are obsolete might be replaced.

Again, Seattle University, with the help of the Stanford Research Institute, studied its possible growth in enrollment; logical direction of its site-acquisition program, building use, and building needs; possible means of financing expansion; and other data necessary for proper curriculum planning.[12] The college anticipated an enrollment of 2,800 to 3,000 students by 1960 and 5,000 by 1970. The crucial items were the availability of land and the financing of its purchase, the university's capacity to finance its building program, the availability of staff with special background of preparation and religious beliefs. The university must have effective building utilization and flexibility for sound educational planning. For 5,000 full-time-equivalent students Seattle University would require building space at a total estimated cost of $10.7 million. More than half would be required for residential building.[13]

The famous Oberlin plan shows how, by increasing the number of students by 50 per cent, tuition income can increase by 75 per cent. This can be done by concentrating three terms in the first year of college instead of two, giving a total of nine terms throughout the four years instead of eight. The result is that the same plant largely serves twice as many students, since students are in residence only two of the four quarters. The rise in the faculty would not be nearly as great as the increase in the number of students. As Dean Stewart has said, " . . . an increase in the faculty by one-third would staff four quarters without increasing the total teaching load of any faculty member." Unfortunately this plan was rejected by the faculty.

PLANNING ENROLLMENT

In a later volume I expect to deal fully with the enrollment issue. But here as part of the discussion of planning I present the results of my questionnaire, to which three-quarters (more than 160) of the IHL, accounting for about 900,000 students, sent replies, Of the 161, 118 were private and 43 public. By enrollment the numbers were as follows:

Group	Enrollment	No. of IHL
1	0–500	13
2	500–1,000	28
3	1,000–3,000	49
4	3,000–7,000	32
5	7,000–10,000	13
6	10,000–20,000	18
7	20,000–30,000	8
Modal range........	300–1,500	
Mean enrollment.....	4,784	

None of the public IHL in the sample had an enrollment of less than 900, while 71 per cent had enrollments between 10,000 and 30,000. While 39 per cent with enrollment under 2,000 had graduate students, every college with enrollment in excess of 2,000 had some graduate students. Within six of the seven size groups, the proportions of colleges in low-, medium-, and high-income states was roughly the same; in the largest group all IHL were in high-income areas. Approximately 100 of the 161 IHL were in high-income areas, and though only 20 per cent of the IHL in high-income areas were public as compared to 36 and 37 per cent in the low- and medium-income areas, the 20 per cent accounted for much more enrollment, for the very large public IHL were in high-income areas.

The replies to questionnaires were not always unambiguous. Anticipated enrollment generally was for a year from 1965 to 1970 and frequently one or the other—that is, seven to twelve years from the date of inquiry. Though the question was meant to elicit the planned enrollment, at times the answer seemed to be the objective or the estimated actual enrollment.

DISTRIBUTION OF COLLEGES ACCORDING TO ESTIMATED PERCENTAGE RISE IN ENROLLMENT

Tables 49-1 through 49-5 summarize the results of the questionnaire. The largest number of IHL plan for increases of 1 to 25 and 26 to 50 per cent (Table 49-1). Of those planning no increase, IHL with enrollment of 1,000 to 3,000 (14 out of 49) especially stand out (Table 49-2). IHL with enrollments of 0 to 500 and those with the highest enrollment plan the largest increases (Table 49-3), the former undoubtedly because economic survival generally depends upon a rise of enrollment. Many of these IHL were still relatively young and had been gradually increasing their enrollment. Of the 23 IHL that expected no increase, the explanation generally was that they were now operating at full capacity and did not anticipate resources for further increases or they were fearful of de-

TABLE 49-1
Distribution according to Range of Estimated Increases

Range of percentage est. increases	No. of colleges	Percentage of total sample
1–25	42	26
26–50	32	23
51–75	23	14
76–100	12	8
101–150	7	4
151–250	3	1
0	23	14
Unable to est..........	15	10

TABLE 49-2
Distribution of Estimated Increases according to Size Group

Group	Size	No. of IHL	No. of IHL planning no increase	No. of IHL planning increases	No. of IHL unable to estimate increase	Range of estimated increases, per cent
1	0–500	13	1	11	1	22–250
2	501–1,000	28	3	23	2	5–95
3	1,001–3,000	49	14	32	3	9–130
4	3,001–7,000	32	2	28	2	12–116
5	7,001–10,000	13	2	11	0	15–95
6	10,001–20,000	18	1	14	3	15–170
7	20,001–30,000	8	0	4	4	50–143
Total.........	....	161	23	123	15	

TABLE 49-3

Group	Size	No. of IHL able to estimate their enr., per cent increase	Mean est. per cent increase	Standard deviation
1	0–500	12	83	80.8
2	501–1,000	26	28	23.5
3	1,001–3,000	46	31	35.6
4	3,001–7,000	30	39	33.6
5	7,001–10,000	13	43	32.9
6	10,001–20,000	15	59	53.9
7	20,001–30,000	4	77	46.2

TABLE 49-4

Distribution of Estimated Increases according to Income Area

Income areas	No. of IHL	No. of IHL planning no increase	No. of IHL planning some increases	No. of IHL unable to estimate increases	Range of est. per cent increases
Low.......................	22	3	18	1	0–120
Medium....................	38	3	33	2	15–230
High.......................	101	17	71	13	4–170
Total.....................	161	23	122	16	

TABLE 49-5

Distribution of Estimated Increases according to Type of Control

Type of control	No. of IHL	No. of IHL planning no increase	No. of IHL planning some increases	No. of IHL unable to est. increases	Range of est. per cent increases	Unweighted average increase
Private.........	117	21	85	11	4–250	31
Public..........	44	2	36	5	20–170	73.5

Source: Replies to my questionnaire. I am greatly indebted to Paul David for summarizing the material in the questionnaires.

stroying the qualities of their institutions by increasing enrollment. Among the largest IHL the general view seemed to be that they were equipped to handle many more, though they often could not say what their maximum would be.

Group 2 (501 to 1,000) plans to increase much less than group 1—in part because resources are not available to expand greatly and in part because they are now operating at a more economic level than IHL in group 1. The greatest resistance to growth is in group 3 (1,001 to 3,000). Here part of the explanation is again lack of resources; but the large number of women's colleges, reluctant to expand, and the special problems of denominational schools are also relevant. The most frequent explanation of resistance to growth is the desire to preserve the peculiar quality of the college.

Group 4 anticipates a rise of enrollment of 39 per cent as compared to 83, 28, and 31 per cent for groups 1 to 3. Large differences in planned rises prevail within this group, though the largest rises are anticipated for the larger units within the group (3,001 to 7,000). Much vagueness is found in the replies to the questionnaire. These IHL are not the classic liberal arts colleges nor large enough to have the appeal of the major universities with a wide choice of graduate and professional schools. The public IHL in this group at least say their expansion will depend on population growth, needs for higher education, and state resources made available.

Expected rises of 43, 59, and 77 per cent are estimated for groups 5, 6, and 7. In group 5, three outstanding private universities anticipate no increase or virtually none. In general it is clear that IHL with enrollments in excess of 10,000 planned larger increases than those in the 5,000-to-10,000 range. Beyond 10,000, if we are to judge from the responses to the questionnaire, it is possible to expand without fundamental changes in the nature of the IHL. In group 6 (10,000 to 20,000) 39 per cent of the IHL are private urban, and their responses clarify the issues: they can expand with large rises in part-time students and depend greatly on increased numbers of part-time faculty.

Whereas groups 1 to 5 include more private than public IHL, groups 6 and 7 are composed of more public than private IHL. The pressure for expansion is much greater for public than for private IHL. Respondents from group 7 virtually assume very large rises, though they are often reluctant to speculate on the size by 1970. The large IHL tend to be increasingly in higher-income areas. The percentages for groups 1 to 7 in high-income areas are 54, 65, 59, 63, 70, 61, 100. More resources may, therefore, be forthcoming for the larger IHL despite the rotten-borough systems.

Here is the relation of expected increase and income levels:

Income	Range, per cent rise	Unweighted mean
Low.............	9–120	48.7
Medium..........	15–130	58.8
High............	4–170	35.6

What explains the low figure for high-income areas? The large numbers of Ivy universities, women's colleges, and small liberal arts colleges; also the reluctance of the large IHL to estimate rises.

What of graduate expansion? Of 115 IHL in our sample with graduate students, 22 were unable to answer; 20 planned no graduate increase; 11, 20, 42 planned increases in graduate enrollment proportionately less than, equal to, and greater than rises in undergraduate enrollment, respectively. Here the largest proportion not expanding graduate work is in the IHL with the lowest enrollment. Thus at 1,000 to 3,000, 10 out of 25 plan no graduate increase; but at 10,000 to 20,000, only 1 of 13 plans no expansion. Again, whereas 5 out of 15 plan expansion in graduate enrollment in the 1,000-to-3,000 group greater proportionately than in undergraduate, the corresponding figures for the 10,000-to-30,000 groups show that, of 19 planning increases, 15 plan to expand more proportionately in graduate than in undergraduate enrollment.

This survey in general suggests that planned enrollment over a seven- to twelve-year period from 1958 is rather less than anticipated enrollment— 31 per cent for private and 73 per cent for public according to my survey (on the basis of 1958 enrollment this means an increase of 56 per cent). The major burden will be carried by public IHL and very large urban IHL.

According to the latest estimates, enrollment in higher education will rise from 3.4 million in 1959 to more than 6 million in 1970, a rise of about 75 per cent. This estimate is based on a *modest* projection of the percentage of college-age enrollment at IHL: 1939 = 14.3; 1959 = 37.1; 1970 = 41.2 (an annual percentage rise from 1959 to 1970 about one-third that of 1939 to 1959).

TABLE 49-6

Distribution of Estimated Increases in Graduate Enrollment
in Relation to Present Size of IHL (by Size Group)

Size group, enrollment	No. of IHL with graduate students	No. of IHL unable to give figures or did not answer	No. planning no graduate increase	No. planning grad. increase proportionately less than undergrad. increase	No. planning grad. increase proportionately equal to undergrad. increase	No. planning grad. increase proportionately greater than undergrad. increase
0–500	2	...	2			
501–1,000	9	...	3	2	1	3
1,001–3,000	33	8	10	2	8	5
3,001–7,000	32	7	1	6	5	13
7,001–10,000	13	1	3	...	3	6
10,001–20,000	18	5	1	1	3	8
20,001–30,000	8	1	...	...	...	7
Total..........	115	22	20	11	20	42

In this connection, note that the high school graduate population grows more than the college-age population—as might be expected with increasing urbanization. Thus in Wisconsin in the years 1956–1960, college-age population rose by 7 per cent, but high school graduates by 19.5 per cent.[14]

From 1956–1959, HEW found no less than 153 official agencies sponsoring special and continuing staff studies in higher education. The subjects under consideration included enrollment (91), programs (80), finance (75), physical facilities (72), organization and administration (62), junior college (61), and faculty (60).[15]

FOOTNOTES

[1] T. L. MacMitchell, "Are Institutions Planning Ahead?" *Journal of Higher Education,* November, 1955, p. 465.

[2] T. R. McConnell, "Diversification of American Higher Education: A Research Program," *The Educational Record,* October, 1957; cf. L. Wilson, "Analyzing and Evaluating Costs in Higher Education," *The Educational Record,* April, 1961, esp. pp. 100, 105, for an excellent statement on the need of planning.

[3] McConnell, *op. cit.,* p. 7.

[4] *Ibid.,* p. 11.

[5] *Ibid.,* pp. 14–15 (paraphrased).

[6] For last few pages see especially *State-supported Higher Education in North Carolina: The Report of the Commission on Higher Education,* 1955, pp. 14–15, 31–32, 54–58, 66, 98–99; *Texas Commission on Higher Education: . . . Report,* 1954, pp. 4–5, 13–17, 24–25; *A Study of the Need for State Colleges in the North Bay Area,* Joint Staff for the Liaison Committee of the California State Board of Education and the Regents of the University of California, November, 1958, appendix A; *A Report of a Survey of the University System in Georgia: Submitted to the Regents . . . ,* 1949, p. 178; *A Report of a Survey of the Needs of California in Higher Education,* 1948, pp. 44, 116; American Council on Education, *A Call for Action,* 1954, pp. 6–9; The *Survey of Higher Education in Michigan,* pp. 114, 178; L. A. Glenny, *Autonomy of Public Colleges,* 1959, esp. chaps. 4, 5, 9, 10; E. F. Potthoff, *History and Functions of the Bureau of Institutional Research, University of Illinois,* May 1, 1960 (mimeographed); Brumbaugh and Sugg, Jr., "Recent Developments in State and Regional Planning of Higher Education," *The Annals, Higher Education under Stress,* September, 1955, pp. 32–40; M. M. Chambers, *The Campus and the People,* 1960, pp. 46–47.

[7] H. J. Heneman, "Planning Comes First; Fund Raising Follows," *College and University Business,* March, 1958, pp. 23, 24; also see his essay in Dexter M. Keezer (ed.), *Financing Higher Education, 1960–70,* McGraw-Hill, New York, 1959, pp. 118–139.

[8] *Tradition and Transition: The President's Report, 1955, University of Pennsylvania,* pp. 15–17.

[9] General Electric, *Higher Education: A 20-Year Look Ahead,* 1957, pp. 8–12; Fretwell, Jr., and Doran, "Higher Education in New York State Faces the Future," *The Educational Record,* April, 1958, pp. 163–164.

[10] *Proposed Cooperative Plan of the Associated Colleges of the Midwest,* June, 1958. (Mimeographed.)

[11] "Space Utilization Study, Marietta College," *Case Book: Education beyond the High School,* November, 1957.

[12] "Future Development Study, Seattle University," *Case Book: Education beyond the High School,* December, 1957.

[13] cf. Case Institute of Technology, *People, Program, Plan: President's Annual Report,* 1957.

[14] HEW, *Ten Year Objectives in Education,* Jan. 17, 1961, pp. 7–9; cf. HEW, *Financing Higher Education 1960–70,* p. 74; and Joint Staff Coordinating Committee, Wisconsin, *Wisconsin's High School Graduates, 1960,* December, 1960, pp. 1–2.

[15] HEW, *Advance Planning to Meet Higher Education Needs,* Recent State Studies, 1956–1959, pp. 3–5.

Chapter 50

COOPERATION AND COORDINATION

Colleges have cooperated in attempts to cut costs and offer a richer curriculum for many years. (Indeed the duplication of schools, courses, library facilities had been scandalous.) Even in the early 1930s North Carolina colleges entered into cooperative agreements in extension work, purchases of supplies, and business management; in both Nebraska and Kansas there were cooperative agreements for scholarships; in New York there were informal agreements between the American Tel. and Tel. and numerous colleges to avoid duplication and waste in engineering education; in Pennsylvania there were cooperative efforts to reduce duplication of courses and departments. Again, colleges often federated to achieve common objectives. In the plan for a greater University of Oklahoma it was even expected that competition would be eliminated entirely. The first objective is to use resources more effectively. One writer distinguishes between the cooperative arrangements which are useful but do not " . . . touch the main stream of institutional individuality . . . " and those which involve specialization and hence involve radical changes in procedure.[1]

But it is especially since the war that large advances have been made in coordination. There are scientific projects which are taken over by the government, because these are not possible fields of exploitation by colleges. The kinds of equipment and machinery needed are so expensive that no college or group of colleges can afford to undertake this kind of work. "The great particle accelerators required by nuclear physics are reaching such size and cost that they no longer can be financed by a university or limited in their use to a single institution. . . . " In a recent report a National Academy of Science committee urged " . . . the establishment of a national institute of Atmospheric Research which could provide the research facilities on a scale required to cope with the global

596

nature of the meteorological problems as described in this report. . . . "
But it is also hoped that many of these projects could be worked out by
cooperative activities on the part of institutions of higher learning.[2]

Progress, especially at the regional level, has been made in recent years.
Examples are the Southern, the Mountain, and the New England Regional Compacts. The extent to which the cooperating states and institutions have moved varies somewhat, but their objectives, accomplishments, and possibilities are suggested best by the Southern Regional Compact.

Here the authorities were impressed by the high cost of higher education and the need for substituting cooperation for costly competition. "Duplication of curricula, laboratory facilities and library facilities have proceeded at a pace and to an extent that may have gone beyond our financial ability to sustain."

Hence, instead of accepting the proliferation of professional schools even where the market was small, the colleges pooled their funds and planned to shift professional students from some states where facilities were inadequate to other states with excess capacity. Freedom of choice was available for the students, and quotas were set up for each program. The 16 states pooled more than $1 million. Several years ago the contract service carried 850 students into 19 institutions.

The purpose of the board was to " . . . serve as a clearinghouse for information about higher education of regional significance, provide continuous assessment of the needs of higher education in the region and make plans to meet them; administer interstate arrangements for educational services; and develop research and consultation services relating to higher education."

Aside from encouraging the migration of students, the conference worked on improving standards of graduate work, obtaining research funds and facilities, and running conferences on higher education with government representatives, especially legislative budget officers.[3]

Many other programs could be mentioned: the New England Compact, which parallels the Southern though on a smaller scale; the Western Compact, a North Central association consisting of 65 colleges operating in a cooperative program to improve training of secondary school teachers; the program of 18 Middle Atlantic universities to " . . . develop improved ways to prepare public school administrators in their graduate schools of education"; the Seven College (women's) plan, which emphasizes " . . . the need of a method of evaluating the product of a liberal arts program and the protection of the states from incompetently trained professional teachers."[4] At the state level also there are increased attempts to cooperate rather than to compete, to avoid excessive duplications of curricula and courses, and to set up new institutions with attention being paid to available resources both within the state and within the region. We discuss this issue more fully elsewhere.[5]

Cooperation among institutions has also gone far. We have, for example, the cooperation of 15 IHL for an interlibrary center in the Middle West; the Richmond experiment with sharing of libraries, research funds, professors, and the like; the Oak Ridge project and the Brookhaven Laboratories, both projects for which many institutions are responsible; an educational television program in the Greater Boston area financed in part by institutions there; a television cooperative program in Oregon; an attempt to treat the problem of teacher education in Southern California through cooperative action by a number of institutions; a cooperative program of seven liberal arts colleges and the Illinois Institute of Technology; a program under which Temple University provides instruction and faculty for two small colleges; a new University Center in Georgia. Furthermore, numerous attempts have been made to cooperate on fund raising and in purchasing of supplies and services. A notable experiment for improving educational practices and achieving a more effective use of resources is the 10 Associated Colleges of the Midwest.[6]

In many instances, for example, in the agreement among Swarthmore, Haverford, and Bryn Mawr, students from these institutions are able to take courses in other institutions where their own colleges cannot provide such instruction. In the Connecticut Valley four participating institutions cooperate in allocating the burden of instruction where demand in one institution is small. This might happen, for example, in such fields as Russian or classics. Professors are also exchanged. These institutions also cooperate in programs for the M.A. and are discussing the possibility of complete cooperative Ph.D. programs. In many programs of this kind, the cooperating institutions bring distinguished lecturers to their campuses. Earlham College and the University of Indiana participate in a program for adult instruction. In this manner much better use is made of the Earlham plant and the faculty of both institutions.[7]

A most interesting cooperative project is the five units associated as the Claremont colleges in Southern California. Here is an advanced form of cooperation. Under pressure of rapid population advances, Pomona College in the 1920s accepted a cooperative program which would put the pressure of numbers on additional units. A new unit, utilizing existing resources of manpower, courses, and even finance of existing units could absorb increased demands and exploit a division of labor, and yet not incur the large unit costs of an entirely new college with an enrollment, say, of but 300.

Finally, I should say a word about an interesting project set up by the four Connecticut Valley colleges.[8] Here four colleges, including Smith, Amherst, Mt. Holyoke, and the University of Massachusetts, proposed a new college plan. Supported by the resources available in these four institutions, the authors of this plan propose a liberal arts college which could provide a high-quality education to 1,000 students at a relatively low unit cost. The proposal involves a revolutionary type of education through the cooperation of these four colleges. Economies would be possible because extracurricular activities of limited educational value would be prohibited in the new college and because courses would be carefully scrutinized and their number kept to a minimum. As a result of this and because of the reduced course requirements for students, the ratio of student to faculty would be 20 to 1 as against the national average of about 13 to 1.*

FOOTNOTES

[1] *Bulletin of the Association of American Colleges,* vol. 19, 1933, p. 291; H. W. K. Fitzroy, in *Current Issues in Higher Education,* 1958, pp. 153–154.

[2] *Science and Technology Act of 1958,* Senate Document no. 90, pp. 44–45; M. W. Ertell, "Towards a Philosophy of Interinstitutional Cooperation," *The Educational Record,* April, 1958, pp. 131–135.

[3] On the Southern Regional Compact, see J. E. Ivey, "An Emerging Regional Program in Higher Education," *The Educational Record,* April, 1952; McG. L. William, "Dreams into Reality: Regional Planning in Education in the South," *School and Society,* Jan. 6, 1951; R. S. Sugg, Jr., "Regionalism in Higher Education," *Journal of Higher Education,* February, 1956; "The Southern Regional Educational Program," *School and Society,* Mar. 8, 1952.

[4] See "Seven College Plan to Cooperate with State Departments of Education," *School and Society,* June 16, 1951; "Middle Atlantic State Universities Cooperate to Improve Educational Administration," *School and Society,* Apr. 21, 1951; "Western Interstate Compact," *Higher Education,* October, 1955; "Western Interstate Compact for Student Exchange Programs," *Higher Education,* January, 1951; New England Board of Education, *Annual Report, 1957;* and *Higher Education,* Oct. 11, 1954; also see L. B. Mayhew, "Interinstitutional Cooperation through Regional Studies," *Higher Education,* March, 1955; Dressel and Mayhew, "Educational Planning and Research," *Educational Record,* April, 1953.

[5] See, for example, A. J. Brumbaugh and R. S. Sugg, Jr., "Recent Developments in State and Regional Planning of Higher Education," *The Annals, Higher Education under Stress,* September, 1955, pp. 32–40.

[6] "Liberal Arts Colleges Cooperate with the Illinois Institute of Technology," *School and Society,* Feb. 6, 1954; "The Minnesota Inter-college Cooperation," *School and Society,* Jan. 26, 1952; "Temple Cooperation with Two Colleges," *School and Society,* December, 1951; "A New University Center in Georgia," *School and Society,* June 10, 1944; R. T. Esterquest, "The Midwest Inter-library Center," *Higher Education,* Jan. 1, 1950; H. W. K. Fitzroy, "The Richmond Area University Center," *The Educational Record,* July, 1957, pp. 241–249; *First Annual Report of the Associated Colleges of the Midwest,* 1960.

[7] See, for example, "Current Issues in Higher Education," *Proceedings of the Eighth Annual National Conference on Higher Education,* 1953, pp. 98–101; "Co-

---

* A recent study (HEW, *Cooperative Projects among Colleges and Universities,* 1961) summarizes current practices.

operative Intercollegiate Program of Graduate Studies in the Humanities and Social Sciences, Seven Southern California Colleges," *Case Book: Education beyond the High School,* Nov. 1, 1957; "Intercollegiate Committee on Cooperation, Amherst College, Mt. Holyoke College, Smith College and the University of Massachusetts," *ibid.,* 1957; "Evening College for Adults: The Earlham College-Indiana University Center," *ibid.,* 1957; "Statewide Study of Higher Education, The Florida Board of Control," *ibid.,* 1957.

  [8] See C. L. Barber, Donald Sheehan, Stuart M. Stoke, and Shannon McCune, *The New College Plan: A Proposal for a Major Departure in Higher Education,* 1958.

Chapter 51

PLANT LOCATION AND UTILIZATION

INTRODUCTION

In 1957–58, the operation and maintenance of physical plant of IHL cost $409 million, or 11 per cent of educational and general expenditures. The physical plant was carried at $11.2 billion, though its real value was probably at least twice as great. At 4 per cent rate of interest and amortization over fifty years, the annual capital charge, inclusive of maintenance, would be about $1.7 billion—as a business firm would estimate it. Of $751 million of gifts in 1957–58, one estimate puts contributions for plant at $181 million.[1] Since the resources involved are so large, it is important to use plant effectively.

ENROLLMENT IN RELATION TO LOCATION OF IHL

To a considerable degree the attendance at college is determined by the proximity of a college to the potential student. Hence it is important if we are to use our IHL effectively to relate our location to sources of population. In an earlier section I discussed this problem briefly.

"The proximity of an institution is an important factor in its per cent of those eligible who attend it. For example, Alameda, Yolo, Santa Barbara, and Riverside Counties, where campuses of the University of California are located, rank high in the per cent of those eligible to enter the University of California."

Similar conclusions are drawn for attendance at state and junior colleges. The percentage of 1955 school graduates who continued their formal education varied from 57 per cent in Napa County to 6.4 per cent in Glenn County, with an over-all figure for the 41 counties of 43 per cent.[2]

Similar conclusions are to be drawn from the experience at Michigan. In 27 counties with IHL, the percentage of college-age population in college in 1955–56 was 32.9 per cent, and the figure for 56 counties with no IHL was 16.8. Location is of course not the only factor. Where there are no colleges, economic status may well be low also. The importance of the economic issue is also suggested by the fact that the largest percentage (46.6) of college-age group at college was in 7 counties with *state* institutions, excluding Wayne (Detroit). In 8 counties with private IHL only, the percentage was but 23.6.[3]

In Minnesota also there is a maldistribution of colleges. Whereas 3 counties in the eastern part of the state had 14 colleges, the remaining 18 colleges were scattered among 12 counties, with the entire western half of the state having but 4 IHL.[4]

LOCATION OF NEW IHL AND NEW SCHOOLS (E.G., LAW)[5]

Our discussion of coordination of state IHL suggests that new IHL are not always located where they ought to be. In order to throw further light on this problem I sent a questionnaire to the heads of 543 new IHL or new schools (e.g., law, engineering, business) founded in a recent period of ten years. In this same period there were of course many IHL that were closed or combined with others. In the 1920s, the 1930s, and the 1940s the number of IHL increased by 368, 299 and 143, respectively, and from 1949–50 to 1955–56 there was a net rise of but 7. Apparently it is becoming more difficult to establish new IHL, and on the whole the deceleration of the rate of increase is a factor making for increased productivity.

From the 543 questionnaires sent I received 269 answers. After eliminating unusable replies and allowing for multiple-campus answers, I found 253 usable replies. The new IHL or schools varied greatly in enrollment: 42, or 16 per cent, had enrollments of less than 100; more than half had less than 500; and almost three-quarters had less than 1,000. On the whole these are uneconomic operations and, unless enrollment increases, are likely to remain high-cost IHL. Two of the IHL had enrollments of more than 10,000, and five had enrollments of from 5,000 to 10,000. The range was 50 for a theological seminary to 13,000 for the Los Angeles City College.

TABLE 51-1
Types of IHL

IHL	Number	Per cent
State...........................	92	36.4
State and local....................	21	8.3
Local...........................	38	15.0
Independent......................	39	15.4
Roman Catholic....................	34	13.4
Protestant.......................	26	10.3
Other...........................	3	1.2
Total..........................	253	100.0

Of the 253 IHL whose replies were used, 40 per cent were private and 60 per cent public.

Of 253 new units over the ten-year period, the breakdown was as shown in Table 51-2. In general, enrollment in business schools of the under-graduate and two-year variety tends to be large, private four-year colleges small, and public colleges large. Graduate schools also tend to be small.

TABLE 51-2

IHL	Number	Per cent
Professional and technical:		
Undergraduate and graduate......	122	48.2
Undergraduate—two-year.........	77	30.4
Undergraduate—four-year........	32	12.6
Theological and bible..............	22	8.7
Total.........................	253	100.0

TABLE 51-3

Manner of Estimating Need for a College or a Curriculum (e.g., Law)

Manner of estimating	Number	Per cent*
State survey of population, demand for higher education...............	36	14.2
Local or institutional survey of pop., demand for higher education.........	49	19.4
Estimate of job needs..	42	16.6
Cursory examination population, jobs, etc.............................	14	5.5
Total studies..	141	55.7
Requests from professional and business groups.......................	37	14.6
Requests from prospective students.................................	44	17.4
Requests related to church needs....................................	39	15.4
Elections and similar public demand.................................	8	3.2
Total requests...	128	50.6
Allow continued segregation in higher education.......................	5	2.0
Other..	22	8.7
No answer or unknown...	6	2.4

* The total percentages add to more than 100 because a number of respondents cited more than one basis for determining need.

The decline of liberal arts is perhaps suggested by this table. In 1955–56 the liberal arts colleges numbered 732, or almost 40 per cent of the total, and enrollment numbered 740,000, or 28 per cent of the total enrollment. It is clear from the small rise of liberal arts colleges vis-à-vis their pro-portion of existing IHL that liberal arts were losing ground relative to total new units and a fortiori in relation to enrollment.

To the question "How did you decide there would be a need for this college?" the replies to my questionnaire were as shown in Table 51-3.

The summary is in some respects misleading, since the institutional surveys of demand for new IHL were often cursory. "Church needs" often meant no college of a particular church in the region. The Protestant IHL tended to be much smaller than the Catholic.

On the whole, the answers to the question "How did you estimate likely enrollment?" were disappointing. More than half gave unsatisfactory answers—e.g., number of applications, cursory examination, guess, none (see Table 51-4). Job opportunity surveys were helpful, but they did

TABLE 51-4
Manner of Estimating Likely Enrollment

Manner of estimating	Number	Per cent
High school population and intent survey........	86	34.0
Job opportunity survey......................	20	7.9
Applications...............................	35	13.8
Total studies............................	141	55.7
Cursory examination available data...........	41	16.2
Guess....................................	27	10.7
None.....................................	22	8.7
Total superficial or nonexistent estimate......	90	35.6
Facilities available as limit..................	16	6.3
No answer or unknown......................	6	2.4

not often take into account the available training facilities. One gets a better impression of the quality of enrollment studies from such surveys as were made by expert state committees in California, New York, Florida, and Michigan.[6]

In response to a related question, 142, or 56 per cent, replied that they studied enrollment in competitive IHL and 31 per cent that they did not; 13 per cent replied that such investigations were irrelevant or made no reply. Often "not relevant" meant that the IHL unit had no serious competition—e.g., a seminary, a sole nursing school in a state. Generally all public graduate and professional and technical institutions made such studies, and more Catholic than Protestant. In general the investigations were not made for the smaller units. One college authority said in effect that an examination of enrollments in competitive institutions would have shown no need for this proposed institution. Hence no attempt was made to study competitive enrollments.

"Was this enrollment figure based on trying to achieve minimum cost per student or on purely educational issues?" The replies (Table 51-5) tended to stress the educational objective. Pennsylvania extension campuses and the New York community colleges accounted for most of those who replied they considered both education and cost. Some respondents were surprised that unit costs varied with enrollment; and in many fields, especially the graduate schools, the reply often was that costs are necessarily high and these high costs cannot be treated by raising enrollment.

One of the questions asked was "Were the founders of professional, graduate, and technical units influenced by the market for graduates?" The answer was "Yes" in 151 instances, "No" in 23 instances, no answer or "Do not know" in 10, and "Not relevant" in 69. A reading of the replies suggests actually that in less than 100 of the 151 "Yes" replies was a serious study of markets made.

TABLE 51-5
Enrollment: Determined How?

Determinant	Number	Per cent
Purely educational issues....................	137	54.2
Both educational issues and cost considered.....	82	32.4
Primarily cost considerations.................	13	5.1
Neither.................................	1	0.4
Unknown, no answer.......................	20	7.9

TABLE 51-6
Manner of Determining Particular Location

Determinant	Number	Per cent	Per cent of those selecting new location (156 IHL)*
Central location in terms of proposed student body......	77	30.4	49.4
Site and/or buildings available......................	57	22.5	36.5
Staff available....................................	11	4.3	7.1
Professional advice...............................	7	2.8	4.5
Donors' wishes...................................	9	3.6	5.8
Other...	13	5.1	8.3
Existing institution determined choice of site............	111	43.9	
No answer.......................................	6	2.4	

* Adds to more than 100 because some mentioned two criteria.

How was a particular location selected? Table 51-6 reveals that, where existing institutions did not determine choice, central location in relation to the student body was especially important. The largest causal overlap was between this and sites and buildings available. Professional advice and staff available as a determinant of site was especially relevant for health institutions. Theological and professional schools, as might be expected, were little concerned with the proximity of potential students.

"Was proximity to potential students crucial?" Apparently, this was a matter of concern frequently (Table 51-7).

TABLE 51-7

Answer	Number	Per cent
Yes.....................	124	49.0
Somewhat..............	33	13.0
No.....................	87	34.4
No answer.............	9	3.6

On the question of the relevance of labor market in choice of site, some respondents seemed to misinterpret the content of the question. The objective was to discover the relation of site chosen and availability of faculty. Some seemed to answer on the theory that the market for graduates was the relevant variable. At any rate, the majority seemed to select their site irrespective of market for faculty or graduates. Medical schools are an important exception.

Availability of plant was a decisive factor in choosing a site in more than 50 per cent of the cases. Where much new construction was necessary—e.g., New York and California—this factor did not appear to be important. But often the availability of estates, abandoned college campuses, former state and Federal institutions, and low-cost land were decisive.

Donors' influence was not generally important in the choice of site— in part because donors were generally not involved. Where there were donors, they made possible the establishment of the institution and generally the metropolitan area to be chosen—e.g., the Rutgers School of Microbiology, the Eastman School of Geography at Johns Hopkins.

TABLE 51-8
Extent to Which Wish of Donor (If Any) Was an Important Consideration

Extent	Number	Per cent
None (virtually all "no donor")..........	182	71.9
Donor(s):		
Low influence......................	13	5.1
Some influence.....................	27	10.7
Major influence....................	23	9.1
Total influence of donor(s).........	63	24.9
No answer.........................	8	3.2

TABLE 51-9
Extent of Influence of Local Politicians, Business, Professional, or Church Groups

Extent	Number	Per cent
Little or no influence..................	110	43.5
Some influence:*		
Church..........................	15	5.9
Business.........................	36	14.2
Political.........................	36	14.2
Professional......................	11	4.3
Total with some influence..........	60	23.7
Considerable influence:*		
Church..........................	27	10.7
Business.........................	32	12.6
Political.........................	39	15.4
Professional......................	13	5.1
Total with considerable influence....	71	28.1
No answer........................	12	4.7

* More than one group in many instances.

Many influenced the choice of sites: local politicians, especially vis-à-vis local and state colleges; businessmen in choice of sites for schools of business; professional groups in choice for medical and technical institutions. Table 51-9 reveals substantial influence by various interests.

* * *

An examination of individual questionnaires reveals how diverse are the factors determining the establishment of a new school or college and its location. At Riverside, California, local politicians and civic leaders exercised much influence in precise location, but the need of a college and prospective enrollment were matters of careful study. In Santa Fe, a new Catholic college was started because an order already was operating a high school, because the view was that there was need of a college for Catholics, and because a Federal hospital was available for plant. Enrollment, not carefully estimated, proved disappointing. A Baptist college in Kentucky was an outgrowth of the church and its location determined by that of the church. The founding of Roosevelt College followed a dispute over the entry of Negroes in a predecessor institution, the central YMCA. The college's location was determined primarily by the availability of students in the downtown area. Mississippi established a medical school because clinical facilities were available in Jackson and the authorities wanted to stop the exodus of Mississippi men going to medical colleges elsewhere and not returning even as shortages of doctors prevailed in the state.

* * *

In reply to the question "Have developments been about as expected?" 61 per cent replied "Yes," 26 per cent reported "Better than expected," and 10 per cent "Poorer than expected" (others = 3 per cent). In view of the large proportion of inadequate examination of likely enrollment, the explanation of the favorable results must be optimism by the respondents or the generally rising trend of enrollments.

A STUDY OF PROFESSIONAL SCHOOLS PER STANDARD METROPOLITAN DISTRICT IN THE UNITED STATES

This study represents an attempt to ascertain the number of professional schools (law, medical, dental, and graduate) per standard metropolitan district in selected categories of states and wherever possible to make note of those areas, if any, where economic inefficiency exists in the form of overcapacity and the concentration of a large number of professional schools in a limited area. Conversely, the study will hope to show those areas in which capacity is most inadequate and where further facilities are most urgently needed.

The primary basis of classification of the several states was that of "wealth." States were ranked both with respect to total income and per capita income, in each instance the 10 top and 10 lowest.

Characteristics of the wealthy group (with respect to *total* income) are as follows:

1. These states are primarily Eastern. Only California and Texas of this group are not found in the Northeastern sector of the United States.

2. It will almost invariably be found that professional schools in these states tend to congregate in and around the one or two largest cities of the state. Pennsylvania and Massachusetts serve to illustrate this point. In Massachusetts, Boston, with a metropolitan area including approximately one-half of the state's population, includes 6 of its 7 law schools, all 3 of its medical schools, both its dental schools, and 9 of its 13 graduate schools. While Massachusetts may be termed monocentric, Pennsylvania is duocentric. Its twin giants at opposite ends of the state, Pittsburgh and Philadelphia, which include slightly more than one-half the state's population, also include 5 of its 6 law schools, its 7 medical schools (6 of which are in Philadelphia), its 3 dental schools, and 7 of its 10 graduate schools.

The one notable exception to the rule stated above is the state of Texas, which has its professional facilities well dispersed among its 15 metropolitan areas. It should be noted, however, that Texas has no one dominant city or center and that its vast expanse would tend to produce a greater diffusion of professional schools than would be found in the more compact Eastern states.

3. With respect to the utilization of capacity in this group of wealthy states, generalization is difficult because of the lack of sufficient data. It is, however, safe to conclude that effective utilization is greatest among the medical schools, next among the law schools, and least among the graduate schools. Whether effective utilization of capacity would be increased by a greater dispersion of these schools is open to question which the data at hand seems insufficient to answer, and greater dispersion would undoubtedly raise unit costs. It must be remembered that attendance at professional schools is not solely a function of the population density of the surrounding area but also depends on prestige, quality, and the like.

If one were to venture a guesstimate of the degree of effective utilization of the various professional schools, it would be somewhat of this order:

	Per cent
Medical schools	95–100
Dental schools	90–95
Law schools	80–85
Graduate schools	75–80

Characteristics of the poor group—i.e., poor with respect to total income, are as follows:

1. These are primarily Southern states; of the 10 states included in this category only North Dakota falls outside of the geographic area of the Southeastern United States.

2. These states, low in per capita income, are also relatively small with respect to population, and accordingly few standard metropolitan areas are to be found within their confines.

3. The generalization that professional schools tend to congregate in and around the one or two largest cities or centers of the state is not as valid with respect to these states as it was found to be for the wealthier group. Georgia, North Carolina, and Tennessee, the largest three states of this group in terms of population tend to follow the Northern pattern, while the remaining seven states would seem to have their graduate facilities dispersed.

4. By almost any practical standard, the professional facilities of these states (except perhaps those of the law schools) must be considered inadequate to meet not only the projected expansion of the future but even present-day needs. Where graduate instruction costs $3,000 or more per unit (e.g., medical schools and arts and science), a great deal is to be said for centralizing this kind of instruction as much as possible and, if neces-

sary, subsidizing transportation costs of students. Additional units may cost $5,000 to $10,000 per student, and medical schools require a state population of at least 2 million for adequate support. While data concerning capacity is perhaps even scarcer here than was the case in the consideration of the wealthier group of states, most effective utilization again would seem to be in the medical and dental area. Another rough guesstimate of capacity utilization would be as follows:

	Per cent
Medical and dental schools	96–100
Graduate schools	70–75
Law schools	50–60

These data indicate a far less efficient allocation of resources than was found for the wealthier states and the ability to absorb a far higher percentage of the projected increases in enrollment. It would seem that existing capacity with regard to graduate and law schools would be, if anything, more adequate than those of the wealthy states, and considered in a narrow sense this is actually the case. However, the excess capacity noted in these states represents economic inefficiency, since the effective utilization of resources is not maximized. That these are the very states where the ratio of students emigrating to other states for professional education over students immigrating to these states is at its highest is relevant here. Here again one may conclude that graduate capacity is excessive in the poorer states, in part because of the pull of the IHL in the wealthy states. Unit costs tend to be high in these states because of low enrollment and despite inferior quality.

Data concerning percentage capacity utilization tend to show that utilization is universally greatest in medical and dental schools and that the number and percentage utilization of professional and graduate schools vary with the wealth of the state, the Northern and wealthier states having a *relatively* greater number of graduate schools and the Southern and poorer states having a relatively greater number of law schools.

The study reveals that economic inefficiency is not marked in those large areas which have a great many professional schools such as New York, Boston, or San Francisco, but rather in those areas of the poorer states where inadequate facilities exist. The problem to be dealt with is usually not one of the existence of a superabundance of professional schools of any one type in one area, but rather how the professional school can meet the demands for higher education without placing upon the student the burden of the necessity of extensive travel to reach adequate professional facilities. In less costly methods of instruction—e.g., law and business—the problem is simple. Decentralization is the most economical approach for the institution and student. But in medicine and graduate arts and science centralization, with transportation subsidies for students living outside of large metropolitan areas, seems the most effective approach.

INSTITUTIONS OF HIGHER LEARNING ESTABLISHED IN THE UNITED STATES BY REGION, STATE, AND INCOME AREA[7]

The decade commencing with the conclusion of World War II has in general been one of intense growth. In large part, however, this generalization is not applicable to the number of IHL established during this period. Only 75 colleges (gross), exclusive of junior colleges and theological seminaries, were instituted in the ten-year period under consideration. Even a cursory glance through *The College Blue Book* or some similar document will serve to highlight the fact that entry into the field of higher learning is a difficult and expensive feat. The general trend, in line with the practice of the American economy, has been for existing institutions to expand both in terms of creation of new capacity and the addition of new schools and departments.

During this ten-year period it is interesting to note that of the newly created professional schools, schools and departments of nursing were more numerous than those of any other type, with graduate schools a close second. To some degree this is merely representative of the demand conditions and the urgent needs of the economy for professional nurses and college teachers, but during this same period only 12 medical and dental schools and 17 schools or departments of engineering were established.

During the 1945–1954 decade, the trends in rate of increase of population and the addition of various schools and colleges tended to correlate fairly well, with the exception of New England, where the rate of growth of total population has been well below the national average but in which 34 institutions were established. In two of the areas where rate of growth of population has been the highest (the South Atlantic and the Pacific Coast regions), the rise of IHL seems not to have kept pace, but the explanation of this phenomenon may lie in the fact that junior or community colleges and the theological and Bible institutes have largely been omitted from the study.

The dispersion of location of colleges and professional schools seems to be a function of many and complex variables. Schools of education, nursing schools, graduate schools, colleges and schools of business or commerce appear to be somewhat uniformly distributed throughout the country in accordance with population, per capita income, etc. A major exception to this statement is the fact that only one school of business or commerce was instituted on the Pacific Coast in the decade 1945–1954. Relatively few law schools were established throughout the nation, and only two in the Northeast sector of the United States. More than one-half of all law schools established (five out of nine), were instituted in the South Atlantic and West South Central states. In large part this seems to be an attempt to remedy the deficiencies of the past.

Medical and dental schools were established rather sporadically throughout the country but tended to cluster in three major areas:

1. Middle Atlantic (largely New York)
2. The South
3. The Pacific Coast (largely California)

Engineering schools tended to appear in three clusters:

1. The East (New England and Middle Atlantic)
2. Southeast (South Atlantic and East South Central)
3. The Pacific Coast

On balance it would seem that the Mountain and the East North Central states have not adequately provided for collegiate and professional training. This generalization, however, must be tempered by the fact that there has been a vast expansion of some of the state schools in this area. Whatever deficiency does exist should not be associated with regional poverty, since neither of these areas is low in income.

The growth of IHL over time in the United States by geographic area is somewhat startling in that since 1939–40 there has been no really appreciable net gain in the number of IHL in the United States. Only some 100 institutions net have been established since that time, and this is all the more remarkable since these figures were obtained from the *Biennial Surveys of Education,* published by the Bureau of the Census, which include data on junior and community colleges. Strange though it may appear at first glance, a period of substantial creations of new IHL in the United States was that of the Great Depression. The only other period of anything resembling expansion of the ranks of IHL was in the four-year period immediately following World War II, and a large part of the expansion during this period stems from growth in the Pacific Coast area and the great number of veterans returning to college under the GI Bill.

The number of IHL within any one area is not always indicative of the educational adequacy of the area. Often these institutions are not accredited, and in some areas a relatively high proportion of them are Bible or theological schools. The South Atlantic states, with a total population of two-thirds that of the Middle Atlantic states, have approximately the same number of institutions, but there are differences in educational quality. If the number of institutions per member of the population were the relevant criterion, New England would rank highest, but such a measure alone would be of little value in assessing the educational adequacy of any one area, since it omits the major relevant factor of the average size of the institution.

Again, the differences among the several states are vast. Massachusetts has far more than doubled the number of IHL within her confines since 1927–28, while Missouri has had a net loss of one institution during the same period. In the case of almost all the states the major period of growth was the decade of the 1930s.

It is extremely difficult to draw any valid conclusions concerning the relation of the number of IHL within any one area, the rate of growth of population in the area, and the increase of personal and per capita income within the area.

Generally we would classify the East North Central, the South Atlantic, the West South Central, the Mountain, and the Pacific Coast states as rapidly expanding, whereas the Middle Atlantic, the New England, the East South Central, and the West North Central might be termed the group of slow expansion. This classification is based on rate of growth of population. In terms of per capita income, the alignment is somewhat different, since the poorer states are growing faster than the richer areas with the effect of a far smaller differential than previously existed.

When rate of growth of number of IHL is considered, New England emerges as the leading area, followed by the Pacific Coast and Middle Atlantic states. It would seem that the rate of growth of the number of IHL is not related to the rate of growth of population, nor even to per capita income over a longer period of time, but to a multitude of factors which might include the number of similar institutions already in the area, the availability of faculty, and the opportunity of attaining sufficient endowment capital.

COUNTY-DATA STUDY

The aim of this county-population–enrollment study was to determine the extent to which IHL tended to "pile up" in high population areas within a state.

We had the following data available: the population, number of IHL, and total IHL enrollment in each county in the United States as of 1950. It was decided to compute each county's population as a percentage of the total state population, and each county's IHL enrollment as a percentage of the total state IHL enrollment. The enrollment percentage divided by the population percentage would thus provide a useful index to determine whether a county had a large or small IHL enrollment in relation to its population. Three examples will suffice to illustrate:

County and state	Percentage of state population	Percentage of state enrollment	Index
1. Aroostook, Maine............	10.5	2.8	0.3
2. Cuyahoga, Ohio.............	17.5	17.1	1.0
3. New York, N.Y..............	13.2	38.6	2.9

The IHL enrollment in Aroostook County, with an index of 0.3, is far below its relative population status, whereas New York County (i.e., Manhattan) houses many more students than even its large population would suggest. Cuyahoga County (which includes Cleveland) has equal proportions of state population and state IHL enrollment.

In terms of the index, our investigation hypothesized the following:

1. A county with a large proportion (more than 15 per cent) of its state's population would have an index "comfortably" greater than unity. (We use the word "comfortably" quite loosely in the following sense: County A with 15 per cent of the state's population may have 30 per cent of the total enrollment. County B with 35 per cent of the state's population may have 50 per cent of the state's enrollment. A's index of 2.0 and B's index of 1.4 are both "comfortably" above unity.)

2. A county with a small proportion (less than 3 per cent) of its state's population would have an index below unity.

The purpose of the study, then, is to see whether or not the deviations are infrequent enough to be properly classed as "deviations from the norm."

It is worthwhile to reproduce here the data obtained for the State of Massachusetts (see Table 51-10). Massachusetts thus seems to conform

TABLE 51–10
Massachusetts

County	Population, per cent	Enrollment, per cent	Index
Berkshire...............	2.8	1.2	0.4
Bristol.................	8.1	0.3	0.04
Essex..................	11.1	1.9	0.2
Hampden..............	7.8	2.9	0.4
Hampshire.............	1.9	8.6	4.5
Middlesex.............	22.7	24.9	1.1
Norfolk................	8.4	2.5	0.3
Plymouth..............	4.0	0.7	0.2
Suffolk................	19.1	51.6	2.7
Worcester.............	11.6	5.3	0.5

quite well to hypotheses 1 and 2 above. Hampshire County (which contains the University of Massachusetts, Amherst College, Smith College, and Mt. Holyoke College) constitutes the only "deviate" in the state.

Unfortunately for our hypotheses, however, Massachusetts is in this respect quite different from the other 47 states. Observing the 2 largest (most populous) counties in each state, the distribution of their indices is 37 counties with indices below 1.0, 23 counties with indices from 1.0 to 1.3 inclusive, and 35 counties with indices greater than 1.3. Perhaps 50 per cent of these 95 counties contained only 3 to 10 per cent of the state population, but they were nevertheless the largest counties with IHL in the state.

Considering all 30 counties in the United States with at least 18 per cent of the state population, the distribution of indices is as follows: 8 counties with indices below 1.0, 12 counties with indices from 1.0 to 1.3 inclusive, and 10 counties with indices greater than 1.3.

At a still higher population level, the indices for all 18 counties with more than 25 per cent of the state population are distributed thus: 5 counties with indices below 1.0, 9 counties with indices from 1.0 to 1.3 inclusive, and 4 counties with indices above 1.3. Table 51-11 shows quite well the apparent *lack of "pile-up"* in the high-population counties.

TABLE 51-11
Distribution of Indices for High-population Counties

County population	Index		
	Below 1.0	1.0–1.3	Above 1.3
Top two per state..........................	37	23	35
18 per cent of population or above.........	8	12	10
More than 25 per cent of population........	5	9	4

Our next thought was to look at counties containing very large cities. The indices for the counties containing the 10 largest cities in the United States are as follows:

TABLE 51-12

City and state	County	Index
New York, N.Y...............	New York	2.9
Chicago, Ill..................	Cook	1.0
Philadelphia, Pa.............	Philadelphia	1.6
Los Angeles, Calif...........	Los Angeles	1.4
Detroit, Mich...............	Wayne	1.4
Baltimore, Md...............	Baltimore City	0.9
Cleveland, Ohio..............	Cuyahoga	1.0
St. Louis, Mo................	St. Louis	2.7
Boston, Mass................	Suffolk	2.7
San Francisco, Calif..........	San Francisco	1.1

This distribution conforms quite well with our hypothesis, with 6 out of the 10 having indices above 1.3 and 9 out of 10 having indices 1.0 or above. It seems quite reasonable that the use of standard metropolitan areas rather than counties would present even more meaningful (and generally higher) indices. Counties are merely arbitrary designations subject to considerable gerrymandering, whereas metropolitan areas have important economic meaning.

CONCLUSION 1

IHL tend to "pile up" in areas of considerable urban agglomeration, i.e., very large cities (not cities which are large merely in relation to the surrounding towns). These are areas of particular economic importance through highly developed distributive and service industries and, in many cases, high productive activity. Historically, IHL have always found large markets in these surroundings. This is still true today, and even with the recent growth of interregional student mobility, the IHL continue to derive benefits from the so-called "tertiary" economic development of very large cities.

CONCLUSION 2

The final fact brought out in this study is that very often large IHL seem to be located in areas of particularly low population. This is the case with agricultural and state universities, which are frequently located in areas with large spatial accommodations. The land-grant institutions have generally been given locales which were not overly important economically and which provided campus-space and farm land when necessary. (Compare Hampshire County in the Massachusetts distribution reproduced above.)

Deficient Utilization of Plant

Undoubtedly, utilization of space can be improved. President John Millett of Miami University has written[8] that

. . . a resident campus ought to set a 70 per cent average utilization per 39-hour week as its goal. Admittedly this is a substantial improvement over the proportion of use which now obtains on most campuses. For laboratories the goal should be 50 to 60 per cent utilization. Many institutions could almost double their enrollment on this basis alone. Such a high degree of utilization means course scheduling so that there will be more students in class on Tuesday, Thursday, and Saturday mornings and every week-day afternoon. . . .

In a similar vein, W. T. Middlebrook, in an able study based on the needs of the University of Minnesota, comments on the possibility of saving on space. Large increases of enrollment can be achieved through improved use of space. Current usage is far from optimal. In order to assess building needs of the college Middlebrook would not accept current use but would take into account also optimal use—though the latter is not easily attained. Building needs depend of course on future enrollment, in turn estimated on the basis of geographical origins of students, and allowances have to be made for crossovers, that is, the use of arts and science facilities, for example, by students in engineering.[9]

John Russell and James Doi, using as a base a study by the American Association of Collegiate Registrars and Admissions Officers, published a helpful study of space utilization.[10] Studies of utilization of space are important, according to these writers, because they reveal uneconomic practices. More effective use, achieved by eliminating costly space or increasing the use of available space, or even by *reducing the number of classes,* can greatly reduce costs of maintaining plant.

What particularly disturbed the writers was the primitive state of utilization studies even though there is an increased recourse to such studies to justify state budgetary requests. A somewhat more optimistic appraisal is made by Moos and Rourke, who pointed to useful studies in Kentucky, New Hampshire, Colorado, Minnesota, and Indiana.[11]

A committee of registrars in the spring of 1956 sent an inquiry to each of its 1,400 members, asking for reports on studies of space utilization. Only 961 responded, of which number 241, or 25 per cent, indicated that a study of plant space utilization had been made. But most studies were inadequate.

"The general impression to be gained from an examination of available space utilization is that relatively few reports showed imaginative planning and skillful execution. For the most part they are limited with respect to the kinds of plant space included, limited in techniques of analysis, and generally lacking in interpretative material. . . . "[12]

Helpful measures of utilization are suggested in the following examples:[13]

1. *Room-period use:* forty-four hour week; 50 instructional rooms, or 2,200 possible room periods. With 1,100 class meetings scheduled, the average "room-period use" would be twenty-two hours, or 50 per cent, on a weekly basis.

2. *Student-station-period use* (the number of hours that stations [e.g., seats] are occupied):

Class occupied, 22 hours
Average class, 45
Student-period use, 990
Student-station room with 60 stations
Student hours per week per station = 16.5 (990/60)

3. *Percentage of possible periods during the week the student stations are occupied:*

Weekly schedule, 44 hours
Stations in room, 60
Possible student-station periods, 2,640
Group of student stations occupied, 990
Percentage of possible student-station periods, 37.5

Most studies reveal an inadequate use of space. For example, a study of space utilization in Michigan reveals that the state IHL have a better record than private IHL in Michigan and of IHL generally in the country. Yet even the public IHL in Michigan reveal wastes.

The total hours (weekly schedule) for public IHL in Michigan varies from forty in Northern Michigan College to sixty-three in Wayne State University. Colleges in large metropolitan areas tend to use their space more efficiently than those without night students. In this connection Julian H. Levi, executive director of the South East Chicago Commission, notes that at the University of Chicago classes start at 7:00 A.M. and continue until 10 to 11 P.M.; but at another university, where the faculty commutes to suburbs, classes have to stop at 4:30 P.M. as a rule.

The percentage of possible student-station-period utilization in general classrooms in state-controlled IHL in Michigan in the fall term of 1956, based on a forty-four hour week, was as follows:[14]

Monday	42.7	Tuesday	33.6
Wednesday	38.5	Thursday	33.3
Friday	36.6	Saturday A.M.	5.9

Even so, classrooms . . . seats and laboratory desks are, on the average, occupied only one-third of the possible hours in a 44-period week in the state-controlled institutions in Michigan. During those periods when rooms are actually in use, about two-thirds of the student stations in these rooms are occupied on the average in state-controlled institutions in Michigan.

In a similar manner a study of the University System of Georgia revealed inadequate utilization of facilities. The writers emphasized especially the need of *centralized* assignment of space as a means toward effective use. One point brought out is the lack of proper relationship between class size and room capacity. For example, 125 class sessions in which enrollment was 20 or less were held in nonspecialized rooms in which the capacity was 20 or less; but 335 class sessions with enrollment under 20 met in classrooms with a capacity of 21 to 40, 126 in those with capacity of 41 to 60, 34 in rooms with a capacity of 61 to 100, and 6 in rooms with a capacity of over 100—or 501 classes were held in rooms with a capacity larger than required. For 12 IHL in Georgia it was found that for 422 nonspecialized rooms, from 8 A.M. to 12 noon only 89 were used at a maximum (90 per cent and up), 136 experienced high use (70 to 89 per cent), 67 normal (60 to 69 per cent), 93 low (45 to 59 per cent), and 37 very low (below 45 per cent). From 1 to 5 P.M. the respective figures were 2, 16, 34, 48, and 322. The scores varied greatly from institution to institution. At Georgia Tech, the rating was normal or higher for 130 out of 135 rooms in the morning, but for the University of Georgia 76 out of 128 rooms were normal and above—differences in location are relevant here.[15]

An interesting and amusing case is that of the study of plumbing-facilities requirements at Purdue University. Here a study of use of facilities by students was made. Apparently plans had been based on use of facilities by students in public schools, where the ratio was 1 facility per 35 students. But habits of college students varied from those of school children. The proper formula at Purdue, based on a questionnaire for Purdue students, was found to be 1 facility per 135 students—a very large saving indeed.[16]

This program of improved utilization has had much study in California: in the *Strayer Report* (1948), in the *Restudy Report* (1955), and in the master plan (1960). For example, the *Restudy Report* recommended that:

> The standard room utilization of classrooms in both the state colleges and the University of California be, on the average, 36 scheduled hours per week with class enrollment after the first month of the term or semester averaging 67 per cent of room capacity, i.e., the number of student stations the room will accommodate.

Similar high standards were to be attained in laboratories—twenty-four scheduled hours and 80 per cent of room capacity utilized. In order to achieve these high standards the writers would schedule three-hour courses on Monday, Wednesday, and Friday and on Tuesday, Thursday, and Saturday forenoon; require departments to schedule as many organized classes between 12 noon and 5 P.M. as between 8 A.M. and 12 noon;[17] offer more two-hour courses on Tuesdays and Thursdays; schedule three-hour courses in two meetings on Tuesdays and Thursdays; start classes on the half hour as a means of reducing resistance to room-hour class periods; schedule more regular classes in the evenings and Saturdays; consider a full four-quarter optimum. (The last is of course a more fundamental change.)[18]

Although the restudy suggested that these standards could be achieved— on the basis of experience at some colleges—the master plan five years later reflected doubts. Very few colleges had achieved such high standards. Hence, for state colleges and the University of California the master plan urged the maximum practical level " . . . but in no case shall [classrooms] average less than 30 scheduled hours per week, with class enrollments after the first month of the term averaging 60 per cent of room capacity."[19]

In California we also find careful estimates of required construction in the years to come. For example, on the basis of assured construction, capacity will rise from 272,719 (full-time enrollment) to 361,429, or an increase of 32.6 per cent. The rise would be 26 per cent for junior colleges, 59 per cent for state colleges, 51 per cent for the University of California, and 18 per cent for independent colleges and universities. Of the total rise of 79,000 the independent colleges and universities would account for only 11,000, or about 14 per cent.

By 1975 the projected enrollments would be 648,650, with 361,429 provided for by funded capacity. Hence construction funds have to be provided for 361,000 additional students.[20]

Conclusion

Plant use is much less efficient than it might be. Resistance of students and faculty to afternoon and Saturday classes is one important cause of waste.[21] But the responsibility lies in part with administration also. They have shown little interest in studying the utilization of plant.

Returns to a questionnaire on new IHL or new schools also reveal that the opening of these institutions or schools and their locations were often not subjects of adequate and careful examination. An over-all survey of professional schools also points to bad distribution. Large economies might be had by greater centralization of schools with high unit costs, combined with transportation subsidies for students.

In the light of the fact that total capital costs on existing plant are approaching $2 billion per year, an improved use of plant through increased access in unpopular hours, through improved matching of size of class and enrollment, through central control of assignment of space, through longer school year, through more considered establishment of new units and location on improved theories of location—through these and other means, savings as large as $1 billion a year by 1970 are within the realm of the possible.

FOOTNOTES

[1] HEW, *Memo to the Board*, 1960 Series, no. 4, 1960; HEW, *Council For Financial Aid to Education, 1958–1959*, 1959, p. 13.

[2] *A Study of the Need for Additional Centers of Public Higher Education in California*, 1957, pp. 131–32.

[3] "Geographic Origins of Michigan College Students," *The Survey of Higher Education in Michigan*, Staff Study no. 2, 1957, p. 31.

[4] Minnesota Commission on Vocational and Higher Education, *Higher Education Looks Ahead*, 1953, p. 13.

[5] I am indebted to Saul Hymans for the statistical work and much of the analysis of the problems of location of new schools and IHL.

[6] For an excellent statement on the relation of situs of new IHL and population and functional needs, distribution of functions and coordination of curricula, see Joint Staff of the Liaison Committee of the . . . California State Board of Education and the Regents of the University of California, *A Study of the Need for State Colleges in the North Bay Area*, 1958, appendix A.

[7] To save space I have omitted the tables upon which this analysis is based.

[8] J. D. Millett, "Colleges Can and Must be More Efficient," *College Admissions*, 5, 1958, p. 56.

[9] W. T. Middlebrook, *How To Estimate the Building Needs of a College or University*, 1958, esp. pp. 1–12.

[10] Russell and Doi, *Manual for Studies of Space Utilization in Colleges and Universities*, 1957, esp. pp. 1–23.

[11] Moos and Rourke, *Campus and the State*, pp. 138–39.

[12] Russell and Doi, *op. cit.*, p. 15.

[13] *Ibid.*, pp. 21–22.

[14] "Space Utilization and Value of Physical Plants in Michigan Institutions of Higher Education," *The Survey of Higher Education in Michigan*, Staff Study no. 9, June, 1958, pp. 82, 96, 124, 128; and *Senate Banking and Currency Hearings, Housing Act of 1959*, p. 503.

[15] *A Report of a Survey of the University System of Georgia*, 1949, pp. 104–112.

[16] *A Sample Survey Design Using the Operations Research Queueing Theory for Establishing Plumbing Facility Requirements*, Purdue University Statistical Laboratory, April, 1954.

[17] Such a requirement at Ohio State University made possible an increase of enrollment from 12,000 to 24,000 with less than 10 per cent increase in floor space.

[18] California State Department of Education, *A Restudy of the Needs of California in Higher Education*, 1955, pp. 319–321.

[19] *A Master Plan for Higher Education in California, 1960–1975*, 1959, p. 117.

[20] *Ibid.*, pp. 104, 109.

[21] President Meredith Wilson has suggested that faculty might be more amenable if in return for longer span of class use they were given adequate office space. American Council for Education, *Expanding Resources for College Education*, 1956. p. 112.

Chapter 52

TELEVISION

Clarence Faust, president of the Fund for the Advancement of Education, has well said: "We could seize upon television as *the* means of education, neglecting the other ingredients of educational processes that are necessary for the development of human intelligence. Or we might, and perhaps the danger of this course is more real, make the equally sad mistake of neglecting this great and powerful means of communication."[1]

There can be no doubt that much progress has been made. A Michigan State University survey made during 1955–56 showed a total of some 280 separate television courses being offered by 69 different colleges and universities. Since that time the total has risen to almost 400 courses.[2]

Carpenter, of Pennsylvania State University, one of the leading experimenters in this field, has said that at the State University they have used " . . . television in chemistry lecture demonstrations, psychology, sociology, economics, business law, speech, German, education, music appreciation, air science, engineering, meteorology, and theatre. On the basis of evidence, systematic observations and critical judgments, we judge television is or can be adapted appropriately for most of these courses. . . ."[3]

The writer of the following passage[4] may be a little too optimistic, but we cannot be sure.

Perhaps by the end of the century the average student will be both living and *learning* in a small but comfortable room into which the world's entire store of knowledge—not only as recorded in books, but also as then recorded on film and tape, in three-dimensional color, with sound, perhaps even touch, taste, smell and essence of thought can be brought to the individual student at his pressing a button on the end of whatever will then have supplanted co-axial cable. We may not have anything quite that fantastic within a decade or two, but we cannot imagine the technological developments that will occur within half the life of the buildings we are constructing today.

What are the objectives of televised education? Obviously television must be used as part of the program of the particular college. It should be fitted to the objectives of the educational institution. One observer has noted that the capacity of television to handle information, both visual and aural, is " . . . analagous to the capacities of high speed digital computers . . . ."[5] Users of television also emphasize that in education the visual techniques have not been used as much as the aural.

As Carpenter puts it, "By linking the distribution capacities of television with the information storage capacities of film, the instructional input resources can be greatly increased and broadened. . . . "[6]

It is obvious that television can make a large contribution, though it would vary greatly with subject matter. For example, at Rensselaer Polytechnic Institute television on a closed circuit has been found very effective in a course on materials. Previously it was difficult for more than five students to be present at a class where the effects of various external influences on materials were studied. With closed-circuit television it is possible to have a class of 50 or 75, each getting a better view of what goes on than was previously possible in a class of 5. In a surgical operation under colored television not only can more students be instructed, but each observer gets a better view of what is happening. Faust has questioned whether the educational world could have enlisted the cooperation of a great physicist like Zacharias if the television were not available to broadcast the results of his revised school physics course. The same applies to White's course in physics.

Others have pointed out further instructional advantages of television. It often makes possible more effective use of teachers for large audiences. Great teachers are scarce, and television makes more use of limited resources. In the light of the increased enrollment expected in the next ten years this will be very important.

It may be asked why large classes could not be held just as well without television. One reason is that physical facilities are not available for these large classes. With television an outstanding instructor can televise his performance and be heard in rooms of varying size with a proctor present in each room. And in the RPI experiment it was pointed out how much cheaper it would be to televise a program from a studio than to reproduce several laboratories for the treatment of materials that would be required otherwise. This is an issue of economy rather than effective teaching, though with the shortage of teachers the two problems are interrelated.

Another great advantage of television is that it can be combined with other aids. Movies, kinescopes, etc., may be used. It may be true, as one observer notes, that so far we have had not televised instruction but rather instruction televised. By this he means that the television instructors have not exploited all the programming possibilities of television.

Still another observer notes that television makes possible, say, a thirty- or forty-minute program followed immediately by discussion in small rooms. In this way the students do not have to wait several days before they deal with the issues raised in the lecture.[7]

Undoubtedly one of the main objectives of using television is to save money. The result, however, may very well be that there are actually no monetary savings but that the faculty does a much more effective job. Faust points out that the use of television may result in much greater demand for the outstanding teachers, and their salaries may rise accordingly. One of the great failures in the structure of pay in colleges is that there are few really large prizes. This may have some effect in recruiting staff, though I would not put great emphasis on it. There is some difference of opinion on the issue of whether television really saves money or not. On the whole, the evidence points to savings.

Before one introduces television, one should make a careful investigation of the unit costs. President Walker of Pennsylvania State University, one of the institutions experimenting widely with television, says that on the basis of one thousand hours of operation, costs are about $26 per hour. The break-even point comes at about 200 students; that is to say, savings are not likely if there are fewer than 200 students in a course.[8]

One observer of the various experiments sponsored by the Fund for the Advancement of Education wrote as follows:

There is no reason, in theory, that the various ideas used in the experimental programs should not enable experienced college instructors to teach much greater numbers of students than they have and just as effectively. *This* should be the result of larger classes, the use of assistants, improved methods, the use of machines and audio-visual aids, independent study and streamlined curricula. . . .

One of the difficult problems is the distance between teacher and student. Television has the effect of removing the teacher from the student. The important problem is "feedback." But feedback is not merely a matter of question and answer. If the televised program is well done, the student may think more and this might be sufficient. At any rate, techniques in television have improved greatly since the early days. At first the tendency was to put a camera on a teacher and the surrounding students. This made the students watching who were not in the studio feel they were spectators rather than participants. A more recent and effective technique is to have the teacher in the studio without students, and the students in other rooms with the possibility of two-way communication. The student may ask questions of the professor in the studio, and the professor may answer these questions.

Many who favor television are nevertheless disappointed that most of the results show no appreciable difference as compared with conventional methods. They think that television should show a considerably better performance. That it does not is undoubtedly in part the result of the rather primitive state of television even today, and we may expect large improvements. As has been shown in our discussion of size of classes, however, many other factors determine the final results as given by tests. One view is that television has given disappointing results because of the failure to integrate television with all the other visual aids. Another factor of some importance is the frequent use of bad equipment and poor technological advice. Still another consideration is that television is an entirely new method of communication for the average college professor. He should have some training in the technique, and more important, he should be given adequate time for preparation. It is even conceivable that a one-hour performance on television where the course is important and reaches large numbers should be a full week's stint for the average lecturer. Moreover, if the results were measured by allowing the best teachers to perform in television—as seems appropriate—then the gains of television might be found to be greater.

Observers of the Fund for the Advancement of Education experiments have raised some interesting questions concerning visual aids.[9]

Visual aids will undoubtedly play an increasing role in the teaching of college students. Therefore their "promise" would seem to be a matter of quality and of teaching effectiveness. Much that is purely expository can be conveyed more clearly by pictures than by words. But the student's knowledge and understanding of the subject are likely to be measured in large part through the use of words, and we may find a falling off, either apparent or real, in the results of visual teaching as compared to verbal teaching. The use of motion pictures and television in place of laboratory experience is a special case which I leave to others for comment.

* * *

Television made considerable progress in the 1950s. (I concentrate here on its use in higher education.) Yet William G. Harley, President of the National Association of Educational Broadcasters, testifying before a Senate committee, pointed out that only 20 great universities had a TV station for educational purposes. Great pressure is being put on the Federal government to finance construction of TV stations for educational purposes. Without this help, it is estimated that 200 of the 250 frequencies allocated for education would lie fallow. (A Senate bill, providing up to $1 million per state for this purpose, was passed unanimously.) Undoubtedly with Federal aid for capital purposes the construction of educational TV would increase greatly.[10]

Among the contributions of TV are large audiences, particularly of extension students working for credit. The Chicago Junior College has been broadcasting a home-television education program since September, 1956. The estimated audience was 30,000 to 50,000 for viewing. In six semesters there were almost 30,000 registrations for courses, more than one-quarter of these on a for-credit basis. These students were more mature and more able than the on-campus students.[11]

"Continental Classroom" in 1960 was reaching an estimated 414,000 viewers for a 6:30 A.M. course in Modern Chemistry. At 6 A.M. 66,000 persons watched the rerun of "Atomic Age Physics," a course which had attracted 400,000 viewers in the preceding year.[12] In 1959 the Fund for the Advancement of Education estimated that since 1953, when the first educational television station began operations, the number had risen to 39, and 12 more were under construction. These of course are not only for higher education. There are more than 150 closed-circuit installations in schools and colleges. The Fund lists 117 IHL that offer televised courses for credit.[13] The estimate by John E. Ivey, Jr., in early 1959 was 256 colleges.[14]

At Penn State, one of the leaders in televised instruction, the university, through closed-circuit television, offered 46 television courses in 1956–57 in fields as diverse as chemistry, music, speech, air science, and sociology.[15]

One of the most interesting projects is one planned by the Southern Regional Education Board (SREB). The proposed network provides " . . . for the interconnection of 309 institutions in 16 states, a route of 10,446 miles. There would be 32 points of program origin serving institutions with a current enrollment of over 600,000 students." Each participating institution could receive five courses simultaneously. These institutions spend about $240 million for instruction and an estimated $360 million by 1970. Capital costs for a 16-state microwave network would be $204 million, and annual costs of operation, inclusive of depreciation, would be $22.5 million. On the assumption that television would provide one-third of the courses, Ivey estimates that the cost per semester-hour by 1967 would be $2.80 as compared to $12 to $18 per semester-hour in some of the larger IHL in the South.[16]

These estimates reflect large savings from televised instruction. Similar conclusions—though not quite so promising—are to be found in the studies at Penn State mentioned earlier. According to a recent study of the Penn State experience, the operating costs of the Dage 320 Vidicon professional system as installed at Penn State, inclusive of depreciation and obsolescence, was $28,552 in 1956–57, or $26.64 per hour of operation. *Total* costs for four courses by conventional methods were $91,000; by TV, $52,000, or a net gain of $39,000. For these courses the student credit-unit costs were $9.48 by conventional methods and $5.44 by television, the largest differences being revealed in the large air science course—$8.47. Obviously, as numbers increase, the gains of televised instruction rise. At an enrollment of 135, conventional instruction costs $2.46 less per student credit unit; at 675, television costs $2.97 less; and at 1,216, $4.05 less.[17]

Despite the great advances made in the use of TV in higher education, I doubt that as much as 1 per cent of total instruction or instructional costs are incurred in the on-campus instructional costs through the use of television. Thus the Educational Facilities Laboratories estimated that 100,000 students received part of their instruction in courses for credit from television. But even if they received such instruction in one full course, this would account for less than 1 per cent of total instruction. Even Penn State, perhaps the outstanding IHL in television instruction, had only 46 courses televised in the spring of 1957. Surely this amounted to a very small percentage of all courses. The current enrollment at this institution is about 20,000 and the number of faculty 1,700. If each faculty member gave only two courses, the televised instruction would account for 1 to 2 per cent of instruction, though a larger part of the student hours in class.

One may ask why so little progress has been made. Television is still a matter of secondary importance in higher education on the campus, that is, without consideration of extension work and broadcasting for the public.

One explanation is the conservatism of faculties. "A distinguished professor once remarked that it took about fifty years for a new idea to gain general acceptance in American education." In one article[18] a professor said frankly that

. . . they [the professors] are dubious of the emphasis currently placed on the capacity of ETV to reach a greater number of students, and if this emphasis is set forth as the major gain of ETV over conventional classroom teaching, the ETV planners will have difficulty in convincing professors that television is a more effective device than loud-speakers in an auditorium.

Faculty members have all kinds of reservations about TV instruction. A survey of the Penn State faculty revealed about thirty objections to TV instruction, the most frequently mentioned being lack of contact and individual attention (26 per cent), no feedback (17), impersonal (14), no student questions (13), not applicable to course (13).

Of a sample of 55 non-TV teachers, 22 per cent believed TV instruction to be better, 38 per cent expressed no preference, and 38 per cent held TV to be worse. Among the TV teachers (a small sample) the respective figures were 61, 23, and 8 per cent. Of 140 non-TV teachers, 14 per cent would very much like to experiment with TV, 31 per cent would probably like to, 23 per cent probably would dislike to, and 23 per cent expressed no special feeling. Of 140 non-TV teachers, 34 per cent preferred television over direct instruction in large classes, 41 per cent preferred large non-TV classes, and 17 per cent had no preference: for 15 TV teachers, the respective figures were 74, 12, and 7 per cent.[19]

In some respects the fears of teachers are to be explained by the assumed effects on employment. But the Penn State analysis reveals that a relatively small number admit to such fears. Though among non-TV teachers the majority clearly are doubtful about TV instruction, a large number would prefer TV instruction by an able teacher to non-TV instruction by less able professors. Yet about three times as many of the non-TV faculty would prefer to send their children to IHL with nontelevised instruction.[20]

One reason for doubt is the effectiveness of TV instruction—and that despite the many studies which show that there is no significant difference in the results between televised and orthodox methods. In 110 different comparisons involving 14,326 television students and 12,666 control students of equal ability, 68 tests favored the former and 42 the latter. Of the 38 cases where there was a statistically significant difference, 29 were in favor of television.[21]

Yet some questions continue to be raised concerning the validity of these tests. On the whole, the tests usually measure accumulation of knowledge. They fail to measure any gains, for example, from the give and take in the usual classrooms. Some of the inadequacies of the usual tests are well described by Henry Dyer, of the Educational Testing Service.

> The goals of achievement fall into three broad classes: informational goals, proficiency goals, and attitudinal goals. . . .
> Most of what I think of as the higher aspects of learning are contained in what I have called the proficiency goals of academic achievement; that is proficiency in various kinds of skills, both manual and mental—manipulative, problem-solving, evaluative, and organizational skills. . . .

Thus in comparisons of TV and ordinary instruction in laboratory work, the favorable results for television are found only because the emphasis is on accumulation of information, not on proficiency.[22]

Students on the whole are not too enthusiastic about television. They prefer small groups and more intimate contact with the faculty. But they make it clear that they prefer a first-class teacher in television to a second-rate one in the classroom. In general the poor students seem to experience greater difficulties with television than the better students. In a study at Penn State where students had an opportunity in a chemistry course to listen under regular procedures and under television, 187 out of 589 students (32 per cent) " . . . preferred instruction over television strongly enough to leave the large class in the lecture hall and return to the TV classrooms for the rest of the semester." What is especially interesting is that, whereas about 15 per cent in the first 6 rows in the conventional science lecture hall preferred television, almost 50 per cent in the last 7 rows (13 to 19) preferred television. Approximately 46 per cent of the students in large TV rooms in a psychology section preferred TV presentation, and 65 per cent who had received instruction in small TV rooms. In general there is increasing evidence that the quality of the instructor, the nature of the materials, and manner of presentation play an increasing part in the attitude of the students—not so much whether the manner of presentation is by TV or direct. At the current writing, however, the students still seem to prefer direct to televised instruction, *ceteris paribus*. But conditions are not always equal. At Miami University, 86 per cent of the students expressed a preference for a teacher of known excellence in a large TV class to a random instructor in a conventional class.[23]

In summary, this is to be said about televised instruction: TV has something to offer. Its contribution is likely to grow and become substantial; but it is only one of many approaches to the solution of our problems.

What are the main contributions of TV? Where an outstanding teacher is available, TV offers a medium for his most effective use—on the assumption that the subject matter can be adapted to TV, that the teacher gets the training required for this task, and that he gets the credit—e.g., two TV hours = full-time teaching—so that he can prepare adequately. The advantage of TV in a sense is similar to that of a well-written and publishable lecture over the rambling lecture generally presented in a classroom. TV teaching also offers an opportunity for the teacher to be observed, both as a source of constructive criticism for him and as training for others.

TV may also contribute toward conservation of resources. Substantial savings are available for the large classes, even with an outlay of $50,000 for closed-circuit equipment. Once, as is anticipated, equipment for video tape recordings becomes available for $10,000 ($50,000 today), then the use of TV may become cost-saving even in moderate-sized classes.[24]

Savings through TV may be similar to those discussed from an increased number of large classes. In some respects the savings may be larger, because large numbers can be handled through distribution of students for viewing in all available classes, irrespective of size. This advantage probably outweighs the diseconomy involved in the cost of TV equipment. The savings in dollars may be considered a contribution toward solving the serious financial problems of higher education, or may be siphoned off for the purpose of improving instruction—e.g., incentive pay for the TV team, the lecturer, the assistants who work directly with the students.

But we should not overweight the contribution of televised instruction. Even if all the instruction in the lower division (first two years) could be televised, only about one-third of the instructional costs would be relevant. Though enrollment in the upper division is substantially less than in the lower division and graduate enrollment only 10 per cent of the total, nevertheless these two account roughly for two-thirds of instructional costs; and these are the areas where TV is not likely to be helpful—at least with current technology and costs.

Moreover, even in the lower division many courses are not likely to gain from television. A large lecture room seating, say, 600, may be just as well taught in the conventional manner as by TV. The latter is advantageous where experiments, many groups, and the like are required—e.g., the chemistry course discussed above—and large lecture rooms are not to be had. To give an example, at Harvard, Economics I enrolls about 600 students, with instruction almost exclusively by section meetings of 25 to 30 in a section, taught primarily by teaching fellows and a few instructors (Ph.D.s). Many of these young men and women are able and are good teachers. But I am reasonably certain that a first-class lecturer could be more effective; and since the amount of visual material is small and a lecture room available, the course could be handled in the conventional method through lectures. Savings would be large, and part could be used to finance small seminars once a week.

What is perhaps most troublesome to students and teachers is the lack of contact and feedback in the televised courses. This is of course a problem in all large classes, and a special problem in televised instruction only in so far as classes are larger and because of the absence of a direct contact with the teacher. In the feedback improvisations in TV, the students still seem dissatisfied; for what they want is direct contact with the lecturer, not with graduate assistants present in their viewing rooms.

The only answer I can give here is one similar to the Ruml reply: We should have a larger number of large classes, and many of these televised. We should eliminate, wherever it is possible—and it often is not in the advanced courses—the intermediate-sized classes, say, from 25 to 75—and increase greatly the number of seminars and—where financially feasible—tutorials. Then the student will have an adequate opportunity to discuss problems with his teachers.[25]

Recently Gordon Ray quoted a statement by Newman of 100 years ago: "A university ideally should be an alma mater, knowing her children one by one, not a foundry, or a mint, or a treadmill." Indeed this is an ideal. But it is not realized today and will be even less so by 1970. The case against television is largely the case against large classes generally. The case for television is the more effective use of the *great* teacher—he is largely wasted on groups of 5 to 25—and the economies made available through large classes to finance much greater recourse to small-group instruction.

FOOTNOTES

[1] American Council on Education, *College Teaching by Television*, 1958, p. 151.
[2] HEW, *Television and Education*, 1957, pp. 71–72.
[3] C. R. Carpenter, "That's Teaching by TV," *College and University Business*, March, 1958, pp. 45 and 46.

[4] D. E. Smith, "Better Utilization—but Watch Out!" *ibid.,* August, 1958, p. 17.

[5] American Council on Education, *op. cit.,* p. 11.

[6] *Ibid.,* p. 12.

[7] See G. F. Freese, "Exploring the Possibilities of Teaching by Closed-circuit TV," *College and University Business,* February, 1958, pp. 24–26.

[8] American Council on Education, *op. cit.,* p. 72; C. R. Carpenter, *op. cit.,* p. 47.

[9] Apart from the items already mentioned in this section, I should note the following: Pennsylvania State University, *Summary, Abstracts and Bibliography of Studies of Class Size;* Fund for the Advancement of Education, *Better Utilization of College Teaching Resources: A Second Year's Experiment: A Report by the Committee on Utilization of College Teaching Resources,* October, 1957; *ibid.,* October, 1956; and also the mimeographed notes of observers which I have quoted in a few instances.

[10] *Senate Committee on Interstate and Foreign Commerce, Hearings on Educational Television,* 1959, p. 68.

[11] C. A. Siepman, *TV and Our Schools,* 1958, pp. 100–105, 130–132; Educational Facilities Laboratories, *Design for ETV: Planning for Schools with Television,* 1960, p. 22.

[12] *Ibid.,* p. 22.

[13] *Teaching by Television,* 1959, pp. 3–4, 69–72.

[14] *Senate . . . Hearings on Educational Television,* 1959, p. 23.

[15] The Pennsylvania State University, *Instructional Television Research,* Report No. 2, *Academic Years 1955–56 and 1956–57,* 1958, p. 5.

[16] *Senate . . . Hearings on Educational Television,* 1959, p. 26.

[17] The Pennsylvania State University, *op. cit.,* pp. 101–105.

[18] W. P. Fidler, "Educational Television: A Faculty Point of View," *AAUP Bulletin,* June, 1959, pp. 209–217, esp. p. 210.

[19] The Pennsylvania State University, *op. cit.,* pp. 67–69.

[20] *Ibid.,* p. 72.

[21] A Report from the Ford Foundation and the Fund for the Advancement of Education, *Teaching by Television,* 1959, pp. 9–10, and The Pennsylvania State University, *op. cit.,* pp. 10–38.

[22] American Council on Education, *op. cit.,* pp. 115–120, esp. pp. 116–117.

[23] The Pennsylvania State University, *op. cit.,* pp. 73–94; C. A. Siepman, *op. cit.,* pp. 125–129, 142–143; Macomber and Siegel, "A Study in Large-group Teaching Procedures," *The Educational Record,* July, 1957, pp. 225–227.

[24] Educational Facilities Laboratories, *op. cit.,* p. 22.

[25] Aside from the references mentioned, the following should be noted: *House Subcommittee on Interstate and Foreign Commerce, Hearings on Educational Television,* May, 1959; Report no. 56, *Educational Television,* February, 1959; J. E. Ivey, Jr., "Television, Educational Quality and Dollars," *The Educational Record,* January, 1959, pp. 53–61; C. H. Faust, *ibid.,* January, 1958, pp. 44–51; W. W. Turnbull, "Making the Most of a Scarce Resource," *Expanding Resources for Education,* 1956, pp. 92–95; E. Earnest, "Must the Technicians Take Over the Colleges?" *AAUP Bulletin,* September, 1958, pp. 575–581; Educational Facilities Laboratories, *Here They Learn,* First Annual Report of 1959, p. 20.

CONCLUSION: COSTS AND ECONOMIES

If we are to obtain the required resources, we must make effective use of what we have or are likely to get. IHL are subject to criticism for operating inefficiently. A former president of a major university told me that a great university could perform better at half the cost if the president had a free hand. This may be optimistic. IHL do not operate like the profit corporations. The faculty are not employees, but rather part of the management. They do not accept orders from the administration on such matters as curriculum or the choice of faculty. If they did, the universities would soon lose their freedom and the uninhibited search for knowledge. Yet it is possible to operate more efficiently through cooperation of trustees, administration, and faculty. Most faculty members have a surprisingly limited knowledge of the relation of economical management and the effectiveness of the task they perform or their own economic status. They do not seem to be aware that, aside from their pay in dollars, they accept compensation in the form of many courses which nobody wants or needs but the one who gives the course. Elimination of excessive courses, or courses too costly in terms of their educational contribution, could make an important source of additional income for faculty.

Hence the importance of improved planning; of rational choices of sites of new colleges and curricula; of cooperation among colleges to avoid excessive duplication through alternation or elimination of courses where not justified by educational contribution; of eliminating concentration of courses at 10 A.M. to 12 noon on Monday, Wednesday, and Friday (at the pleasure of the instructor); of careful scrutiny of outlays not directly related to the educational process; of exploitation of mechanical aids; of discontinuing the practice of requiring (say) a $20,000 faculty member to spend a substantial part of his time on tasks that should cost at the rate of $2,000 to $4,000 (e.g., research, secretarial, paper grading); of providing cost data for all programs as a guide to administrators in choosing alternative educational programs or the roads to educational objectives; of improved counseling to reduce the attrition of students at college and to enhance the chances of a choice related to the students' abilities and needs; and of adapting the size of the college to minimizing costs, or at least justifying uneconomic size by educational gains.

To supplement the above, I summarize the results of 160 replies to my questionnaire on economies. The respondents on the whole did not systematically survey courses in relation to educational objectives. Course alternation as a program to reduce wastes was used infrequently. Apparently one-quarter used visual aids, but most on a small scale. As a rule, the college administrators considered a cut in classroom hours by students as a deterioration in the quality of instruction. But about 50 per cent of the private IHL, and a somewhat larger percentage of public IHL, had started or expanded programs for independent studies. More than half of the IHL claimed that they had introduced economies in the utilization of existing facilities.

PART EIGHT

FACULTY

Chapter 53

FACULTY STATUS

DECLINE OF ECONOMIC STATUS

At the outset I should say that college teachers do not put as much emphasis on economic status as most members of the working population. They will often stay at one institution or move to another when there are substantial economic disadvantages involved. They do not primarily seek high economic rewards, or they would not have chosen teaching in the first place. Big prizes might attract some who otherwise would not teach but would they be the dedicated researchers and teachers? The college teacher often values the quality of his colleagues and students, time for research, the privilege of seeking the truth without interference, and genuine tenure, a condition for noninterference in the quest for truth, more than his pay scale.

But he must have an adequate income to be free to teach and search without serious financial obstacles. He needs working conditions free of material worries, and a home to entertain students, faculty, and his friends. And since he prizes education so highly, he should have money enough to provide his own children with the best schooling available. Moreover, he does not want to be pitied nor, as Barber has said, does he wish to operate like a monk in a society where the ethos to support the austere life is no longer present.

We cannot disregard competitive issues. If industry or practice (e.g., medical) offers material rewards greatly exceeding those in teaching, the result may be serious losses of potential teachers. Even the California Institute of Technology finds it difficult to compete with an offer to one of its faculty members of $750,000 in stock options as an inducement to join a business firm.

In a statement from Harvard to Harvard alumni of May 18, 1905, the issues were well put. At that time 13 members of the Harvard faculty received $5,000 or more; all professors (57) received an average of $3,980; 38 assistant professors, $2,130; and 88 instructors, $990.

The heart of the University is the College, the Alma Mater which receives the boys from their homes and leads them into her spirit and high traditions. The heart of the College is the teachers. The position of Harvard today among American Universities is due not so much to its age, traditions, or able administration as to its noble line of teachers. That the teachers in the College should be the best in the land; that the older professors should be free from the cares of a straitened income; that the younger teachers should be able to give themselves without distraction to their work; that the best men should not be drawn away to other Colleges but should see before them reasonable promotion in work and salary, is essential to the leadership of Harvard and the culture of her sons.

Great gifts have been made for special objects and different departments of the University in recent years, but the addition to the endowment of the teaching force of the old College has been comparatively small. Meanwhile students, teachers, subjects and courses have multiplied. The classics, philosophy, modern languages, history, mathematics, the standard studies, have all increased their corps of teachers.

With what results?

Facing deficits in seven of the past nine years, the Corporation has now cut down the general expenses to the danger point, has refused the usual advance in salaries and reduced the standard of salaries of new teachers until on December 14, 1904, the Overseers passed this vote:

"That it is the sense of this Board that salaries of professors and instructors should be maintained and that the customary and expected increase of salary be paid in every instance, irrespective of any other economies."

In these days of increasing cost of living and of higher salaries in commercial and industrial pursuits, the Alumni and friends of Harvard will not allow the men who teach their boys and who fill the chairs of the great teachers of the past to receive these meagre wages.

The time has now come when the sons of Harvard may rally to her help and in grateful love make her the gift of an endowment of at least $2,500,000, to increase the present totally inadequate amount available for the salaries of the teaching staff of the College.

There have been periods when the teacher has gained ground relative to the rest of the community, such as the last part of the nineteenth century. George Stigler holds that then teachers' salaries rose more over a period of fifty years than did the income of the rest of the community.[1] But Ruml's statistics for the Fund for the Advancement of Education show that since the beginning of the twentieth century the college teacher has lost ground in relation to the country as a whole.

In the early years of his regime, President Eliot made quite an impression by increasing the salary of a Harvard professor to $4,000. Before the Civil War a figure of $2,000 was considered very high. We should compare the $4,000 soon after the Civil War with the average of $16,000[2] for professors at Harvard today. If one allows for the average rise of per capita income during this period, however, it is clear that there has been no gain for the Harvard professor in relation to the rest of the population. In fact, in 1960–61 the pay of a full professor in dollars of stable purchasing power is less at Harvard and other prestige universities than it was in 1930.

In fact, some crude statistics show the following rises in 90 years:

Rise of salary of full professor at Harvard.... 4   times*
Rise of prices............................ 2.2 times
Rise of per capita income.................. 13   times

* The rise is close to 4¾ times if allowance is made for the increase of fringe benefits. (Almost $19,000 in 1962)

Real income for the senior faculty members rose over this period, but the gains of income for the whole population greatly exceeded those of professors at Harvard. This is even more true if allowance is made for the larger taxes today on higher incomes.

Nelson of Amherst reveals[3] that the average Amherst professor in 1904 was receiving roughly $200 more in 1956–57 dollars, than in 1956–57, a decline from $9,915 to $9,724. The associate professor's pay increased by $900, about 15 per cent, and the instructor's by $540, about 13 per cent. If we allow for the rise in real income for the average American, it is quite clear that the Amherst professor suffered a serious relative decline in his economic position over this period. What is more, and this is of course a most relevant consideration, the proportion of full professors at Amherst declined from 50 to 37 per cent of the total faculty, associate professors from 29 to 16 per cent, with little change in instructors and an increase of assistant professors from 0 to 24½ per cent. A decline in the proportion of senior faculty members suggests a greater deterioration in economic status than is shown by a comparison of average income by rank. From 1946 to 1956, the proportion of senior members at Amherst actually rose, however.[4]

What is more, Nelson points out that in this period of fifty years there was a *real* increase (i.e., in stable dollars) of tuition of more than 100 per cent and a rise of national income per capita much in excess of this; yet the real income of the Amherst faculty had changed very little. Apparently the demands on tuition income, other than for faculty salary, had risen greatly.

Since before World War II, in the nation generally, the average age of faculty seems to have declined, a trend explained in part by the large increase in numbers. In so far as this is true, the economic status of faculty has not deteriorated as much as might be suggested by crude figures. (This conclusion on the trend toward a more youthful faculty is based on interviews in more than one hundred IHL.)

In 1920, according to one study,[5] the median salary of a president or chancellor was $6,000, of a dean or director $3,500, of a professor $3,000, of an associate professor $2,500, an assistant professor $2,000, an instructor $1,500, and an assistant $750. These were indeed low salaries at the peak of an inflation. In 1915–16 the maximum pay for a professor was $2,423 in institutions with less than 26 faculty members, and the rate of pay varied little for larger institutions until the number of faculty members rose above 200, when the maximum salary increased to an amount in excess of $4,000.[6]

Incidentally, it is relevant to point out that there is a positive correlation between the size of the institution and faculty salaries. Since the average IHL today is several times as large as early in the century (a factor making for lower unit costs), the rise of salary may well be associated in part with this trend toward bigness. Hence it is of some relevance to show that at any one time salaries are higher in bigger IHL.

Differences are especially large for the bigger institutions in the higher ranks. Since small colleges are economically less efficient, the higher salaries in the larger institutions may be explained to some extent by economies of scale and to some extent by their capacity to bid for higher paid and perhaps better faculty members[7] (see Table 53-1).

TABLE 53-1

Comparison of Mean Salaries by Size of Enrollment and by Teaching Ranks
for Those Employed No More Than Ten Months, 1957–58

Enrollment	Professor		Assoc. prof.		Asst. prof.		Instructor	
	Public	Private	Public	Private	Public	Private	Public	Private
200–499	$5,920	$5,310	$5,250	$4,710	$4,960	$4,230	$5,050	$3,810
500–999	7,110	6,400	6,030	5,360	5,100	4,650	5,160	4,010
1,000–1,999	7,380	6,980	6,300	5,750	5,550	5,000	5,160	4,390
2,000–4,999	7,370	7,380	6,240	6,000	5,470	5,070	4,870	4,320
5,000–9,999	8,410	8,600	6,790	6,600	5,860	5,470	5,260	4,560
10,000–19,999	9,530	9,140	7,460	6,650	6,240	5,600	5,070	4,520
20,000 and more	10,420	10,040	7,830	7,270	6,480	5,730	5,350	4,530

Source: W. Robert Bokelman, *Higher Education Planning and Management Data, 1957–58*, U.S. Office of Education Circular 517, 1958, p. 27.

* * *

The great inflation in World War I seriously reduced the real income of college faculties. It was not until 1932 that the college professor had achieved a purchasing power equivalent to what it had been before the World War I inflation. From 1940 to 1957, the purchasing power of faculty pay again declined, though in the latter part of this period the *abso-*

lute losses were recouped to a considerable extent. A rough estimate reveals that faculty members lost about $2 billion in purchasing power. Had their incomes kept up with that of the population, their gain would have been about $5 to $6 billion in seventeen years.[8] Hence even if the college teacher once more obtains an income equal to prewar purchasing power, he has nonetheless suffered a serious deterioration in his standard of living for many years, and a more or less permanent relative loss. But I add that by 1939–40 *real* Faculty salaries were about 20 per cent higher than in 1929–30.

From 1939 to 1956 the national per capita *disposable* personal income (i.e., after direct taxes) in dollars of stable purchasing power rose by 62 per cent, and in relation to 1930, by 73 per cent. If one considers income before taxes, one notes that the *real* income of the average American rose by more than 100 per cent, at the same time that that of the college teacher fell.

In still another respect, the costs to the academic profession were greater than so far suggested: the rise of salaries in current dollars was not the same in different areas. Where competition for teachers was keen (e.g., the competition between medical faculty and practitioners), there was a relatively large salary increase. Faculty members at public institutions lost less ground than those at private institutions. Thus, from 1940 to 1950, the pay at four ranks rose as shown in Table 53-2.

TABLE 53-2
Percentage Rise in Faculty Salaries, 1940 to 1950

Rank	Land-grant colleges	32 selected private colleges and universities
Professors................	68	40
Associate professors........	68	43
Assistant professors.........	74	47
Instructors................	83	60

Source: J. D. Millett, *Financing Higher Education in the United States*, pp. 134–35.

In 1952, salaries in 70 public institutions exceeded those in private institutions by 27 per cent for full professors, by 15 per cent for associate professors, by 16 per cent for assistant professors, and by 7 per cent for instructors. But a national study reveals much smaller excesses for public IHL for 1959–60. The excess pay in public IHL was 12 per cent (dean), 1 (professor), 6 (associate professor), 3 (assistant professor), less than 1 (instructor), 6 (all).[9]

A study by a Columbia University committee reveals some interesting facts shown in Table 53-3.

TABLE 53-3

Mean Income Improvement for Faculty in 27 Privately Owned Colleges and Universities

Rank	Mean income, 1955–56	Mean income, 1939–40	Dollar ratio	Real salary ratio
All ranks.................	$6,564	$3,999	1.64	0.85
Professors................	8,938	5,827	1.53	0.79
Associate professors.......	6,597	4,075	1.62	0.84
Assistant professors........	5,187	3,189	1.63	0.84
Instructors...............	4,060	2,184	1.86	0.96

Source: *Educational Future of Columbia University*, 1957.

These are figures for a highly selected group of colleges and universities. Note that from 1939–40 to 1955–56 the college faculties experienced a substantial decline in their real income while the real income of the rest of the population had greatly increased. College faculties experienced a deterioration of close to 50 per cent of their real income as against the rest of the population. This report also points out that the real salary ratio (1955–56 vis-à-vis 1939–40) for professors at Columbia was 0.65, for associate professors 0.67, and for assistant professors 0.72. Whereas the *real* salary ratio of professional, technical, and kindred workers had risen in 1955 to 1.44 (1939 = 100) and that of managers, officials, and proprietors to 1.28, of clerical and kindred to 1.41, of sales to 1.75, of craftsmen, foremen, and kindred workers to 1.72, and of laborers except farm to 1.84, the college professor had experienced a decline in his real income.[10] In a brilliant public service advertisement in *The New York Times* of March 21, 1955, the McGraw-Hill Book Company, Inc., showed that whereas the real income of faculty members had declined by 5 per cent from 1940 to 1954, that of lawyers, industrial workers, and physicians had increased by 10, 48, and 80 per cent respectively.

Yale reports as follows:[11]

Percentage Increase from 1939–40 to 1955–56

Cost of living..	93
Weekly earnings of workers in manufacturing industries.............	220
Average annual earnings of all full-time employees................	206
Faculty salaries, other institutions................................	75
Hourly wages, Yale operating and maintenance employees.........	156
Faculty salaries, Yale...	54

I find similar trends at Harvard. In 1957 the average salary of a full professor at Harvard was about $14,000, and of all members of the faculty about $9,500. From 1930 to 1956 the real income of a full professor fell by 15 to 20 per cent in a period when that of the average employed member of the labor market rose by 80 per cent and the real per capita income of the nation by 75 per cent. That is to say, the full professor at Harvard experienced a *relative* deterioration in his position of more than 50 per cent in relation to the working population. (In the years 1957–1961, however, there was a further rise in Harvard professors' salaries. This increase was about twice the estimated increase for the working population.)

At Johns Hopkins the evidence is along the same lines. A full professor's salary in the early 1950s had been reduced to 73 per cent of the 1940 level in dollars of stable purchasing power.[12]

Indeed, in the years 1956–1958, according to one study the average pay of a full professor in the nation rose by about $2,000, or 15 per cent. This is a substantial gain, but it should be noted that the average gain of income of the working population was about 7 per cent a year and that therefore even this 15 per cent rise makes up only a small part of the losses since the thirties.

When we compare the senior faculties of such institutions as Yale, Harvard and Johns Hopkins, we are considering the highest-paid 1 per cent in the profession. Yet the Harvard full professor (average age about fifty), with an income of $14,000 (in 1957), earned less than the *average* doctor of a lower median age. The comparison is not with the top 2 per cent of the doctors, who earned more than $50,000, but with all doctors—incompetent, average, and successful. In 1949, 41 per cent of the male physicians and surgeons, 28 per cent of the lawyers and judges, 25 per cent of the dentists, 18 per cent of the architects, and only 5 per cent of college presidents, professors, and instructors were earning $10,000 or more. In 1953, the professors in large state universities, with incomes of $7,000, were earning less than railroad engineers; associate professors in these institutions, less than railroad firemen; assistant professors and instructors, 24 to 30 per cent less than railroad conductors and switch tenders.[13]

The 1950 U.S. Census revealed that college professors were earning considerably less than members of other professions with similar periods of training. In 1955–56, the average net income for physicians, after deducting expenses, was $16,000, against the $5,200 median income of college teachers. Whereas 0.4 per cent of college teachers received $14,000 or more, 57 per cent of the physicians earned $15,000 or more; whereas 14 per cent of the college teachers earned $4,000 or less, only 4 per cent of the physicians received $5,000 or less.[14] Incidentally, the dispersion of college salaries in the entire academic market is much greater than has been suggested by Stigler.[15]

We can conclude that faculty members have experienced serious declines in their economic status, both absolute and relative. On the other hand, school teachers in public elementary and secondary schools in the 1950s ultimately matched the gains of the rest of the population.[16]

Yet in all fairness we may have overstated our position. I owe to Robert Bokelman of the Office of Education some helpful statistics on pay for faculty of land-grant colleges on a nine- to ten-month basis. These statistics are especially helpful because they compare salaries in *identical* IHL over a period of twenty-nine years. In Table 53-4 I have adapted this material for my use.

TABLE 53-4

Land-grant-college Salaries (Nine- to Ten-month Basis), Weekly Manufacturing Wages, and Index Numbers of Prices and Salaries (1928–29 = 100), Various Years to 1957–58

Year	BLS cost-of-living index	Weekly mfg. wage index	Professors—land-grant colleges		Instructors	
			Salaries	Index	Salaries	Index
1928–29	100	100	$4,278	100	$2,047	100
1939–40	81	99	4,245	99	1,937	95
1949–50	140	231	6,132	143	3,202	156
1957–58	167	334	8,750	205	4,720	230

Source: HEW, unpublished statistics, adapted by S. E. H.

What conclusions can we draw from this table?

Note salaries rose vis-à-vis prices in the 1930s. Hence the salary level is not so low when compared with 1929 as with 1939. By 1949–50, salaries were somewhat higher in real terms than in 1928–29, but substantially less than in 1939–40. By 1957–58, in relation to 1928–29 (and also to 1939–40), manufacturing wages had risen more than twice as much as professors' salaries and about 80 per cent more than instructors' salaries. By 1957–58, faculty salaries vis-à-vis 1928–29 had risen more than prices; but from 1939–40 the increase roughly paralleled that of prices for professors and exceeded it for instructors. This analysis to some extent is more favorable to faculty than is justified, because in recent years land-grant salaries seem to have risen more than those in private IHL.

Just a word about the relative rises of pay within the profession: as has been noted, the low-rank members improved their position in relation to the high-rank members, a likely development in periods of great economic stress. As a result the range for the nation of average professor and instructor salaries was but 2 to 1, a degree of dispersion too low to assure an adequate flow of talent. Increases at the lower levels undoubtedly reflect the great need for junior faculty members in a period of rising demand for education. From 1939 to 1950 the numbers of faculty rose from about 132,000 to 210,000,[17] increasing the number of teachers in the lower ranks disproportionately; and for this reason the small rise in over-all pay must to some extent be discounted. But we cannot disregard the fact that at each rank, and particularly at the higher ranks, the increase in the cost of living exceeded that in pay, especially in private colleges and universities.[18]

An indication of recent trends is given in a study by Imlah.[19] This report reveals that the average gain of salaries from 1955–56 to 1957–58 for 33 private institutions was 13.6 per cent, and for 5 state universities 13.5 per cent. The average salary of a professor in the private IHL was $10,315 in the latter year, in the public IHL $10,593. A larger sample shows, however, for 1957–58 an excess of pay in public over private institutions of 5.7, 9.6, 11.0, and 17.5 per cent for professors, associate professors, assistant professors, and instructors, respectively. The private universities, however, had a larger proportion of full professors in 1957–58: 28.1 versus 25.0 per cent (also see the 1959–60 comparison quoted earlier).

TABLE 53-5

Percentage Rise of Faculty Salaries from 1957–59 to 1959–60, Selected Private IHL

IHL	Professors	Instructors
New England and Middle Atlantic IHL:		
6 small...........................	+22	+15
5 medium.........................	+10	+18
5 large...........................	+14	+11
3 women's........................	+18	+20
North Central and Pacific IHL:		
5 small...........................	+24	+14
4 medium.........................	+15	+12
Southern IHL:		
4 medium and large..............	+10	+14
2 institutes of technology..........	+18	+12

Source: Adapted from "Instructional Salaries in 39 Selected Colleges and Universities for the Academic Year 1959–60," AAUP Bulletin, December, 1959, pp. 479–495.

The Bokelman statistics for identical IHL reveal a rise of all faculty salaries of 11.6 and 16.3 per cent for public and private IHL respectively for the two years ending 1959–60.

This salary gain of about 14 per cent did not vary greatly by ranks and reflects a rise substantially greater than that in the whole population. To a small extent some lost ground was made up in these two years. But the report also showed that from 1939–40 to 1957–58 the mean salary

TABLE 53-6
Salaries and Percentage Rise 1958–59 to 1959–60, Four-year Undergraduate IHL

Year	All	Public	Private
1958–59	$6,630	$6,780	$6,350
1959–60	$6,810	$7,040	$6,510
Percentage rise.........	2.7%	3.8%	2.5%

Source: HEW, *Higher Education: Planning and Management Data, 1958–59* and *1959–60*.

TABLE 53-7
Salaries and Percentage Rise 1958–59 to 1959–60, AAUP Study of 188 IHL

1958–59	$7,545
1959–60	$8,046
Percentage rise, average.....................	6.64%
Percentage rise, professors...................	7.07%
Percentage rise, instructors..................	6.19%

Source: AAUP, "The Economic Status of the Profession, 1959–60," *Annual Report by Committee Z*, p. 36. (Mimeographed.)

TABLE 53-8
Increases of Salary, 60 Colleges, 1953–54 to 1957–58

	Per cent
Minimum salaries.............	+11.7
Maximum salaries.............	+68.3

Source: *A Second Look at the Sixty College Student*, 1957–58.

in stable dollars of professors in 28 privately controlled institutions had declined to 84.6 per cent of the prewar level. For associate professors salaries declined to 88.5, for assistant professors to 90.7 per cent. Instructors' salaries rose to 105.3 per cent. For all ranks there had been a decline of 8.5 per cent.[20] (This supports an earlier statement of the better record of land-grant IHL.)

Imlah notes that from 1957–58 to 1959–60 the increase in salaries was greater for high ranks than for low. But the picture is not a consistent one. Moreover, his 34 selected private institutions reveal a greater rise than seems to be apparent from a more general view.

An average increase of 9 per cent for the selected 32 private IHL (Imlah) is comforting. At this rate salaries would double in about eight years. The AAUP study of 188 IHL yields an average rise of 6.64 per cent, or a doubling in less than eleven years. The Bokelman figures for more than 500 identical IHL suggest a doubling in twelve years. But the more general statistics of HEW—an average rise of less than 3 per cent in the year 1958–59 to 1959–60—would require twenty-five years for doubling of salaries.

Another approach which can yield only *very rough* results is to compare expenditures for instruction and number of faculty working with resident degree students. For the two years 1955–56 to 1957–58, this yields a rise of 13+ per cent, or a doubling in about eleven years.

* * *

This survey does reveal that college faculty has lost ground over both a short and long period. The college professor has not shared the gains of the economy and for many years even experienced a decline in his *real* income. These absolute and relative losses do not necessarily yield the appropriate salary for college faculties, but they are relevant data. I have heard the dean of the Harvard faculty say that average salaries for professors at the 50 leading universities today ought to be $20,000 to $25,000 and top salaries $30,000. In setting these goals, the dean is thinking in terms of the income that would be required to give the college professor the prestige and freedom from financial worries that would yield maximum efficiency. But, in a sense, he is also saying that had the college full professor in the 50 leading institutions maintained his relative position since 1929, he would now be earning about $20,000. The guide, in his view, is not the earnings of doctors or railroad conductors nor their relative positions in 1900 or 1929 or 1939, though in fact the rise to $20,000 to $25,000 would largely reestablish earlier relationships. Average salaries for professors of $20,000 to $25,000 and ceilings of $30,000 would strengthen the competitive position of IHL in the market for talent—aside from the need of higher salaries to improve the competitive position of college faculty.

Whatever the criterion, the general conclusion is that substantial increases are needed. A rise of 100 per cent by 1970 (assumption of stable prices) should improve the competitive position of college teachers sufficiently even if the prewar relations would not be reestablished. Something could be said for a somewhat smaller increase as we shall see. In fact, comparisons with 1929–30 rather than 1939–40 point to smaller rises.

PAY STRUCTURE

In assessing the present economic status of the faculty, one should take into account the distribution of faculty members by rank, by age, and by various other factors as well.

For example, one should consider the work load of the faculty. My strong impression is that this has declined over the years. In some institutions faculty members are now given relief for time devoted to research, a relatively new development which probably has not affected many. Incidentally, we should not assume that the work load is given by the number of classes. Hughes of the University of Chicago has even suggested that there is an inverse relation between the number of classes and the work load—as hours of teaching increase, the time given to each class declines disproportionately.

Another issue of some importance is the average age of faculty members. As enrollment increases and more faculty members are needed, younger men and women will be appointed, and the average age of the faculty will decline. If this happens, the average salary for the whole faculty may well understate the real increase in salaries. In the postwar years, average age has fallen and promotions have been accelerated. On the other hand, if the average member of the faculty is more highly trained than in the past, the recorded rise in pay will overstate the true rise. But with the great demands currently and in the future, the reverse is likely. It has been estimated that as compared to 40 per cent of the faculty members with Ph.D.s today, the proportion may decline to 30 per cent in the next ten to twelve years.[21]

In some respects, a better indication of faculty pay is given by the average pay for each rank rather than by an average of the whole faculty irrespective of rank. If there is a larger number of instructors and the instructors are relatively young, an average wage for the whole faculty would suggest a lower wage average than in fact prevails. But it would be wrong to infer the salary trends by comparing average wages in different ranks where the proportion of teachers in different ranks is changing. The AAUP noted in one of its reports that the *minimum* at any rank might seem high for some IHL; but these institutions, with many at or near the minimum, would show low *averages*.

Over the years, the proportion in different ranks does not *seem* to have changed greatly, but the information is scanty.

During eleven recent years at one major university, we found an increase in pay of 44 per cent for identical members of the faculty; but the average pay rose only 18 per cent for all faculty members. The first is not an accurate measure of the rise, because it includes promotions; the second is inadequate, because it does not reveal the decline in the age of assistant and associate professors over this period.

The relation between increases in scale and normal increase of income with age is suggested by the following:[22]

If the salaries at Amherst on July 1, 1956, are compared with those of July 1, 1946, it will be found that the average salary of instructors has risen

68%; of assistant professors and associate professors 56% and of professors 55%. If attention is centered on those members of the faculty who were here on July 1, 1940, and are still here it will be found that the salaries of those who were, in 1940, already full professors had increased by July 1, 1956, an average of 97%, while the salaries of those who have in the interim received one or more promotions have increased an average of 168%. But, for the latter, the increases represent, in considerable part, normal growth in earning power rather than an increase in the salary scale.

It has been widely believed that promotions have been relatively rapid in recent years, and to that extent the average pay tends to rise. This increase disappears, however, if one compares on the basis of average pay in each rank.

Former President Charles Cole of Amherst pointed out to me that an unusually large number of promotions from instructors to assistant professors and hiring of new instructors resulted in higher incomes, yet the average pay for instructors (with a large proportion of new ones) and assistant professors would be reduced (higher proportion of low-pay entrants). However, the status of the individuals involved had been improved. Undoubtedly the reduction in average pay for assistant professors conceals an improvement associated with the promotions.

Another issue often raised is that the average salary paid by the large universities is not nearly so high as it seems to be, since they use large numbers of teaching fellows or graduate students. At Harvard I made a rough estimate and found that 15 to 20 per cent of the *student hours* in classrooms were in the care of teaching fellows (generally graduate students with two or more years of graduate work behind them).

In its 1959–60 report on *The Economic Status of the Profession,* the AAUP studied the faculty cost per full-time student, an approach which allows for the use of low-paid faculty, e.g., graduate students. They found that of the 12 IHL with high unit costs ($800 or more), 11 were small— with faculties of less than 200. Princeton was the exception. Wesleyan was first with $1,626; then Princeton, $1,283; Gallaudet College, $1,196; and Amherst College, $1,056. The range was from less than $199 to $1,626.

On the basis of the Imlah study referred to above, I find that for 39 selected IHL the increase of instructional costs per student was more than 160 per cent (unweighted) from 1940 to 1960, a rise greatly exceeding that in salaries. The explanation of this excess must lie in a reduction of work load, and large *relative* rises in laboratory and other teaching aids, clerical and secretarial pay and numbers, and in departmental research. Budgetary rises in the nonfaculty parts of the instructional budget, e.g., more secretarial, grading, or research help, may reflect a reduction of work loads or at least freedom from chores and, in that sense, improved working conditions.

In one first-class liberal arts college a self-evaluation report read as follows: "There have been many promotions in rank during this period. For example, an average assistant professor of 1950–51 receiving $3,800 is now an associate professor receiving $5,800 or an increase of nearly 53 per cent in six years."

It was also pointed out that the average number in higher ranks was 67 per cent, that is, in 1955–56, as compared with 56 per cent in 1950–51.

An interesting study by M. Bronfenbrenner and L. D. Orr[23] of Michigan State University deals with the problem of upgrading of professors (a dry raise, i.e., giving an increase in rank rather than in pay). It shows that in 29 private institutions the proportion of professors and associate professors both increased from 1939–40 to 1957–58, the former from 34.3 to 35.7 per cent, the latter from 15.4 to 21.5 per cent. In the 5 largest state universities the rise for these two groups was from 47.3 per cent to 53.3 per cent. This suggests the possibility of some upgrading. In order to test this possibility more fully, the writers sent a questionnaire to members of the Michigan State Chapter of the American Association of University Professors. Three hundred faculty members received the questionnaire and approximately 40 per cent responded. The results were as follows:

These results indicate unequivocally that at least one large university faculty does not believe that there has been upgrading in rank over the past 20 years. As regards present rank, some 35 per cent believe they would have been further along 20 years ago as against 15 per cent who suspect that they may have been beneficiaries of some upgrading. (The other 50 per cent feel their ranks would have been the same.) With regard to outside professional incomes the results are much less clearcut.

Many have been impressed by the fact that under economic pressures college administrators often upgrade. The head of one of the largest private universities in the country told me that upgrading was a common practice in his institution until recently. (A survey of the HEW reveals that 22 per cent of IHL upgraded in rank.) Professor Machlup writes as follows:[24]

Professional ranks and titles should have meanings in terms of professional qualifications and attainments. These meanings have in recent years been distorted by bad promotion practices adopted by many, perhaps most colleges and universities. Some of them, unable to offer competitive salaries, have tried to compete for academic personnel by awarding higher ranks and titles to teachers who, by formerly accepted standards would not have been ready for such promotion. In other words, these institutions of higher education have tried to substitute "payments in prestige" for the pecuniary awards they could not afford; and in so doing, they reduce the prestige of the professional rank and title. Other institutions prepared to pay higher salaries to scholars they want to attract or keep from leaving but confronted with the inflexible salary ceiling they have themselves fixed for various ranks have chosen to promote these scholars in ranks that "justify" the highest salaries. In other words, instead of breaking through the ceilings of obsolete salary scales they have preferred to lower the standards customarily applied in promotions to higher ranks. . . .

Stigler argues on somewhat different lines. His point is that

. . . when the workers in an occupation are classified by grade or rank the employer may increase the salaries of individuals by within-grade increments or by promotions to a higher grade, without changing the nominal schedule of salaries by rank. This time pattern of an individual's salary is then governed by three factors: the initial levels of salary for persons of given qualifications; the rate of in-grade increments; and the rate of promotions. Any discussion of salary changes is concentrated on the first factor, tacitly treating the second and third factors as stable or unimportant.

Stigler then goes on to point out that the acceleration of in-grade increments and promotions are of some importance. He finds some evidence that this acceleration exists.[25]

Another related factor is the relative salaries of those who are in universities, those who are brought in, and those who are promoted from lower ranks. In a period of intense competition for faculty, there is a tendency to raise the incomes of young professors in relation to the older professors. This is not universal, but the tendency is clear to many who have watched the trend of faculty salaries over many years.[26]

A comparison of pay for each rank by institutions is not decisive, however. The proportion of faculty members in different ranks is also relevant. For example, a comparison of faculty members in nine engineering schools shows that the proportion of professors varies from 28 to 57 per cent, of associate professors from 19 to 32 per cent, of assistant professors from 12 to 36 per cent, and instructors from 4 to 27 per cent.[27] Obviously a comparison of the average pay in each rank would not be nearly as significant for this particular purpose as a comparison of the average pay for *all* ranks together.

President Cole noted that at Amherst 40 per cent of the faculty are full professors, but at least one urban university had only 10 per cent of its staff in the full-professor category. Many urban universities tend to have a relatively small number of high-ranking professors. For them, the average pay by rank is misleading: faculty members are not as well off as it might seem. A college where 40 per cent of the faculty are professors is better off than it seems to be from an analysis of pay by rank.

For all IHL a rough equality in the four main grades is found (Table 53-9). A few other facts should be noted about pay structure. Work loads tend to fall with time. Hence it may be concluded that pay of teachers

TABLE 53-9
Per Cent of Faculty Members in Different Ranks

Rank	Public universities	Private universities
Professor.........................	25.0	28.1
Associate professor................	23.6	23.0
Assistant professor................	30.7	29.8
Instructor........................	20.7	19.1

Source: HEW, *Higher Education: Planning and Management Date,*
1957–58, p. 23.

tends to rise per student and hence, on a "piece-rate" basis, the rise of pay is larger than it seems. But a reservation is necessary here. Even though the average teacher may be responsible for 10 students today as compared to 12 twenty years ago, his work load is not necessarily cut correspondingly. The fact is he may spend the time saved on research, or he may give each student more time. For example, 100 teachers may give as many or more courses to 800 students as earlier to 1,000 students.

TABLE 53-10
Mean Student-Teacher Ratio, Selected Institutions

IHL	1939–40	1957–58	1959–60
Private:			
New England and North Atlantic:			
6 small........................	11.8	9.1	9.0
5 medium......................	12.6	12.4	12.9
5 large........................	14.0	15.7	14.4
3 women's.....................	9.5	9.6	9.1
North Central and Pacific:			
5 small........................	14.5	11.1	11.2
4 medium and large.............	16.3	15.2	15.0
South:			
4 medium and large.............	17.8	15.4	14.9
2 institutes of technology..........	9.2	8.8	8.7
Public:			
North Central and Pacific:			
5 large state...................	22.5	17.2	17.3

Source: Adapted from AAUP, "Instructional Salaries in 39 Selected Colleges
and Universities for the Academic Year 1959–60," *AAUP Bulletin,*
December, 1959, pp. 479–492.

Table 53-10 presents some facts on teacher/student ratio. But compensation varies too by types of institutions, by size (as noted earlier), and also by regions. For example, incomes are higher in the North than in the

South; in public than in private institutions; in men's than in women's institutions. Within the public IHL, pay in large state institutions is higher than in teachers' colleges and junior colleges.

Mabel Newcomer, in her able study (*A Century of Higher Education for American Women,* 1959, p. 165) notes that in 1940 average salaries in 21 men's colleges were 27 per cent higher than in women's colleges— the latter employed 72 per cent women, the former only 3 per cent. The explanation of the difference stems from prejudices against women and, to some extent, availability of women for shorter periods (and hence less productivity), smaller student/faculty ratio (again less productivity?), and perhaps the unavailability of as large resources in women's colleges as in the corresponding men's colleges.

Some examples of differentials are given in Table 53-11. A few observations from this table:

TABLE 53-11

Miscellaneous Statistics on Faculty Salaries, 1959–60

IHL	All	Public	Private
Four-year.....................	$ 6,810	$7,040	$6,510
Two-year.....................	6,110	6,560	4,640
All..........................	6,720	6,960	6,380
North Atlantic..................	7,150		
Southeast.....................	6,690		
Teachers colleges, public..........	.....	6,650	
Liberal arts....................	.....	6,990	5,940
Universities....................	.....	7,340	7,720
AAUP:			
323 IHL.....................	7,970		
63 grade C or better..........	9,194		
Professors.................	13,007		
Instructors.................	5,910		

Average Compensation, AAUP, 1959–60

$11,000 and above	Harvard
10,500–10,999	Cal Tech, Princeton
10,000–10,499	California, CCNY, Johns Hopkins, Michigan
9,500–9,999	Amherst, Brooklyn, Chicago, Columbia, Dartmouth, Duke, Northwestern, Swarthmore, Wesleyan, Yale

Source: HEW, *Planning and Management Data, 1959–60;* AAUP, "The Economic Status of the Profession, 1959–60," *Annual Report by Committee Z.* (Mimeographed.)

1. Salaries are much higher in four-year than in two-year IHL; in public than in private; in the Northeast than in the Southeast. But *in re* the last, note that whereas per capita incomes in the Southeast are 40 per cent

less than in the North Atlantic, pay of faculty is only 6½ per cent less in the Southeast. Hence, in relation to general standards, faculty pay in the Southeast is very high.

2. Whereas in the public liberal arts colleges salaries are 17 per cent higher than in private liberal arts colleges, in universities the pay in the private exceeds that in the public by 5 per cent. A possible explanation is that in the public liberal arts college average enrollment is about three times that of the private liberal arts college; the average enrollment in the public university is about equal to that in the private. (In liberal arts colleges the student/faculty ratio is much higher in public IHL.)

3. Average pay for all IHL ($6,810) is much below that in selected groups—e.g., $7,970 for 323 IHL, $9,194 for 63 IHL, in excess of $11,000 for Harvard.

4. A marked difference prevails in the average salary in public junior colleges ($6,560) and private ($4,640). Here undoubtedly the competition of public IHL with large resources is relevant.

WHY THE DETERIORATION?

How does one explain the deterioration in the position of the college teachers? One relevant point is the inflexibility of income of IHL in periods of rising prices. The yields of tuition, endowment income, and government appropriations do not respond adequately to rising prices and increasing national income, and the faculty tends to receive a smaller part of the educational dollar. This is notably true when enrollments are rising. Construction costs and maintenance and operation of plant especially reflect the inflation, and as enrollment rises, the demand for plant and equipment grows disproportionately. And, as we just noted, faculty salaries tend to become a declining part of the omnibus item, instruction and departmental research.

R. H. Ostheimer has presented some figures on the payment of nonfaculty staff and workers which bear on the issue. During the 1940s, payment to nonacademic employees was only two-thirds as large as salaries for faculty members; the former rose so much that they contributed one-third more than did faculty salaries to the rise in outlays of institutions of higher learning.

The nonfaculty members of the academic community are better organized, and more sensitive to market conditions, than are the faculty.[28]

The prices of the goods and services institutions must buy for educational and general purposes were, in the aggregate, 76 per cent higher in 1950 than in 1940. This increase is based on a 54 per cent increase in faculty salaries, weighted as 43 per cent of the total educational expense, a 110 per cent increase in nonacademic salaries, weighted as 28 per cent of the total, and a

76 per cent increase in the prices of other items, which accounted for 29 per cent of the expenditures. The 43 per cent increase in per student expenditures by private institutions, therefore, amounted to a 19 per cent decrease in dollars of the purchasing power of 1940. The implication is, of course, a serious deterioration in the quality of the service, which is to say that there was less opportunity for personal contact between student and teacher and that library materials and facilities of all kinds were less available to the individual student. There were, for example, about one-fifth more students in private institutions for each faculty member in 1950 than 1940.

Instructional salaries, then, became a less important part of educational expenditures in the 1940s:

Percentage Resident Instruction in Relation to
All Educational and General Expenditures

1930	1940	1950
63.1	53.1	45.1

Source: Campbell, English, and Lampros, *Current Operating Expenditures and Income of Higher Education in the United States, 1930, 1940 and 1950*, Staff Technical Paper of the Commission on Financing Higher Education, p. 9.

At the same time, the amount of money made available to IHL increased greatly between 1939 and 1958. Moreover, the amounts of educational and general income divided by the number of faculty members has increased substantially (Table 53-12). Obviously, on the basis of ad-

TABLE 53-12

Year	Educational and general income (millions)	Numbers, faculty (thousands)	Educational income allocated over faculty members, dollars per member
1929–30	$ 483	82.4	$ 5,862
1939–40	571	146.9	3,890
1951–52	2,020	246.3	8,210
1957–58	3,634	348.5	10,430

Source: Calculated from HEW, *Statistical Summary of Education, 1956–57*, p. 6; HEW, *Memo to the Board, 1960 Series*, no. 4; HEW, *Statistics of Higher Education, 1955–56: Receipts, Expenditures and Property*, p. 6; HEW, *Faculty and Other Professional Staff in Institutions of Higher Education, 1957–58*, p. 3.

ditional resources made available, faculty salaries might have risen by about 170 per cent from 1939–40 to 1957–58. In fact, they rose by little more than one-half that amount, a measure of the greater drain of other expenditures.

Long puts the whole matter in a different way. For 85 institutions, he finds a rise of enrollment of 88 per cent, of income per student of 55 per cent, of administration costs per student of 76 per cent, of maintenance per student of 84 per cent, and of instruction per student of 47 per cent.[29]

We have given an over-all picture, and of course the problem varies from college to college and type of school. For example, in the volume of the American Institute of Architects the following appears: "It is true that despite public demand for education of high quality, support for adequate teaching budgets is difficult to secure at all levels and for all disciplines. Few areas of education, however, are faced with such competition for qualified personnel as are professional fields and in none is the situation more severe than in architecture."[30]

TABLE 53-13

Mean Salaries of Deans and Professors of 10 Professional and Graduate
Schools and 3 Undergraduate Colleges, 1957–58

School	Dean, over 10 months	Professor, no more than 10 months
Medicine....................	$18,100	$12,240
Graduate business............	16,940	12,100
Dentistry....................	14,730	9,960
Veterinary medicine...........	13,750	8,950
Graduate education...........	13,720	10,760
Engineering..................	12,960	9,250
Osteopathy..................	12,870	*
Law........................	12,800	10,860
Graduate school..............	11,740	9,190
Social work..................	11,440	9,800
Pharmacy...................	11,240	8,430
Nursing.....................	9,000	7,670
Theology....................	7,440	7,090

* Not available.

Source: HEW, *Higher Education Planning and Management Data,*
1957–58, p. 50.

In this connection, note the variations in Table 53-13 in average pay for deans and professors in various professional schools—differences of about 100 per cent. Where salaries are low, e.g., in theology, the deterioration is much more costly than where salaries are high, e.g., in medicine.

This problem of deterioration is related to the recent trends in salaries for public school teachers and for faculty of IHL. It is now clear that the average pay in the public schools, both elementary and secondary, is roughly in the same relationship to other pay as in the 1930s. In other words, school teachers have recouped losses associated not only with inflation but also with the relatively greater rise of the real income of the average member of the labor market. The college faculty has experienced no such good fortune.

Why is there this difference? Even in the public IHL this serious relative deterioration has taken place. It has occurred despite a large increase in the student body and an expected rise in the demand for college teachers in the future for both public and private institutions. The availability of tax power behind the public school perhaps counts for something; but tax support is not reflected in adequate pay in the public IHL.

There are various possible explanations. First, more people are concerned with pay in public schools and consider this a more serious problem than pay in colleges. Second, public schools are financed to a considerable extent by local government, and here the relationship between the taxpayer and the parent is close. Third, public school teachers are better organized than college teachers. College faculties, considering themselves not as employees but as part of the governing powers of the IHL, are not disposed to organize, or to seek higher pay aggressively; in recent years, however, the American Association of University Professors has launched a campaign to improve the economic status of faculty. Depending heavily on private funds, private institutions undoubtedly find it difficult to pay large salaries, and to some extent they set the pace in salary scales. Fourth, college faculty with pay above that of the average member of the labor market has shared to some extent the losses suffered by all relatively high-income groups since 1940.

Faculty has experienced a deterioration in economic position. Sound leadership might have pressed for higher tuition, which could have been had without serious effects on enrollment, quality, or expansion of new programs. Other college employees, including nonteaching departments and ordinary labor, were able to appropriate an increased share of the educational dollar. Riesman has pointed out to me that this is the same problem as the well-organized electrician or stagehand squeezing the theatrical producer, with the result that the actors are underpaid or the play does not go on. I am not arguing that the labor component is overpaid—rather that resources must be found for the professionals as well as labor.

In studying income structures in IHL, one must be cautious. A concentration of trends in pay by ranks may be misleading where the proportionate numbers in ranks vary substantially. Average pay for faculty

may reflect not only upward trends but also a change in age distribution
and in educational achievement of the faculty; that is to say, the "basket"
of faculty members has changed.

HOW MUCH SHOULD FACULTY PAY RISE?

We have discussed the goal for pay increases. Official commissions and
associations generally propose a 100 per cent rise in five to twelve years.
They generally do not make clear the reasoning behind this objective.
Equity obtained by restoring past relative rates of pay and the need of
higher pay to attract adequate numbers of good men into teaching are
the most plausible arguments. Generally these experts do not tell us where
the money will come from.

The 100 per cent rise applies generally. Where large increases have
been granted, the rise required may be substantially less. Moreover, in
view of the declining average age of faculty, the probable deterioration of
average quality, and the shift to relatively low-cost operations and colleges,
a rise of 100 per cent would in fact be a greater rise than 100 per cent
for the "identical basket of professors." Hence we would need substantially less than a 100 per cent rise to achieve a genuine gain of 100
per cent. Greater outside earnings and a tendency for fringe benefits to
rise more than regular pay also point to the need of increases of less than
100 per cent. But the arithmetic doubling of salaries may still be necessary
to induce the required supply of able teachers. A rising productivity as
measured by student/faculty ratios, with deterioration of quality, may
not only contribute to large rises in pay but may also help justify such
increases.

It is necessary to distinguish objectives from resources. In an earlier
chapter I estimated that a 100 per cent rise in pay would cost about
$2½ billion as compared with a current total budget of $3+ billion.* The
major resources from which this large bill can be financed are increased
tuition (or, for state IHL, government appropriations) and/or economies.
Hence the large emphasis we put upon number of courses and classes,
course requirements for students, the use of plant, etc.

Objectives are of little use without action. It is not enough to contend
that the market will inevitably press faculty salaries up. In the absence of
aggressive measures, the resources will not be forthcoming, and the adjustments will be made through heavier teaching loads, inadequate rises of
pay, and a deterioration of the product. I am reminded that Justice Holmes

* The HEW estimates the professional salary bill at $6 billion in 1968 as com-
pared to $2 billion in 1958. This allows for a rise of staff somewhat less than in en-
rollment (HEW, *Ten Year Objectives in Education*, January, 1961, pp. 16–17).

once said that " . . . the mold by which the inevitable comes to pass is effort."

How much should the pay of college faculty members rise? I have suggested some possibilities above. Earlier I had suggested a rise of 50 per cent, as soon as possible, which would bring faculty pay back closer to the prewar relationship with the general population. In addition, the pay of the faculty should rise as prices and real income rise.

In its report the President's Commission of 1947 recommended a rise of 50 per cent for faculty salaries and instruction, or an increase to $1½ billion by 1952 (in 1947 dollars) and to $1.675 billion by 1960. But by 1951–52 expenditures on resident instruction had risen to only $828 million. (In dollars of 1947 purchasing power, the figure is $702 million.) By 1952 the total *instructional* budget had risen only 10 per cent to an amount only one-half of that recommended by the President's Commission —$702 million versus the objective of $1.5 billion. Yet the *over-all* expansion of expenditures proposed by the Commission had been exceeded. Hence, it is clear that the faculty had continued to be squeezed.[31]

Several writers have indicated that the loss of economic status of faculties is exaggerated.[32] In particular, Stigler contends that promotions have been accelerated (but is this not reflected in average pay?), tenure is relatively safe with long vacations, outside earnings are substantial, fringe benefits are large, incomes are relatively stable, and, since incomes are lower, taxes are lower. (Is the fact that higher incomes pay higher taxes relevant?) He does not comment on tax avoidance in other professions, or longer working life in the law and the medical professions. He fails also to compare the incomes of college teachers with those of all workers. I find it difficult to accept the contention that, with the corrections suggested by Stigler (in excess of 50 per cent vis-à-vis the independent professions), the income of college teachers is above that of dentists and almost equal to that in law and medicine. The correction is excessive. The U.S. Census figures, which include the more important items given by Stigler, give averages for the year 1949 of $4,941 for college professors and presidents, $8,704 for physicians, $6,544 for lawyers, and $6,637 for dentists.[33] Elsewhere I presented more recent figures which reveal, for example, faculty salaries at approximately one-third those of physicians.

In the staff report of the *Commission on Financing Higher Education* (1953) it was proposed that salaries in liberal arts colleges ought to rise from $3,800 to $5,836, an increase of 53 per cent.[34] But the Educational Policies Commission proposed as a reasonable goal a rise of 75 to 125 per cent in faculty pay within the next fifteen years. In its final report, President Eisenhower's Committee on Education beyond the High School gave teachers' pay the top priority and criticized the practice of teachers subsidizing students. Its goal was a doubling of average salary within five to ten years. I also suggested at an earlier time a 50 per cent rise in the next few years and 30 per cent additionally to match the growth of real income per capita, or 95 per cent over ten years.[35]

*   *   *

Are there any general principles that may guide policy makers in this area? I have already suggested base-period comparisons and the improved competitive position as possible guides. Why an increase of 100 per cent, for example? It should be pointed out right here that even an increase of 100 per cent would still leave the college faculty at a disadvantage in relation to the rest of the population.

	Real income, 1956 (money income corrected for price change) (1930 = 100)	Proposed pay in 10 years (1930 = 100)
College faculty..........	85	170*
Average American.......	175	227*

* I assume a 100 per cent rise for college faculty and the expected 30 per cent increase for the general population (average rise of productivity of a little more than 2 per cent compounded for ten years).

With an increase of 100 per cent in ten years, the index of the average college faculty salary would be 170 and of the average American would be 227 (1930 = 100). One guide is the idea that the college faculty should maintain the position in relation to the rest of the population which existed in a more normal period untouched by large inflation.

In one of its excellent public announcements, the McGraw-Hill Book Company, Inc., wrote as follows:[36]

In the United States the average faculty salary is little more than the average income of industrial workers. . . .

According to the National Education Association, the average salary is about $5,240. . . . The average income of the United States factory workers in 1956 was $4,580. . . .

In Russia, on the other hand, the young Soviet graduate can see that it pays —and pays very well—to choose teaching as a career. The head of a department at a Russian university can command the salary of about 6,000 rubles a month. This is about eight times the income of the average Russian worker who earns 750 rubles a month.

It is clear that the Soviet professor enjoys a higher real income than that offered his American counterpart by a much more prosperous economy.

These comparisons suggest that the college professor is treated less well here than in the Soviet Union. Here is another guide that has some relevance in any quest for the appropriate pay for college teachers.

Another relevant consideration is a comparison of the pay of the college professor with the pay of the other professions. For example, the average doctor in private practice receives about 2½ times as much as the average college teacher. These incomes, for example, may be put in 1959–60 at $6,800 for college teachers and $20,000 for doctors. It is not necessary to raise the average pay today of the college teacher to $20,000. The doctor gives eleven or even twelve months to his occupation, and his work is probably more trying than teaching. But the difference should be reduced. A reasonable position might be to pay the average college teacher $12,000, as compared to about $7,000 paid currently, and the doctor $20,000. Then pay would be adequate to assure the standard of living expected of college teachers and wanted by them, and this level would help establish their prestige and give colleges a more competitive position.

In the actual situation what will determine the income of the teacher is the resources that go into higher education; the proportion of resources that go into the teachers' budget, the productivity of college administrations and the teachers, and the competition among the colleges, the last influencing the flow of resources.

We have already pointed out that the instructional budget has tended to decline in importance in relation to the total budget, and faculty salaries vis-à-vis the instructional budget. Imlah has shown that for three different colleges from 1935 to 1946 the percentage of instructional salaries and expenses to total expenditures fell from 49 to 43 per cent in one instance, from 45 to 43 in another, and from 57 to 44 in still another.[37]

I have already discussed competition among colleges, and teaching productivity is considered more fully elsewhere.

As we have noted, the salary of the teacher is determined by the resources available, the nonteaching expenditures, and the number of teachers. The last is especially related to the manner of operating—number of courses required of students, size of classes, number of courses, work loads of teachers, and, related to these, the ratio of students to teachers. Obviously, the larger the teaching load or the larger the classes, the higher the average salary might be. Increases in course requirements per student, without other changes, tend to increase teaching costs and reduce average salaries.

Several years ago Beardsley Ruml contended that with a tuition of $600, 20 students per faculty member, and an equal number in the three faculty ranks, salaries could be raised to an average of $12,000. This would provide an average of $6,000, $12,000, and $18,000 for assistant, associate, and full professor. Ruml argues that tuition alone could finance these faculty salaries. Actually, in a recent year for all IHL tuition accounted for only 60 per cent of instructional expenditures, although in 1959 the percentage is probably somewhat higher. But it should be noted that Ruml was primarily interested in private liberal arts colleges. In these institutions tuition income exceeded instructional costs by 23 per cent. An equality of the two is rather unusual, but Ruml considers it to be a possible goal.

The instructional costs are influenced by the relation of the average number of hours spent by the student in the classroom to the total number of hours of teaching per full-time teacher. For example, at Harvard (arts and sciences) I would estimate the teaching load at six hours and the student load at twelve hours a week. High ratios of student hours in the classroom to faculty teaching load prevail, especially in the sciences and certain professional schools. At California Institute of Technology, a student in mechanical engineering has forty-three hours of work in the classroom or laboratory, a fact suggesting why engineering instruction is costly. At a 2 to 1 ratio in student-faculty classes instead of 4 to 1, the ratio of students to faculty would be reduced from 20 to 1 to 10 to 1 if the average class size is not changed.

To offset the high cost of instruction and maintain adequate salaries when student loads are high in relation to faculty class hours, a college can raise its tuition. But it should not be assumed that, once tuition has risen, other income will rise correspondingly; and other noninstructional expenditures might drain the teaching budget.

Let us assume that we want high salaries in the top rank in order to attract talent. Several authorities have suggested a ratio of 4 to 1 from top salaries to minimum ones. It is of some interest that in 1957–58 the median salaries for instructors in all institutions was $4,562 and for professors $8,072, a rather narrow range. Actually, as President Meredith Wilson of the University of Minnesota has pointed out to me, the range should be given by citing the ratio of minimum and maximum pay in each IHL. At major private universities today the ratio of pay for full professors to that of instructors is about 3 to 1; for all private universities and land-grant colleges, somewhat less.

In an excellent paper, Hutchisson of Case Institute discussed just this problem.[38] To deal with the problem of heavy course requirements for students and yet preclude large classes, to assure an adequate number of high salaries, reasonable rates of promotion and a mean salary of $7,750, Hutchisson established a model ratio of 4 to 3 to 2 to 1 of numbers in the faculty ranks, from bottom to top; with this model, it is possible to achieve a 5 to 1 student/faculty ratio. He assumed in this tuition of $1,000, other income equal to 50 per cent of tuition income, and an average class size of 15.5 (or 20 with a tuition of $750)[39] (Table 53-14).

Though prestige in the academic and nonacademic community determines to a considerable extent the flow of numbers and talent into the teaching profession, it is not the only reason that high wages, a prestige factor, seem imperative. Higher pay is also important because in the next ten or fifteen years the relative increase in the numbers of teachers needed will be much greater than for all professions or for all workers; we should expect an improvement in the relative pay of teachers, not a deterioration.

In practice, teachers' salaries will rise in response to the market mechanism, but recall the reservations made earlier on the excessive reliance on market response. As the need for teachers increases, colleges will compete for the limited supply. For example, Columbia University's MacMahon report proposes that within ten years salaries ought to double, the rise being financed by increasing tuition as much as possible. Their objective is not only to double salaries but to achieve at the same time a median pay equivalent to the maximum median pay of any other university.

TABLE 53-14
Salaries, Numbers, and Progression on Assumptions Above *

Rank	Relative no. in rank	No. of years in rank	Relative no. advancing each year	Relative no. leaving each year
Instructor................	40	4	5 out of 10	5 out of 10
Assistant professor........	30	6	1 out of 5	4 out of 5
Associate professor........	20	10 or 30	1 in 2 years	None
Professor................	10	20	....	1 by retirement

Salary	
Minimum...............	$ 4,000
Average...............	7,750
Maximum...............	16,000

* An alternative more nearly acceptable in present competitive conditions is $4,000 to $7,000 for instructors, $7,000 to $10,000, $10,000 to $15,000, and $15,000 to $25,000 for the other ranks, and the over-all average now becomes $9,250.

Unfortunately the competition among colleges and universities for talent may very well result in a great inflation of salaries and no increase in numbers. IHL that refuse to yield to the pressures of rising demand and hence do not expand may well find it difficult to hold on to their staffs; for the growing IHL—and especially the public IHL—will offer increased competition for faculty. Moreover, expanding private institutions, with tuition a large part of total costs, also will improve their competitive power.

One would hope that the general rise of income will have the ultimate effect of inducing more and more people to come into the teaching profession, but this will take time. The immediate effect is likely to be a long overdue rise of salaries.

In the campaign to raise faculty salaries William A. Neiswanger, chairman of Committee Z of the AAUP, stated:[40]

Individual institutions cannot expect to protect their educational standards and maintain levels of staff competency consistent with the requirements of our era without substantial salary increases, the formulation of long-range salary plans, and the establishment of priorities for the use of American resources in harmony with these objectives. . . .

The AAUP urged:[41]

. . . that absolute highest priority in the use of available funds be given to raising faculty salaries with the goal of doubling the average level within five to ten years and with particular attention to increasing the spread between the bottom and top of each institution's salary structure.

The committee also suggested through one spokesman, Machlup:

. . . the employment of skilled organizers and of high calibre public relations experts making national salary minima a criterion of institutional accreditation; launching special investigations of the salary situations in institutions against which complaints are received, publication of the reports of the investigation committees and possibly censure by the Association.

But these were suggestions rather than policy. It was hoped that special incentives might be provided through a salary schedule, rating institutions on the basis of this schedule. This would provide, it was hoped, a stronger incentive to obtain additional funds and to allocate a larger part to salaries. Yet the grade of AA was not adequate to raise minimum professors' salaries at the top universities to the 1930 level *in dollars of stable value.* A salary of $14,000, for example, (AA ranking) was much below the $10,000 minimum in the 1930s at Harvard. In the same period, *real* income of the working population had risen about 75 per cent.

The association was also critical of the tendency to indulge in what they call "discriminatory exploitation": the increase of pay of mobile teachers and new appointees while keeping immobile teachers at low pay.

The association's Committee on the Economic Status of the Profession set up a table of minimum salaries in IHL for the academic year 1958–59 on a nine-month basis; specified benefits were included, notably annuity payments by the institution. The scale was as follows:

Rank	AA	A	B	C	D	E	F
Professor..............	$14,000	$12,000	$10,000	$8,750	$7,500	$6,250	$5,250
Associate professor......	10,000	8,750	7,750	6,750	6,000	5,250	4,500
Assistant professor.......	7,750	6,750	6,000	5,250	4,750	4,250	3,750
Instructor..............	6,000	5,000	4,500	4,000	3,750	3,500	3,250

Source: "Economic Status of the Profession: A Statement of Policy," AAUP *Bulletin,* 1957, pp. 217, 236. In 1958–59 no institution met the AA standards.

* * *

In summary, there is a widespread view that college salaries have to rise substantially, whatever the measure of the extent of the needed rise. How much they will rise will depend upon the total amount of resources going into higher education, the competing claims on these resources (academic salaries have been losing in this competition), and the productivity of the system. In this regard, of special importance is the number of contact hours required by students, (related) the number of courses, and size of classes—all factors determining student/faculty ratios and influencing the productivity of the system and the teacher.

Former President Hutchins of the University of Chicago was optimistic that adequate salaries could be paid if economy was practiced. But in a great inflationary and growth period this is not enough. The able young men, as President Keeney of Brown noted, want a chance at high incomes to provide adequate standards of living. Faculty are not money grubbers; but it requires publicity (the AAUP approach), rising productivity, and a conscious effort to divert an increasing share of the educational dollar to faculty to assure an adequate flow of talent.[42]

MERIT VERSUS SCALE INCREASES

One can raise the average salary paid to faculty members of a given rank in one of two ways: either with an across-the-board salary increase, or by an increase in the salaries of certain individual members according to their merit. The method chosen makes a great difference in the final effectiveness and attractiveness of the salary increase. Consider a college with a $5 million payroll, for example, with 500 faculty members and an average salary of $10,000. Suppose an additional $1 million becomes available for salaries. Now the administrator may give a salary increase of $2,000 to each faculty member, or he may provide increases from 0 to $4,000 to certain faculty members judged according to merit. Obviously the merit increases reward those who contribute more, and obviously the failure of many to receive increases causes much dissatisfaction.

In the public schools the use of merit increases is a great issue. In general the teachers oppose them, arguing that the increases are not in fact based on merit but on political influence and the like. In the private colleges at least some attempts are made to introduce merit increases, and I have been told by the head of one private university that very little attention is paid by his institution to anything but market forces. By that he means that he pays a member of the faculty more if there is demand for his services from the outside which might result in losing him. Market forces of course do not necessarily measure merit. No one assumes that because a professor receives more offers from the outside, he is to that extent better than the next member of the faculty. Caplow and McGee in *The Academic Market-*

place had much to say about this problem of outside offers and the extent to which they really measure merit.

Policies of different institutions vary a great deal on these issues. One college administrator told me that the average pay in three large divisions, natural sciences, social sciences, and humanities, is roughly equal, but that the scientists on the average are not quite as old as the other members of the faculty. This particular administrator evidently thinks that pay schedule should not be determined by market demand but rather by merit as measured by some internal measuring rod. But on the other hand, the institution that reserves its salary increases for those who receive outside offers uses its income more effectively and efficiently, for it pays only what it clearly must. Yet there are, as I have suggested, some disadvantages to a pay schedule determined by market demand. Moreover, it is very difficult for any college administrator to avoid across-the-board increases in a period when inflation works havoc with the economic system and real incomes decline.

(One result of the recent AAUP formula for classifying institutions on the basis of minimum pay in different ranks may well be a tendency to stress more across-the-board rather than merit increases. The AAUP is, it may be said, paying increasing attention to average pay.)

Perhaps the best solution, particularly in a period of rising prices, is to reserve a substantial sum to offset the increased cost of living and also to deal with possible merit increases. A reduction of real income, e.g., a fixed income in the face of rising prices, is surely justified for *some* faculty members on tenure.

In discussing the problem of merit versus across-the-board increases with college administrators in at least one hundred IHL, I came to the conclusion that merit increases absorb an inadequate proportion of rising salary funds. Particularly is this true in public institutions. With inflation and the growth of the economy there is a natural tendency to raise minima in each rank. But even this only means an across-the-board increase if all members in each rank, inclusive of those previously above the new minimum, also receive increases in pay. In a period when per capita incomes rise, as in the last twenty years, a substantial part of the increased resources necessarily goes to general rises. In a period when prices rise by 100 per cent and per capita incomes in the nation by 200 per cent, and resources are available for an increase of pay of 100 per cent, an acceptable procedure might be to increase all incomes by 50 to 60 per cent (say) and use the remainder of the resources required to raise the average by 100 per cent in *merit* increases. In periods of relative price stability a larger proportion could be used for merit increases.

At one institution in 1956–57, according to its self-evaluation report, the average salary for faculty members was $6,000. The minima were

$4,000 for the librarians, and $5,200 for teachers of physical education, athletics, and history. The maxima were $7,200 in philosophy and $6,400 in electrical engineering. These differences do not suggest the usual higher pay for the sciences.

In some universities salary structures are roughly the same for the various colleges, though medicine often experiences a higher maximum, and divinity and home economics, etc., lower maxima. Where the maxima are roughly equal, differentials occur in the proportions at various ranks and salaries. Divinity and education, for example, are likely to have lower average pay than medicine and law, reflecting supply and demand, the latter related to available resources.[43]

I find that generally college administrators are disposed to take the view that they do not operate on a policy of paying higher salaries to those teachers who are subjected to large market demand. But under pressure of questioning, they are inclined to admit that they generally pay their physics professors more than (say) their professors of classics; or they will suggest that in order to get a young physics member on the faculty they offer him an assistant professorship but that they can get faculty for the humanities at the instructor level.

Opposition tends to develop where pay differentials become large, and notably in public institutions. For example, a report of the commissioner on higher education in North Carolina had this to say:

"It is widely recognized that the responsibility assigned to faculty members will vary widely among the institutions and that variations in compensation because of this are justified. . . . Even so, it is hard to justify substantial differences in faculty salaries among those who have substantially equal competence and responsibilities."

Again, the range of average salaries of 18 public IHL in Texas was $4,156 to $5,728, or an excess of 38 per cent at the University of Texas over Texas Southern University; but by 1958–59, the range was from $5,047 for Arlington State College to $6,462 for the University of Texas, or an excess of only 28 per cent.

A problem is how to measure merit. In a large university, promotions and salaries are determined largely if not almost exclusively by contributions to knowledge; in the usual liberal arts college, by teaching qualifications. In attempts to weight teaching for undergraduates more heavily, some major universities (e.g., Chicago and Columbia) have appointed separate faculties at the graduate and undergraduate levels, with the more scholarly and higher paid at the graduate level. Some years ago an expert discovered in a study of 64 IHL that the determinants of salaries were degrees held, length of service, and academic preparation. Teaching was the sixth factor of importance.

At the University of New Mexico

The differences in average teachers' salaries are set by the board to be "appropriate" to the differences in the three types of institutions; that is, those offering doctors' degrees, those offering masters' degrees, and those limited to undergraduate degrees. The determination of salaries takes into consideration the salaries paid in previous years, the costs resulting from increases in faculty load, average class size, and student-faculty ratios, the salaries paid in neighboring states, and an estimate of anticipated state appropriation.

Finally, Fouraker, in an interesting article, proposes that the market prices should be decisive—as in the pay of private docents in European Universities.[44] He wants pay on the basis of merit and the market reveals merit. He finds the current system yields excessive pay for administrators and an excessive supply, and inadequate numbers and pay for faculty.

The administrator is budget-oriented and budget-justified, the faculty member is budget-justified but market-oriented. This structure has resulted in a system of regards consistent with Weber's Budgetary Principle and, consequently, a misallocation of human resources. It would seem that the most direct means of restoring equilibrium would be to make the faculty market justified as well as market-oriented. The objective would be to find an alternative, non-budgetary means of determining faculty salaries, so that the cultural carnage wrought by paying a budgetary subordinate more than his budgetary superior could be avoided; Weber's Principle must be skirted, not assaulted frontally. . . .

Most significantly, this method would permit the payment of teachers on some scale proportionate to their teaching effectiveness. In the long run, the best judge of a product is the consumer; if examinations and grades are assigned by an external agent, students will eventually select those instructors whom they judge to be most effective in preparing them for the examinations. The teaching portion of a faculty member's salary would be proportional to the undergraduate and (weighted) graduate enrollment in his courses. Admittedly, the student market is an imperfect mechanism for evaluating teaching ability, but the alternative is not perfection but the present system, whereby teaching effectiveness is judged administratively. I submit administrative evaluation is less perfect than that of the students, particularly if the students are motivated by their own self-interest to be objective.

The tendency for salaries to be compressed, particularly in the upper ranks, under the pressure of economic need and shortage of resources is related to this problem.[45] In the 1940s to 1950s, for instance, the range of salaries was narrowed; under pressure, teachers who already had tenure got relatively small increases while newer faculty members (particularly from the outside) tended to receive higher pay. In order to meet the pressure from the outside, there was a tendency to promote more rapidly and to create a larger number of full professors. (At one institution 60 per cent of the faculty were full professors.) In such a situation, a large part of the budget is absorbed in the payment of a large number of top-ranking professors, resulting in reduced incomes for others, including the average full professor. In other words, under pressure we get a rise in the number of teachers at the higher levels, but relatively low incomes for them. The gap between the minimum and maximum pay for faculties was clearly reduced in the years after 1940. Under the pressure of deficient resources, the low-income groups improve their relative position.

Decisions about salaries and promotions are made by both administrators and faculty, and it may well be that the latter has more authority here than the former. The problem is to make the most effective use of the teaching budget, given the educational objectives.

One approach is to increase salaries and promote as required by outside offers. Administered in this way, a given budget buys the maximum amount of talent. But the result of this system may well be reduced morale for those whom Harvard's Dean Bundy called "the invisibles," those who serve the university, given its objectives, but are unknown 15 miles beyond. The "visibles" get the offers.

The market approach seemed to be especially favored at the University of Chicago under President Hutchins, though there now seems to be departure from it. The nonmarket approach is characterized by former President Harold Taylor of Sarah Lawrence, who tells me that his college considers only teaching effectiveness, with no regard for outside offers. The "invisibles" at Sarah Lawrence often receive the highest pay.

At Harvard the approach is somewhere in between these two policies: some attention is paid to outside offers, but the "invisibles" share in improved economic status almost as much as the "visibles." This is suggested by the fact that those in the forty-five to sixty-five age bracket, generally not approached by outside seekers of talent, share in the rise of pay though in the market situation of the 1950s those in the thirty to forty-five age bracket moved along much more rapidly than their seniors and much more rapidly than their seniors did when they were in the thirty to forty-five age bracket. The Harvard attention to market forces is also reflected in high bids for promising young scholars from the outside.

I also detect an increasing use of a vigorous market approach by state universities. They are beginning to repay the "prestige universities" for their past raids. One outstanding man was bid away from a "prestige university" by a public IHL with an offer to double his present salary, a promise of no teaching requirements, and a large research budget. All his colleagues at the state university, many years older, were receiving much less; in fact they were suffering from a relative deterioration much greater than prevails, say, at Harvard, where the older faculty members still command higher pay than those in their forties. Again, a state university offered another professor at a private university $25,000 a year (almost three times his current pay) for four years on a research project, and then the maximum pay of the university as a full professor after four years—estimated at $17,000 to $18,000.

In an earlier discussion I raised the question of pay versus tenure for members of the faculty. There are some who contend that tenure means little when the college promotes a teacher to a higher level with tenure (a "dry" raise) rather than raising his pay and leaving his rank unchanged. Tenure appointments can come too early and hence be costly; the problem of motivation is a serious one. They generally come at around age thirty-five. If the path to maximum income and rank is clear at that point, important incentives are abandoned. Professors do not require incentives as much as unskilled workers, but they are not entirely immune to them. The civil service system of Japan, where increases are automatic and the professor appoints his assistant, does not produce good results.

Not only is it possible to deny increases of pay to tenure members, but under the pressure of inflation it is possible to impose demerits on the incompetent or poorly motivated tenure professors. It is only necessary not to adjust pay to the rising cost of living while others experience increases much beyond the rise in the cost of living. Many object to reductions in real pay (i.e., a greater rise in the cost of living than in pay) as an infringement of the rights of tenure members. In practice, tenure members profit from any upward revision of the minimum pay for tenure rank. Any administration that wishes to invoke the incentive system tends to limit over-all increases of minima and to concentrate on merit increases. Actually most colleges introduce both across-the-board and merit increases, but in varying degrees. The failures and the immobile profit from the across-the-board increases, and the motivated and able still more from merit rises. It should be noted that if teachers in fixed positions profit from merit increases substantially in relation to the mobile, then the costs of instruction are much greater than otherwise, and the range from minimum to maximum is reduced.

In summary, IHL waste resources by devoting an excessive part of their incremental pay budgets to across-the-board increases. Undoubtedly equal treatment, despite varying merit, is the easy way out, and the rising price level increases the need of general increases. Moreover, it is not always easy to measure merit. Many college administrators stress excessively market pressures and in particular outside offers.

OUTSIDE INCOME

A study of academic salaries should take into account the fact that members of the academic professions are able to supplement their incomes to a greater degree than others. To understand their economic status, we must consider their outside activities.

According to a study at the University of Minnesota,[46] the average faculty member spends about 48 hours per week at work. Half of this time constitutes his teaching hours: one-third spent on classes, one-third on preparation, and one-third on meeting students outside of formal classes. The University of California has also, through questionnaires, tried to discover the allocation of time of faculty, notably for instruction and research. But these studies can be accepted only with reservations. Faculty members answering these questionnaires have told me about their doubts concerning their knowledge of time allocation. When the faculty member is not teaching, two-thirds of his "free" time is spent on what the Minnesota report calls "research, writing and general professional development," and the other third is devoted to administrative and office responsibilities attendance at staff meetings, committee work, and the like.

Obviously the college teacher can cut his work load for the university much below 48 hours if he wishes, especially if he has tenure. If classes account for 4 to 15 hours a week, a college teacher can easily spend no more than 20 to 25 hours a week on his university duties; he is then free to earn income for 20 or 30 hours, from outside activities, including writing books.

The problem of monitoring the outside activities of faculty members, so that they do not abuse the system by taking advantage of it, has a long history. In 1857 the president of the University of Wisconsin, John Lathrop, wrote a letter to the Governor of Wisconsin. In discussing a man who had dedicated his life to the educational profession, he said:[47]

Such a man does not belong to himself. He has been bought with a price; his time, his talents, his energies, his true allegiance constitute the precise consideration which he has yielded up for the honors and emoluments of his position. . . . He owes to the institution, even his vacations, for what is the philosophy, and what the justification of the vacation, save that it is needed, both by instructor and pupil, to restore the tone of the system exhausted by the overdrafts of the varied life. Whatever is more than this is in fraud of the good cause.

In accordance with this common sense of the subject, the doctrine that the professor on full pay shall not engage in the practice of any profession, art or calling in the business world, shall assume no position in church or state exacting time and thought, has found its way into the statutes of our best universities. . . .

In the 1890s, however, when the University of Wisconsin began to feel the competition for faculty from Chicago and other institutions, the vice president announced: "To meet the threat of losses of outstanding professors . . . (several men of prominence) . . . were permitted to supplement their salaries and to broaden their experience by teaching at Chicago and Michigan State while at the same time maintaining their connection with Wisconsin."[48]

In 1914 a report by the State Board of Public Affairs for the Wisconsin Legislature said, "The members of the faculty are sacrificing instructional work to write books, to lecture and do other work for outside pay."[49]

Competition makes it difficult for any institution to deny its faculty outside income. The University of Chicago plan, introduced a generation ago, which severely limited the outside activities of the faculty, irritated and annoyed many faculty members. But at the medical school, where the plan requires the medical school faculty to devote its full time and energies to the university at relatively high pay and to turn over to the university all fees received, the plan seemed to work well.[50] In other departments of the university the program has not been equally successful. Earlier (1919) the board of the university had concluded that "It is the sense of this committee that the present practice appears to lead to no embarrassment on the part of the University, while the enforcing of rigid rules preventing outside service would doubtless cause dissatisfaction."[51]

In 1908 Henry Pritchet, President of the Carnegie Foundation for the Advancement of Teaching, wrote as follows:

A large proportion of teachers in American universities are engaged in turning to the grindstone of some outside employment with one hand whilst they carry on the work of the teacher with the other. Owing to the rise in the cost of living, the proportion of teachers who seek to increase their income in this way is very large. The method of organization in the American university also throws a large amount of executive work upon the members of the faculty. For this, extra compensation is sometimes paid. Both processes cut down the opportunity for scholarly study and take away from the dignity, simplicity and highmindedness of the teacher's calling.

Pritchet also pointed out one reason for outside activities: one-third of the colleges and universities at that time paid less than $1,000 on the average to full professors, and in 35 institutions the average was $500.[52]

Undoubtedly the inadequacy of teachers' salaries contributes toward outside activities. In acquiescing to outside activities the college administrator finds the means of bringing faculty income closer to minimum needs. I recall a rather pathetic letter I had from the chairman of a department of a small college in Texas who was prepared to pay $5,000 for an assistant professor but feared that he could not obtain the product of a major university at that level. He assured me that he could persuade a large bank in that part of the country to employ the prospective faculty member, so that his income would be increased by 50 per cent.

One liberal arts college, in a self-evaluation report made recently, had this to say:

We have adopted the general policy of permitting a faculty member to serve as a consultant to an outside organization or firm for the equivalent of one day each week during the college year and of course during the summers and vacations. Appointments to the teaching faculty are in general for the nine-months year. At the present time our Evening Division courses are treated as extra teaching for extra income. We do this because faculty members need the extra income to increase their earning capacity and because we could not include these as part of the normal 12 hours teaching load without diluting the salary scale by adding to the staff; also the demand for Evening Division courses is so uncertain that it is practically impossible to be sure what courses will develop. . . .

Disturbed by the tendency of members of the Columbia faculty to devote an excessive amount of time to outside activities, the MacMahon Committee wrote as follows:[53]

The number and scope of these outside services are apparently increasing. They raise an issue that calls for comment. The paramount responsibilities of the faculty member are clearly to his teaching and to the other scholarly pursuits that are likewise part of the obligation of his position. Within the limits of this principle, the Committee accepts as normal and desirable that the knowledge and skills of the individual faculty member be at the disposal of those outside the University who turn to him for professional advice and guidance. Such occasions contribute both to the standing and usefulness of the individual and of his institution. . . . It is difficult to frame a general rule that will sharply separate most "outside" activities from those directly related to the professor's contribution as scholar and teacher. Undoubtedly a distinction exists between activities that arise as a natural extension of a scholar's competence, and which enlarges experience, capacity, and influence, and activities that have no such function and may be carried on solely for the sake of the remuneration involved. . . .

The committee then went on to discuss the results of the questionnaire sent to 15 universities and the restrictions put upon outside activities by these institutions, and concluded[54]

. . . that the faculty member makes an obvious commitment when he accepts a full-time position on the University faculty, and that he should regard this position as primary and by far his major responsibility. In recognition of this commitment, it should be normal practice for any individual who plans to assume a regular commitment or a large unit of obligation outside the University to inform the executive officer of his department—or if the person is himself an executive officer, his dean—of his intention to do so, together with such evident information about the outside obligation as is pertinent.

At New York University recently the problem arose because the president announced a substantial increase in pay; the increase was accompanied by restrictions on the amount of outside work permitted to full-time faculty members. In a self-study of their situation, a faculty group wrote:[55]

The enthusiasm for this long-awaited action has been somewhat tempered by the limitations imposed upon other remunerative activities of the full-time faculty. There is no basic disagreement with the principle that full-time faculty members should devote their major energies to University teaching, research, student advisement and related duties. The measure of maximum outside compensated activities has been set at not more than one day per week. There is some concern lest this limitation deprive the University of the service of distinguished faculty members who are in demand as consultants in their specialties. . . .

Another reason that a large amount of outside activities on the part of faculty members is often permitted is that administrators fear they will lose faculty members to other institutions if they put rigid limits on outside activities. A third factor, one that particularly concerns the professional schools—engineering or medical schools, for instance—is the awareness that the faculty serves the public as well as the institution. I estimated that the medical schools only pay about 5 per cent of the total income of their staffs (including part-time members). Of the more than eighty medical schools which must deal with this problem of policing outside activities, there are almost eighty different solutions. Some of them limit the amount of time allowed for outside practice; others restrict the amount of outside income; others set the distribution of the extra income between the medical school and the faculty member.

TABLE 53-15

Distribution of Supplemental Earnings from Additional Professional Work
of University Faculty Members beyond the Budgeted Salary

Amount of yearly additional earning	Henderson and Davies (Yale study, 1928), per cent	Arnett* (369 institutions, 1926–27), per cent	Peixotto* (California study, 1925–26), per cent	Boothe* (27 state universities 1925–26), per cent	Private university study, 1948–49, per cent
0	34	34	25	21	27
$1–$499	25	32	38	39	21
$500–$999	19	19	26	22	20
$1,000–$1,999	12	10	3	11	11
$2,000–$3,999	4				
$4,000–$7,999	5	5	8	7	21
Above $8,000	1				

* Figures shown here for these studies were calculated from the data given for the distributions among those who supplemented their incomes, corrected for those who did not do so.

Source: H. E. Longenecker, *University Faculty Compensation Policies and Practices in the United States*, Association of American Universities, 1956, p. 147. (Mimeographed.)

It would be helpful to know how large outside incomes really are. In the Michigan State survey, 20 per cent of the faculty members thought that they earned a higher percentage of their normal income in outside professional income than they could have done in 1937–38; 17½ per cent thought the opposite.[56] A study of another university made about ten years ago showed that the average outside income, excluding property income, was about $1,000 per year for the average professor. This was roughly 10 per cent of his income.

Several comprehensive studies, summarized in Table 53-15, have been made of the distribution of supplementary earnings.

The case for active contact between the faculty member and the outside world is given by Longenecker:[57]

In summary, then, consulting arrangements with private industry or government have these favorable attributes for the faculty member, aside from the monetary consideration:

1. Provision of an opportunity to develop understanding of modern industrial processes and organization.

2. Opens up areas previously unknown and otherwise unavailable to the faculty member and leading to ideas for research.

3. In several fields, e.g., business administration and education, opportunities for team approaches are developed utilizing the skills of persons from different fields.

4. Increased confidence is developed for the faculty member's assignment to teaching and research as a result of the recognition of his successful accomplishment in the business world or government.

5. An opportunity is provided to assist and share in the development of industry or industrial processes.

6. Access to extensive literature reviews is an aid to research.

7. Not infrequently, opportunity for travel is part of the arrangement.

8. Continuing contacts with industry help the faculty member to inform students more accurately concerning opportunities in industry.

Longenecker also quotes Newton Edwards on "town and gown":[58]

The success of universities, as well as that of lower institutions, is measured by the degree to which they sense and serve the needs of the community upon which they rely for spiritual and financial support. Town and gown may have their quarrels, they may indulge in the exchange of epithets that explode emotional mine fields, but they dare not ignore each other. When the university severs itself from the problems which men must solve as they work in isolation or in groups, in field or factory, in market place or legislative hall, it chooses a course that leads to social ineffectiveness and, in the long run, to moral and intellectual sterility.

Because fixed commitments in the college represent a relatively small number of hours per week for the faculty member, there may be serious conflicts of interest with university obligations. Longenecker discusses these in great detail.[59]

Conflicts may also arise for other reasons. Once a governing board ruled that a consulting fee from a private corporation could not be accepted by a faculty member working for it because the institution was testing the corporation's products. At another time a faculty member had been steering graduate students to problems in which a particular company was interested. He was a consultant for that company. Seligman referred to a situation " . . . involving a scholar of repute who was reluctant to participate in a reinvestigation of his own published results because of the possibility of injurious effects upon the industry that was then retaining him on a purely technical problem."[60]

Another problem arising from outside activities is the resentment of those who carry their full teaching load and in addition often undertake responsibilities that should be those of the errant members of the faculty. Members of humanities departments, for example, complain not only because their average salary is lower but also because those in the sciences and social sciences may well have large outside income and be away from the university a great deal.[61]

Another relevant point is that if outside sources of income are available, the administrator does not try as hard to increase salaries. This charge has been made time and again.[62]

The abuse of the policy of allowing outside activities is especially important when a university grants a faculty member time for research. If he sacrifices that research to increase his outside income, the administration may justly question the professor's right to receive the grant.

In allowing time for research the universities have progressed greatly since the early days of President Eliot when he refused to allow a distinguished member of his Harvard faculty time to carry on research. He said this was the problem of the individual member of the faculty. But the Hopkins example soon changed President Eliot's mind.

In short, the great flexibility in working hours of faculties, the low pay, the competition of IHL for personnel and hence an unwillingness to hold faculty to account for abuses of the privilege of outside work, the relation of outside work and the effectiveness of teaching and research— these explain the wide recourse to outside earnings. Once we allow for this income, faculty pay is higher than it otherwise seems, and the relative decline somewhat less.

FACULTY PAY AND ECONOMIES

It has been said many times that a more economical arrangement of faculty members and their work load would make larger resources available for pay, a theory that Ruml had presented many times. He had tried to show that a proper use of faculty services would make it possible to double the salary of the average faculty member. He also contended that it is possible to reduce teaching staffs by 200,000 teachers by 1969–70 at a $12,000 average pay, or a saving of around $2.5 billion if we increase the student/teacher ratio 50 per cent. This is, however, too optimistic. Rules of tenure would reduce the savings and cut the junior staff disproportionately. Appointments, particularly in leading universities, are made not only on the basis of student/faculty ratios but also to cover fields of knowledge. But even so, in ten years the savings could be at least $1 billion, and in fifteen to twenty years considerably larger.[63]

One most interesting study has been done by E. E. Edwards.[64] Edwards makes it quite clear that the reservoir from which faculty pay comes can be increased only by diverting more resources into higher education, or by cutting down the funds for nonfaculty purposes. In general, he doubts that much more can be made available from additional resources, though he anticipates a budget of $7 billion within ten years. He is not hopeful of cutting down on nonfaculty salary appropriations and concludes that many possible economies would make the position of the faculty member more difficult, since they would remove aids such as secretaries and assistants. I think he is unduly pessimistic here. It is possible that smaller sums might be spent on construction, for example. Also, there has been a tendency for nonfaculty personnel to squeeze the faculty personnel, partly because of their better organization, a situation which could be improved.

One interesting point Edwards makes is that executives account for a relatively small part of the total payroll in colleges as compared to business. But in another sense the faculty is the executive counterpart, and obviously any cutting of cost to be rewarded by higher pay cannot be on the same scale as the rewards to executives in a corporation, who account for a relatively small part of the total employment.

Edwards therefore concludes that the most effective way of dealing with the faculty salary is to increase the number of students per faculty. He assumes a faculty salary of $5,590 and a student/faculty ratio of 13 to 1, average resources per student of $1,400, and other expenses per student, $970. Edwards finds that by raising the student/faculty ratio to 20 without affecting either the resources or other expenses per student, average salaries could advance to $8,600. He also argues that by providing aid to the faculty equal to $1,000 per faculty member for assistants, equipment, and other aid, one could increase the student/faculty ratio to 20 without impairing quality or decreasing support; then the faculty salaries could rise to an average of $7,600.

Among the proposed economies, Edwards suggests a reduction in the number of hours of classroom work by students. A reduction from fifteen to twelve hours would result in a 25 per cent increase in enrollment with no increase in faculty and no added classrooms. He also proposes that the students should rent books from a central place and not depend so much upon the library. "We might at least put into students' hands and remove from libraries the first 5, 10, 25 or 50 titles on our reading list, all of which could be made available for purchase or rental at a bookstore." Why should not the student write, inquires Edwards, four essays instead of one, and the teacher grade and go over one of these four essays instead of grading each one?

Often in discussions of economies in teaching the point is made that the student should be asked to do more independent work, one expected result being a reduction in the student/faculty ratio. Originally the honors programs were supposed to give the student time to do more independent work, but faculty members complain that they spend more time with their honors students than with others. A discussion in the seminar on higher education[65] revealed that in a half-dozen experimental colleges, much emphasis was put both on reduced course requirements and more independent work.

There seem to be a great many set ideas about the proper size of classes.[66] Ruml's studies show that it is possible to introduce large economies even with a large number of very small groups for instruction and an increased number of large lectures. Many of us believe that the medium-sized class, say between 25 to 75, is the least effective form of teaching and should be largely eliminated.[67,68]

The conclusion that seems to emerge from several hundreds of studies is that, in general, the use of pertinent illustrative materials of any sort enhances learning and that, in fact, the content and instruction can be carried about as well by a good film as by the average instructor. Similarly films appear to be as effective as speakers on the average in influencing attitudes. It is my impression that the use of films in stimulating deep political thinking has been less fully explored.

One would think that this finding would point directly to the conclusion that relatively small classes are desirable in order to avoid dehumanizing the instruction. Guthrie has found contrary evidence on this point however. He finds no relation between class size and student ratings of either the overall effectiveness of instruction or of the friendliness of the instructor and his interest in the students as people. It seems that a platform style of a warm and sympathetic instructor can convey a personal relationship even in a large class. Presumably this can also be done, but perhaps with greater difficulty, via films.

Since various functions have to be fulfilled in education, we should consider variable sizes for class meetings. One expert put it as follows:[69]

There are some tasks when an individual student is the unit and maybe we should dispense with class meetings unless students work who are interested. There are other cases in a class of maybe 30 where student groups of five each could approach the task more creatively than 30 students working as a group. There are other cases where we can put together a number of sections of about 30 or 50 students and do that task with 500 or 1000. So if we would work as a team, utilizing the best insights of our staff, we who do the teaching and the administrators who help coordinate the endeavor could get away from the stereotype of a large class or small class and we would think in terms of class groups appropriate to the particular purposes that at that time this learning group ought to be carrying on.

That economies are possible is also suggested by the breakdown of law school data in Table 53-16. This table shows quite clearly rising costs per

TABLE 53-16

Law school enrollment	Direct teaching cost per full-time student	Direct teaching cost per hour credit offered	Full-time faculty/ student ratio	Median salaries
Law schools with enrollment in excess of 1,000....	$ 221	$ 895	1–56	$10,110
Law schools with enrollment between 500 and 1,000	347	588	1–45	8,506
Law schools with enrollment less than 100........	1,253	498	1–10	6,148
Nine leading law schools.....................	595	1,510	1–24	13,091

Source: Material put at my disposal by Law Schools Association.

student as enrollment declines, even though costs per credit hour are higher for the large schools. Salaries tend to be much higher where the schools are larger. The leading law schools (defined for me by an expert) pay the highest salaries, are presumably the most productive, and have a 24 to 1 student/faculty ratio. The large schools obviously can attract high-priced faculty.

One study of 14 large private universities for 1956–57 shows a weighted average of student/faculty ratio of 9.6 to 1. But the variations are from 7.0 to 16.4 These statistics are subject to error, because they do not allow for part-time students. But they suggest a large range of student/faculty ratios and, on the assumption that the average ratio is appropriate, that the ratios could be increased in a number of institutions.

Other, perhaps more radical, economies are suggested in a report by the Committee on Utilization of College Teaching Resources. The committee first cites the common assumptions about college education which it is setting out to examine:[70,71]

It is generally assumed that colleges could not teach anything unless it were "packaged" in a course meeting regularly throughout an academic quarter or semester three or more hours a week. Also it is assumed that students cannot learn unless there is a professor in charge. With few exceptions, we have presumed that the college experience of a student could be carried on only for nine months a year, and that all the students' "credit work" must be gained while in residence at the college.

Another approach is to shift burdens from teachers to assistants wherever possible.[72]

As the situation stands now, it is clear that we do not use our teachers in the manner dictated by their abilities. As a rule, each teacher is required to teach for four to fifteen hours weekly, depending on his college. It makes no difference if he is primarily a research man; he still teaches the same (say) four to fifteen hours. It would be much more effective if each teaching task, be it graduate or undergraduate teaching, lecturing, or small-group instruction, seminars, or research, were given to the faculty members on the basis of their ability to perform one or the other task. Research men, for example, could avoid an inordinate amount of teaching; the teacher who does no research might well teach fifteen hours a week rather than the normal load of nine.

Dean Woodburne of the University of Washington says:[73]

The scholar should not be expected to teach as much as the non-research person and still be expected to prosecute important investigations. Neither should the pure teacher be allowed to limit his contribution to the student body to a schedule which is calculated to allow a reasonable time for research. The establishment of a light teaching schedule carries with it an obligation of serious scholarly investigation, and those who do not fulfil this obligation should expect their load to be increased.

Allocating personnel according to their abilities and interests may not result in an increase in average salaries, but it certainly would contribute to a much more effective teaching program with current teaching budgets. Not only do we want higher salaries for teachers, but also we want a given salary budget to do the most effective job.

One significant factor in determining the average pay of faculty is the number of jobs taken on by the institution. One writer has suggested that the faculty should oppose additional programs undertaken by the university until faculty pay rises to a level that is considered adequate. Undoubtedly, as more resources become available, they go disproportionately into new enterprises. This is one reason why the unit cost of education continues to rise. In view of the increased responsibilities of the college and the changing world, one should not necessarily object to new programs, but there must be a balance.[74]

In their interesting book, *The Academic Marketplace,* Caplow and McGee emphasize that often when members of the faculty leave, replacements are not necessary but occur nevertheless. They find that though 38 per cent of the vacancies did not call for direct replacement, the replacements were always made.[75]

This finally calls to mind an episode at one of the universities in our sample when, several years ago, requests for suggestions for the establishment of a new position and the abolition of all positions were circulated to departments on parallel forms. Several million dollars worth of new positions were proposed, whereas the total recommendations for abolition covered only one clerical position with an annual salary of $2,100 located in the department other than the one which suggested its abolition.

It is much easier to add a man than to get rid of one, and it is much easier to add a new program than to get rid of those that are no longer necessary.[76]

* * *

In an interesting chapter, Woodburne discusses tenure, and the wastes it involves.[77] Pointing out that tenure is necessary to assure academic freedom, he nevertheless suggests that tenure may be given too hastily and without adequate consideration. Tenure is, after all, he points out, often a commitment by the college administration to spend $150,000 to $200,000. (Each time a permanent appointment is made today in a large private university, it is an obligation to spend about $750,000, I would estimate, in terms of expected income.) This kind of appointment, therefore, requires the most careful scrutiny. One might also question whether the wastes of tenure are so great as to weaken the validity, even the noneconomic validity, of the tenure appointment system. Supporters of the tenure system rest their case largely on the point that it yields a better faculty than a nontenure system, and tenure protects the teacher's right to seek the truth and report it. But undoubtedly many of those who receive tenure do not merit it; to that extent the wastes of higher education are increased. The question is: how numerous are the mistakes?

What of retirement? Retirement age has varied from about sixty-five to seventy, tending in recent years to be reduced from seventy toward sixty-five. This development is somewhat surprising, since we expect to be faced with a large shortage of faculty members. At the University of Texas, retirement now is at age seventy, and faculty members are generally kept on an annual basis at half time for many years beyond seventy. Once annuities exceed half-time pay, the temptation is to retire.

To meet the problem of numbers we may very well have to reverse the trend and increase the age limit. Even now, when the large flood of students has not yet occurred, many retired professors find it easy to get jobs in other institutions. But the age of retirement raises certain problems about the economic status of the faculty. Late retirements are due in part from a desire to increase the annual annuity once the professor retires, for a difference of four years makes a large difference in the proportion of retirement pay. If a college wants an early retirement age for its faculty members, this problem could be attacked in part by providing larger annuities compared to current pay. The net result would be an improved economic status of the professor, who often suffers a severe drop in income when he retires.

On the other hand, any tendency to move retirement to a later age also raises serious problems. It may mean that the highly paid members of the faculty may be more numerous, promotions less frequent, and the average faculty pay may well be higher. But a higher average pay for the faculty is not necessarily an improvement in the situation, for it occurs because younger faculty members have been squeezed out.

In contrast to the tendency to increase the number of permanent appointments, I present here statistics for a large urban university from 1955 to 1970. Enrollment is to rise by 154 per cent, but the full-time faculty by only 54 per cent. The proportion of full professors to total instructional staff is to decline from 21 to 14 per cent, the part-time faculty to increase from 44 to 67 per cent of the faculty total, and the graduate assistants (largely part-time) to rise from 15 to 36 per cent. In other words, the college will depend much more on the junior members of the faculty, thereby saving money and providing the senior professors with more help. The plan also emphasizes a much greater use of part-time faculty, which is less costly than a full-time faculty and which is especially appropriate for an urban university. The president of one such institution told me that city colleges cannot survive without the extensive use of part-time teachers, and also that they can survive only by growing.

* * *

In summary, economies are possible. The reduction of unnecessary courses, alternation of small courses, and the like can make an important contribution. (As Dean Bundy of Harvard urged, courses must not be considered in terms of the number of students enrolled, but " . . . in terms of the total educational impact of a given number of teachers on a given number of students. . . . ") A saving on courses can also result in more time for conferences or research; a more effective and economical job can thus be done with the same outlays.

I am impressed by Caplow's statistics relating to the growth of non-academic departments. They bear out the truth of a remark made to me by President Glennan of Case Institute of Technology in Cleveland that despite the protests against a $200,000 public relations budget, the annual additional revenue it provided was $1 million. But even here we must be sure that marginal revenue exceeds marginal cost.

Caplow is also persuasive when he speaks of the waste involved in the

38 per cent of vacancies which needed to be filled even though no need existed. Reallocation of resources when values and needs change is necessary for economical operation. Indeed taking one professorship away from a department may be costly in morale, but if the case is good, it need not be.

Again, one of the greatest wastes is the use of faculty time for non-professional tasks. The faculty member is generally required to do his own filing, paper correcting, typing, and other chores. At present pay the faculty in the average college receives $3 per hour, and in high quality institutions, $6 an hour. Is it economic for work to be done at $3 or $6 an hour when much of it can be done at $1.25 per hour? One faculty member hired at a liberal arts college was required to help with the parking of cars at football games. Why does the young graduate student in his first government post find research and secretarial help which his professor is not likely to command until he is forty or forty-five years of age, if then?

Treatment of the student/faculty ratio, in part related to the size of the institution as well as to the number of courses, course requirements, etc., use of manpower on the basis of exploitation of special abilities, more careful scrutiny of tenure appointments, and retirement regulations tied to the changing market conditions—all these should contribute to a more effective use of teaching resources and generally either to a more effective teaching job or (and) higher pay.

FRINGE BENEFITS

An understanding of the economic status of the faculty is not complete without a discussion of fringe benefits. Fringe benefits include almost anything. A Columbia report includes the following: retirement programs, Federal old-age and survivors insurance (OASI), group life insurance; medical benefits, both noninsured and insured; salary during disability and group disability insurance; tuition exchange and tuition exemption; nursery school, elementary school, and high school benefits; place to live; travel expenses to meetings; subscriptions to journals; grants or loans for summer study and travel; research leaves or money for research and publication; sabbatical leaves and grants or loans for sabbaticals; emergency loans; discounts on expensive items; individual offices: private secretaries; research assistants; paper readers; parking facilities.[78]

What is the case for fringe benefits? One important point is the tax advantage. If the university carries the burden of annuity benefits, a large tax saving is made. The annuitant later has to pay taxes on income, but he has special advantages both because of exemptions and because of low rates at low income during retirement. The contribution of the university to the annuity is exempt from taxes. Many other fringe benefits profit from tax exemption. Moreover, a dollar of taxes paid in 1985 (say) is much less costly to an individual than a dollar paid in 1960.

Another advantage is that fringe benefits often use the insurance principle and thereby lighten the burdens of those who suffer from sickness or disability. The burden is shared among many rather than concentrated on a few.

Still another advantage of the fringe benefit is that help is given at times when the economic burden is particularly great. This is particularly

TABLE 53-17
Availability of Fringe Benefits, 1957–58, Per Cent of Institutions

Special fringe benefits	Provided by the institution		Cost shared		Service available but not subsidized by institution*	
	Public	Private	Public	Private	Public	Private
Social security (OASI).............	....	....	70.1	89.5		
Retirement annuity other than OASI..	3.6	11.9	77.9	65.1	11.2	1.6
Group hospitalization.............	1.3	8.8	16.7	23.9	74.1	59.1
Major medical coverage..........	1.6	5.8	8.5	10.7	42.0	16.1
Accident insurance................	15.9	20.3	8.0	9.1	26.3	8.7
Health service provided by the institution......................	7.1	12.9	4.7	7.0		
Life insurance....................	2.7	12.8	18.8	34.0		
Sabbatical leaves................	23.4	24.3	25.2	19.0		
Vacations with pay...............	87.5	89.8				
Sick leave with pay..............	91.1	79.0	3.8	5.1		
Reduction of tuition of employees' dependents...................	7.8	55.5	3.4	19.2		
Discounts on purchases...........	5.8	35.8	.7	5.7		
Providing housing for many employees......................	....	....	6.9	21.3	11.2	11.8
Loan fund for sizable purchases.....	2.2	15.8				
Significant recreation facilities......	14.3	17.2	4.5	3.8		

* Blanks in columns apparently mean service is not available on an unsubsidized basis.
Source: HEW, Higher Education Planning and Management Data, 1957–58, p. 56.

true of free-tuition benefits for children of faculty members. This sort of advantage, gained through the use of fringe benefits, is especially important when the economic status of a teacher is reduced because of inflation or financial difficulties. If it is not possible to distribute large sums among all members of the faculty, there is still much to be said for distributing some part of the total funds available to those teachers who need it most. Unfortunately, faculty members tend to underweight fringe benefits. They prefer, and especially young members, to maximize their monthly regular salaries. One college president, aware of opposition to fringe benefits by young members, would concentrate fringes on others. Former President Charles Cole of Amherst holds that fringe benefits are not considered part of pay once the initial announcement is made.

An indication of the extent to which fringe benefits are used is given by Table 53-17. This table reveals that institutions do not generally provide fringe benefits paid for exclusively by the institution. The important exceptions are vacations and sick leave with pay, and roughly one-quarter of them provide sabbatical leaves. The reduction of tuition for employees' dependents is provided by about 55 per cent of private IHL and by only 8 per cent of public ones; but the necessity for such a benefit is not so pressing at public institutions. (In a more restricted study that I prepared for the dean of the faculty at Harvard on the problem of tuition discounts or exchange, I found that about 80 per cent of a selected group of institutions provided this benefit.)

Only a small proportion of the institutions provide retirement annuities made through donations exclusively by the institutions. But most of them do share these costs, as is evident in the "Cost shared" columns of Table 53-17. Group hospitalization is largely financed by the members of the faculty, and only to a small extent shared by the institution.

In a study of 49 selected colleges and universities for 1956–57 the Columbia group presented the results shown in Table 53-18.

TABLE 53-18
Numbers of IHL Providing Benefits

Retirement programs	48	Grants for summer study and travel	29
Federal OASI	41	Research leaves	42
Group life insurance	48	Money for research and publications	38
Medical benefits, not insured	8	Sabbatical leaves	35
Medical benefits, insured	46	Grants for sabbaticals	17
Salary during disability	47	Individual offices	40
Group disability insurance	14	Private secretary	0
Tuition exchange incorporated	21	Research assistance	35
Tuition exemption, faculty	22	Paper readers	38
Tuition exemption, families	32	Parking facilities	39
Place to live	35	Serv'ces for retired	43
Travel expense to meetings	48		

In a survey an adviser of the Teachers Insurance and Annuity Association writes that 90 per cent of college teachers are now covered by retirement plans, 60 per cent by life insurance plans, 30 per cent by major-medical-expense insurance, 97 per cent in private IHL and 84 per cent in public IHL by social security. This writer anticipates that retirement income will be equal to 50 per cent of income before retirement. But this will be achieved only if prices and money income do not rise rapidly. These fringe benefits paid by the IHL now cover 15 to 20 per cent of pay (according to this estimate). This may be high. I estimate the Harvard contribution at less than 15 per cent.[79]

There are still serious gaps in fringe benefits: it is surprising that less than half of the colleges provide a program of adequate medical coverage. Again, even when funds are not available, group insurance can be financed by the faculty with great savings in cost; very few institutions provide health service; there is surely no excuse for the fact that only 21 per cent of the public institutions and 47 per cent of the private institutions provide life insurance, for even where IHL are unable to contribute, the institution through a group program can save considerable sums of money for its faculty; discounts or free tuition are still not widely provided.

Here are some details on the progress of various programs of fringe benefits. First, housing. According to the management survey[80] the proportion of public institutions with 5 per cent or more full-time employees living in college-owned housing facilities varied from 10 to 29 per cent in different parts of the country, with the maximum in the South. For private institutions the proportions were between 14 and 40 per cent, with the maximum again in the South. The percentage of employees covered at public IHL varied from 5 to 29 per cent in the North Central states and 5 to 95 per cent in the South. For private institutions, the proportions were from 7 to 100 per cent in the Northeast and 5 to 98 in the South.

The institution providing housing (generally at a discount below the market rate) will to some extent attract faculty members who would otherwise not be interested. But the system is not an easy one to administer. Several college administrators have told me that they have had to raise their rents to, or close to, the market level in order to reduce the friction among potential tenants resulting from rentals at a level much below market prices.

Related to this problem is another one concerning the neighborhood in which the college is located. A number of outstanding institutions have been embarrassed by the gradual deterioration of their neighborhoods, and the resultant tendency for members of the faculty to move away. Because of this, some institutions, Columbia and the University of Chicago, for example, are having increasing difficulties in holding their faculty. But both Chicago and Columbia have undertaken programs to improve the situation. At Columbia 89 per cent of the faculty lived in Manhattan or in New York City at the turn of the century. But by 1956–57 the respective percentages were 57 and 65. Aside from, though related to, its neighborhood-development program, Columbia is trying to acquire more apartments for the use of the faculty, giving the faculty priorities, or possibly discounts, in rentals.[81]

Annuities are another important problem faced by college administrators. On the whole the progress made in this area has not been adequate. Recent surveys show that for a large number of institutions the average annuity was only about $100 a month, scarcely a living wage even for one. This sharp decline in the income of the average faculty member once he retires has serious economic and medical effects. A distinguished retired professor at Harvard about ten years ago complained bitterly to me when I raised the issue of economic status. His salary just before retirement was at a peak of $12,000, but his annuity with retirement only $4,000. Inflation was reducing the value of his annuity, and serious medical bills consumed a large part of his $4,000.

A weakness of most of the annuity programs is the inadequate projections upon which they are based. The general assumption is that income twenty-five or forty years from now will be at the same average level as it is today. The result is that the retirement program working on this assumption proves most inadequate when the insured collects his annuity. The minimum estimate of a rise of per capita income over a period of twenty-five years should be 100 per cent. Even this does not allow for the probable inflation over a period of twenty-five years, but it at least allows for the rise of per capita income associated with increased productivity.

In 1950, to examine a case in point, Harvard revised its pension program. I was a member of the committee involved. We were seeking an average retirement income equal to 50 per cent of income just before retirement. The rise of prices and income since that period has already indicated that this was a miscalculation. For if provision is made for income to be had forty years from now, one ought to assume that income will rise at least 200 per cent (3 per cent compounded for forty years brings a rise of 226 per cent).

The annuity problem can be solved to some extent by a later retirement age; this would require smaller amounts *in all* for annuities, but larger amounts per year. Otherwise the solution must lie in larger contributions. Certainly at the present time a total contribution of 15 per cent of faculty salaries should be a minimum.

Perhaps the best solution is to be found in systems where annuities are *tied* to the teaching income in the late years of teaching. A unique and generous program is that available to faculty members at the University of California. Teachers serving around thirty years are entitled to 80 per cent of pay. This is not, however, a funded program. In other IHL in California some annuitants have received in excess of 100 per cent of their last income.

William Greenough of the Teachers Insurance and Annuity Association discusses the recent improvement (e.g., more coverage and larger benefits) in annuity programs; the need of full vesting (no loss if employer is changed); of a minimum of 50 per cent of last pay; and of protection against inflation through investments in equities.[82]

If a late-retirement policy seems unrealistic but necessary, a sensible program would be gradually to taper off the work for older members of the faculty. For example, instead of retiring members of the faculty at sixty-five, why not reduce them to half-time work from sixty-five to seventy? This not only would ease the physical transition from a full work load to none at all but also would contribute significantly to a treatment of the annuity problem and shortage of teachers.

I turn now to the issue of free tuition, or tuition at a discount, for children of faculty members, a fringe benefit which has become increasingly important. It is difficult to measure the costs, for they vary with the benefits provided and with the number of children of college age at each institution. The costs would vary for another reason: at a college with excess capacity, the taking on of a number of faculty children involves very small additional costs, but where the increase in faculty children displaces other students, there is a corresponding loss of tuition.

In the 1930s, when there was excess capacity in most institutions, the faculty-children program was relatively costless. The faculty exchange system so ably introduced and managed by Dean R. R. R. Brooks of Williams College was, therefore, easily justified. This excellent program has gradually lost support because it proved too costly for some of the colleges in the group of cooperating institutions. What tended to happen was that some of the colleges in the group developed an excess of imports over exports and accumulated credits which were of little use to them. In the 1930s, when the program was relatively costless, this did not matter; but later on, when the faculty children displacing other applicants cost the colleges substantial losses of tuition, the system did not work. Now these colleges seem to prefer to give this fringe benefit in the form of a cash grant, allowing the faculty children to choose their college.

These programs for free tuition of faculty children have, however, aroused opposition. Many believe that a faculty member should be paid whatever his appropriate salary is and that how he spends his money is his business: the free-market approach. If a faculty member wants to consume his resources by raising a large family, the argument runs, that is his business; he should not be subsidized by other members of the faculty who have few or no children. President Phillips of Bates College has supported this position. He shows that at Bates 38 per cent of the faculty, either because their children are beyond college age or because they have no children, would be subsidizing the rest of the faculty. He would much prefer a general increase in salary. My value judgments support the program.

Comprehensive medical programs, or catastrophic insurance programs, have made considerable progress in recent years. Such programs can be financed by the faculty, particularly if it is well paid, or by the university.

If the average income of the faculty is $8,000 or more, then a program paid at least in part by the faculty makes a great deal of sense.

Generally the program provides corridors; that is, an initial payment has to be made by the faculty member before the insurance program bears part of the cost of medical bills, and, of course, there is coinsurance, so that, for example, if the total bill for an illness is $15,000, the faculty member may have to pay $2,500. These "corridor" and coinsurance features reduce the premium. They also have the adverse effect of discouraging use of medical services when they may be needed. An adequate medical program of this kind may well cost more than $100 a year to each faculty member, which may be a serious burden for the average teacher. In instances where salaries are below $5,000, substantial subsidies from the college could be required.

I will mention one last issue here. It appears that faculty members now find it much easier than they did in the past to obtain leaves, trips to Europe, and the like. Perhaps this is a result of the increased activity of foundations. It means that essentially the faculty member has a higher income than he did before. I am sure that in the major universities, particularly for their faculties of social and natural sciences, these programs have contributed to the teachers' economic status. But even today only a small proportion of the teaching profession experience this improvement in economic status.

*   *   *

In summary, fringe benefits are an important supplement to regular pay; and for each dollar disbursed by the IHL the faculty members gain substantially more because of tax gains and the distribution of the expense of illness, catastrophes, and other concentrated costs among the many and over time. But unfortunately faculty members tend to underweight the relevant advantages, and important gaps in these programs are still to be found. Perhaps the greatest deficiency is in annuity programs where coverage is not adequate, plans not sufficiently geared to the rising incomes during the working period of faculty, and stipends generally inadequate.

THE PROBLEM OF SUPPLY

In 1947, the President's Commission on Higher Education estimated that by 1960, 55,000 new teachers would be required, and replacement demand would be 195,000 (the current number of teachers is about 350,000). In 1955, the Fund for the Advancement of Education estimated that, on the basis of fairly conservative projections, in 1956–1960, 1961–1965, and 1966–1970, respectively, 84,000, 111,000, and 144,000 new college teachers would be needed; the figures were 97,000, 153,000, and

236,000 when more generous estimates of future enrollment were used. For " . . . every 10 college teachers now employed, somewhere between 16 and 25 new ones will have to be found between now and 1970." Yet the anticipated increase in Ph.Ds who will teach is considerably less.[83] (In 1953–54, only 40 per cent of the college teachers had Ph.D. degrees.) The low pay of the academic profession undoubtedly explains in part the fact that only a small percentage of persons with adequate mental endowments obtain Ph.D. degrees and go into teaching.

An estimate of 1961 puts the *full-time* teachers in 1958–59 at 250,000, the new full-time teachers required in 1959–1970 at 346,800. Yet as compared to 40.5 per cent of staff with Ph.Ds in 1953–54, the Ph.Ds and new staff was 31.4 per cent in 1953–54 and only 25.8 per cent in 1960–61.[84]

An average projection is a *net rise* of 100 per cent in numbers of college teachers in fifteen years. This greatly exceeds the expected rise in all employment, or that in competitive occupations. The increase of college teachers, according to projections, should be 4 times that in all employments, 2½ times that in white-collar markets, and almost twice that for professional persons. We should therefore expect an improvement in the relative pay of college teachers, not a deterioration.

In 1953–54, according to a survey of the National Education Association,[85] the number of college teachers added was 4,300, and 8,308 in 1956–57. The greater rise in the latter year is associated in part with the rise of enrollment in 1956–57.

Where do the new teachers come from?[86] The sources for 1953–54 and 1954–55 are given in Table 53-19. For 1955–56 and 1956–57 a

TABLE 53-19
Sources of New Teachers, 1953–54 and 1954–55

	Per cent
Graduate schools...............................	51.5
Educational service other than full-time teachers....	22.2
Business occupations............................	10.4
Government service.............................	3.5
Military service................................	2.0
Other...	10.4
All...	100.0

Source: *Teacher Supply and Demand in Colleges and Universities, 1955–56 and 1956–57*, p. 20.

somewhat different classification reveals a decline in the graduate school contribution to 45 per cent, and high school teaching provides 13.8 per cent.[87] Here the shortages are revealed in the greater dependence upon sources other than graduate schools, unfortunately sources like high schools which suffer themselves from serious shortages.

Of the new Ph.Ds each year, it is well to remember that one-third continue in their previous occupations and in this sense do not add to the teaching profession; 57.3 per cent of the Ph.D.s entering *new* occupations in 1954–55 and 1955–56 chose educational services. (In these years, the maximum percentage of Ph.D.s entering *noneducational* services was chemistry with 74.3. In general, the graduates in the natural sciences tended to desert the educational field.)[88]

Women constitute only a small proportion of college teachers. In 1938 they accounted for 15 per cent of the number of Ph.D. candidates; by 1956, only 10 per cent; but in recent years women account for about one-quarter of new teachers employed. Evidently women fill the lower ranks disproportionately.[89] The main reason for this is probably a prejudice against women in colleges, and also relatively short careers.

Part-time teachers also offer a solution to the shortage of college teachers. They are increasingly used. Much is to be said for using them, though an excessive proportion of them would raise problems of integration of programs, faculty-student relations, and the like. Part-time teachers seem to be used especially in nonpublic municipal universities, probably because part-time faculties are particularly helpful for institutions with large enrollments, night classes, and difficult financial problems. Part-time teachers account for two-sevenths of all teachers.[90]

TABLE 53-20

Ratio of Full-time to Part-time Teachers

Type of Institution	Ratio
State universities	3.8:1
Nonpublic universities	1.1:1
Municipal universities	1.4:1
Land-grant colleges	5.4:1
State colleges	8.2:1
Teachers colleges	8.7:1
Nonpublic colleges (by enrollment):	
1,000 and over	3.6:1
500–999	4.2:1
Under 500	3.3:1
All institutions	2.5:1

Source: See previous table.

In primary and secondary public schools, it is not too difficult to judge the qualifications of teachers: all one need use is legal requirements. I am not implying that this is the best way to judge. But in the colleges it is an entirely different matter. Acceptable educational achievement and qualities vary from college to college; there is no organized market for college teachers. The Caplow book reveals the extent of imperfections in the market. At a meeting of the American Economic Association in 1958, the U.S. Employment Security Officer who helped organize a market for economists complained bitterly about these imperfections, about the unwillingness to choose the best candidates, and about the fact that potential teachers and administrators refused to use the facilities provided.

A few years ago, as chairman of an economics department, I organized the chairmen of the 25 universities which produce most of the Ph.D.s in economics. For the first time we had a central organization to present potential teachers and to announce openings. But even this elementary attack evoked protests and was dubbed the Harris cartel. It is still considered bad taste for a prospective teacher to apply for a position, and prospective American employers, unlike the British, will not advertise an opening. On one occasion, I proposed a public advertisement of major openings to the dean of the faculty, who approved; but, alas, my colleagues envisaged all kinds of difficulties. One chairman of a leading university said that there was probably no such thing as a general market for economists but rather that special markets were tied to each institution. The University of Chicago, for example, has one market and Stanford has another.

The large variation in degrees held by teachers suggests that qualifications vary widely. In private universities, in a recent year, 52 per cent of the teachers held doctorates; in public universities, 44 per cent; in teachers colleges, only 30 per cent. The differences were also very large within each group, as they were among departments.[91]

Table 53-21, which covers most IHL, shows the techniques used by college administrators to obtain more teachers and use them more effectively.[92] Not all these measures represent attempts to overcome teacher shortage, nor are the economies introduced as successful as they sometimes appear.

It may be estimated that 44 per cent of the IHL now employ faculty members not as well qualified as formerly. The declining proportion of Ph.D.s among the new faculty members shows that the formal standards for qualification are changing. This is not necessarily a deterioration. Much can be said for providing teachers with an M.A. rather than a Ph.D. Most teachers do not want to do research, and many are incapable of it. Much of the teaching in junior colleges, liberal arts colleges, and teachers colleges can be done well by those who do not have the experience in research required for a Ph.D. degree. More important for such teachers is a good command of their subjects and the ability to teach. In an able essay in a *Symposium on Basic Research* (1959) President Laurence Gould of Carleton College emphasized more than I do here the need of research experience for teachers in liberal arts colleges. A two-year M.A. (or even a one-year program) is frequently adequate for college teachers.[93] Yet we usually require of our teachers excessive graduate work and research training that they do not want or need. We demand too much teaching of others who want to work at the frontiers of knowledge. Conflicts arise between those who train the teachers and their consumers. We tend to drag out the preparation for the Ph.D. excessively.[93a]

In assessing research potential of faculty members in New York State IHL, the writers of a report complain of excessive teaching loads and paper work, lack of secretarial and filing assistance, rigid teaching schedules, absence of faculty summer research appointments, burdens of committee assignments, pressures of extension and summer teaching, and the lack of graduate students for assistance.[94]

* * *

To solve the problem of supply, we shall have to depend on streamlining and improving preparation; improved income status; economies in the use of teachers; greater use of part-time teachers, women, and retired faculty; accelerated promotions; improved organization of the market; etc.

Much will depend on the student/faculty ratio. In the NEA study, Maul assumes that the current ratio of 13 to 1 will become 16 to 1 by 1970. Even with this rise of numbers per faculty member, he anticipates the need of 206,000 for replacement and 140,000 for additional students. The ratio will depend on number of classes, size of classes, extent of the development of community colleges, which have large student/faculty ratios, and trends in teaching load. Earlier I presented some evidence of declining work loads. One study shows a rise of enrollment of 194 per cent for the country and of 203 per cent of faculty from 1939 to 1955, but in Pennsylvania, 205 and 169 per cent respectively.[95]

After this long discussion mainly of economical aspects, I remind the reader of the significance of nonacademic factors. Many are fearful that solutions, both of pay and number of recruits, through the economy path would deteriorate the product: less time with faculty, elimination of the written papers, less discussion, etc. Another approach to the supply problem would be to restrict enrollment, a solution that appeals to some. One writer anticipates a rise in student/faculty ratio as the most likely solution of the faculty-supply-and-salary problem. Higher tuition would not, in his view, be politically acceptable.[96]

A Minnesota survey revealed that five-sixths of the faculties in the state would do it again, that is, choose teaching as a career. Indeed they are troubled by inadequate pay; but they are attracted by such factors as the pleasure of working with young minds, intellectually stimulating associations, freedom and independence in work. The appeal would be greater if salaries were higher, students better, and work less routine. Almost half complained of low pay.[97]

The Conference on Improving the Effectiveness of College Faculties in December, 1950, listed ten factors which can " . . . contribute sig-

TABLE 53-21
Extent of Use of Various Faculty and Instructional Practice in Institutions of Higher Education

Practice	Number of institutions reporting on practice*	Reporting institutions following practice in 1957–58		Reporting institutions following practice in 1954–1957 and continuing but not increasing it in 1957–58‡						Reporting institutions introducing or increasing practice in 1957–58					
				Due primarily to faculty shortage		Due equally to faculty shortage and other reasons		Due primarily to other reasons		Due primarily to faculty shortage		Due equally to faculty shortage and other reasons		Due primarily to other reasons	
		Num-ber	Per cent	Num-ber	Per cent	Num-ber	Per cent	Num-ber	Per cent	Num-ber	Per cent	Num-ber	Per cent	Num-ber	Per cent
Employment of retired professors and other retired persons...	1,459	597	†40.9	106	7.3	118	8.1	101	6.9	105	7.2	112	7.7	55	3.8
Employment part-time of persons whose incomes are mainly from other occupations...	1,449	952	65.7	113	7.8	155	10.7	263	18.2	93	6.4	158	10.9	170	11.7
Sharing instructors and instructional facilities with other institutions...	1,404	517	36.8	56	4.0	51	3.6	157	11.2	45	3.2	81	5.8	127	9.0
Employment of new faculty less qualified than formerly for positions occupied...	1,459	649	44.5	287	19.7	31	2.1	16	1.1	226	15.5	69	4.7	20	1.4
Employment of new faculty at salaries (ranks same) relatively higher than formerly...	1,448	909	62.8	232	16.0	101	7.0	62	4.3	213	14.7	206	14.2	95	6.6
Employment of new faculty at ranks (salaries same) relatively higher than formerly...	1,366	306	22.4	72	5.3	26	1.9	19	1.4	108	7.9	52	3.8	29	2.1
Employment of new faculty at both ranks and salaries relatively higher than formerly...	1,356	430	31.7	101	7.4	44	3.2	27	2.0	135	10.0	84	6.2	39	2.9
Accelerated promotion of faculty...	1,323	335	25.3	67	5.1	27	2.0	35	2.6	76	5.7	64	4.8	66	5.0
Employment of some faculty members beyond mandatory retirement age...	1,403	512	36.5	115	8.2	62	4.4	84	6.0	90	6.4	77	5.5	84	6.0
Increase of the established mandatory age limit...	1,330	120	9.0	27	2.0	4	0.3	11	0.8	34	2.6	24	1.8	20	1.5
New fringe benefits established or existing ones increased...	1,397	852	61.0	26	1.9	60	4.3	196	14.0	40	2.9	196	14.0	334	23.1
Salary increases of at least 5 per cent per annum for faculty as a whole...	1,416	1,197	84.5	35	2.5	135	9.5	231	16.3	42	3.0	365	25.8	389	27.5

TABLE 53-21 (Continued)

Practice	Number of institutions reporting on practice* (Number)	Reporting institutions following practice in 1957–58		Reporting institutions following practice in 1954–57 and continuing but not increasing it in 1957–58‡						Reporting institutions introducing or increasing practice in 1957–58					
				Due primarily to faculty shortage		Due equally to faculty shortage and other reasons		Due primarily to other reasons		Due primarily to faculty shortage		Due equally to faculty shortage and other reasons		Due primarily to other reasons	
	Number	Number	Per cent	Number	Per cent	Number	Per cent	Number	Per cent	Number	Per cent	Number	Per cent	Number	Per cent
Increase in the size of lecture sessions	1,439	651	45.3	115	8.0	75	5.2	73	5.1	97	6.7	170	11.8	121	8.3
Reduction of duplicating and overlapping course offerings	1,380	805	58.3	59	4.3	84	6.1	175	12.7	48	3.5	158	11.4	281	20.4
A significantly larger responsibility placed on student for his own learning	1,367	500	36.6	24	1.8	32	2.3	89	6.5	20	1.5	116	8.5	219	16.0
Use of nonprofessional assistants to help relieve faculty of nonteaching duties	1,401	488	34.8	48	3.4	43	3.1	92	6.6	54	3.8	142	10.1	109	7.8
Reduction in number of smaller classes	1,398	764	54.6	82	5.9	99	7.1	115	8.2	65	4.7	196	14.0	207	14.8
Elimination, curtailment, or postponement of some programs of study	1,413	671	47.5	69	4.9	68	4.8	117	8.3	72	5.1	155	11.0	190	13.4
Reduction in the number of subcollegiate courses of instruction	1,311	277	21.1	15	1.1	21	1.6	58	4.4	30	2.3	63	4.8	90	6.9
Courses given completely or primarily by television	1,378	71	5.2	0	0.0	5	0.4	14	1.0	2	0.1	11	0.8	39	2.8
Courses given completely or primarily by films	1,373	27	2.0	2	0.1	0	0.0	6	0.4	2	0.1	6	0.4	11	0.8

* Some practices (e.g., practices concerning ranks, mandatory retirement age, subcollegiate instruction) were not applicable to all institutions. Some forms were not fully completed. Hence, the total number of responses to various practices differs. The percentages for each practice in this table are based upon the total number of responses by institutions which have reported on each practice.

† Due to rounding off, the sum of the percentages in the following columns may differ slightly from the percentage in this column.

‡ Some institutions in 1957–58 decreased use of practices followed during 1954–1957. However, the number of such cases is relatively small, and it is thought inadvisable in this preliminary report to expand the tables to show them.

Source: C. D. Lindquist, "Recent Practices Relating to Faculty in Institutions of Higher Learning: Preliminary Report," *Higher Education*, November, 1958, p. 44.

nificantly to faculty morale and to better college teaching." These would of course also improve the supply situation. Among the items: " . . . an atmosphere of freedom of thought: . . . extensive faculty participation in the planning and management; . . . generous recognition for faculty services; . . . policies of promotion, tenure and retirement that will reduce the fear and frustration arising from economic and social insecurity; . . . sufficient clerical and technical help. . . . "[98]

The President's Science Advisory Committee said in its report (May 24, 1959):

> But what do we offer in return? We are often less concerned with their [teachers'] successes than we are with those of the football coach, whom we customarily pay more money as well. We impose a load of class hours and student numbers which make it almost impossible for teachers to do their best either as stimulators or as guides, critics or judges—or to find the time and energy for their own scholarship and self-development. It is small wonder that good teachers are in short supply.
>
> The attractiveness of teaching careers at all levels from secondary school to postgraduate university depends on many things beyond the mere general attractiveness of the surrounding community. The weight put upon each may vary from teacher to teacher and from institution to institution, but all are important. They include, among other things, a reasonable work load, a reasonable salary, adequate research or scholarly facilities and opportunities, good and interested students, associates interested in the same field, a favorable community attitude toward intellectual achievement which provides recognition of good teaching and the opportunity for professional development. None of these is trivial. They are commonly most favorable in graduate schools and in universities, next in colleges, and least of all in the majority of secondary schools.

A NOTE ON NUMBERS OF Ph.D.s

A further word about Ph.D.s. It is generally assumed that a Ph.D. should be required for college teaching. In my view, the M.A. can do as effective a job as the Ph.D. in junior colleges, many liberal arts colleges, and many professional schools.

But leaving this consideration aside, how many Ph.D.s will be available? The estimate of the manpower studies was 135,000 over the years from 1954 to 1970; of the Graduate School Deans, 235,000; of President Meredith Wilson of the University of Minnesota for the Ford Foundation, 220,000 (a preliminary estimate).

During the years 1937 to 1947, the average yearly number of Ph.D.s was 2,540; in the eight years from 1948 to 1955, 7,050; in the three years from 1956 to 1958, 8,650.[99]

The trend is clearly upward. Aside from the campaigns to enlist more graduate students and improvements in economic status, we may expect a substantial rise merely because college enrollments will be roughly 50 per cent higher in the years from 1958 to 1970 than in 1956 to 1958. Hence we may assume that the annual flow of Ph.D.s from 1958 to 1970 would be about 13,000. This figure is somewhat inflated because the lag in the rise of graduate numbers following the increase of undergraduates is not considered. But this is a low estimate, because we do not allow adequately for any upward trend vis-à-vis total college enrollment. Hence I estimate the flow of Ph.D.s of at least 200,000 from 1954 to 1970. The figure may be substantially higher. Only one-half of these will be available for teaching, and even this figure must be substantially reduced, since many of the future Ph.D.s are already in the teaching profession. But the further we look ahead, the greater is the proportion of new Ph.D.s who are a net addition to the teaching force. One report gives the estimates shown in Table 53-22.

TABLE 53-22
Estimated Full-time University, College, and Junior College Teachers

Year	Total enrollment (thousands)	Number of full-time teachers (thousands)	Student/ teacher ratio	New teachers needed		
				Replacements at 6 per cent	Additions to meet increased enrollment	Total
1959–60	3,470	262	13.25:1	15,000	12,200	27,200
1969–70	6,150	390	15.77:1	22,600	13,100	35,700
Total, 1958–59 to 1969–70......	.....	...	....	206,400	140,400	346,800

Source: NEA Research Report, *Teacher Supply and Demand in Universities, Colleges, and Junior Colleges, 1957–58 and 1958–59*, p. 50.

In conclusion, faculty salaries are too low given the numbers and quality needed. A serious relative deterioration of faculty pay still prevails. A comparison of income trends by rank simplifies the problem excessively. We also have to consider trends in numbers by ranks, average age, and training, increases in fringe benefits, and outside work. And we stress the relation of economies, to which faculty can contribute, to the mobilization of resources needed to finance the rise of pay.

FOOTNOTES

[1] G. J. Stigler, *Employment and Compensation in Education*, 1950, p. 26.

[2] $18,000 plus $2,000 in fringes in 1960–61.

[3] *Report to the Amherst Chapter of the AAUP*, December, 1957. (Mimeographed.)

[4] *Amherst College Bulletin,* 1946–1956; *The President's Report,* 1956, p. 8.

[5] *Salaries in Universities and Colleges in 1920,* U.S. Bureau of Education Bulletin 20.

[6] U.S. Bureau of Education Bulletin 36, 1922.

[7] W. Robert Bokelman, *Higher Education Planning and Management Data, 1957–58,* U.S. Office of Education Circular 517, p. 27; also see *Bulletin of the Association of American Colleges,* 1932, p. 441 for similar trends in 1930.

[8] This estimate is obtained by relating faculty salaries to what they would have been had they kept up with rising prices and incomes. The calculations are based on materials in *A Study of Income and Expenditures in Sixty Colleges;* HEW, *Statistics of Higher Education: Receipts, Expenditures and Property, 1951–52; Summary of 1953–54 Financial Statistics of Institutions of Higher Education; Economic Report of the President,* January, 1957; and various sources for estimates of faculty pay in individual years from 1940 on. (In some instances interpolations were necessary.) Cf. also G. J. Stigler, *op. cit.,* p. 44.

[9] J. D. Millett, *Financing Higher Education in the United States,* p. 135; HEW, *Higher Education: Planning and Management Data, 1959–60,* p. 19.

[10] *The Educational Future of Columbia University: Report of the President's Committee on the Educational Future of the University,* New York, 1957, p. 206.

[11] I am indebted to Edward Budd of Yale University for this material.

[12] See C. D. Long, "Professors' Salaries and the Inflation," *AAUP Bulletin,* Winter, 1952–53, pp. 577–78, and S. E. Harris, "Salary of a Full Professor at Harvard, 1930, to 1954–55," *Harvard Alumni Bulletin,* Apr. 9, 1955, pp. 513–14.

[13] Fund for the Advancement of Education, *Teachers for Tomorrow,* 1955, p. 37.

[14] See 1950 U.S. Census of Population, *Occupational Characteristics,* table 19; *Survey of Current Business,* July, 1952, and December, 1956; "How Much Are Physicians Earning?" *Medical Economics,* October, 1956; and National Education Association Research Bulletin, *Salaries Paid and Salary Practices in Universities, Colleges and Junior Colleges, 1955–56,* 1956.

[15] G. J. Stigler, *op. cit.,* pp. 48–49; cf. The Ohio College Association, *Meeting Ohio's Needs in Higher Education,* 1956, p. 54; and National Education Association, *op. cit.,* p. 20.

[16] Cf. my John Dewey Lecture, *More Resources for Education,* Harper, 1960.

[17] U.S. Department of Health, Education, and Welfare, *Statistical Summary of Education, 1951–52,* p. 40.

[18] J. D. Millett, *op. cit.,* pp. 134–35.

[19] "A Final Report on Instructional Salaries in 39 Selected Colleges and Universities for the Academic Year 1957–58," *AAUP Bulletin,* March, 1958, pp. 237–69.

[20] *Ibid.,* pp. 238 and 241; cf. *Trends in Higher Education: Planning and Management Data, 1957–58 to 1959–60,* p. 4.

[21] This view has been contested: see S. E. Harris (ed.), *Higher Education in the United States: The Economic Problems,* 1960, pp. 180–184.

[22] Cf. footnotes 3 and 4.

[23] *Comparability of Prewar and Postwar Teachers' Income Data: Two Point Survey,* 1957. (Mimeographed.)

[24] F. Machlup, "Grading of Academic Salary Scales," *AAUP Bulletin,* March, 1958, p. 224.

[25] G. J. Stigler, *op. cit.,* pp. 46–47.

[26] T. Caplow and R. J. McGee, *The Academic Marketplace,* 1958, pp. 43–44.

[27] I am indebted to President Glennan of the Case Institute of Technology for putting these statistics at my disposal.

[28] R. H. Ostheimer, *Student Charges and Financing Higher Education*, 1953, pp. 39, 48–49.

[29] C. D. Long, *op. cit.*, p. 582.

[30] *The Architect of Mid-century: Evolution and Achievement*, 1954, p. 262.

[31] President's Commission V, *Financing Higher Education*, p. 14; and HEW, *Summary of 1953–54 Financial Statistics of Institutions of Higher Learning*.

[32] On these issues, see Soltow, "Are College Teachers Really Underpaid?" *AAUP Bulletin*, Autumn, 1956, pp. 504–506; and G. J. Stigler, *op. cit.*, pp. 42–63.

[33] U.S. Census of 1950: U.S. Census of Population, *Occupational Characteristics*, vol. 20, 1953.

[34] J. D. Millett, *op. cit.*, pp. 194–200.

[35] *Ibid.*, pp. 137, 138; *Higher Education in a Decade of Decision*, 1957, pp. 130–32; and *Committee on Education Beyond the High School: Second Report*, 1957, p. 6.

[36] Various newspapers, Nov. 17 and Nov. 24, 1957.

[37] A. H. Imlah, "Three Case Histories in College Budgeting," *AAUP Bulletin*, Summer, 1947, pp. 319–321 and 327.

[38] E. Hutchisson, "An Economic Study of College Salaries and Academic Rank Distribution," *Educational Record*, 1956, pp. 277–84.

[39] The model given by Hutchisson cannot be generally used. Attrition is altogether too high for most institutions, and the rate of promotion too slow. But these are necessary (in his model) to attain the high salaries and a low ratio of students to faculty. At a major university, however, the attrition rate from instructor to full professor may well exceed 10 to 1; that is, only 1 out of 10 or more instructors ever reaches the final rank.

[40] "Association Activity for the Improvement of the Economic Status of the Profession," *AAUP Bulletin*, March, 1958, p. 12.

[41] "Economic Status of the Professor: A Statement of Policy," *ibid.*, p. 215.

[42] See *The Educational Future of Columbia University*, p. 207; *The Carnegie Conference on Higher Education*, 1957, p. 20; R. Brandis, "A College Teacher Looks at the Future," *Journal of Higher Education*, April, 1957, pp. 188–193; R. M. Hutchins, *The State of the University, 1929–1949*, p. 14.

[43] Cf. Table 53-13.

[44] For the last few paragraphs see L. A. Glenny, *Autonomy of Public Colleges*, 1959, p. 118; *The Report of the Commission on Higher Education: State-supported Higher Education in North Carolina*, 1955, p. 74; L. E. Fouraker, "Trouble in the Technique Industry," *The Journal of Business of the University of Chicago*, October, 1959, esp. pp. 332–38; Texas Commission on Higher Education, *Report to the Honorable Price Daniel and the Legislature of the State of Texas*, December, 1958, p. 39; *Encyclopedia of Educational Research*, 1950, p. 243.

[45] Cf. L. S. Woodburne, *Faculty Personnel Policies in Higher Education*, 1950, pp. 45–61.

[46] American Council on Education, *Expanding Resources for College Teaching*, 1956, pp. 91–92.

[47] H. E. Longenecker, *University Faculty Compensation Policies and Practices in the United States*, Association of American Universities, 1956, pp. 3 and 4. (Mimeographed.)

[48] *Ibid.*, pp. 5 and 6.

[49] *Ibid.*, p. 6.

[50] I have been told by the chancellor of the university that one professor with a salary of over $20,000 obtains for the university fees much in excess of $100,000.

[51] Reeves, Henry, Kelly, Klein, and Russell, *The University of Chicago Survey,* vol. III, *The University Faculty,* 1933, pp. 101–113.

[52] H. E. Longenecker, *op. cit.,* pp. 10–11.

[53] *The Educational Future of Columbia University,* pp. 207–208.

[54] *Ibid.,* pp. 208–210.

[55] *The New York University Self-study Interim Report,* New York University Bulletin 55, 1955, p. 75.

[56] *Comparability of Prewar and Postwar Teachers' Income Data: Two Point Survey,* 1957. (Mimeographed.)

[57] H. E. Longenecker, *op. cit.,* p. 51.

[58] *Ibid.,* p. 52.

[59] *Ibid.,* p. 54 *et seq.*

[60] *Ibid.,* p. 58.

[61] *Ibid.,* pp. 72–73.

[62] *Ibid.,* p. 74.

[63] E. Hutchisson, *op. cit.,* pp. 277–83; S. E. Harris, "College Salaries, Financing of Higher Education, and Management of Institutions of Higher Learning," *AAUP Bulletin,* Summer, 1958, p. 595.

[64] E. E. Edwards, "Problem: How Professors Can Earn More Pay," *Business Horizons of the Indiana Business Review,* June, 1957, pp. 78–89.

[65] See S. E. Harris (ed.), *Higher Education in the United States: The Economic Problems,* 1960, Chap. 5.

[66] This issue is discussed fully in Chap. 44.

[67] American Council on Education, *op. cit.,* pp. 92–93.

[68] *Ibid.,* p. 121.

[69] *Ibid.*

[70] Fund for the Advancement of Education, *Better Utilization of College Teaching Resources,* 1957.

[71] *Ibid.,* p. 8.

[72] *Ibid.,* pp. 8–9.

[73] L. S. Woodburne, *op. cit.,* p. 144; cf. American Council on Education, *op. cit.,* p. 110.

[74] M. A. Rauh, "Louder, Please, Professor!" *College and University Business,* July, 1956, p. 17.

[75] *Ibid.,* p. 143.

[76] For a fuller discussion of these matters, see Chap. 44.

[77] L. S. Woodburne, *op. cit.,* chap. 6.

[78] *The Educational Future of Columbia University,* p. 211; cf. *Second Report of the Committee on Education beyond the High School.*

[79] *The Educational Future of Columbia University,* p. 211; G. F. Keane, "A Look at the Professor's Personal Finances . . . ," *College and University Business,* February, 1961, pp. 42–43.

[80] Bokelman, *op. cit.,* 1957–58, p. 56.

[81] *The Educational Future of Columbia University,* pp. 217–19. In part, of course, the tendency to live away from the site of the university is explained by improved communications. But undoubtedly a serious factor in recent years has been the deterioration of the neighborhood.

[82] For some of the details on annuity planning, see E. S. Babbitt, "The Mechanics of Pension Planning," *College and University Business,* January, 1957, pp. 22–24; "Faculty Retirement Problems," *AAUP Bulletin,* Spring, 1950; *Academic Retirement and Related Subjects: Report on the Study Conducted by a Joint Committee of the*

American Associations of University Professors and the Association of American Colleges, p. 97; W. C. Greenough, and F. P. King, *Retirement and Insurance Plans in American Colleges,* 1959; and "Recent Developments in Retirement Planning," *AAUP Bulletin,* December, 1959, pp. 502–512.

[83] Experts disagree on the likely numbers.

[84] See especially Fund for the Advancement of Education, *Teachers for Tomorrow,* 1955, pp. 18–19, 60–62; NEA, *Teacher Supply and Demand in Degree-granting Institutions, 1954–55,* December, 1955, esp. chap. 3 and pp. 158–163; and President's Commission, *Higher Education for Democracy,* IV, *Staffing Higher Education,* p. 27.

[85] *Teacher Supply and Demand in Colleges and Universities, 1955–56 and 1956–57,* 1957, p. 18. *Ibid., 1959–60 and 1960–61,* 1961, pp. 12–55.

[86] *Ibid.,* p. 20.

[87] *Ibid.,* p. 21.

[88] *Ibid.,* pp. 29–31. See "A Note on Numbers of Ph.D.'s" at end of Chapter.

[89] *Ibid.,* pp. 28–33.

[90] *Ibid.,* p. 36; and *1957–58 and 1958–59,* pp. 25–26.

[91] NEA, *ibid.,* p. 138.

[92] C. D. Lindquist, "Recent Practices Relating to Faculty in Institutions, of Higher Learning: Preliminary Report," *Higher Education,* November, 1958, p. 44.

[93] Woodburne, *op. cit.,* pp. 10–11; American Council on Education, *College Teaching as a Career,* 1958, pp. 7–8, 20–23.

[93a] In a survey of the influence of Hollis's book *Toward Improving the Ph.D.* much criticism was made by administrators of teachers more interested in subject matter per se than in communicating it to students. A survey of 300 heads of departments revealed the following proposed distribution of time of graduate students as meeting their needs: major area, 35 per cent; related areas, 21; education, 5; dissertation and research, 15; elective, 13; structural techniques, etc., 7; miscellaneous, 4. "Training of College Teachers," *Journal of Higher Education,* 1954, p. 153.

[94] T. C. Blegero, *The Harvest of Knowledge,* The Research Foundation of State University of New York, 1957, pp. 20–21.

[95] NEA, *Teacher Supply and Demand in Universities, Colleges, and Junior Colleges, 1957–58 and 1958–59,* pp. 50–53; and Commonwealth of Pennsylvania, Joint State Government Commission Advisory Panel, *Higher Education in Pennsylvania,* Jan. 2, 1959, p. 37; also see *Ten Year Objectives in Education,* pp. 11–13 for estimates of professional staff for 1969–70; teachers, administrators, and research workers.

[96] B. R. Morris, "Faculty Salaries, Class Size, and Sound Education," *AAUP Bulletin,* June 1959, pp. 195–202.

[97] Eckert, Stecklein, and Sagen, "College Faculty Members View Their Jobs," *ibid.,* December, 1959, pp. 513–536.

[98] H. J. Corman, "Campus Issues and Problems," *The Annals, Higher Education under Stress,* September, 1955, p. 53.

[99] I am indebted to President O. Meredith Wilson of the University of Minnesota and Robert E. Iffert of HEW for these estimates.

CONCLUSION

Here at least I shall be brief. A substantial summary appears at the beginning, and numerous summaries are to be found at the end of sections or chapters.

I have tried to deal with the tough economic problems of higher education, but with my eye on the educational product as well. Unfortunately the measurement of the product is full of difficulties.

In view of the size of our economy, its expected growth, the large contributions of education to our growth, and the possibilities of raising the productivity of the educational dollar, there should be enough resources available for higher education to provide an education for 6 to 7 million students by 1970 at an average quality higher than the current one. Moreover, this could be achieved without putting a burden on students that would close higher education to many of those who should benefit. When one compares the input of labor, capital, and management of our economy with the output, one is struck by the much greater increase in output vis-à-vis input in the years since the Civil War. The difference is in no small way explained by the rising relative investment in education.

The costs of education are large, and they must rise more than GNP in the years to come. Hence the need of tapping all possible sources: government, philanthropy, students where the resources are available, improved techniques for financing, modifications in tax structure that reduce the *real costs* of tax receipts, and more economical management. Much will depend on the public relations performance of those responsible for higher education and the increased flexibility of faculty once they understand the issues.

INDEX